D1479578

*Students learn best when they atten*

*and assignments...but learning*

## MyEconLab *Picks Up Wher*

**Instructors choose MyEconLab:**

"MyEconLab's e-text is great. Particularly in that it helps offset the skyrocketing cost of textbooks. Naturally, students love that."

**—Doug Gehrke, Moraine Valley Community College**

"MyEconLab offers them a way to practice every week. They receive immediate feedback and a feeling of personal attention. As a result, my teaching has become more targeted and efficient."

**—Kelly Blanchard, Purdue University**

"Students tell me that offering them MyEconLab is almost like offering them individual tutors."

**—Jefferson Edwards, Cypress Fairbanks College**

"Chapter quizzes offset student procrastination by ensuring they keep on task. If a student is having a problem, MyEconLab indicates exactly what they need to study."

"MyEconLab helps both students and instructors. There's something there for everyone."

"Someone has already pulled out articles that relate to economics and to the chapter at hand. As much as MyEconLab helps the student, that helps the instructor."

**—Diana Fortier, Waubonsee Community College**

*Get Ahead of the Curve*

# *ectures and Office Hours Leave Off*

**Students choose MyEconLab:**

*In a Fall 2005 study, 87 percent of students who used MyEconLab regularly felt it improved their grade.*

"It was very useful because it had EVERYTHING, from practice exams to exercises to reading. Very helpful."

—**student, Northern Illinois University**

"I like how every chapter is outlined by vocabulary and flash cards. It helped me memorize equations and definitions. It was like having a study partner."

—**student, Temple University**

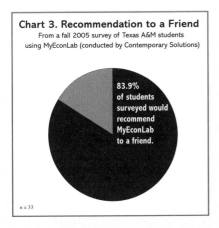

**Chart 2. Helpfulness of Study Plan Practice Questions and Feedback**
From a fall 2005 nationwide survey of students using MyEconLab (conducted by Contemporary Solutions)

90% of students surveyed who used the Study Plan practice questions and feedback felt it helped them to prepare for tests.

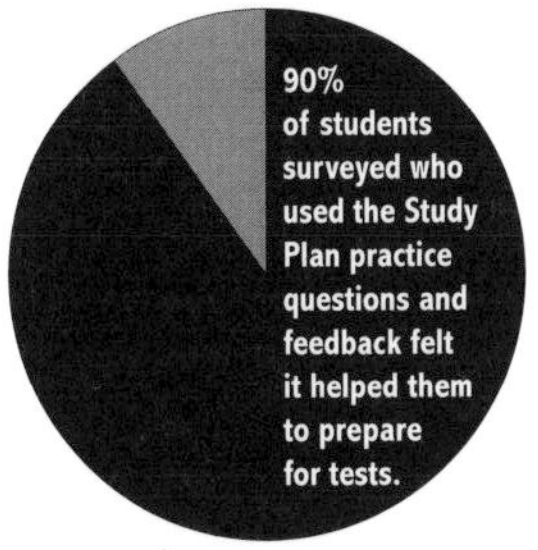

*n = 227*

"It made me look through the book to find answers so I did more reading."

—**student, Northern Illinois University**

"It was very helpful to get instant feedback. Sometimes I would get lost reading the book, and these individual problems would help me focus and see if I understood the concepts."

—**student, Temple University**

**Chart 3. Recommendation to a Friend**
From a fall 2005 survey of Texas A&M students using MyEconLab (conducted by Contemporary Solutions)

83.9% of students surveyed would recommend MyEconLab to a friend.

*n = 33*

"I really like the way MyEconLab took me through the graphs step-by-step. The Fast Track tutorials were the most helpful for the graph questions. I used the 1-2-3 buttons all the time."

—**student, Stephen F. Austin State University**

"I would recommend MyEconLab to a friend. It was really easy to use and helped in studying the material for class."

—**student, Northern Illinois University**

"I would recommend taking the quizzes on MyEconLab because it gives you a true account of whether or not you understand the material."

—**student, Montana Tech**

# Survey of Economics

## PRINCIPLES, APPLICATIONS, AND TOOLS

THIRD EDITION

# Survey of Economics

## PRINCIPLES, APPLICATIONS, AND TOOLS

### THIRD EDITION

**Arthur O'Sullivan**
*Lewis and Clark College*

**Steven M. Sheffrin**
*University of California, Davis*

**Stephen J. Perez**
*California State University, Sacramento*

PEARSON

Prentice
Hall

Upper Saddle River, NJ 07458

**Library of Congress Cataloging-in-Publication Data**

O'Sullivan, Arthur
   Survey of economics / Arthur O'Sullivan, Steven M. Sheffrin, Stephen J. Perez.—3rd ed.
    p. cm.
   Includes bibliographical references and index.
   ISBN 0-13-244702-9
   1. Economics. I. Sheffrin, Steven M. II. Perez, Stephen J. III. Title.
HB171.5.O843 2007
330—dc22

AVP/Executive Editor: *David Alexander*
VP/Director of Development: *Steve Deitmer*
Senior Development Editor: *Lena Buonanno*
Director, Product Development: *Pamela Hersperger*
Senior Media Project Manager: *Peter Snell*
AVP/Executive Marketing Manager: *Sharon Koch*
Associate Director, Production Editorial: *Judy Leale*
Senior Managing Editor: *Cynthia Zonneveld*
Production Editor: *Suzanne Grappi*
Permissions Coordinator: *Charles Morris*
Associate Director, Manufacturing: *Vinnie Scelta*
Manufacturing Buyer: *Diane Peirano*
Creative Director: *Maria Lange*
Design/Composition Manager: *Christy Mahon*

Composition Liaison: *Suzanne Duda*
Interior Design: *MLM Graphics*
Cover Illustration/Photo: *Image Bank*
Illustration (Interior): *Rob Aleman*
Director, Image Resource Center: *Melinda Patelli*
Manager, Rights and Permissions: *Zina Arabia*
Manager, Visual Research: *Beth Brenzel*
Manager, Cover Visual Research
& Permissions: *Karen Sanatar*
Image Permission Coordinator: *Angelique Sharps*
Photo Researcher: *Diane Austin*
Composition/Full-Service Project Management: *Prepare, Inc.*
Printer/Binder: *Courier-Kendalville*
Typeface: *Janson Text 10/12*

Credits and acknowledgments borrowed from other sources and reproduced, with permission, in this textbook appear on appropriate page within text.

Microsoft® and Windows® are registered trademarks of the Microsoft Corporation in the U.S.A. and other countries. Screen shots and icons reprinted with permission from the Microsoft Corporation. This book is not sponsored or endorsed by or affiliated with the Microsoft Corporation.

**Copyright © 2008, 2005, 2002 by Pearson Education, Inc., Upper Saddle River, New Jersey 07458.**

Pearson Prentice Hall. All rights reserved. Printed in the United States of America. This publication is protected by Copyright and permission should be obtained from the publisher prior to any prohibited reproduction, storage in a retrieval system, or transmission in any form or by any means, electronic, mechanical, photocopying, recording, or likewise. For information regarding permission(s), write to: Rights and Permissions Department.

**Pearson Prentice Hall**™ is a trademark of Pearson Education, Inc.
**Pearson**® is a registered trademark of Pearson plc
**Prentice Hall**® is a registered trademark of Pearson Education, Inc.

Pearson Education LTD.
Pearson Education Singapore, Pte. Ltd.
Pearson Education, Canada, Ltd.
Pearson Education–Japan

Pearson Education Australia PTY, Limited
Pearson Education North Asia Ltd
Pearson Educación de Mexico, S.A. de C.V.
Pearson Education Malaysia, Pte. Ltd

10 9 8 7 6 5 4 3 2

ISBN-13: 978-0-13-244702-7
ISBN-10: 0-13-244702-9

TO OUR CHILDREN

CONOR, MAURA, MEERA, KIRAN, DAVIS, AND TATE

# About the Authors

### ARTHUR O'SULLIVAN

Is a professor of economics at Lewis and Clark College in Portland, Oregon. After receiving his B.S. in economics at the University of Oregon, he spent two years in the Peace Corps, working with city planners in the Philippines. He received his Ph.D. in economics from Princeton University in 1981 and has taught at the University of California, Davis, and Oregon State University, winning several teaching awards at both schools. He recently accepted an endowed professorship at Lewis and Clark College, where he teaches microeconomics and urban economics. He is the author of the best-selling textbook *Urban Economics*, currently in its sixth edition.

Professor O'Sullivan's research explores economic issues concerning urban land use, environmental protection, and public policy. His articles have appeared in many economics journals, including the *Journal of Urban Economics*, *Journal of Environmental Economics and Management*, *National Tax Journal*, *Journal of Public Economics*, and *Journal of Law and Economics*.

Professor O'Sullivan lives with his family in Lake Oswego, Oregon. For recreation, he enjoys hiking, boogie-boarding, paragliding, and squash.

### STEVEN M. SHEFFRIN

Is dean of the division of social sciences and professor of economics at the University of California, Davis. He has been a visiting professor at Princeton University, Oxford University, and the London School of Economics and has served as a financial economist with the Office of Tax Analysis of the United States Department of the Treasury. He has been on the faculty of the University of California, Davis, since 1976 and has served as the chairman of the department of economics. He received his B.A. from Wesleyan University and his Ph.D. in economics from the Massachusetts Institute of Technology.

Professor Sheffrin is the author of 10 other books and monographs and over 100 articles in the fields of macroeconomics, public finance, and international economics. His most recent books include *Rational Expectations* (second edition) and *Property Taxes and Tax Revolts: The Legacy of Proposition 13* (with Arthur O'Sullivan and Terri Sexton).

Professor Sheffrin has taught macroeconomics at all levels, from large introduction to principles classes (enrollments of 400) to graduate classes for doctoral students. He is the recipient of the Thomas Mayer Distinguished Teaching Award in economics.

He lives with his wife Anjali (also an economist) in Davis, California, and has two daughters who have studied economics. In addition to a passion for current affairs and travel, he plays a tough game of tennis.

### STEPHEN J. PEREZ

Is chair of the economics department at California State University, Sacramento. After receiving his B.A. in economics at the University of California, San Diego, he was awarded his Ph.D. in economics from the University of California, Davis, in 1994. He taught economics at Virginia Commonwealth University and Washington State University before coming to California State University, Sacramento, in 2001. He teaches macroeconomics at all levels as well as econometrics, sports economics, labor economics, and mathematics for economists.

Professor Perez's research explores most macroeconomic topics. In particular, he is interested in evaluating the ability of econometric techniques to discover the truth, issues of causality in macroeconomics, and sports economics. His articles have appeared in many economics journals, including the *Journal of Monetary Economics*, *Econometrics Journal*, *Economics Letters*, *Journal of Economic Methodology*, *Public Finance and Management*, *Journal of Economics and Business*, *Oxford Bulletin of Economics and Statistics*, *Journal of Money, Credit, and Banking*, *Applied Economics*, and *Journal of Macroeconomics*.

# Brief Contents

# Contents

# Preface

## ▶ ONE-SEMESTER BOOK

This book is a one-semester version of our full-length introductory text, *Economics: Principles, Applications, and Tools*, now in its fifth edition. This text has been a success in classrooms around the country, but many colleges and universities teach a one-semester economics course that covers both microeconomics and macroeconomics. This book preserves the key features of *Economics: Principles, Applications, and Tools*, including its organization around the five key principles of economics to explain the most important concepts of economics, and the extensive use of practical applications to reinforce the learning process.

In designing a one-semester book, we knew that we had to focus on the essential concepts of economics. We start with the five key principles of economics and move quickly into the heart of microeconomics: demand and supply. We then turn to production and cost, competition and market structure, market failure from imperfect information and externalities, and the labor market. Macroeconomics begins with chapters that introduce national income, unemployment, and inflation. We then explore the issues of economic growth and economic fluctuations. We cover monetary and fiscal policy, in both the short run and long run. The book concludes with international trade and finance. We've strived to make all explanations of key ideas and key concepts as simple as possible. In a one-semester book, the student will be introduced to a wide range of ideas. It is important that these ideas be as straightforward and transparent as possible.

## 3.7 | APPLICATIONS OF DEMAND AND SUPPLY

We can apply what we've learned about demand and supply to real markets. We can use the model of demand and supply to *predict* the effects of various events on equilibrium prices and quantities. We can also *explain* some observed changes in equilibrium prices and quantities.

1

## APPLICATION

### HURRICANE KATRINA AND BATON ROUGE HOUSING PRICES

**APPLYING THE CONCEPTS #1:**
How do changes in demand affect prices?

In the late summer of 2005, Hurricane Katrina caused a storm surge and levee breaks that flooded much of New Orleans and destroyed a large fraction of the city's housing. Hundreds of thousands of residents were displaced, and about 250,000 relocated to nearby Baton Rouge. The increase in population was so large that Baton Rouge became the largest city in the state, and many people started calling the city "New Baton Rouge."

Figure 3.14 shows the effects of Hurricane Katrina on the housing market in Baton Rouge. Before Katrina, the average price of a single-family home was $130,000, as shown by point *a*. The increase in the city's population shifted the demand curve to the right, causing excess demand for housing at the original price. Just before the hurricane, there were 3,600 homes listed for sale in the city, but a week after the storm, there were only 500. The excess demand caused fierce competition among buyers for the limited supply of homes, increasing the price. Six months later, the average price had risen to $156,000 as shown by point *b*. *Related to Exercises 7.1 and 7.6.*

SOURCE: Federal Deposit Insurance Corporation, *Louisiana State Profile—Fall 2005.*

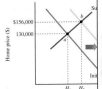

▲ **FIGURE 3.14**
**Hurricane Katrina and Housing in Ba[...]**
An increase in the population of Baton Rouge [...]
demand for housing, shifting the demand curve [...]
librium price increases from $130,000 (point [...]
(point *b*).

68

---

▶ # APPLYING THE CONCEPTS

This is an applications-driven textbook. We carefully selected dozens of real-world Applications that help students develop and master essential economic concepts. We start each chapter with several thought-provoking questions that convey important economic concepts. Once we present the economic concept and the logic behind it, we illustrate its use with a real-world Application. For each Application, we provide exercises that test students' understanding of the concepts and give them opportunities to do their own economic analysis. Here is an example of our approach from Chapter 3, "Demand, Supply, and Market Equilibrium."

---

## SUMMARY

In this chapter, we've seen how demand and supply determine prices. We also learned how to predict the effects of changes in demand or supply on prices and quantities. Here are the main points of the chapter:

1 A *market demand curve* shows the relationship between the quantity demanded and price, *ceteris paribus.*

2 A *market supply curve* shows the relationship between the quantity supplied and price, *ceteris paribus.*

3 *Equilibrium* in a market is shown by the intersection of the demand curve and the supply curve. When a market reaches equilibrium, there is no pressure to change the price.

4 A *change in demand* changes price and quantity in the same direction: An increase in demand increases the equilibrium price and quantity; a decrease in demand decreases the equilibrium price and quantity.

5 A *change in supply* changes price and quantity in opposite directions: An increase in supply decreases price and increases quantity; a decrease in supply increases price and decreases quantity.

### KEY TERMS

change in demand, p. 59
change in quantity demanded, p. 51
change in quantity supplied, p. 54
change in supply, p. 63
complements, p. 60
demand schedule, p. 50
excess demand (shortage), p. 57
excess supply (surplus), p. 58

individual demand curve, p. 51
individual supply curve, p. 54
inferior good, p. 59
law of demand, p. 51
law of supply, p. 54
market demand curve, p. 51
market equilibrium, p. 57
market supply curve, p. 55

minimum supply price, p. 54
normal good, p. 59
perfectly competitive market, p. 50
quantity demanded, p. 50
quantity supplied, p. 53
substitutes, p. 59
supply schedule, p. 53

### EXERCISES  myeconlab
*Get Ahead of the Curve*   Visit www.myeconlab.com to complete these exercises online and get instant feedback.

#### 3.1 | The Demand Curve

1.1 Arrow up or down: According to the law of demand, an increase in price _____ the quantity demanded.

[...]at are

1.3 From the following list, choose the variables that change as we draw a market demand curve.
• The price of the product
• Consumer income
• The price of other related goods
• Consumer expectations about future prices
• The quantity of the product purchased

1.4 The market demand curve is the _____ (horizontal/vertical) sum of the individual demand curves.

---

## 3.7 | Applications of Demand and Supply

7.1 Arrow up or down: Hurricane Katrina _____ the demand for housing in Baton Rouge, so the price of housing _____ and the quantity of housing _____. (Related to Application 1 on page 68.)

7.2 Ted Koppel's analysis of the drug market was incorrect because he failed to notice that the _____ of drugs decreased at the same time that the _____ of drugs decreased. (Related to Application 2 on page 69.)

7.3 Innovations in wind technology decrease the price of electricity from wind from 50 cents per kilowatt-hour to _____ cents. (Related to Application 3 on page 70.)

7.4 Arrow up or down: The development of a sun-tolerant variety of the vanilla plant _____ the supply of vanilla and _____ its price. (Related to Application 4 on page 71.)

7.5 Arrow up or down: The increase in the price of platinum _____ recycling of used platinum and _____ the quantity of platinum used for jewelry. (Related to Application 5 on page 72.)

7.6 **Katrina Victims Move Back.** Suppose that 5 years

7.7 **Decrease in the Price of Heroin.** Between 1990 and 2003, the price of heroin decreased from $235 per gram to $76. Over the same period, the quantity of heroin consumed increased from 376 metric tons to 482 metric tons. Use a demand and supply graph to explain these changes in price and quantity. (Related to Application 2 on page 69.)

7.8 **Electricity from Fuel Cells.** Suppose that initially the cost of the capital required to generate electricity from fuel cells is $4,500 per kilowatt capacity, compared to $800 per kilowatt capacity for a diesel generator. The goal of the U.S. Department of Energy (DOE) is to cut the cost of fuel-cell generators to $400 per kilowatt capacity. Consider the market for electricity from fuel cells. Use a demand and supply graph to show the effects of meeting the DOE goal on the price and quantity of electricity from fuel cells. (Related to Application 3 on page 70.)

7.9 **Artificial Versus Natural Vanilla.** An artificial alternative to natural vanilla is cheaper to produce but doesn't taste as good. Suppose the makers of artificial vanilla discover a new recipe that improves its taste. Use a demand and supply graph to show the effects on the equilibrium price and quantity of natural vanilla.

We tested our approach of using questions to open each chapter and presenting related real-world Applications with economics instructors. Here is what some of them had to say about our approach:

> [The book] provides wonderful Applications for each principle presented. The introductory questions at the beginning of each chapter should create enough interest to get students to dig a little deeper into the subject.
>
> ARLENA SULLIVAN, *Jones County Junior College*

> The chapters have some incredible real-life examples that students will easily relate to; makes the math behind economics less scary and more approachable.
>
> GRETCHEN MESTER, *Anne Arundel Community College*

> I liked the use of the Katrina natural disaster [in Chapter 3] as a means of discussing the effect on market equilibrium price and quantity due to changes in demand, in the particular case of the textbook example the housing market in "new" Baton Rogue.
>
> CRAIG ROGERS, *Canisius College*

> The Applications go beyond just illustrating concepts. They develop/reinforce the core principles by taking a nontechnical applied approach. They should enable students to understand the relevance of economics in everyday life and hopefully will arouse curiosity and interest.
>
> RATHA RAMOO, *Diablo Valley College*

> I think that the inclusion of this feature could both help the instructor in teaching and facilitate the understanding of the material by the students.
>
> MIKAYEL VARDANYAN, *Oregon State University*

> The book engages today's students by relating their world to economic theory. Our students of today need to know why the information is important before they undertake learning. Each chapter opens with intriguing, real-world resource allocation questions which economic principles can answer.
>
> DAVID SHOROW, *Richland College*

## ▶ WHY FIVE KEY PRINCIPLES?

In Chapter 2, "The Key Principles of Economics," we introduce the following five key principles and then apply them throughout the book:

1. **The Principle of Opportunity Cost.** The opportunity cost of something is what you sacrifice to get it.

2. **The Marginal Principle.** Increase the level of an activity as long as its marginal benefit exceeds its marginal cost. Choose the level at which the marginal benefit equals the marginal cost.

3. **The Principle of Diminishing Returns.** If we increase one input while holding the other inputs fixed, output will increase, but at a decreasing rate.

4. **The Principle of Voluntary Exchange.** A voluntary exchange between two people makes both people better off.

5. **The Real–Nominal Principle.** What matters to people is the real value of money or income—its purchasing power—not the face value of money or income.

This approach of repeating five key principles gives students the big picture—the framework of economic reasoning. We make the key concepts unforgettable by using them repeatedly, illustrating them with intriguing examples, and giving students many opportunities to practice what they've learned. Throughout the text, economic concepts are connected to the five key principles:

PRINCIPLE OF OPPORTUNITY COST
The opportunity cost of something is what you sacrifice to get it.

## ▶ HOW IS THE MARKET EQUILIBRIUM CHAPTER ORGANIZED?

Students need to have a solid understanding of demand and supply to be successful in the course. Many students have difficulty understanding movement along a curve versus shifts of a curve. To address this difficulty, we developed an innovative way to organize topics in Chapter 3, "Demand, Supply, and Market Equilibrium." We examine the law of demand and changes in quantity demanded, the law of supply and changes in quantity supplied, and then the notion of market equilibrium. After students have a firm grasp of equilibrium concepts, we explore the effects of changes in demand and supply on equilibrium prices and quantities. Here is what reviewers have said about our organization of Chapter 3:

> This treatment is innovative and effective. It covers equilibrium before changing demand and supply. This will greatly reduce the confusion about distinguishing between changes in quantity demanded and changes in demand (and, similarly, about changes in quantity supplied and changes in supply). . . . It makes good sense.
>
> GEOFFREY BLACK, *Boise State University*

> As I was reading the chapter, I thought to myself . . . this is a good approach: it takes one important economic idea to a conclusion: forces of demand and supply determine price and along the way, it covers quantity demanded, quantity supplied, demand curve, supply curve, etc. And now we're going to expand the model and look at the effects of the other determinants. . . .
>
> RATHA RAMOO, *Diablo Valley College*

The organization has the advantage of focusing attention early upon the key concept of market equilibrium, so that the reasons demand and supply shifts become important can be discussed before getting into the details of the shifts themselves. . . .

DAVID SCHUTTE, *Mountain View College*

# ▶ WHAT'S NEW TO THIS EDITION?

Based on our teaching experiences and extensive feedback from economics instructors, we have revised selected key term definitions, added new graphs, updated existing graphs, and presented new examples and Applications. Compared to the last edition, we now have entire separate chapters devoted to the Key Principles of Economics and to Fiscal Policy. This helps keep the focus on key ideas and concepts in economics.

In addition to these changes, we also have made three major revisions to the end-of-chapter exercises. First, we responded to market requests to group exercises together at the end of the chapter. Second, we revised the end-of-chapter exercises to correspond with new content and Applications in the chapters. Third, we now give students the option of completing exercises online at www.myeconlab.com, where they receive instant feedback, tutorial instruction, and additional practice exercises.

A new coauthor, Stephen J. Perez of California State University, Sacramento, joins the third edition. In addition to providing guidance on the macroeconomics chapters, Professor Perez is the organizing force behind MyEconLab and ensured the seamless integration of MyEconLab with the book. He also served as advisor and coordinator for the extensive print and technology supplement package that accompanies the book. Professor Perez ensured that each supplement met the highest standards of quality. (For more on the supplements, please see pages xx.)

# ▶ WHAT IS MYECONLAB?

*Get Ahead of the Curve*

Everyone benefits when students arrive to class confident and prepared. MyEconLab is the only online assessment system that gives students the tools they need to learn from their mistakes right at the moment they are struggling. MyEconLab has a variety of online features that solve problems for students and professors.

## Problem Solving for Students

Each chapter in this text ends with a wide selection of summary and practice exercises to appeal to a variety of learning styles. Students have the option of completing these exercises online at www.myeconlab.com. MyEconLab identifies students' weak spots and provides tutorial help to help students master those areas:

- **Help Beyond Homework.** Student learning begins in the classroom. But instructors know that's only the start. Students need practice with theories and models to master key concepts. Instructors need a way to hold students accountable for getting that practice and to provide targeted support as they work through assessments.

- **Tests and Quizzes.** MyEconLab comes with two pre-loaded Sample Tests for each chapter so that students can self-assess their understanding of the material. Instructors can assign the Sample Tests or create their own from publisher-supplied content or their own custom exercises. Many Sample Test problems contain algorithmically generated values to increase practice opportunities.

- **Study Plan.** MyEconLab generates a Study Plan from each student's results on assigned and Sample Tests. Students can clearly see which topics they have mastered—and more importantly, where they need remediation. The Study Plan links them to additional practice problems and tutorial help on those topics.

- **Unlimited Practice.** Study Plan exercises and instructor-assigned homework problems provide students with valuable opportunities for practice and remediation. Each problem includes links to learning resources so that students can focus on the concepts they need to master.

- **Learning Resources.** Students can get help from a host of interactive, targeted resources. Links to eText pages secure the connection between online practice and key chapter concepts. MyEconLab also has a suite of graphing tools that help students draw and interpret graphs and chapter-specific, current news articles that tie economic concepts to everyday topics.

## Problem Solving for Instructors

Instructors choose how much, or how little, energy they want to spend setting up the course and gain back precious time with MyEconLab's automatic grading. MyEconLab helps instructors track student performance and assess their progress by offering:

- **Graded Homework.** Instructors can create and assign tests, quizzes, or graded homework assignments.

- **Graded Graphing Problems.** MyEconLab can even grade assignments that require students to draw a graph.

- **Gradebook.** MyEconLab saves time by automatically grading all questions and tracking results in an online grade book.
- **Supplementary Questions.** Test Item File # 1 for both Macroeconomics and Microeconomics are also preloaded into MyEconLab, giving instructors ample material from which they can create assignments.
- **Weekly News Updates.** Weekly news feeds with links to related Web sites, accompanied by homework and discussion questions, are provided and archived for use in class or as homework.
- **Teaching Resources.** Once registered for MyEcon-Lab, instructors have access to downloadable supplements such as Instructor's Manuals, PowerPoint® lecture notes, and Test Banks.

For more information about MyEconLab or to request an Instructor Access Code, visit www.myeconlab.com or ask your local Prentice Hall representative.

## ▶ WHAT INSTRUCTOR'S SUPPLEMENTS DID WE DEVELOP?

A fully integrated teaching and learning package is necessary for today's classroom. Our supplement package helps you provide new and interesting real-world Applications and assess student understanding of economics. The supplements are coordinated with the main text through the numbering system of the headings in each section. The major sections of the chapters are numbered (1.1, 1.2, 1.3, and so on), and that numbering system is used consistently in the supplements to make it convenient and flexible for instructors to develop assignments.

### Test-Item File

*Survey of Economics, Third Edition,* is supported by a test-item file created by Randy Methenitis of Richland College and James Swofford of the University of South Alabama. To ensure the highest level of quality, an accuracy review board of 30 professors carefully examined each test bank question for accuracy, consistency with the text, balance of difficulty level and question type, and overall functionality for the purpose of testing student knowledge of the material. Ben Paris, Prentice Hall's executive producer of assessment programs, provided the test bank authors with guidance on how to write effective questions.

The test bank offers multiple-choice, true/false, and short-answer questions. The questions are referenced by topic and are presented in sequential order. Each question is keyed by degree of difficulty as *easy, moderate,* or *difficult.* Easy questions involve straightforward recall of information in the text. Moderate questions require some analysis on the student's part. Difficult questions usually entail more complex analysis and may require the student to go one step further than the material presented in the text. Questions are also classified as

*fact, definition, conceptual,* and *analytical.* Fact questions test a student's knowledge of factual information presented in the text. Definition questions ask the student to define an economic concept. Conceptual questions test a student's understanding of a concept. Analytical questions require the student to apply an analytical procedure to answer the question.

The test bank includes tables and a series of questions asking students to solve for numeric values, such as profit or equilibrium output. There are also numerous questions based on graphs: Several questions ask students to interpret data presented in a graph, draw a graph on their own, and answer related questions.

New to the third edition test bank are several questions that support the Applications in the main book. Each test bank chapter also includes a *new* Application based on a newspaper, journal, or online news story. There are also new questions to support the updated and new content in the main book.

### TestGen

*Survey of Economics* Test Item File appears in print and as a computer file that may be used with this TestGen test-generating software, which permits instructors to edit, add, or delete questions from the test bank; analyze test results; and organize a database of tests and student results. This software allows for flexibility and ease of use. It provides many options for organizing and displaying tests, along with a search and sort feature.

### Instructor's Manual

The Instructor's Manual, revised by Daniel Condon of Dominican University, follows the textbook's organization, incorporating extra Applications questions. The manual also provides detailed outlines (suitable for use as lecture notes) and solutions to all questions in the textbook. The solutions were prepared by David Schutte of Mountain View College. The Instructor's Manual is also designed to help the instructor incorporate applicable elements of the supplement package. The Instructor's Manual contains the following for each chapter:

- Summary: A bullet list of key topics in the chapter
- Approaching the Material: Student-friendly examples to introduce the chapter
- Chapter Outline: Summary of definitions and concepts
  - Teaching Tips on how to encourage class participation
  - Summary and discussion points for the Applications in the main text
  - New Applications and discussion questions
- Solutions to all end-of-chapter exercises

The Instructor's Manual is also available for download from the Instructor's Resource Center.

### PowerPoint® Lecture Presentation

Prepared by Fernando and Yvonn Quijano, with assistants Kyle Thiel and Aparna Subramanian, the comprehensive set of PowerPoint® slides can be used by instructors for class presentations or by students for lecture preview or review. The set includes summaries of the key concepts in each major section and all the graphs, tables, and equations in the textbook. The set also includes summaries and figures of each Application. It displays figures in two versions—in step-by-step mode so that you can build graphs as you would on a blackboard, and in an automated mode, using a single click per slide.

Instructors and students may download these Power-Point® presentations from www.prenhall.com/osullivan.

## Instructor's Resource Center Online

This password-protected site is accessible from www.prenhall.com/osullivan and hosts all of the resources listed above: Test Bank Instructor's Manual, and Power-Point®. Instructors can click on the "Help downloading Instructor Resources" link for easy-to-follow instructions on getting access or contact their sales representative for further information.

## Online Courses: Blackboard and WebCT

Prentice Hall offers fully customizable course content for the Blackboard and WebCT course management systems that includes a link to the MyEconLab software hosting all of the course materials.

## Classroom Response Systems

Classroom Response Systems (CRS) is an exciting new wireless polling technology that makes large and small classrooms even more interactive because it enables instructors to pose questions to their students, record results, and display those results instantly. Students can answer questions easily using compact remote-control transmitters. Prentice Hall has partnerships with leading Classroom Response Systems providers and can show you everything you need to know about setting up and using a CRS system. We'll provide the classroom hardware, text-specific PowerPoint® slides, software, and support, and we'll also show you how your students can benefit! Learn more at www.prenhall.com/crs.

## ▶ WHAT STUDENT SUPPLEMENTS DID WE DEVELOP?

To accommodate different learning styles and busy student lifestyles, we provide a variety of print and online supplements.

## Study Guide

The Study Guide, created by David Eaton of Murray State University and Dan Martinez of Salt Lake Community College, reinforces economic concepts and Applications from the main book and help students assess their learning. Each chapter of the Study Guide includes the following features:

- Chapter Summary: Provides a summary of the chapter, key term definitions, and review of the Applications from the main book.
- Study Tip: Provides students with tips on understanding key concepts.
- Key equations: Alerts students to equations they are likely to see throughout the class.
- Caution!: Alerts students about potential pitfalls and key figures or tables that deserve special attention.
- Activity: Encourages students to think creatively about an economic problem. An answer is provided so students can check their work.
- Practice Test: Includes approximately 25 multiple-choice and short-answer questions that help students test their knowledge. Select questions include a graph or table for students to analyze. Some of these questions support the Applications in the main book.
- Solutions to the Practice Test.

## The Companion Web Site (www.prenhall.com/osullivan)

This free Web site, www.prenhall.com/osullivan, gives students access to an interactive study guide with instant feedback, economics news updates, and student PowerPoint® slides to promote success in the Principles of Economics news course.

## SafariX WebBooks

SafariX WebBooks (online versions of the printed texts) will be available for students to purchase in lieu of a standard print text, without any modifications needed to how the instructor or professor teaches the course. Learn more at www.prenhall.com/safariX.

## VangoNotes

Students can study on the go with VangoNotes—chapter reviews from the text in downloadable MP3 format from www.vangonotes.com. Now wherever students are—whatever they're doing—they can study by listening to the following for each chapter of the book:

- **Big Ideas.** The "need to know" for each chapter
- **Practice Tests.** A gut check for the Big Ideas; tells students if they need to keep studying
- **Key Terms.** Audio "flashcards" to help students review key concepts and terms
- **Rapid Review.** A quick drill session that students can use right before a test

VangoNotes are **flexible**. Students can download all the material directly to their MP3 player or only the chapters they need. VangoNotes are also **efficient**. Students can use them in the car, at the gym, walking to class, wherever they want to go.

## ▶ HOW CAN YOU KEEP UP-TO-DATE WITH THE NEWS?

Analyzing current events is an important skill for economics students to develop. To sharpen this skill and further support the book's Applications theme, Prentice Hall offers you and your students three news subscription.

### The *Wall Street Journal* Print and Interactive Editions Subscription

Prentice Hall has formed a strategic alliance with the *Wall Street Journal*, the most respected and trusted daily source for information on business and economics. For a small additional charge, Prentice Hall offers your students a 10- or 15-week subscription to the *Wall Street Journal* print edition and the *Wall Street Journal* interactive edition.

Upon adoption of a special package containing the book and the subscription booklet, professors will receive a free one-year subscription of the print and interactive versions as well as weekly subject-specific *Wall Street Journal* educators' lesson plans.

### *The Financial Times*

We are pleased to announce a special partnership with *The Financial Times*. For a small additional charge, Prentice Hall offers your students a 15-week subscription to *The Financial Times*. Upon adoption of a special package containing the book and the subscription booklet, professors will receive a free one-year subscription. Please contact your Prentice Hall representative for details and ordering information.

### Economist.com

Through a special arrangement with Economist.com, Prentice Hall offers your students a 12-week subscription to Economist.com for a small additional charge. Upon adoption of a special package containing the book and the subscription booklet, professors will receive a free six-month subscription. Please contact your Prentice Hall representative for further details and ordering information.

## ▶ ACCURACY BOARD, CONSULTANTS, AND REVIEWERS

A long road exists between the initial vision of an innovative principles text and the final product. Along our journey we participated in a structured process to reach our goal. We wish to acknowledge the assistance of the many people who participated in this process.

### Accuracy Board

A dedicated team of economics professors checked the figures, equations, and text in the book and supplements package:

DIANE ANSTINE, *North Central College*
LEN ANYANWU, *Union County College*
BHARATI BASU, *Central Michigan University*
JAMES BRUMBAUGH, *Lord Fairfax Community College*
MICHAEL COHICK, *Collin County Community College*
DAVID EATON, *Murray State University*
HAROLD ELDER, *University of Alabama-Tuscaloosa*
MICHAEL GOODE, *Central Piedmont Community College*
WILLIAM HALLAGAN, *Washington State University*
HADLEY HARTMAN, *Santa Fe Community College*
MICHAEL G. HESLOP, *Northern Virginia Community College*
TONY LIMA, *California State University, East Bay*
SOLINA LINDAHL, *California Polytechnic State University-San Luis Obispo*
MICHAEL MCILHON, *Century College*
SHAH MEHRABI, *Montgomery College*
GRETCHEN MESTER, *Anne Arundel Community College*
RANDY METHENITIS, *Richland College*
JOHN S. MIN, *Northern Virginia Community College*
LYDIA ORTEGA, *Palo Alto College*
DEBORAH PAIGE, *Santa Fe Community College*
TIM PAYNE, *Shoreline Community College*
STANLEY J. PETERS, *Southeast Community College*
JOHN L. PISCIOTTA, *Baylor University*
RATHA RAMOO, *Diablo Valley College*
CRAIG ROGERS, *Canisius College*
JOSEPH SANTOS, *South Dakota State University*
STEVEN M. SCHAMBER, *St. Louis Community College, Meramec*
DAVID SCHUTTE, *Mountain View College*
JERRY SCHWARTZ, *Broward Community College*
MOURAD SEBTI, *Central Texas College*
PETER SHAW, *Tidewater Community College*
ROBERT L. SCHOFFNER III, *Central Piedmont Community College*
LARRY SINGELL, *University of Oregon*
ARLENA SULLIVAN, *Jones County Junior College*
ERIC TAYLOR, *Central Piedmont Community College*
KEITH ULRICH, *Valencia Community College*
MICHAEL VARDANYAN, *Binghamton University*
ROBERT WHAPLES, *Wake Forest University*
MARK WEINSTOCK, *Pace University*
WENDY WYSOCKI, *Monroe County Community College*

## ▶ CONSULTANT BOARD

We received guidance on content, organization, figure treatment, and design from a dedicated Consultant Board:

GEOFFREY BLACK, *Boise State University*
JEFF BOOKWALTER, *University of Montana*
AMY CRAMER, *Pima Community College and University of Arizona*
HERB ELLIOTT, *Allan Hancock College*
HARRY ELLIS, *University of North Texas*
WILLIAM HALLAGAN, *Washington State University*
R. PETER PARCELLS, *Whitman College*
TED SCHEINMAN, *Mount Hood Community College*
DAVID SCHUTTE, *Mountain View College*
PETER MARK SHAW, *Tidewater Community College*

## ▶ REVIEWERS OF THE CURRENT EDITION

The guidance and recommendations from the following professors helped us develop the revision plans for this new edition:

### California
ANTONIO AVALOS, *California State University, Fresno*
PETER BOELMAN-LOPEZ, *Riverside Community College*
PEGGY CRANE, *Southwestern College*
JOSE L. ESTEBAN, *Palomar College*
E. B. GENDEL, *Woodbury University*
RATHA RAMOO, *Diablo Valley College*
GREG ROSE, *Sacramento City College*

### Florida
ERIC P. CHIANG, *Florida Atlantic University*
GEORGE GREENLEE, *St. Petersburg College, Clearwater*
STEPHEN MORRELL, *Barry University*
CARL SCHMERTMANN, *Florida State University*
MICHAEL VIERK, *Florida International University*
ANDREA ZANTER, *Hillsborough Community College*

### Georgia
ASHLEY HARMON, *Southeastern Technical College*

### Illinois
DIANE ANSTINE, *North Central College*
ROSA LEA DANIELSON, *College of DuPage*
CHUCK SICOTTE, *Rock Valley College*

### Iowa
SAUL MEKIES, *Kirkwood Community College, Iowa City*

### Maryland
GRETCHEN MESTER, *Anne Arundel Community College*

### Massachusetts
BRIAN DEURIARTE, *Middlesex Community College*
MARLENE KIM, *University of Massachusetts, Boston*

### Michigan
BHARATI BASU, *Central Michigan University*

SCANLON ROMER, *Delta College*
WENDY WYSOCKI, *Monroe Community College*

### Minnesota
MIKE McILHON, *Augsburg College*
RICHARD MILANI, *Hibbing Community College*

### Mississippi
ARLENA SULLIVAN, *Jones County Junior College*

### Missouri
DENISE KUMMER, *St. Louis Community College*
STEVEN M. SCHAMBER, *St. Louis Community College, Meramec*
ELIAS SHUKRALLA, *St. Louis Community College, Meramec*
KEITH ULRICH, *Valencia Community College*

### Nebraska
THEODORE LARSEN, *University of Nebraska, Kearney*
TIMOTHY R. MITTAN, *Southeast Community College*

### Nevada
CHARLES OKEKE, *College of Southern Nevada*

### New Jersey
LEN ANYANWU, *Union County College*
RICHARD COMERFORD, *Bergen Community College*
BRIAN DE URIARTE, *Middlesex County College*

### New York
FARHAD AMEEN, *State University of New York, Westchester Community College*
BARBARA CONNELLY, *Westchester Community College*
SERGE S. GRUSHCHIN, *ASA College of Advanced Technology*
MARIE KRATOCHVIL, *Nassau Community College*
CRAIG ROGERS, *Canisius College*
MICHAEL VARDANYAN, *Binghamton University*

### North Carolina
MICHAEL G. GOODE, *Central Piedmont Community College*
DIANE TYNDALL, *Craven Community College*

### Ohio
JEFF ANKROM, *Wittenberg University*

### Oregon
LARRY SINGELL, *University of Oregon*

### South Carolina
FRANK GARLAND, *Tri-County Technical College*
WOODROW W. HUGHES, JR., *Converse College*

### Tennessee
NIRMALENDU DEBNATH, *Lane College*
QUENTON PULLIAM, *Nashville State Technical College*
ROSE RUBIN, *University of Memphis*

### Texas
JACK BUCCO, *Austin Community College*
MICHAEL I. DUKE, *Blinn College*

S. Aun Hassan, *Texas Tech University*
Randy Methenitis, *Richland College*
Lydia Ortega, *Palo Alto College*
Joshua Pickrell, *South Plains College*
John Pisciotta, *Baylor University*
Dave Shorrow, *Richland College*
Inske Zandvliet, *Brookhaven College*

## Utah
Ali Hekmat, *College of Eastern Utah*

## Virginia
James Brumbaugh, *Lord Fairfax Community College, Middleton Campus*
Michael G. Heslop, *North Virginia Community College*
George Hoffer, *Virginia Commonwealth University*
John Min, *North Virginia Community College, Alexandria*
Shannon K. Mitchell, *Virginia Commonwealth University*

## Washington
William Hallagan, *Washington State University*
Mark Wylie, *Spokane Falls Community College*

# ▶ REVIEWERS OF PREVIOUS EDITIONS

We benefited from the assistance of many dedicated professors who reviewed all or parts of previous editions in various stages of development:

## Alabama
James Swofford, *University of South Alabama*

## Alaska
Paul Johnson, *University of Alaska, Anchorage*

## Arizona
Pete Mavrokordatos, *Tarrant County College/University of Phoenix*
Evan Tanner, *Thunderbird, The American Graduate School of International Management*
Donald Wells, *University of Arizona*

## California
Collette Barr, *Santa Barbara Community College*
Matthew Brown, *Santa Clara University*
Peggy Crane, *San Diego State University*
Albert B. Culver, *California State University, Chico*
E.B. Gendel, *Woodbury University*
Charles W. Haase, *San Francisco State University*
John Henry, *California State University, Sacramento*
George Jensen, *California State University, Los Angeles*
Janis Kea, *West Valley College*
Rose Kilburn, *Modesto Junior College*
Philip King, *San Francisco State University*

Anthony Lima, *California State University, Hayward*
Bret McMurran, *Chaffey College*
Rahmat Mozayan, *Heald College, California*
Jon J. Nadenichek, *California State University, Northridge*
Alex Obiya, *San Diego City College*
Jack W. Osman, *San Francisco State University*
Stephen Perez, *California State University, Sacramento*
Kurt Schwabe, *University of California, Riverside*
Terri Sexton, *California State University, Sacramento*
Xiaochuan Song, *San Diego Mesa College*
Ed Sorensen, *San Francisco State University*
Rodney Swanson, *University of California, Los Angeles*
Daniel Villegas, *California Polytechnic State University*

## Connecticut
John A. Jascot, *Capital Community Technical College*

## Delaware
Lawrence Stelmach, *Delaware Valley College*

## Florida
Irma de Alonso, *Florida International University*
Jay Bhattacharya, *Okaloosa-Walton Community College*
Edward Bierhanzl, *Florida A&M University*
David Figlio, *University of Florida*
Martine Duchatelet, *Barry University*
Martin Markovich, *Florida A&M University*
Thomas McCaleb, *Florida State University*
Garvin Smith, *Daytona Beach Community College*
Noel Smith, *Palm Beach Community College*
Virginia York, *Gulf Coast Community College*

## Georgia
Steven F. Koch, *Georgia Southern University*
L. Wayne Plumly, Jr., *Valdosta State University*
Greg Trandel, *University of Georgia*

## Hawaii
Barbara Ross-Pfeiffer, *Kapiolani Community College*

## Idaho
Charles Scott Benson Jr. , *Idaho State University*
Tesa Stegner, *Idaho State University*

## Illinois
Sel Dibooglu, *Southern Illinois University*
Linda Ghent, *Eastern Illinois University*
Gary Langer, *Roosevelt University*
Nampeang Pingkarawat, *Chicago State University*
Dennis Shannon, *Belleville Area College*

## Indiana
John L. Conant, *Indiana State University*
Mousumi Duttaray, *Indiana State University*

JAMES T. KYLE, *Indiana State University*
VIRGINIA SHINGLETON, *Valparaiso University*

## Iowa
JONATHAN O. IKOBA, *Scott Community College*

## Kansas
CARL PARKER, *Fort Hays State University*
JAMES RAGAN, *Kansas State University*
TRACY M. TURNER, *Kansas State University*

## Kentucky
DAVID EATON, *Murray State University*
JOHN ROBERTSON, *University of Kentucky*

## Louisiana
JOHN PAYNE BIGELOW, *Louisiana State University*
SANG LEE, *Southeastern Louisiana University*
RICHARD STAHL, *Louisiana State University*

## Maine
GEORGE SCHATZ, *Maine Maritime Academy*

## Maryland
IRVIN WEINTRAUB, *Towson State University*

## Massachusetts
DAN GEORGIANNA, *University of Massachusetts, Dartmouth*
JAMES E. HARTLEY, *Mount Holyoke College*
MARK SIEGLER, *Williams College*
GILBERT WOLFE, *Middlesex Community College*

## Michigan
CHRISTINE AMSLER, *Michigan State University*
NORMAN CURE, *Macomb Community College*
SUSAN LINZ, *Michigan State University*
ROBERT TANSKY, *St. Clair County Community College*

## Missouri
DUANE EBERHARDT, *Missouri Southern State College*
DAVID GILLETTE, *Truman State University*
BRAD HOPPES, *Southwest Missouri State University*

## Nebraska
STANLEY J. PETERS, *Southeast Community College*
BROCK WILLIAMS, *Metropolitan Community College*

## Nevada
STEPHEN MILLER, *University of Nevada, Las Vegas*

## New Jersey
JOHN GRAHAM, *Rutgers University*
PAUL C. HARRIS, JR., *Camden County College*
CALVIN HOY, *County College of Morris*
TAGHI RAMIN, *William Paterson University*

## New Mexico
CARL ENOMOTO, *New Mexico State University*

## New York
KARIJIT K. ARORA, *Le Moyne College*
ALEX AZARCHS, *Pace University*
KATHLEEN K. BROMLEY, *Monroe Community College*
SUSAN GLANZ, *St. John's University*
ROBERT HERMAN, *Nassau Community College*
MARIANNE LOWERY, *Erie Community College*
JEANNETTE MITCHELL, *Rochester Institute of Technology*
TED MUZIO, *St. John's University*
FRED TYLER, *Fordham University*

## North Carolina
KATIE CANTY, *Cape Fear Community College*
LEE CRAIG, *North Carolina State University*
HOSSEIN GHOLAMI, *Fayetteville Technical Community College*
CHARLES M. OLDHAM, JR., *Fayetteville Technical Community College*
LINDA GHENT, *East Carolina University*
HOSSEIN GHOLAMI, *Fayetteville Technical Community College*
RANDALL PARKER, *East Carolina University*
CHESTER WATERS, *Durham Technical Community College*
JAMES WHEELER, *North Carolina State University*

## North Dakota
SCOTT BLOOM, *North Dakota State University*

## Ohio
FATMA ABDEL-RAOUF, *Cleveland State University*
TAGHI T. KERMANI, *Youngstown State University*

## Oklahoma
JEFF HOLT, *Tulsa Community College*
MARTY LUDLUM, *Oklahoma City Community College*
DAN RICKMAN, *Oklahoma State University*

## Oregon
TOM CARROLL, *Central Oregon Community College*
JOHN FARRELL, *Oregon State University*
DAVID FIGLIO, *University of Oregon*
RANDY R. GRANT, *Linfield College*

## Pennsylvania
KEVIN A. BAIRD, *Montgomery County Community College*
ED COULSON, *Pennsylvania State University*
TAHANY NAGGAR, *West Chester University*
ABDULWAHAB SRAIHEEN, *Kutztown University*

## South Carolina
DONALD BALCH, *University of South Carolina*
CALVIN BLACKWELL, *College of Charleston*
JANICE BOUCHER BREUER, *University of South Carolina*
CHARLOTTE DENISE HIXSON, *Midlands Technical College*
MIREN IVANKOVIC, *Southern Wesleyan University*
CHIRINJEV PETERSON, *Greenville Technical College*
DENISE TURNAGE, *Midlands Technical College*
CHAD TURNER, *Clemson University*

### South Dakota
JOSEPH SANTOS, *South Dakota State University*

### Texas
RASHID AL-HMOUD, *Texas Technical University*
MAHAMUDU BAWUMIA, *Baylor University*
CINDY CANNON, *North Harris College*
DAVID L. COBERLY, *Southwest Texas State University*
GHAZI DUWAJI, *University of Texas, Arlington*
HARRY ELLIS, *University of North Texas*
THOMAS JEITSCHKO, *Texas A&M University*
JESSICA MCCRAW, *University of Texas, Arlington*
WILLIAM NEILSON, *Texas A&M University*
MICHAEL NELSON, *Texas A&M University*
PAUL OKELLO, *University of Texas, Arlington*
JAMES R. VANBEEK, *Blinn College*

### Utah
JEFF DAVIS, *ITT Techinical Institute, Utah*
LOWELL GLENN, *Utah Valley State College*

### Virginia
SHERYL BALL, *Virginia Polytechnic Institute and State University*
BRUCE BRUNTON, *James Madison University*
MELANIE MARKS, *Longwood College*
THOMAS J. MEEKS, *Virginia State University*

### Australia
HAK YOUN KIM, *Monash University*

## ▶ CLASS TESTERS

A special acknowledgment goes to the instructors who were willing to class-test drafts of early editions in different stages of development. They provided us with instant feedback on parts that worked and parts that needed changes:

SHERYL BALL, *Virginia Polytechnic Institute and State University*
JOHN CONSTANTINE, *University of California, Davis*
JOHN FARRELL, *Oregon State University*
JAMES HARTLEY, *Mt. Holyoke College*
KAILASH KHANDKE, *Furman College*
PETER LINDERT, *University of California, Davis*
LOUIS MAKOWSKI, *University of California, Davis*
BARBARA ROSS-PFEIFFER, *Kapiolani Community College*

Our greatest appreciation goes out to Carlos Aguilar and his economics students from El Paso Community College, who gave us their feedback and evaluations with comparable textbooks. The students provided us with positive feedback and constructive criticism that helped us prepare the Third Edition:

ERIK ACONA
ERICA AVILA

JAIME BERMUDEZ
ISRAEL CASTILLO
MARIBELL CASTILLO
SARAH DAVIS
REBEKAH DENNIS
MICHELE DONOHOE
EMMANUEL ECK
PATRICK ESPINOZA
EDWARD ESTRADA
KIM GARDNER
ALEISA GARZA
DANIEL HEITZ
LAURA HEREBIA
HILDA HOWARD
MELANIE JOHNSON
BRENDA JORDAN
EUGENE JORDAN
VANESSA LARA
HARMONY LOPEZ
STACEY LUCAS
MARIA LYNCH
SINDY MCELVANY
ROGER MITCHELL
BENNY ONTIVEROS
LOUIE ORTEGA
KAREN SEITZ
ANA SMITH
BEVERLY STEPHENS
ADRIAN TERRAZAS
CHRIS WRIGHT

## ▶ FOCUS GROUPS

We want to thank the participants who took part in the focus groups for the first and second editions; they helped us see the manuscript from a fresh perspective:

CARLOS AQUILAR, *El Paso Community College*
JIM BRADLEY, *University of South Carolina*
THOMAS COLLUM, *Northeastern Illinois University*
DAVID CRAIG, *Westark College*
JEFF HOLT, *Tulsa Junior College*
THOMAS JEITSCHKO, *Texas A & M University*
GARY LANGER, *Roosevelt University*
MARK MCCLEOD, *Virginia Polytechnic Institute and State University*
TOM MCKINNON, *University of Arkansas*
AMY MEYERS, *Parkland Community College*
HASSAN MOHAMMADI, *Illinois State University*
JOHN MORGAN, *College of Charleston*
NORM PAUL, *San Jancinto Community College*

NAMPEANG PINGKARATWAT, *Chicago State University*
SCANLAN ROMER, *Delta Community College*
BARBARA ROSS-PFEIFFER, *Kapiolani Community College*
ZAHRA SADERION, *Houston Community College*
VIRGINIA SHINGLETON, *Valparaiso University*

JIM SWOFFORD, *University of South Alabama*
JANET WEST, *University of Nebraska–Omaha*
LINDA WILSON, *University of Texas–Arlington*
MICHAEL YOUNGBLOOD, *Rock Valley Community College*

# A WORLD OF THANKS . . .

We would also like to acknowledge the team of dedicated authors who contributed to the various ancillaries that accompany this book: Daniel Condon of Dominican University, David Eaton of Murray State University, Hadley Hartman of Santa Fe Community College, Randy Methenitis of Richland College, Dan Martinez of Salt Lake Community College, David Schutte of Mountain View College, James Swofford of the University of South Alabama, and Fernando Quijano of Dickinson State University, and Yvonn Quijano.

For the Third Edition, Suzanne Grappi, Cindy Zonneveld, and Maria Lange turned our manuscript pages into a beautiful published book. Ben Paris, executive producer of assessment programs, critiqued the test-item files and helped the supplement authors improve the quality of those supplements. Karen Misler coordinated the extensive supplement package that accompanies the book. We want to single out two people for special mention. Our development editor, Lena Buonanno, did a terrific job identifying parts of the book that could be improved for the third edition and had many suggestions on how to improve it. Finally, we are indebted to David Alexander, executive editor at Prentice Hall, who guided the project from start to finish.

From the start, Prentice Hall provided us with first-class support and advice. In the first two editions, many people contributed to the project, including Leah Jewell, Rod Banister, P. J. Boardman, Marie McHale, Gladys Soto, Lisa Amato, Victoria Anderson, Cynthia Zonneveld, Kathleen McLellan, Sharon Koch, David Theisen, Steve Deitmer, and Christopher Bath.

Last but not least, we must thank our families, who have seen us disappear, sometimes physically and other times mentally, to spend hours wrapped up in our own world of principles of economics. A project of this magnitude is very absorbing, and our families have been particularly supportive in this endeavor.

ARTHUR O'SULLIVAN
STEVEN SHEFFRIN
STEPHEN PEREZ

# Survey of Economics

PRINCIPLES, APPLICATIONS, AND TOOLS

# 1

# Introduction: What Is Economics?

Economics is the science of choice, exploring the choices made by individuals and organizations. Over the last few centuries, these choices have led to substantial gains in the standard of living around the globe. The typical American household today has roughly seven times the income and purchasing power of a household 100 years ago. Our prosperity is the result of choices made by all sorts of people, including inventors, workers, entrepreneurs, and the people who saved money and loaned it to others to invest in machines and other tools of production. One reason we have prospered is greater efficiency: We have discovered better ways to use our resources—raw materials, time, and energy—to produce the goods and services we value.

As an illustration of changes in the standard of living and our growing prosperity, let's compare the way people listened to music in 1891 with how we listen today. You can buy an iPod Nano for $199 and fill it with 1,000 songs at $0.99 each. If you earn a wage of $15 per hour, it would take you about 80 hours of work to earn enough money to purchase and then fill an iPod. Back in 1891, the latest technological marvel was Thomas Edison's cylinder phonograph, which played music recorded on 4-inch cylinders. Imagine that you lived back then and wanted to get just as much music as you could fit on an iPod. Given the wages and prices in 1891, it would take you roughly 800 hours of work to earn enough money to buy the phonograph and all the cylinders. And if you wanted to keep your music with you, you would need 14 backpacks to carry all the cylinders.

Although prosperity and efficiency are widespread, they are not universal. In some parts of the world, many people live in poverty. For example, in sub-Saharan Africa, 290 million people—almost half the population—live on less than $1 per day. And in all nations of the world, inefficiencies still exist, with valuable resources being wasted. For example, each year the typical urban commuter in the United States wastes more than 47 hours and $84 worth of gasoline trapped in rush hour traffic.

- **scarcity**
  The resources we use to produce goods and services are limited.

- **economics**
  The study of choices when there is scarcity.

- **factors of production**
  The resources used to produce goods and services; also known as *production inputs*.

- **natural resources**
  Resources provided by nature and used to produce goods and services.

- **labor**
  The physical and mental effort people use to produce goods and services.

- **physical capital**
  The stock of equipment, machines, structures, and infrastructure that is used to produce goods and services.

- **human capital**
  The knowledge and skills acquired by a worker through education and experience.

- **entrepreneurship**
  The effort used to coordinate the factors of production—natural resources, labor, physical capital, and human capital—to produce and sell products.

Economics provides a framework to diagnose all sorts of problems faced by society and then helps create and evaluate various proposals to solve them. Economics can help us develop strategies to replace poverty with prosperity, and to replace waste with efficiency. In this chapter, we explain what economics is and how we all can use economic analysis to think about practical problems and solutions.

# 1.1 | WHAT IS ECONOMICS?

Economists use the word **scarcity** to convey the idea that resources—the things we use to produce goods and services—are limited, while human wants are unlimited. Therefore, we cannot produce everything that everyone wants. In the words of the Rolling Stones, "You can't always get what you want." **Economics** studies the choices we make when there is scarcity; it is all about trade-offs. Here are some examples of scarcity and the trade-offs associated with making choices:

- You have a limited amount of time. If you take a part-time job, each hour on the job means one less hour for study or play.
- A city has a limited amount of land. If the city uses an acre of land for a park, it has one less acre for housing, retailers, or industry.
- You have limited income this year. If you spend $17 on a music CD, that's $17 less you have to spend on other products or to save.

People produce goods (music CDs, houses, and parks) and services (the advice of physicians and lawyers) by using one or more of the following five **factors of production**, or *production inputs*, or simply *resources*:

- **Natural resources** are provided by nature. Some examples are fertile land, mineral deposits, oil and gas deposits, and water. Some economists refer to all types of natural resources as *land*.
- **Labor** is the physical and mental effort people use to produce goods and services.
- **Physical capital** is the stock of equipment, machines, structures, and infrastructure that is used to produce goods and services. Some examples are forklifts, machines, computers, factories, airports, roads, and fiber-optic cables.
- **Human capital** is the knowledge and skills acquired by a worker through education and experience. Every job requires some human capital: To be a surgeon, you must learn anatomy and acquire surgical skills. To be an accountant, you must learn the rules of accounting and acquire computer skills. To be a musician, you must learn to play an instrument.
- **Entrepreneurship** is the effort used to coordinate the factors of production—natural resources, labor, physical capital, and human capital—to produce and sell products. An entrepreneur comes up with an idea for a product, decides how to produce it, and raises the funds to bring it to the market. Some examples of entrepreneurs are Bill Gates of Microsoft, Steve Jobs of Apple Computer, Inc., Howard Schultz of Starbucks, and McDonald's founder Ray Kroc.

Given our limited resources, we make our choices in a variety of ways. Sometimes we make our decisions as individuals, and other times we participate in collective decision making, allowing the government and other organizations to choose for us. Many of our choices happen within *markets*, institutions or arrangements that enable us to buy and sell things. For example, most of us participate in the labor market, exchanging our time for money, and we all participate in consumer markets, exchanging money for food and clothing. But we make other choices outside markets—from our personal decisions about everyday life to our political choices about matters that concern society as a whole. What unites all these decisions is the notion of scarcity: We can't have it all; there are trade-offs.

Economists are always reminding us that there is scarcity—that there are trade-offs in everything we do. Suppose that in a conversation with your economics instructor you share your enthusiasm about an upcoming launch of the space shuttle. The economist may tell you that the resources used for the shuttle could have been used instead for an unmanned mission to Mars.

By introducing the notion of scarcity into your conversation, your instructor is simply reminding you that there are trade-offs, that one thing (a shuttle mission) is sacrificed for another (a Mars mission). Talking about alternatives is the first step in a process that can help us make better choices about how to use our resources. For example, we could compare the scientific benefits of a shuttle mission to the benefits of a Mars mission and choose the mission with the greater benefit.

## Positive Versus Normative Analysis

Economics doesn't tell us what to choose—shuttle mission or Mars mission—but simply helps us to understand the trade-offs. President Harry S. Truman once remarked,

> All my economists say, "On the one hand, . . .; On the other hand, . . ." Give me a one-handed economist!

An economist might say, "On the one hand, we could use a shuttle mission to do more experiments in the gravity-free environment of Earth's orbit; on the other hand, we could use a Mars mission to explore the possibility of life on other planets." In using both hands, the economist is not being evasive, but simply doing economics, discussing the alternative uses of our resources. The ultimate decision about how to use our resources—shuttle mission or Mars exploration—is the responsibility of citizens or their elected officials.

Most modern economics is based on **positive analysis**, which predicts the consequences of alternative actions by answering the question "What *is*?" or "What *will be*?" A second type of economic reasoning is normative in nature. **Normative analysis** answers the question "What *ought to be*?"

In Table 1.1, we compare positive questions to normative questions. Normative questions lie at the heart of policy debates. Economists contribute to policy debates by conducting positive analyses of the consequences of alternative actions. For example, an economist could predict the effects of an increase in the minimum wage on the number of people employed nationwide, the income of families with minimum-wage workers, and consumer prices. Armed with the conclusions of the

• **positive analysis**
Answers the question "What is?" or "What will be?"

• **normative analysis**
Answers the question "What *ought to be*?"

## Table 1.1 | COMPARING POSITIVE AND NORMATIVE QUESTIONS

| Positive Questions | Normative Questions |
|---|---|
| • If the government increases the minimum wage, how many workers will lose their jobs? | • Should the government increase the minimum wage? |
| • If two office-supply firms merge, will the price of office supplies increase? | • Should the government block the merger of two office-supply firms? |
| • How does a college education affect a person's productivity and earnings? | • Should the government subsidize a college education? |
| • How do consumers respond to a cut in income taxes? | • Should the government cut taxes to stimulate the economy? |
| • If a nation restricts shoe imports, who benefits and who bears the cost? | • Should the government restrict imports? |

economist's positive analysis, citizens and policy makers could then make a normative decision about whether to increase the minimum wage. Similarly, an economist could study the projects that could be funded with $1 billion in foreign aid, predicting the effects of each project on the income per person in an African country. Armed with this positive analysis, policy makers could then decide which projects to support.

Economists don't always reach the same conclusions in their positive analyses. The disagreements often concern the magnitude of a particular effect. For example, most economists agree that an increase in the minimum wage will cause unemployment, but there is disagreement about how many people would lose their jobs. Similarly, economists agree that spending money to improve the education system in Africa will increase productivity and income, but there is disagreement about the size of the increase in income.

## The Three Key Economic Questions: What, How, and Who?

Economic decisions are made at every level in society. Individuals decide what products to buy, what occupations to pursue, and how much money to save. Firms decide what goods and services to produce and how to produce them. Governments decide what projects and programs to complete and how to pay for them. The choices made by individuals, firms, and governments answer three questions:

**1** *What products do we produce?* Trade-offs exist: If a hospital uses its resources to perform more heart transplants, it has fewer resources to care for premature infants.

**2** *How do we produce the products?* Alternative means of production are available: Power companies can produce electricity with coal, natural gas, or wind power. Professors can teach in large lecture halls or small classrooms.

**3** *Who consumes the products?* We must decide how the products of society are distributed. If some people earn more money than others, should they consume more goods? How much money should the government take from the rich and give to the poor?

As we'll see later in the book, most of these decisions are made in markets, with prices playing a key role in determining what products we produce, how we produce them, and who gets the products.

## Economic Models

Economists use *economic models* to explore the choices people make and the consequences of those choices. An economic model is a simplified representation of an economic environment, with all but the essential features of the environment eliminated. An **economic models** is an abstraction from reality that enables us to focus our attention on what really matters. As we'll see throughout the book, most economic models use graphs to represent the economic environment.

To see the rationale for economic modeling, consider an architectural model. An architect builds a scale model of a new building and uses the model to show how the building will fit on a plot of land and blend with nearby buildings. The model shows the exterior features of the building, but not the interior features. We can ignore the interior features because they are unimportant for the task at hand—seeing how the building will fit into the local environment.

Economists build models to explore decision making by individuals, firms, and other organizations. For example, we can use a model of a profit-maximizing firm to predict how a firm will respond to increased competition. If a new car-stereo store opens up in your town, will the old firms be passive and simply accept smaller market shares, or will they aggressively cut their prices to try to drive the new rival

• **economic model**
A simplified representation of an economic environment, often employing a graph.

out of business? The model of the firm includes the monetary benefits and costs of doing business, and assumes that firms want to make as much money as possible. Although there may be other motives in the business world—to have fun or help the world—the economic model ignores these other motives. The model focuses our attention on the profit motive and how it affects a firm's response to increased competition.

# 1.2 | ECONOMIC ANALYSIS AND MODERN PROBLEMS

Economic analysis provides important insights into real-world problems. To explain how we can use economic analysis in problem solving, we provide three examples. You'll see these examples again in more detail later in the book.

## Economic View of Traffic Congestion

Consider first the problem of traffic congestion. According to the Texas Transportation Institute, the typical U.S. commuter wastes about 47 hours per year because of traffic congestion.[1] In some cities, the time wasted by the typical commuter is much greater: 93 hours in Los Angeles, 72 hours in San Francisco, and 63 hours in Houston. In addition to time lost, we also waste 2.3 billion gallons of gasoline and diesel fuel each year.

To an economist, the diagnosis of the congestion problem is straightforward. When you drive onto a busy highway during rush hour, your car takes up space and decreases the distance between the vehicles on the highway. The normal reaction to a shorter distance between moving cars is to slow down. So when you enter the highway, you force other commuters to spend more time on the highway. If each of your 900 fellow commuters spends just 2 extra seconds on the highway, you will increase the total travel time by 30 minutes. In deciding whether to use the highway, you will presumably ignore these costs that you impose on others. Similarly, your fellow commuters ignore the cost they impose on you and others when they enter the highway. Because no single commuter pays the full cost, too many people use the highway, and everyone wastes time.

One possible solution to the congestion problem is to force people to pay for using the road, just as they pay for gasoline and tires. The government could impose a congestion tax of $8 per trip on rush-hour commuters and use a debit card system to collect the tax: Every time a car passes a checkpoint, a transponder would charge the commuter's card. Traffic volume during rush hours would then decrease as travelers (a) shift their travel to off-peak times, (b) switch to ride sharing and mass transit, and (c) shift their travel to less congested routes. The job for the economist is to compute the appropriate congestion tax and predict the consequences of imposing the tax.

## Economic View of Poverty in Africa

Consider next the issue of poverty in Africa. In the final two decades of the twentieth century, the world economy grew rapidly, and the average per capita income (income per person) increased by about 35 percent. By contrast, the economies of poverty-stricken sub-Saharan Africa shrank, and per capita income decreased by about 6 percent. Africa is the world's second-largest continent in both area and population and accounts for more than 12 percent of the world's human population. Figure 1.1 shows a map of Africa. The countries of sub-Saharan Africa are highlighted in yellow.

Economists have found that as a nation's economy grows, its poorest households share in the general prosperity.[2] Therefore, one way to reduce poverty in sub-Saharan

Africa is the world's second-largest continent in both area and population, and
accounts for more than 12 percent of the
world's human population. The countries
of sub-Saharan Africa are highlighted in
yellow.
*SOURCE: web.worldbank.org/WBSITE/
EXTERNAL/COUNTRIES/AFRICA*

Sub-Saharan
Africa

Africa would be to increase economic growth. Economic growth occurs when a country expands its production facilities (machinery and factories), improves its public
infrastructure (highways and water systems), widens educational opportunities, and
adopts new technology.

The recent experience of sub-Saharan Africa is somewhat puzzling because in
the last few decades the region has expanded educational opportunities and
received large amounts of foreign aid. Some recent work by economists on the
sources of growth suggests that institutions such as the legal system and the regulatory environment play key roles in economic growth.[3] In sub-Saharan Africa, a
simple legal dispute about a small debt takes about 30 months to resolve, compared
to five months in the United States. In Mozambique, it takes 174 days to complete
the procedures required to set up a business, compared to just two days in Canada.
In many cases, institutions impede rather than encourage the sort of investment
and risk taking—entrepreneurship—that causes economic growth and reduces
poverty. As a consequence, economists and policy makers are exploring ways to
reform the region's institutions. They are also challenged with choosing among
development projects that will generate the biggest economic boost per dollar
spent—the biggest bang per buck.

### Economic View of Japan's Economic Problems

Consider next the economic problems experienced by Japan in the last decade. Following World War II, Japan grew rapidly, with per capita income increasing by about
4 percent per year between 1950 and 1992. But in 1992, the economy came to a
screeching halt. For the next 10 years, per capita income either decreased or
increased slightly. In 1995, the prices of all sorts of goods—including consumer
goods and housing—actually started to decrease, and the downward slide continued
for years. In an economy with declining prices, consumers expect lower prices
tomorrow, so they are reluctant to buy goods and services today. Business managers
are reluctant to borrow money to invest in production facilities, because if the prices
of their products drop they might not have enough money to repay the loans.

The challenge for economists was to develop a set of policies to get the Japanese economy moving again. Economists responded by designing policies to stimulate spending by consumers and businesses and to make needed changes to the Japanese financial system. Although it was a slow process, economic and political reforms have put the Japanese economy on a sound footing that will support future economic growth.

# 1.3 | THE ECONOMIC WAY OF THINKING

How do economists think about problems and decision making? The economic way of thinking is best summarized by British economist John Maynard Keynes (1883–1946)[4]:

> The theory of economics does not furnish a body of settled conclusions immediately applicable to policy. It is a method rather than a doctrine, an apparatus of the mind, a technique of thinking which helps its possessor draw correct conclusions.

Let's look at the four elements of the economic way of thinking.

## 1. Use Assumptions to Simplify

Economists use assumptions to make things simpler and focus attention on what really matters. If you use a road map to plan a car trip from Seattle to San Francisco, you make two unrealistic assumptions to simplify your planning:

- The earth is flat: The flat road map doesn't show the curvature of Earth.
- The roads are flat: The standard road map doesn't show hills and valleys.

Instead of a map, you could use a globe that shows all the topographical features between Seattle and San Francisco, but you don't need those details to plan your trip. A map, with its unrealistic assumptions, will suffice, because the curvature of the earth and the topography of the highways are irrelevant to your trip. Although your analysis of the road trip is based on two unrealistic assumptions, that does not mean your analysis is invalid. Similarly, if economic analysis is based on unrealistic assumptions, that doesn't mean the analysis is faulty.

What if you decide to travel by bike instead of by automobile? Now the assumption of flat roads really matters, unless of course you are eager to pedal up and down mountains. If you use a standard map, and thus assume there are no mountains between the two cities, you may inadvertently pick a mountainous route instead of a flat one. In this case, the simplifying assumption makes a difference. The lesson is that we must think carefully about whether a simplifying assumption is truly harmless.

## 2. Isolate Variables—*Ceteris Paribus*

Economic analysis often involves *variables* and how they affect one another. A **variable** is a measure of something that can take on different values. Economists are interested in exploring relationships between two variables—for example, the relationship between the price of apples and the quantity of apples consumers purchase. Of course, the quantity of apples purchased depends on many other variables, including the consumer's income. To explore the relationship between the quantity and price of apples, we must assume that the consumer's income—and anything else that influences apple purchases—doesn't change.

Alfred Marshall (1842–1924) was a British economist who refined the economic model of supply and demand and provided a label for this process.[5] He picked one

• **variable**
A measure of something that can take on different values.

• *ceteris paribus*
The Latin expression meaning other variables being held fixed.

variable that affected apple purchases (price) and threw the other variable (income) into what he called the "pound" (in Marshall's time, the "pound" was an enclosure for holding stray cattle; nowadays, a pound is for stray dogs). That variable waited in the pound while Marshall examined the influence of the first variable. Marshall labeled the pound ***ceteris paribus***, the Latin expression meaning that other variables are held fixed:

> . . . the existence of other tendencies is not denied, but their disturbing effect is neglected for a time. The more the issue is narrowed, the more exactly can it be handled.

This book contains many statements about the relationship between two variables. For example, the quantity of computers produced by Dell depends on the price of computers, the wage of computer workers, and the cost of microchips. When we say, "An increase in the price of computers increases the quantity of computers produced," we are assuming that the other two variables—the wage and the cost of microchips—do not change. That is, we apply the *ceteris paribus* assumption.

## 3. Think at the Margin

Economists often consider how a small change in one variable affects another variable and what impact that has on people's decision making. In other words, if circumstances change only slightly, how will people respond? A small, one-unit change in value is called a **marginal change**. The key feature of marginal change is that the first variable changes by only one unit. For example, you might ask, "If I study just one more hour, by how much will my exam score increase?" Economists call this process "thinking at the margin." Thinking at the margin is like thinking on the edge. You will encounter marginal thinking throughout this book. Here are some other marginal questions:

• marginal change
A small, one-unit change in value.

- If I study one more hour for an exam, by how much will my grade increase?
- If I stay in school and earn another degree, by how much will my lifetime earnings increase?
- If a car dealer hires one more sales associate, how many more cars will the dealer sell?

As we'll see in the next chapter, economists use the answer to a marginal question as a first step in deciding whether to do more or less of something.

## 4. Rational People Respond to Incentives

A key assumption of most economic analysis is that people act rationally, meaning that they act in their own self-interest. Scottish philosopher Adam Smith (1723–1790), who is also considered the founder of economics, wrote that he discovered within humankind:[6]

> a desire of bettering our condition, a desire which, though generally calm and dispassionate, comes with us from the womb, and never leaves us until we go to the grave.

Smith didn't say that people are motivated exclusively by self-interest, but rather that self-interest is more powerful than kindness or altruism. In this book, we will assume that people act in their own self-interest. Rational people respond to incentives. When the payoff, or benefit, from doing something changes, people change their behavior to get the benefit.

# APPLICATION

## PEDALING FOR TELEVISION TIME

Do people respond to incentives?

To illustrate the notion that people are rational and respond to incentives, consider an experiment conducted by researchers at St. Luke's Roosevelt Hospital in New York City. The researchers addressed the following question: If a child must pedal a stationary bicycle to run a television set, will he watch less TV? The researchers randomly assigned obese children, ages 8 to 12, to two types of TVs. The first type of TV had a stationary bicycle in front of it, but the TV operated independently of the bicycle: No pedaling was required to operate the TV. In contrast, the second type of TV worked only if the child pedaled a bike facing the TV. The kids in the control group (no pedaling required) watched an average of 21 hours of TV per week, while the kids in the treatment group (pedaling required) watched only 2 hours per week. In other words, kids respond to incentives, watching less TV when the cost of watching is higher.
*Related to Exercise 3.4.*

SOURCE: Myles Faith et al., "Effects of Contingent Television on Physical Activity and Television Viewing in Obese Children," *Pediatrics*, vol. 107, May 2001, pp. 1043–1048; Nanci Hellmich, "Pedaling a Solution for Couch-Potato Kids," *USA Today*, April 19, 1999, p. 1.

# 1.4 | PREVIEW OF COMING ATTRACTIONS: MACROECONOMICS

The field of economics is divided into two categories: macroeconomics and microeconomics. **Macroeconomics** is the study of the nation's economy as a whole; it focuses on the issues of inflation, unemployment, and economic growth. These issues are regularly discussed on Web sites, in newspapers, and on television. Macroeconomics explains why economies grow and change and why economic growth is sometimes interrupted. Let's look at three ways we can use macroeconomics.

- **macroeconomics**
  The study of the nation's economy as a whole; focuses on the issues of inflation, unemployment, and economic growth.

## To Understand Why Economies Grow

As we discussed earlier in the chapter, the world economy has been growing in recent decades, with per capita income increasing by about 1.5 percent per year. Increases in income translate into a higher standard of living for consumers—better cars, houses, and clothing and more options for food, entertainment, and travel. People in a growing economy can consume more of all goods and services because the economy has more of the resources needed to produce these products. Macroeconomics explains why some of these resources increase over time and how an increase in resources translates into a higher standard of living. Let's look at a practical question about economic growth.

## LONDON SOLVES ITS CONGESTION PROBLEM

**APPLYING THE CONCEPTS #2:** What is the role of prices in allocating resources?

To illustrate the economic way of thinking, let's consider again how an economist would approach the problem of traffic congestion. Recall that each driver on the highway slows down other drivers but ignores these time costs when deciding whether to use the highway. If the government imposes a congestion tax to reduce congestion during rush hour, the question for the economist is: How high should the tax be?

To determine the appropriate congestion tax, an economist would assume that people respond to incentives and use the three other elements of the economic way of thinking:

- **Use assumptions to simplify.** To simplify the problem, we would assume that every car has the same effect on the travel time of other cars. Of course, this is unrealistic, because people drive cars of different sizes in different ways. But the alternative—looking at the effects of each car on travel speeds—would needlessly complicate the analysis.

- **Isolate variables—*ceteris paribus*.** To focus attention on the effects of a congestion tax on the number of cars using the highway, we would make the *ceteris paribus* assumption that everything else that affects travel behavior—the price of gasoline, bus fares, and consumer income—remains fixed.

- **Think at the margin.** To think at the margin, we would estimate the effects of adding one more car to the highway. The marginal question is: If we add one more car to the highway, by how much does the total travel time for commuters increase?

Once we answer this question, we could determine the cost imposed by the marginal driver. If the marginal driver forces each of the 900 commuters to spend two extra seconds on the highway, total travel time increases by 30 minutes. If the value of time is, say, $16 per hour, the appropriate congestion tax would be $8.

If the idea of charging people for using roads seems odd, consider the city of London, which for decades had experienced the worst congestion in Europe. In February 2003, the city imposed an $8 tax per day to drive in the city between 7:00 A.M. and 6:30 P.M. The tax reduced traffic volume and cut travel times for cars and buses in half. The congestion tax reduced the waste and inefficiency of congestion, and the city's economy thrived. Given the success of London's ongoing congestion tax, other cities, including Toronto, Singapore, and San Diego, have implemented congestion pricing. *Related to Exercise 3.5.*

Why do some countries grow much faster than others? Between 1960 and 2001, the economic growth rate was 2.2 percent per year in the United States, compared to 2.3 percent in Mexico and 2.7 percent in France. But in some countries, the economy actually shrunk, and per capita income dropped. Among the countries with declining income were Romania, Sierra Leone, Haiti, and Zambia.

In the fastest-growing countries, citizens save a large fraction of the money they earn. Firms can then borrow the funds saved to purchase machinery and equipment that make their workers more productive. The fastest-growing countries also have well-educated workforces, allowing firms to quickly adopt new technologies that increase worker productivity.

## To Understand Economic Fluctuations

All economies, including ones that experience a general trend of rising per capita income, are subject to economic fluctuations, including periods when the economy shrinks. During an economic downturn, some of the economy's resources—natural resources, labor, physical capital, human capital, and entrepreneurship—are idle. Some workers are unemployed, and some factories and stores are closed. By contrast, sometimes the economy grows too rapidly, causing prices to rise. Macroeconomics helps us understand why these fluctuations occur—why the economy sometimes cools and sometimes overheats—and what the government can do to moderate the fluctuations. Let's look at a practical question about economic fluctuations.

Should Congress and the president do something to reduce the unemployment rate? For example, should the government cut taxes to stimulate consumer spending and thus encourage firms to hire more workers to produce the additional goods and services? If unemployment is very high, the government may want to reduce it. However, it is important not to reduce the unemployment rate too much, because, as we'll see later in the book, a low unemployment rate will cause inflation.

## To Make Informed Business Decisions

A third reason for studying macroeconomics is to make informed business decisions. As we'll see later in the book, the government uses various policies to influence interest rates and the inflation rate. A manager who intends to borrow money for a new factory or store could use knowledge of macroeconomics to predict the effects of current public policies on interest rates and then decide whether to borrow the money now or later. Similarly, a manager must keep an eye on the inflation rate to help decide how much to charge for the firm's products and how much to pay workers. A manager who studies macroeconomics will be better equipped to understand the complexities of interest rates and inflation and how they affect the firm.

## 1.5 | PREVIEW OF COMING ATTRACTIONS: MICROECONOMICS

**Microeconomics** is the study of the choices made by households (an individual or a group of people living together), firms, and government and how these choices affect the markets for goods and services. Let's look at three ways we can use microeconomic analysis.

• **microeconomics**
The study of the choices made by households, firms, and government and how these choices affect the markets for goods and services.

## To Understand Markets and Predict Changes

One reason for studying microeconomics is to better understand how markets work and to predict how various events affect the prices and quantities of products in markets. In this book, we answer many practical questions about markets and how they operate. Let's look at one practical question that can be answered with some simple economic analysis.

How would a tax on beer affect the number of highway deaths among young adults? Research has shown that the number of highway fatalities among young adults is roughly proportional to the total amount of beer consumed by that group. A tax on beer would make the product more expensive, and young adults, like other beer drinkers, would therefore consume less of it. Consequently, a tax that decreases beer consumption by 10 percent will decrease highway deaths among young adults by about 10 percent, too.

### To Make Personal and Managerial Decisions

On the personal level, we use economic analysis to decide how to spend our time, what career to pursue, and how to spend and save the money we earn. As workers, we use economic analysis to decide how to produce goods and services, how much to produce, and how much to charge for them. Let's use some economic analysis to look at a practical question confronting someone considering starting a business.

If the existing music stores in your city are profitable and you have enough money to start your own music store, should you do it? If you enter this market, the competition among the stores for consumers will heat up, causing some stores to drop their CD prices. In addition, your costs may be higher than the costs of the stores that are already established. It would be sensible to enter the market only if you expect a small drop in price and a small difference in costs. Indeed, entering what appears to be a lucrative market may turn out to be a financial disaster.

### To Evaluate Public Policies

Although modern societies use markets to make most of the decisions concerning production and consumption, the government does fulfill several important roles. We can use economic analysis to determine how well the government performs its roles in the market economy. We can also explore the trade-offs associated with various public policies. Let's look at a practical question about public policy.

Like other innovations, prescription drugs are protected by government patents, giving the developer the exclusive right to sell the drug for a fixed period of time. Once the patent expires, other pharmaceutical companies can legally produce and sell generic versions of a drug, causing prices to drop. Should drug patents be shorter? Shortening the patent has trade-offs. The good news is that a shorter patent means that generic versions of the drug will be available sooner, so prices will be lower and more people will use the drug to improve their health. The bad news is that a shorter patent means that the payoff from developing new drugs will be smaller, so pharmaceutical companies won't develop as many new drugs. The question is whether the benefit of shorter patents (lower prices) exceeds the cost (fewer drugs developed).

# SUMMARY

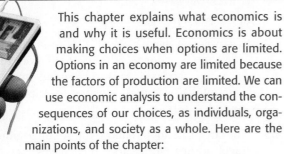

This chapter explains what economics is and why it is useful. Economics is about making choices when options are limited. Options in an economy are limited because the factors of production are limited. We can use economic analysis to understand the consequences of our choices, as individuals, organizations, and society as a whole. Here are the main points of the chapter:

1 Most of modern economics is based on *positive analysis*, which answers the question "What *is*?" or "What *will be*?" Economists contribute to policy debates by conducting positive analyses about the consequences of alternative actions.

2 The choices made by individuals, firms, and governments answer three questions: What products do we produce?

How do we produce the products? Who consumes the products?

3 *Normative analysis* answers the question "What *ought to be*?"

4 To think like an economist, we (a) use assumptions to simplify, (b) use the notion of *ceteris paribus* to focus on the relationship between two variables, (c) think in marginal terms, and (d) assume that rational people respond to incentives.

5 We use *macroeconomics* to understand why economies grow, to understand economic fluctuations, and to make informed business decisions.

6 We use *microeconomics* to understand how markets work, to make personal and managerial decisions, and to evaluate the merits of public policies.

## KEY TERMS

*ceteris paribus*, p. 10
economics, p. 4
economic model, p. 6
entrepreneurship, p. 4
factors of production, p. 4
human capital, p. 4

labor, p. 4
macroeconomics, p. 11
marginal change, p. 10
microeconomics, p. 13
natural resources, p. 4
normative analysis, p. 5

physical capital, p. 4
positive analysis, p. 5
scarcity, p. 4
variable, p. 9

## EXERCISES

*Get Ahead of the Curve*

Visit www.myeconlab.com to complete these exercises online and get instant feedback.

### 1.1 | What Is Economics?

**1.1** The three basic economic questions a society must answer are: _____ products do we produce? _____ do we produce the products? _____ consumes the products?

**1.2** Which of the following statements is true?
   **a.** Positive statements answer questions like "What will happen if . . ."; normative economic statements answer questions like "What ought to happen to . . ."
   **b.** Normative statements answer questions like "What will happen if . . ."; positive economic statements answer questions like "What ought to happen to . . ."
   **c.** Most modern economics is based on normative analysis.

**1.3.** Indicate whether each of the following questions is normative or positive.
   **a.** Should your city build levees strong enough to protect the city from Class-5 hurricanes?

   **b.** How did Hurricane Katrina affect housing prices in New Orleans and Baton Rouge?
   **c.** Who should pay for a new skate park?
   **d.** Should a school district increase teachers' salaries by 20 percent?
   **e.** Would an increase in teachers' salaries improve the average quality of teachers?

### 1.2 | Economic Analysis and Modern Problems

**2.1** What is the economist's solution to the congestion problem?
   **a.** Require people to carpool.
   **b.** Charge a toll during rush hour.
   **c.** Require people to move closer to their jobs.
   **d.** No economist would suggest any of the above.

**2.2** Some recent work by economists on the sources of growth suggests that institutions such as the _____ and the _____ play key roles in economic growth.

**3.1** A road map incorporates two unrealistic assumptions: (1) _____ and (2) _____

**3.2** The four elements of the economic way of thinking are: (1) use _____ to simplify the analysis; (2) explore the relationship between two variables by _____; (3) think at the _____; and (4) rational people respond to _____.

**3.3** Which of the following is the Latin expression meaning *other things being held fixed*?

    **a.** *ceteriferous proboscis*

    **b.** *ceteris paribus*

    **c.** *e pluribus unum*

    **d.** *tres grand fromage*

**3.4** When researchers hooked TVs to stationary bikes as a power source, the cost of watching TV _____, and the kids responded by _____ the hours of TV watched. (Related to Application 1 on page 11.)

**3.5** The city of London reduced traffic congestion and cut travel times for cars and buses in half by _____. (Related to Application 2 on page 12.)

## NOTES

1. Texas Transportation Institute, *2005 Urban Mobility Study* (http://mobility.tamu.edu/ums/).

2. William Easterly, *The Elusive Quest for Growth* (Cambridge, MA: MIT Press, 2001), Chapter 1.

3. William Easterly, *The Elusive Quest for Growth* (Cambridge, MA: MIT Press, 2001); World Bank, *World Development Report 2000/2001: Attacking Poverty* (New York: Oxford University Press, 2000).

4. John Maynard Keynes, *The Collected Writings of John Maynard Keynes, Volume 7*, edited by Donald Moggridge (London: Macmillan, 1973), p. 856.

5. Alfred Marshall, *Principles of Economics*, 9th ed., edited by C.W. Guillebaud (London: Macmillan, 1961 [first published in 1920]), p. 366.

6. Adam Smith, *An Inquiry into the Nature and Causes of the Wealth of Nations* (First published in 1776; New York: Random House, 1973), Book 2, Chapter 3.

# APPENDIX A
## USING GRAPHS AND PERCENTAGES

Economists use several types of graphs to present data, represent relationships between variables, and explain concepts. In this appendix, we review the mechanics of graphing variables. We'll also review the basics of computing percentage changes and using percentages to compute changes in variables.

## USING GRAPHS

A quick flip through the book will reveal the importance of graphs in economics. Every chapter has at least several graphs, and many chapters have more. Although it is possible to do economics without graphs, it's a lot easier with them in your toolbox.

### Graphing Single Variables

As we saw earlier in Chapter 1, a *variable* is a measure of something that can take on different values. Figure 1A.1 shows two types of graphs, each presenting data on a single variable. Panel A uses a pie graph to show the breakdown of U.S. music sales by type of music. The larger the sales of a type of music, the larger the pie slice. For example, the most popular type is Rock music, comprising 24 percent of the market. The next largest type is Rap/Hip-hop, followed by R&B/Urban, Country, and so on. Panel B of Figure 1A.1 uses a bar graph to show the revenue from foreign sales (exports) of selected U.S. industries. The larger the revenue, the taller the bar. For example, the bar for computer software, with export sales of about $60 billion, is over three times taller than the bar for motion pictures, TV, and video, with export sales of $17 billion.

A third type of single-variable graph shows how the value of a variable changes over time. Panel A of Figure 1A.2 shows a time-series graph, with the total dollar

► **FIGURE 1A.1**
**Graphs of Single Variables**

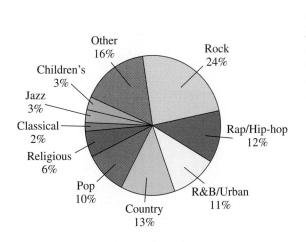

**(A) Pie Graph for Types of Recorded Music Sold in the United States**

SOURCE: Author's calculations based on Recording Industry Association of America, "2004 Consumer Profile."

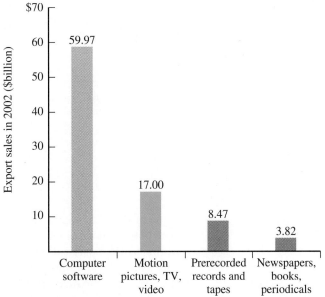

**(B) Bar Graph for U.S. Export Sales of Copyrighted Products**

SOURCE: Author's calculations based on International Intellectual Property Alliance, "Copyright Industries in the U.S. Economy, 2004 Report."

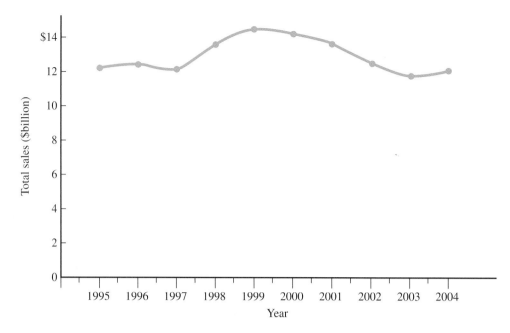

**(A) Total Sales of the U.S. Sound Recording Industry, 1995–2004**

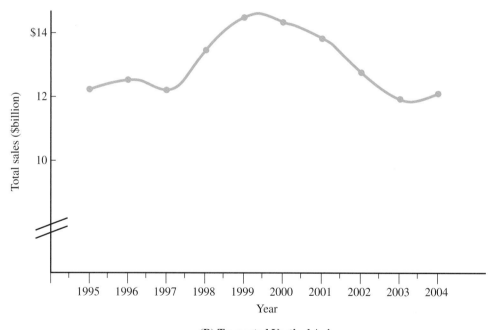

**(B) Truncated Vertical Axis**

value of the U.S. sound-recording industry from 1995 through 2004. Time is measured on the horizontal axis, and sales are measured on the vertical axis. The height of the line in a particular year shows the value in that year. For example, in 1995 the value was $12.32 billion. After reaching a peak of $14.59 billion in 1999, the value dropped over the next several years.

Panel B of Figure 1A.2 shows a truncated version of the graph in Panel A. The double hash marks in the lower part of the vertical axis indicate that the axis doesn't start from zero. The truncation of the vertical axis exaggerates the fluctuations in the value of production.

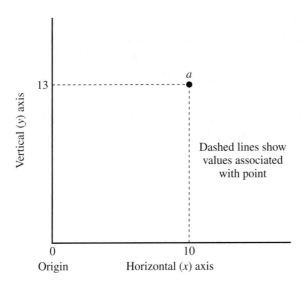

**Basic Elements of a Two-Variable Graph**

One variable is measured along the horizontal, or *x*, axis, while the other variable is measured along the vertical, or *y*, axis. The origin is defined as the intersection of the two axes, where the values of both variables are zero. The dashed lines show the values of the two variables at a particular point.

## Graphing Two Variables

We can also use a graph to show the relationship between two variables. Figure 1A.3 shows the basic elements of a two-variable graph. One variable is measured along the horizontal, or *x*, axis, while the other variable is measured along the vertical, or *y*, axis. The *origin* is defined as the intersection of the two axes, where the values of both variables are zero. Dashed lines show the values of the two variables at a particular point. For example, for point *a*, the value of the horizontal, or *x*, variable is 10, and the value of the vertical, or *y*, variable is 13.

To see how to draw a two-variable graph, suppose that you have a part-time job and you are interested in the relationship between the number of hours you work and your weekly income. The relevant variables are the hours of work per week and your weekly income. In Figure 1A.4, the table shows the relationship between the hours

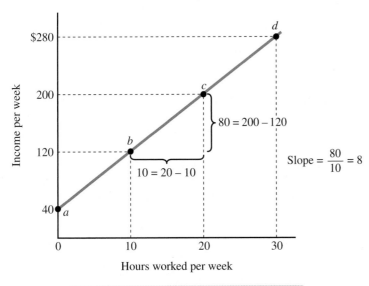

◄ **FIGURE 1A.4**
**Relationship between Hours Worked and Income**

There is a positive relationship between work hours and income, so the income curve is positively sloped. The slope of the curve is $8: Each additional hour of work increases income by $8.

| Hours Worked per Week | Income per Week | Point on the Graph |
|---|---|---|
| 0 | $ 40 | a |
| 10 | 120 | b |
| 20 | 200 | c |
| 30 | 280 | d |

worked and income. Let's assume that your weekly allowance from your parents is $40 and your part-time job pays $8 per hour. If you work 10 hours per week, for example, your weekly income is $120 ($40 from your parents and $80 from your job). The more you work, the higher your weekly income: If you work 20 hours, your weekly income is $200; if you work 30 hours, it is $280.

Although a table with numbers is helpful in showing the relationship between work hours and income, a graph makes it easier to see the relationship. We can use data in a table to draw a graph. To do so, we perform five simple steps:

1 Draw a horizontal line to represent the first variable. In Figure 1A.4, we measure hours worked along the horizontal axis. As we move to the right along the horizontal axis, the number of hours worked increases, from zero to 30 hours.

2 Draw a vertical line intersecting the first line to represent the second variable. In Figure 1A.4, we measure income along the vertical axis. As we move up along the vertical axis, income increases from zero to $280.

3 Start with the first row of numbers in the table, which shows that with zero hours worked, income is $40. The value of the variable on the horizontal axis is zero, and the value of the variable on the vertical axis is $40, so we plot point *a* on the graph. This is the *vertical intercept*—the point where the curve cuts or intersects the vertical axis.

4 Pick a combination with a positive number for hours worked. For example, in the second row of numbers, if you work 10 hours, your income is $120.

    4.1 Find the point on the horizontal axis with that number of hours worked—10 hours—and draw a dashed line vertically straight up from that point.

    4.2 Find the point on the vertical axis with the income corresponding to those hours worked—$120—and draw a dashed line horizontally straight to the right from that point.

    4.3 The intersection of the dashed lines shows the combination of hours worked and income. Point *b* shows the combination of 10 hours worked and $120 in income.

5 Repeat step 4 for different combinations of work time and income shown in the table. Once we have a series of points on the graph (*a*, *b*, *c*, and *d*), we can connect them to draw a curve that shows the relationship between hours worked and income.

- **positive relationship**
  A relationship in which two variables move in the same direction.

There is a **positive relationship** between two variables if they move in the same direction. As you increase your work time, your income increases, so there is a positive relationship between the two variables. In Figure 1A.4, as the number of hours worked increases, you move upward along the curve to higher income levels. Some people refer to a positive relationship as a *direct relationship*.

- **negative relationship**
  A relationship in which two variables move in opposite directions.

There is a **negative relationship** between two variables if they move in opposite directions. For example, there is a negative relationship between the amount of time you work and the time you have available for other activities such as recreation, study, and sleep. Some people refer to a negative relationship as an *inverse relationship*.

## Computing the Slope

- **slope of a curve**
  The vertical difference between two points (the *rise*) divided by the horizontal difference (the *run*).

How sensitive is one variable to changes in the other variable? We can use the slope of the curve to measure this sensitivity. To compute the **slope of a curve**, we pick two points and divide the vertical difference between the two points (the *rise*) by the horizontal difference (the *run*):

$$\text{Slope} = \frac{\text{Vertical difference between two points}}{\text{Horizontal difference between two points}} = \frac{\text{rise}}{\text{run}}$$

To compute the slope of a curve, we take four steps:

1 Pick two points on the curve, for example, points *b* and *c* in Figure 1A.4.
2 Compute the vertical difference between the two points (the rise). For points *b* and *c*, the vertical difference between the points is $80 ($200 – $120).
3 Compute the horizontal distance between the same two points (the run). For points *b* and *c*, the horizontal distance between the points is 10 hours (20 hours – 10 hours).
4 Divide the vertical distance by the horizontal distance to get the slope. The slope between points *b* and *c* is $8 per hour:

$$\text{Slope} = \frac{\text{Vertical difference}}{\text{Horizontal difference}} = \frac{\$200 - 120}{20 - 10} = \frac{\$80}{10} = \$8$$

In this case, a 10-hour increase in time worked increases income by $80, so the increase in income per hour of work is $8, which makes sense because this is the hourly wage. Because the curve is a straight line, the slope is the same at all points along the curve. You can check this yourself by computing the slope between points *c* and *d*.

We can use some shorthand to refer to the slope of a curve. The mathematical symbol Δ (delta) represents the change in a variable. So the slope of the curve in Figure 1A.4 could be written as

$$\text{Slope} = \frac{\Delta \text{ Income}}{\Delta \text{ Work hours}}$$

In general, if the variable on the vertical axis is *y* and the variable on the horizontal axis is *x*, we can express the slope as

$$\text{Slope} = \frac{\Delta y}{\Delta x}$$

## Moving Along the Curve Versus Shifting the Curve

Up to this point, we've explored the effect of changes in variables that cause movement along a given curve. In Figure 1A.4, we see the relationship between hours of work (on the horizontal axis) and income (on the vertical axis). Because the total income also depends on the allowance and the wage, we can make two observations about the curve in Figure 1A.4:

1 To draw this curve, we must specify the weekly allowance ($40) and the hourly wage ($8).
2 The curve shows that an increase in time worked increases the student's income, *ceteris paribus*. In this case, we are assuming that the allowance and the wage are both fixed.

A change in the weekly allowance will shift the curve showing the relationship between work time and income. In Figure 1A.5, when the allowance increases from $40 to $90, the curve shifts upward by $50: For a given number of work hours, income increases by $50. For example, the income associated with 10 hours of work is $170 (point *f*), compared to $120 with the original allowance (point *b*). The upward shift also means that to reach a given amount of income, fewer work hours are required. In other words, the curve shifts upward and to the left.

We can distinguish between movement along a curve and a shift of the entire curve. In Figure 1A.5, an increase in the hours worked causes movement along a single income curve. For example, if the allowance is $40, we are operating on the lower of the two curves, and if the hours worked increases from 10 to 20, we move from point *b* to point *c*. In contrast, if something other than the hours worked changes, we shift the entire curve, as we've seen with an increase in the allowance.

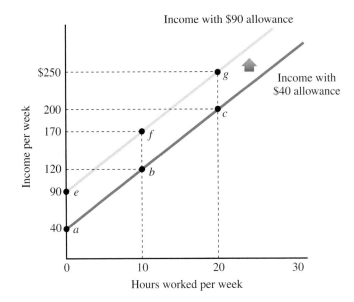

► **FIGURE 1A.5**

**Movement Along a Curve Versus Shifting the Curve**

To draw a curve showing the relationship between hours worked and income, we fix the weekly allowance ($40) and the wage ($8 per hour). A change in the hours worked causes movement along the curve, for example, from point *b* to point *c*. A change in any other variable shifts the entire curve. For example, a $50 increase in the allowance (to $90) shifts the entire curve upward by $50.

This book uses dozens of two-dimensional curves, each of which shows the relationship between *only two* variables. A common error is to forget that a single curve tells only part of the story. In Figure 1A.5, we needed two curves to explore the effects of changes in three variables. Here are some simple rules to keep in mind when you use two-dimensional graphs:

- A change in one of the variables shown on the graph causes movement along the curve. In Figure 1A.5, an increase in work time causes movement along the curve from point *a* to point *b*, to point *c*, and so on.

- A change in one of the variables that is not shown on the graph—one of the variables held fixed in drawing the curve—shifts the entire curve. In Figure 1A.5, an increase in the allowance shifts the entire curve upward.

### Graphing Negative Relationships

We can use a graph to show a negative relationship between two variables. Consider a consumer who has an annual budget of $360 to spend on CDs at a price of $12 per CD and downloaded music at a price of $1 per song. The table in Figure 1A.6 shows the relationship between the number of CDs and downloaded songs. A consumer who doesn't buy any CDs has $360 to spend on downloaded songs and can get 360 of them at a price of $1 each. A consumer who buys 10 CDs at $12 each has $240 left to spend on downloaded songs (point *b*). Moving down through the table, as the number of CDs increases, the number of downloaded songs decreases.

The graph in Figure 1A.6 shows the negative relationship between the number of CDs and the number of downloaded songs. The vertical intercept (point *a*) shows that a consumer who doesn't buy any CDs can afford 360 downloaded songs. There is a negative relationship between the number of CDs and downloaded songs, so the curve is negatively sloped. We can use points *b* and *c* to compute the slope of the curve:

$$\text{Slope} = \frac{\text{Vertical difference}}{\text{Horizontal difference}} = \frac{240 - 120}{10 - 20} = \frac{120}{-10} = -12$$

The slope is 12 downloaded songs per CD: For each additional CD, the consumer sacrifices 12 downloaded songs.

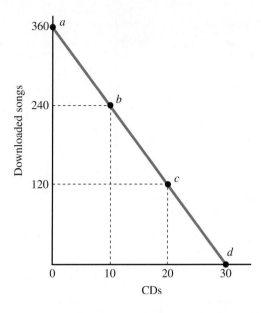

| Number of CDs Purchased | Number of Songs Downloaded | Point on the Graph |
|:---:|:---:|:---:|
| 0 | 360 | a |
| 10 | 240 | b |
| 20 | 120 | c |
| 30 | 0 | d |

▲ **FIGURE 1A.6**

**Negative Relationship Between CD Purchases and Downloaded Songs**

There is a negative relationship between the number of CDs and downloaded songs that a consumer can afford with a budget of $360. The slope of the curve is $12: Each additional CD (at a price of $12 each) decreases the number of downloadable songs (at $1 each) by 12 songs.

## Graphing Nonlinear Relationships

We can also use a graph to show a nonlinear relationship between two variables. Panel A of Figure 1A.7 shows the relationship between hours spent studying for an exam and the grade on the exam. As study time increases, the grade increases, but at a decreasing rate. In other words, each additional hour increases the exam grade by a smaller and smaller amount. For example, the second hour of study increases the grade by 4 points—from 6 to 10 points—but the ninth hour of study increases the grade by only 1 point—from 24 points to 25 points. This is a nonlinear relationship: The slope of the curve changes as we move along the curve. In Figure 1A.7, the slope decreases as we move to the right along the curve: The slope is 4 points per hour between points *a* and *b* but only 1 point per hour between points *c* and *d*.

Another possibility for a nonlinear curve is that the slope increases as we move to the right along the curve. Panel B of Figure 1A.7 shows the relationship between the amount of grain produced on the horizontal axis and the total cost of production on the vertical axis. The slope of the curve increases as the amount of grain increases, meaning that production cost increases at an increasing rate. On the lower part of the curve, increasing output from 1 ton to 2 tons increases production cost by $5, from $10 to $15. On the upper part of the curve, increasing output from 10 to 11 tons increases production cost by $25, from $100 to $125.

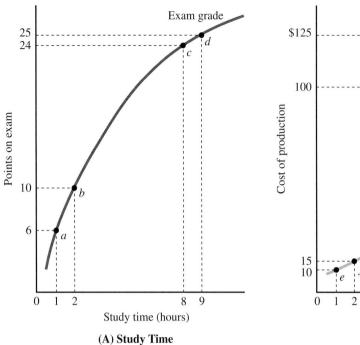

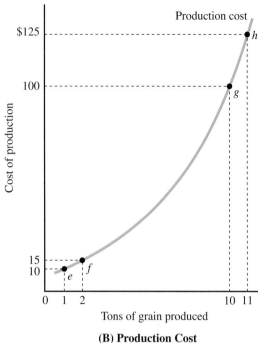

(A) Study Time

(B) Production Cost

▲ **FIGURE 1A.7**
**Nonlinear Relationships**

(**A**) **Study time** There is a positive and nonlinear relationship between study time and the grade on an exam. As study time increases, the exam grade increases at a decreasing rate. For example, the second hour of study increased the grade by 4 points (from 6 points to 10 points), but the ninth hour of study increases the grade by only 1 point (from 24 points to 25 points).

(**B**) **Production cost** There is a positive and nonlinear relationship between the quantity of grain produced and total production cost. As the quantity increases, the total cost increases at an increasing rate. For example, to increase production from 1 ton to 2 tons, production cost increases by $5 (from $10 to $15) but to increase the production from 10 to 11 tons, total cost increases by $25 (from $100 to $125).

## COMPUTING PERCENTAGE CHANGES AND USING EQUATIONS

Economists often express changes in variables in terms of percentage changes. This part of the appendix provides a brief review of the mechanics of computing percentage changes. It also reviews some simple rules for solving equations to find missing values.

### Computing Percentage Changes

In many cases, the equations that economists use involve percentage changes. In this book, we use a simple approach to computing percentage changes: We divide the change in the variable by the initial value of the variable and then multiply by 100:

$$\text{Percentage change} = \frac{\text{New value} - \text{initial value}}{\text{Initial value}} \times 100$$

For example, if the price of a book increases from $20 to $22, the percentage change is 10 percent:

$$\text{Percentage change} = \frac{22 - 20}{20} \times 100 = \frac{2}{20} \times 100 = 10\%$$

Going in the other direction, suppose the price decreases from $20 to $19. In this case, the percentage change is –5 percent:

$$\text{Percentage change} = \frac{19 - 20}{20} \times 100 = -\frac{1}{20} \times 100 = -5\%$$

The alternative to this simple approach is to base the percentage change on the average value, or the midpoint, of the variable:

$$\text{Percentage change} = \frac{\text{New value} - \text{initial value}}{\text{Average value}} \times 100$$

For example, if the price of a book increases from $20 to $22, the computed percentage change under the midpoint approach would be 9.52 percent:

$$\text{Percentage change} = \frac{22 - 20}{(20 + 22) \div 2} \times 100 = \frac{2}{42 \div 2} \times 100 = \frac{2}{21} \times 100 = 9.52\%$$

If the change in the variable is relatively small, the extra precision associated with the midpoint approach is usually not worth the extra effort. The simple approach allows us to spend less time doing tedious arithmetic and more time doing economic analysis. In this book, we use the simple approach to compute percentage changes: If the price increases from $20 to $22, the price has increased by 10 percent.

If we know a percentage change, we can translate it into an absolute change. For example, if a price has increased by 10 percent and the initial price is $20, then we add 10 percent of the initial price ($2 is 10 percent of $20) to the initial price ($20), for a new price of $22. If the price decreases by 5 percent, we subtract 5 percent of the initial price ($1 is 5 percent of $20) from the initial price ($20), for a new price of $19.

## Using Equations to Compute Missing Values

It will often be useful to compute the value of the numerator or the denominator of an equation. To do so, we use simple algebra to rearrange the equation to put the missing variable on the left side of the equation. For example, consider the relationship between time worked and income. The equation for the slope is

$$\text{Slope} = \frac{\Delta \, \text{Income}}{\Delta \, \text{Work hours}}$$

Suppose you want to compute how much income you'll earn by working more hours. We can rearrange the slope equation by multiplying both sides of the equation by the change in work hours:

$$\text{Work hours} \times \text{Slope} = \Delta \, \text{Income}$$

By swapping sides of the equation, we get:

$$\Delta \text{ Income} = \Delta \text{ Work hours} \times \text{Slope}$$

For example, if you work seven extra hours and the slope is $8, your income will increase by $56:

$$\Delta \text{ Income} = \Delta \text{Work hours} \times \text{Slope} = 7 \times \$8 = \$56$$

We can use the same process to compute the difference in work time required to achieve a target change in income. In this case, we multiply both sides of the slope equation by the change in work time and then divide both sides by the slope. The result is

$$\Delta \text{Work hours} = \frac{\Delta \text{ Income}}{\text{Slope}}$$

For example, to increase your income by $56, you need to work seven hours:

$$\Delta \text{Work hours} = \frac{\Delta \text{ Income}}{\text{Slope}} = \frac{\$56}{\$8} = 7$$

## KEY TERMS

negative relationship, p. 20          positive relationship, p. 20          slope of a curve, p. 20

## EXERCISES

*Get Ahead of the Curve*   Visit www.myeconlab.com to complete these exercises online and get instant feedback.

**A1.** Suppose you belong to a tennis club that has a monthly fee of $100 and a charge of $5 per hour to play tennis.

   **a.** Using Figure 1A.4 on page 19 as a model, prepare a table and draw a curve to show the relationship between the hours of tennis (on the horizontal axis) and the monthly club bill (on the vertical axis). For the table and graph, use 5, 10, 15, and 20 hours of tennis.

   **b.** The slope of the curve is _____ per _____.

   **c.** Suppose you start with 10 hours of tennis and then decide to increase your tennis time by 3 hours. On your curve, show the initial point and the new point. By how much will your monthly bill increase?

   **d.** Suppose you start with 10 hours and then decide to spend an additional $30 on tennis. On your curve, show the initial point and the new point. How many additional hours can you get?

**A2.** The following graph shows the relationship between the number of Frisbees produced and the cost of production. The vertical intercept is $____, and the slope of the curve is $____ per Frisbee. Point *b* shows that the cost of producing ____ Frisbees is $____. The cost of producing 15 frisbees is $____.

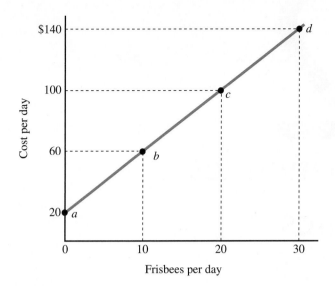

**A3.** Suppose you have $120 to spend on CDs and movies. The price of a CD is $12, and the price of a movie is $6.
  **a.** Using Figure 1A.6 on page 23 as a model, prepare a table and draw a curve to show the relationship between the number of CDs (on the horizontal axis) and movies (on the vertical axis) you can afford to buy.
  **b.** The slope of the curve is _____ per _____.

**A4.** You manage Gofer Delivery Service. You rent a truck for $50 per day, and each delivery takes an hour of labor time. The hourly wage is $8.

  **a.** Draw a curve showing the relationship between the number of deliveries (on the horizontal axis) and your total cost (on the vertical axis). Draw the curve for between zero and 20 deliveries.
  **b.** The slope of the cost curve is _____ per _____.
  **c.** To draw the curve, what variables are held fixed?
  **d.** A change in _____ would cause a movement upward along the curve.
  **e.** Changes in _____ would cause the entire curve to shift upward.

**A5.** A change in a variable measured on an axis of a graph causes movement _____ a curve, while a change in a relevant variable that is not measured on an axis _____ the curve.

**A6.** Compute the percentage changes for the following :

| Initial Value | New Value | Percentage Change |
| --- | --- | --- |
| 10 | 11 | _____ |
| 100 | 98 | _____ |
| 50 | 53 | _____ |

**A7.** Compute the new values for the following changes.

| Initial Value | Percentage Change | New Value |
| --- | --- | --- |
| 100 | 12% | _____ |
| 50 | 8 | _____ |
| 20 | 15 | _____ |

# 2

## The Key Principles of Economics

Your student film society is looking for an auditorium to use for an all-day Hitchcock film program and is willing to pay up to $200. Your college has a new auditorium that would be perfect for your event. However, according to the campus facility manager, "The daily rent on the auditorium is $450, an amount that includes $300 to help pay for the cost of building the auditorium, $50 to help pay for insurance, and $100 to cover the extra costs of electricity and janitorial services for a one-day event."

How should you respond to the facility manager? As we'll see, if you could persuade the manager to use the marginal principle—one of the five key principles of economics—you should be able to get the facility for an amount between $100 and $200.

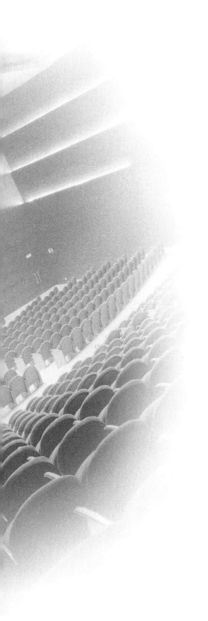

• **opportunity cost**
What you sacrifice to get something.

I n this chapter, we introduce five key principles that provide a foundation for economic analysis. A *principle* is a self-evident truth that most people readily understand and accept. For example, most people readily accept the principle of gravity. As you read through the book, you will see the five key principles of economics again and again as you do your own economic analysis.

# 2.1 | THE PRINCIPLE OF OPPORTUNITY COST

Economics is all about making choices, and to make good choices we must compare the benefit of something to its cost. **Opportunity cost** incorporates the notion of scarcity: No matter what we do, there is always a trade-off. We must trade off one thing for another because resources are limited and can be used in different ways. By acquiring something, we use up resources that could have been used to acquire something else. The notion of opportunity cost allows us to measure this trade-off.

## PRINCIPLE OF OPPORTUNITY COST

The opportunity cost of something is what you sacrifice to get it.

Most decisions involve several alternatives. For example, if you spend an hour studying for an economics exam, you have one less hour to pursue other activities. To determine the opportunity cost of an activity, we look at what you consider the best of these "other" activities. For example, suppose the alternatives to studying economics are studying for a history exam or working in a job that pays $10 per hour. If you consider studying for history a better use of your time than working, then the opportunity cost of studying economics is the 4 extra points you could have received on a history exam if you studied history instead of economics. Alternatively, if working is the best alternative, the opportunity cost of studying economics is the $10 you could have earned instead.

The principle of opportunity cost can also be applied to decisions about how to spend money from a fixed budget. For example, suppose that you have a fixed budget to spend on music. You can either buy your music at a local music store for $15 per CD or you can buy your music online for $1 per song. The opportunity cost of 1 CD is 15 one-dollar online songs. A hospital with a fixed salary budget can increase the number of doctors only at the expense of nurses or physician's assistants. If a doctor costs five times as much as a nurse, the opportunity cost of a doctor is 5 nurses.

In some cases, a product that appears to be free actually has a cost. That's why economists are fond of saying, "There's no such thing as a free lunch." Suppose someone offers to buy you lunch if you agree to listen to a sales pitch for a time-share condominium. Although you don't pay any money for the lunch, there is an opportunity cost because you could spend that time in another way—such as studying for your economics or history exam. The lunch isn't free because you sacrifice an hour of your time to get it.

## The Cost of College

What is the opportunity cost of a college degree? Consider a student who spends a total of $40,000 for tuition and books. Instead of going to college, the student could have spent this money on a wide variety of goods, including housing, stereo equipment, and world travel. Part of the opportunity cost of college is the $40,000 worth of other goods the student sacrifices to pay for tuition and books. Also, instead of going to college, the student could have worked as a bank clerk for $20,000 per year and earned

# APPLICATION

## THE OPPORTUNITY COSTS OF TIME AND INVESTED FUNDS

**APPLYING THE CONCEPTS #1:** What is the opportunity cost of running a business?

The principle of opportunity cost also applies to the cost of running a business. Suppose you inherit $10,000 and decide to use the money to start a lawn-care business. You purchase a truck and a mower for $10,000 and start mowing lawns. If your annual cost for fuel and other supplies is $2,000, what's your annual cost of doing business?

We can use the principle of opportunity cost to compute your costs. In addition to the $2,000 expense for fuel and other supplies, we must include two other sorts of costs:

- **Opportunity cost of funds invested**. You could have invested the $10,000 in a bank account. If the interest rate on a bank account is 8 percent, the annual cost of the truck and mower is the $800 you could have earned in a bank account during the year.

- **Opportunity cost of your time**. Suppose that you could have earned $30,000 in another job. The opportunity cost of your time is the $30,000 you sacrificed by being your own boss.

Adding the $800 cost of funds and the $30,000 cost of your time to the $2,000 fuel cost, the cost of doing business is $32,800 per year.

*Related to Exercise 1.6.*

$80,000 over four years. That makes the total opportunity cost of this student's college degree $120,000:

| | |
|---|---|
| Opportunity cost of money spent on tuition and books | $ 40,000 |
| Opportunity cost of college time (four years working for $20,000 per year) | 80,000 |
| Economic cost or total opportunity cost | $120,000 |

We haven't included the costs of food or housing in our computations of opportunity cost. That's because a student must eat and live somewhere even if he or she doesn't go to college. But if housing and food are more expensive in college, then we would include the extra costs of housing and food in our calculations.

There are other things to consider in a person's decision to attend college. As we'll see later, a college degree can increase a person's earning power, so there are benefits from a college degree. In addition, college offers the thrill of learning and the pleasure of meeting new people. To make an informed decision about whether to attend college, we must compare the benefits to the opportunity costs.

## Opportunity Cost and the Production Possibilities Curve

Just as individuals face limits, so do entire economies. As we saw in Chapter 1, the ability of an economy to produce goods and services is determined by its factors of production, including labor, natural resources, physical capital, human capital, and entrepreneurship.

Figure 2.1 shows a production possibilities graph for an economy that produces wheat and steel. The horizontal axis shows the quantity of wheat produced by the economy, and the vertical axis shows the quantity of steel produced. The shaded area shows all the possible combinations of the two goods that can be produced. At point *a*,

**Scarcity and the Production
Possibilities Curve**

The production possibilities curve illustrates
the principle of opportunity cost for an
entire economy. An economy has a fixed
amount of resources. If these resources
are fully employed, an increase in the production of wheat comes at the expense of
steel.

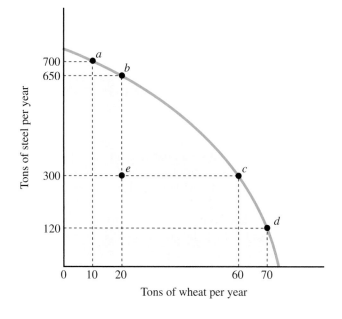

• **production possibilities curve**
A curve that shows the possible
combinations of products that an
economy can produce, given that its
productive resources are fully
employed and efficiently used.

for example, the economy can produce 700 tons of steel and 10 tons of wheat. In contrast, at point *e*, the economy can produce 300 tons of steel and 20 tons of wheat. The
set of points on the border between the shaded and unshaded area is called the **production possibilities curve** (or *production possibilities frontier*), because it separates the
combinations that are attainable from those that are not. The attainable combinations
are shown by the shaded area within the curve and the curve itself. The unattainable
combinations are shown by the unshaded area outside the curve. The points on the
curve show the combinations that are possible if the economy's resources are fully
employed.

The production possibilities curve illustrates the notion of opportunity cost. If
an economy is fully utilizing its resources, it can produce more of one product only if
it produces less of another product. For example, to produce more wheat, we must
take resources away from steel. As we move resources out of steel, the quantity of
steel will decrease. For example, if we move from point *a* to point *b* along the pro-

► **FIGURE 2.2**

**Shifting the Production
Possibilities Curve**

An increase in the quantity of resources or
technological innovation in an economy
shifts the production possibilities curve outward. Starting from point *f*, a nation could
produce more steel (point *g*), more wheat
(point *h*), or more of both goods (points
between *g* and *h*).

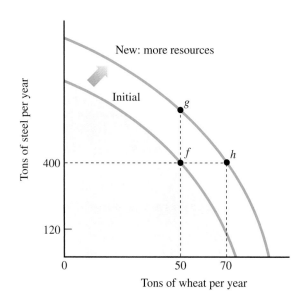

duction possibilities curve in Figure 2.1, we sacrifice 50 tons of steel (700 tons − 650 tons) to get 10 more tons of wheat (20 tons − 10 tons). Further down the curve, if we move from point *c* to point *d*, we sacrifice 180 tons of steel to get the same 10-ton increase in wheat.

Why is the production possibilities curve bowed outward, with the opportunity cost of wheat increasing as we move down the curve? The reason is that resources are not perfectly adaptable for the production of both goods. Some resources are more suitable for steel production, while others are more suitable for wheat production. Starting at point *a*, the economy uses its most fertile land to produce wheat. Here, a 10-ton increase in wheat reduces the quantity of steel by only 50 tons, because plenty of fertile land is available for conversion to wheat farming. As the economy moves downward along the production possibilities curve, farmers will be forced to use land that is progressively less fertile, so to increase wheat output by 10 tons, more and more resources must be diverted from steel production. In the move from point *c* to point *d*, the land converted to farming is so poor that increasing wheat output by 10 tons decreases steel output by 180 tons.

The production possibilities curve shows the production options for a given set of resources. As shown in Figure 2.2, an increase in the amount of resources available to the economy shifts the production possibilities outward. For example, if we start at point *f*, and the economy's resources increase, we can produce more steel (point *g*), more wheat (point *h*), or more of both goods (points between *g* and *h*). The curve will also shift outward as a result of technological innovations that enable us to produce more output with a given quantity of resources.

# 2.2 | THE MARGINAL PRINCIPLE

Economics is about making choices, and we rarely make all-or-nothing choices. For example, if you sit down to read a book, you don't read the entire book in a single sitting, but instead decide how many pages or chapters to read. Economists think in marginal terms, considering how a one-unit change in one variable affects the value of another variable and people's decisions. When we say *marginal*, we're looking at the effect of a small, or incremental, change.

The marginal principle is based on a comparison of the marginal benefits and marginal costs of a particular activity. The **marginal benefit** of an activity is the additional benefit resulting from a small increase in the activity. For example, the marginal benefit of keeping a bookstore open for one more hour equals the additional revenue from book sales. Similarly, the **marginal cost** is the additional cost resulting from a small increase in the activity. For example, the marginal cost of keeping a bookstore open for one more hour equals the additional expenses for workers and utilities. Applying the marginal principle, the bookstore should stay open for one more hour if the marginal benefit (the additional revenue) is at least as large as the marginal cost (the additional cost). For example, if the marginal benefit is $80 of additional revenue and the marginal cost is $30 of additional cost for workers and utilities, staying open for the additional hour increases the bookstore's profit by $50.

- **marginal benefit**
  The additional benefit resulting from a small increase in some activity.

- **marginal cost**
  The additional cost resulting from a small increase in some activity.

## MARGINAL PRINCIPLE

Increase the level of an activity as long as its marginal benefit exceeds its marginal cost. Choose the level at which the marginal benefit equals the marginal cost.

Thinking at the margin enables us to fine-tune our decisions. We can use the marginal principle to determine whether a one-unit increase in a variable would make us better off. Just as a bookstore owner could decide whether to stay open for one

# APPLICATION

## THE OPPORTUNITY COST OF MILITARY SPENDING

**APPLYING THE CONCEPTS #2:** What are society's trade-offs between different goods?

We can also use the principle of opportunity cost to explore the cost of military spending. In 1992, Malaysia bought two warships. For the price of the warships, the country could have provided safe drinking water for 5 million citizens who lacked it. In other words, the opportunity cost of the warships was safe drinking water for 5 million people. The policy question is whether the benefits of the warships exceed their opportunity cost.

In the United States, economists have estimated that the cost of the Iraq War will be at least $540 billion. The economists' calculations go beyond the simple budgetary costs and quantify the opportunity cost of the war. For example, the resources used in the war could have been used in various government programs for children—to enroll more children in preschool programs, to hire more science and math teachers to reduce class sizes, or to immunize more children in poor countries. For example, each $100 billion spent on the war could instead support one of the following programs:

- Enroll 13 million preschool children in the Head Start program for one year.
- Hire 1.8 million additional teachers for one year.
- Immunize all the children in less-developed countries for the next 33 years.

The fact that the war had a large opportunity cost does not necessarily mean that it was unwise. The policy question is whether the benefits from the war exceed its opportunity cost. Taking another perspective, we can measure the opportunity cost of war in terms of its implications for domestic security. The resources used in the Iraq War could have been used to improve domestic security by securing ports and cargo facilities, hiring more police officers, improving the screening of airline passengers and baggage, improving fire departments and other first responders, upgrading the Coast Guard fleet, and securing our railroad and highway systems.

The cost of implementing the domestic-security recommendations of various government commissions would be about $31 billion, a small fraction of the cost of the war. The question for policy makers is whether money spent on domestic security would be more beneficial than money spent on the war.

*Related to Exercises 1.5 and 1.7.*

SOURCES: United Nations Development Program, *Human Development Report 1994* (New York: Oxford University Press, 1994); Linda Blimes and Joseph Stiglitz, "The Economic Costs of the Iraq War: An Appraisal Three Years After the Beginning of the Conflict," *Faculty Research Working Papers*, Harvard University, January 2006; Center for American Progress, "The Opportunity Costs of the Iraq War," August 25, 2004; Scott Wallsten and Katrina Kosec, "The Economic Costs of the War in Iraq," AEI-Brookings Joint Center for Regulatory Studies, September 2005.

more hour, you could decide whether to study one more hour for a psychology midterm. When we reach the level where the marginal benefit equals the marginal cost, we cannot do any better, and the fine-tuning is done.

## How Many Movie Sequels?

To illustrate the marginal principle, let's consider movie sequels. When a movie is successful, its producer naturally thinks about doing another movie, continuing the story line with the same set of characters. If the first sequel is successful, too, the producer thinks about producing a second sequel, then a third, and so on. We can use the marginal principle to explore the decision of how many movies to produce.

Figure 2.3 shows the marginal benefits and marginal costs for movies. On the benefit side, a movie sequel typically generates about 30 percent less revenue than the original movie, and revenue continues to drop for additional movies. In the second column of the table, the first movie generates $300 million in revenue, the second generates $210 million, and the third generates $135 million. This is shown in the graph as a negatively sloped marginal-benefit curve, with the marginal benefit decreasing from $300 for the first movie (point *a*), to $210 (point *b*), and then to $135 (point *c*). On the cost side, the typical movie in the United States costs about $50 million to produce and about $75 million to promote.[1] In the third column of the table, the cost of the first movie (the original) is $125 million. In the graph, this is shown as point *d* on the marginal-cost curve. The marginal cost increases with the number of movies because film stars typically demand higher salaries to appear in sequels. For example, Angelina Jolie was paid more for *Tomb Raider 2* than for *Tomb Raider*, and the actors in *Charlie's Angels 2* received raises, too. In the table and the graph, the marginal cost increases to $150 million for the second movie (point *e*) and to $175 for the third (point *f*).

In this example, the first two movies are profitable, but the third is not. For the original movie, the marginal benefit ($300 million at point *a*) exceeds the marginal

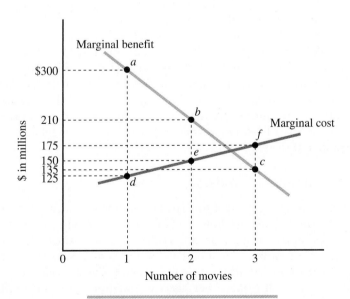

◄ **FIGURE 2.3**
**The Marginal Principle and Movie Sequels**
The marginal benefit of movies in a series decreases because revenue falls off with each additional movie, while the marginal cost increases because actors demand higher salaries. The marginal benefit exceeds the marginal cost for the first two movies, so it is sensible to produce two, but not three, movies.

| Number of Movies | Marginal Benefit ($ millions) | Marginal Cost ($ millions) |
|---|---|---|
| 1 | $300 | $125 |
| 2 | 210 | 150 |
| 3 | 135 | 175 |

cost ($125 million at point *d*), generating a profit of $175 million. Although the second movie has a higher cost and a lower benefit, it is profitable because the marginal benefit still exceeds the marginal cost, so the profit on the second movie is $60 million ($210 million − $150 million). In contrast, the marginal cost of the third movie of $175 million exceeds its marginal benefit of only $135 million, so the third movie *loses* $40 million. In this example, the movie producer should stop after the second movie.

Although this example shows that only two movies are profitable, other outcomes are possible. If the revenue for the third movie were larger, making the marginal benefit greater than the marginal cost, it would be sensible to produce the third movie. Similarly, if the marginal cost of the third movie were lower—if the actors didn't demand such high salaries—the third movie could be profitable. Many movies have had multiple sequels, such as *The Matrix* and *Star Wars*. Conversely, many profitable movies, such as *Rushmore* and *Groundhog Day*, didn't result in any sequels. In these cases, the expected drop-off in revenues and the run-up in costs for the second movie were large enough to make a sequel unprofitable.

### Renting College Facilities

Recall the chapter opener about renting a college auditorium for your student film society. Suppose the society offers to pay $150 for using the auditorium. Should the college accept the offer? The college could use the marginal principle to make the decision.

To decide whether to accept your group's offer, the college should determine the marginal cost of renting out the auditorium. The marginal cost equals the extra costs the college incurs by allowing the student group to use an otherwise vacant auditorium. In our example, the extra cost is $100 for additional electricity and janitorial services. It would be sensible for the college to rent the auditorium, because the marginal benefit ($150 offered by the student group) exceeds the marginal cost ($100). In fact, the college should be willing to rent the facility for any amount greater than $100. If the students and the college's facility manager split the difference between the $200 the students are willing to pay and the $100 marginal cost, they would agree on a price of $150, leaving both parties better off by $50.

Most colleges do not use this sort of logic. Instead, they use complex formulas to compute the perceived cost of renting out a facility. In most cases, the perceived cost includes some costs that are unaffected by renting out the facility for the day. In our example, the facility manager included $300 worth of construction costs and $50 worth of insurance, for a total cost of $450 instead of just $100. Because many colleges include costs that aren't affected by the use of a facility, they overestimate the actual cost of renting out their facilities, missing opportunities to serve student groups and make some money at the same time.

### Automobile Emissions Standards

We can use the marginal principle to analyze emissions standards for automobiles. The U.S. government specifies how much carbon monoxide a new car is allowed to emit per mile. The marginal question is: "Should the standard be stricter, with fewer units of carbon monoxide allowed?" On the benefit side, a stricter standard reduces health-care costs resulting from pollution: If the air is cleaner, people with respiratory ailments will make fewer visits to doctors and hospitals, have lower medication costs, and lose fewer work days. On the cost side, a stricter standard requires more expensive control equipment on cars and may also reduce fuel efficiency. Using the marginal principle, the government should make the emissions standard stricter as long as the marginal benefit (savings in health-care costs and work time lost) exceeds the marginal cost (the cost of additional equipment and extra fuel used).

# APPLICATION

### CONTINENTAL AIRLINES USES THE MARGINAL PRINCIPLE

**APPLYING THE CONCEPTS #3:** How do firms think at the margin?

In the 1960s, Continental Airlines puzzled observers of the airline industry and dismayed its stockholders by running flights with up to half the seats empty. The average cost of running a flight was about $4,000, and a half-full aircraft generated only $3,100 of revenue. So why did the airline run such flights? Were the managers of the airline irrational?

The managers of Continental Airlines ran half-full flights because they correctly applied the marginal principle. Although the average cost of a flight was $4,000, half of this cost involved fixed costs, such as airport fees and the cost of running the reservation system. The airline paid these costs regardless of how many flights it ran. The other half of the average cost involved costs that varied with the number of flights, including the cost of a flight crew, jet fuel, and food service. These other costs added up to $2,000 per flight. In other words, the marginal cost of a flight was only $2,000, so running a flight that generated $3,100 in revenue was sensible. Using the marginal principle, Continental ran flights with up to half the seats empty, earning profit in the process. *Related to Exercises 2.4 and 2.5.*

SOURCE: "Airline Takes the Marginal Bone," *BusinessWeek*, April 20, 1963, pp. 111–114.

# 2.3 | THE PRINCIPLE OF VOLUNTARY EXCHANGE

The principle of voluntary exchange is based on the notion that people act in their own self-interest. Self-interested people won't exchange one thing for another unless the trade makes them better off.

## PRINCIPLE OF VOLUNTARY EXCHANGE

A voluntary exchange between two people makes both people better off.

Here are some examples.

- If you voluntarily exchange money for a college education, you must expect you'll be better off with a college education. The college voluntarily provides an education in exchange for your money, so the college must be better off, too.

- If you have a job, you voluntarily exchange your time for money, and your employer exchanges money for your labor services. Both you and your employer are better off as a result.

### Exchange and Markets

Adam Smith stressed the importance of voluntary exchange as a distinctly human trait.[2] He noticed a propensity in human nature. . . to truck, barter, and exchange one thing for another. . . It is common to all men, and to be found in no other. . . animals. . . Nobody ever saw a dog make a fair and deliberate exchange of one bone for another with another dog.

As we saw in Chapter 1, a market is an institution or arrangement that enables people to exchange goods and services. If participation in a market is voluntary and people are well informed, both people in a transaction—buyer and seller—will be better off. The next time you see a market transaction, listen to what people say after money changes hands. If both people say "Thank you," that's the principle of voluntary exchange in action: The double thank you reveals that both people are better off.

What is the rationale for voluntary exchange? The alternative to exchange is *self-sufficiency:* Each of us could produce everything for ourselves. For most of us it is more sensible to specialize, doing what we do best and then buying products from other people, who in turn are doing what they do best. For example, if you are good with numbers but an awful carpenter, you could specialize in accounting and buy furniture from Woody, who could specialize in making furniture and pay someone to do his bookkeeping. In general, exchange allows us to take advantage of differences in people's talents and skills.

### Online Games and Market Exchange

As another illustration of the power of exchange, consider the virtual world of online games. EverQuest is a role-playing game that allows thousands of people to interact online, moving their characters through a landscape of survival challenges. Each player constructs a character—called an *avatar*—by choosing some initial traits for it. The player then navigates the avatar through the game's challenges, where it acquires skills and accumulates assets, including clothing, weapons, armor, and even magic spells. The currency in EverQuest is a *platinum piece* (PP). Avatars can earn PPs by performing various tasks and can use PPs to buy and sell assets.

The curious part about EverQuest is that players use real-life auction sites, including eBay and Yahoo! Auctions, to buy products normally purchased in the game with PPs.[3] Byron, who wants a piece of armor for his avatar (say, a Rubicite girdle), can use eBay to buy one for $50 from Selma. The two players then enter the online game, and Selma's avatar transfers the armor to Byron's avatar. It is even possible to buy another player's avatar, with all of its skills and assets. Given the time required to acquire various objects such as Rubicite girdles in the game versus the prices paid for them on eBay, the implicit wage earned by the typical online player auctioning them off is $3.42 per hour: That's how much the player could earn by first taking the time to acquire the assets in the game and then selling them on eBay.

## $2.4$ | THE PRINCIPLE OF DIMINISHING RETURNS

Xena has a small copy shop, with one copying machine and one worker. When the backlog of orders piled up, she decided to hire a second worker, expecting that doubling her workforce would double the output of her copy shop from 500 pages per hour to 1,000. She was surprised when output increased to only 800 pages per hour. If she had known about the principle of diminishing returns, she would not have been surprised.

### PRINCIPLE OF DIMINISHING RETURNS

Suppose output is produced with two or more inputs, and we increase one input while holding the other input or inputs fixed. Beyond some point—called the *point of diminishing returns*—output will increase at a decreasing rate.

# APPLICATION

## TIGER WOODS AND WEEDS

**APPLYING THE CONCEPTS #4:** What is the rationale for specialization and exchange?

Should Tiger Woods whack his own weeds? The swinging skills that make Tiger Woods one of the world's best golfers also make him a skillful weed whacker. His large estate has a lot of weeds, and it would take the best gardener 20 hours to take care of all of them. With his powerful and precise swing, Tiger could whack down all the weeds in just one hour. Since Tiger is 20 times more productive than the best gardener, should he take care of his own weeds?

We can use the principle of voluntary exchange to explain why Tiger should hire the less productive gardener. Suppose Tiger earns $1,000 per hour playing golf—either playing in tournaments or giving lessons. For Tiger, the opportunity cost of weed whacking is $1,000—the income he sacrifices by spending an hour cutting weeds rather than playing golf. If the gardener charges $10 per hour, Tiger could hire him to take care of the weeds for only $200. By switching one hour of his time from weed whacking to golf, Tiger earns $1,000 and incurs a cost of only $200, so he is better off by $800. Tiger Woods specializes in what he does best, and then buys goods and services from other people.
*Related to Exercise 3.5.*

Xena added a worker (one input) while holding the number of copying machines (the other input) fixed. Because the two workers shared a single copying machine, each worker spent some time waiting for the machine to be available. As a result, adding the second worker increased the number of copies, but did not double the output. With a single worker and a single copy machine, Xena has reached the point of diminishing returns: That is, as she increases the number of workers, output increases, but at a decreasing rate. The first worker increases output by 500 pages (from 0 to 500), but the second worker increases output by only 300 pages (from 500 to 800).

## Diminishing Returns from Sharing a Production Facility

This principle of diminishing returns is relevant when we try to produce more output in an existing production facility (a factory, a store, an office, or a farm) by increasing the number of workers sharing the facility. When we add a worker to the facility, each worker becomes less productive because he or she works with a smaller piece of the facility: More workers share the same machinery, equipment, and factory space. As we pack more and more workers into the factory, total output increases, but at a decreasing rate.

It's important to emphasize that diminishing returns occurs because one of the inputs to the production process is fixed. When a firm can vary all of its inputs, including the size of the production facility, the principle of diminishing returns is not relevant. For example, if a firm doubled all of its inputs, building a second

# APPLICATION

## FERTILIZER AND CROP YIELDS

**APPLYING THE CONCEPTS #5:** Do farmers experience diminishing returns?

The notion of diminishing returns applies to all inputs to the production process. For example, one of the inputs in the production of corn is nitrogen fertilizer. Suppose a farmer has a fixed amount of land (an acre) and must decide how much fertilizer to apply. The first 50-pound bag of fertilizer will increase the crop yield by a relatively large amount, but the second bag is likely to increase the yield by a smaller amount, and the third bag is likely to have an even smaller effect. Because the farmer is changing just one of the inputs, the output will increase, but at a decreasing rate. Eventually, additional fertilizer will actually decrease output as the other nutrients in the soil are overwhelmed by the fertilizer.

Table 2.1 shows the relationship between the amount of fertilizer and the corn output. The first 50-pound bag of fertilizer increases the crop yield from 85 to 120 bushels per acre, a gain of 35 bushels. The next bag of fertilizer increases the yield by only 15 bushels (from 120 to 135), followed by a gain of 9 bushels (from 135 to 144) and then a gain of only 3 bushels (from 144 to 147). The farmer experienced diminishing returns because the other inputs to the production process are fixed.
*Related to Exercises 4.5 and 4.6.*

**Table 2.1 | FERTILIZER AND CORN YIELD**

| Bags of Nitrogen Fertilizer | Bushels of Corn Per Acre |
| :---: | :---: |
| 0 | 85 |
| 1 | 120 |
| 2 | 135 |
| 3 | 144 |
| 4 | 147 |

factory and hiring a second workforce, we would expect the total output of the firm to at least double. The principle of diminishing returns does not apply when a firm is flexible in choosing all its inputs.

# 2.5 | THE REAL-NOMINAL PRINCIPLE

One of the key ideas in economics is that people are interested not just in the amount of money they have but also in how much their money will buy.

## REAL-NOMINAL PRINCIPLE

What matters to people is the real value of money or income—its purchasing power—not the "face" value of money or income.

To illustrate this principle, suppose you work in your college bookstore to earn extra money for movies and newspapers. If your take-home pay is $10 per hour, is this a high wage or a low wage? The answer depends on the prices of the goods you buy. If

# APPLICATION

**6**

## THE DECLINING REAL MINIMUM WAGE

**APPLYING THE CONCEPTS #6:** How does inflation affect the real minimum wage?

Between 1974 and 2005, the federal minimum wage increased from $2.00 to $5.15. Was the typical minimum-wage worker better or worse off in 2005? We can apply the real-nominal principle to see what's happened over time to the real value of the federal minimum wage.

As shown in the first row of Table 2.2, the minimum wage was $2.00 per hour in 1974, and by 2005 it had risen to $5.15. These are nominal figures, indicating the face value of the minimum wage. By working 40 hours per week, a minimum-wage worker could earn $80 in 1974 and $206 in 2005. The third row of Table 2.2 shows the cost of a standard basket of consumer goods, which includes a standard mix of housing, food, clothing, and transportation. In 1974, consumer prices were relatively low, and the cost of buying all the goods in the standard basket was only $49. Between 1974 and 2005, consumer prices increased, and the cost of this standard basket of goods increased to $193.

The last row in Table 2.2 shows the purchasing power of the minimum wage in 1974 and 2005. In 1974, the $80 in weekly income could buy 1.63 standard baskets of goods. Between 1974 and 2005, the weekly income more than doubled, but the cost of the standard basket of goods nearly quadrupled, from $49 to $193. As a result, the weekly income of $206 in 2005 could buy only 1.07 baskets of goods. Because prices increased faster than the nominal wage, the real value of the minimum wage actually decreased over this period. *Related to Exercises 5.4 and 5.6.*

**Table 2.2** | THE REAL VALUE OF THE MINIMUM WAGE, 1974–2005

|  | 1974 | 2005 |
|---|---|---|
| Minimum wage per hour | $2.00 | $5.15 |
| Weekly income from minimum wage | 80.00 | 206.00 |
| Cost of a standard basket of goods | 49.00 | 193.00 |
| Number of baskets per week | 1.63 | 1.07 |

a movie costs $4 and a newspaper costs $1, with 1 hour of work you could afford to see 2 movies and buy 2 papers. The wage may seem high enough for you. But if a movie costs $8 and a newspaper costs $2, an hour of work would buy only 1 movie and 1 paper, and the same $10 wage doesn't seem so high. This is the real-nominal principle in action: What matters is not how many dollars you earn, but what those dollars will purchase.

The real-nominal principle can explain how people choose the amount of money to carry around with them. Suppose you typically withdraw $40 per week from an ATM to cover your normal expenses. If the prices of all the goods you purchase during the week double, you would have to withdraw $80 per week to make the same purchases. The amount of money people carry around depends on the prices of the goods and services they buy.

• **nominal value**
The face value of an amount of money.

• **real value**
The value of an amount of money in terms of what it can buy.

Economists use special terms to express the ideas behind the real-nominal principle:

• The **nominal value** of an amount of money is simply its face value. For example, the nominal wage paid by the bookstore is $10 per hour.

• The **real value** of an amount of money is measured in terms of the quantity of goods the money can buy. For example, the real value of your bookstore wage would fall as the prices of movies and newspapers increase, even though your nominal wage stayed the same.

Government officials use the real-nominal principle when they design public programs. For example, Social Security payments are increased each year to ensure that the checks received by the elderly and other recipients will purchase the same amount of goods and services, even if prices have increased.

The government also uses this principle when it publishes statistics about the economy. For example, when the government issues reports about changes in "real wages" in the economy over time, these statistics take into account the prices of the goods purchased by workers. Therefore, the real wage is stated in terms of its buying power, rather than its face value or nominal value.

# APPLICATION

## REPAYING STUDENT LOANS

**APPLYING THE CONCEPTS #7:** How does inflation affect lenders and borrowers?

Suppose you finish college with student loans that must be repaid in 10 years. Which is better for you, inflation (rising prices) or deflation (falling prices)? As an example, suppose you finish college this year with $20,000 in student loans and start a job that pays a salary of $40,000 in the first year. In 10 years, you will repay your college loans. Which would you prefer, stable prices, rising prices, or falling prices?

We can use the real-nominal principle to compute the real cost of repaying your loans. The first row of Table 2.3 shows the cost of the loan when all prices in the economy are stable—including the price of labor, your salary. In this case, your nominal salary in 10 years is $40,000, and the real cost of repaying your loan is the half year of work you must do to earn the $20,000. However, if all prices double over the 10-year period, your nominal salary will double to $80,000, and, as shown in the second row of Table 2.3, it will take you only a quarter of a year to earn $20,000 to repay the loan. In other words, a general increase in prices lowers the real cost of your loan. In contrast, if all prices decrease and your annual salary drops to $20,000, it will take you a full year to earn the money to repay the loan. In general, people who owe money prefer inflation to deflation.
*Related to Exercises 5.5 and 5.8.*

**Table 2.3** | EFFECT OF INFLATION AND DEFLATION ON LOAN REPAYMENT

| Change in Prices and Wages | Annual Salary | Years of Work to Repay $20,000 Loan |
|---|---|---|
| Stable | $40,000 | 1/2 year |
| Inflation: Salary doubles | 80,000 | 1/4 year |
| Deflation: Salary cut in half | 20,000 | 1 year |

# SUMMARY

This chapter covers five key principles of economics, the simple, self-evident truths that most people readily accept. If you understand these principles, you are ready to read the rest of the book, which will show you how to do your own economic analysis.

1 **Principle of opportunity cost.** The opportunity cost of something is what you sacrifice to get it.

2 **Marginal principle.** Increase the level of an activity as long as its marginal benefit exceeds its marginal cost.

Choose the level at which the marginal benefit equals the marginal cost.

3 **Principle of voluntary exchange.** A voluntary exchange between two people makes both people better off.

4 **Principle of diminishing returns.** Suppose that output is produced with two or more inputs, and we increase one input while holding the other inputs fixed. Beyond some point—called the *point of diminishing returns*—output will increase at a decreasing rate.

5 **Real-nominal principle.** What matters to people is the real value of money or income—its purchasing power—not the face value of money or income.

# KEY TERMS

marginal benefit, p. 33

marginal cost, p. 33

nominal value, p. 42

opportunity cost, p. 30

production possibilities curve, p. 32

real value, p. 42

# EXERCISES

 *Get Ahead of the Curve*

Visit www.myeconlab.com to complete these exercises online and get instant feedback.

## 2.1 | The Principle of Opportunity Cost

**1.1** Consider Figure 2.1 on page 32. Between points *c* and *d*, the opportunity cost of _____ tons of wheat is _____ tons of steel.

**1.2** Arrow up or down: An increase in the wage for high-school graduates _____ the opportunity cost of college.

**1.3** Arrow up or down: An increase in the market interest rate _____ the economic cost of holding a $500 collectible for a year.

**1.4** Oprah just inherited a house with a market value of $200,000, and she does not expect the market value to change. Each year, she will pay $500 for utilities and $3,000 in taxes. She can earn 6 percent interest on money in a bank account. Her cost of living in the house for a year is $_____.

**1.5** What is the cost of a pair of warships purchased by Malaysia? (Related to Application 2 on page 34.)

**1.6** **The Cost of a Flower Business.** Jen left a job paying $50,000 per year to start her own florist shop in a building she owns. The market value of the building is $100,000. She pays $30,000 per year

for flowers and other supplies, and has a bank account that pays 8 percent interest. What is the economic cost of Jen's business? (Related to Application 1 on page 31.)

**1.7** **The Opportunity Cost of a Mission to Mars.** The United States has plans to spend billions of dollars on a mission to Mars. List some of the possible opportunity costs of the mission. What resources will be used to execute the mission, and what do we sacrifice by using these resources on a mission to Mars? (Related to Application 2 on page 34.)

**1.8** **Interest Rates and ATM Trips.** Carlos, who lives in a country where interest rates are very high, goes to an ATM every day to get $10 of spending money. Art, who lives in a country with relatively low interest rates, goes to the ATM once a month to get $300 of spending money. Why does Carlos use the ATM more frequently?

**1.9** **Correct the Cost Statements.** Consider the following statements about cost. For each incorrect statement, provide a correct statement about the relevant cost.

**a.** One year ago, I loaned a friend $100, and she just paid me back the whole $100. The loan didn't cost me anything.

**b.** Our sawmill bought a truckload of logs one year ago for $20,000. If we use the logs to build tables today, the cost of the logs is $20,000.

**c.** Our new football stadium was built on land donated to the university by a wealthy alum. The cost of the stadium equals the $50 million construction cost.

**1.10** **Production Possibilities Curve.** Consider a nation that produces MP3 players and bicycles. The following table shows the possible combinations of the two products.

| MP3 players (millions) | 0 | 3 | 6 | 9 | 12 |
|---|---|---|---|---|---|
| Bicycles (millions) | 60 | 54 | 42 | 24 | 0 |

**a.** Draw a production possibilities curve with MP3 players on the horizontal axis and bicycles on the vertical axis.

**b.** Suppose the technology for producing MP3 players improves, meaning that fewer resources are needed for each MP3 player. In contrast, the technology for producing bicycles does not change. Draw a new production possibilities curve.

**c.** The opportunity cost of the first 3 million MP3 players is _____ million bicycles and the opportunity cost of the last 3 million MP3 players is _____ million bicycles.

## 2.2 | The Marginal Principle

**2.1** If a bus company adds a third daily bus between two cities, the company's total cost will increase from $500 to $600 and its total revenue will increase by $150 per day. Should the company add the third bus? _____ (Yes/No)

**2.2** In Figure 2.3 on page 35, suppose the marginal cost of movies is constant at $125 million. Is it sensible to produce the third movie? _____ (Yes/No)

**2.3** Suppose that stricter emissions standards would reduce health-care costs by $50 million but increase the costs of fuel and emissions equipment by $30 million. Is it sensible to tighten the emissions standards? _____ (Yes/No)

**2.4** Continental Airlines ran flights with up to half the seats empty because _____ was greater than _____. (Related to Application 3 on page 37.)

**2.5** **Marginal Airlines.** Marginal Airlines runs 10 flights per day at a total cost of $50,000, including $30,000 in fixed costs for airport fees and the reservation system and $20,000 for flight crews and food service. (Related to Application 3 on page 37.)

**a.** If an 11th flight would have 25 passengers, each paying $100, would it be sensible to run the flight?

**b.** If the 11th flight would have only 15 passengers, would it be sensible to run the flight?

**2.6** **How Many Police Officers?** In your city, each police officer has a budgetary cost of $40,000 per year. The property loss from each burglary is $4,000. The first officer hired will reduce crime by 40 burglaries, and each additional officer will reduce crime by half as much as the previous one. How many officers should the city hire? Illustrate with a graph with a marginal-benefit curve and a marginal-cost curve.

**2.7** **How Many Hours at the Barber Shop?** Your opportunity cost of cutting hair at your barbershop is $20 per hour. Electricity costs $6 per hour, and your weekly rent is $250. You normally stay open nine hours per day.

**a.** What is the marginal cost of staying open for one more hour?

**b.** If you expect to give two haircuts in the 10th hour and you charge $15 per haircut, is it sensible to stay open for the extra hour?

**2.8** **How Many Pints of Blackberries?** The pleasure you get from each pint of freshly picked blackberries is $2.00. It takes you 12 minutes to pick the first pint, and each additional pint takes an additional 2 minutes (14 minutes for the second pint, 16 minutes for the third pint, and so on). The opportunity cost of your time is $0.10 per minute.

**a.** How many pints of blackberries should you pick? Illustrate with a complete graph.

**b.** How would your answer to (a) change if your pleasure decreased by $0.20 for each additional pint ($1.80 for the second, $1.60 for the third, and so on)? Illustrate with a complete graph.

## 2.3 | The Principle of Voluntary Exchange

**3.1** When two people involved in an exchange say "thank you" afterwards, they are merely being polite. _____ (True/False)

**3.2** Consider a transaction in which a consumer buys a book for $15. The value of the book to the buyer is at least $_____, and the cost of producing the book is no more than $_____.

**3.3** Arrow up or down: Andy buys and eats one apple per day, and smacks his lips in appreciation as he eats it. The greater his satisfaction with the exchange of money for an apple, the larger the number of smacks. If the price of apples decreases, the number of smacks per apple will _____.

**3.4** Sally sells one apple per day to Andy, and says "ca-ching" to show her satisfaction with the transaction. The greater her satisfaction with the exchange, the louder her "ca-ching." If the price of apples decreases, her "ca-ching" will become _____. (louder/ softer)

**3.5 Should a Heart Surgeon Do Her Own Plumbing?** A heart surgeon is skillful at unplugging arteries and rerouting the flow of blood, and these skills also make her a very skillful plumber. She can clear a clogged drain in 6 minutes, about 10 times faster than the most skillful plumber in town. (Related to Application 4 on page 39.)
   **a.** Should the surgeon clear her own clogged drains? Explain.
   **b.** Suppose the surgeon earns $20 per minute in heart surgery, and the best plumber in town charges $50 per hour. How much does the surgeon gain by hiring the plumber to clear a clogged drain?

**3.6 Fishing Versus Boat Building.** Half the members of a fishing tribe catch 2 fish per day and half catch 8 fish per day. A group of 10 members could build a boat for another tribe in 1 day and receive a payment of 40 fish for the boat.
   **a.** Suppose the boat builders are drawn at random from the tribe. From the tribe's perspective, what is the expected cost of building the boat?
   **b.** How could the tribe decrease the cost of building the boat, thus making it worthwhile?

**3.7 Solving a Smoking Problem.** Consider a restaurant in a city with no restrictions on smoking. When one patron lights up a cigar in the full restaurant, an uproar occurs because other diners object to the smoke. You leave the restaurant, and when you return five minutes later the air is clear, but everyone is happy. On the table in front of the person who extinguished his cigar is a pile of cash. Use the principle of voluntary exchange to explain what happened.

## 2.4 | The Principle of Diminishing Returns

**4.1** Consider the example of Xena's copy shop. If she added a third worker, her output would increase by fewer than _____ pages.

**4.2** If a firm is subject to diminishing marginal returns, an increase in the number of workers decreases the quantity produced. _____(True/False)

**4.3** Fill in the blanks with "at least" or "less than": If a firm doubles one input but holds the other inputs fixed, we normally expect output to _____ double; if a firm doubles all inputs, we expect output to _____ double.

**4.4** Fill in the blanks with "flexible" or "inflexible": Diminishing returns is applicable when a firm is _____ in choosing inputs, but does not apply when a firm is _____ in choosing its inputs.

**4.5** Arrows up or down: As a farmer adds more and more fertilizer to the soil, the crop yield _____, but at a _____ rate. (Related to Application 5 on page 40.)

**4.6 Feeding the World from a Flowerpot?** Comment on the following statement: "If agriculture did not experience diminishing returns, we could feed the world using the soil from a small flowerpot." (Related to Application 5 on page 40.)

**4.7 When to Use the Principle of Diminishing Returns?** You are the manager of a firm that produces memory chips for mobile phones.
   **a.** In your decision about how much output to produce this week, would you use the principle of diminishing returns? Explain.
   **b.** In your decision about how much output to produce two years from now, would you use the principle of diminishing returns? Explain.

**4.8 Diminishing Returns in a Coffee Shop?** Your coffee shop produces espressos, using an espresso machine and workers.
   **a.** If you double the number of workers but don't add a second espresso machine, would you expect your output (espressos per hour) to double? Explain.
   **b.** If you double the number of workers and add a second espresso machine, would you expect your output (espressos per hour) to double? Explain.

**4.9 Diminishing Returns and the Marginal Principle.** Molly's Espresso Shop has become busy, and the more hours Ted works, the more espressos Molly can sell. The price of espressos is $2 and Ted's hourly wage is $11. Complete the following table.

| Hours for Ted | Espressos Sold | Marginal Benefit from Additional Hour | Marginal Cost from Additional Hour |
|---|---|---|---|
| 0 | 100 | — | — |
| 1 | 130 | $60 = $2 × 30 additional espressos | $11 = hourly wage |
| 2 | 154 | _____ | _____ |
| 3 | 172 | _____ | _____ |
| 4 | 184 | _____ | _____ |
| 5 | 190 | _____ | _____ |
| 6 | 193 | _____ | _____ |

If Molly applies the marginal principle, how many hours should Ted work?

**5.1** Your savings account pays 4 percent per year: Each $100 in the bank grows to $104 over a one-year period. If prices increase by 3 percent per year, by keeping $100 in the bank for a year you actually gain $_____.

**5.2** Suppose that over a one-year period, the nominal wage increases by 2 percent and consumer prices increase by 5 percent. Fill in the blanks: The real wage _____ by _____ percent.

**5.3** Suppose you currently live and work in Cleveland, earning a salary of $60,000 per year and spending $10,000 for housing. You just heard that you will be transferred to a city in California where housing is 50 percent more expensive. In negotiating a new salary, your objective is to keep your real income constant. Your new target salary is $_____.

**5.4** Between 1974 and 2005, the federal minimum wage increased from $2.00 to $5.15. Was the typical minimum-wage worker better off in 2005? _____ (Yes/No) (Related to Application 6 on page 41.)

**5.5** Suppose you graduate with $20,000 in student loans and repay the loans 10 years later. Which is better for you, inflation (rising prices) or deflation (falling prices)? _____ (Related to Application 7 on page 42)

**5.6** **Changes in Welfare Payments.** Between 1970 and 1988, the average monthly welfare payment to single mothers increased from $160 to $360. Over the same period, the cost of a standard basket of consumer goods (a standard bundle of food, housing, and other goods and services) increased from $39 to $118. Fill the blanks in the following table. Did the real value of welfare payments increase or decrease over this period? (Related to Application 6 on page 41.)

| | 1970 | 1988 |
|---|---|---|
| Monthly welfare payment | $160 | $360 |
| Cost of a standard basket of goods | 39 | 118 |
| Number of baskets per week | _____ | _____ |

**5.7** **Changes in Wages and Consumer Prices.** The following table shows for 1980 and 2004 the cost of a standard basket of consumer goods (a standard bundle of food, housing, and other goods and services) and the nominal average wage (hourly earnings) for workers in several sectors of the economy.

| Year | Cost of Consumer Basket | Nominal Wage: Manufacturing | Nominal Wage: Professional Services | Nominal Wage: Leisure and Hospitality | Nominal Wage: Information |
|---|---|---|---|---|---|
| 1980 | $82 | $7.52 | $7.48 | $4.05 | $9.83 |
| 2004 | 189 | 16.34 | 17.69 | 9.01 | 21.70 |
| Percent change from 1980 to 2004 | _____ | _____ | _____ | _____ | _____ |

**a.** Complete the table by computing the percentage changes of the cost of the basket of consumer goods and the nominal wages.

**b.** How do the percentage changes in nominal wages compare to the percentage change in the cost of consumer goods?

**c.** Which sectors experienced an increase in real wages, and which sectors experienced a decrease in real wages?

**5.8** **Repaying a Car Loan.** Suppose you borrow money to buy a car and must repay $20,000 in interest and principal in 5 years. Your current monthly salary is $4,000. (Related to Application 7 on page 42.)

**a.** Complete the following table.

**b.** Which environment has the lowest real cost of repaying the loan?

| Change in Prices and Wages | Monthly Salary | Months of Work to Repay $20,000 Loan |
|---|---|---|
| Stable | $4,000 | |
| Inflation: Prices rise by 25% | _____ | _____ |
| Deflation: Prices drop by 50% | _____ | _____ |

**5.9** **Inflation and Interest Rates.** Len consumes only music, with an initial price of $10 per CD. Like other people, he prefers music now to music later and is willing to accept 1.10 units of music in 1 year for each unit of music he sacrifices today.

**a.** Suppose Len loans $100 to Barb, and Len sacrifices 10 CDs to make the loan. How much must Barb repay Len a year later to make him indifferent about making the loan? What is the implied interest rate?

**b.** Suppose that over the one-year period of the loan, all prices (including the price of CDs) increase by 20 percent. If Len and Barb anticipate the inflation, what is the appropriate loan arrangement? What is the implied interest rate?

# ECONOMIC EXPERIMENT

## Producing Fold-Its

Here is a simple economic experiment that takes about 15 minutes to run. The instructor places a stapler and a stack of paper on a table. Students produce "fold-its" by folding a page of paper in thirds and stapling both ends of the folded page. One student is assigned to inspect each fold-it to be sure that it is produced correctly. The experiment starts with a single student, or worker, who has 1 minute to produce as many fold-its as possible. After the instructor records the number of fold-its produced, the process is repeated with 2 students, 3 students, 4 students, and so on. The question is, "How does the number of fold-its change as the number of workers increases?"

## NOTES

1. Colin Kennedy, "Lord of the Screens," *Economist: The World in 2003*, p. 29 (London, 2003).

2. Adam Smith, *An Inquiry into the Nature and Causes of the Wealth of Nations* (First published in 1776; New York: Random House, 1973), Book 1, Chapter 2.

3. Edward Castronova, *Synthetic Worlds: The Business and Culture of Online Games* (Chicago: University of Chicago Press, 2005).

# 3

# Demand, Supply, and Market Equilibrium

The price of vanilla is bouncing. A kilogram (2.2 pounds) of vanilla beans sold for $50 in 2000, but by 2003 the price had risen to $500 per kilogram. The price soared because a devastating cyclone hit Madagascar, the African nation that leads the world in vanilla production. Three years later in 2006, the price of vanilla beans had sunk to only $25 per kilogram. What caused the price to go from $50 to $500 to $25? As we'll see in this chapter, the answer is "demand and supply." We'll use the model of demand and supply, the most popular tool of economic analysis, to explain the bouncing price of vanilla and other market phenomena.

• **perfectly competitive market**
A market with so many buyers and sellers that no single buyer or seller can affect the market price.

• **quantity demanded**
The amount of a product that consumers are willing and able to buy.

• **demand schedule**
A table that shows the relationship between the price of a product and the quantity demanded, *ceteris paribus*.

This chapter explores the mechanics of markets. We use the model of demand and supply—the most important tool of economic analysis—to see how markets work. We'll see how the prices of goods and services are affected by all sorts of changes in the economy, including bad weather, higher income, technological innovation, bad publicity, and changes in consumer preferences. This chapter will prepare you for the applications of demand and supply you'll see in the rest of the book.

The model of demand and supply explains how a perfectly competitive market operates. A **perfectly competitive market** has many buyers and sellers of a product, and no single buyer or seller can affect the market price. The classic example of a perfectly competitive firm is a wheat farmer, who produces a tiny fraction of the total supply of wheat. No matter how much wheat an individual farmer produces, the farmer can't change the market price of wheat.

# 3.1 | THE DEMAND CURVE

On the demand side of a market, consumers buy products from firms. The main question concerning the demand side of the market is: How much of a particular product are consumers willing to buy during a particular period? A consumer who is willing to buy a particular product is willing to sacrifice enough money to purchase it. The consumer doesn't merely have a desire to buy the good, but is willing and able to sacrifice something to get it. Notice that *demand* is defined for a particular period, for example, a day, a month, or a year.

We'll start our discussion of demand with the individual consumer. How much of a product is an individual willing to buy? It depends on a number of variables. Here is a list of the variables that affect an individual consumer's decision, using the pizza market as an example:

- The price of the product (for example, the price of a pizza)
- The consumer's income
- The price of substitute goods (for example, the prices of tacos or sandwiches)
- The price of complementary goods (for example, the price of lemonade)
- The consumer's preferences or tastes and advertising that may influence preferences
- The consumer's expectations about future prices

Together, these variables determine how much of a particular product an individual consumer is willing and able to buy, the **quantity demanded**. We'll start our discussion of demand with the relationship between the price and quantity demanded, a relationship that is represented graphically by the demand curve. Later in the chapter, we will discuss the other variables that affect the individual consumer's decision about how much of a product to buy.

## The Individual Demand Curve and the Law of Demand

The starting point for a discussion of individual demand is a **demand schedule**, which is a table of numbers showing the relationship between the price of a particular product and the quantity that an individual consumer is willing to buy. The demand schedule shows how the quantity demanded by an individual changes with the price, *ceteris paribus* (everything else held fixed). The variables that are held fixed in the demand schedule are the consumer's income, the prices of substitutes and complements, the consumer's tastes, and the consumer's expectations about future prices.

The table in Figure 3.1 shows Al's demand schedule for pizza. At a price of $2, Al buys 13 pizzas per month. As the price rises, he buys fewer pizzas: 10 pizzas at a price of $4, 7 pizzas at a price of $6, and so on, down to only 1 pizza at a price of $10. It's important to remember that in a demand schedule, any change in quantity results from a change in price alone.

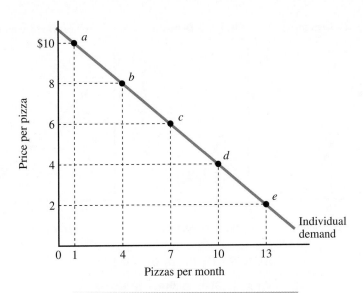

**The Individual Demand Curve**
According to the law of demand, the higher the price, the smaller the quantity demanded, everything else being equal. Therefore, the demand curve is negatively sloped: When the price increases from $6 to $8, the quantity demanded decreases from 7 pizzas per month (point *c*) to 4 pizzas per month (point *b*).

**AL'S DEMAND SCHEDULE FOR PIZZAS**

| Point | Price | Quantity of Pizzas per Month |
|-------|-------|------------------------------|
| *a* | $10 | 1 |
| *b* | 8 | 4 |
| *c* | 6 | 7 |
| *d* | 4 | 10 |
| *e* | 2 | 13 |

The **individual demand curve** is a graphical representation of the demand schedule. By plotting the numbers in Al's demand schedule—various combinations of price and quantity—we can draw his demand curve for pizza. The demand curve shows the relationship between the price and the quantity demanded by an individual consumer, *ceteris paribus*. To get the data for a single demand curve, we change only the price of pizza and observe how a consumer responds to the price change. In Figure 3.1, Al's demand curve shows the quantity of pizzas he is willing to buy at each price.

Notice that Al's demand curve is negatively sloped, reflecting the **law of demand**. This law applies to all consumers:

*There is a negative relationship between price and quantity demanded,* **ceteris paribus.**

The words *ceteris paribus* remind us that to isolate the relationship between price and quantity demanded, we *must* assume that income, the prices of related goods such as substitutes and complements, and tastes are unchanged. As the price of pizza increases and nothing else changes, Al moves upward along his demand curve and buys a smaller quantity of pizza. For example, if the price increases from $8 to $10, Al moves upward along his demand curve from point *b* to point *a*, and he buys only 1 pizza per month, down from 4 pizzas at the lower price. A movement along a single demand curve is called a **change in quantity demanded**, a change in the quantity a consumer is willing to buy when the price changes.

## From Individual Demand to Market Demand

The **market demand curve** shows the relationship between the price of the good and the quantity demanded by *all* consumers, *ceteris paribus*. As in the case of the individual demand curve, when we draw the market demand curve we assume that the other

• **individual demand curve**
A curve that shows the relationship between the price of a good and quantity demanded by an individual consumer, *ceteris paribus*.

• **law of demand**
There is a negative relationship between price and quantity demanded, *ceteris paribus*.

• **change in quantity demanded**
A change in the quantity consumers are willing and able to buy when the price changes; represented graphically by movement along the demand curve.

• **market demand curve**
A curve showing the relationship between price and quantity demanded by all consumers, *ceteris paribus*.

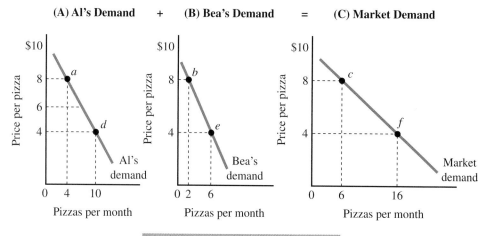

| QUANTITY OF PIZZA DEMANDED | | | |
|---|---|---|---|
| **Price** | **Al +** | **Bea =** | **Market Demand** |
| $8 | 4 | 2 | 6 |
| 6 | 7 | 4 | 11 |
| 4 | 10 | 6 | 16 |
| 2 | 13 | 8 | 21 |

▲ **FIGURE 3.2**

**From Individual to Market Demand**

The market demand equals the sum of the demands of all consumers. In this case, there are only two consumers, so at each price, the market quantity demanded equals the quantity demanded by Al plus the quantity demanded by Bea. At a price of $8, Al's quantity is 4 pizzas (point *a*) and Bea's quantity is 2 pizzas (point *b*), so the market quantity demanded is 6 pizzas (point *c*). Each consumer obeys the law of demand, so the market demand curve is negatively sloped.

variables that affect individual demand (income, the prices of substitute and complementary goods, tastes, and price expectations) are fixed. In addition, we assume that the number of consumers is fixed.

Figure 3.2 shows how to derive the market demand curve when there are only 2 consumers. Panel A shows Al's demand curve for pizza, and Panel B shows Bea's demand curve. At a price of $8, Al will buy 4 pizzas (point *a*) and Bea will buy 2 pizzas (point *b*), so the total quantity demanded at this price is 6 pizzas. In Panel C, point *c* shows the point on the market demand curve associated with a price of $8. At this price, the market quantity demanded is 6 pizzas. If the price drops to $4, Al will buy 10 pizzas (point *d*) and Bea will buy 6 pizzas (point *e*), for a total of 16 pizzas (shown by point *f* on the market demand curve). The market demand curve is the horizontal sum of the individual demand curves.

The market demand is negatively sloped, reflecting the law of demand. This is sensible, because if each consumer obeys the law of demand, consumers as a group will too. When the price increases from $4 to $8, there is a change in quantity demanded as we move along the demand curve from point *f* to point *c*. The movement along the demand curve occurs if the price of pizza is the only variable that has changed.

# 3.2 | THE SUPPLY CURVE

On the supply side of a market, firms sell their products to consumers. Suppose you ask the manager of a firm, "How much of your product are you willing to produce and sell?" The answer is likely to be "It depends." The manager's decision about how much to produce depends on many variables, including the following, using pizza as an example:

- The price of the product (for example, the price per pizza)
- The wage paid to workers
- The price of materials (for example, the price of dough and cheese)
- The cost of capital (for example, the cost of a pizza oven)
- The state of production technology (for example, the knowledge used in making pizza)
- Producers' expectations about future prices
- Taxes paid to the government or *subsidies* (payments from the government to firms to produce a product)

Together, these variables determine how much of a product firms are willing to produce and sell, the **quantity supplied**. We'll start our discussion of market supply with the relationship between the price of a good and the quantity of that good supplied, a relationship that is represented graphically by the supply curve. Later in the chapter, we will discuss the other variables that affect the individual firm's decision about how much of a product to produce and sell.

• **quantity supplied**
The amount of a product that firms are willing and able to sell.

## The Individual Supply Curve and the Law of Supply

Consider the decision of an individual producer. The starting point for a discussion of individual supply is a **supply schedule**, a table that shows the relationship between the price of a particular product and the quantity that an individual producer is willing to sell. The supply schedule shows how the quantity supplied by an individual producer changes with the price, *ceteris paribus*. The variables that are held fixed in the supply schedule are input costs, technology, price expectations, and government taxes or subsidies.

The table in Figure 3.3 shows the supply schedule for pizza at Lola's Pizza Shop. At a price of $2, she doesn't produce any pizzas, indicating that a $2 price is not high enough to cover her cost of producing a pizza. In contrast, at a price of $4 she supplies

• **supply schedule**
A table that shows the relationship between the price of a product and quantity supplied, *ceteris paribus*.

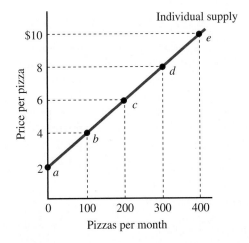

**◀ FIGURE 3.3**
**The Individual Supply Curve**
The supply curve of an individual supplier is positively sloped, reflecting the law of supply. As shown by point *a*, the quantity supplied is zero at a price of $2, indicating that the minimum supply price is just above $2. An increase in price increases the quantity supplied, to 100 pizzas at a price of $4, to 200 pizzas at a price of $6, and so on.

### INDIVIDUAL SUPPLY SCHEDULE FOR PIZZA

| Point | Price | Quantity of Pizzas per Month |
|-------|-------|------------------------------|
| *a* | $2 | 0 |
| *b* | 4 | 100 |
| *c* | 6 | 200 |
| *d* | 8 | 300 |
| *e* | 10 | 400 |

• **individual supply curve**
A curve showing the relationship between price and quantity supplied by a single firm, *ceteris paribus*.

• **law of supply**
There is a positive relationship between price and quantity supplied, *ceteris paribus*.

• **change in quantity supplied**
A change in the quantity firms are willing and able to sell when the price changes; represented graphically by movement along the supply curve.

• **minimum supply price**
The lowest price at which a product will be supplied.

100 pizzas. In this example, each $2 increase in price increases the quantity supplied by 100 pizzas—to 200 at a price of $6, to 300 at a price of $8, and so on. It's important to remember that in a supply schedule, a change in quantity results from a change in price alone.

The **individual supply curve** is a graphical representation of the supply schedule. By plotting the numbers in Lola's supply schedule—different combinations of price and quantity—we can draw her supply curve for pizza. The individual supply curve shows the relationship between the price of a product and the quantity supplied by a single firm, *ceteris paribus*. To get the data for a supply curve, we change only the price of pizza and observe how a producer responds to the price change.

Figure 3.3 shows the supply curve for Lola, which shows the quantity of pizzas she is willing to sell at each price. The individual supply curve is positively sloped, reflecting the **law of supply**, a pattern of behavior that we observe in producers:

*There is a positive relationship between price and quantity supplied, **ceteris paribus**.*

The words *ceteris paribus* remind us that to isolate the relationship between price and quantity supplied we assume that the other factors that influence producers are unchanged. As the price of pizza increases and nothing else changes, Lola moves upward along her individual supply curve and produces a larger quantity of pizza. For example, if the price increases from $6 to $8, Lola moves upward along her supply curve from point *c* to point *d*, and the quantity supplied increases from 200 to 300. A movement along a single supply curve is called a **change in quantity supplied**, a change in the quantity that a producer is willing and able to sell when the price changes.

The **minimum supply price** is the lowest price at which a product is supplied. A firm won't produce a product unless the price is high enough to cover the marginal cost of producing it. In the case of pizza, the price must be high enough to cover the cost of producing the first pizza. As shown in Figure 3.3, a price of $2 is not high enough to cover the cost of producing the first pizza, so Lola's quantity supplied is zero (point *a*). But when the price rises above $2, she produces some pizzas, indicating that her minimum supply price is just above $2.

### Why Is the Individual Supply Curve Positively Sloped?

The individual supply curve is positively sloped, consistent with the law of supply. To explain the positive slope, consider how Lola responds to an increase in price. A higher price encourages a firm to increase its output by purchasing more materials and hiring more workers. To increase her workforce, Lola might be forced to pay overtime or hire workers who are more costly or less productive than the original workers. But the higher price of pizza makes it worthwhile to incur these higher costs.

The supply curve shows the marginal cost of production for different quantities produced. We can use the marginal principle to explain this.

## MARGINAL PRINCIPLE

Increase the level of an activity as long as its marginal benefit exceeds its marginal cost. Choose the level at which the marginal benefit equals the marginal cost.

For Lola, the marginal benefit of producing a pizza is the price she gets for it. When the price is only $2.00, she doesn't produce any pizza, which tells us that the marginal cost of the first pizza must be greater than $2.00; otherwise, she would have produced it. But when the price rises to $2.01, she produces the first pizza because now the marginal benefit (the $2.01 price) exceeds the marginal cost. This tells us that the marginal cost of the first pizza is less than $2.01; otherwise, she wouldn't produce it at a price of $2.01. To summarize, the marginal cost of the first pizza is between $2.00 and $2.01, or just over $2.00. Similarly, point *b* on the supply curve in Figure 3.3 shows that Lola won't produce her 100<sup>th</sup> pizza at a price of $3.99, but will produce at a price of $4.00, indicating that her marginal cost of producing that pizza is between $3.99 and $4.00, or just under $4.00. In general, the supply curve shows the marginal cost of production.

## From Individual Supply to Market Supply

The **market supply curve** for a particular good shows the relationship between the price of the good and the quantity that all producers together are willing to sell, *ceteris paribus*. To draw the market supply curve, we assume that the other variables that affect individual supply are fixed. The market quantity supplied is simply the sum of the quantities supplied by all the firms in the market. To show how to draw the market supply curve, we'll assume that there are only two firms in the market. Of course, a perfectly competitive market has a large number of firms, but the lessons from the two-firm case generalize to a case of many firms.

Figure 3.4 shows how to derive a market supply curve from individual supply curves. In Panel A, Lola has relatively low production costs, as reflected in her relatively low minimum supply price ($2 at point *a*). In Panel B, Hiram has higher production costs, so he has a higher minimum price ($6 at point *f*). As a result, his supply curve lies above Lola's. To draw the market supply curve, we add the individual supply curves horizontally. This gives us two segments for the market supply curve:

- **Prices between $2 and $6:** Segment connecting points *i* and *k*. Hiram's high-cost firm doesn't supply any output, so the market supply is the same as the individual supply from Lola. For example, at a price of $4 Lola supplies 100 pizzas (point *b*) and Hiram does not produce any pizzas, so the market supply is 100 pizzas (point *j*).

- **market supply curve**
  A curve showing the relationship between the market price and quantity supplied by all firms, *ceteris paribus*.

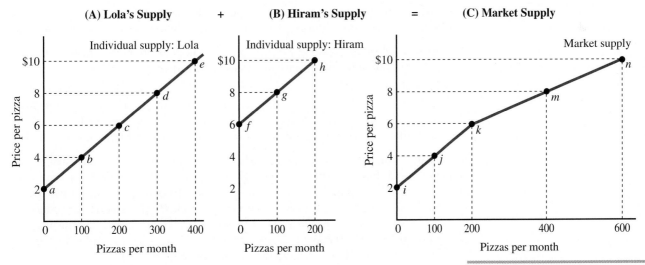

▲ **FIGURE 3.4**
**From Individual to Market Supply**
The market supply is the sum of the supplies of all firms. In Panel A, Lola is a low-cost producer who produces the first pizza once the price rises above $2 (shown by point *a*). In Panel B, Hiram is a high-cost producer who doesn't produce pizza until the price rises above $6 (shown by point *f*). To draw the market supply curve, we sum the individual supply curves horizontally. At a price of $8, market supply is 400 pizzas (point *m*), equal to 300 from Lola (point *d*) plus 100 from Hiram (point *g*)

**QUANTITY OF PIZZA SUPPLIED**

| Price | Lola + | Hiram = | Market Supply |
|---|---|---|---|
| 2 | 0 | 0 | 0 |
| 4 | 100 | 0 | 100 |
| 6 | 200 | 0 | 200 |
| 8 | 300 | 100 | 400 |
| 10 | 400 | 200 | 600 |

► **FIGURE 3.5**

**The Market Supply Curve with Many Firms**

The market supply is the sum of the supplies of all firms. The minimum supply price is $2 (point *a*), and the quantity supplied increases by 10,000 for each $2 increase in price, to 10,000 at a price of $4 (point *b*), to 20,000 at a price of $6 (point *c*), and so on.

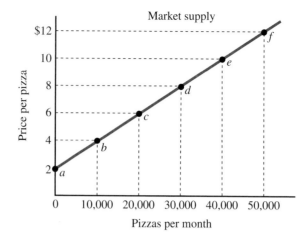

- **Prices above $6:** Segment above point *k*. At higher prices, the high-cost firm produces some output, and the market supply is the sum of the quantities supplied by the two firms. For example, at a price of $8 Lola produces 300 pizzas (point *d*) and Hiram produces 100 pizzas (point *g*), so the market quantity supplied is 400 pizzas (point *m*).

A perfectly competitive market has hundreds of firms rather than just two, but the process of going from individual supply curves to the market supply curve is the same. We add the individual supply curves horizontally by picking a price and adding up the quantities supplied by all the firms in the market. In the more realistic case of many firms, the supply curve will be smooth rather than kinked. This smooth line is shown in Figure 3.5. In this case, we assume that there are 100 firms identical to Lola's firm. The minimum supply price is $2, and for each $2 increase in price, the quantity supplied increases by 10,000 pizzas.

### Why Is the Market Supply Curve Positively Sloped?

The market supply curve is positively sloped, consistent with the law of supply. To explain the positive slope, consider the two responses by firms to an increase in price:

- **Individual firm.** As we saw earlier, a higher price encourages a firm to increase its output by purchasing more materials and hiring more workers.

- **New firms.** In the long run, new firms can enter the market and existing firms can expand their production facilities to produce more output. The new firms may have higher production costs than the original firms, but the higher output price makes it worthwhile to enter the market even with higher costs.

Like the individual supply curve, the market supply curve shows the marginal cost of production for different quantities produced. In Figure 3.5, the marginal cost of the first pizza is the minimum supply price for the firm with the lowest cost (just over $2.00). Similarly, point *d* on the supply curve shows that the 30,000th pizza won't be produced at a price of $7.99, but will be produced at a price of $8.00. This indicates that the marginal cost of producing the 30,000th pizza is just under $8.00. Like the individual supply curve, the market supply curve shows the marginal cost of production.

## 3.3 | MARKET EQUILIBRIUM: BRINGING DEMAND AND SUPPLY TOGETHER

A market is an arrangement that brings buyers and sellers together. So far in this chapter, we've seen how the two sides of a market—demand and supply—work. In this part of the chapter, we bring the two sides of the market together to show how prices and quantities are determined.

When the quantity of a product demanded equals the quantity supplied at the prevailing market price, this is called a **market equilibrium**. When a market reaches an equilibrium, there is no pressure to change the price. For example, if pizza firms produce exactly the quantity of pizza consumers are willing to buy, there will be no pressure for the price of pizza to change. In Figure 3.6, the equilibrium price is shown by the intersection of the demand and supply curves. At a price of $8, the supply curve shows that firms will produce 30,000 pizzas, which is exactly the quantity that consumers are willing to buy at that price.

- **market equilibrium**
  A situation in which the quantity demanded equals the quantity supplied at the prevailing market price.

## Excess Demand Causes the Price to Rise

If the price is below the equilibrium price, there will be excess demand for the product. **Excess demand** (sometimes called a *shortage*) occurs when, at the prevailing market price, the quantity demanded exceeds the quantity supplied, meaning that consumers are willing to buy more than producers are willing to sell. In Figure 3.6, at a price of $6, there is an excess demand equal to 16,000 pizzas: Consumers are willing to buy 36,000 pizzas (point *c*), but producers are willing to sell only 20,000 pizzas (point *b*). This mismatch between demand and supply will cause the price of pizza to rise. Firms will increase the price they charge for their limited supply of pizza, and anxious consumers will pay the higher price to get one of the few pizzas that are available.

- **excess demand (shortage)**
  A situation in which, at the prevailing price, the quantity demanded exceeds the quantity supplied.

An increase in price eliminates excess demand by changing both the quantity demanded and quantity supplied. As the price increases, the excess demand shrinks for two reasons:

- The market moves upward along the demand curve (from point *c* toward point *a*), decreasing the quantity demanded.
- The market moves upward along the supply curve (from point *b* toward point *a*), increasing the quantity supplied.

Because the quantity demanded decreases while the quantity supplied increases, the gap between the quantity demanded and the quantity supplied narrows. The price will continue to rise until excess demand is eliminated. In Figure 3.6, at a price of $8 the quantity supplied equals the quantity demanded, as shown by point *a*.

In some cases, government creates an excess demand for a good by setting a maximum price (sometimes called a *price ceiling*). If the government sets a maximum price that is less than the equilibrium price, the result is a permanent excess demand for the good. Later in the book, we will explore the market effects of such policies.

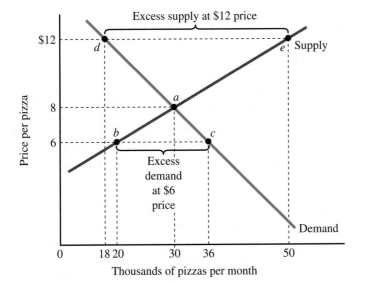

◄ **FIGURE 3.6**
**Market Equilibrium**
At the market equilibrium (point *a*, with price = $8 and quantity = 30,000), the quantity supplied equals the quantity demanded. At a price below the equilibrium price ($6), there is excess demand— the quantity demanded at point *c* exceeds the quantity supplied at point *b*. At a price above the equilibrium price ($12), there is excess supply—the quantity supplied at point *e* exceeds the quantity demanded at point *d*).

• **excess supply (surplus)**
A situation in which at the prevailing price the quantity supplied exceeds the quantity demanded.

## Excess Supply Causes the Price to Drop

What happens if the price is above the equilibrium price? **Excess supply** (sometimes called a *surplus*) occurs when the quantity supplied exceeds the quantity demanded, meaning that producers are willing to sell more than consumers are willing to buy. This is shown by points *d* and *e* in Figure 3.6. At a price of $12, the excess supply is 32,000 pizzas: Producers are willing to sell 50,000 pizzas (point *e*), but consumers are willing to buy only 18,000 pizzas (point *d*). This mismatch will cause the price of pizzas to fall as firms cut the price to sell them. As the price drops, the excess supply will shrink for two reasons:

- The market moves downward along the demand curve from point *d* toward point *a*, increasing the quantity demanded.
- The market moves downward along the supply curve from point *e* toward point *a*, decreasing the quantity supplied.

Because the quantity demanded increases while the quantity supplied decreases, the gap between the quantity supplied and the quantity demanded narrows. The price will continue to drop until excess supply is eliminated. In Figure 3.6, at a price of $8, the quantity supplied equals the quantity demanded, as shown by point *a*.

The government sometimes creates an excess supply of a good by setting a minimum price (sometimes called a *price floor*). If the government sets a minimum price that is greater than the equilibrium price, the result is a permanent excess supply. We'll discuss the market effects of minimum prices later in the book.

# 3.4 | MARKET EFFECTS OF CHANGES IN DEMAND

We've seen that a market equilibrium occurs when the quantity supplied equals the quantity demanded, shown graphically by the intersection of the supply curve and the demand curve. In this part of the chapter, we'll see how changes on the demand side of the market affect the equilibrium price and equilibrium quantity.

## Change in Quantity Demanded Versus Change in Demand

Earlier in the chapter, we listed the variables that determine how much of a particular product consumers are willing to buy. One of the variables is the price of the product. The demand curve shows the negative relationship between price and quantity demanded, *ceteris paribus*. In Panel A of Figure 3.7, when the price decreases from $8 to $6, we move down-

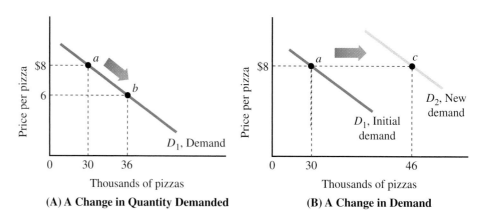

**(A) A Change in Quantity Demanded**     **(B) A Change in Demand**

▲ **FIGURE 3.7**
**Change in Quantity Demanded Versus Change in Demand**
(**A**) A change in price causes a change in quantity demanded, a movement along a single demand curve. For example, a decrease in price causes a move from point *a* to point *b*, increasing the quantity demanded.
(**B**) A change in demand, caused by changes in a variable other than the price of the good, shifts the entire demand curve. For example, an increase in demand shifts the demand curve from $D_1$ to $D_2$.

ward along the demand curve from point *a* to point *b*, and the quantity demanded increases. As noted earlier in the chapter, this is called a *change in quantity demanded*. Now we're ready to take a closer look at the other variables that affect demand besides price—income, the prices of related goods, tastes, advertising, and the number of consumers—and see how changes in these variables affect the demand for the product and the market equilibrium.

If any of these other variables change, the relationship between the product's price and quantity—shown numerically in the demand schedule and graphically in the demand curve—will change. That means we will have an entirely different demand schedule and an entirely different demand curve. In Panel B of Figure 3.7, this is shown as a *shift* of the entire demand curve from $D_1$ to $D_2$. This shift means that at any price consumers are willing to buy a larger quantity of the product. For example, at a price of $8 consumers are willing to buy 46,000 pizzas (point *c*), up from 30,000 with the initial demand curve. To convey the idea that changes in these other variables change the demand schedule and the demand curve, we say that a change in any of these variables causes a **change in demand**.

## Increases in Demand Shift the Demand Curve

What types of changes will increase the demand and shift the demand curve to the right, as shown in Figure 3.7? An increase in demand like the one represented in Figure 3.7 can occur for several reasons, which are listed in Table 3.1:

- **Increase in income.** Consumers use their income to buy products, and the more money they have, the more money they spend. For a **normal good**, there is a positive relationship between consumer income and the quantity consumed. When income increases, a consumer buys a larger quantity of a normal good. Most goods fall into this category—including new clothes, movies, and pizza.

- **Decrease in income.** An **inferior good** is the opposite of a normal good. Consumers buy larger quantities of inferior goods when their income *decreases*. For example, if you lose your job you might make your own coffee instead of buying it in a coffee shop, rent DVDs instead of going to the theater, and eat more macaroni and cheese. In this case, home-made coffee, DVDs, and macaroni and cheese are examples of inferior goods.

- **Increase in price of a substitute good.** When two goods are **substitutes**, an increase in the price of the first good causes some consumers to switch to the second good. Tacos and pizzas are substitutes, so an increase in the price of tacos increases the demand for pizzas as some consumers substitute pizza for tacos, which are now more expensive relative to pizza.

- **change in demand**
  A shift of the demand curve caused by a change in a variable other than the price of the product.

- **normal good**
  A good for which an increase in income increases demand.

- **inferior good**
  A good for which an increase in income decreases demand.

- **substitutes**
  Two goods for which an increase in the price of one good increases the demand for the other good.

## Table 3.1 | INCREASES IN DEMAND SHIFT THE DEMAND CURVE TO THE RIGHT

| When this variable... | increases or decreases... | the demand curve shifts in this direction... |
|---|:---:|---|
| Income, with normal good | ↑ | |
| Income, with inferior good | ↓ | |
| Price of a substitute good | ↑ | |
| Price of complementary good | ↓ | |
| Population | ↑ | |
| Consumer preferences for good | ↑ | |
| Expected future price | ↑ | |

**An Increase in Demand Increases the Equilibrium Price**

An increase in demand shifts the demand curve to the right: At each price, the quantity demanded increases. At the initial price ($8), there is excess demand, with the quantity demanded (point *b*) exceeding the quantity supplied (point *a*). The excess demand causes the price to rise, and equilibrium is restored at point *c*. To summarize, the increase in demand increases the equilibrium price to $10 and increases the equilibrium quantity to 40,000 pizzas.

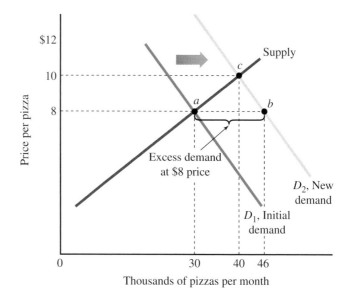

• **complements**
Two goods for which a decrease in the price of one good increases the demand for the other good.

• **Decrease in price of a complementary good.** When two goods are **complements**, they are consumed together as a package, and a decrease in the price of one good decreases the cost of the entire package. As a result, consumers buy more of both goods. Pizza and lemonade are complementary goods, so a decrease in the price of lemonade decreases the total cost of a lemonade-and-pizza meal, increasing the demand for pizza.

• **Increase in population.** An increase in the number of people means that there are more potential pizza consumers—more individual demand curves to add up to get the market demand curve—so market demand increases.

• **Shift in consumer preferences.** Consumers' preferences or tastes can change over time. If consumers' preferences shift in favor of pizza, the demand for pizza increases. One purpose of advertising is to change consumers' preferences, and a successful pizza advertising campaign will increase the demand for pizza.

• **Expectations of higher future prices.** If consumers think next month's pizza price will be higher than they had initially expected, they may buy a larger quantity today and a smaller quantity next month. That means that the demand for pizza today will increase.

We can use Figure 3.8 to show how an increase in demand affects the equilibrium price and equilibrium quantity. An increase in the demand for pizza resulting from one or more of the factors listed in Table 3.1 shifts the demand curve to the right, from $D_1$ to $D_2$. At the initial price of $8, there will be excess demand, as indicated by points *a* and *b*: Consumers are willing to buy 46,000 pizzas (point *b*), but producers are willing to sell only 30,000 pizzas (point *a*). Consumers want to buy 16,000 more pizzas than producers are willing to supply, and the excess demand causes upward pressure on the price. As the price rises, the excess demand shrinks because the quantity demanded decreases while the quantity supplied increases. The supply curve intersects the new demand curve at point *c*, so the new equilibrium price is $10 (up from $8), and the new equilibrium quantity is 40,000 pizzas (up from 30,000).

### Decreases in Demand Shift the Demand Curve

What types of changes in the pizza market will decrease the demand for pizza? A decrease in demand means that at each price consumers are willing to buy a smaller quantity. In Figure 3.9, a decrease in demand shifts the market demand curve from $D_1$ to $D_0$. At the initial price of $8, the quantity demanded decreases

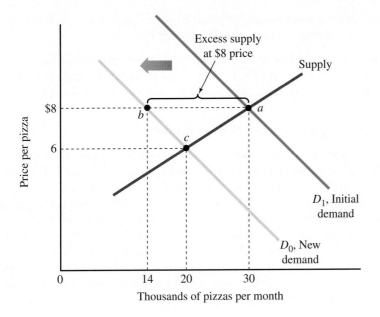

A decrease in demand shifts the demand curve to the left: At each price, the quantity demanded decreases. At the initial price ($8), there is excess supply, with the quantity supplied (point *a*) exceeding the quantity demanded (point *b*). The excess supply causes the price to drop, and equilibrium is restored at point *c*. To summarize, the decrease in demand decreases the equilibrium price to $6 and decreases the equilibrium quantity to 20,000 pizzas.

from 30,000 pizzas (point *a*) to 14,000 pizzas (point *b*). A decrease in demand like the one represented in Figure 3.9 can occur for several reasons, which are listed in Table 3.2:

- **Decrease in income.** A decrease in income means that consumers have less to spend, so they buy a smaller quantity of each normal good.

- **Decrease in the price of a substitute good.** A decrease in the price of a substitute good such as tacos makes pizza more expensive relative to tacos, causing consumers to demand less pizza.

- **Increase in the price of a complementary good.** An increase in the price of a complementary good such as lemonade increases the cost of a lemonade-and-pizza meal, decreasing the demand for pizza.

- **Decrease in population.** A decrease in the number of people means that there are fewer pizza consumers, so the market demand for pizza decreases.

**Table 3.2** ⏐ DECREASES IN DEMAND SHIFT THE DEMAND CURVE TO THE LEFT

| When this variable... | increases or decreases... | the demand curve shifts in this direction... |
|---|:---:|---|
| Income, with normal good | ↓ | |
| Income, with inferior good | ↑ | |
| Price of a substitute good | ↓ | |
| Price of complementary good | ↑ | |
| Population | ↓ | |
| Consumer preferences for good | ↓ | |
| Expected future price | ↓ | |

- **Shift in consumer tastes.** When consumers' preferences shift away from pizza in favor of other products, the demand for pizza decreases.

- **Expectations of lower future prices.** If consumers think next month's pizza price will be lower than they had initially expected, they may buy a smaller quantity today, meaning the demand for pizza today will decrease.

### A Decrease in Demand Decreases the Equilibrium Price

We can use Figure 3.9 to show how a decrease in demand affects the equilibrium price and equilibrium quantity. The decrease in the demand for pizza shifts the demand curve to the left, from $D_1$ to $D_0$. At the initial price of $8, there will be an excess supply, as indicated by points *a* and *b*: Producers are willing to sell 30,000 pizzas (point *a*), but given the lower demand consumers are willing to buy only 14,000 pizzas (point *b*). Producers want to sell 16,000 more pizzas than consumers are willing to buy, and the excess supply causes downward pressure on the price. As the price falls, the excess supply shrinks because the quantity demanded increases while the quantity supplied decreases. The supply curve intersects the new demand curve at point *c*, so the new equilibrium price is $6 (down from $8), and the new equilibrium quantity is 20,000 pizzas (down from 30,000).

# $3.5$ | MARKET EFFECTS OF CHANGES IN SUPPLY

We've seen that changes in demand shift the demand curve and change the equilibrium price and quantity. In this part of the chapter, we'll see how changes on the supply side of the market affect the equilibrium price and equilibrium quantity.

## Change in Quantity Supplied Versus Change in Supply

Earlier in the chapter, we listed the variables that determine how much of a product firms are willing to sell. Of course, one of these variables is the price of the product. The supply curve shows the positive relationship between price and quantity, *ceteris paribus*. In Panel A of Figure 3.10, when the price increases from $6 to $8 we move

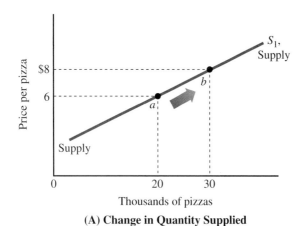

**(A) Change in Quantity Supplied**

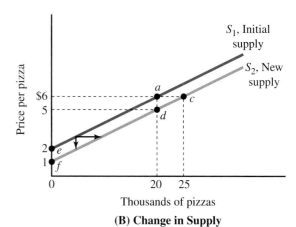

**(B) Change in Supply**

▲ **FIGURE 3.10**

**Change in Quantity Supplied Versus Change in Supply**

(**A**) A change in price causes a change in quantity supplied, a movement along a single supply curve. For example, an increase in price causes a move from point *a* to point *b*.

(**B**) A change in supply (caused by a change in something other than the price of the product) shifts the entire supply curve. For example, an increase in supply shifts the supply curve from $S_1$ to $S_2$. For any given price (for example, $6), a larger quantity is supplied (25,000 pizzas at point *c* instead of 20,000 at point *a*). The price required to generate any given quantity decreases. For example, the price required to generate 20,000 pizzas drops from $6 (point *a*) to $5 (point *d*).

along the supply curve from point *a* to point *b*, and the quantity of the product supplied increases. As noted earlier in the chapter, this is called a *change in quantity supplied*. Now we're ready to take a closer look at the other variables that affect supply—including wages, material prices, and technology—and see how changes in these variables affect the supply curve and the market equilibrium.

If any of these other variables changes, the relationship between price and quantity—shown numerically in the supply schedule and graphically in the supply curve—will change. That means that we will have an entirely different supply schedule and a different supply curve. In Panel B of Figure 3.10, this is shown as a shift of the entire supply curve from $S_1$ to $S_2$. In this case, the supply curve shifts downward and to the right:

- The shift to the right means that at any given price (for example, $6), a larger quantity is produced (25,000 pizzas at point *c*, up from 20,000 at point *a*).
- The shift downward means that the price required to generate a particular quantity of output is lower. For example, the new minimum supply price is just over $1 (point *f*), down from just over $2 (point *e*). Similarly, the price required to generate 20,000 pizzas is $5 (point *d*), down from $6 (point *a*).

To convey the idea that changes in these other variables change the supply curve, we say that a change in any of these variables causes a **change in supply**.

### Increases in Supply Shift the Supply Curve

What types of changes increase the supply of a product, shifting the supply curve downward and to the right? Consider first the effect of a decrease in the wage paid to pizza workers. A decrease in the wage will decrease the cost of producing pizza and shift the supply curve:

- **Downward shift.** When the cost of production decreases, the price required to generate any given quantity of pizza will decrease. In general, a lower wage means a lower marginal cost of production, so each firm needs a lower price to cover its production cost. In other words, the supply curve shifts downward.
- **Rightward shift.** The decrease in production costs makes pizza production more profitable at a given price, so producers will supply more at each price. In other words, the supply curve shifts to the right.

A decrease in the wage is just one example of a decrease in production costs that shifts the supply curve downward and to the right. These supply shifters are listed in Table 3.3. A reduction in the costs of materials (dough, cheese) or capital (pizza

• **change in supply**
A shift of the supply curve caused by a change in a variable other than the price of the product.

**Table 3.3** | CHANGES IN SUPPLY SHIFT THE SUPPLY CURVE DOWNWARD AND TO THE RIGHT

| When this variable... | increases or decreases... | the supply curve shifts in this direction... |
|---|---|---|
| Wage | ↓ | |
| Price of materials or capital | ↓ | |
| Technological advance | ↑ | |
| Government subsidy | ↑ | |
| Expected future price | ↓ | |
| Number of producers | ↑ | |

oven) decreases production costs, decreasing the price required to generate any particular quantity (downward shift) and increasing the quantity supplied at any particular price (rightward shift). An improvement in technology that allows the firm to economize on labor or material inputs cuts production costs and shifts the supply curve in a similar fashion. The technological improvement could be a new machine or a new way of doing business—a new layout for a factory or store, or a more efficient system of ordering inputs and distributing output. Finally, if a government subsidizes production by paying the firm some amount for each unit produced, the net cost to the firm is lowered by the amount of the subsidy, and the supply curve shifts downward and to the right.

Two other possible sources of increases in supply are listed in Table 3.3. First, if firms believe that next month's price will be lower than they had initially expected, they may try to sell more output now at this month's relatively high price, increasing supply this month. Second, because the market supply is the sum of the quantities supplied by all producers, an increase in the number of producers will increase market supply.

As summarized in Table 3.3, the language of shifting supply is a bit tricky. An increase in supply is represented graphically by a shift to the right (a larger quantity supplied at each price) and down (a lower price required to generate a particular quantity). The best way to remember this is to recognize that the *increase* in "increase in supply" refers to the increase in quantity supplied at a particular price—the horizontal shift of the supply curve to the right.

## An Increase in Supply Decreases the Equilibrium Price

We can use Figure 3.11 to show the effects of an increase in supply on the equilibrium price and equilibrium quantity. An increase in the supply of pizza shifts the supply curve to the right, from $S_1$ to $S_2$. At the initial price of $8, the quantity supplied increases from 30,000 pizzas (point *a*) to 46,000 (point *b*).

The shift of the supply curve causes excess supply that eventually decreases the equilibrium price. At the initial price of $8 (the equilibrium price with the initial supply curve), there will be an excess supply, as indicated by points *a* and *b*: Producers are willing to sell 46,000 pizzas (point *b*), but consumers are willing to buy only 30,000 (point *a*). Producers want to sell 16,000 more pizzas than consumers are willing to buy, and the excess supply causes pressure to decrease the price. As the price

▶ **FIGURE 3.11**

**An Increase in Supply Decreases the Equilibrium Price**

An increase in supply shifts the supply curve to the right: At each price, the quantity supplied increases. At the initial price ($8), there is excess supply, with the quantity supplied (point *b*) exceeding the quantity demanded (point *a*). The excess supply causes the price to drop, and equilibrium is restored at point *c*. To summarize, the increase in supply decreases the equilibrium price to $6 and increases the equilibrium quantity to 36,000 pizzas.

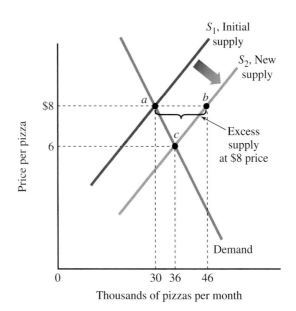

decreases, the excess supply shrinks, because the quantity supplied decreases while the quantity demanded increases. The new supply curve intersects the demand curve at point $c$, so the new equilibrium price is $6 (down from $8) and the new equilibrium quantity is 36,000 pizzas (up from 30,000).

## Decreases in Supply Shift the Supply Curve

Consider next the changes that cause a decrease in supply. As shown in Table 3.4, anything that increases a firm's production costs will decrease supply. An increase in production cost increases the price required to generate a particular quantity (an upward shift of the supply curve) and decreases the quantity supplied at each price (a leftward shift). Production costs will increase as a result of an increase in the wage, an increase in the price of materials or capital, or a tax on each unit produced. As we saw earlier, the language linking changes in supply and the shifts of the supply curve is tricky. In the case of a decrease in supply, the *decrease* refers to the change in quantity at a particular price—the horizontal shift of the supply curve to the left.

A decrease in supply could occur for two other reasons. First, if firms believe next month's pizza price will be higher than they had initially expected, they may be willing to sell a smaller quantity today and a larger quantity next month. That means that the supply of pizza today will decrease. Second, because the market supply is the sum of the quantities supplied by all producers, a decrease in the number of producers will decrease market supply, shifting the supply curve to the left.

## A Decrease in Supply Increases the Equilibrium Price

We can use Figure 3.12 to show the effects of a decrease in supply on the equilibrium price and equilibrium quantity. A decrease in the supply of pizza shifts the supply curve to the left, from $S_1$ to $S_0$. At the initial price of $8 (the equilibrium price with the initial supply curve), there will be an excess demand, as indicated by points $a$ and $b$: Consumers are willing to buy 30,000 pizzas (point $a$), but producers are willing to sell only 14,000 pizzas (point $b$). Consumers want to buy 16,000 more pizzas than producers are willing to sell, and the excess demand causes upward pressure on the price. As the price increases, the excess demand shrinks because the quantity demanded decreases while the quantity supplied increases.

Table 3.4 | CHANGES IN SUPPLY SHIFT THE SUPPLY CURVE UPWARD AND TO THE LEFT

| When this variable... | increases or decreases... | the supply curve shifts in this direction... |
|---|---|---|
| Wage | ↑ | |
| Price of materials or capital | ↑ | |
| Tax | ↑ | $S_0$, New supply; $S_1$, Initial supply |
| Expected future price | ↑ | |
| Number of producers | ↓ | Price / Quantity |

A decrease in supply shifts the supply
curve to the left: At each price, the quantity
supplied decreases. At the initial price ($8),
there is excess demand, with the quantity
demanded (point *a*) exceeding the quantity supplied (point *b*). The excess demand
causes the price to rise, and equilibrium is
restored at point *c*. To summarize, the
decrease in supply increases the equilibrium price to $8 and decreases the equilib-
rium quantity to 24,000 pizzas.

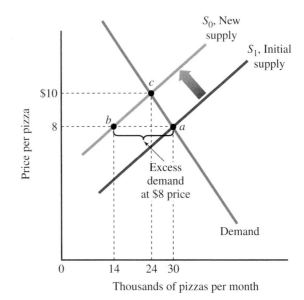

The new supply curve intersects the demand curve at point *c*, so the new equilibrium price is $10 (up from $8), and the new equilibrium quantity is 24,000 pizzas
(down from 30,000).

## Simultaneous Changes in Demand and Supply

What happens to the equilibrium price and quantity when both demand and supply
increase? It depends on which change is larger. In Panel A of Figure 3.13, the increase
in demand is larger than the increase in supply, meaning the demand curve shifts by a
larger amount than the supply curve. The market equilibrium moves from point *a* to
point *b*, and the equilibrium price increases from $8 to $9. This is sensible because an
increase in demand tends to pull the price up, while an increase in supply tends to
push the price down. If demand increases by a larger amount, the upward pull will be
stronger than the downward push, and the price will rise.

We can be certain that when demand and supply both increase, the equilibrium
quantity will increase. That's because both changes tend to increase the equilibrium
quantity. In Panel A of Figure 3.13, the equilibrium quantity increases from 30,000 to
44,000 pizzas.

► **FIGURE 3.13**
**Market Effects of Simultaneous
Changes in Demand and Supply**
(**A**) Larger increase in demand. If the
increase in demand is larger than the
increase in supply (if the shift of the
demand curve is larger than the shift of the
supply curve), both the equilibrium price
and the equilibrium quantity will increase.
(**B**) Larger increase in supply. If the
increase in supply is larger than the
increase in demand (if the shift of the supply curve is larger than the shift of the
demand curve), the equilibrium price will
decrease and the equilibrium quantity will
increase.

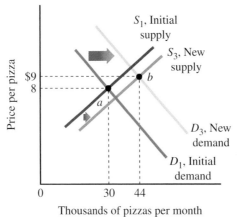

**(A) Larger Increase in Demand**

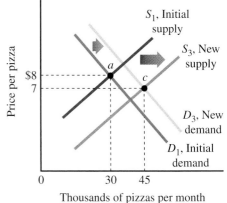

**(B) Larger Increase in Supply**

Panel B of Figure 3.13 shows what happens when the increase in supply is larger than the increase in demand. The equilibrium moves from point *a* to point *c*, meaning that the price falls from $8 to $7. This is sensible because the downward pull on the price resulting from the increase in supply is stronger than the upward pull from the increase in demand. As expected, the equilibrium quantity rises from 30,000 to 45,000 pizzas.

What about simultaneous *decreases* in demand and supply? In this case, the equilibrium quantity will certainly fall because both changes tend to decrease the equilibrium quantity. The effect on the equilibrium price depends on which change is larger, the decrease in demand, which pushes the price downward, or the decrease in supply, which pulls the price upward. If the decrease in demand is larger, the price will fall because the force pushing the price down will be stronger than the force pulling it up. In contrast, if the decrease in supply is larger, the price will rise because the force pulling the price up will be stronger than the force pushing it down.

# 3.6 | PREDICTING AND EXPLAINING MARKET CHANGES

We've used the model of demand and supply to show how equilibrium prices are determined and how changes in demand and supply affect equilibrium prices and quantities. Table 3.5 summarizes what we've learned about how changes in demand and supply affect equilibrium prices and quantities:

- When demand changes and the demand curve shifts, price and quantity change in the *same* direction: When demand increases, both price and quantity increase; when demand decreases, both price and quantity decrease.
- When supply changes and the supply curve shifts, price and quantity change in *opposite* directions: When supply increases, the price decreases but the quantity increases; when supply decreases, the price increases but the quantity decreases.

We can use these lessons about demand and supply to predict the effects of various events on the equilibrium price and equilibrium quantity of a product.

We can also use the lessons listed in Table 3.5 to explain the reasons for changes in prices or quantities. Suppose we observe changes in the equilibrium price and quantity of a particular good, but we don't know what caused these changes. Perhaps it was a change in demand, or maybe it was a change in supply. We can use the information in Table 3.5 to work backwards, using what we've observed about changes in prices and quantities to determine which side of the market—demand or supply—caused the changes:

- If the equilibrium price and quantity move in the same direction, the changes were caused by a change in demand.
- If the equilibrium price and quantity move in opposite directions, the changes were caused by a change in supply.

**Table 3.5** | MARKET EFFECTS OF CHANGES IN DEMAND OR SUPPLY

| Change in Demand or Supply | How does the equilibrium price change? | How does the equilibrium quantity change? |
|---|---|---|
| Increase in demand | ↑ | ↑ |
| Decrease in demand | ↓ | ↓ |
| Increase in supply | ↓ | ↑ |
| Decrease in supply | ↑ | ↓ |

# 3.7 | APPLICATIONS OF DEMAND AND SUPPLY

We can apply what we've learned about demand and supply to real markets. We can use the model of demand and supply to *predict* the effects of various events on equilibrium prices and quantities. We can also *explain* some observed changes in equilibrium prices and quantities.

# APPLICATION

## HURRICANE KATRINA AND BATON ROUGE HOUSING PRICES

### APPLYING THE CONCEPTS #1:
How do changes in demand affect prices?

In the late summer of 2005, Hurricane Katrina caused a storm surge and levee breaks that flooded much of New Orleans and destroyed a large fraction of the city's housing. Hundreds of thousands of residents were displaced, and about 250,000 relocated to nearby Baton Rouge. The increase in population was so large that Baton Rouge became the largest city in the state, and many people started calling the city "New Baton Rouge."

Figure 3.14 shows the effects of Hurricane Katrina on the housing market in Baton Rouge. Before Katrina, the average price of a single-family home was $130,000, as shown by point *a*. The increase in the city's population shifted the demand curve to the right, causing excess demand for housing at the original price. Just before the hurricane, there were 3,600 homes listed for sale in the city, but a week after the storm, there were only 500. The excess demand caused fierce competition among buyers for the limited supply of homes, increasing the price. Six months later, the average price had risen to $156,000 as shown by point *b*. *Related to Exercises 7.1 and 7.6.*

SOURCE: Federal Deposit Insurance Corporation, *Louisiana State Profile—Fall 2005.*

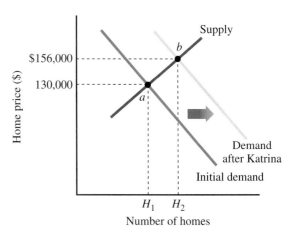

▲ **FIGURE 3.14**
**Hurricane Katrina and Housing in Baton Rouge**
An increase in the population of Baton Rouge increases the demand for housing, shifting the demand curve to right. The equilibrium price increases from $130,000 (point *a*) to $156,000 (point *b*).

# APPLICATION

## TED KOPPEL TRIES TO EXPLAIN LOWER DRUG PRICES

**APPLYING THE CONCEPTS #2:** What could explain a decrease in price?

Ted Koppel, host of the ABC news program *Nightline*, once said, "Do you know what's happened to the price of drugs in the United States? The price of cocaine, way down, the price of marijuana, way down. You don't have to be an expert in economics to know that when the price goes down, it means more stuff is coming in. That's supply and demand." According to Koppel, the price of drugs dropped because the government's efforts to control the supply of illegal drugs had failed. In other words, the lower price resulted from an increase in supply. According to the U.S. Department of Justice, the quantity of drugs consumed actually decreased during the period of dropping prices. Is Koppel's economic detective work sound?

In this case, both the price and the quantity decreased. As shown in the second row of Table 3.5, when both the price and the quantity decrease, that means demand has decreased. For example, in Figure 3.15, a decrease in demand shifts the demand curve to the left, and the market moves from point *a* (price = $15 and quantity = 400 units per day) to point *b* (price = $10 and quantity = 300 units per day). Koppel's explanation (an increase in supply) would be correct if the quantity of drugs increased at the same time that the price decreased. However, because the quantity of drugs consumed actually decreased during the period of dropping prices, Koppel's explanation is incorrect. Lower demand—not a failure of the government's drug policy and an increase in supply—was responsible for the decrease in drug prices.
*Related to Exercises 7.2 and 7.7.*

SOURCES: Kenneth R. Clark, "Legalize Drugs: A Case for Koppel," *Chicago Tribune*, August 30, 1988, sec. 5, p. 8; U.S. Department of Justice, "Drugs, Crime, and the Justice System" (Washington, DC: U.S. Government Printing Office, 1992), p. 30.

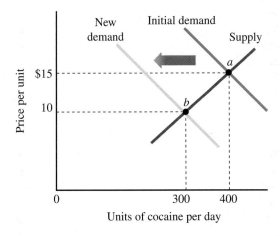

▲ **FIGURE 3.15**
**Ted Koppel and the Falling Price of Drugs**
At the same time that the price of cocaine decreased (from $15 to $10), the quantity of cocaine consumed decreased (from 400 to 300 units). Therefore the decrease in price was caused by a decrease in demand, not an increase in supply.

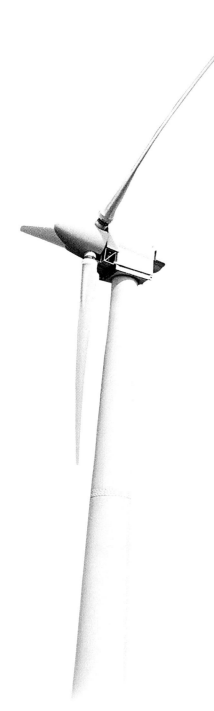

# APPLICATION

## ELECTRICITY FROM THE WIND

**APPLYING THE CONCEPT #3:** How does the adoption of new technology affect prices?

In recent years, the supply of electricity generated from wind power has increased dramatically. Between 2000 and 2006, total wind power in the United States increased from 620 megawatts to 9,200 megawatts, enough power to serve the equivalent of 2.4 million households. Over the same period, the price of electricity generated from wind power decreased from 50 cents per kilowatt-hour to 4 cents.

Figure 3.16 shows the changes in the wind electricity market in recent years. Several design innovations, including the replacement of small, rapid rotors with large, slow-moving blades and the development of monitoring systems that change the direction and the angle of the blades to more efficiently harness the wind, have decreased the cost of producing electricity, shifting the supply curve downward and to the right. In Figure 3.16, the shift of the supply curve decreases the equilibrium price and increases the equilibrium quantity.

The innovations in wind generation have made wind power more competitive with conventional power sources such as coal and natural gas. The price of electricity from natural gas and coal is about 2 cents per kilowatt-hour. The producers of wind electricity receive a federal tax credit of almost 2 cents per kilowatt-hour, making the net price of wind power close to the price of conventional power.
*Related to Exercises 7.3 and 7.8.*

SOURCE: *Christian Science Monitor*, "A New Gust of Wind Projects Across the U.S.," January 19, 2006, p. 1.

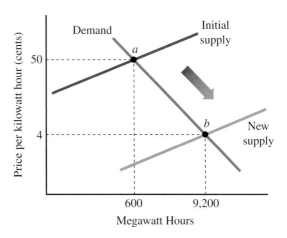

▲ **FIGURE 3.16**
**Wind Power and Electricity**
Technological innovations in generating electricity from the wind decreased production costs, shifting the supply curve downward and to the right. The equilibrium price decreased and the equilibrium quantity increased. (To represent the large changes in price and quantity, the graph is not drawn to scale.)

# APPLICATION

## THE BOUNCING PRICE OF VANILLA BEANS

**APPLYING THE CONCEPTS #4:** How do changes in supply affect prices?

As we saw in the chapter opener, the price of vanilla beans has been bouncing around a lot. The price was $50 per kilo (2.2 pounds) in 2000, then rose to $500 in 2003, then dropped to $25 in 2006. We can use the model of demand and supply to explain the bouncing price.

Figure 3.17 shows the changes in the vanilla market in recent years. Point *a* shows the initial equilibrium in 2000, with a price of $50 per kilo. The 2000 cyclone that hit Madagascar, the world's leading producer, destroyed that year's crop and a large share of the vines that produce vanilla beans. Although the vines were replanted, new plants don't bear usable beans for three to five years, so the supply effects of the cyclone lasted several years. In Figure 3.17, the cyclone shifted the supply curve upward and to the left, generating a new equilibrium at point *b*, with a higher price and a smaller quantity.

In Figure 3.17, the changes between 2003 and 2006 are shown by a shift of the supply curve downward and to the right. In 2006, the vines replanted in Madagascar in 2001 started to produce vanilla beans. In addition, other countries, including India, Papua New Guinea, Uganda, and Costa Rica, entered the vanilla market. The vines planted in these other countries started to produce beans in 2006, so the world supply curve for 2006 lies below and to the right of the original supply curve (in 2000). Given the larger supply of vanilla beans in 2006, the price dropped to about half of its 2000 level, to $25 per kilo. The increase in supply from other countries was facilitated by the development of a sun-tolerant variety of the vanilla plant that allows it to be grown as a plantation crop. The new variety is an example of technological progress. *Related to Exercises 7.4 and 7.9.*

SOURCES: Rhett Butler, "Collapsing Vanilla Prices Will Affect Madagascar," mongabay.com (May 9, 2005); Noel Paul, "Vanilla Sky High," *Christian Science Monitor,* csmonitor.com (August 11, 2003); G.K. Nair, "Vanilla Prices fall on Under-cutting," *Hindu Business Line,* (April 03, 2006).

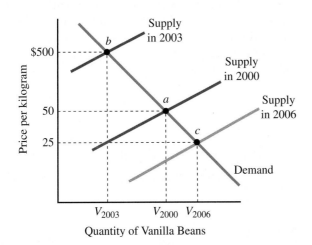

**▲ FIGURE 3.17**
**The Bouncing Price of Vanilla Beans**
A cyclone destroyed much of Madagascar's crop in 2000, shifting the supply curve upward and to the left. The equilibrium price increased from $50 per kilogram (point *a*) to $500 per kilo-gram (pont *b*). By 2005, the vines replanted in Madagascar—along with new vines planted in other countries— started producing vanilla beans, and the supply curve shifted downward and to the right, beyond the supply curve for 2000. The price dropped to $25 per kilogram (point *c*), half the price that prevailed in 2000. (To represent the large changes in price and quantity, the graph is not drawn to scale.)

## APPLICATION

## PLATINUM, JEWELRY, AND CATALYTIC CONVERTERS

**APPLYING THE CONCEPTS #5:** How do changes in one market affect other markets?

In early 2004, the price of platinum reached $937 per ounce—up from $440 in 1999 and $700 in 2003. The two largest sources of demand for platinum are jewelry and the catalytic converters used in automobiles to control emissions. In recent years, the tightening of emissions standards for automobiles and trucks increased the demand for platinum. In rapidly growing Asian countries, the demand for automobiles increased, and many countries adopted stricter emissions standards. In Latin America, Brazil and Chile recently mandated the use of catalytic converters in their automobiles.

Table 3.6 shows the changes in the demand for platinum from 1999 to 2004. The demand for platinum for use in catalytic converters more than doubled, from 1.19 million ounces to 2.81 million ounces. The increase in demand increased the equilibrium price of platinum. The other numbers in the table illustrate the laws of demand and supply:

1 *The law of demand for jewelry.* The increase in the price of platinum increased the equilibrium price of platinum jewelry, and consumers responded by purchasing less platinum jewelry. As a result, the amount of platinum used in jewelry decreased, from 2.88 million ounces to 2.20 million ounces.

2 *The law of supply for recycling.* The increase in the price of platinum increased the payoff from recycling used platinum, increasing the quantity of platinum supplied through recycling from 0.42 million ounces to 0.70 million ounces.

What's next for the platinum market? Another potential source of increased demand is the development of fuel cells. This environmentally friendly technology combines oxygen and hydrogen to produce electricity. Platinum is a core material in fuel cells, and if fuel cells emerge as an important source of electricity the resulting increase in the demand for platinum will increase its price.
*Related to Exercises 7.5 and 7.10.*

SOURCE: Johnson Matthy, *Platinum 2005* (London, 2005).

**Table 3.6 | SOURCES OF DEMAND FOR PLATINUM**

| Source of Demand | 1999 (million ounces) | 2004 (million ounces) |
|---|---|---|
| Catalytic converters | 1.19 | 2.81 |
| Jewelry | 2.88 | 2.20 |
| Chemical and electrical | 0.69 | 0.58 |
| Other | 0.83 | 0.99 |
| **Total** | **5.59** | **6.58** |
| **Supply from recycling** | 0.42 | 0.70 |

# SUMMARY

In this chapter, we've seen how demand and supply determine prices. We also learned how to predict the effects of changes in demand or supply on prices and quantities. Here are the main points of the chapter:

1 A *market demand curve* shows the relationship between the quantity demanded and price, *ceteris paribus*.

2 A *market supply curve* shows the relationship between the quantity supplied and price, *ceteris paribus*.

3 *Equilibrium* in a market is shown by the intersection of the demand curve and the supply curve. When a market reaches equilibrium, there is no pressure to change the price.

4 A *change in demand* changes price and quantity in the same direction: An increase in demand increases the equilibrium price and quantity; a decrease in demand decreases the equilibrium price and quantity.

5 A *change in supply* changes price and quantity in opposite directions: An increase in supply decreases price and increases quantity; a decrease in supply increases price and decreases quantity.

# KEY TERMS

change in demand, p. 59

change in quantity demanded, p. 51

change in quantity supplied, p. 54

change in supply, p. 63

complements, p. 60

demand schedule, p. 50

excess demand (shortage), p. 57

excess supply (surplus), p. 58

individual demand curve, p. 51

individual supply curve, p. 54

inferior good, p. 59

law of demand, p. 51

law of supply, p. 54

market demand curve, p. 51

market equilibrium, p. 57

market supply curve, p. 55

minimum supply price, p. 54

normal good, p. 59

perfectly competitive market, p. 50

quantity demanded, p. 50

quantity supplied, p. 53

substitutes, p. 59

supply schedule, p. 53

# EXERCISES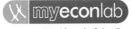

*Get Ahead of the Curve*

Visit www.myeconlab.com to complete these exercises online and get instant feedback.

## 3.1 | The Demand Curve

**1.1** Arrow up or down: According to the law of demand, an increase in price _____ the quantity demanded.

**1.2** From the following list, choose the variables that are held fixed in drawing a market demand curve:
- The price of the product
- Consumer income
- The price of other related goods
- Consumer expectations about future prices
- The quantity of the product purchased

**1.3** From the following list, choose the variables that change as we draw a market demand curve.
- The price of the product
- Consumer income
- The price of other related goods
- Consumer expectations about future prices
- The quantity of the product purchased

**1.4** The market demand curve is the _____ (horizontal/vertical) sum of the individual demand curves.

**1.5** **Draw a Demand Curve.** Your state has decided to offer its citizens vanity license plates for their cars and wants to predict how many vanity plates it will sell at different prices. The price of the state's regular license plates is $20 per year, and the state's per-capita income is $30,000. A recent survey of other states with approximately the same population (3 million people) generated the following data on incomes, prices, and vanity plates:

| State | B | C | D | E |
|---|---|---|---|---|
| Price of vanity plate | $60 | $55 | $50 | $40 |
| Price of regular plates | 20 | 20 | 35 | 20 |
| Income | 30,000 | 25,000 | 30,000 | 30,000 |
| Quantity of vanity plates | 6,000 | 6,000 | 16,000 | 16,000 |

a. Use the available data to identify some points on the demand curve for vanity plates and connect the points to draw a demand curve. Don't forget *ceteris paribus*.

b. Suppose the demand curve is linear. If your state set a price of $50, how many vanity plates would be purchased?

## 3.2 | The Supply Curve

2.1 Arrow up or down: According to the law of supply, an increase in price _____ the quantity supplied.

2.2 From the following list, choose the variables that are held fixed when drawing a market supply curve.
   • The price of the product
   • Wages paid to workers
   • The price of materials used in production
   • Taxes paid by producers
   • The quantity of the product purchased

2.3 The minimum supply price is the _____ price at which a product is supplied.

2.4 The market supply curve is the _____ (horizontal/vertical) sum of the individual supply curves.

2.5 **Marginal Cost of Housing.** When the price of a standard three-bedroom house increases from $150,000 to $160,000, a building company increases its output from 20 houses per year to 21 houses per year. What does the increase in the quantity of housing reveal about the cost of producing housing?

2.6 **Imports and Market Supply.** Two nations supply sugar to the world market. Lowland has a minimum supply price of 10 cents per pound, while Highland has a minimum supply price of 24 cents per pound. For each nation, the slope of the supply curve is 1 cent per million pounds.
   a. Draw the individual supply curves and the market supply curve. At what price and quantity is the supply curve kinked?

b. The market quantity supplied at a price of 15 cents is _____ million pounds. The market quantity supplied at a price of 30 cents is _____ million pounds.

## 3.3 | Market Equilibrium: Bringing Demand and Supply Together

3.1 The market equilibrium is shown by the intersection of the _____ curve and the _____ curve.

3.2 Excess demand occurs when the price is _____ (less/greater) than the equilibrium price; excess supply occurs when the price is _____ (less/greater) than the equilibrium price.

3.3 Arrow up or down: An excess demand for a product will cause the price to _____. As a consequence of the price change, the quantity demanded will _____ and the quantity supplied will _____.

3.4 Arrow up or down: An excess supply of a product will cause the price to _____. As a consequence of the price change, the quantity demanded will _____, and the quantity supplied will _____.

3.5 **Interpreting the Graph.** The graph below shows the demand and supply curves for CD players. Complete the following statements.

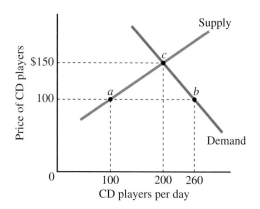

a. At the market equilibrium (shown by point _____), the price of CD players is _____ and the quantity of CD players is _____.

b. At a price of $100, there would be excess _____, so we would expect the price to _____.

c. At a price exceeding the equilibrium price, there would be excess _____, so we would expect the price to _____.

3.6 **Draw and Find the Equilibrium.** The following table shows the quantities of corn supplied and demanded at different prices.

| Price per Ton | Quantity Supplied | Quantity Demanded |
|---|---|---|
| $80 | 600 | 1,200 |
| 90 | 800 | 1,100 |
| 100 | 1,000 | 1,000 |
| 110 | 1,200 | 900 |

a. Draw the demand curve and the supply curve.
b. The equilibrium price of corn is _____, and the equilibrium quantity is _____.

## 3.4 | Market Effects of Changes in Demand

**4.1** A change in demand causes a _____ (movement along/shift of) the demand curve. A change in quantity demanded causes a _____ (movement along/shift of) the demand curve.

**4.2** Circle the variables that change as we move along the demand curve for pencils and cross out those that are assumed to be fixed.
- Quantity of pencils demanded
- Number of consumers
- Price of pencils
- Price of pens
- Consumer income

**4.3** A decrease in the price of online music shifts the demand curve for CDs to the _____ (right/left); an increase in the price of CD players shifts the demand curve for CDs to the _____ (right/left).

**4.4** Arrow up or down: The market demand curve for a product will shift to the right when the price of a substitute good _____, the price of a complementary good _____, consumer income _____, population _____.

**4.5** Arrow up or down: An increase in demand for a product _____ the equilibrium price and _____ the equilibrium quantity.

**4.6** **Market Effects of Increased Income.** Consider the market for restaurant meals. Use a demand and supply graph to predict the market effects of an increase in consumer income. Arrow up or down: The equilibrium price of restaurant meals will _____, and the equilibrium quantity of restaurant meals will _____.

**4.7** **Public Versus Private Colleges.** Consider the market for private college education. Use a demand and supply graph to predict the market effects of an increase in the tuition charged by public colleges. Arrow up or down: The equilibrium price of a private college education will _____, and the equilibrium quantity will _____.

## 3.5 | Market Effects of Changes in Supply

**5.1** A change in supply causes a _____ (movement along/shift of) the supply curve. A change in quantity supplied causes a _____ (movement along/shift of) the supply curve.

**5.2** Circle the variables that change as we move along the supply curve for pencils and cross out those that are assumed to be fixed:
- Quantity of pencils supplied
- Price of wood
- Price of pencils
- Production technology

**5.3** Arrow up or down: An increase in the price of wood shifts the supply curve for pencils _____; an improvement in pencil-production technology shifts the supply curve for pencils _____; a tax on pencil production shifts the supply curve for pencils _____.

**5.4** Arrow up or down: An increase in the supply of a product _____ the equilibrium price and _____ the equilibrium quantity.

**5.5** If both demand and supply increase simultaneously, the equilibrium price will increase if the change in _____ is relatively large.

**5.6** **Effect of Weather on Prices.** Suppose a freeze in Florida wipes out 20 percent of the orange crop. How will this affect the equilibrium price and quantity of Florida oranges? Illustrate your answer with a graph.

**5.7** **Immigration Control and Prices.** Consider the market for raspberries. Suppose a new law outlaws the use of foreign farm workers on raspberry farms, and the wages paid to farm workers increase as a result. Use a demand and supply graph to predict the effects of the higher wage on the equilibrium price and quantity of raspberries. Arrow up or down: The equilibrium price of raspberries will _____, and the equilibrium quantity of raspberries will _____.

**5.8** **Market Effects of Import Ban.** Consider the market for shoes in a nation that initially imports half the shoes it consumes. Use a demand and supply graph to predict the market effect of a ban on shoe imports. Arrow up or down: The equilibrium price will _____, and the equilibrium quantity will _____.

**5.9** **Market Effects of a Tax.** Consider the market for fish. Use a demand and supply graph to predict the effect of a tax paid by fish producers of $1 per pound of fish. Use a demand and supply graph to predict the market effect of the tax. Arrow up or down: The equilibrium price will _____, and the equilibrium quantity will _____.

5.10 **Innovation and the Price of Mobile Phones.** Suppose that the initial price of a mobile phone is $100 and that the initial quantity demanded is 500 phones per day. Use a graph to show the effects of a technological innovation that decreases the cost of producing mobile phones. Label the starting point with "*a*" and the new equilibrium with "*b*."

## 3.6 | Predicting and Explaining Market Changes

6.1 Fill the blanks in the following table. Note that the ordering of the first column has been scrambled.

| Change in Demand or Supply | How does the equilibrium price change? | How does the equilibrium quantity change? |
|---|---|---|
| Increase in supply | | |
| Decrease in demand | | |
| Decrease in supply | | |
| Increase in demand | | |

6.2 When _____ (supply/demand) changes, the equilibrum price and equilibrum price change in the same direction. When _____ (supply/demand) changes, the equilibrium price and equilibrium price change in opposite directions.

6.3 Suppose the equilibrium price of accordions recently increased while the equilibrium quantity decreased. These changes were caused by a(n) _____ (increase/decrease) in _____ (supply/demand).

6.4 Suppose the equilibrium price of housing recently increased, and the equilibrium quantity increased as well. These changes were caused by a(n) _____ (increase/decrease) in _____ (supply/demand).

6.5 **What Caused the Higher Gasoline Price?** In the last month, the price of gasoline increased by 20 percent. Your job is to determine what caused the increase in price, a change in demand or a change in supply. Ms. Info has all the numbers associated with the gasoline market, and she can answer a single factual question. (She cannot answer the question: "Was the higher price caused by a change in demand or a change in supply?")
   a. What single question would you ask?
   b. Provide an answer to your question that implies that the higher price was caused by a change in demand. Illustrate with a complete graph.
   c. Provide an answer to your question that implies that the higher price was caused by a change in supply. Illustrate with a complete graph.

6.6 **Rising Price of Used Organs.** Over the last few years, the price of used organs (livers, kidneys,

hearts) has increased dramatically. Why? What additional information about the market for used organs would allow you to prove that your explanation is the correct one?

6.7 **The Price of Summer Cabins.** As summer approaches, the equilibrium price of rental cabins increases and the equilibrium quantity of cabins rented increases. Draw a demand and supply graph that explains these changes.

6.8 **Simplest Possible Graph.** Consider the market for juice oranges. Draw the simplest possible demand and supply graph consistent with the following observations. You should be able to draw a graph with no more than 4 curves. Label each of your curves as "supply" or "demand" and indicate the year (1, 2, or 3).

| Year | 1 | 2 | 3 |
|---|---|---|---|
| Price | $5 | $7 | $4 |
| Quantity | 100 | 80 | 110 |

6.9 **Zero Price for Used Newspapers.** In 1987, you could sell a ton of used newspaper for $60. Five years later, you couldn't sell them at any price. In other words, the price of used newspapers dropped from $60 to zero in just 5 years. Over this period, the quantity of used newspapers bought and sold increased. What caused the drop in price? Illustrate your answer with a complete graph.

## 3.7 | Applications of Demand and Supply

7.1 Arrow up or down: Hurricane Katrina _____ the demand for housing in Baton Rouge, so the price of housing _____ and the quantity of housing _____. (Related to Application 1 on page 68.)

7.2 Ted Koppel's analysis of the drug market was incorrect because he failed to notice that the _____ of drugs decreased at the same time that the _____ of drugs decreased. (Related to Application 2 on page 69.)

7.3 Innovations in wind technology decrease the price of electricity from wind from 50 cents per kilowatt-hour to _____ cents. (Related to Application 3 on page 70.)

7.4 Arrow up or down: The development of a sun-tolerant variety of the vanilla plant _____ the supply of vanilla and _____ its price. (Related to Application 4 on page 71.)

7.5 Arrow up or down: The increase in the price of platinum _____ recycling of used platinum and _____ the quantity of platinum used for jewelry. (Related to Application 5 on page 72.)

7.6 **Katrina Victims Move Back.** Suppose that 5 years after Hurricane Katrina, half the people who had relocated to Baton Rouge move back to a rebuilt New Orleans. Use a demand and supply graph of the Baton Rouge housing market to show the market effects of the return of people to New Orleans. (Related to Application 1 on page 68.)

**7.7** **Decrease in the Price of Heroin.** Between 1990 and 2003, the price of heroin decreased from $235 per gram to $76. Over the same period, the quantity of heroin consumed increased from 376 metric tons to 482 metric tons. Use a demand and supply graph to explain these changes in price and quantity. (Related to Application 2 on page 69.)

**7.8** **Electricity from Fuel Cells.** Suppose that initially the cost of the capital required to generate electricity from fuel cells is $4,500 per kilowatt capacity, compared to $800 per kilowatt capacity for a diesel generator. The goal of the U.S. Department of Energy (DOE) is to cut the cost of fuel-cell generators to $400 per kilowatt capacity. Consider the market for electricity from fuel cells. Use a demand and supply graph to show the effects of meeting the DOE goal on the price and quantity of electricity from fuel cells. (Related to Application 3 on page 70.)

**7.9** **Artificial Versus Natural Vanilla.** An artificial alternative to natural vanilla is cheaper to produce but doesn't taste as good. Suppose the makers of artificial vanilla discover a new recipe that improves its taste. Use a demand and supply graph to show the effects on the equilibrium price and quantity of natural vanilla. (Related to Application 4 on page 71.)

**7.10** **Platinum Price and Jewelry.** Consider the market for platinum jewelry. Use a demand and supply graph to illustrate the following statement: "The increase in the price of platinum increased the price of platinum jewelry, and consumers responded by purchasing less platinum jewelry." (Related to Application 5 on page 72.)

# ECONOMIC EXPERIMENT

## Market Equilibrium

This simple experiment takes about 20 minutes. We start by dividing the class into two equal groups: consumers and producers.

- The instructor provides each consumer with a number indicating the maximum amount he or she is willing to pay (WTP) for a bushel of apples: The WTP is a number between $1 and $100. Each consumer has the opportunity to buy 1 bushel of apples per trading period. The consumer's score for a single trading period equals the gap between the WTP and the price actually paid for apples. For example, if the consumer's WTP is $80 and he or she pays only $30 for apples, the consumer's score is $50. Each consumer has the option of not buying apples. This will be sensible if the best price the consumer can get exceeds the WTP. If the consumer does not buy apples, his or her score will be zero.

- The instructor provides each producer with a number indicating the cost of producing a bushel of apples (a number between $1 and $100). Each producer has the opportunity to sell 1 bushel per trading period. The producer's score for a single trading period equals the gap between the selling prices and the cost of producing apples. So if a producer sells apples for $20, and the cost is only $15, the producer's score is $5. Producers have the option of not selling apples, which is sensible if the best price the producer can get is less than the cost. If the producer does not sell apples, his or her score is zero.

Once everyone understands the rules, consumers and producers meet in a trading area to arrange transactions. A consumer may announce how much he or she is willing to pay for apples and wait for a producer to agree to sell apples at that price. Alternatively, a producer may announce how much he or she is willing to accept for apples and wait for a consumer to agree to buy apples at that price. Once a transaction has been arranged, the consumer and producer inform the instructor of the trade, record the transaction, and leave the trading area.

Several trading periods are conducted, each of which lasts a few minutes. After the end of each trading period, the instructor lists the prices at which apples sold during the period. Then another trading period starts, providing consumers and producers another opportunity to buy or sell apples. After all the trading periods have been completed, each participant computes his or her score by adding the scores from the trading periods.

# 4

# Elasticity: A Measure of Responsiveness

In every large city in the United States, the public bus system runs a deficit: Operating costs exceed revenues from passenger fares. Suppose your city wants to reduce its bus deficit and is trying to decide whether to increase fares by 10 percent. Consider the following exchange between two city officials:

BUSTER: "A fare increase is a great idea. We'll collect more money from bus riders, so revenue will increase, and the deficit will shrink."

BESSIE: "Wait a minute, Buster. Haven't you heard about the law of demand? The increase in the bus fare will decrease the number of passengers taking buses, so we'll collect less money, not more, and the deficit will grow."

Who is right? As we'll see in this chapter, we can't predict how an increase in price will affect total revenue unless we know just how responsive consumers are to an increase in price. Like other consumers, bus riders obey the law of demand, but that doesn't necessarily mean that total fare revenue will fall.

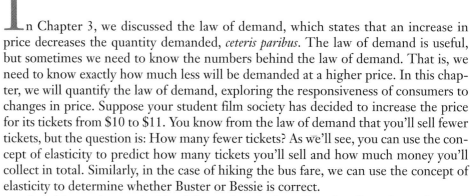

In Chapter 3, we discussed the law of demand, which states that an increase in price decreases the quantity demanded, *ceteris paribus*. The law of demand is useful, but sometimes we need to know the numbers behind the law of demand. That is, we need to know exactly how much less will be demanded at a higher price. In this chapter, we will quantify the law of demand, exploring the responsiveness of consumers to changes in price. Suppose your student film society has decided to increase the price for its tickets from $10 to $11. You know from the law of demand that you'll sell fewer tickets, but the question is: How many fewer tickets? As we'll see, you can use the concept of elasticity to predict how many tickets you'll sell and how much money you'll collect in total. Similarly, in the case of hiking the bus fare, we can use the concept of elasticity to determine whether Buster or Bessie is correct.

Switching to the supply side of the market, the law of supply tells us that an increase in price increases the quantity supplied, *ceteris paribus*. Sometimes the question is: By how much? We'll quantify the law of supply, showing how to predict just how much more of a product will be supplied at a higher price. For example, if the world price of oil increases from $70 to $80 per barrel, we know from the law of supply that domestic producers will supply more oil, but the question is: How much more? We can use the concept of elasticity to predict how much more domestic oil will be supplied at the higher price.

# 4.1 | THE PRICE ELASTICITY OF DEMAND

- **price elasticity of demand ($E_d$)**
A measure of the responsiveness of the quantity demanded to changes in price; equal to the absolute value of the percentage change in quantity demanded divided by the percentage change in price.

The **price elasticity of demand** ($E_d$) measures the responsiveness of the quantity demanded to changes in price. To compute the price elasticity of demand, we divide the percentage change in the quantity demanded by the percentage change in price, and then take the absolute value of the ratio:

$$E_d = \left| \frac{\text{percentage change in quantity demanded}}{\text{percentage change in price}} \right|$$

The vertical bars indicate that we take the absolute value of the ratio, so the price elasticity is always a positive number. For example, suppose the price of milk *increases* by 10 percent and the quantity demanded *decreases* by 15 percent. The price elasticity of demand is 1.5:

$$E_d = \left| \frac{\text{percentage change in quantity demanded}}{\text{percentage change in price}} \right| = \left| \frac{-15\%}{10\%} \right| = 1.50$$

The law of demand tells us that price and quantity demanded move in opposite directions. Therefore, the percentage change in quantity will always have the opposite sign of the percentage change in price. In our example, a positive 10-percent change in price results in a negative 15-percent change in quantity. The ratio of the percentage changes is −1.50, and taking the absolute value of this ratio, the elasticity is 1.50. Although it is conventional to use the absolute value to compute the price elasticity, the practice is not universal. So you may encounter a negative price elasticity, which means that the elasticity is reported as its numerical value rather than its absolute value.

When the price elasticity is listed as a positive number, the interpretation of the elasticity is straightforward. If the elasticity number is large, it means that the demand for the product is very elastic, or very responsive to changes in price. In contrast, a small number indicates that the demand for a product is very inelastic.

## Computing Percentage Changes and Elasticities

As we saw in the Appendix to Chapter 1, a percentage change can be computed in two ways. Using the initial-value method, we divide the change in the value of a variable by its initial value. For example, if a price increases from $20 to $22, the percentage change is $2 divided by $20, or 10 percent:

$$\text{percent change with initial value} = \frac{22-20}{20} \times 100 = \frac{2}{20} \times 100 = 10\%$$

Alternatively, we could use the midpoint method. We divide the change in the variable by its average value, that is, the midpoint of the two values. For example, if the price increases from $20 to $22, the average or midpoint value is $21 and the percentage change is 9.52 percent:

$$\text{percent change with midpoint value} = \frac{2}{\frac{20+22}{2}} \times 100 = \frac{2}{21} \times 100 = 9.52\%$$

The advantage of the midpoint approach is that it generates the same absolute percentage change whether the variable has increased or decreased. That's because the denominator is the same in both cases. In contrast, the initial-value computation is based on the initial value, so it depends on the direction of the change—which of the two values is the initial value.

Table 4.1 shows the calculation of the price elasticity of demand with the two approaches. When the price increases from $20 to $22, the quantity demanded decreases from 100 to 80 units. Using the initial-value method, we get an elasticity of 2.0, equal to the 20-percent change in quantity divided by the 10-percent change in price. As shown in the lower part of the table, the midpoint method generates an elasticity of 2.33.

Why do the two approaches generate different elasticity numbers? The midpoint approach measures the percentage changes more precisely, so we get a more precise measure of price elasticity. In this case, the percentage changes are relatively small, so the two elasticity numbers are close to one another. If the percentage changes were larger, however, the elasticity numbers generated by the two approaches would be quite different, and it would be wise to use the midpoint approach. In this book, we use the initial-value approach because it generates nice round numbers and allows us to focus on economics rather than arithmetic. But anytime you want to be more precise, you can use the midpoint formula.

**Table 4.1** | COMPUTING PRICE ELASTICITY WITH INITIAL VALUES AND MIDPOINTS

|  |  | **Price** | **Quantity** |
|---|---|---|---|
| Data | Initial | $20 | 100 |
|  | New | 22 | 80 |
|  |  | **Price** | **Quantity** |
| Computation with Initial-value method | Percentage change | $10\% = \dfrac{\$2}{\$20} \times 100$ | $-20\% = -\dfrac{20}{100} \times 100$ |
|  | Price elasticity of demand | $2.0 = \left\lvert \dfrac{-20\%}{10\%} \right\rvert$ |  |
|  |  | **Price** | **Quantity** |
| Computation with Midpoint method | Percentage change | $9.52\% = \dfrac{\$2}{\$21} \times 100$ | $-22.22\% = -\dfrac{20}{90} \times 100$ |
|  | Price elasticity of demand | $2.33 = \left\lvert \dfrac{-22.22\%}{9.52\%} \right\rvert$ |  |

## Price Elasticity and the Demand Curve

Figure 4.1 shows five different demand curves, each with a different elasticity. We can divide products into five types, depending on their price elasticities of demand.

• **elastic demand**
The price elasticity of demand is greater than one.

• **inelastic demand**
The price elasticity of demand is less than one.

• **unit elastic demand**
The price elasticity of demand is one.

• **perfectly inelastic demand**
The price elasticity of demand is zero.

• **perfectly elastic demand**
The price elasticity of demand is infinite.

- **Elastic demand** (Panel A). In this case, a 20-percent increase in price (from $5 to $6) decreases the quantity demanded by 40 percent (from 20 to 12), so the price elasticity of demand is 2.0. When the price elasticity is greater than 1.0, we say that demand is "elastic," or highly responsive to changes in price. Some examples of goods with elastic demand are restaurant meals, air travel, and movies.

- **Inelastic demand** (Panel B). The same 20-percent increase in price decreases the quantity demanded by only 10 percent (from 20 to 18), so the price elasticity of demand is 0.50. When the elasticity is less than 1.0, we say that demand is *inelastic*, or not very responsive to changes in price. Some examples of goods with inelastic demand are salt, eggs, coffee and cigarettes.

- **Unit elastic demand** (Panel C). A 20-percent increase in price decreases the quantity demanded by exactly 20 percent, so the price elasticity of demand is 1.0. Some examples of goods with unit elasticity are housing and fruit juice.

- **Perfectly inelastic demand** (Panel D). When demand is perfectly inelastic, the quantity doesn't change as the price changes, so the demand curve is vertical at the fixed quantity. The price elasticity of demand is zero. This extreme case is rare because for most products, consumers can either switch to a substitute good or do without. For example, although there are no direct substitutes for household water, as the price of water rises, people install low-flow shower-heads, water their lawns less frequently, and clean their cars less frequently. The rare cases of perfectly inelastic demand are medicines—such as insulin for diabetics—that have no substitutes.

- **Perfectly elastic demand** (Panel E). In this case, the price elasticity is infinite and the demand curve is horizontal, meaning that only one price is possible. At that price, the quantity demanded could be any quantity, from one unit to millions of units. If the price were to increase even a penny, the quantity demanded would drop to zero. As we'll see later in the book, firms in a perfectly competitive market face this sort of demand curve. For example, each wheat farmer can sell as much as he or she wants at the market price but would sell nothing at any price above the market price.

## Elasticity and the Availability of Substitutes

The key factor in determining the price elasticity for a particular product is the availability of substitute products. Consider the substitution possibilities for insulin (a medicine for diabetics) and cornflakes. There are no good substitutes for insulin, so consumers are not very responsive to changes in price. When the price of insulin increases, diabetics cannot switch to another medicine, so the demand for insulin is inelastic. In contrast, there are many substitutes for cornflakes, including different types of corn cereals, as well as cereals made from wheat, rice, and oats. Faced with an increase in the price of cornflakes, consumers can easily switch to substitute products, so the demand for cornflakes is relatively elastic.

Table 4.2 on page 84 shows the price elasticities of demand for various products. The different elasticities illustrate the importance of substitutes in determining the price elasticity of demand. Because there are no good substitutes for water and salt, it is not surprising that the elasticities are small. For example, the price elasticity of demand for water is 0.20, meaning that a 10-percent increase in price decreases the quantity demanded by 2 percent. The demand for coffee is inelastic (0.30), because although there are alternative beverages and caffeine-delivery systems (tea, infused soft drinks, and pills), coffee provides a unique combination of taste and caffeine. Although there is an artificial substitute for eggs (for people concerned about dietary cholesterol), there are no natural substitutes, so the demand for eggs is relatively inelastic (0.30).

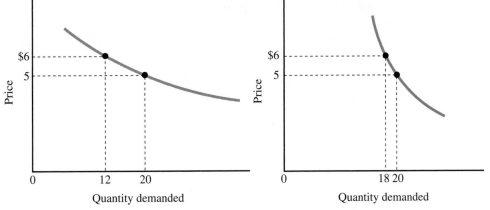

**◄ FIGURE 4.1**
**Elasticity and Demand Curves**

**(A) Elastic Demand:** $E_d = \left|\dfrac{-40\%}{20\%}\right| = 2.0 > 1$      **(B) Inelastic Demand:** $E_d = \left|\dfrac{-10\%}{20\%}\right| = 0.50 < 1$

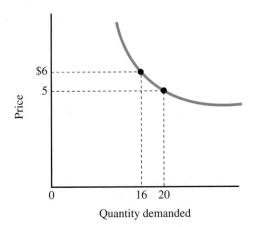

**(C) Unit Elastic Demand:** $E_d = \left|\dfrac{-20\%}{20\%}\right| = 1$

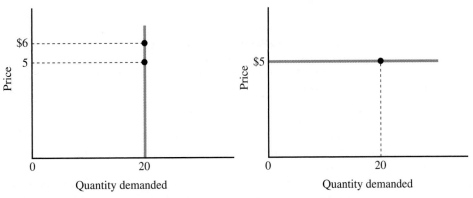

**(D) Perfectly Inelastic Demand:** $E_d = \left|\dfrac{0\%}{20\%}\right| = 0$      **(E) Perfectly Elastic Demand:** $E_d = \infty$

Alternative brands of a product are good substitutes for one another, so the demand for a specific brand of a product is typically elastic. For example, the elasticity of demand for a specific brand of coffee is 5.6, compared to an overall elasticity for coffee of 0.30. This means that a 10-percent increase in the price of coffee in general (all brands) will decrease the quantity of coffee sold by 3 percent, but a 10-percent increase in the price of a specific brand will decrease the quantity of that brand sold by 56 percent. Each brand of coffee is a substitute for the other

Table 4.2 | PRICE ELASTICITIES OF DEMAND FOR SELECTED PRODUCTS

|  | Product | Price Elasticity of Demand |
|---|---|---|
| Inelastic | Salt | 0.1 |
|  | Food (wealthy countries) | 0.15 |
|  | Weekend canoe trips | 0.19 |
|  | Water | 0.2 |
|  | Coffee | 0.3 |
|  | Physician visits | 0.25 |
|  | Sport fishing | 0.28 |
|  | Gasoline (short run) | 0.3 |
|  | Eggs | 0.3 |
|  | Cigarettes | 0.3 |
|  | Food (poor countries) | 0.34 |
|  | Shoes and footwear | 0.7 |
|  | Gasoline (long run) | 0.7 |
| Unit elastic | Housing | 1.0 |
|  | Fruit juice | 1.0 |
| Elastic | Automobiles | 1.2 |
|  | Foreign travel | 1.8 |
|  | Motorboats | 2.2 |
|  | Restaurant meals | 2.3 |
|  | Air travel | 2.4 |
|  | Movies | 3.7 |
|  | Specific brands of coffee | 5.6 |

*SOURCES:* Frank Chaloupka, "Rational Addictive Behavior and Cigarette Smoking," *Journal of Political Economy,* August 1991, pp. 722–742; Gregory Chow, *Demand for Automobiles in the United States* (Amsterdam: North-Holland, 1957); David Ellwood and Mitchell Polinski, "An Empirical Reconciliation of Micro and Grouped Estimates of the Demand for Housing," *Review of Economics and Statistics,* vol. 61, 1979, pp. 199–205; H. F. Houthakker and Lester B. Taylor, *Consumer Demand in the United States: Analysis and Projections,* 2nd ed. (Cambridge, MA: Harvard University Press, 1970); John R. Nevin, "Laboratory Experiments for Estimating Consumer Demand: A Validation Study," *Journal of Marketing Research,* vol. 11, August 1974, pp. 261–268; Herbert Scarf and John Shoven, *Applied General Equilibrium Analysis* (New York: Cambridge University Press, 1984); Phil Goodwin, "Review of New Demand Elasticities with Special Reference to Short and Long Run Effects of Price Changes," *Journal of Transport Economics* 26 (1992), pp. 155–171; Chin-Fun Cling and James Peale, Jr., "Income and Price Elasticities," in *Advances in Econometrics Supplement,* edited by Henri Theil (Greenwich, CT: JAI Press, 1989); R. L. Adams, R. C. Lewis, and B. H. Drake, "Estimated Price Elasticity of Demand for Selected Outdoor Recreation Activities, United States," *Recreation Economic Decisions,* 2d ed., edited by J. B. Loomis and R. G. Walsh (State College, PA: Venture Publishing, Inc., 1973), p. 20; U.S. Army Corps of Engineers, Walla Walla District, "Sport Fishery Use and Value on the Lower Snake River Reservoirs," May 1999; Rand Health, "The Elasticity of Demand for Health Care: A Review of the Literature and Its Application to the Military Health System" (Santa Monica, CA, 2001).

brands, so consumers are very responsive to a change in the price of a specific brand. Similarly, the demand for specific brands of tires is more elastic than the demand for tires in general.

The availability of substitutes increases over time, so the longer the time consumers have to respond to a price change, the more elastic the demand. Because it often takes time for consumers to respond to price changes, the short-run price elasticity of demand is typically smaller than the long-run elasticity. For example, when the price of gasoline increases, consumers can immediately drive fewer miles in their existing cars or switch to public transportation. As shown in Table 4.2, the short-run price elasticity of demand for gasoline is 0.30. In the long run, consumers can buy more fuel-efficient cars and move closer to work-places. As time passes, consumers have more options to cut gasoline consumption—more substitution possibilities—so demand becomes more elastic. In Table 4.2, the long-run price elasticity of demand for gasoline is 0.70, over twice as large as the short-run elasticity.

## Other Determinants of the Price Elasticity of Demand

Two other factors help determine the price elasticity of demand for a product. First, the elasticity is generally larger for goods that take a relatively large part of a consumer's budget. If a good represents a small part of the budget of the typical consumer, demand is relatively inelastic. For example, suppose the price of pencils is 20 cents and then increases by 10 percent, or 2 cents. Because the price change is tiny compared to the income of the typical consumer, we would expect a relatively small decrease in the quantity of pencils demanded. In contrast, if the price of a car is $20,000 and then increases 10 percent ($2,000), we would expect a bigger response because the change in price is large relative to the income of the typical consumer.

International comparisons of the price elasticity of demand for food suggest that demand is more price elastic when the good represents a large part of the consumer's budget. As shown in Table 4.2, in wealthy countries such as the United States, Canada, and Germany, the price elasticity of demand for food is around 0.15. In poor countries such as India, Nigeria, and Bolivia, people spend a larger fraction of their budget on food, so they are more responsive to changes in food prices. In these poor countries, the price elasticity of demand is around 0.34.

Another factor in determining the elasticity of demand is whether the product is a necessity or a luxury good. As shown in Table 4.2, the demand for food, a necessity, is relatively low in both wealthy and poor countries. Similarly, the demand for physician visits is inelastic (elasticity = 0.25). In contrast, the elasticity of demand for luxury goods such as restaurant meals, foreign travel, and motorboats is relatively elastic. Of course, not all goods that are considered luxuries have elastic demand. For example, the price elasticity of demand for weekend canoe trips is 0.19, and the demand elasticity for sport fishing is 0.28. These elasticities suggest that one person's luxury is another person's necessity.

Table 4.3 summarizes our discussion of the determinants of the price elasticity of demand. Demand is relatively elastic if there are many good substitutes, if we allow consumers a long time to respond, if spending on the product is a large part of the consumer's budget, and if the product is a luxury as opposed to a necessity.

## 4.2 | USING PRICE ELASTICITY TO PREDICT CHANGES IN QUANTITY

The price elasticity of demand is a very useful tool for economic analysis. If we know the elasticity of demand for a particular good, we can quantify the law of demand, predicting the change in quantity resulting from a change in price.

If we have values for two of the three variables in the elasticity formula, we can compute the value of the third. The three variables are (1) the price elasticity of demand itself, (2) the percentage change in quantity, and (3) the percentage change in price. So if we know the values for the price elasticity and the percentage change in price, we can compute the value for the percentage change in quantity. Specifically, we can rearrange the elasticity formula:

$$\text{percentage change in quantity demanded} = \text{percentage change in price} \times E_d$$

### Table 4.3 | DETERMINANTS OF ELASTICITY

| Factor | Demand is relatively elastic if . . . | Demand is relatively inelastic if . . . |
|---|---|---|
| Availability of substitutes | there are many substitutes. | there are few substitutes. |
| Passage of time | a long time passes. | a short time passes. |
| Fraction of consumer budget | is large. | is small. |
| Necessity | the product is a luxury. | the product is a necessity. |

For example, suppose you run a campus film series and you've decided to increase your admission price by 15 percent. If you know the elasticity of demand for your movies, you could use it to predict how many fewer tickets you'll sell at the higher price. If the elasticity of demand is 2.0 and you increase the price by 15 percent, we would predict a 30-percent decrease in the quantity of tickets demanded:

$$\text{percentage change in quantity demanded} = \text{percentage change in price} \times E_d$$
$$= 15\% \times 2.0 = 30\%$$

# APPLICATION

## BEER TAXES AND HIGHWAY DEATHS

APPLYING THE CONCEPTS #1: How can we use the price elasticity of demand to predict the effects of taxes?

We can use the concept of price elasticity to predict the effects of a change in the price of beer on drinking and highway deaths among young adults. The law of demand tells us that an increase in the price of beer will decrease beer consumption, and if we know the price elasticity of demand for beer, we can predict just how much less beer will be consumed at the higher price.

The price elasticity of demand for beer among young adults is about 1.30. If a state imposes a beer tax that increases the price of beer by 10 percent, how will the price hike affect beer consumption among young adults? Using the elasticity formula, we predict that beer consumption will decrease by 13 percent:

$$\text{percentage change in quantity demanded} = \text{percentage change in price} \times E_d$$
$$= 10\% \times 1.30 = 13\%$$

The number of highway deaths among young adults is roughly proportional to their beer consumption, so the number of deaths will also decrease by 13 percent. Of course, if young adults switch from beer to other alcoholic beverages, the number of highway deaths will decrease by a smaller amount.

A recent study provides support for the notion that increasing the beer tax will reduce highway deaths. The authors predict that a doubling of the beer tax from $0.16 to $0.32 per six-pack would decrease highway deaths among 18- to 20-year-olds by about 12 percent. Larger taxes would decrease beer consumption and highway deaths by larger amounts. For example, raising the tax on beer to make it equivalent to the taxes on alcoholic spirits (rum, vodka, tequila) would cut highway deaths among young adults by 35 percent. Raising the beer tax back to where it was in 1951 would cut highway deaths by 32 percent. *Related to Exercises 2.1 and 2.5.*

SOURCES: Henry Saffer and Michael Grossman, "Beer Taxes, the Legal Drinking Age, and Youth Motor Vehicle Fatalities," *Journal of Legal Studies*, vol. 16, June 1987, pp. 351–374; Frank Chaloupka, Henry Saffer, and Michael Grossman, "Alcohol Control Policies and Motor Vehicle Fatalities," *Journal of Legal Studies*, vol. 22, January 1993, pp. 161–183.

# APPLICATION

**2**

## SUBSIDIZED MEDICAL CARE IN CÔTE D'IVOIRE AND PERU

**APPLYING THE CONCEPTS #2:** Does the responsiveness of consumers to changes in price vary by income?

If the price of medical care increases, how will consumers respond? The rising cost of medical care has forced many nations to take a closer look at programs that subsidize medical care for their citizens. If prices are increased to cover more of the costs of providing medical care, how will this affect poor and wealthy households?

Many developing nations subsidize medical care, charging consumers a small fraction of the cost of providing the services. If a nation were to cut its subsidies and thus increase the price of medical care for consumers, how would the higher price affect its poor and wealthy households? In Côte d'Ivoire in Africa, the price elasticity of demand for hospital services is 0.47 for poor households and 0.29 for wealthy households. This means that a 10-percent increase in the price of hospital services would cause poor households to cut back their hospital care by 4.7 percent:

$$\text{percentage change in quantity demanded} = 10\% \times 0.47 = 4.7\%$$

In contrast, wealthy households would cut back by only 2.9 percent:

$$\text{percentage change in quantity demanded} = 10\% \times 0.29 = 2.9\%$$

In Peru, the differences between poor and wealthy households are even larger: The price elasticity is 0.67 for poor households but only 0.03 for wealthy households. The same pattern occurs in the demand for the medical services provided in outpatient clinics. The poor are much more sensitive to price, so when prices increase, they experience much larger reductions in medical care. *Related to Exercises 2.2 and 2.8.*

SOURCE: Paul Gertler and Jacques van der Gaag, *The Willingness to Pay for Medical Care: Evidence from Two Developing Countries* (Baltimore, MD: Johns Hopkins University Press, 1990).

## 4.3 | PRICE ELASTICITY AND TOTAL REVENUE

Firms use the concept of price elasticity to predict the effects of changing their prices. A firm produces products to sell, and a firm's **total revenue** equals the money it generates from selling products. If a firm sells its product for the same price to every consumer, total revenue equals the price per unit times the quantity sold:

**• total revenue**
The money a firm generates from selling its product.

$$\text{total revenue} = \text{price per unit} \times \text{quantity sold}$$

# APPLICATION

## HOW TO CUT TEEN SMOKING BY 60 PERCENT

**APPLYING THE CONCEPTS #3:** How can we use the price elasticity of demand to predict the effects of public policies?

Under the 1997 federal tobacco settlement, if smoking by teenagers does not decline by 60 percent by the year 2007, cigarette makers will be fined $2 billion. The settlement increased cigarette prices by about 62 cents per pack, a percentage increase of about 25 percent. Will the price hike be large enough to meet the target reduction of 60 percent? The demand for cigarettes by teenagers is elastic, with an elasticity of 1.3. Therefore, a 25-percent price hike will reduce teen smoking by only 32.5 percent, far short of the target reduction:

$$\text{percentage change in quantity demanded} = 25\% \times 1.30 = 32.5\%$$

About half of the decrease in consumption occurs because fewer teenagers will become smokers, and the other half occurs because each teenage smoker will smoke fewer cigarettes. To meet the target reduction of teenage smoking, the price of cigarette prices must increase by about 46 percent:

$$\text{percentage change in quantity demanded} = 46\% \times 1.3 = 60\%$$

Tobacco companies recognize this problem and have taken other measures to reduce teen smoking, including antismoking campaigns aimed at teens.
*Related to Exercises 2.3 and 2.9.*

SOURCES: Michael M. Phillips and Suein L. Hwang, "Why Tobacco Pact Won't Hurt Industry," *Wall Street Journal*, September 12, 1997, p. A2; Frank J. Chaloupka and Michael Grossman, "Price, Tobacco Control Policies, and Smoking Among Young Adults," *Journal of Health Economics*, vol. 16, 1997, pp. 359–373.

Suppose a firm increases the price of its product. Will its total sales revenue increase or decrease? The answer depends on the price elasticity of demand for the product. If you know the price elasticity, you can determine whether a price hike will increase or decrease the firm's total revenue.

Let's return to the example of the campus film series. Suppose you are thinking about increasing the price of tickets by 10 percent, from $10 to $11. An increase in the ticket price brings good news and bad news:

- Good news: You get more money for each ticket sold.
- Bad news: You sell fewer tickets.

Your total revenue will decrease if the bad news (fewer tickets sold) dominates the good news (more money per ticket). The elasticity of demand tells us how the good news compares to the bad news. If demand is elastic, consumers will respond to the higher price by purchasing many fewer tickets, so although you will collect more money per ticket, you'll sell so few tickets that your total revenue will decrease.

## Elastic Versus Inelastic Demand

The upper part of Table 4.4 shows an example of the effects of a price hike when the demand for a product is elastic. In this case, the price elasticity of demand is 2.0, so a 10-percent increase in price decreases the quantity demanded by 20 percent, from 100 to 80 tickets. Because the percentage decrease in quantity (the bad news) exceeds the percentage increase in price (the good news), total revenue decreases, from $1,000 to $880. In general, an elastic demand means that the percentage change in quantity (the bad news from a price hike) will exceed the percentage change in price (the good news), so an increase in price will decrease total revenue.

We get the opposite result if the demand for the good is inelastic: An increase in price increases total revenue. If demand is inelastic, consumers are not very responsive to an increase in price, so the good news (more money per unit sold) dominates the bad news (fewer units sold). The lower part of Table 4.4 shows an example of the effects of a price hike when demand is inelastic (equal to 0.50). Suppose that your campus bookstore starts with a textbook price of $100 and sells 10 books per minute. If the bookstore increases its price by 20 percent (from $100 to $120 per book) and the elasticity of demand for textbooks is 0.50, the quantity of textbooks sold will decrease by only 10 percent (from 10 to 9 per minute). Therefore, the store's total revenue will increase from $1,000 per minute ($100 × 10 books) to $1,080 per minute ($120 × 9 books). In general, an inelastic demand means that the percentage change in quantity will be smaller than the percentage change in price, so an increase in price will increase total revenue.

Table 4.5 summarizes the revenue effects of changes in prices for different types of goods:

- *Elastic demand.* The relationship between price and total revenue is negative: An increase in price decreases total revenue; a decrease in price increases total revenue.

- *Inelastic demand.* The relationship between price and total revenue is positive: An increase in price increases total revenue; a decrease in price decreases total revenue.

- *Unit elastic demand.* Total revenue does not vary with price.

**Table 4.4 | PRICE AND TOTAL REVENUE WITH DIFFERENT ELASTICITIES OF DEMAND**

**Elastic Demand: $E_d = 2.0$**

| Price | Quantity Sold | Total Revenue |
|---|---|---|
| $10 | 100 | $1,000 |
| 11 | 80 | 880 |

**Inelastic Demand: $E_d = 0.50$**

| Price | Quantity Sold | Total Revenue |
|---|---|---|
| 100 | 10 | $1,000 |
| 120 | 9 | 1,080 |

**Table 4.5** | PRICE ELASTICITY AND TOTAL REVENUE

| | | Elastic Demand: $E_d > 1.0$ |
|---|---|---|
| **If price . . .** | **Total revenue . . .** | **Because the percentage change in quantity is . . .** |
| ↑ | ↓ | Larger than the percentage change in price. |
| ↓ | ↑ | Larger than the percentage change in price. |
| | | **Inelastic: $E_d < 1.0$** |
| **If price . . .** | **Total revenue . . .** | **Because the percentage change in quantity is . . .** |
| ↑ | ↑ | Smaller than the percentage change in price. |
| ↓ | ↓ | Smaller than the percentage change in price. |

We can use the relationships summarized in Table 4.5 to work backwards. If we observe the relationship between the price of a product and total sales revenue of the product, we can determine whether the demand for the product is elastic or inelastic. Suppose that when a music store increases the price of its CDs, its total revenue from CDs drops. The negative relationship between price and total revenue means that demand for the store's CDs is elastic: Total revenue decreases because consumers are very responsive to an increase in price, buying a much smaller quantity. In contrast, suppose that when a city increases the price it charges for water, the total revenue from water sales increases. The positive relationship between price and total revenue suggests that the demand for the city's water is inelastic: Total revenue increases because consumers are not very responsive to an increase in price.

## Market Elasticity Versus Elasticity for a Firm

The manager of a DVD rental store has asked you to solve a puzzle. According to national studies of the DVD rental market, the price elasticity of demand for DVD rentals is 0.80: A 10-percent increase in price decreases the quantity of DVDs demanded by about 8 percent. In other words, the demand for DVDs is inelastic. Based on this information, the manager of the DVD store increased prices by 20 percent, expecting total revenue to increase. The manager expected the good news (more money per rental) to dominate the bad news (fewer rentals). But in fact total revenue decreased. Why?

The key to solving this puzzle is to recognize that the manager can't use the results of a national study to predict the effects of increasing a single store's price. The national study suggests that if all DVD stores in the nation increased their prices by 10 percent, the nationwide quantity of DVDs demanded would drop by 8 percent. But when a single DVD store in a city increases its price, consumers can easily rent DVDs at other competing stores in the city. As a result, a 10-percent increase in the price of DVD rentals at one store will decrease the quantity sold by that store by much more than 8 percent. The demand facing an individual store is elastic, so an increase in price will decrease total revenue.

## Transit Fares and Deficits

At the beginning of the chapter, we considered the question of whether increasing the price of bus rides would reduce a city's transit deficit. Here is the exchange between two city officials:

- *Buster:* "A fare increase is a great idea. We'll collect more money from bus riders, so revenue will increase, and the deficit will shrink."

- *Bessie*:"Wait a minute, Buster. Haven't you heard about the law of demand? The increase in the bus fare will decrease the number of passengers taking buses, so we'll collect less money, not more, and the deficit will grow."

Who's right? It depends on the price elasticity of demand for bus ridership.

The price elasticity of demand for bus ridership in the typical city is 0.33, meaning that a 10-percent increase in fares will decrease ridership by only about 3.3 percent.[1] Because demand for bus travel is inelastic, the good news associated with a fare hike (10 percent more revenue per rider) will dominate the bad news (3.3 percent fewer riders), and total fare revenue will increase. In other words, an increase in fares will reduce the transit deficit, so Buster is right.

# APPLICATION

## A BUMPER CROP IS BAD NEWS FOR FARMERS

**APPLYING THE CONCEPTS #4:** If demand is inelastic, how does an increase in supply affect total expenditures?

Suppose that favorable weather generates a "bumper crop" for soybeans that is 30 percent larger than last year's harvest. The bumper crop generates good news and bad news for farmers. The good news is that they will sell more bushels of soybeans. The bad news is that the increase in supply will decrease the equilibrium price of soybeans, so they will get less money per bushel. Which will be larger, the increase in quantity or the decrease in price?

Unfortunately for farmers, the demand for soybeans and many other agricultural products is inelastic. Therefore, to increase the quantity demanded by 30 percent to meet the higher supply, the price must decrease by more than 30 percent. With inelastic demand, consumers need a large price reduction to buy more of the product. For example, if the price elasticity of demand is 0.75, the price must decrease by 40 percent to increase the quantity demanded by 30 percent. To show this, we can rearrange the elasticity formula:

$$\text{percentage change in price} = \frac{\text{percentage change in quantity demanded}}{E_d}$$

$$= \frac{30\%}{0.75} = 40\%$$

Although soybean farmers will sell 30 percent more bushels, they will receive 40 percent less per bushel, so their total revenue will decrease. In general, a bumper crop will make farmers worse off if the demand for their product is inelastic.
*Related to Exercises 3.1 and 3.8.*

# APPLICATION

## DRUG PRICES AND PROPERTY CRIME

**APPLYING THE CONCEPTS #5:** If demand is inelastic, how does a decrease in supply affect total expenditures?

What's the connection between antidrug policies and property crimes such as robbery, burglary, and auto theft? The government uses search-and-destroy tactics to restrict the supply of illegal drugs. If this approach succeeds, drugs become scarce, and the price of drugs increases. Because the demand for illegal drugs is inelastic, the increase in price will increase total spending on illegal drugs. Many drug addicts support their habits by stealing personal property—robbing people, stealing cars, and burglarizing homes. This means that drug addicts will commit more property crimes to support the higher total spending level associated with pricier drugs. Given the inelastic demand for illegal drugs and the connection between drug consumption and property crime, there is a trade-off: A policy that increases drug prices will reduce drug consumption and the number of drug addicts, but will also increase the amount of property crime committed by addicts who continue to abuse drugs. *Related to Exercises 3.2 and 3.9.*

SOURCE: L. P. Silverman and N. L. Sprull, "Urban Crime and the Price of Heroin," *Journal of Urban Economics*, vol. 4, 1977, pp. 80–103.

## 4.4 | ELASTICITY AND TOTAL REVENUE FOR A LINEAR DEMAND CURVE

It is often useful to represent the demand for a product with a linear demand curve. A linear demand curve—a straight line—has a constant slope, but that does not mean that it has a constant elasticity of demand. In fact, the price elasticity of demand decreases as we move downward along a linear demand curve. On the upper half of a linear demand curve, demand is elastic; on the lower half of the curve, demand is inelastic. At the midpoint of a linear demand curve, demand is unit elastic.

### Price Elasticity Along a Linear Demand Curve

We can use Panel A of Figure 4.2 to show how price elasticity varies along a linear demand curve. The slope of the demand curve is –$2 per unit quantity. We see this by picking any two points and computing the slope as the vertical difference between the two points (the "rise") divided by the horizontal difference between the two points (the "run"). For example, between points $e$ and $u$, the vertical difference is –$30 and the horizontal difference is 15, so the slope is –$30/15 = –$2. That means a $2 decrease in price increases the quantity demanded by one unit.

Table 4.6 shows how to compute the price elasticity of demand with three starting points: $e$ (for elastic demand), $u$ (for unit elastic), and $i$ (for inelastic). As shown in

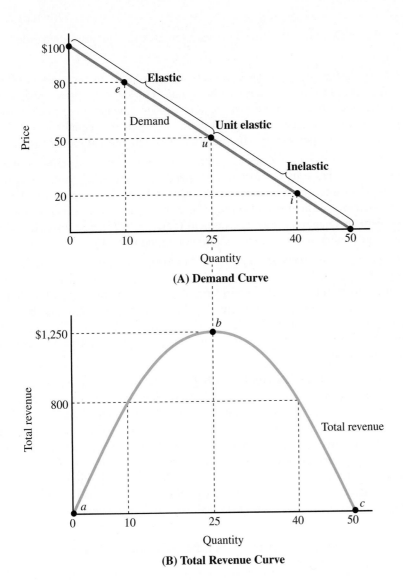

**(A) Demand Curve**

**(B) Total Revenue Curve**

Demand is elastic along the upper half of a linear demand curve, so an increase in quantity from a decrease in price increases total revenue (between points *a* and *b* on the total-revenue curve). Demand is inelastic along the lower half of a linear demand curve, so an increase in quantity from a decrease in price decreases total revenue (between points *b* and *c*). Total revenue is maximized at the midpoint of a linear demand curve (point *u*), where demand is unit elastic.

**Table 4.6 | ELASTICITY OF DEMAND ALONG A LINEAR DEMAND CURVE**

| A | B | C | D | E | F |
|---|---|---|---|---|---|
| Starting Point | Change in Price | Percentage Change in Price | Change in Quantity | Percentage Change in Quantity | Elasticity of Demand |
| *e: Elastic* | −$2 | $\dfrac{-\$2}{\$80} = -2.5\%$ | +1 | $\dfrac{1}{10} = 10\%$ | $\left|\dfrac{10\%}{-2.5\%}\right| = 4$ |
| *u: Unit elastic* | −$2 | $\dfrac{-\$2}{\$50} = -4\%$ | +1 | $\dfrac{1}{25} = 4\%$ | $\left|\dfrac{4\%}{-4\%}\right| = 1$ |
| *i: Inelastic* | −$2 | $\dfrac{-\$2}{\$20} = -10\%$ | +1 | $\dfrac{1}{40} = 2.5\%$ | $\left|\dfrac{2.5\%}{-10\%}\right| = 0.25$ |

columns B and D, a $2 reduction in price increases the quantity demanded by one unit.

- *Column C: Percentage change in price.* Starting from point *e*, we cut $2 off an $80 price, resulting in a 2.5-percent price cut. The same $2 price cut is larger in percentage terms farther down the demand curve, where the price is lower. For point *u*, the percentage change in price is –4 percent (equal to –$2/$50), and for point *i*, the percentage change in price is –10 percent (equal to –$2/$20).
- *Column E: Percentage change in quantity.* At point *e*, we start with 10 units, so a one-unit increase in quantity is a 10-percent increase. Moving down the column, the same one-unit increase in quantity is smaller in percentage terms as we move down the demand curve, where the quantity is larger. For point *u*, the percentage change in price is 4 percent (equal to 1/25), and for point *i* the percentage change in quantity is 2.5 percent (equal to 1/40).
- *Column F: Price elasticity of demand.* Starting from point *e*, the price elasticity is large (4.0) because the percentage change in quantity (10%) is four times the percentage change in price (2.5%). Starting at point *u*, demand is unit elastic because the percentage change in quantity equals the percentage change in price. Starting from point *i*, demand is inelastic (0.25), because the percentage change in quantity is one-fourth the percentage change in price.

Why does the price elasticity vary along a linear demand curve? It's tempting to think the elasticity will be constant because a straight line has a constant slope. But that's incorrect, because elasticity is measured by percentage changes, not absolute changes. As we move downward along the demand curve, we're moving in the direction of larger quantities, so the same absolute change in quantity (one unit) becomes a smaller *percentage* change in quantity. At the same time, as we move downward along the curve, we are moving to lower prices, so a $2 price reduction leads to a larger *percentage* change in price. As a result, the elasticity (the ratio of the percentage changes) decreases as we move downward along the demand curve.

### Elasticity and Total Revenue for a Linear Demand Curve

Panel B of Figure 4.2 shows the relationship between total revenue and the quantity sold for the linear demand curve. Demand is elastic along the upper half of a linear demand curve, which means that a decrease in price will increase the quantity sold by a larger percentage amount. As a result, total revenue will increase, as shown by the positively sloped total-revenue curve between points *a* and *b*. In contrast, demand is inelastic along the lower half of a linear demand curve, which means that a decrease in price will increase the quantity sold by a smaller percentage amount. As a result, total revenue will decrease, as shown by the negatively sloped total-revenue curve between points *b* and *c*. The total-revenue curve reaches its maximum at the midpoint of the linear demand curve, where demand is unit elastic. In Figure 4.2, demand is unit elastic at point *u* on the demand curve, so total revenue reaches its maximum at $1,250 at point *b* on the total-revenue curve.

# 4.5 | OTHER ELASTICITIES OF DEMAND

We've seen that the price elasticity of demand measures the responsiveness of consumers to changes in the price of a particular good. Of course, the demand for a particular product also depends on other variables such as consumer income and the prices of related goods—substitutes and complements. We can use two other elasticities to measure the responsiveness of consumers to changes in these other variables that affect demand: income elasticity of demand and cross-price elasticity of demand.

## Income Elasticity of Demand

We saw in Chapter 3 that the demand for a particular product depends in part on the consumer's income. The **income elasticity of demand** measures the responsiveness of demand to changes in income, indicating how much more or less of a particular product is purchased as income changes. The income elasticity of demand is defined as the percentage change in quantity demanded divided by the percentage change in income:

$$E_i = \frac{\text{percentage change in quantity demanded}}{\text{percentage change in income}}$$

For example, if a 10-percent increase in income increases the quantity of books demanded by 15 percent, the income elasticity of demand for books is 1.50 (equal to 15% divided by 10%).

We can use the income elasticities of demand for various products to categorize the products into different types. Recall from Chapter 3 that when a consumer's income increases, he or she buys more of a "normal" good. If the income elasticity is positive—indicating a positive relationship between income and demand—we say that the good is normal. New cars and new clothes are products that have positive income elasticities and are thus considered normal goods. In contrast, if the income elasticity is negative—indicating a negative relationship between income and demand—we say the good is "inferior." Some examples of inferior goods are intercity bus travel, used clothing, and used cars.

- **income elasticity of demand** A measure of the responsiveness of demand to changes in consumer income; equal to the percentage change in the quantity demanded divided by the percentage change in income.

## Cross-Price Elasticity of Demand

We saw in Chapter 3 that the demand for a particular product also depends in part on the prices of related goods—substitutes and complements. The **cross-price elasticity of demand** measures the responsiveness of demand to changes in the prices of other goods, indicating how much more or less of a particular product is purchased as other prices change. The cross-price elasticity is defined as the percentage change in quantity demanded of one good (X) divided by the percentage change in the price of another good (Y):

$$E_{xy} = \frac{\text{percentage change in quantity of } X \text{ demanded}}{\text{percentage change in price of } Y}$$

- **cross-price elasticity of demand** A measure of the responsiveness of demand to changes in the price of a another good; equal to the percentage change in the quantity demanded of one good (X) divided by the percentage change in the price of another good (Y).

As we saw in Chapter 3, two goods are considered substitutes if there is a positive relationship between the quantity demanded of one good and the price of the other good. For example, an increase in the price of bananas increases the demand for apples as consumers substitute apples for the now relatively expensive bananas. For substitute goods, the cross-price elasticity is positive. In contrast, two goods are considered complements if there is a negative relationship between the quantity demanded of one good and the price of the other. For example, an increase in the price of ice cream increases the cost of apple pie with ice cream, causing consumers to demand fewer apples. For complementary goods, the cross-price elasticity is negative. Table 4.7 summarizes the signs (positive or negative) for different types of goods.

**Table 4.7** | INCOME AND CROSS-PRICE ELASTICITIES FOR DIFFERENT TYPES OF GOODS

| This elasticity . . . | Is positive for . . . | Is negative for . . . |
| --- | --- | --- |
| Income elasticity | Normal goods | Inferior goods |
| Cross-price elasticity | Substitute goods | Complementary goods |

Estimates of cross-price elasticity of demand are useful to retailers in their pricing decisions. For example, when a grocery store cuts the price of peanut butter by 10 percent, the store will sell more peanut butter but will also sell more complementary goods such as jelly and bread. If the cross-price elasticity of demand for jelly is 0.5, a 10-percent decrease in the price of peanut butter will increase the demand for jelly by 5 percent. Retailers use coupons for one product to promote sales of that good as well as complementary goods. Armed with the relevant cross elasticities, retailers can predict just how much more of a complementary good consumers will buy.

# 4.6 | THE PRICE ELASTICITY OF SUPPLY

• **price elasticity of supply**
A measure of the responsiveness of the quantity supplied to changes in price; equal to the percentage change in quantity supplied divided by the percentage change in price.

We've used the concept of elasticity to measure the responsiveness of consumers to changes in prices. We now look at elasticity on the supply side of the market. The **price elasticity of supply** measures the responsiveness of the quantity supplied to changes in price. We compute this elasticity by dividing the percentage change in quantity supplied by the percentage change in price:

$$E_s = \frac{\text{percentage change in quantity supplied}}{\text{percentage change in price}}$$

We can use some of the numbers in Figure 4.3 to compute the price elasticity of supply of milk. Consider Panel A, with a relatively steep supply curve. When the price of milk increases from $1.00 to $1.20, the quantity supplied increases from 100 million gallons (point $a$) to 102 million gallons (point $b$). The percentage change in quantity is the change (2) divided by the initial value (100), or 2 percent:

$$\text{percentage change in quantity supplied} = \frac{2}{100} = 2\%$$

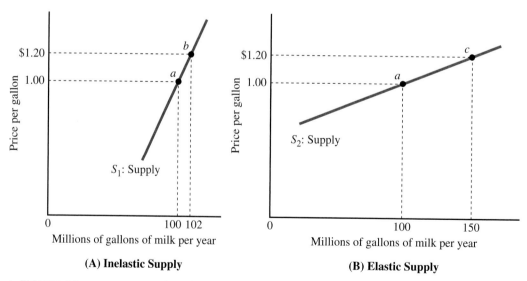

**(A) Inelastic Supply**

**(B) Elastic Supply**

▲ **FIGURE 4.3**
**The Slope of the Supply Curve and Supply Elasticity**
(**A**) The supply curve is relatively steep. A 20% increase in price increases the quantity supplied by 2%, implying a supply elasticity of 0.10.
(**B**) The supply curve is relatively flat. A 20% increase in price increases the quantity supplied by 50%, implying a supply elasticity of 2.5.

The percentage change in price is the change ($0.20) divided by the initial value ($2.00), or 10 percent:

$$\text{percentage change in price} = \frac{\$0.20}{\$1.00} = 20\%$$

Dividing the percentage change in quantity supplied by the percentage change in price, the price elasticity of supply is 0.10:

$$E_s = \frac{\text{percentage change in quantity supplied}}{\text{percentage change in price}} = \frac{2\%}{20\%} = 0.10$$

## What Determines the Price Elasticity of Supply?

What's the connection between the slope of the supply curve and the price elasticity of supply? With a steep curve, a given increase in price (in the denominator of the elasticity formula) generates a small increase in quantity supplied (in the numerator of the elasticity formula). In Panel A of Figure 4.3, an increase in price from $1.00 to $1.20 increases the quantity supplied from 100 to 102, so the price elasticity of supply is 0.10 (equal to 2% divided by 10%). In contrast, with a relatively flat supply curve the same increase in price generates a larger increase in quantity supplied, so the supply elasticity is relatively large. In Panel B of Figure 4.3, an increase in price from $1.00 to $1.20 increases the quantity supplied from 100 to 150, so the price elasticity of supply is 2.50 (equal to 50% divided by 20%).

Why is the market supply curve positively sloped? As we saw in Chapter 3, the market supply curve shows the marginal cost of production. A positively sloped supply curve tells us that the marginal cost of production increases as the total output of the industry increases. In other words, if we want to get more output out of an industry, the price must rise to cover the higher production costs associated with a larger industry. For example, as the total output of the gasoline industry increases, the worldwide demand for crude oil increases, pushing up its price. So to get more gasoline, the price of gasoline must increase to cover the higher cost of crude oil. The more rapidly crude-oil prices rise, the larger the increase in the gasoline price required to get more gasoline—and the steeper the gasoline supply curve.

The price elasticity of supply is determined by how rapidly production costs increase as the total output of the industry increases. If the marginal cost increases rapidly, the supply curve is relatively steep and the price elasticity is relatively low. For example, if crude-oil prices increase rapidly as the total amount of gasoline increases, the supply curve for gasoline will be relatively steep and the price elasticity of supply of gasoline will be relatively low. In contrast, as the output of the pencil industry increases the prices of wood and other inputs used to produce pencils are unlikely to increase by much, so the supply curve will be relatively flat and the price elasticity of supply will be relatively large.

## The Role of Time: Short-Run Versus Long-Run Supply Elasticity

Time is an important factor in determining the price elasticity of supply for a product. As we saw in Chapter 3, the market supply curve is positively sloped because of two responses to an increase in price:

- *Short run.* A higher price encourages existing firms to increase their output by purchasing more materials and hiring more workers.
- *Long run.* New firms enter the market and existing firms expand their production facilities to produce more output.

The short-run response is limited because of the principle of diminishing returns.

# PRINCIPLE OF DIMINISHING RETURNS

Suppose output is produced with two or more inputs, and we increase one input while holding the other input or inputs fixed. Beyond some point—called the *point of diminishing returns*—output will increase at a decreasing rate.

In the short run, the fixed input is the firm's production facility. Although a higher price will induce firms to produce more, the response is limited by the fixed capacity of the firms' production facilities. As a result, the short-run supply curve is relatively steep and the short-run supply elasticity is relatively small.

The long-run supply response to an increase in price is not limited by diminishing returns because production facilities are not fixed. Over time, new firms enter the market with new production facilities and old firms build new facilities. As a result, a given increase in price generates a larger increase in quantity supplied. The long-run supply curve will be relatively flat and the elasticity of supply will be relatively large.

The milk industry provides a good example of the difference between the short-run and long-run price elasticity of supply. In Panel A of Figure 4.3, the steep curve is a short-run supply curve, showing the relationship between price and quantity supplied over a one-year period. The price elasticity of supply over a one-year period is about 0.10: If the price of milk increases by 20 percent and stays there for a year, the quantity of milk supplied will rise by only 2 percent.[2] In the short run, dairy farmers can squeeze just a little more output from their existing production facilities.

In Panel B of Figure 4.3, the long-run supply curve shows the relationship between price and quantity supplied over a 10-year period. In the long run, dairy farmers can expand existing facilities and build new ones, so farmers are more responsive to a higher price—the supply curve is flatter and the supply elasticity is larger. The price elasticity of supply is 2.5, so the same 20-percent rise in price increases the quantity supplied by 50 percent.

### Extreme Cases: Perfectly Inelastic Supply and Perfectly Elastic Supply

Figure 4.4 shows the extreme cases of supply elasticity. The supply curve in Panel A is a vertical line, indicating that regardless of price, the quantity supplied is 50 units. This is the case of **perfectly inelastic supply**, with a price elasticity of supply equal to zero. The numerator in the elasticity expression (the percentage change in quantity supplied) is zero, regardless of the percentage change in the price of the good. Land is

• **perfectly inelastic supply**
The price elasticity of supply equals zero.

▶ **FIGURE 4.4**
**Perfectly Inelastic Supply and Perfectly Elastic Supply**
In Panel A, the quantity supplied is the same at every price, so the price elasticity of supply is zero. In Panel B, the quantity supplied is infinitely responsive to changes in price, so the price elasticity of supply is infinite.

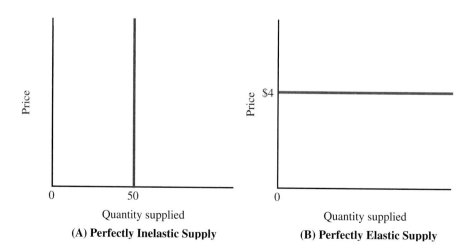

**(A) Perfectly Inelastic Supply**          **(B) Perfectly Elastic Supply**

an example of a product that has a perfectly inelastic supply. In the words of American humorist and author Will Rogers, "The trouble with land is that they're not making it any more."

The supply curve in Panel B of Figure 4.4 is a horizontal line, indicating that the quantity supplied is infinitely responsive to any change in price. This is the case of **perfectly elastic supply**, with a price elasticity of supply equal to infinity. The numerator in the elasticity expression (the percentage change in quantity supplied) is infinite, regardless of the percentage change in the price. One implication of this supply curve is that if the price were to drop below $4, the quantity supplied would fall to zero.

What is the economic logic behind a horizontal supply curve? Recall that the supply curve shows the marginal cost of production. A horizontal supply curve indicates that the marginal cost of production doesn't change as the total output of the industry increases. For example, if the production cost per pencil is $0.20 no matter how many pencils the industry produces, the supply curve will be horizontal at $0.20.

• **perfectly elastic supply**
The price elasticity of supply is equal to infinity.

### Predicting Changes in Quantity Supplied

We can use the price elasticity of supply to predict the effect of price changes on the quantity supplied. For example, suppose that the elasticity of supply is 0.80 and the price increases by 5 percent. Rearranging the elasticity formula, we would predict a 4-percent increase in the quantity supplied:

$$\text{percentage change in quantity supplied} = E_s \times \text{percentage change in price}$$
$$= 0.80 \times 5\% = 4\%$$

As we saw in Chapter 3, many governments establish minimum prices for agricultural products. The higher the minimum price, the larger the quantity supplied, consistent with the law of supply. If we know the price elasticity of supply, we can predict just how much more will be supplied at a higher minimum price. For example, if the minimum price of cheese increases by 10 percent and the price elasticity is 0.60, the quantity of cheese supplied will rise by 6 percent:

$$\text{percentage change in quantity supplied} = E_s \times \text{percentage change in price}$$
$$= 0.60 \times 10\% = 6\%$$

## 4.7 | USING ELASTICITIES TO PREDICT CHANGES IN EQUILIBRIUM PRICE

When demand or supply changes—that is, when the demand curve or the supply curve shifts—we can draw a demand and supply graph to predict whether the equilibrium price will increase or decrease. In many cases, the simple graph will show all we need to know about the effects of a change in supply or demand. But what if we want to predict how much a price will increase or decrease? We can use a simple formula to predict the change in the equilibrium price resulting from a change in demand or a change in supply.

### The Price Effects of a Change in Demand

In Figure 4.5, an increase in demand shifts the demand curve to the right and increases the equilibrium price. We explained in Chapter 3 that a demand curve shifts as a result of a change in something other than the price of the product—for example, a change in income, tastes, or the price of a related good. When demand increases, the immediate effect is excess demand: At the original price ($1.00), the quantity demanded exceeds the quantity supplied by 35 million gallons

**An Increase in Demand Increases the Equilibrium Price**

An increase in demand shifts the demand curve to the right, increasing the equilibrium price. In this case, a 35-percent increase in demand increases the equilibrium price by 10 percent. Using the price-change formula, 10% = 35%/(2.5 + 1.0).

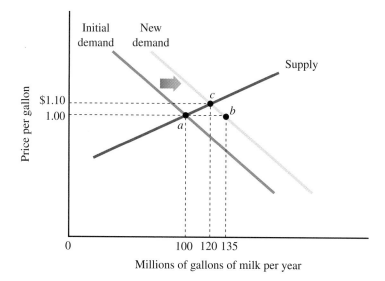

Millions of gallons of milk per year

(135 million – 100 million). As the price increases, both consumers and producers help to eliminate the excess demand: Consumers buy less (the law of demand), and firms produce more (the law of supply).

Under what conditions will an increase in demand cause a relatively small increase in price?

- *Small increase in demand.* If the shift of the demand curve is relatively small, the gap between the new demand and the old supply will be relatively small, and the small excess demand can be eliminated with a relatively small increase in price.

- *Highly elastic demand.* If consumers are very responsive to changes in price, the increase in price caused by excess demand will cause a large reduction in the quantity demanded. As a result, the excess demand will be eliminated with a relatively small increase in price.

- *Highly elastic supply.* If producers are very responsive to changes in price, the increase in price caused by excess demand will cause a large increase in the quantity supplied. As a result, the excess demand will be eliminated with a relatively small increase in price.

We can use the following *price-change formula* to predict the change in the equilibrium price resulting from a change in demand. We divide the percentage change in demand by the sum of the price elasticities of supply and demand:

$$\text{percentage change in equilibrium price} = \frac{\text{percentage change in demand}}{E_s + E_d}$$

The numerator is the rightward shift of the demand curve in percentage terms. In Figure 4.5, the initial quantity demanded at a price of $1.00 is 100 million gallons (shown by the initial demand curve), and the new quantity demanded at the same price is 135 million gallons (shown by the new demand curve). The change in demand is 35 percent (35/100). The larger the increase in demand (the larger the rightward shift of the demand curve), the larger the increase in the equilibrium price. It makes sense that the change in demand is in the numerator of the price-change formula. The two price elasticities appear in the denominator. This is sensible because if consumers and producers are very responsive to changes in price (the elasticities are large numbers), excess demand will be eliminated with a relatively small increase in price.

We can use a simple example to see how to use the price-change formula. Suppose that demand increases by 35 percent (the demand curve shifts to the right by 35 percent). If the supply elasticity is 2.5 and the demand elasticity is 1.0, the predicted change in the equilibrium price is 10 percent:

$$\text{percentage change in equilibrium price} = \frac{35\%}{2.5+1.0} = \frac{35\%}{3.5} = 10\%$$

In Figure 4.5, the equilibrium price increases by 10 percent, from $1.00 to $1.10. If either demand or supply were less elastic (if either of the elasticity numbers were smaller), the predicted change in price would be larger. For example, if the supply elasticity were 0.75 instead of 2.5, we would predict a 20-percent increase in price (35% divided by 1.75).

What about the direction of the price change? We know from Chapter 3 that an increase in demand increases the equilibrium price, and a decrease in demand decreases the equilibrium price. Therefore, the percentage change in price is positive when the change in demand is positive (when demand increases and the demand curve shifts to the right), and negative when the change in demand is negative (when demand decreases and the demand curve shifts to the left). For example, suppose the demand for a product decreases by 12 percent (the demand curve shifts to the left by 12 percent). If the supply elasticity is 1.6 and the demand elasticity is 0.40, the price-change formula shows that the equilibrium price will decrease by 6 percent:

$$\text{percentage change in equilibrium price} = \frac{-12\%}{1.6+0.4} = \frac{-12\%}{2.0} = -6\%$$

### The Price Effects of a Change in Supply

Consider next the effects of a change in supply on the equilibrium price. In Figure 4.6, a decrease in supply shifts the supply curve to the left and increases the equilibrium price. We explained in Chapter 3 that a change in supply results from changes in

# APPLICATION

## METROPOLITAN GROWTH AND HOUSING PRICES

**APPLYING THE CONCEPTS #6:** How does population growth affect prices?

We can use the price-change formula to predict the effects of changes in demand on equilibrium prices. The Portland metropolitan area is expected to grow by 12 percent in the next decade. Suppose planners want to predict the effects of population growth on the equilibrium price of housing. At the metropolitan level, the price elasticity of supply is about 5.0 and the price elasticity of demand is 1.0. If the demand for housing is proportional to population, a 12-percent increase in population will increase the equilibrium price of housing by 2 percent:

$$\text{percentage change in equilibrium price} = \frac{12\%}{5.0+1.0}$$

$$= \frac{12\%}{6.0} = 2\%$$

*Related to Exercises 7.5 and 7.6.*

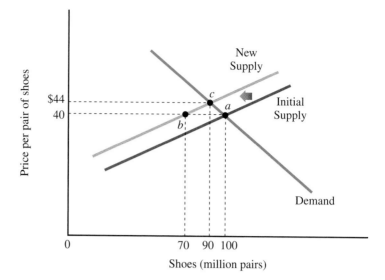

► **FIGURE 4.6**

**A Decrease in Supply Increases the Equilibrium Price**

An import restriction on shoes decreases the supply of shoes, shifting the market supply curve to the left and increasing the equilibrium price from $40 to $44. In this case, a 30% reduction in supply increases the equilibrium price by 10%. Using the price-change formula,

$10\% = -(-30\% / (2.3 + 0.70))$.

something other than the price of the product—for example, a change in the cost of labor or raw materials, a change in production technology, or a change in the number of firms. The immediate effect of a decrease in supply is excess demand: At the original price, the quantity demanded exceeds the quantity supplied. In response to the excess demand, the price increases. Consumers respond to the higher price by purchasing less, and producers respond by producing more, so the gap between the quantity demanded and the quantity supplied narrows.

Under what conditions will a decrease in supply cause a relatively small increase in price?

- *Small decrease in supply.* If the shift of the supply curve is relatively small, the gap between the new supply and the old demand will be relatively small, and the small excess demand can be eliminated with a relatively small increase in price.

- *Highly elastic demand.* If consumers are very responsive to changes in price, the increase in price caused by excess demand will cause a large reduction in the quantity demanded. As a result, the excess demand will be eliminated with a relatively small increase in price.

- *Highly elastic supply.* If producers are very responsive to changes in price, the increase in price caused by excess demand will cause a large increase in the quantity supplied. As a result, the excess demand will be eliminated with a relatively small increase in price.

We can use a variation on the price-change formula to predict the price effects of a change in supply. We modify the numerator of the formula by substituting the percentage change in supply for the percentage change in demand and then add a minus sign. The minus sign indicates a negative relationship between supply and the equilibrium price: When supply decreases (when the supply curve shifts to the left), the price increases; when supply increases, the price decreases:

$$\text{percentage change in equilibrium price} = -\frac{\text{percentage change in supply}}{E_s + E_d}$$

# APPLICATION

## AN IMPORT BAN AND SHOE PRICES

**APPLYING THE CONCEPTS #7:** How do import restrictions affect prices?

We can use the supply version of the price-change formula to predict the effects of import restrictions on equilibrium prices. Consider a nation that limits shoe imports. Suppose the import restrictions decrease the supply of shoes by 30 percent. As shown in Figure 4.6, the policy shifts the supply curve to the left by 30 percent: At the original price of $40, the quantity supplied decreases from 100 million pairs (point *a*) to 70 million pairs (point *b*). The decrease in supply increases the equilibrium price, and the price-change formula tells us just how much the price will increase.

To use the price-change formula, we need the price elasticities of supply and demand. Suppose the supply elasticity is 2.3 and, as shown in Table 4.2, the demand elasticity is 0.70. Plugging these numbers into the price-change formula, we predict a 10-percent increase in price:

$$\text{percentage change in equilibrium price} = -\frac{-30\%}{2.3 + 0.70} = \frac{30\%}{3.0} = 10\%$$

In Figure 4.6, the price rises by 10 percent, from $40 to $44 per pair.
*Related to Exercise 7.7.*

# SUMMARY

This chapter explored the numbers behind the laws of demand and supply. The law of demand tells us that an increase in price decreases the quantity demanded, *ceteris paribus*. If we know the price elasticity of demand for a particular product, we can determine just how much less of it will be purchased at the higher price. Similarly, if we know the price elasticity of supply for a product, we can determine just how much more of it will be supplied at a higher price. Here are the main points of the chapter:

1 The *price elasticity of demand*—defined as the percentage change in quantity demanded divided by the percentage change in price—measures the responsiveness of consumers to changes in price.

2 Demand is relatively elastic if there are good substitutes.

3 If demand is *elastic*, the relationship between price and total revenue is negative. If demand is *inelastic*, the relationship between price and total revenue is positive.

4 The *price elasticity of supply*—defined as the percentage change in quantity supplied divided by the percentage change in price—measures the responsiveness of producers to changes in price.

5 If we know the elasticities of demand and supply, we can predict the percentage change in price resulting from a change in demand or supply.

# KEY TERMS

cross-price elasticity of demand, p. 95

elastic demand, p. 82

income elasticity of demand, p. 95

inelastic demand, p. 82

perfectly elastic demand, p. 82

perfectly elastic supply, p. 99

perfectly inelastic demand, p. 82

perfectly inelastic supply, p. 98

price elasticity of demand ($E_d$), p. 80

price elasticity of supply, p. 96

total revenue, p. 87

unit elastic demand, p. 82

# EXERCISES  ⨉ myeconlab

*Get Ahead of the Curve*

Visit www.myeconlab.com to complete these exercises online and get instant feedback.

## 4.1 | The Price Elasticity of Demand

**1.1** To compute the price elasticity of demand, we divide the percentage change in _____ by the percentage change in _____ and then take the _____ value of the ratio.

**1.2** If a 10-percent increase in price decreases the quantity demanded by 12 percent, the price elasticity of demand is _____.

**1.3** When the price of CDs increased from $10 to $11, the quantity of CDs demanded decreased from 100 to 80. The price elasticity of demand for CDs is _____, and demand is _____ (elastic/inelastic).

**1.4** As the number of substitutes for a particular product increases, the price elasticity of demand for the product _____ (increases/decreases).

**1.5** Over time, the price elasticity of demand for gasoline _____ (increases/decreases).

## 4.2 | Using Price Elasticity to Predict Changes in Quantity

**2.1** A doubling of the tax on beer will reduce the number of highway deaths among young adults by _____ percent. (Related to Application 1 on page 86.)

**2.2** Suppose Peru increases the price of hospital care by 10 percent. The quantity of medical care demanded in low-income areas will _____ by _____ percent. (Related to Application 2 on page 87.)

**2.3** A 20-percent increase in the price of cigarettes will reduce the quantity of cigarettes demanded by teenagers by _____ percent. (Related to Application 3 on page 88.)

**2.4** If the price elasticity of demand is 0.60, a 10-percent increase in price will _____ the quantity demanded by _____ percent.

**2.5** **MADD Beer Tax.** The organization Mothers Against Drunk Driving (MADD) has a target of reducing the number of highway deaths among young adults by

39 percent. Assume that the number of highway deaths for young adults is proportional to their beer consumption. By what percentage must the price of beer increase to meet the MADD target? (Related to Application 1 on page 86.)

**2.6** **Use the Correct Elasticity.** Your company currently sells 50 units of salt per year and has decided to increase its price from $1.00 to $1.20. In a meeting, one person says, "As shown in Table 4.2 on page 84, the price elasticity of demand for salt is 0.10, so if we increase the price of salt by 20 percent, the quantity demanded will decrease by 2 percent." What's wrong with this statement?

**2.7** **Projecting Transit Ridership.** As a transit planner, your job is to predict ridership and total fare revenue. Suppose the short-run elasticity of demand for commuter rail (over a one-month period) is 0.60, and the long-run elasticity (over a two-year period) is 1.60. The current ridership is 100,000 people per day. Suppose the transit authority decides to increase its fares from $2.00 to $2.20.
   **a.** Predict the changes in train ridership over a one-month period (the short run) and a two-year period (the long run).
   **b.** Over the one-month period, will total fare revenue increase or decrease? What about the two-year period?

**2.8** **X-ray Film to Peru.** Last year your charitable organization donated 100 rolls of x-ray film to hospitals in low-income areas of Peru, just enough to meet the country's need for X-ray film in those areas. Suppose Peru increases the price of hospital care by 30 percent. How many rolls of X-ray film should you send to Peru this year? (Related to Application 2 on page 87.)

**2.9** **Meeting the Teen Smoking Target with Prices and Persuasion.** Suppose an antismoking campaign reduces teen smoking by 8 percent, meaning that the price of cigarettes must increase by an amount large enough to reduce teenage smoking by 52 percent to achieve an overall reduction of 60 percent. The required percentage increase in price is _____ percent. (Related to Application 3 on page 88.)

**3.1** A bumper crop is bad news for farmers because _____ is _____. (Related to Application 4 on page 91.)

**3.2** A policy that limits the supply of illegal drugs increases the number of burglaries and robberies because _____ is _____. (Related to Application 5 on page 92.)

**3.3** If demand is elastic, when the price increases, the percentage change in _____ (quantity/price) exceeds the percentage change in _____ (quantity/price).

**3.4** If demand is elastic, an increase in price _____ (increases/decreases) total revenue; if demand is inelastic, an increase in price _____ (increases/decreases) total revenue.

**3.5** If a decrease in the price of accordions increases total revenue from accordion sales, the demand for accordions is _____.

**3.6** Suppose at the current price, the price elasticity of demand for a campus film series is 2.0. If the price is cut, total revenue will _____ (increase/decrease).

**3.7** You observe a positive relationship between the price your store charges for CDs and the total revenue from CDs. The demand for your CDs is _____.

**3.8** **Revenue Effects of a Bumper Crop.** Your job is to predict the total revenue generated by the nation's corn crop. Last year's crop was 100 million bushels, and the price was $5 per bushel. This year's weather was favorable throughout the country, and this year's crop will be 110 million bushels, or 10 percent larger than last year's. The price elasticity of demand for corn is 0.50. (Related to Application 4 on page 91.)
   **a.** Predict the effect of the bumper crop on the price of corn. Assume that the entire crop is sold this year, meaning that the price elasticity of supply is zero. Illustrate with a complete graph.
   **b.** Predict the total revenue from this year's corn crop.
   **c.** Did the favorable weather increase or decrease the total revenue from corn? Why?

**3.9** **The Price of Heroin and Property Crime.** The price elasticity of demand for heroin is 0.27. Suppose that half of heroin users support their habits with property crime, so the loss from property crimes committed by heroin users equals half the total spending (total revenue) on the drug. Suppose the government reduces the supply of heroin, increasing the equilibrium price by 20 percent. Fill the blanks in the following table. (Related to Application 5 on page 92.)

| Price | Quantity of Heroin | Total Spending (Total Revenue) | Property Crime |
|---|---|---|---|
| $10 | 1,000 | $10,000 | $5,000 |
| 12 | _____ | _____ | _____ |

**3.10** **Revenue from Mobile Phones.** Consider the demand for mobile phones. Suppose the price elasticity of demand for the market as a whole is 0.80.
   **a.** If all mobile-phone companies simultaneously increased their prices, will total revenue in the industry increase or decrease?
   **b.** If a single mobile-phone company increased its price, would you expect the company's total revenue to increase or decrease? Explain.

**3.11** **Price Hikes and Cable TV Revenue.** Four years ago the cable company in your city increased its price by 20 percent, and its total revenue increased. Last year, a new company started providing TV service with satellite dishes. This year, the cable company increased its price by 20 percent, but its total revenue decreased. Provide an explanation for the different revenue consequences of the cable company's price hikes.

## 4.4 | Elasticity and Total Revenue for a Linear Demand Curve

**4.1** Demand is _____ on the upper portion of a linear demand curve and _____ on the lower portion of a linear demand curve.

**4.2** Suppose we are on the upper portion of a linear demand curve. If the price increases by 10 percent, the quantity demanded will decrease by _____ (more/less) than 10 percent and total revenue will _____ (increase/decrease).

**4.3** At the midpoint of a linear demand curve, the price elasticity of demand is _____ .

**4.4** If we are on the lower part of a linear demand curve, a decrease in price _____ (increases/decreases) total revenue.

**4.5** **Revenue from Vanity Plates.** The objective of your state is to maximize the total revenue from the sale of vanity license plates. The current price is $25. The demand for vanity license plates is linear, and a price of $80 would drive the quantity demanded to zero. What is the appropriate price? Illustrate with a complete graph.

**4.6** **Where on the Demand Curve?** The demand curve for your firm's product is linear. Based on recent sales data, you have determined that at the current price, the price elasticity of demand is 0.80.
   **a.** Is the current price on the upper or lower portion of the demand curve?
   **b.** If you want to increase your total revenue, should you increase or decrease your price?
   **c.** Will you move upward or downward along the demand curve?

## 4.5 | Other Elasticities of Demand

**5.1** The income elasticity of demand is _____ (positive/negative) for normal goods and _____ (positive/negative) for inferior goods.

**5.2** If a 20-percent increase in income increases the quantity of iPods demanded by 30 percent, the income elasticity of demand is _____.

**5.3** The cross-price elasticity of demand is _____ (positive/negative) for substitute goods and _____ (positive/negative) for complementary goods.

**5.4** If a 10-percent increase in the price of natural gas increases the quantity of residential electricity demanded by 18 percent, the cross-price elasticity of demand is _____.

**5.5** If a 10-percent increase in the price of tennis rackets decreases the quantity of tennis balls demanded by 15 percent, the cross-price elasticity of demand is _____.

**5.6** **Income and Starbucks Coffee Shops.** Starbucks just hired you to determine whether your city could support a new Starbucks coffee shop. There are currently four Starbucks coffee shops in the city, and each has just enough customers to survive. The average household income in the city is expected to increase by 10 percent per year for the next few years. Suppose the income elasticity of demand for Starbucks' coffee products is 1.25. The population of the city is constant.
   **a.** By what percentage will the demand for coffee increase each year?
   **b.** How soon will the area have enough demand to support a fifth Starbucks?

**5.7** **iPods and iTunes.** You have been hired to predict the effects of increasing the price of iTunes songs by 10 percent, from $0.99 to $1.09. You are interested in the effects of the price hike on the number of songs downloaded legally from iTunes, the number of songs downloaded legally from other online music stores, the number of iPod players sold, and the number of CDs sold in stores. Given the hypothetical elasticities in the following table, fill in the blanks. Recall that conventional practice for the price elasticity of demand of a product uses the absolute value of the elasticity.

| Product | Price Elasticity or Cross-Price Elasticity | Predicted Percentage Change in Quantity Demanded |
| --- | --- | --- |
| iTunes songs | 1.50 (absolute value) | _____ |
| Songs from other online stores | +2.00 | _____ |
| iPod players | −0.70 | _____ |
| CDs in stores | +1.80 | _____ |

## 4.6 | The Price Elasticity of Supply

**6.1** When the price of paper increases from $100 to $104 per ton, the quantity supplied increases from 200 to 220 tons per day. The price elasticity of supply is _____.

**6.2** Suppose the price elasticity of a supply of cheese is 0.80. If the price of cheese rises by 20 percent, the quantity of cheese supplied will increase by _____ percent.

**6.3** The short-run elasticity of supply is _____ (smaller/larger) than the long-run elasticity of supply because the principle of _____ is applicable in the short run.

**6.4** As the supply curve becomes flatter, the price elasticity of supply _____ (increases/decreases).

## 4.7 | Using Elasticities to Predict Changes in Equilibrium Price

**7.1** Assume that the elasticity of demand for chewing tobacco is 0.70 and the elasticity of supply is 2.30. Suppose an antichewing campaign decreases the demand for chewing tobacco by 18 percent. The equilibrium price of chewing tobacco will _____ (decrease/increase) by _____ percent.

**7.2** Suppose the elasticity of demand for motel rooms is 1.0 and the elasticity of supply is 0.50. If the demand for motel rooms increases by 15 percent, the equilibrium price of motel rooms will _____ (decrease/increase) by _____ percent.

**7.3** Suppose the price elasticity of demand for apples is 1.0 and the supply elasticity is 3.0. If the supply of apples decreases by 12 percent, the equilibrium price will _____ (decrease/increase) by _____ percent.

**7.4** Suppose the price elasticity of demand for accordions is 2.0 and the supply elasticity is 3.0. If a subsidy on accordions increases supply by 20 percent, the equilibrium price will _____ (decrease/increase) by _____ percent.

**7.5** **College Enrollment and Apartment Prices.** Consider a college town where the initial price of apartments is $400 and the initial quantity is 1,000 apartments. The price elasticity of demand for apartments is 1.0, and the price elasticity of supply of apartments is 0.50. (Related to Application 6 on page 101.)
   **a.** Use demand and supply curves to show the initial equilibrium, and label the equilibrium point *a*.
   **b.** Suppose that an increase in college enrollment is expected to increase the demand for apartments in a college town by 15 percent. Use your graph to show the effects of the increase in demand on the apartment market. Label the new equilibrium point *b*.

**c.** Predict the effect of the increase in demand on the equilibrium price of apartments.

**7.6** **The Cost of Wood and the Price of Housing**. Suppose the price of wood increases the cost of building new houses by 4 percent and shifts the supply curve to the left by 12 percent. The initial price of new housing is $100,000, the price elasticity of demand is 1.0, and the price elasticity of supply is 3.0. Predict the effect of the higher wood prices on the equilibrium price of new housing. Illustrate your answer with a graph that shows the initial point (*a*) and the new equilibrium (*b*). (Related to Application 6 on page 101.)

**7.7** **Import Restrictions and the Price of Steel**. Suppose import restrictions on steel decrease the supply of steel by 24 percent. The initial price of steel is $100 per unit, the elasticity of demand is 0.70, and the elasticity of supply is 2.3. Predict the effect of the import restrictions on the equilibrium price of steel. Illustrate your answer with a graph that shows the initial point (*a*) and the new equilibrium (*b*). (Related to Application 7 on page 103.)

NOTES

1. Kenneth A. Small, *Urban Transportation Economics* (Philadelphia, PA: Harwood Academic Publishers, 1992).

2. Richard Klemme and Jean-Paul Chavas, "The Effects of Changing Milk Price on Milk Supply and National Dairy Herd Size," *Economic Issues*, no. 92, June 1985, University of Wisconsin.

# 5

# Production Technology
and Cost

A few years ago the price of a hardback version of *Encyclopedia Britannica*, the world's leading encyclopedia, was $1,600. Now you can get a CD version of the encyclopedia, along with a dictionary, thesaurus, and world atlas, for only $69.95. Why did the price drop to less than one-twentieth of its former value?

An encyclopedia is an information good because its production involves collecting information—facts, figures, and images—and packaging them for use by consumers. The cost of compiling the information for the first copy of an encyclopedia is huge, but the cost of reproducing the encyclopedia in digital format (CDs) is tiny. The move from hardback encyclopedias to digital ones decreased the cost of production, pulling down the price. In addition, heated competition among rival encyclopedia firms pulled the price down further.

- **economic profit**
  Total revenue minus economic cost.

- **economic cost**
  The opportunity cost of the inputs used in the production process; equal to explicit cost plus implicit cost.

- **explicit cost**
  The actual monetary payment for inputs.

- **implicit cost**
  The opportunity cost of inputs that do not require a monetary payment.

This chapter explores the relationship between the quantity of output produced and the cost of production. As we'll see, a firm's production cost is determined by its production technology—the way the firm combines capital, labor, and materials to produce output. After we explain the link between technology and costs, we'll look at the actual cost curves of several products, including aluminum, hospital services, wind power, truck freight, and airplanes.

As we saw in Chapter 2, economists distinguish between the short run and the long run. The long run is a period long enough that a firm is perfectly flexible in its choice of all inputs, including its production facility. In contrast, when a firm cannot modify its facility, it is operating in the short run. In this chapter, we'll explore both short-run and long-run costs. In later chapters, we'll show how firms use short-run and long-run cost curves to make decisions about whether to enter a market and how much output to produce.

## 5.1 | ECONOMIC COST AND ECONOMIC PROFIT

This is the first of several chapters on the decisions firms make. A firm's objective is to maximize its **economic profit**, which equals its total revenue minus its economic cost:

$$\text{economic profit} = \text{total revenue} - \text{economic cost}$$

As we saw earlier in the book, a firm's total revenue is the money it gets from selling its product. If a firm charges the same price to every consumer, its total revenue equals the price per unit of output times the quantity sold.

This chapter explores the firm's cost of production. A firm's **economic cost** equals the cost of all the inputs used in the production process; it is measured as the opportunity cost of the inputs. Recall the first key principle of economics.

## PRINCIPLE OF OPPORTUNITY COST

The opportunity cost of something is what you sacrifice to get it.

To compute a firm's economic cost, we must determine what the firm sacrifices to use inputs in the production process. Economic cost is opportunity cost.

As shown in the first column of numbers in Table 5.1, a firm's economic cost can be divided into two types. A firm's **explicit cost** is its actual monetary payments for inputs. For example, if a firm spends a total of $10,000 per month on labor, capital, and materials, its explicit cost is $10,000. This is an opportunity cost because money spent on these inputs cannot be used to buy something else. A firm's **implicit cost** is the opportunity cost of the inputs that do not require a monetary payment. Here are two examples of inputs whose cost is implicit rather than explicit:

- *Opportunity cost of the entrepreneur's time.* If an entrepreneur could earn $5,000 per month in another job, the opportunity cost of the time spent running the firm is $5,000 per month.

**Table 5.1** | ECONOMIC COST VERSUS ACCOUNTING COST

| | Economic Cost | Accounting Cost |
|---|---|---|
| Explicit: monetary payments for labor, capital, materials | $10,000 | $10,000 |
| Implicit: opportunity cost of entrepreneur's time | 5,000 | — |
| Implicit: opportunity cost of funds | 2,000 | — |
| **Total** | 17,000 | 10,000 |

- *Opportunity cost of the entrepreneur's funds.* Many entrepreneurs use their own funds to set up and run their businesses. If an entrepreneur starts a business with $200,000 withdrawn from a savings account, the opportunity cost is the interest income the funds could have earned, for example, $2,000 per month.

Economic cost equals explicit cost plus implicit cost:

$$economic\ cost = explicit\ cost + implicit\ cost$$

In the first column of Table 5.1, the firm's economic cost is $17,000, equal to $10,000 in explicit cost plus $7,000 in implicit cost.

Accountants have a different approach to computing costs. Their narrower definition of cost includes only the explicit cost of inputs:

$$accounting\ cost = explicit\ cost$$

In other words, **accounting cost** includes the monetary payments for inputs, but ignores the opportunity cost of inputs that do not require an explicit monetary payment. In the second column of Table 5.1, the accounting cost is the $10,000 in monetary payments for labor, capital, and materials. **Accounting profit** equals total revenue minus accounting cost:

$$accounting\ profit = total\ revenue - accounting\ cost$$

A firm's accounting cost is always lower than its economic cost, so its accounting profit is always *higher* than its economic profit. For the rest of this book, when we refer to cost and profit, we mean *economic* cost and *economic* profit.

- **accounting cost**
  The explicit costs of production.

- **accounting profit**
  Total revenue minus accounting cost.

# 5.2 | A FIRM WITH A FIXED PRODUCTION FACILITY: SHORT-RUN COSTS

Consider first the case of a firm with a fixed production facility. Suppose that you have decided to start a small firm to produce plastic paddles for rafts. The production of paddles requires a workshop where workers use molds to form plastic material into paddles. Before we can discuss the cost of production, we need information about the nature of the production process.

## Production and Marginal Product

The table in Figure 5.1 shows how the quantity of paddles produced varies with the number of workers. A single worker in the workshop produces one paddle per day. Adding a second worker increases the quantity produced to five paddles per day. The **marginal product of labor** is the change in output from one additional unit of labor. In the table, the marginal product of the first worker is one paddle, compared to a marginal product of four paddles for the second worker.

Why does the marginal product increase as output increases? As we saw earlier in the book, when a firm increases its workforce, workers can specialize in production tasks. Productivity increases because of the benefits of continuity—each worker spends less time switching between production tasks. In addition, there are benefits from repetition—each worker becomes more proficient at an assigned task. A two-worker operation produces more than twice as many paddles as a one-person operation because the two workers can specialize, one being responsible for preparing the plastic for the mold and the other responsible for working the mold.

Starting with the third worker, the production process is subject to **diminishing returns**, one of the key principles of economics.

- **marginal product of labor**
  The change in output from one additional unit of labor.

- **diminishing returns**
  As one input increases while the other inputs are held fixed, output increases at a decreasing rate.

# PRINCIPLE OF DIMINISHING RETURNS

Suppose that output is produced with two or more inputs and we increase one input while holding the other inputs fixed. Beyond some point—called the *point of diminishing returns*—output will increase at a decreasing rate.

The third worker adds three paddles to total output, down from four paddles for the second worker. As the firm continues to hire more workers, the marginal product drops to two paddles for the fourth worker and one paddle for the fifth worker. As we saw earlier in the book, diminishing returns occurs because workers share a production facility. A larger workforce means that each worker gets a smaller share of the production facility. In the paddle example, the workers share a mold; as the number of workers increases, they will spend more time waiting to use the mold.

Figure 5.1 shows the firm's **total-product curve**, which represents the relationship between the quantity of labor (on the horizontal axis) and output (on the vertical axis), *ceteris paribus*. The total-product curve shows the effects of labor specialization as well as diminishing returns. For the first two workers, output increases at an increasing rate because labor specialization increases the marginal product of labor. Starting with the third worker, however, total output increases at a decreasing rate because of diminishing returns.

## Short-Run Total Cost

We've seen the production relationship between labor input and output, so we're ready to show the relationship between output and production cost. Suppose the opportunity cost of your time is $50 per day, and you can hire workers for your workshop at the market wage of $50 per day. You can purchase your workshop, including the building and the paddle mold, for $365,000. If the interest rate you could have earned on that money is 10 percent per year, the opportunity cost of tying up your $365,000 in the workshop is $36,500 per year, or $100 per day.

> • **total-product curve**
> A curve showing the relationship between the quantity of labor and the quantity of output produced, ceteris paribus.

▶ **FIGURE 5.1**
**Total-Product Curve**
The total-product curve shows the relationship between the quantity of labor and the quantity of output, given a fixed production facility. For the first 2 workers, output increases at an increasing rate because of labor specialization. Diminishing returns occurs for 3 or more workers, so output increases at a decreasing rate.

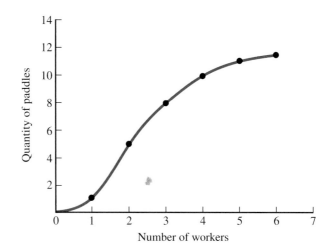

| Labor | Quantity of Output Produced | Marginal Product of Labor |
|-------|------------------------------|----------------------------|
| 1 | 1 | 1 |
| 2 | 5 | 4 |
| 3 | 8 | 3 |
| 4 | 10 | 2 |
| 5 | 11 | 1 |
| 6 | 11.5 | 0.5 |

In the short-run analysis of costs, we divide production costs into two types, fixed cost and variable cost.

- **Fixed cost (FC)** is the cost that does not vary with the quantity produced. In our example, the fixed cost is the cost of the workshop, including the cost of the building and the mold. As shown in the third column of Table 5.2, the fixed cost is $100 per day, regardless of how much output is produced.

- **Variable cost (VC)** is the cost that varies with the quantity produced. For example, to produce more paddles, you must hire more workers. If the cost per worker is $50 per day, your daily variable cost is $50 times the number of workers, including you. As shown in the fourth column of Table 5.2, variable cost is $50 for one worker, $100 for two workers, and so on.

To compute the firm's total cost, we simply add the fixed and variable costs. The firm's **short-run total cost (TC)** equals the sum of fixed and variable costs:

$$TC = FC + VC$$

The fifth column in Table 5.2 shows the total cost for different quantities of output. For example, 1 worker produces 1 paddle at a total cost of $150, equal to the fixed cost of $100 plus a variable cost of $50. Hiring a second worker increases output to 5 paddles and increases total cost to $200, equal to $100 in fixed cost and $100 in variable cost. Moving down the fifth column, the total cost rises to $250 for 8 units of output, $300 for 10 units, and so on.

Figure 5.2 shows the short-run cost curves corresponding to columns 3, 4, and 5 of Table 5.2. The horizontal line on the graph shows the fixed cost of $100. The lower of the two positively sloped curves shows the variable cost (*VC*), and the higher of the two positively sloped curves is total cost (*TC*). Total cost is the sum of fixed cost and

**• fixed cost (FC)**
Cost that does not vary with the quantity produced.

**• variable cost (VC)**
Cost that varies with the quantity produced.

**• short-run total cost (TC)**
The total cost of production when at least one input is fixed; equal to fixed cost plus variable cost.

**Table 5.2** | **SHORT-RUN COSTS**

| 1<br>Labor | 2<br>Output | 3<br>Fixed Cost (FC) | 4<br>Variable Cost (VC) | 5<br>Total Cost (TC) | 6<br>Average Fixed Cost (AFC) | 7<br>Average Variable Cost (AVC) | 8<br>Average Total Cost (ATC) | 9<br>Marginal Cost (MC) |
|---|---|---|---|---|---|---|---|---|
| 0 | 0 | $100 | $ 0 | $100 | — | — | — | — |
| 1 | 1 | 100 | 50 | 150 | $100.00 | $50.00 | $150.00 | $50.00 |
| 2 | 5 | 100 | 100 | 200 | 20.00 | 20.00 | 40.00 | 12.50 |
| 3 | 8 | 100 | 150 | 250 | 12.50 | 18.75 | 31.25 | 16.67 |
| 4 | 10 | 100 | 200 | 300 | 10.00 | 20.00 | 30.00 | 25.00 |
| 5 | 11 | 100 | 250 | 350 | 9.09 | 22.73 | 31.82 | 50.00 |
| 6 | 11.5 | 100 | 300 | 400 | 8.70 | 26.09 | 34.78 | 100.00 |

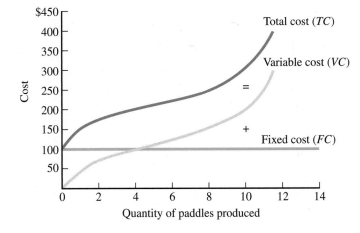

**◄ FIGURE 5.2**
**Short-Run Costs: Fixed Cost, Variable Cost, and Total Cost**
The short-run total-cost curve shows the relationship between the quantity of output and production costs, given a fixed production facility. Short-run total cost equals fixed cost (the cost that does not vary with the quantity produced) plus variable cost (the cost that varies with the quantity produced).

• **average fixed cost (AFC)**
Fixed cost divided by the quantity produced.

• **average variable cost (AVC)**
Variable cost divided by the quantity produced.

variable cost, so the vertical distance between the *TC* curve and the *VC* curve equals the firm's fixed cost. Notice that this distance is the same at any level of output.

## Short-Run Average Costs

There are three types of average cost. **Average fixed cost (AFC)** equals the fixed cost divided by the quantity produced:

$$AFC = \frac{FC}{Q}$$

To compute *AFC* for our paddle company, we simply divide the fixed cost ($100) by the quantity of paddles produced. In Table 5.2, we divide the number in column 3 by the number in column 2. This calculation gives us the values for *AFC*, which are shown in column 6. For example, the output in the second row is 1 paddle, so the average fixed cost is $100 = $100/1. In the third row, output is 5 paddles, so the average fixed cost is $5 = $100/5. As output increases, the $100 fixed cost is spread over more units, so *AFC* decreases.

A firm's **average variable cost (AVC)** incorporates the costs that vary with the quantity produced. Average variable cost equals the variable cost divided by the quantity produced:

$$AVC = \frac{VC}{Q}$$

To compute *AVC* for our paddle company, we simply divide the number in column 4 of Table 5.2 by the number in column 2. That calculation gives us the values for *AVC*, shown in column 7. For example, the output in the third row is 5 paddles and the variable cost is $100, so the average variable cost is $100/5 paddles, or $20. Notice that for small quantities of output, the *AVC* decreases as the quantity produced increases—from $50 for one paddle, $20 for 2 paddles, and so on. The *AVC* declines because of the benefits of labor specialization. Adding workers to a small workforce makes workers more productive on average, so the amount of labor required per unit of output drops, pushing down the average variable cost. In contrast, for large quantities of output, average variable cost increases as output increases because of diminishing returns. Adding workers to a large workforce makes workers less productive on average, pulling up the average variable cost. In Figure 5.3, the *AVC* curve is negatively sloped for small quantities, but positively sloped for large quantities.

▶ **FIGURE 5.3**
**Short-Run Average Costs**
The short-run average-total-cost curve (*ATC*) is U-shaped. As the quantity produced increases, fixed costs are spread over more and more units, pushing down the average total cost. In contrast, as the quantity increases, diminishing returns eventually pulls up the average total cost. The gap between *ATC* and *AVC* is the average fixed cost (*AFC*).

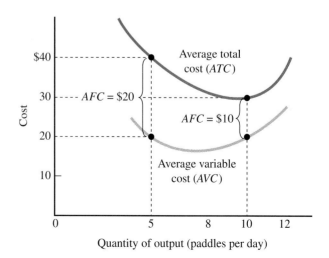

A firm's total cost is the sum of its fixed cost and variable cost, so the **short-run average total cost (ATC)**, or what we'll simply call "average cost," is the sum of the average fixed cost and the average variable cost:

$$ATC = \frac{TC}{Q} = \frac{FC}{Q} + \frac{VC}{Q} = AFC + AVC$$

In Figure 5.3, we go from the *AVC* to *ATC* by adding the average fixed cost to *AVC*. For example, for five paddles *AFC* is $20 and *AVC* is $20, so *ATC* is equal to $40, the sum of $20 + $20. For 10 paddles, the average fixed cost is lower—only $10—while the average variable cost is $20, so *ATC* is $30, the sum of $10 + $20. In Figure 5.3, the gap between the *AVC* and *ATC* curves is the average fixed cost.

The *ATC* curve in Figure 5.2 is negatively sloped at quantities less than 10 paddles. The negative slope results from two forces that work together to push average cost down as output increases:

- *Spreading the fixed cost.* For small quantities of output, a one-unit increase in output reduces *AFC* by a large amount because the fixed cost is pretty "thick," being spread over just a few units of output. For example, going from 1 paddle to 5 paddles decreases *AFC* from $100 to $20 per paddle.
- *Labor specialization.* For small quantities of output, *AVC* decreases as output increases because labor specialization increases worker productivity.

These two forces both push *ATC* downward as output increases, so the curve is negatively sloped for small quantities of output.

What happens once the firm reaches the point at which the benefits of labor specialization are exhausted? As the firm continues to increase output beyond that point, the average variable cost increases because of diminishing returns. There is a tug-of-war between two forces: The spreading of fixed cost continues to push *ATC* down, while diminishing returns and rising average variable cost pull *ATC* up. The outcome of the tug-of-war varies with the quantity produced, giving the *ATC* curve its U shape:

- *Intermediate quantities of output, such as output between 3 and 10 paddles.* The tug-of-war is won by the spreading of fixed cost, because the fixed cost is still relatively "thick" and diminishing returns are not yet very strong. As a result, *ATC* decreases as output increases. For example, at 5 paddles *ATC* is $40, but at 10 paddles *ATC* drops to only $30.
- *Large quantities of output, such as 11 or more paddles.* The tug-of-war is won by diminishing returns and rising average variable cost. In this case, the reductions in *AFC* are relatively small because the fixed cost is already spread pretty thinly and diminishing returns are severe. As a result, *ATC* increases as output increases. For example, at 10 paddles *ATC* is $30, but at 11.5 paddles *ATC* jumps to $34.78.

## Short-Run Marginal Cost

The **short-run marginal cost (MC)** is the change in short-run total cost per unit change in output. In other words, it is the increase in total cost resulting from a one-unit increase in output. Mathematically, marginal cost is calculated by dividing the change in total cost (*TC*) by the change in output (*Q*):

$$MC = \frac{\Delta TC}{\Delta Q} = \frac{\text{change in } TC}{\text{change in output}}$$

The marginal cost of the first paddle is the increase in cost when the firm produces the first paddle. To produce the first unit of output, the firm hires a single worker at $50. As shown in column 9 of Table 5.2, the marginal cost of the first paddle is $50. Moving down the ninth column, hiring the second worker for $50 increases

• **short-run average total cost (ATC)**
Short-run total cost divided by the quantity of output; equal to *AFC* plus *AVC*.

• **short-run marginal cost (MC)**
The change in short-run total cost resulting from a one-unit increase in output.

► **FIGURE 5.4**

**Short-Run Marginal and Average Cost**

The marginal-cost curve (*MC*) is negatively sloped for small quantities of output, because of the benefits of labor specialization, and positively sloped for large quantities, because of diminishing returns. The *MC* curve intersects the average-cost curve (*ATC*) at the minimum point of the average curve. At this point *ATC* is neither falling nor rising.

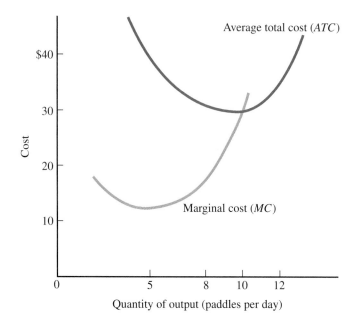

output to 5 paddles. A $50 increase in total cost increases output by 4 paddles, so the marginal cost is $12.50:

$$MC = \frac{\Delta TC}{\Delta Q} = \frac{\text{change in } TC}{\text{change in output}} = \frac{\$50}{4} = \$12.50$$

In this case, marginal cost decreases as output increases because of labor specialization and rising worker productivity. The first worker produces just one paddle, but adding a second worker increases output by four paddles. The $50 expense of adding the second worker translates into a $12.50 expense for each of the four extra paddles produced. We saw earlier that specialization leads to increasing marginal productivity. Now we know that specialization also leads to decreasing marginal cost. In Figure 5.4, the short-run marginal-cost curve is negatively sloped for the first five paddles.

The positively sloped portion of the marginal-cost curve is a result of diminishing returns. Hiring the third worker increases output from 5 to 8, so the $50 expense translates into a $16.67 expense for each of the 3 extra paddles produced. Diminishing returns has set in, so marginal cost increases as output increases. The marginal cost increases to $25 for between 8 and 10 paddles ($50/2 paddles), then increases to $50 for between 10 and 11 paddles ($50/1 paddle), and so on. In general, diminishing returns decreases labor productivity and causes rising marginal cost.

## The Relationship Between Marginal Cost and Average Cost

Figure 5.4 shows the relationship between short-run marginal cost and short-run average total cost. Whenever the marginal cost is less than the average cost (for fewer than 10 paddles), the average cost is falling. In contrast, whenever the marginal cost exceeds the average cost (for more than 10 paddles), the average cost is rising. Finally, when the marginal cost equals the average cost, the average cost is neither rising nor falling. Therefore, the marginal-cost curve intersects the short-run average total cost curve at its minimum point.

We can use some simple logic to explain the relationship between average and marginal cost. Suppose that you start the semester with 9 completed courses and a cumulative grade-point average of 3.0. In the first row of Table 5.3, you have 27 grade points (4 points for each A, 3 points for each B, and so on), so your GPA is 3.0, which is 27 points divided by 9 courses. You enroll in a single course this semester—a history course. Your new GPA will depend on your grade in the history course, the marginal grade. There are three possibilities:

**Table 5.3** | MARGINAL GRADE AND AVERAGE GRADE

| | Marginal Grade | Number of Courses | Grade Points | Grade Point Average |
|---|---|---|---|---|
| Starting point | — | 9 | 27 | 3.0 = 27/9 |
| Marginal grade < GPA | D | 10 | 28 = 27 + 1 | 2.8 = 28/10 |
| Marginal grade = GPA | B | 10 | 30 = 27 + 3 | 3.0 = 30/10 |
| Marginal grade > GPA | A | 10 | 31 = 27 + 4 | 3.1 = 31/10 |

- *Marginal grade less than the average grade.* In the second row of Table 5.3, if you get a D in history, your grade point total increases from 27 points to 28 points. Dividing the new total by 10 courses, your new GPA is 2.80. It's lower because your marginal grade of 1.0 is less than the old average grade of 3.0.

- *Marginal grade equal to the average grade.* In the second row of Table 5.3, if you get a B in history, your grade point total increases from 27 points to 30 points. Dividing the new total by 10 courses, your new GPA is 3.0. It hasn't changed because your marginal grade of 3.0 equals the old average grade of 3.0.

- *Marginal grade greater than the average grade.* In the second row of Table 5.3, if you get an A in history, your grade point total increases from 27 points to 31 points, so your new GPA is 3.10. It's higher because your marginal grade of 4.0 is greater than the old average grade of 3.0.

To summarize, whenever the marginal grade is less than the average grade, the average will fall; whenever the marginal grade exceeds the average grade, the average will rise; whenever the marginal grade equals the average grade, the average will not change.

# 5.3 | PRODUCTION AND COST IN THE LONG RUN

Up to this point, we've been exploring short-run cost curves, which show the cost of producing different quantities of output in a given production facility. We turn next to long-run cost curves, which show production costs in facilities of different sizes. The *long run* is defined as the period of time over which a firm is perfectly flexible in its choice of all inputs. In the long run, a firm can build a new production facility such as a factory, store, office, or restaurant. Another option in the long run is to modify an existing facility.

The key difference between the short run and the long run is that there are no diminishing returns in the long run. Recall that diminishing returns occur because workers share a fixed production facility, so the larger the number of workers in the facility, the smaller the share of the facility available for each worker. In the long run, a firm can expand its production facility as its workforce grows, so there are no diminishing returns.

## Expansion and Replication

Continuing the example of paddle production, suppose that you have decided to replace your existing workshop with a new one. You have been producing 10 paddles per day at a total cost of $300 per day, or an average cost of $30 per paddle. Suppose a company that sponsors rafting adventures orders new paddles, and you decide to produce twice as much output in your new facility. What should you do?

One possibility is simply to double the original operation. You could build two workshops that are identical to the original shop and hire two workforces, each identical to the original workforce. In the table in Figure 5.5, your firm moves from the third row of numbers (4 workers and $100 worth of capital produces 10 paddles per

**The Long-Run Average-Cost Curve and Scale Economies**

The long-run average-cost curve (*LAC*) is negatively sloped for up to 10 paddles per day, a result of indivisible inputs and the effects of labor specialization. If the firm replicates the operation that produces 10 paddles per day, the long-run average-cost curve will be horizontal beyond 10 paddles per day.

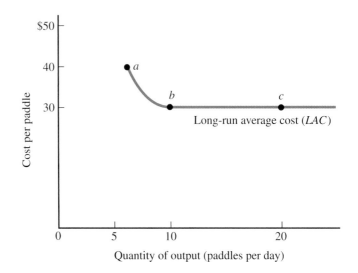

| | 1 | 2 | 3 | 4 | 5 |
|---|---|---|---|---|---|
| **Labor** | **Capital** | **Output** | **Labor Cost** | **Long-Run Total Cost (LTC)** | **Long-Run Average Cost (LAC)** |
| 1 | $100 | 1 | $50 | $150 | $150 |
| 2 | 100 | 5 | 100 | 200 | 40 |
| 4 | 100 | 10 | 200 | 300 | 30 |
| 8 | 200 | 20 | 400 | 600 | 30 |
| 12 | 300 | 30 | 600 | 900 | 30 |

• **long-run total cost (LTC)**
The total cost of production when a firm is perfectly flexible in choosing its inputs.

• **long-run average cost (LAC)**
The long-run cost divided by the quantity produced.

• **constant returns to scale**
A situation in which the long-run total cost increases proportionately with output, so average cost is constant.

day) to the fourth row, with twice as much labor, capital, and output. A firm's **long-run total cost (LTC)** is the total cost of production when the firm is perfectly flexible in choosing its inputs, including its production facility. As shown in column 5 of the table in Figure 5.5, if your firm doubles its output from 10 paddles to 20 paddles, the long-run total cost doubles too, from $300 to $600.

The firm's **long-run average cost (LAC)** equals the long-run cost divided by the quantity produced. As shown in column 6 of the table in Figure 5.5, doubling output from 10 to 20 paddles doesn't change the long-run average cost because doubling output by doubling both labor and capital increases costs proportionately. In the graph in Figure 5.5, point *b* shows the average cost with 10 paddles and point *c* shows the average cost with 20 paddles. As the quantity produced increases, the average cost doesn't change, so the average-cost curve is horizontal over this range of output. This is the case of **constant returns to scale**: As a firm scales up its operation, costs increase proportionately with output, so average cost is constant.

The same logic applies to larger output levels. Your firm could build a third workshop identical to the first two workshops, and its production costs will increase proportionately, from $600 to $900. In the table in Figure 5.5, the average cost for 30 paddles is $30, the same as for 10 and 20 paddles. In general, the replication process means the long-run total cost increases proportionately with the quantity produced, so the average cost is constant. In Figure 5.5, the long-run average-cost curve is horizontal for 10 or more paddles per day. In other words, there are constant returns to scale for output levels of 10 or more paddles.

We've seen that if a firm wants to double its output in the long run, replication is one option. By simply replicating an existing operation, a firm can double its output and its total costs, leaving average cost unchanged. Another possibility is to build a single larger workshop, one that can produce twice as much output at a lower cost than would be possible by simply replicating the original. If so, the long-run average cost of producing 20 or 30 paddles would be less than $30 per paddle.

A firm's **long-run marginal cost (*LMC*)** is the change in long-run cost resulting from producing one more unit of output. In the long run, the firm is perfectly flexible in choosing its inputs. Therefore, *LMC* is the increase in cost when the firm can change its production facility as well as its workforce.

- **long-run marginal cost (*LMC*)**
  The change in long-run cost resulting from a one-unit increase in output.

## Reducing Output with Indivisible Inputs

What would happen if you decide to produce only 5 paddles per day instead of 10? Although it's tempting to think that your total costs would be cut in half, that's not necessarily the case. Remember that you use a single mold to produce 10 paddles per day. If you cut your output in half, you would still need the mold, so your capital costs won't be cut in half. In addition, if each mold requires a fixed amount of floor space, you would still need the same floor space. Therefore, cutting output in half wouldn't decrease the cost of your production facility at all. You would still have a cost of $100 per day for the mold and the workspace. Because cutting output in half doesn't cut capital costs in half, the average cost for producing 5 paddles will exceed the average cost for 10 paddles.

The mold is an example of an **indivisible input**, one that cannot be scaled down to produce a smaller quantity of output. When a production process requires the use of indivisible inputs, the average cost of production increases as output decreases, because the cost of the indivisible inputs is spread over a smaller quantity of output. Most production operations use some indivisible inputs, but the costs of these inputs vary. Here are some examples of firms and their indivisible inputs:

- **indivisible input**
  An input that cannot be scaled down to produce a smaller quantity of output.

- A railroad company uses tracks to provide freight service between two cities. The company cannot scale down by laying a half set of tracks—a single rail.
- A shipping firm uses a large ship to carry TV sets from Japan to the United States. The company can't scale back by transporting TVs in rowboats.
- A steel producer uses a large blast furnace. The company can't scale back by producing steel in a toaster oven.
- A hospital uses imaging machines for x-rays, CAT scans, and MRIs. The hospital can't scale back by getting mini-MRI machines.
- A pizzeria uses a pizza oven. The company can't scale back by making pizza in a toaster oven.

The second row of the table in Figure 5.5 on page 118 shows labor and capital costs in the smaller operation. Suppose that to produce 5 paddles, you'll need 2 workers, including yourself. In this case, your labor cost will be $100. Adding the $100 cost of the indivisible input (the mold and shop space), the total cost of producing 5 paddles per day will be $200, or $40 per paddle. This cost exceeds the average cost of 10 paddles because in the smaller operation you still need the same amount of capital. In Figure 5.5 on page 118, point *a* shows that the average cost of 5 paddles per day exceeds the average cost for larger quantities.

## Scaling Down and Labor Specialization

A second possible reason for higher average long-run costs in a smaller operation is that labor will be less specialized in the small operation. As we saw earlier in the chapter, the labor specialization—each worker specializing in an individual production task—makes workers more productive because of continuity and repetition. Reversing this process, when we reduce the workforce each worker will become less specialized, performing a wider variety of production tasks. The loss of specialization will decrease labor productivity, leading to higher average cost.

To see the role of labor specialization, consider the first row of numbers in the table in Figure 5.6. To produce one paddle per day, the firm needs a full day of work by one worker. The single worker performs all production tasks and is less productive than the

● **economies of scale**
A situation in which the long-run average cost of production decreases as output increases.

● **minimum efficient scale**
The output at which scale economies are exhausted.

● **diseconomies of scale**
A situation in which the long-run average cost of production increases as ouput increases.

specialized workers in larger operations. This is one reason for the relatively high average cost in a one-paddle operation ($150). The second reason is that the cost of the indivisible input is spread over fewer paddles.

## Economies of Scale

A firm experiences **economies of scale** if the long-run average cost of production decreases as output increases, meaning that the long-run average-cost curve is negatively sloped. In Figure 5.5 on page 118, the paddle producer experiences economies of scale between points *a* and *b*. At point *a*, the long-run average cost is $40, compared to $30 at point *b* and beyond. An increase in output from 5 to 10 paddles decreases the long-run average cost of production because the firm spreads the cost of an indivisible input over a larger quantity, decreasing average cost. In other words, there are some economies—cost savings—associated with scaling up the firm's operation.

One way to quantify the extent of scale economies in the production of a particular good is to determine the minimum efficient scale for producing the good. The **minimum efficient scale** is defined as the output at which scale economies are exhausted. In Figure 5.5, the long-run average-cost curve becomes horizontal at point *b*, so the minimum efficient scale is 10 paddles. If a firm starts out with a quantity of output below the minimum efficient scale, an increase in output will decrease the average cost. Once the minimum efficient scale has been reached, the average cost no longer decreases as output increases.

## Diseconomies of Scale

A positively sloped long-run average-cost curve indicates the presence of **diseconomies of scale**. In this case, average cost increases as output increases. Diseconomies of scale can occur for two reasons:

● *Coordination problems.* One of the problems of a large organization is that it requires several layers of management to coordinate the activities of the different parts of the organization. A large organization requires more meetings, reports, and administrative work, leading to higher unit cost. If an increase in the firm's output requires additional layers of management, the long-run average-cost curve may be positively sloped.

● *Increasing input costs.* When a firm increases its output, it will demand more of each of its inputs and *may* be forced to pay higher prices for some of these inputs.

For example, an expanding construction firm may be forced to pay higher wages to attract more workers. Alternatively, an expanding firm may be forced to hire workers who are less skilled than the original workers. An increase in wages or a decrease in productivity will increase the average cost of production, generating a positively sloped long-run average-cost curve.

Firms recognize the possibility of diseconomies of scale and adopt various strategies to avoid them. An example of a firm that adjusts its operations to avoid diseconomies of scale is 3M, a global technology company that produces products ranging from Post-it® notes to pharmaceuticals and telecommunications systems. The company makes a conscious effort to keep its production units as small as possible to keep them flexible. When a production unit gets too large, the company breaks it apart.

## Actual Long-Run Average-Cost Curves

Figure 5.6 shows the actual long-run average-cost curves for three products: aluminum production, truck freight, and hospital services.[1] In each case, the long-run average cost curve is negatively sloped for small quantities of output and relatively flat—almost horizontal—over a large range of output. In other words, these curves are L-shaped.

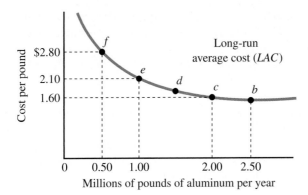

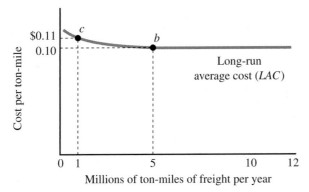

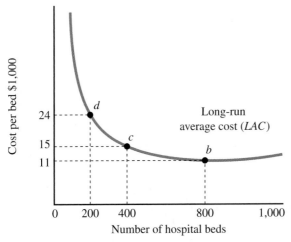

Other studies suggest that the long-run cost curves of a wide variety of goods and services have the same shape.

Why is the typical long-run average-cost curve L-shaped? The long-run average-cost curve is negatively sloped for small quantities of output because there are economies of scale resulting from indivisible inputs and labor specialization. As output increases, the average-cost curve eventually becomes horizontal and remains horizontal for a wide range of output. Over the horizontal portion of the cost curve, increases in inputs lead to proportionate increases in output, so the average cost doesn't change. In other words, the long-run average total cost (*LAC*) is constant and production is subject to constant returns to scale.

## Short-Run Versus Long-Run Average Cost

Why is the firm's short-run average-cost curve U-shaped, while the long-run average-cost curve is L-shaped? For large quantities of output, the short-run curve is positively sloped because of diminishing returns and the resulting decrease in labor productivity and increase in marginal cost. If a firm increases its output while at least one input is held fixed, diminishing returns eventually occur, pulling up the average cost of production.

The difference between the short run and long run is a firm's flexibility in choosing inputs. In the long run, a firm can increase all of its inputs, scaling up its operation by building a larger production facility. As a result, the firm will not suffer from diminishing returns. In most cases, the long-run average-cost curve will be negatively sloped or horizontal. In some cases, firms experience diseconomies of scale, so the long-run average-cost curve will be positively sloped for high output levels. Nonetheless, the long-run average cost will not be as steep as the short-run curve, which is relatively steep because of diminishing returns.

# 5.4 | APPLICATIONS OF PRODUCTION COST

In this chapter, we've explored the links between production technology and the cost of production. We've seen the firm's short-run cost curves, which show how production costs vary with the quantity produced when at least one input is fixed. We've also seen the long-run cost average-cost curve, which shows how the average cost of production varies when the firm is perfectly flexible in choosing its inputs. In this part of the chapter, we look at actual production costs for several products.

# APPLICATION

## THE PRODUCTION COST OF AN iPOD NANO

APPLYING THE CONCEPTS #1: What are the cost components for electronic products?

What's the cost of producing an iPod Nano, the ultra-thin digital music player with a storage capacity of 2 GB? As shown in Table 5.4, the cost per iPod is $98, which is divided between flash memory, other electronic components, other materials and parts, and assembly cost. The largest part of the cost is the $54 spent on flash memory.

Apple has sold millions of iPods, and its large sales volume gives the company an advantage in negotiating with its suppliers. For example, the flash memory that costs Apple $54 would cost smaller companies about $90. The large volume also provides a large reward for cost cutting. When the company switched the computer chip controlling the click wheel from a $1 chip from Synaptics to a $0.55 chip from Cypress Semiconductor, it saved only $0.45 per iPod, but with millions of units sold, that small savings per unit added up to a large increase in profit. *Related to Exercises 4.1 and 4.6.*

**Table 5.4 | THE AVERAGE COST OF AN iPOD NANO**

| Component | Cost per iPod |
|---|---|
| Flash memory | $54 |
| Other electronic components | 15 |
| Other materials and parts | 21 |
| Assembly | 8 |
| **TOTAL** | **98** |

SOURCE: Arik Hesseldahl, "Unpeeling Apple's Nano," *BusinessWeek Online*, September 22, 2005, available online at www.businessweek.com/technology/, accessed June 27, 2006.

# APPLICATION

## INDIVISIBLE INPUTS AND THE COST OF FAKE KILLER WHALES

**APPLYING THE CONCEPTS #2:** How do indivisible inputs affect production costs?

Sea lions off the Washington coast eat steelhead and other fish, depleting some species threatened with extinction and decreasing the harvest of the commercial fishing industry. Rick Funk is a plastics manufacturer who has offered to build a life-sized fiberglass killer whale, mount it on a rail like a roller-coaster, and send the whale diving through the water to scare off the sea lions, their natural prey. According to Funk, it would cost about $16,000 to make the first whale, including $11,000 for the mold and $5,000 for labor and materials. Once the mold is made, each additional whale would cost an additional $5,000. In other words, the cost of producing the first fake killer whale is more than three times the cost of producing the second. In terms of total cost, producing 2 whales would cost a total of $21,000, while 3 whales would cost a total of $26,000, and so on.

This little story illustrates the effects of indivisible inputs on the firm's cost curves. The mold is an indivisible input, because it cannot be scaled down and still produce whales. If Funk wants to cut his production from 2 whales per month down to 1, he still needs the mold; he cannot simply produce half as many whales with a mold that is half the size. The cost of producing the first whale, $16,000, includes the cost of the mold, the indivisible input. Once the firm has the mold, the marginal cost for each whale is only $5,000, so the average cost per whale decreases as the number of whales increases. *Related to Exercises 4.2 and 4.7.*

SOURCE: Sandi Doughton, "Killer Whale Latest Idea on Sea Lions," *The Oregonian*, January 7, 1995, p. B2.

# APPLICATION

## SCALE ECONOMIES IN WIND POWER

**APPLYING THE CONCEPTS #3:** What are the sources of scale economies in production?

There are scale economies in the production of electricity from wind because electricity can be generated from turbines of different size. Although large wind turbines are more costly than small ones, the higher cost is more than offset by greater generating capacity. The scale economies occur because the cost of purchasing, installing, and maintaining a wind turbine increases less than proportionately with the turbine's generating capacity. Table 5.5 shows the costs of a small turbine (150-kilowatt capacity) and a large turbine (600-kilowatt capacity), each with an assumed lifetime of 20 years.

The large turbine has four times the generation capacity of the small turbine—20 million kilowatt hours versus 5 million kilowatt hours—but its purchase price is less than three times as much. The two turbines have the same installation cost, and the operating and maintenance cost of the larger turbine is less than twice as large. Adding the various costs, the larger turbine, with four times the generating capacity, has less than twice the cost. As a result, the average cost per kilowatt-hour is only $0.032 for the large turbine, compared to $0.065 for the smaller turbine. *Related to Exercises 4.3 and 4.8.*

**Table 5.5** | WIND TURBINES AND THE AVERAGE COST OF ELECTRICITY

|  | Small Turbine (150 kilowatt) | Large Turbine (600 kilowatt) |
|---|---|---|
| Purchase price of turbine | $150,000 | $420,000 |
| Installation cost | $100,000 | $100,000 |
| Operating and maintenance cost | $75,000 | $126,000 |
| **Total cost** | **$325,000** | **$646,000** |
| Electricity generated (kilowatt-hours) | 5 million | 20 million |
| Average cost (per kilowatt-hour) | $0.065 | $0.032 |

SOURCE: Danish Wind Turbine Manufacturers Association, "Guided Tour of Wind Energy" (2003), available online at www.windpower.dk, accessed June 27, 2006.

# APPLICATION

## INFORMATION GOODS AND FIRST-COPY COST

**APPLYING THE CONCEPTS #4:** What is the cost structure for information goods?

Consider the cost of producing an information good such as a music CD, a movie on DVD, or a book. In all three cases, the cost of producing the first copy is very high, but the marginal cost of reproduction is very low. Suppose that your band, Adam Smith and the Invisible Hands, has decided to produce a music CD. The cost of recording a set of songs is $100,000. This amount includes the band's opportunity cost of time spent in the recording studio and the cost of studio time at $200 per hour. Once the tracks are recorded and put in a digital format, you can have CDs burned at a cost of $1 per CD, regardless of the number burned.

The table in Figure 5.7 shows the relationships between the quantity of CDs produced and the production cost. In this case, you are using the production facilities of other firms, so the distinction between short run and long run is not important. The marginal cost is constant at $1, but the average cost decreases with the quantity produced. For example, the cost of the first CD is a whopping $100,001, but the average cost drops to $11 for the 10,000th CD and $3 for the 50,000th CD. In Figure 5.7, the average-cost curve is negatively sloped and gets closer and closer to the horizontal marginal-cost curve as the quantity produced increases. The gap decreases as the fixed recording cost is spread over a larger number of CDs. *Related to Exercises 4.4 and 4.9.*

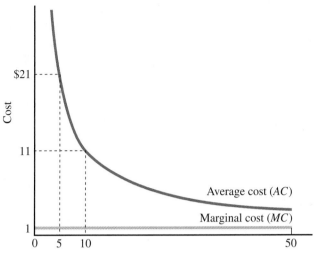

| Quantity of CDs | Recording Cost | Burning Cost | Total Cost | Average Cost | Marginal Cost |
|---|---|---|---|---|---|
| 0 | $100,000 | $0 | $100,000 | — | — |
| 1 | 100,000 | 1 | 100,001 | $100,001 | $1 |
| 1,000 | 100,000 | 1,000 | 101,000 | 101 | 1 |
| 5,000 | 100,000 | 5,000 | 105,000 | 21 | 1 |
| 10,000 | 100,000 | 10,000 | 110,000 | 11 | 1 |
| 50,000 | 100,000 | 50,000 | 150,000 | 3 | 1 |

▲ **FIGURE 5.7**
**Average-Cost Curve for an Information Good**
For an information good such as a music CD, the cost of producing the first copy is very high, but the marginal cost of reproduction is low and constant.

# APPLICATION

## THE AVERAGE COST OF PRODUCING AIRPLANES

**APPLYING THE CONCEPTS #5:** Why does average cost decrease as the quantity produced increases?

Suppose you want to design and manufacture a new airplane, one with a performance level comparable to the Boeing 737. To get a rough idea of how much it would cost to design the new aircraft and then produce a particular quantity of airplanes, you could use the Airframe Cost Model developed by U.S. National Aeronautics and Space Administration (NASA).

Figure 5.8 shows the average cost of production for up to 100 airplanes. The fixed cost includes the cost of designing the aircraft and the cost of capital used in the production process, including the machine tools used to fabricate the components of the aircraft. Together these fixed costs add up to about $2.45 billion. The variable cost includes the costs of the materials and labor used to produce the components and then assemble the aircraft. The NASA cost model suggests that the average variable cost decreases as the number of airplanes increases because of labor specialization. The average-

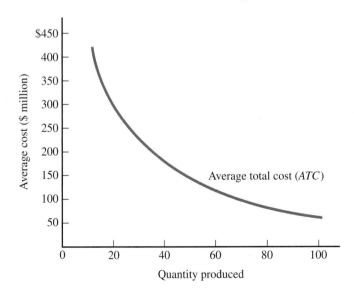

▲ **FIGURE 5.8**
**Average-Cost Curve of Aircraft**
The average cost per airplane decreases as the number produced increases because the cost of designing the aircraft and the cost of capital are spread over more units and labor specialization reduces variable cost.

cost curve in Figure 5.8 is negatively sloped because as the quantity of aircraft increases, the fixed cost is spread over more units *and* labor specialization pulls down the average variable cost. The average cost decreases from $435 million for a quantity of 10 aircraft, to $257 for 20 aircraft, and so on down to $86 million for 100 aircraft.

The average-cost curve is negatively sloped, implying that there are no diminishing returns in the production of airplanes. This occurs because the cost model assumes that as output increases, production occurs over a longer period of time. Diminishing returns normally occur if an increase in output requires an increase in the number of workers in a given production facility. In the normal case, each worker becomes less productive because each worker gets a smaller share of the production facility—plant and equipment such as machine tools. But if doubling output means that we operate a given production facility twice as long, diminishing returns won't occur: Each worker still gets the same share of the facility, but simply uses the facility for twice as much time.   *Related to Exercises 4.5 and 4.10.*

SOURCE: National Aeronautics and Space Administration, "Cost Estimating Web Site," available online at cost.jsc.nasa.gov/airframe.html, accessed June 27, 2006.

# SUMMARY

In this chapter, we explored the cost side of a firm, explaining the shapes of the firm's short-run and long-run cost curves. Table 5.6 summarizes the definitions of various types of costs. Here are the main points of the chapter:

1 The negatively sloped portion of the *short-run marginal-cost curve (MC)* results from input specialization that causes increasing marginal returns.

2 The positively sloped portion of the short-run marginal-cost curve (MC) results from *diminishing returns*.

3 The *short-run average-total-cost curve (ATC)* is U-shaped because of the conflicting effects of (a) fixed costs being spread over a larger quantity of output and (b) diminishing returns.

4 The *long-run average-cost curve (LAC)* is horizontal over some range of output because replication is an option, so doubling output will no more than double long-run total cost.

5 The long-run average-cost curve (LAC) is negatively sloped for small quantities of output because (a) there are indivisible inputs that cannot be scaled down and (b) a smaller operation has limited opportunities for labor specialization.

6 *Diseconomies of scale* arise if there are problems in coordinating a large operation or higher input costs in a larger organization.

## Table 5.6 | THE LANGUAGE AND MATHEMATICS OF COSTS

| Type of Cost | Definition | Symbols and Equations |
|---|---|---|
| Economic cost | The opportunity cost of the inputs used in the production process; equal to explicit cost plus implicit cost | — |
| Explicit cost | The actual monetary payment for inputs | — |
| Implicit cost | The opportunity cost of inputs that do not require a monetary payment | — |
| Accounting cost | Explicit cost | — |
| **Short-Run Costs** | | |
| Fixed cost | Cost that does not vary with the quantity produced | $FC$ |
| Variable cost | Cost that varies with the quantity produced | $VC$ |
| Short-run total cost | The total cost of production when at least one input is fixed | $TC = FC + VC$ |
| Short-run marginal cost | The change in short-run total cost resulting from a one-unit increase in output | $MC = \Delta TC / \Delta Q$ |
| Average fixed cost | Fixed cost divided by the quantity produced | $AFC = FC / Q$ |
| Average variable cost | Variable cost divided by the quantity produced | $AVC = VC / Q$ |
| Short-run average total cost | Short-run total cost divided by the quantity of output | $ATC = AFC + AVC$ |
| **Long-Run Costs** | | |
| Long-run total cost | The total cost of production when a firm is perfectly flexible in choosing its inputs | $LTC$ |
| Long-run average cost | Long-run total cost divided by the quantity produced | $LAC = LTC / Q$ |
| Long-run marginal cost | The change in long-run cost resulting from a one-unit increase in output | $LMC = \Delta LTC / \Delta Q$ |

## KEY TERMS

accounting cost, p. 111
accounting profit, p. 111
average fixed cost (*AFC*), p. 114
average variable cost (*AVC*), p. 114
constant returns to scale, p. 118
diminishing returns, p. 111
diseconomies of scale, p. 120
economic cost, p. 110

economic profit, p. 110
economies of scale, p. 120
explicit cost, p. 110
fixed cost (*FC*), p. 113
implicit cost, p. 110
indivisible input, p. 119
long-run average cost (*LAC*), p. 118
long-run marginal cost (*LMC*), p. 119

long-run total cost (*LTC*), p. 118
marginal product of labor, p. 111
minimum efficient scale, p. 120
short-run average total cost
    (*ATC*), p. 115
short-run marginal cost (*MC*), p. 115
short-run total cost (*TC*), p. 113
total-product curve, p. 112
variable cost (*VC*), p. 113

## EXERCISES

Get Ahead of the Curve

Visit www.myeconlab.com to complete these exercises online and get instant feedback.

### 5.1 | Economic Cost and Economic Profit

**1.1** The computation of economic cost is based on the principle of _____.

**1.2** A firm's implicit cost is defined as the _____ cost of nonpurchased inputs, such as the entrepreneur's _____ and _____.

**1.3** Suppose a person quits a job earning $40,000 per year and starts a business with $100,000 withdrawn from a money-market account earning 8 percent per year. The implicit cost of the business is _____ for the entrepreneur's time plus _____ for the entrepreneur's funds.

**1.4** The _____ run is defined as a period over which a firm cannot change its production facility.

**1.5** When a firm is perfectly flexible in its choice of all inputs, the firm is operating in the _____ run.

**1.6** **Computing Cost.** Edward the entrepreneur takes 2 hours to cut a lawn, and he cuts 1,000 lawns per year. He uses solar-powered equipment (truck and mower) that will last forever—and could be sold at any time for $20,000. Edward could earn $12 per hour as a pedicurist. The interest rate is 10 percent.
   **a.** Given his current output level, compute his marginal cost and average cost of cutting lawns.
   **b.** Suppose he decides to reduce the number of lawns cut by half, to 500 per year. Compute the new marginal cost and average cost.

### 5.2 | A Firm with a Fixed Production Facility: Short-Run Costs

**2.1** The short-run marginal cost curve is shaped like the letter _____.

**2.2** The negatively sloped portion of the short-run marginal-cost curve is explained by _____.

**2.3** The positively sloped portion of the short-run marginal cost curve is explained by _____.

**2.4** The short-run average cost curve is shaped like the letter _____.

**2.5** Over the positively sloped portion of the short-run average-cost curve, the effect of _____ dominates the effect of _____.

**2.6** At the current level of output, the marginal cost of chairs is less than the average cost. If you increase output, the average cost will _____ (increase/decrease).

**2.7** A marginal-cost curve intersects the average-cost curve at the minimum point of the _____ cost curve.

**2.8** The short-run average cost of production is the same for two different quantities. _____ (True/False).

**2.9** **Compute the Costs.** Consider a firm that has a fixed cost of $60. Complete the following table:

| Output | Fixed Cost (*FC*) | Variable Cost (*VC*) | Total Cost (*TC*) | Marginal Cost (*MC*) | Average Fixed Cost (*AFC*) | Average Variable Cost (*AVC*) | Average Total Cost (*ATC*) |
|---|---|---|---|---|---|---|---|
| 1 | | $10 | — | — | — | — | — |
| 2 | | 18 | — | — | — | — | — |
| 3 | | 30 | — | — | — | — | — |
| 4 | | 45 | — | — | — | — | — |
| 5 | | 65 | — | — | — | — | — |

**2.10** **Changing Costs.** Consider the paddle production example shown in Table 5.2 on page 113. Compute the short-run average cost for 10 paddles with the following changes.
   **a.** Your opportunity cost of work time triples, from $50 to $150.
   **b.** The interest rate for invested funds is cut in half, from 10 to 5 percent.
   **c.** Labor productivity—the quantity produced by each workforce—doubles.

**2.11 Compute the Short-Run Costs.** Consider a firm with the following short-run costs:

| Quantity | Variable Cost (VC) | Total Cost (TC) | Marginal Cost (MC) | Average Variable Cost (AVC) | Average Total Cost (ATC) |
|---|---|---|---|---|---|
| 1 | $30 | $90 | ____ | ____ | ____ |
| 2 | 50 | 110 | ____ | ____ | ____ |
| 3 | 90 | 150 | ____ | ____ | ____ |
| 4 | 140 | 200 | ____ | ____ | ____ |
| 5 | 200 | 260 | ____ | ____ | ____ |

a. What is the firm's fixed cost?
b. Compute short-run marginal cost (*MC*), short-run average variable cost (*AVC*), and short-run average total cost (*ATC*) for the different quantities of output.
c. Draw the three cost curves. Explain the relationship between the *MC* curve and the *ATC* curve and the relationship between the *AVC* curve and the *ATC* curve.

**2.12 Same Average Cost with Different Quantities?** Suppose there are two pencil producers with identical production facilities—identical factories and equipment. The firms pay the same wages and pay the same prices for materials. Sam has a small workforce and produces 1,000 pencils per minute; Marian has a medium-size workforce and produces 2,000 pencils per minute. The two firms have the same average total cost of 10 cents per pencil. Suppose you build a production facility identical to the ones used by the other firms and hire enough workers and buy enough materials to produce 2,500 pencils per minute. Would you expect your average cost to be 10 cents per pencil (like the other two firms), less than 10 cents, or more than 10 cents?

## 5.3 | Production and Cost in the Long Run

**3.1** The presence of indivisible inputs explains the _____ portion of a long-run average-cost curve.

**3.2** The notion of replication explains the _____ portion of a long-run average-cost curve.

**3.3** Consider the information provided in Figure 5.6 on page 121. Suppose the output of a large aluminum firm drops from 2 million pounds to 1 million pounds per year. The long-run average cost of producing aluminum will go from $_____ to $_____.

**3.4** The typical *short-run* average-cost curve is shaped like the letter U, while the typical *long-run* average-cost curve is shaped like the letter L because _____ are not applicable in the _____ run.

**3.5 Deregulation and the Cost of Trucking.** Suppose the government initially limits the number of trucking firms that can haul freight. The market for truck freight is initially served by a single firm that produces 5 million ton miles of service per year, where 1 ton mile is the hauling of 1 ton of freight 1 mile. The newly elected governor has proposed that other firms be allowed to enter the market. At a public hearing on the issue of eliminating the entry restrictions, the manager of the existing firm issued a grim warning: "If you allow entry into the market, 4 or 5 firms will enter, and the unit cost of truck freight will at least triple. There are big economies of scale in trucking services, so a single large firm is much more cost-efficient than several small firms would be." What's your reaction to this statement?

**3.6 Draw the Long-Run Cost Curve.** Consider the long-run production of shirts. The cost of the indivisible inputs used in the production of shirts is $400 per day. To produce 1 shirt per day, the firm must also spend a total of $5 on other inputs—labor, materials, and other capital. For each additional shirt, the firm incurs the same additional cost of $5.
a. Compute the average cost for 40 shirts, 100 shirts, 200 shirts, and 400 shirts.
b. Draw the long-run average-cost curve for 40 to 400 shirts per day.

**3.7 Diminishing Returns Versus Diseconomies of Scale.** Explain the difference between diseconomies of scale and diminishing returns. Based on the cost curves you've seen in this chapter, which is more likely in firms?

## 5.4 | Applications of Production Cost

**4.1** The average cost of producing an iPod Nano is about $_____. (Related to Application 1 on page 122.)

**4.2** The cost of producing the first fake killer whale is about three times the cost of producing the second because the firm uses _____ inputs. (Related to Application 2 on page 123.)

**4.3** The average cost of electricity _____ (increases/decreases) as the size of the wind turbine increases. (Related to Application 3 on page 124.)

**4.4** For information goods such as CDs and DVDs, the cost of producing the first copy is very _____, but the marginal cost of reproduction is _____. (Related to Application 4 on page 124.)

**4.5** The average cost per airplane _____ (increases/decreases) as the number of airplanes produced increases. (Related to Application 5 on page 125.)

**4.6 Changing the Cost of iPods.** Suppose a new flash-memory chip for the iPod Nano has two-thirds the cost of the original chip. The new chip doubles the assembly cost. How does the cost of an iPod with the new chip compare to the cost of the iPod with the original chip? (Related to Application 1 on page 122.)

**4.7 A Better Whale Mold?** Suppose a new mold is developed for producing fake killer whales. The new mold has twice the cost of the original mold, but cuts the marginal cost of whales to $1,000.

   **a.** How does the cost of the first whale produced with the new mold compare to the cost with the original mold?

   **b.** At what quantity of whales will production with the new mold be less costly than production with the original mold? (Related to Application 2 on page 123.)

**4.8 The Average Cost of a Super-Sized Turbine.** Suppose a new super-sized wind turbine is developed. Fill the blanks in the following table.

| | Super-Sized Turbine (1,000 kilowatt) |
|---|---|
| Purchase price of turbine | $500,000 |
| Installation cost | $100,000 |
| Operating and maintenance cost | $200,000 |
| **Total cost** | _____ |
| Electricity generated (kilowatt-hours) | 40 million |
| Average cost (per kilowatt-hour) | _____ |

(Related to Application 3 on page 124.)

**4.9 The Average Cost of Drama DVDs.** You have been hired to produce a DVD of a play put on by a high-school drama club. It will take you about 50 hours to make the master that is stored on a hard drive on your computer. The opportunity cost of your time is $20 per hour. The marginal cost of burning DVDs is constant at $2. Draw the average-cost curve for producing the DVD, with quantities up to 100 DVDs. (Related to Application 4 on page 124.)

**4.10 Limited Time to Produce Airplanes.** Suppose you have one year to produce airplanes in a given production facility. Using Figure 5.8 on page 125 as a starting point, draw a hypothetical average cost for producing airplanes. Why does it differ from the curve shown in Figure 5.8? (Related to Application 5 on page 125.)

NOTES

1. Laurits Christensen and William H. Greene, "Economies of Scale in U.S. Electric Power Generation," *Journal of Political Economy*, vol. 84, 1976, pp. 655–676. Reprinted by permission of The University of Chicago Press; Joel P. Clark and Merton C. Flemings, "Advanced Materials and the Economy," *Scientific American*, vol. 255, October 1986, pp. 51–60. Copyright © 1986 by Scientific American, Inc. All rights reserved; Roger Koenker, "Optimal Scale and the Size Distribution of American Trucking Firms," *Journal of Transport Economics and Policy*, January 1977, p. 62; Harold A. Cohen, "Hospital Cost Curves with Emphasis on Measuring Patient Care Output," in *Empirical Studies in Health Economics*, edited by Herbert E. Klarman (Baltimore, MD: Johns Hopkins University Press, 1970); John Johnson, *Statistical Cost Analysis* (New York: McGraw-Hill, 1960).

# 6

# Perfect Competition

In 1992, Hurricane Andrew struck the southeastern United States, leaving millions of people without electricity for several days. Refrigerators stopped working, and thousands of people suddenly needed a lot of ice to cool and preserve their food. The price of a bag of ice immediately rose from $1 to $5. Similar price hikes occurred for bottled

1 What is the break-even price?
    *The Break-Even Price for a Corn Farmer*

2 How do entry costs affect the number of firms in a market?
    *Wireless Women in Pakistan*

3 How do producers respond to an increase in price?
    *Wolfram Miners Obey the Law of Supply*

4 When production costs vary across producers, what are the implications for the market supply curve?
    *The Worldwide Supply of Sugar*

5 When input prices increase with the total output of the industry, what are the implications for the market supply curve?
    *Zoning, Land Prices, and the Supply Curve for Apartments*

water, chain saws to clear downed trees, and tarpaper for roof repairs.

If you had been the governor of Florida in 1992, what would you have

done about the price hikes?

- **perfectly competitive market**
  A market with many sellers and buyers of a homogeneous product and no barriers to entry.

- **price taker**
  A buyer or seller that takes the market price as given.

- **firm-specific demand curve**
  A curve showing the relationship between the price charged by a specific firm and the quantity the firm can sell.

This is the first of three chapters exploring the decisions firms make in different types of markets. Markets differ in the number of firms that compete against one another for customers. In this chapter, we'll look at a perfectly competitive market. In a **perfectly competitive market**, hundreds, or even thousands, of firms sell a homogeneous product. Each firm is such a small part of the market that it takes the market price as given: Each firm is a **price taker**. For example, each soybean farmer takes the market price as given. There is no reason to cut the price to sell more soybeans, because the farmer can sell as much as he wants at the market price. There is no reason to increase the price, because the farmer would lose all of his customers to other farmers selling at the market price.

A perfectly competitive market has two other features. First, on the demand side of the market there are hundreds, or even thousands, of buyers, each of whom takes the market price as given. Second, there are no barriers to market entry, so firms can easily enter or exit the market. To summarize, here are the five features of a perfectly competitive market:

1 There are many sellers.
2 There are many buyers.
3 The product is homogeneous.
4 There are no barriers to market entry.
5 Both buyers and sellers are price takers.

If you're thinking that the model of perfect competition is unrealistic, you're right. Most firms have some flexibility over their prices. For example, when Target increases its price of DVDs, it will certainly sell fewer DVDs, but the quantity sold will probably not drop to zero. Although perfect competition is rare, it's a good starting point for analyzing a firm's decisions, because a price-taking firm's decisions are easy to understand. The firm doesn't have to pick a price; it just decides how much to produce, given the market price. Once you understand this simple case, you will be ready to tackle the more complex decisions made by firms that are *price makers*—able to affect prices. We'll discuss this scenario in later chapters.

In this chapter, we'll see how price-taking firms use information on revenues and costs to decide how much output to produce. The output decisions of price-taking firms underlie the market supply curve and the law of supply. In other words, this chapter reveals the economic logic behind the market supply curve and the law of supply.

# 6.1 | PREVIEW OF THE FOUR MARKET STRUCTURES

Before we delve into perfect competition, it will be useful to see how our discussion of perfect competition fits into the general scheme of the book. After discussing perfect competition in this chapter, we'll look at three other market structures in the next two chapters. The key difference between perfect competition and these other market structures is that perfectly competitive firms are price takers, while firms in these other market structures are price makers.

Let's start by distinguishing between a market demand curve and the demand curve for an individual firm. As we saw earlier in the book, the market demand curve shows the relationship between the price and the quantity that can be sold in the market, assuming that all firms charge the same price. In contrast, the **firm-specific demand curve** shows the relationship between the price charged by a specific firm and the quantity the firm can sell. In a *monopoly*, a single firm serves the entire market, so the firm-specific demand curve is the same as the market demand curve. As shown in Panel A of Figure 6.1, the monopolist can choose any point on the market demand curve, recognizing that the higher the price, the smaller the quantity the firm will sell.

As shown in Panel B of Figure 6.1, things are different for a perfectly competitive firm. The firm-specific demand curve is horizontal—perfectly elastic. A perfectly competitive firm can sell as much as it wants at the market price of $12, but if it raises its price even a penny, it will sell nothing.

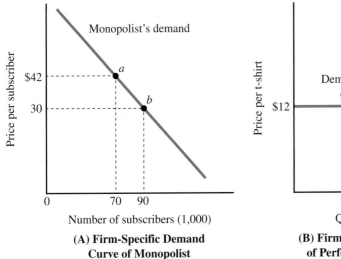

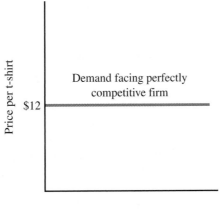

**(A) Firm-Specific Demand
Curve of Monopolist**

**(B) Firm-Specific Demand Curve
of Perfectly Competitive Firm**

◄ **FIGURE 6.1**
**Monopoly Versus Perfect
Competition**
In Panel A, the demand curve facing a
monopolist is the market demand curve. In
Panel B, a perfectly competitive firm takes
the market price as given, so the firm-specific demand curve is horizontal. The firm
can sell all it wants at the market price, but
would sell nothing if it charged a higher
price.

Most markets lie between the extremes of monopoly and perfect competition.
Table 6.1 provides a preview of three alternative market structures, which we discuss
in the next two chapters:

- **Monopoly.** A single firm serves the entire market. A monopoly occurs when the
  barriers to market entry are very large. This can result from very large
  economies of scale or a government policy that limits the number of firms.
  Some examples of monopolies that result from large economies of scale are
  local phone service, cable TV, and electric power transmission. Some examples
  of monopolies established by government policy are drugs covered by patents,
  the selling of firewood in national parks, and the U.S. Postal Service.
- **Monopolistic competition.** There are no barriers to entering the market, so
  there are many firms, and each firm sells a slightly different product. For example, coffee shops in your city provide slightly different goods and compete for
  customers. Your local grocery store sells many brands of toothbrushes, with
  slight differences in size, shape, color, and style.
- **Oligopoly.** The market consists of just a few firms because economies of scale or
  government policies limit the number of firms. Some product examples are automobiles, computer processor chips, airline travel, and breakfast cereals. The large
  economies of scale in automobile production result from the large startup costs,
  with billions of dollars required to build a factory or assembly plant. Similarly, a
  fabrication plant for computer processor chips costs several billion dollars.

**Table 6.1 | CHARACTERISTICS OF THE FOUR MARKET STRUCTURES**

| Characteristic | Perfect Competition | Monopolistic Competition | Oligopoly | Monopoly |
|---|---|---|---|---|
| Number of firms | Many | Many | Few | One |
| Type of product | Homogeneous | Differentiated | Homogeneous or differentiated | Unique |
| Firm-specific demand curve | Demand is perfectly elastic | Demand is elastic but not perfectly elastic | Demand is less elastic than demand facing monopolistically competitive firm | Firm faces market demand curve |
| Entry conditions | No barriers | No barriers | Large barriers from economies of scale or government policies | Large barriers from economies of scale or government policies |
| Examples | Corn, plain T-shirts | Toothbrushes, music stores, groceries | Air travel, automobiles, beverages, cigarettes, mobile phone service | Local phone service, patented drugs |

# 6.2 | THE FIRM'S SHORT-RUN OUTPUT DECISION

We'll start our discussion of perfect competition with an individual firm's decision about how much output to produce. The firm's objective is to maximize *economic profit*, which as we saw in the previous chapter, equals total revenue minus economic cost. Recall that economic cost includes all the opportunity costs of production, including both explicit costs (cash payments) and implicit costs (the entrepreneur's opportunity costs). In the previous chapter, we saw that the cost of production varies with the quantity produced. In this chapter, we'll see how economic profit varies with the quantity produced and then show how a firm can pick the quantity that maximizes its economic profit.

It's important to note that economic profit differs from the conventional notion of profit. As we saw in the previous chapter, when accountants compute a firm's cost, they include explicit costs, but ignore implicit costs. Accountants focus on the flow of money into and out of a firm, so they ignore costs that do not involve explicit transactions. *Accounting profit* equals total revenue minus explicit costs. Because accountants ignore implicit costs, accounting profit usually exceeds economic profit.

We will use the market for plain T-shirts to illustrate decision making in a perfectly competitive market. Some plain T-shirts are sold directly to consumers, and others are sold to firms that imprint words and images on the T-shirts and then sell the finished shirts to consumers. Plain T-shirts are produced in countries around the world by a large number of producers.

## The Total Approach: Computing Total Revenue and Total Cost

One way for a firm to decide how much to produce is to compute the economic profit at different quantities and then pick the quantity that generates the highest profit. As we've seen, economic profit equals total revenue minus economic cost. We looked at the cost side of the profit equation in in the previous chapter. The revenue side for a perfectly competitive market is straightforward. A firm's total revenue is the money it gets by selling its product. Total revenue is equal to the price of the product times the quantity sold. For example, if a firm sells 8 T-shirts at $12 per shirt, total revenue is $96 (equal to $8 \times $12$). If our T-shirt producer has an economic cost of $63, the firm's profit would be $33 (equal to $96 - $63$).

Table 6.2 shows the total revenue and total costs of a hypothetical producer of plain cotton T-shirts. Follow the row for an output of 8 shirts. As shown in the second and third columns, the fixed cost is $17, and the variable cost increases with the

**Table 6.2 | DECIDING HOW MUCH TO PRODUCE WHEN THE PRICE IS $12**

| 1 | 2 | 3 | 4 | 5 | 6 | 7 | 8 |
|---|---|---|---|---|---|---|---|
| Output: Shirts per Minute (Q) | Fixed Cost (FC) | Variable Cost (VC) | Total Cost (TC) | Total Revenue (TR) | Marginal Revenue Profit = TR − TC | Marginal Revenue (Price) (MR) | Cost (MC) |
| 0 | $17 | $0 | $17 | $0 | −$17 | | |
| 1 | 17 | 5 | 22 | 12 | −10 | $12 | $5 |
| 2 | 17 | 6 | 23 | 24 | 1 | 12 | 1 |
| 3 | 17 | 9 | 26 | 36 | 10 | 12 | 3 |
| 4 | 17 | 13 | 30 | 48 | 18 | 12 | 4 |
| 5 | 17 | 18 | 35 | 60 | 25 | 12 | 5 |
| 6 | 17 | 25 | 42 | 72 | 30 | 12 | 7 |
| 7 | 17 | 34 | 51 | 84 | 33 | 12 | 9 |
| **8** | **17** | **46** | **63** | **96** | **33** | **12** | **12** |
| 9 | 17 | 62 | 79 | 108 | 29 | 12 | 16 |
| 10 | 17 | 83 | 100 | 120 | 20 | 12 | 21 |

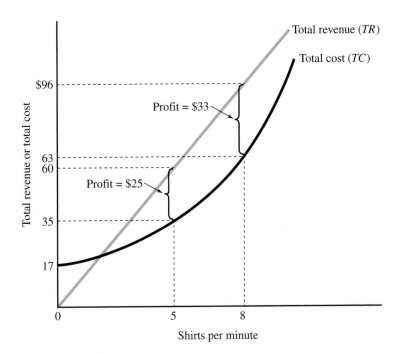

◄ **FIGURE 6.2**
**Using the Total Approach to Choose an Output Level**
Economic profit is shown by the vertical distance between the total-revenue curve and the total-cost curve. To maximize profit, the firm chooses the quantity of output that generates the largest vertical difference between the two curves.

amount produced. The fourth column shows total cost, the sum of the fixed and variable costs. As shown in the fifth column, at a price of $12 per shirt, the firm's total revenue is $12 times the number of shirts produced. The sixth column shows economic profit, equal to total revenue minus total cost.

Figure 6.2 shows one way to choose the quantity of output that maximizes profit. We're looking for the largest profit, shown by the biggest gap between total revenue and total cost. For example, for 5 shirts, the gap is $25: Total revenue (*TR*) equals $60, and total cost (*TC*) equals $35. Moving down the table and across the figure, we see that profit increases to $30 for 6 shirts:

$$TR - TC = \$72 - \$42 = \$30$$

Profit is maximized at $33 when the firm produces either 7 or 8 shirts:

$$TR - TC = 84 - 51 = \$33$$
$$TR - TC = 96 - 63 = \$33$$

When profit reaches its highest level with two different quantities (7 and 8 shirts in this example), we assume that the firm produces the larger quantity. When the firm produces 8 shirts, its total revenue is $96 and its total cost is $63, leaving a profit of $33.

## The Marginal Approach

The other way for a firm to decide how much output to produce involves the marginal principle, the general decision-making rule that is one of the key principles of economics.

## MARGINAL PRINCIPLE

Increase the level of an activity as long as its marginal benefit exceeds its marginal cost. Choose the level at which the marginal benefit equals the marginal cost.

Because our firm is in the business to make money, the "benefit" it gets from producing shirts is revenue. The *marginal* benefit—or **marginal revenue**—of producing shirts is the change in total revenue that results from selling one more shirt. A perfectly

• **marginal revenue**
The change in total revenue from selling one more unit of output.

**135**

competitive firm takes the market price as given, so the marginal revenue—the change in total revenue from one more shirt—is simply the price:

marginal revenue = price

The marginal principle tells us that the firm will maximize its profit by choosing the quantity at which price equals marginal cost:

To maximize profit, produce the quantity where price = marginal cost.

In Figure 6.3, the horizontal line shows the market price for T-shirts, which our shirt producer takes as given. The price line intersects the marginal-cost curve at 8 shirts per minute, so that's the quantity that satisfies the marginal principle and maximizes profit.

To see that an output of 8 shirts per minute maximizes the firm's profit, imagine the firm initially produced only 5 shirts per minute. Could the firm make more profit by producing more—that is, 6 shirts instead of 5?

- From the seventh row of numbers in Table 6.2 and point *c* in Figure 6.3, we know that the marginal cost of the sixth shirt is $7.
- The price of shirts is $12, so the marginal revenue is $12.

Because the extra revenue from the sixth shirt (price = $12) exceeds the extra cost (marginal cost = $7), the production and sale of the sixth shirt increases the firm's total profit by $5 (equal to $12 − $7). Therefore, it is sensible to produce the sixth shirt. The same logic applies, with different numbers for marginal cost, for the seventh shirt. For the eighth shirt, marginal revenue equals marginal cost, so the firm's profit doesn't change. To be consistent with the marginal principle, we'll assume that the firm produces to the point where marginal revenue equals marginal cost. In this case, the firm chooses point *a* and produces 8 shirts.

If the firm produced more than 8 shirts, it would earn less than the maximum profit. Imagine the firm initially produced 9 shirts. From Table 6.2 and the marginal-cost curve in Figure 6.3, we see that the marginal cost of the ninth shirt is $16 (point *d*), which exceeds the marginal revenue (the market price) of $12. The ninth shirt adds more to cost ($16) than it adds to revenue ($12), so producing the shirt decreases the firm's profit by $4. The marginal principle suggests that the firm should choose point *a*, with an output of 8 shirts. The output decision is the same whether the firm uses the marginal approach or the total approach.

The advantage of the marginal approach is that it is easier to apply. To use the total approach, a firm needs information on the total revenue and total cost for all possible

▶ **FIGURE 6.3**

**The Marginal Approach to Picking an Output Level**

A perfectly competitive firm takes the market price as given, so the marginal benefit, or marginal revenue, equals the price. Using the marginal principle, the typical firm will maximize profit at point *a*, where the $12 market price equals the marginal cost. Economic profit equals the difference between the price and the average cost ($4.125 = $12 − $7.875) times the quantity produced (8 shirts per minute), or $33 per minute.

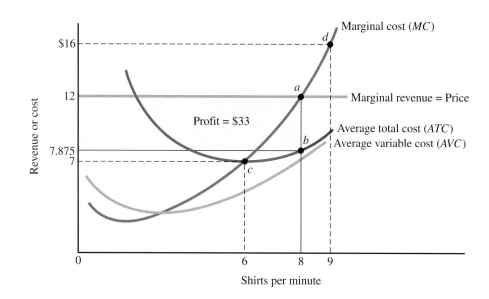

output levels. In contrast, a firm can apply the marginal principle by simply increasing its output by one unit and computing the marginal revenue (the price) and the marginal cost. Using the marginal principle, the firm should produce more output if the price exceeds the marginal cost, or produce less if the opposite is true. The firm can use the marginal principle to fine-tune its decision until the price equals the marginal cost.

## Economic Profit and the Break-Even Price

We've seen that the perfectly competitive firm maximizes its profit by producing the quantity at which its marginal revenue (price) equals its marginal cost. How much profit does the firm earn? The firm's economic profit equals its total revenue minus its total cost. One way to compute a firm's total economic profit is to multiply the average profit per unit produced—the gap between the price and the average cost—by the quantity produced:

economic profit = (price − average cost) × quantity produced

In Figure 6.3, the average cost of producing 8 shirts is $7.875 (point *b*), so the economic profit is $33:

economic profit = ($12 − $7.875) × 8 = $4.125 × 8 = $33

In Figure 6.3, the firm's profit is shown by the area of the shaded rectangle. The area of a rectangle is the height of the rectangle times its width. In Figure 6.3, the height of the profit rectangle is the average profit of $4.125 per shirt (equal to $12 − $7.875) and the width is the 8 shirts produced, so the profit is $33.

How would a decrease in price affect the firm's output decision? A decrease in price shifts the marginal-revenue (price) line downward, so it will intersect the marginal-cost curve at a smaller quantity. In Figure 6.3, suppose the price drops to $7. The marginal-revenue line will shift downward, causing it to intersect the marginal-cost curve at point *c*, so the firm will produce only 6 shirts per minute. In other words, when the price decreases from $12 to $7 the quantity produced decreases from 8 to 6 shirts. This is the law of supply in action: The lower the price, the smaller the quantity supplied.

What about the firm's economic profit at a price of $7? At point *c*, average total cost is $7, the same as the price. Therefore, economic profit is zero. We have discovered the **break-even price**, the price at which economic profit is zero. The break-even price is shown by the minimum point of the *ATC* curve, where marginal cost equals average total cost. Remember that zero economic profit means that the firm is making just enough money to cover all its costs, including the opportunity costs of the entrepreneur.

• **break-even price**
The price at which economic profit is zero; price equals average total cost.

# 6.3 | THE FIRM'S SHUT-DOWN DECISION

Consider next the decisions faced by a firm that is losing money. Suppose the price of shirts drops to $4, which is so low that the firm's total revenue is less than its total cost. In Table 6.3, the marginal principle tells the firm to produce 4 shirts at this price, but the firm's total cost of $30 exceeds its total revenue of $16, so the firm will lose $14 per minute. Should the firm continue to operate at a loss or shut down?

## Total Revenue, Variable Cost, and the Shut-Down Decision

The decision to operate or shut down is a short-run decision, a day-to-day decision to temporarily halt production in response to market conditions. Suppose our shirt factory hires workers by the day, so the decision is made at the beginning of each day. The decision-making rule is:

operate if total revenue > variable cost

shut down if total revenue < variable cost

Table 6.3 DECIDING HOW MUCH TO PRODUCE WHEN THE PRICE IS $4

| 1 | 2 | 3 | 4 | 5 | 6 | 7 | 8 |
|---|---|---|---|---|---|---|---|
| Output: Shirts per Minute (Q) | Fixed Cost (FC) | Variable Cost (VC) | Total Cost (TC) | Total Revenue (TR) | Marginal Revenue Profit (P) | Marginal (Price) (MR) | Cost (MC) |
| 0 | $17 | $0 | $17 | $0 | −$17 | | |
| 1 | 17 | 5 | 22 | 4 | −18 | $4 | $5 |
| 2 | 17 | 6 | 23 | 8 | −15 | 4 | 1 |
| 3 | 17 | 9 | 26 | 12 | −14 | 4 | 3 |
| **4** | **17** | **13** | **30** | **16** | **−14** | **4** | **4** |
| 5 | 17 | 18 | 35 | 20 | −15 | 4 | 5 |
| 6 | 17 | 25 | 42 | 24 | −18 | 4 | 7 |

As we saw in the previous chapter, a firm's variable cost includes all the costs that vary with the quantity produced. In the case of the shirt firm, it includes the costs of workers, raw materials, such as cotton, and the cost of heating and powering the factory for the day. The variable cost does not include the $17 fixed cost of the production facility—for example, the cost of the machines or the factory itself—because these costs are not affected by the decision to operate or shut down.

Although the decision is made at the beginning of each day, we can use the revenue and costs per minute to compare total revenue to variable cost. From Table 6.3, when the price is $4, the best quantity is 4 shirts and the variable cost is $13. The total revenue from selling 4 shirts at $4 per shirt is $16, which exceeds the $13 variable cost. By operating the factory, the firm pays $13 in variable cost to generate $16 in revenue, so the firm is better off operating the facility. The benefit of operating the facility exceeds the variable cost, so it is sensible to produce 4 shirts per minute.

Figure 6.4 shows the firm's choice when the price of shirts is $4. The marginal principle is satisfied at point *a*, where the price equals the marginal cost. As shown by point *b*, the average cost of producing 4 shirts is $7.50, so the firm loses $3.50 per shirt. The shaded rectangle shows the firm's loss of $14. The height of the rectangle is the $3.50 loss per shirt, and the width of the rectangle is the 4 shirts produced.

Of course, if the price drops to a low enough level, the firm will shut down the factory. For example, if the price drops to $1, the firm would be better off shutting the factory down for the day. In this case, the marginal principle is satisfied with 2 shirts

▶ **FIGURE 6.4**

**The Shut-Down Decision and the Shut-Down Price**

When the price is $4, marginal revenue equals marginal cost at 4 shirts (point *a*). At this quantity, average cost is $7.50, so the firm loses $3.50 on each shirt, for a total loss of $14. Total revenue is $16 and the variable cost is only $13, so the firm is better off operating at a loss rather than shutting down and losing its fixed cost of $17. The shut-down price, shown by the minimum point of the *AVC* curve, is $3.00.

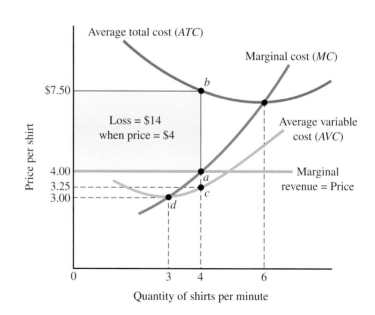

per day. At this quantity, the variable cost is $6, which exceeds $2 revenue ($1 per shirt times 2 shirts). With this low price, the firm's total revenue is not high enough to cover the firm's variable cost from operating the facility, so it is better to shut down for the day.

## The Shut-Down Price

There is a shortcut to determine whether it is sensible to continue to operate—compare the price to the average variable cost. Total revenue equals the price times the quantity produced, and the variable cost equals the average variable cost times the quantity produced. Therefore, total revenue will exceed variable cost if the price exceeds the average variable cost. If that happens, the firm should continue to operate. Otherwise, the firm should shut down.

operate if price > average variable cost

shut down if price < average variable cost

In Figure 6.4, with a price of $4, the marginal principle is satisfied at point *a*, and the average variable cost of producing 4 shirts is $3.25 (point *c*). The price exceeds the average variable cost, so it is sensible to continue operating, even at a loss.

The firm's **shut-down price** is the price at which the firm is indifferent between operating and shutting down. To find the shut-down price, we find the minimum point on the *AVC* curve. In Figure 6.4, *AVC* reaches its minimum of $3 at a quantity of 3 shirts per minute, so the shut-down price is $3 (shown by point *d*). The average variable cost never drops below $3, so if the price drops below $3 it would be impossible to generate enough revenue to cover the firm's variable cost. When the price equals the shut-down price, the firm is generating just enough revenue to cover its variable costs, so it is just as well off either operating or shutting down.

> • **shut-down price**
> The price at which the firm is indifferent between operating and shutting down; equal to the minimum average variable cost.

How long will a firm continue to operate at a loss? Let's think about what happens when the firm must decide whether or not to build a new production facility. The firm will build a new facility—and stay in the market—only if the price of shirts exceeds the average total cost of production. In other words, the firm will stay in the market only if the market price is high enough for its total revenue to cover *all* the costs of production, including the cost of the new facility. In other words, the price must be greater than or equal to the firm's break-even price. Although a firm might make a short-run decision to operate an existing facility at a loss, the firm won't replace the facility unless a new facility will be profitable.

## Fixed Costs and Sunk Costs

It's important to note that the decision whether to operate or shut down does not incorporate the fixed costs of the production facility. If we assume that the facility cannot be rented out to some other firm while the shirt firm isn't using it, the fixed cost is a **sunk cost**, a cost that a firm has already paid or committed to pay, so it cannot be recovered. Once the firm incurs this cost, it cannot be avoided by shutting down the factory. Therefore, the firm should ignore the cost of the facility when deciding whether to operate or shut down.

> • **sunk cost**
> A cost that a firm has already paid or committed to pay, so it cannot be recovered.

Rent is just one example of an irrelevant sunk cost. The marginal principle tells us that decisions are based on the costs that depend on what we do, not on costs that we can do nothing about. Suppose a dairy farmer spills two-thirds of a 300-gallon load of milk on the way to an ice-cream plant. Should the farmer return to the farm or deliver the remaining 100 gallons? As long as the marginal cost of delivering the milk—the opportunity cost of the farmer's time and the cost of fuel—is less than the amount the farmer will be paid for the remaining 100 gallons, it is sensible to deliver the milk. The spilt milk is a sunk cost that is irrelevant to the farmer's delivery decision. The farmer should not cry over spilt milk, but deliver the rest.

## THE BREAK-EVEN PRICE FOR A CORN FARMER

**APPLYING THE CONCEPTS #1:** What is the break-even price?

To illustrate the notions of break-even and shut-down prices, let's look at these prices for the typical corn farmer. The break-even, or zero-profit, price is $0.72 per bushel. At this price, the farmer will produce at the minimum point of the average total-cost curve, with the average cost equal to the market price of $0.72. At a higher price, the farmer will make a positive economic profit. For example, if the price is $0.92 per bushel and the farmer produces 50,000 bushels, the economic profit will be $10,000:

$$\text{economic profit} = (\$0.92 - \$0.72) \times 50,000 = \$0.20 \times 50,000 = \$10,000$$

The corn farmer's shut-down price is $0.44. At this price, total revenue equals the farmer's variable cost, so the farmer is indifferent about operating as opposed to shutting down. At a price between the shut-down price ($0.44) and the break-even price ($0.72), the farmer will lose money but will continue to operate at a loss because total revenue will exceed the variable cost of growing corn. For example, if the price is $0.50, the farmer will operate at a loss in the short run. However, if the price drops below the shut-down price of $0.44, the farmer will shut down, not bringing any crops to market in a particular year.

In the long run, farmers will exit the corn market if the price is not high enough to cover all the costs of growing corn, including the costs of the production facility. In the long run, the price must be high enough to cover the costs of land, machinery, and vehicles. In other words, farmers will exit the market if the price stays below the break-even price of $0.72. If the price is below this level, the farmer will not raise enough revenue to cover all the costs of growing corn and will exit the market. *Related to Exercises 3.5 and 3.6.*

SOURCE: Walter Adams, *The Structure of the American Economy*, 8th ed. (Upper Saddle River, NJ: Prentice Hall, 1990).

## 6.4 | SHORT-RUN SUPPLY CURVES

Now that we've explored the output decision of a price-taking firm, we're ready to show how a firm responds to changes in the market price of its product. We'll show the relationship between price and quantity supplied with two short-run supply curves, one for the individual firm and one for the entire market.

### The Firm's Short-Run Supply Curve

**• short-run supply curve**
A curve showing the relationship between the market price of a product and the quantity of output supplied by a firm in the short run.

The firm's **short-run supply curve** shows the relationship between the market price and the quantity supplied by the firm in the short run, over a period of time during

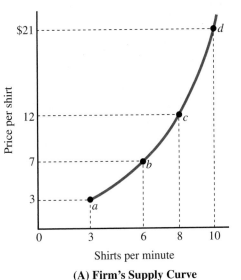

**(A) Firm's Supply Curve**

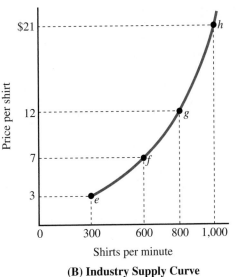

**(B) Industry Supply Curve**

◄ **FIGURE 6.5**
**Short-Run Supply Curves**
In Panel A, the firm's short-run supply curve is the part of the marginal-cost curve above the shut-down price. In Panel B, there are 100 firms in the market, so the market supply at a given price is 100 times the quantity supplied by the typical firm. At a price of $7, each firm supplies 6 shirts per minute (point b), so the market supply is 600 shirts per minute (point f).

which one input— the production facility—cannot be changed. In the case of shirt producers, the firm's supply curve answers the following question: At a given market price for shirts, how many shirts will the firm produce? In Figures 6.3 and 6.4, we used the marginal principle to answer this question for several different prices: At a price of $3, the quantity is 3 shirts; at a price of $7, the quantity is 6 shirts; at a price of $12, the quantity is 8 shirts.

The firm's short-run supply curve is the part of the firm's short-run marginal-cost curve above the shut-down price. The shut-down price for the shirt firm is $3, so as shown by point *a* in Figure 6.5 the short-run supply curve is the marginal-cost curve starting at $3. For any price above the shut-down price, the firm will choose the quantity at which price equals marginal cost, so we can read the firm's quantity supplied directly from its marginal-cost curve. If the price is $7, the firm will supply 6 shirts per minute (point *b*). As the price increases, the firm responds by supplying more shirts: 8 shirts at a price of $12 (point *c*) and 10 shirts at a price of $21 (point *d*).

What about prices below the shut-down price? If the price drops below the shut-down price, the firm's total revenue will not be high enough to cover its variable cost, so the firm will shut down and produce no output. In Panel A of Figure 6.5, the firm's supply curve starts at point *a*, indicating that the quantity supplied is zero for any price less than $3.

## The Short-Run Market Supply Curve

The **short-run market supply curve** shows the relationship between the market price and the quantity supplied by firms as a whole in the short run. Panel B of Figure 6.5 shows the short-run market supply curve when there are 100 identical shirt firms. For each price, we get the quantity supplied for the entire market by multiplying the quantity supplied by the typical firm (from the individual supply curve) by 100. At a price of $7, each firm produces 6 shirts (point *b* in Panel A), so the market supply is 600 shirts (point *f* in Panel B). If the price increases to $12, each firm increases production to 8 shirts (point *c* in Panel A), so the market supply is 800 shirts (point *g* in Panel B).

What happens if firms are not identical but instead have different individual supply curves? To compute the market supply in this case, we would add the quantities supplied by the hundreds of firms in the market. The assumption that firms are identical is harmless: It makes it easier to derive the market supply curve from the supply curve of the typical firm, but it does not change the analysis.

- **short-run market supply curve**
  A curve showing the relationship between market price and the quantity supplied in the short run.

## Market Equilibrium

Figure 6.6 shows a perfectly competitive market in equilibrium. For a short-run equilibrium, two conditions are satisfied:

1 At the market level, the quantity of the product supplied equals the quantity demanded. The demand curve intersects the short-run market supply curve at a price of $7 and a quantity of 600 shirts per minute (Panel A).

2 The typical firm in the market maximizes its profit, given the market price. Given the market price of $7, each of the 100 firms maximizes profit by producing 6 shirts per minute (Panel B).

In Figure 6.6, the market has reached a short-run equilibrium because the price of $7 generates a total of 600 shirts per minute, exactly the quantity demanded by consumers at this price.

In the long run, firms can enter or leave an industry, and existing firms can modify their facilities or build new facilities. The market reaches a long-run equilibrium when the two conditions for short-run equilibrium are met, and a third long-run condition holds as well.

3 Each firm in the market earns zero economic profit, so there is no incentive for existing firms to leave the market and no incentive for other firms to enter the market.

In Figure 6.6, at the quantity chosen by the typical firm (6 shirts), the price ($7) equals the average total cost, so each firm makes zero economic profit, with total revenue equal to total cost. In other words, the market price equals the break-even price. When economic profit is zero, the firm's revenue is high enough to cover all its costs—including the opportunity costs of the entrepreneur—but not high enough to cause additional firms to enter the market. Each firm that is already in the market makes just enough money to stay in business, so there is no incentive for new firms to enter the market, and no incentive for existing firms to leave.

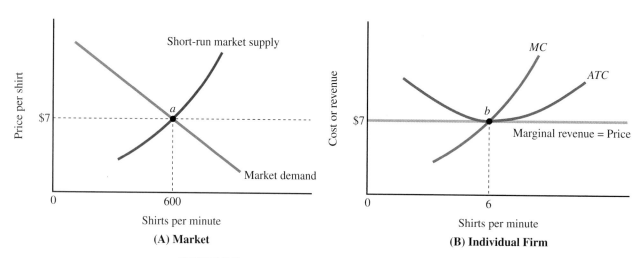

**(A) Market**  **(B) Individual Firm**

▲ **FIGURE 6.6**

**Market Equilibrium**

In Panel A, the market demand curve intersects the short-run market supply curve at a price of $7. In Panel B, given the market price of $7, the typical firm satisfies the marginal principle at point *b*, producing 6 shirts per minute. The $7 price equals the average cost at the equilibrium quantity, so economic profit is zero, and no other firms will enter the market.

# APPLICATION

**WIRELESS WOMEN IN PAKISTAN**

**APPLYING THE CONCEPTS #2:** How do entry costs affect the number of firms in a market?

For another example of a competitive market, consider phone service in the developing world. In many parts of the developing world, people cannot afford their own phones and have traditionally relied on pay phones. The recent development of mobile phones has generated a new competitive industry in many developing nations.

In Pakistan, many poor villagers cannot afford their own phones, and phone service is provided by thousands of "wireless women," entrepreneurs who invest $310 in wireless phone equipment (transceiver, battery, charger), a signboard, a calculator, and a stopwatch. Then they sell phone service to their neighbors, charging by the minute and second. On average, their net income is about $2 per day, about three times the average per capita income in Pakistan. The market for phone service has the features of a perfectly competitive market, with easy entry, a standardized good, and a large enough number of suppliers that each takes the market price as given. In contrast, to enter the phone business in the United States, your initial investment would be millions, or perhaps billions, of dollars, so the market for phone service is not perfectly competitive. *Related to Exercise 4.5.*

SOURCE: TeleCommons Development Group, "Grameen Telecom's Village Phone Programme: A Multi-Media Case Study," 2000, available online at www.telecommons.com/villagephone, accessed June 27, 2006.

## 6.5 | THE LONG-RUN SUPPLY CURVE FOR AN INCREASING-COST INDUSTRY

Let's look at the **long-run market supply curve**, which shows the relationship between the market price and the quantity supplied by all firms in the long run, a period long enough that firms can enter or leave the market. Suppose the typical shirt firm produces 6 shirts per minute, using a standard set of inputs, including a factory, some workers, and raw materials of cotton and thread. In a perfectly competitive industry, there are no restrictions on entry, so anyone can use the standard set of inputs to produce 6 shirts per minute.

We'll start with the case of an **increasing-cost industry**, an industry in which the average cost of production increases as the total output of the industry increases. The average cost increases as the industry grows for two reasons:

- *Increasing input price.* As an industry grows, it competes with other industries for limited amounts of various inputs, and this competition drives up the prices of these inputs. For example, suppose that the shirt industry competes against other industries for a limited amount of cotton. To get more cotton to produce more shirts, firms in the shirt industry must outbid other industries for the limited amount available, and this drives up the price of cotton.

- **long-run market supply curve**
A curve showing the relationship between the market price and quantity supplied in the long run.

- **increasing-cost industry**
An industry in which the average cost of production increases as the total output of the industry increases; the long-run supply curve is positively sloped.

**143**

• *Less productive inputs.* A small industry will use only the most productive inputs, but as the industry grows, firms may be forced to use less productive inputs. For example, a small shirt industry will use only the most skillful workers, but as the industry grows, it will hire workers with lower skills. As the average skill level of the industry's workforce decreases, the average cost of production increases: A firm will require more labor time—and pay more in labor costs—to produce each shirt.

Another example of progressively less productive inputs is the production of agricultural products such as sugar. Because of variation in climate and soil conditions, it is cheaper to grow sugar in some areas than in others. As the quantity of sugar produced increases, growers are forced to produce sugar in areas with less favorable climates and soil conditions, and this results in higher costs.

### Production Cost and Industry Size

Table 6.4 shows hypothetical data on the cost of producing shirts. Let's start with the first row, which shows the firm's production costs in an industry with 100 firms and a total of 600 shirts produced per day (6 shirts per firm). To compute the total cost for the typical firm, we add the cost of the firm's production facility (the cost of the shirt factory), the cost of labor, and the cost of materials. In the first row, the total cost of the typical firm producing 6 shirts per minute is $42, and the average cost is $7 per shirt ($42 divided by 6 shirts). In the second row, if the number of firms doubles to 200 and each firm continues to produce 6 shirts per minute, the total output of the industry will double to 1,200 shirts per minute. For the two reasons listed earlier (higher input prices and less productive inputs), the total cost per firm increases to $60, so the average cost per shirt increases to $10. In the last row, when the total output of the industry increases to 1,800 shirts per minute, the average cost per shirt increases to $13.

The shirt industry is an example of an increasing-cost industry. In the last column of Table 6.4, the average cost increases from $7 for an industry that produces 600 shirts, to $10 for an industry that produces 1,200 shirts, and so on. The average cost increases because firms in a larger industry pay higher input prices and use less productive inputs.

### Drawing the Long-Run Market Supply Curve

The long-run supply curve tells us how much output will be produced at each price in the long run, when the number of firms in the market can change. Recall that in the long-run equilibrium, each firm makes zero economic profit, meaning that the price equals the average cost of production.

The data in Table 6.4 shows three points on the long-run supply curve. At a price of $7, a total of 100 firms will be in the market, with each producing 6 shirts per hour. This combination (price = $7 and quantity = 600 shirts) is on the long-run supply curve because the price equals the average cost. Each firm makes zero economic profit, so there is no incentive for firms to either enter or exit the market. This is shown by point *a* in Figure 6.7. Suppose the price of shirts increases. At the higher price, shirt making will be more profitable, and firms will enter the market, increasing total output. Firms will continue to enter the market until the economic profit becomes zero again, which happens when the average cost again equals the price. From Table 6.4, we see that entry will continue until the market reaches 200 firms producing 1,200 shirts at an average cost and price of $10. This is shown by point *b* in Figure 6.7. Point *c* shows another point on the long-run supply curve, with a price of $13 and a quantity of 1,800 shirts.

**Table 6.4** | INDUSTRY OUTPUT AND AVERAGE PRODUCTION COST

| Number of Firms | Industry Output | Shirts per Firm | Total Cost for Typical Firm | Average Cost per Shirt |
|---|---|---|---|---|
| 100 | 600 | 6 | $42 | $ 7 |
| 200 | 1,200 | 6 | 60 | 10 |
| 300 | 1,800 | 6 | 78 | 13 |

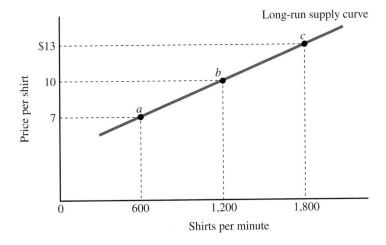

Long-run supply curve

**◀ FIGURE 6.7**
**Long-Run Market Supply Curve**
The long-run market supply curve shows the relationship between the price and quantity supplied in the long run, when firms can enter or leave the industry. At each point on the supply curve, the market price equals the long-run average cost of production. Because this is an increasing-cost industry, the long-run market supply curve is positively sloped.

The long-run supply curve in Figure 6.7 is positively sloped, as it will be for any increasing-cost industry. This is another example of the law of supply. An increase in the price of shirts initially makes shirt production profitable, so firms enter the market and produce more shirts. As industry-wide output increases, the greater demand for cotton and labor increases input prices, which in turn increases the average cost of producing shirts. Firms will continue to enter the market until the average cost rises to the point where it equals the price of shirts. The positively sloped supply curve tells us that the market won't produce a larger quantity of shirts unless the price rises to cover the higher average cost associated with the larger industry.

# A P P L I C A T I O N

## WOLFRAM MINERS OBEY THE LAW OF SUPPLY

**APPLYING THE CONCEPTS #3:** How do producers respond to an increase in price?

For an example of the law of supply with market entry, consider the market for wolfram during World War II. Wolfram is an ore of tungsten, an alloy required to make heat-resistant steel for armor plate and armor-piercing shells. During World War II, the United States and its European allies bought up all the wolfram produced in Spain, thus denying the Axis powers—Germany and Italy—this vital military input. However, the wolfram-buying program was very costly to the Allied powers for two reasons:

- The Allied powers had to outbid the Axis powers for the wolfram, so the price increased from $1,144 per ton to $20,000 per ton.

- Spanish firms responded to the higher prices by supplying more wolfram. Workers poured into the Galatia area in Spain, where they used simple tools to gather wolfram from the widely scattered outcroppings of ore. Because of this market entry, the quantity of wolfram supplied increased tenfold. Because wolfram miners obeyed the law of supply, the Allied powers were forced to buy a huge amount of wolfram, much more than they had expected. *Related to Exercises 5.6 and 5.8.*

SOURCE: D. I. Gordon and R. Dangerfield, *The Hidden Weapon* (New York: Harper & Brothers, 1947), pp. 105–116.

# 4

# APPLICATION

## THE WORLDWIDE SUPPLY OF SUGAR

**APPLYING THE CONCEPTS #4:** When production costs vary across producers, what are the implications for the market supply curve?

The sugar industry is another example of an increasing-cost industry. If the price of sugar is only 11 cents per pound, sugar production is profitable in areas with relatively low production costs, including the Caribbean, Latin America, Australia, and South Africa. At a price of 11 cents, the world supply of sugar equals the amount produced in these areas. As the price increases, sugar production becomes profitable in areas where production costs are higher, and as these areas enter the world market, the quantity of sugar supplied increases. For example, at a price of 14 cents per pound, sugar production is profitable in some countries in the European Union too. At a price of 24 cents, production is profitable even in the United States. *Related to Exercises 5.7 and 5.9.*

SOURCE: Frederic L. Hoff and Max Lawrence, "Implications of World Sugar Markets, Policies, and Production Costs for U.S. Sugar," *Agricultural Economic Research Report* 543 (Washington, D.C.: U.S. Department of Agriculture, Economic Research Service, November 1985).

## 6.6 | SHORT-RUN AND LONG-RUN EFFECTS OF CHANGES IN DEMAND

We can use what we've learned about the short-run and long-run supply curves to get a deeper understanding of perfectly competitive markets. Let's use the two supply curves to explore the short-run and the long-run effects of a change in demand in a perfectly competitive market.

### The Short-Run Response to an Increase in Demand

Figure 6.8 shows the short-run effects of an increase in the demand for shirts. Panel A shows what's happening at the market level. Let's start with the initial equilibrium shown by point *a*: The original demand curve intersects the short-run market supply curve at a price of $7 per shirt and a quantity of 600 shirts. When demand increases, the new demand curve intersects the supply curve at a price of $12 and a quantity of 800 shirts (point *b*). In Panel B, an increase in price from $7 to $12 increases the output per firm from 6 shirts to 8 shirts. At this quantity, the $12 price now exceeds the average total cost, so the typical firm makes an economic profit, as shown by the shaded rectangle.

Point *b* is not a long-run equilibrium, because each firm is making a positive economic profit. Firms will enter the profitable market, and as they compete for customers the price of shirts will decrease. New firms will continue to enter the market until the price drops to the point at which economic profit is zero. How far will the price drop?

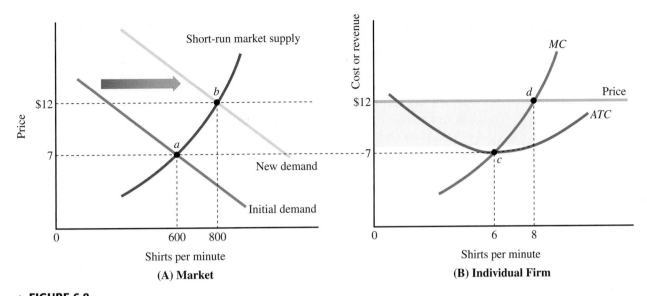

▲ **FIGURE 6.8**
**Short-Run Effects of an Increase in Demand**
An increase in demand for shirts increases the market price to $12, causing the typical firm to produce 8 shirts instead of 6. Price exceeds the average total cost at the 8-shirt quantity, so economic profit is positive. Firms will enter the profitable market.

## The Long-Run Response to an Increase in Demand

We can use the long-run supply curve to determine the long-run price after an increase in demand. In Figure 6.9, the short-run effect of the increase in demand is shown by the move from point *a* to point *b*: The price increases from $7 to $12, and the quantity increases from 600 to 800. Economic profit is positive, so firms will enter the market. As shown by the long-run supply curve, entry will continue until the price drops to $10 and the quantity is 1,200 shirts per minute. The new long-run equilibrium is shown by point *c*, where the new demand curve intersects the long-run supply curve. At this price and quantity, each of the 200 firms produces six shirts per minute and earns zero economic profit.

Figure 6.9 shows how the price of shirts changes over time. An increase in demand causes a large upward jump in the price from $7 to $12 in the short run,

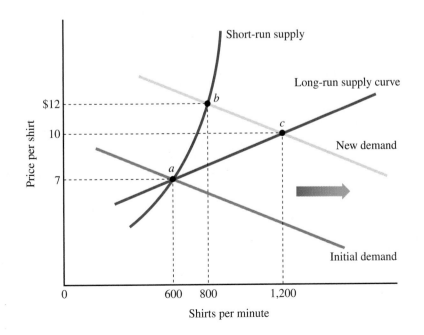

◄ **FIGURE 6.9**
**Short-Run and Long-Run Effects of an Increase in Demand**
The short-run supply curve is steeper than the long-run supply curve because of diminishing returns in the short run. In the short run, an increase in demand increases the price from $7 (point *a*) to $12 (point *b*). But in the long run, firms can enter the industry and build more production facilities, so the price eventually drops to $10 (point *c*). The large upward jump in price after the increase in demand is followed by a downward slide to the new long-run equilibrium price.

followed by a slide downward to the new long-run equilibrium price of $10. In the short run, firms respond to an increase in price by squeezing more output from their existing production facilities. Because of diminishing returns, it is very costly to increase output in the short run, so the price must increase by a large amount to cover these much higher production costs. The higher price causes new firms to enter the market, and as they enter, the price gradually drops to the point at which each firm makes zero economic profit. The long-run supply curve is relatively flat because firms enter the industry and build new factories, so there are no diminishing returns to increase production costs.

# 5

# APPLICATION

## ZONING, LAND PRICES, AND THE SUPPLY CURVE FOR APARTMENTS

**APPLYING THE CONCEPTS #5:** When input prices increase with the total output of the industry, what are the implications for the market supply curve?

In many communities, the rental-apartment industry is an increasing-cost industry. Most communities use zoning laws to restrict the amount of land available for apartments. As the industry expands by building more apartments, competition is fierce among firms for the small amount of land zoned for apartments. Housing firms bid up the price of land, increasing the cost of producing apartments. Producers can cover these higher production costs only by charging higher rents to tenants.

What are the implications of zoning for a market that experiences an increase in demand? In the short run, the stock of housing is fixed. An increase in demand for apartments will increase the price of apartments (the monthly rent), and firms will convert some owner-occupied houses to rental apartments. This short-run supply response will be relatively small, so the price will increase by a relatively large amount, just as we saw in Figure 6.9 as the movement from point *a* to point *b*. In the long run, firms will enter the market by building more apartments. As we saw at point *c* in Figure 6.9, the new long-run equilibrium is shown by the intersection of the new demand curve and the long-run supply curve. The increase in demand leads to a net increase in price because zoning restricts the supply of apartment land, leading to higher land prices and a higher cost of producing apartments.

*Related to Exercises 6.4 and 6.5.*

SOURCE: Frank De Leeuw and Nkanta Ekanem, "The Supply of Rental Housing," *American Economic Review*, vol. 61, 1971, pp. 806–817.

# 6.7 | LONG-RUN SUPPLY FOR A CONSTANT-COST INDUSTRY

So far we have examined products that are produced by increasing-cost industries, whose average cost increases as the industry expands. We turn next to a **constant-cost industry**, an industry whose average cost is constant—it doesn't change as the industry expands. That is, the prices of inputs such as labor and materials do not change as the total output of the industry increases. This happens when the industry uses a relatively small amount of the available labor and materials, meaning that events in the industry—increases or decreases in output—do not affect the price of the input. As a result, the average cost of production for the typical firm doesn't change as the industry grows. In Table 6.4, the shirt industry would be a constant-cost industry if the average cost of shirts were constant at $7, regardless of how many shirts were produced.

• **constant-cost industry**
An industry in which the average cost of production is constant; the long-run supply curve is horizontal.

## Long-Run Supply Curve for a Constant-Cost Industry

As an example of a constant-cost industry, consider the production of birthday-cake candles. As the industry grows, it will use more workers, wicks, and wax, but because the industry is such a small part of the markets for labor and materials, the prices of these inputs won't change. As a result, the average cost of production won't change as the industry grows.

The long-run supply curve for a constant-cost industry is horizontal at the constant average cost of production. If the average cost of birthday-cake candles is $0.05 per candle, the long-run supply curve for candles will be horizontal at $0.05, as shown by Figure 6.10. At any lower price, the quantity of candles supplied would be zero, because in the long run no rational firm would provide candles at a price less than the average cost of production. At any higher price, firms would enter the candle industry in droves, and entry would continue until the price dropped to the constant average cost of $0.05 per candle.

## Hurricane Andrew and the Price of Ice

For an example of the effects of an increase in demand in a constant-cost industry, let's look at the short-run and long-run effects of a hurricane. In 1992, Hurricane Andrew struck the southeastern United States, leaving millions of people without electricity for several days. Figure 6.11 shows the short-run and long-run effects of the hurricane on the price of ice, which was used to cool and preserve food in areas without electricity. Before the hurricane, the market was at point *a*, with a price of $1 per bag of ice. The long-run supply curve is horizontal, indicating that the ice industry is a constant-cost industry.

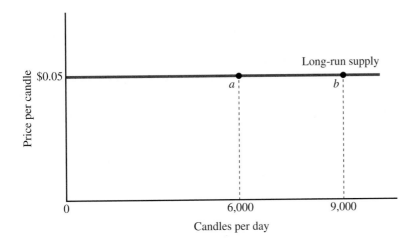

◀ **FIGURE 6.10**
**Long-Run Supply Curve for a Constant-Cost Industry**

In a constant-cost industry, input prices do not change as the industry grows. Therefore, the average production cost is constant and the long-run supply curve is horizontal. For the candle industry, the cost per candle is constant at $0.05, so the supply curve is horizontal at $0.05 per candle.

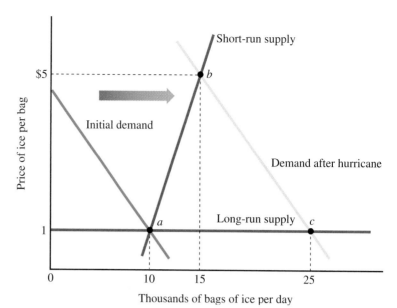

▲ **FIGURE 6.11**
**Hurricane Andrew and the Price of Ice**
A hurricane increases the demand for ice, shifting the demand curve to the right. In the short run, the supply curve is relatively steep, so the price rises by a large amount—from $1 to $5. In the long run, firms enter the industry, pulling the price back down. Because ice production is a constant-cost industry, the supply is horizontal, and the large upward jump in price is followed by a downward slide back to the original price.

In the short run (a day or two), the number of ice suppliers is fixed. The increase in demand caused by the hurricane moved the market from point *a* to point *b*, and the price rose to $5 per bag of ice. In the long run, firms responded to the higher price by entering the market. Many people trucked ice from distant locations and sold it from trucks parked on streets and highways. As these firms entered the ice market in the days after the hurricane, the price of ice gradually dropped, and the market eventually reached the intersection of the new demand curve and the long-run supply curve (point *c*), with a price equal to the prehurricane price. In the case of the retail ice industry, the long run is just a few days.

This pattern of price changes following the hurricane was observed in other markets. Immediately after the hurricane, $200 chain saws were sold for $900, but the price dropped steadily as new roadside firms entered the market. The same sort of price changes occurred for bottled water, tarpaper, and plywood. The basic pattern was a large upward jump in price followed by a downward slide to the long-run equilibrium price.

If you had been the governor of Florida in 1992, what would you have done about the price hikes? Public officials are often tempted to pass laws prohibiting what's called *price gouging*, charging high prices for scarce goods after a natural disaster. One effect of such laws is to slow the transition from the short run to the long run. The people who set up roadside stands to sell ice were motivated by the high price. If the price were controlled at $1 per bag, few people would have incurred the large expenses associated with trucking the ice from distant locations and setting up roadside stores. The result would have been less ice and more spoiled food. An alternative to a law regulating prices is to leave prices to the market and help to ease the transition from short run to long run by making it easier for entrepreneurs to enter the market.

## SUMMARY

In this chapter, we explored the decisions made by perfectly competitive firms and the implications of these decisions for the supply side of the market. In the short run, a firm uses the marginal principle to decide how much output to produce. In the long run, a firm will enter a market if the price exceeds the average cost of production. Here are the main points of this chapter:

1 A *price-taking* firm should produce the quantity of output at which the marginal revenue (the price) equals the marginal cost of production.

2 An unprofitable firm should continue to operate if its total revenue exceeds its total variable cost.

3 The long-run supply curve will be positively sloped if the average cost of production increases as the industry grows.

4 The long-run supply curve is flatter than the short-run supply curve because there are diminishing returns in the short run, but not in the long run.

5 An increase in demand causes a large upward jump in price, followed by a downward slide to the new long-run equilibrium price.

## KEY TERMS

break-even price, p. 137
constant-cost industry, p. 149
firm-specific demand curve, p. 132
increasing-cost industry, p. 143

long-run market supply curve, p. 143
marginal revenue, p. 135
perfectly competitive market, p. 132
price taker, p. 132

short-run supply curve, p. 140
short-run market supply curve, p. 141
shut-down price, p. 139
sunk cost, p. 139

## EXERCISES

Visit www.myeconlab.com to complete these exercises online and get instant feedback.

*Get Ahead of the Curve*

### 6.1 | Preview of the Four Market Structures

**1.1** The firm-specific demand curve shows the relationship between the _____ charged by the firm and the _____ by the firm.

**1.2** For a perfectly competitive firm, the firm-specific demand curve is _____ (horizontal/negatively sloped).

**1.3** For a monopolist, the firm-specific demand curve is the same as the _____ demand curve.

**1.4** For a monopolist, the firm-specific demand curve is _____ (horizontal/negatively sloped).

### 6.2 | The Firm's Short-Run Output Decision

**2.1** Economic profit equals _____ minus _____.

**2.2** Economic cost equals _____ cost plus _____ cost.

**2.3** For a perfectly competitive firm, marginal revenue equals _____.

**2.4** A perfectly competitive firm produces the quantity of output at which _____ equals _____.

**2.5** At the current output level, a farmer's marginal cost of producing sugar is $0.30. If the price of sugar is $0.22 per pound, the farmer should _____ (increase/decrease) production. If the price of sugar is $0.32 per pound, the farmer should _____ (increase/decrease) production.

**2.6** A firm produces 20 units of output at a market price of $5, a marginal cost of $5, and an average cost of $3. The firm's economic profit is $_____, and the firm _____ (is/is not) maximizing its economic profit.

**2.7** For the break-even price, _____ equals the price, so the firm earns _____ economic profit.

**2.8** Your firm delivers packages by bicycle. If you want to determine whether you are maximizing your profit, you need to know your _____ and your _____.

**2.9** **How Many Deliveries?** Consider a delivery firm that delivers packages by bicycle, charging $13 per package and paying each of its workers $12 per hour. One day, one of the workers was two hours late to work, and the number of packages delivered that day decreased by one package.
   **a.** Did the tardiness of the worker increase or decrease the firm's profit?

**b.** Based on the new information provided by the tardy worker, should the firm produce more deliveries by hiring more workers, or produce fewer deliveries by reducing its workforce? Explain, using the marginal principle.

**2.10 Advice for a Firm.** You've been hired as an economic consultant by a price-taking firm that produces scarves. The firm already has a factory, so it is operating in the short run. The price of scarves is $9, the hourly wage is $24, and each scarf requires $1 worth of material. The following table shows the relationship between the number of workers and the output of scarves.

| Workers | 10 | 11 | 12 | 13 | 14 | 15 |
|---|---|---|---|---|---|---|
| Output | 5 | 29 | 41 | 47 | 50 | 52 |
| Labor cost | — | — | — | — | — | — |
| Material cost | — | — | — | — | — | — |
| Fixed cost | $2 | $2 | $2 | $2 | $2 | $2 |
| Total cost | — | — | — | — | — | — |
| Marginal cost | — | — | — | — | — | — |

**a.** Fill the blanks in the table.

**b.** What is the profit-maximizing output?

## 6.3 | The Firm's Shut-Down Decision

**3.1** A firm will shut down an unprofitable business if _____ revenue is less than _____ cost.

**3.2** Your firm has a total revenue of $500, a total cost of $700, and a variable cost of $400. You should _____ (operate/shut down) because _____ exceeds _____.

**3.3** A firm that is losing money should continue to operate in the short run if the market price exceeds _____.

**3.4** Your firm has a price of $5, an average total cost of $7, and an average variable cost of $4. In the short run, you should _____ (operate/shut down) because _____ exceeds _____. In the long run, you should _____ (stay in the market/exit) because _____ exceeds _____.

**3.5** The typical corn farmer makes zero economic profit at a price of $_____. (Related to Application 1 on page 140.)

**3.6 Changes in the Break-Even and Shut-Down Prices.** Consider a corn farmer whose initial production costs are the ones reported in the application, "The Break-Even Price for a Corn Farmer." For each of the following changes, explain the effects on the farmer's break-even price and shut-down price. Specifically, will the price increase, decrease, or remain the same? (Related to Application 1 on page 140.)

**a.** The fixed cost of production increases.

**b.** The cost of fertilizer increases.

**c.** The opportunity cost of the farmer's time increases.

**3.7 Advice for an Unprofitable Firm.** You've been hired as an economic consultant by a price-taking firm that produces baseball caps. The firm already has a factory, so it is operating in the short run. The price of caps is $5, the hourly wage is $12, and each cap requires $1 worth of material. The firm has experimented with different workforces and the results are shown in the first two columns of the table below.

| Workers | Caps | Labor Cost | Material Cost | Variable Cost | Total Revenue | Marginal Cost of Caps |
|---|---|---|---|---|---|---|
| 14 | 56 | — | — | — | — | — |
| 15 | 60 | — | — | — | — | — |

**a.** Fill the blanks in the table.

**b.** Is it sensible to continue to operate at a loss with 14 workers?

**c.** Would it be better to operate with 15 workers? Explain, using the marginal principle.

**3.8 A Bluffing Farmer?** Consider the following statement from a wheat farmer to his workers: "The price of wheat is very low this year, and the most I can get from the crop is $35,000. If I paid you the same amount as I paid you last year ($30,000), I'd lose money because I also have to worry about the $20,000 I paid three months ago for seed and fertilizer. I'd be crazy to pay a total of $50,000 to harvest a crop I can sell for only $35,000. If you are willing to work for half as much as last year ($15,000), my total cost will be $35,000, so I'll break even. If you don't take a pay cut, I won't harvest the wheat." Is the farmer bluffing, or will the farm workers lose their jobs if they reject the proposed pay cut?

## 6.4 | Short-Run Supply Curves

**4.1** A firm's short-run supply curve shows the relationship between _____ (on the horizontal axis) and _____ (on the vertical axis).

**4.2** To draw a firm's short-run supply curve, you need its _____ curve and its _____ price.

**4.3** A perfectly competitive industry has 100 identical firms. At a price of $8, the typical firm supplies seven units of output, so the market quantity supplied is _____ units of output.

**4.4** Figure 6.6 on page 142 shows a long-run equilibrium because (1) the quantity _____ equals the quantity _____; (2) the typical firm maximizes _____ by picking the quantity at which _____ equals _____; (3) each firm makes _____ economic profit because _____ equals _____.

**4.5** In Pakistan, the market for phone service is perfectly _____, because a person can enter the market with a relatively small initial investment—only $310. (Related to Application 2 on page 143.)

**4.6 Soybeans Versus Processor Chips.** Why is the market for soybeans perfectly competitive, with thousands of soybean farmers, while the market for computer processor chips is dominated by a few large firms?

**4.7 Draw the Supply Curves.** The following table shows short-run marginal costs for a perfectly competitive firm:

| Output | 100 | 200 | 300 | 400 | 500 |
|---|---|---|---|---|---|
| Marginal cost | $5 | $10 | $20 | $40 | $70 |

   a. Use this information to draw the firm's marginal-cost curve.
   b. Suppose the shut-down price is $10. Draw the firm's short-run supply curve.
   c. Suppose there are 100 identical firms with the same marginal-cost curve. Draw the short-run industry supply curve.

**4.8 Maximizing the Profit Margin?** According to the marginal principle, the firm should choose the quantity of output at which price equals marginal cost. A tempting alternative is to maximize the firm's profit margin, defined as the difference between price and short-run average total cost. Use the firm's short-run cost curves to evaluate this approach. Draw the firm's short-run supply curve and compare it to the supply curve of a firm that maximizes its profit.

**4.9 Expand If Profit Margin Is Positive?** Consider a firm that uses the following rule to decide how much output to produce: If the profit margin (price minus short-run average total cost) is positive, the firm will produce more output. Use the firm's short-run cost curves to evaluate this approach. Draw the firm's short-run supply curve and compare it to the short-run supply curve of a profit-maximizing firm.

## 6.5 | The Long-Run Supply Curve for an Increasing-Cost Industry

**5.1** The long-run supply curve shows the relationship between _____ (on the horizontal axis) and _____ (on the vertical axis).

**5.2** Arrows up or down: As the total output of an increasing-cost industry increases, the average cost of production _____ because input prices _____ and the productivity of inputs used by firms _____.

**5.3** As the total output of an increasing-cost industry increases, the average cost of production _____ (increases/decreases), so the supply curve is _____ (horizontal/positively sloped/negatively sloped).

**5.4** In Table 6.4 on page 144, suppose the relationship between industry output and the total cost for the typical firm is linear, and each firm produces six shirts. If there are 400 firms in the industry, the total cost for the typical firm is $_____, and the average cost per shirt is $_____. Another point on the supply curve is a price of $_____ and a quantity of _____ shirts.

**5.5** An increase in the price of shirts will cause firms to _____ the industry, and as output increases the _____ cost of production increases. Entry will continue until _____ equals _____.

**5.6** During World War II, the quantity of wolfram supplied increased because the Allies' buying program increased the _____ of wolfram. (Related to Application 3 on page 145.)

**5.7** As the price of sugar increases, the quantity of sugar produced increases because areas with relatively high _____ enter the market. (Related to Application 4 on page 146.)

**5.8 Wolfram Elasticity.** Consider the Application, "Wolfram Miners Obey the Law of Supply." Suppose the initial equilibrium price is $1,144 per ton and the output is 100 tons. (Related to Application 3 on page 145.)
   a. Using the numbers related in the application, draw a supply and demand graph showing the effects of the Allies' wolfram buying program. Your supply curve should be a long-run curve, which incorporates the entry and exit of firms.
   b. Using the formula for the elasticity of supply in the earlier chapter on elasticity, compute the price elasticity of supply.

**5.9 Sugar Import Ban.** Suppose that initially there are no controls on sugar imported into the United States, so the price paid in the United States equals the prevailing world price. (Related to Application 4 on page 146.)
   a. If the world price is 13 cents per pound, what areas of the world supply sugar to the world market and the United States?
   b. Suppose the United States bans sugar imports. Predict the new price of sugar.

**5.10 Long-Run Supply Curve of Lamps.** Suppose each lamp manufacturer produces 10 lamps per hour. Complete the following table. Then use the data in the table to draw the long-run supply curve for lamps.

| Number of Firms | Industry Output | Total Cost for Typical Firm | Average Cost per Lamp |
|---|---|---|---|
| 40 | _____ | $300 | _____ |
| 80 | _____ | 360 | _____ |
| 120 | _____ | 420 | _____ |

**6.1** The short-run supply curve is steeper than the long-run supply curve because of the principle of _____.

**6.2** Arrows up or down: Suppose the demand for shirts increases. In the short run, the price _____ by a relatively large amount. As firms enter the market, the price _____. In the new long-run equilibrium, there is a net _____ in price relative to the old equilibrium.

**6.3** An increase in demand causes a large initial upward _____ (jump/slide) in price, followed by a downward _____ (jump/slide) to the new long-run equilibrium price.

**6.4** Land-use zoning that limits the amount of land for apartments generates a relatively _____ (flat/steep) supply curve for housing, so an increase in the demand for apartments leads to a relatively _____ (large/small) increase in price. (Related to Application 5 on page 148.)

**6.5** **Market Effects of an Increase in Apartment Demand.** Consider the market for apartments in a small city. In the initial equilibrium, the monthly rent (the price) is $500, and the quantity is 10,000 apartments. Suppose that the population of the city suddenly increases by 24 percent. The price elasticity of demand for apartments is 1.0. The short-run price elasticity of supply is 0.20, and the long-run price elasticity of supply is 0.50. (Related to Application 5 on page 148.)
**a.** Draw demand and supply graphs to show the short-run and long-run effects of the increase in population.
**b.** Use the price-change formula from the elasticity chapter to compute the new prices in the short run and the long run.

## 6.7 | Long-Run Supply for a Constant-Cost Industry

**7.1** As the total output of a constant-cost industry increases, the _____ cost does not change, so the long-run supply curve is _____ (horizontal/positively sloped/negatively sloped).

**7.2** A constant-cost industry consumes a relatively _____ (small/large) amount of inputs such as labor and materials, so as industry output increases the prices of these inputs _____ (increase/decrease/don't change).

**7.3** Arrow up, down, or horizontal: In a constant-cost industry, when demand increases the long-run equilibrium price _____.

**7.4** Arrows up, down, or horizontal: Hurricane Andrew _____ the demand for ice. In the short run, the price _____ by a relatively large amount. In the long run, the price _____ relative to the prehurricane price.

**7.5** **The Price of Haircuts.** The haircutting industry in your city uses a tiny fraction of the electricity, scissors, and commercial space available on the market. In addition, the industry employs only about 100 of the 50,000 people who could cut hair.

**a.** Draw a long-run supply curve for haircutting in your city.

**b.** Suppose the initial equilibrium price of haircuts is $12. Draw demand and supply graphs to show the short-run and long-run effects of an increase in population. Does population growth affect the long-run equilibrium price of haircuts?

**7.6** **Butter Prices.** Several years ago, people became concerned about the undesirable health effects of eating butter. The demand for butter dropped, decreasing its price. Some time later, the price of butter started rising steadily, although demand hadn't been changing. After several months of price hikes, the price of butter reached the price observed before demand decreased. According to a consumer watchdog organization, the rising price of butter was evidence of a conspiracy on the part of butter producers. Provide an alternative explanation for the rising price of butter and its eventual return to the original price.

# 7

# Monopoly and Price Discrimination

The Coca-Cola Company recently built a new football scoreboard for a large state university. Now football fans can enjoy the latest in scoreboard graphics as they watch the game. In addition, Coca-Cola gave $2.3 million to remodel the university's student center, providing students with a comfortable place to meet, eat, talk, and relax.[1] What explains this outburst of apparent generosity? Does it have anything to do with the fact that Coca-Cola was recently given the exclusive right to sell beverages on campus—a monopoly? Who is really paying for the scoreboard and the student center?

**monopoly**
A market in which a single firm sells a product that does not have any close substitutes.

**market power**
The ability of a firm to affect the price of its product.

**barrier to entry**
Something that prevents firms from entering a profitable market.

**patent**
The exclusive right to sell a new good for some period of time.

**network externalities**
The value of a product to a consumer increases with the number of other consumers who use it.

**natural monopoly**
A market in which the economies of scale in production are so large that only a single large firm can earn a profit.

In the previous chapter, we explored the decisions made by firms in a perfectly competitive market, a market in which there are many firms. This chapter deals with the opposite extreme: a **monopoly**, a market in which a single firm sells a product that does not have any close substitutes. In contrast with a perfectly competitive, or price-taking, firm, a monopolist controls the price of its product, so we can refer to a monopolist as a *price maker*. A monopolist has **market power**, the ability to affect the price of its product. Of course, consumers obey the law of demand, and the higher the monopolist's price, the smaller the quantity it will sell.

A monopoly occurs when a **barrier to entry** prevents a second firm from entering a profitable market. Among the possible barriers to entry are patents, network externalities, government licensing, the ownership or control of a key resource, and large economies of scale in production:

- A **patent** grants an inventor the exclusive right to sell a new product for some period of time, currently 20 years under international rules.
- When the value of a product to a consumer increases with the number of consumers who use it, **network externalities** are at work. For example, the larger the number of people on an online chat network, the greater the opportunities for interaction. Similarly, the larger the number of people using a software application such as a word processor, the greater the opportunities to share files. Network externalities provide an advantage to existing firms and may inhibit the entry of new ones.
- Under a licensing policy, the government chooses a single firm to sell a particular product. Some examples are licensing for radio and television stations, off-street parking in cities, and vendors in national parks.
- If a firm owns or controls a key resource, the firm can prevent entry by refusing to sell the input to other firms. The classic example is DeBeers, the South African company that controls about 80 percent of the world's production of diamonds. Before the 1940s, the Aluminum Company of America—ALCOA—had long-term contracts to buy most of the world's available bauxite, a key input to the production of aluminum.
- A **natural monopoly** occurs when the scale economies in production are so large that only a single large firm can earn a profit. The market can support only one profitable firm because if a second firm entered the market, both firms would lose money. Some examples are cable TV service, electricity transmission, and water systems.

In this chapter we will discuss "unnatural" monopolies, which result from artificial barriers to entry. Later in the book, we'll explore the reasons for natural monopolies and various public policies to control them.

This chapter examines the production and pricing decisions of a monopoly and explores the implications for society as a whole. As we'll see, monopoly is inefficient from society's perspective because it produces too little output. We'll also discuss the trade-offs with patents, which lead to monopoly and higher prices but also encourage innovation. We'll also explore the issue of price discrimination, which occurs when firms such as airlines and movie theaters charge different prices to different types of consumers. Although we discuss price discrimination in a monopoly, it also happens in markets with more firms, including oligopoly (a few firms) and monopolistic competition (many firms selling differentiated products).

# 7.1 | THE MONOPOLIST'S OUTPUT DECISION

Like other firms, a monopolist must decide how much output to produce, given its objective of maximizing its profit. We learned about production costs in an earlier chapter, so we start our discussion of the monopolist's output decision with the revenue side of the profit picture. Then we show how a monopolist picks the profit-maximizing quantity.

## Total Revenue and Marginal Revenue

A firm's total revenue—the money it gets by selling its product—equals the price times the quantity sold. In this part of the chapter, we'll assume that the monopolist charges the same price to each customer. The table in Figure 7.1 shows how to use a demand schedule (in columns 1 and 2) to compute a firm's total revenue (in column 3). At a price of $16, the firm doesn't sell anything, so its total revenue is zero. To sell the first unit, the firm must cut its price to $14, so its total revenue is $14. To get consumers to buy 2 units instead of just 1, the firm must cut its price to $12, so the total revenue for selling 2 units is $24. As the price continues to drop and the quantity sold increases, total revenue increases for a while, but then starts falling. To sell 5 units instead of 4, the firm cuts its price from $8 to $6, and total revenue decreases from $32 to $30. The total revenue for selling 6 units is even lower, only $24.

The firm's marginal revenue is defined as the change in total revenue that results from selling one more unit of output. This is shown in column 4 of the table in Figure 7.1. For example, the marginal revenue for the third unit is $6, equal to the total revenue from selling 3 units ($30) minus the total revenue from selling only 2 units ($24). As shown in the table, marginal revenue is positive for the first 4 units sold. Beyond that point, selling an additional unit actually decreases total revenue, so marginal revenue is negative. For example, the marginal revenue for the fifth unit is −$2, and the marginal revenue for the sixth unit is −$6.

The table in Figure 7.1 illustrates the trade-offs faced by a monopolist in cutting the price to sell a larger quantity. When the firm cuts its price from $12 to $10, there is good news and bad news:

- **Good news:** The firm collects $10 from the new customer (the third), so revenue increases by $10.

- **Bad news:** The firm cuts the price for all its customers, so it gets less revenue from the customers who would have been willing to pay the higher price of $12. Specifically, the firm collects $2 less from each of the two original customers, so revenue from the original customers decreases by $4.

The combination of good news and bad news leads to a net increase in total revenue of only $6, equal to $10 gained from the new customer minus the $4 lost on the first two customers.

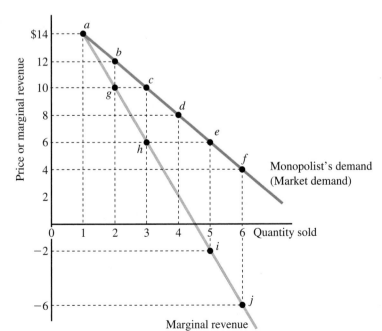

◄ **FIGURE 7.1**
**The Demand Curve and the Marginal-Revenue Curve**
Marginal revenue equals the price for the first unit sold, but is less than the price for additional units sold. To sell an additional unit, the firm cuts the price and receives less revenue on the units that could have been sold at the higher price. The marginal revenue is positive for the first 4 units, and negative for larger quantities.

| (1) Price (P) | (2) Quamtity Sold (Q) | (3) Total Revenue (TR = P × Q) | (4) Marginal Revenue (MR = Δ TR/Δ Q) |
|---|---|---|---|
| $ 16 | 0 | 0 | — |
| 14 | 1 | $14 | $14 |
| 12 | 2 | 24 | 10 |
| 10 | 3 | 30 | 6 |
| 8 | 4 | 32 | 2 |
| 6 | 5 | 30 | −2 |
| 4 | 6 | 24 | −6 |

Our discussion of good news and bad news has revealed a key feature of a monopoly: *Marginal revenue is less than price.* To sell one more unit, the monopolist must cut its price, and the difference between marginal revenue and price is the bad news—the loss in revenue from consumers who would have bought the good at the higher price. In fact, this is true for any firm that must cut its price to sell more.

You may recall from the previous chapter that marginal revenue is different for a perfectly competitive firm, which can sell as much as it wants at the market price. If a perfectly competitive firm sells one unit at $12, it can sell a second unit at the same price, so its marginal revenue is $12 for the second unit sold, just as it was $12 for the first unit sold. For a perfectly competitive firm, marginal revenue is always equal to the price, no matter how many units the firm sells. A perfectly competitive firm does not cut the price to sell more, so there is no bad news associated with selling more.

### A Formula for Marginal Revenue

We can use a simple formula to compute marginal revenue. The formula quantifies the good news and bad news from selling one more unit:

marginal revenue = new price + (slope of demand curve × old quantity)

The first part of the formula is the good news, the money received for the extra unit sold. The second part is the bad news from selling one more unit, the revenue lost by cutting the price for the original customers. The revenue change equals the price change required to sell one more unit—the slope of the demand curve, which is a negative number—times the number of original customers who get a price cut.

We can illustrate this formula with a few examples. Suppose the monopolist wants to increase the quantity sold from 2 to 3, so it cuts the price from $12 to $10. The new price is $10, the old quantity is 2 units, and the slope of the demand curve is –$2, so marginal revenue is $6:

marginal revenue = $10 – ($2 per unit × 2 units) = $6

Similarly, to sell the fifth unit, the firm would cut the price from $8 to $6, and marginal revenue is actually negative:

marginal revenue = $6 – ($2 per unit × 4 units) = –$2

Marginal revenue is negative because the $8 revenue lost from the original customers exceeds the $6 gain from the new customer. This happens because there are so many original customers who get a price cut. If a monopolist continues to cut its price, marginal revenue will eventually become negative because there will be so many consumers who get price cuts.

The graph in Figure 7.1 shows the demand curve and marginal-revenue curve for the data shown in the table. For the first unit sold, the marginal revenue equals the price. Because the firm must cut its price to sell more output, the marginal-revenue curve lies below the demand curve. For example, the demand curve shows that the firm will sell 3 units at a price of $10 (point *c*), but the marginal revenue for this quantity is only $6 (point *h*). The firm will sell 5 units at a price of $6 (point *e*), but the marginal revenue for this quantity is –$2 (point *i*). The marginal revenue is positive for the first 4 units and negative for larger quantities.

### Using the Marginal Principle

A monopolist can use the marginal principle to decide how much output to produce. Suppose a firm called Curall holds a patent on a new drug that cures the common cold, and must decide how much of the drug to produce.

# MARGINAL PRINCIPLE

Increase the level of an activity as long as its marginal benefit exceeds its marginal cost. Choose the level at which the marginal benefit equals the marginal cost.

The firm's activity is producing the cold drug, and it will pick the quantity at which the marginal revenue from selling one more dose equals the marginal cost of production.

In Figure 7.2, the first two columns of the table show the relationship between the price of the cold drug and the quantity demanded. We can use these numbers to draw the market demand curve, as shown in the graph in Figure 7.2. Because the firm is a monopolist—the only seller of the drug—the market demand curve shows how much the firm will sell at each price. The demand curve is negatively sloped, consistent with the law of demand. For example, at a price of $18 per dose, the quantity demanded is 600 doses per hour (point *f*), compared to 900 doses at a price of $15 (point *b*).

Like other monopolists, the firm must cut its price to sell a larger quantity, so marginal revenue is less than price. This is shown in the third column of the table as well as the graph. We can use the marginal-revenue formula explained earlier to compute marginal revenue for different quantities of output. The slope of the demand curve is $0.01 per dose. To simplify the arithmetic, rather than using the "new" price and "old" quantity, we can use a matched pair of price and quantities from the demand curve to get an approximation of marginal revenue. When the change in price is relatively small, for example, $0.01, the difference between the new and old price is small enough to be ignored. For example, at a price of $18, the quantity sold is 600 doses, so marginal revenue is $12:

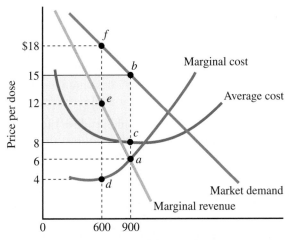

**◄ FIGURE 7.2**

**The Monopolist Picks a Quantity and a Price**

To maximize profit, the monopolist picks point *a*, where marginal revenue equals marginal cost. The monopolist produces 900 doses per hour at a price of $15 (point *b*). The average cost is $8 (point *c*), so the profit per dose is $7 (equal to the $15 price minus the $8 average cost) and the total profit is $6,300 (equal to $7 per dose times 900 doses). The profit is shown by the shaded rectangle.

| (1)<br>Price (*P*) | (2)<br>Quantity<br>Sold (*Q*) | (3)<br>Marginal<br>Revenue<br>($MR = \Delta TR/\Delta Q$) | (4)<br>Marginal<br>Cost<br>($MC = \Delta TC/\Delta Q$) | (5)<br>Total<br>Revenue<br>($TR = P \times Q$) | (6)<br>Total<br>Cost (*TC*) | (7)<br>Profit<br>($TR - TC$) |
|---|---|---|---|---|---|---|
| $18 | 600 | $12 | $4.00 | $10,800 | $5,710 | $5,090 |
| 17 | 700 | 10 | 4.60 | 11,900 | 6,140 | 5,760 |
| 16 | 800 | 8 | 5.30 | 12,800 | 6,635 | 6,165 |
| **15** | **900** | **6** | **6.00** | **13,500** | **7,200** | **6,300** |
| 14 | 1,000 | 4 | 6.70 | 14,000 | 7,835 | 6,165 |
| 13 | 1,100 | 2 | 7.80 | 14,300 | 8,560 | 5,740 |
| 12 | 1,200 | 0 | 9.00 | 14,400 | 9,400 | 5,000 |

$$\text{marginal revenue} = \$18 - (\$0.01 \times 600 \text{ doses}) = \$12$$

Similarly, at a price of $15, the quantity is 900 doses and marginal revenue is $6:

$$\text{marginal revenue} = \$15 - (\$0.01 \times 900 \text{ doses}) = \$6$$

We're ready to show how a monopolist can use the marginal principle to pick a quantity to produce. To maximize its profit, the firm will produce the quantity at which the marginal revenue equals marginal cost. As shown in the fourth row in the table in Figure 7.2, this happens with a quantity of 900 doses. In the graph, the marginal-revenue curve intersects the marginal-cost curve at point *a*, with a quantity of 900 doses, so that's the quantity that maximizes profit. To get consumers to buy this quantity, the price must be $15 (point *b* on the demand curve). The average cost of production is $8 per dose (shown by point *c*).

We can compute the firm's profit in two ways. First, profit equals total revenue minus total cost:

$$\text{profit} = \text{total revenue} - \text{total cost}$$
$$\text{profit} = \$15 \text{ per dose} \times 900 \text{ doses} - \$8 \text{ per dose} \times 900 \text{ doses} = \$6,300$$

Second, we can compute the profit per dose and multiply it by the number of doses:

$$\text{profit} = \text{profit per dose} \times \text{quantity of doses}$$

The profit per dose is the price minus the average cost: $7 = $15 − $8:

$$\text{profit} = \$7 \text{ per dose} \times 900 \text{ doses} = \$6,300$$

To show that a quantity of 900 doses maximizes the firm's profit, let's see what would happen if the firm picked some other quantity. Suppose the firm decided to produce 599 doses per hour at a price just above $18 (just above point *f* on the demand curve). Could the firm make more profit by cutting the price by enough to sell one more dose? The firm should answer two questions:

- What is the extra cost associated with producing dose number 600? As shown by point *d* on the marginal-cost curve, the marginal cost of the 600th dose is $4.
- What is the extra revenue associated with dose number 600? As shown by point *e* on the marginal-revenue curve, the marginal revenue is $12.

If the firm wants to maximize its profit, it should produce the 600th dose because the $12 extra revenue exceeds the $4 extra cost, meaning that the firm's profit will increase by $8. The same argument applies, with different numbers for marginal revenue and marginal cost, for doses 601, 602, and so on, up to 900 doses. The firm should continue to increase the quantity produced as long as the marginal revenue exceeds the marginal cost. The marginal principle is satisfied at point *a*, with a total of 900 doses.

Why should the firm stop at 900 doses? Beyond 900 doses, the marginal revenue from an additional dose will be less than the marginal cost associated with producing it. Although the firm could cut its price and sell a larger quantity, an additional dose would add less to revenue than it adds to cost, so the firm's total profit would decrease. As shown in the fifth row in the table in Figure 7.2, the firm could sell 1,000 doses at a price of $14, but the marginal revenue at this quantity is only $4, while the marginal cost at this quantity is $6.70. Producing the 1,000th dose would decrease the firm's profit by $2.70. For any quantity exceeding 900 doses, the marginal revenue is less than the marginal cost. Therefore, the firm should produce exactly 900 doses.

Let's review what we've learned about how a monopolist picks a quantity and how to compute the monopoly profit. The three-step process is as follows:

1 Find the quantity that satisfies the marginal principle, that is, the quantity at which marginal revenue equals marginal cost. In the example shown in Figure

7.2, marginal revenue equals marginal cost at point *a*, so the monopolist produces 900 doses.

**2** Using the demand curve, find the price associated with the monopolist's chosen quantity. In Figure 7.2, the price required to sell 900 doses is $15 (point *b*).

**3** Compute the monopolist's profit. The profit per unit sold equals the price minus the average cost, and the total profit equals the profit per unit times the number of units sold. In Figure 7.2, the profit is shown by the shaded rectangle, with height equal to the profit per unit sold and width equal to the number of units sold.

# 7.2 | THE CONSEQUENCES OF MONOPOLY

Why should we as a society be concerned about monopoly? Most people are not surprised to hear that a monopolist uses its market power to charge a relatively high price. If this were the end of the story, a monopolist would simply gain at the expense of consumers. As we'll see in this part of the chapter, the social consequences of monopoly go beyond a higher price: A monopolist produces less output.

## Monopoly versus Perfect Competition

How does a monopoly differ from a perfectly competitive market? To show the difference, let's consider an example of an arthritis drug that could be produced by a monopoly or a perfectly competitive industry. Let's take the long-run perspective—a period of time long enough that a firm is perfectly flexible in its choice of inputs and can enter or leave the market.

Consider the monopoly outcome first. Let's assume that the long-run average cost of producing the arthritis drug is constant at $8 per dose. As we saw in the chapter on production and cost, if average cost is constant, the marginal cost equals the average cost. In Panel A of Figure 7.3, the long-run marginal-cost curve is the same as the long-run average-cost curve. Given the demand and marginal-revenue curves in Panel A of Figure 7.3, the monopolist will maximize profit where marginal revenue equals marginal cost (point *a*), producing 200 doses per hour at a price of $18 per dose (point *b*). The monopolist's profit is $2,000 per hour—a $10 profit per dose ($18 – $8) times 200 doses.

Consider next the market for the arthritis drug under perfect competition. We're assuming that the arthritis drug industry is a constant-cost industry: Input prices do not change as the industry grows, so the long-run market supply curve is horizontal at the long-run average cost of producing the drug, which is $8 per dose.

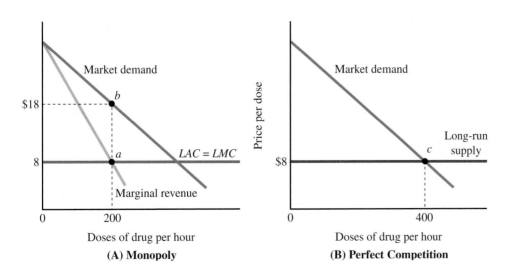

**(A) Monopoly**

**(B) Perfect Competition**

◄ **FIGURE 7.3**
**Monopoly Versus Perfect Competition: Its Effect on Price and Quantity**

**(A)** The monopolist picks the quantity at which the long-run marginal cost equals marginal revenue—200 does per hour, as shown by point *a*. As shown by point *b* on the demand curve, the price required to sell this quantity is $18 per dose.

**(B)** The long-run supply curve of a perfectly competitive, constant-cost industry intersects the demand curve at point *c*. The equilibrium price is $8, and the equilibrium quantity is 400 doses.

# APPLICATION

## ENDING THE MONOPOLY ON INTERNET REGISTRATION

What happens when a monopoly ends?

For an illustration of the consequences of monopoly, we can look at what happens when a government-sanctioned monopoly ends. In February 1999, the U.S. government announced plans to end the five-year monopoly held by Network Solutions Inc. for registering Internet addresses. Network Solutions had an exclusive government contract to register Web addresses, also known as *domain names*, ending in .net, .org, .edu, and .com. The company registered almost 2 million names in 1998, collecting $70 for each address and charging an annual renewal fee of $35. The government's plan to introduce competition had some restrictions—an entering firm had to meet strict requirements for security and backup measures and liability insurance. Two new competitors, Register.com and Tucows.com, cut prices to between $10 and $15 per year. In addition, the new firms offered longer registration periods and permitted more characters in each domain name. Network Solutions, the original monopolist, quickly matched its competitors' lower prices and expanded service options. *Related to Exercises 2.4 and 2.5.*

SOURCE: "Tucows.com to Slash Domain Name Registration Rates," *Newsbytes News Network*, January 11, 2000; "Network Solutions Offers 10-Year. Com Registrations," *Newsbytes News Network*, January 18, 2000; "Register.com Latest to Offer Long Domain Names," *Newsbytes News Network*, January 11, 2000. http://www.newsbytes.com; Accessed June 28, 2006.

In Panel B of Figure 7.3, the horizontal long-run supply curve intersects the demand curve at point *c*, with an equilibrium price of $8 and an equilibrium quantity of 400 doses per hour. Compared to a monopoly outcome, the perfectly competitive outcome has a lower price ($8 instead of $18 per dose) and a larger quantity (400 doses instead of 200).

## Rent Seeking: Using Resources to Get Monopoly Power

Another consequence of monopoly is the use of resources to acquire monopoly power. Because a monopoly is likely earn a profit, firms are willing to spend of money to persuade the government to erect barriers to entry that grant monopoly power through licenses, franchises, and tariffs. One way to get monopoly power is to hire lobbyists to persuade legislators and other policy makers to grant monopoly power. **Rent seeking** is the process of using public policy to gain economic profit. Rent seeking is inefficient because it uses resources that could be used in other ways. For example, the people employed as lobbyists could instead produce goods and services. A classic study of rent seeking by economist Richard Posner found that firms in some industries spent up to 30 percent of their total revenue to get monopoly power.[2]

At the beginning of this chapter, we saw that Coca-Cola helped a state university build a new football scoreboard and remodel its student center. Was this an act of generosity? In return for the scoreboard and the remodeled student center, Coca-Cola earned the exclusive right to sell beverages on campus. Like any monopolist, Coca-Cola will use its monopoly power to charge higher prices for beverages, so the cost of

• **rent seeking**
The process of using public policy to gain economic profit.

the scoreboard and student center actually comes out of the pockets of students. Although Coca-Cola has a monopoly on beverages, some of the profit from the monopoly goes to the university to pay for the scoreboard and the student center.

## Monopoly and Public Policy

Given the consequences of monopoly, governments use a number of policies to intervene in markets that are dominated by a single firm or could become a monopoly. We'll examine these policies later in the book. In the case of natural monopoly—a market that can support only a single firm—the government can intervene by regulating the price charged by the natural monopolist. In other markets, the government uses antitrust policies to break up monopolies into smaller companies and prevent corporate mergers that would lead to a monopoly. These policies are designed to promote competition, leading to lower prices and more production.

# 7.3 | PATENTS AND MONOPOLY POWER

One source of monopoly power is a government patent that gives a firm the exclusive right to produce a product for 20 years. As we'll see, a patent encourages innovation because the innovators know they will earn monopoly profits on a new product over the period covered by the patent. If the monopoly profits are large enough to offset the substantial research and development costs of a new product, a firm will develop the product and become a monopolist. Granting monopoly power through a patent may be efficient from the social perspective because it may encourage the development of products that would otherwise not be developed.

## Incentives for Innovation

Let's use the arthritis drug to show why a patent encourages innovation. Suppose that a firm called Flexjoint hasn't yet developed the drug, but believes the potential benefits and costs of developing the drug are as follows:

- The economic cost of research and development would be $14 million, including all of the opportunity costs of the project.
- The estimated annual economic profit from a monopoly would be $2 million (in today's dollars).
- Flexjoint's competitors will need three years to develop and produce their own versions of the drug, so if Flexjoint isn't protected by a patent, its monopoly will last only three years.

Based on these numbers, Flexjoint won't develop the drug unless the firm receives a patent that lasts at least seven years. That's the length of time the firm needs to recover the research and development costs of $14 million ($2 million per year times seven years). If there is no patent and the firm loses its monopoly in three years, it will earn a profit of $6 million, which is less than the cost of research and development. By comparison, with a 20-year patent the firm will earn $40 million, which is more than enough to recover the $14 million cost.

## Trade-Offs from Patents

Is the patent for Flexjoint's drug beneficial from the social perspective? The patent grants monopoly power to the firm, and it responds by charging a higher price and producing less than the quantity that would be produced in a perfectly competitive market. Looking back at Figure 7.3, a monopolist produces 200 doses per hour instead of 400. From society's perspective, 400 doses would be better than 200 doses, but we don't have that choice. Flexjoint won't develop the drug unless a patent protects the firm from competition for at least seven years. Therefore, society's choice is between the monopoly outcome of 200 doses or zero doses. Because a quantity of 200 doses is clearly better than none, the patent is beneficial from society's perspective.

What about a product that a firm would develop without the protection of a patent? Suppose we change the Flexjoint example by changing one number: The cost of research and development is only $5 million, not $14 million. Suppose that it still takes Flexjoint's competitors three years to develop a substitute, and Flexjoint's profit per year is still $2 million. Without a patent, Flexjoint would earn an economic profit of $6 million during its three-year monopoly ($2 million per year times three years), which is more than the $5 million cost of research and development. Therefore, the firm would develop the new drug even without a patent. In this case, a patent would merely prolong a monopoly, and so it would be inefficient from society's perspective.

What are the general conclusions about the merits of the patent system? It is sensible for a government to grant a patent for a product that would otherwise not be developed, but it is not sensible for other products. Unfortunately, no one knows in advance whether a particular product would be developed without a patent, so the government can't be selective in granting patents. In some cases, patents lead to new products, while in other cases patents merely prolong monopoly power.

# APPLICATION

## BRIBING THE MAKERS OF GENERIC DRUGS

**APPLYING THE CONCEPTS #2:** What is the value of a monopoly?

When a patent expires, new firms enter the market, and the resulting competition for consumers decreases prices and increases quantities. In the pharmaceutical drug market, when the patent for a brand-name drug expires, other firms introduce generic versions of the drug. The generics are virtually identical to the original branded drug, but they sell at a much lower price. The producers of branded drugs have an incentive to delay the introduction of generic drugs and sometimes use illegal means to do so.

In recent years, the Federal Trade Commission (FTC) has investigated allegations that the makers of branded drugs made deals with generic suppliers to keep generics off the market. The alleged practices included cash payments and exclusive licenses for new versions of the branded drug. In 2003, the FTC ruled that Schering-Plough and Upsher-Smith Laboratories entered into an illegal agreement to keep a generic version of a heart medicine off the market. Schering-Plough paid Upsher-Smith $60 million to delay the introduction of a low-price alternative to its prescription drug K-Dur-20, which is used to treat people with low potassium.

Another tactic used by the producers of branded drugs is to claim that generics are not as good as the branded drug. DuPont has claimed that generic versions of its Coumadin (a blood thinner) are not equivalent to Coumadin, and may pose risks to patients. Because generic versions are virtually identical to the branded drugs, such claims are not based on science. *Related to Exercises 3.3 and 3.4.*

SOURCE: Federal Trade Commission, "Commission Rules Schering-Plough, Upsher, and AHP Illegally Delayed Entry of Lower-Cost Generic Drug," http://www.ftc.gov/opa/2003/12/schering.htm; accessed July 9, 2006.

# 7.4 | PRICE DISCRIMINATION

Up to this point in the book, we've assumed that a firm charges the same price to all of its consumers. As we'll see in this part of the chapter, a firm may be able to divide consumers into two or more groups and sell the good at a different price to each group, a practice known as **price discrimination**. For example, airlines offer discount tickets to travelers who are flexible in their departure times, and movie theaters have lower prices for senior citizens.

• **price discrimination**
The practice of selling a good at different prices to different consumers.

Although price discrimination is widespread, it is not always possible. A firm has an opportunity for price discrimination if three conditions are met:

**1 Market power.** The firm must have some control over its price, facing a negatively sloped demand curve for its product. Although we will discuss price discrimination by a monopolist, any firm that faces a negatively sloped demand curve can charge different prices to different consumers. In fact, the only type of firm that cannot engage in price discrimination is a perfectly competitive price-taking firm. Such a firm faces a horizontal demand curve, taking the market price as given. For all other types of markets—monopoly, oligopoly, and monopolistic competition—price discrimination is possible.

**2 Different consumer groups.** Consumers must differ in their willingness to pay for the product or in their responsiveness to changes in price, as measured by the price elasticity of demand. In addition, the firm must be able to identify different groups of consumers. For example, an airline must be able to distinguish between business travelers and tourists, and a movie theater must be able to distinguish between seniors and nonseniors.

**3 Resale is not possible.** It must be impractical for one consumer to resell the product to another consumer. Airlines prohibit consumers from buying and reselling tickets. If airlines allowed consumers to sell discount tickets to each other, you could go into the business as a ticket broker, buying discount airline tickets one month ahead and then selling them to business travelers one week before the travel date. In general, the possibility of resale causes price discrimination to break down.

One approach to price discrimination is to offer a discount, a lower price to some types of consumers. The firm identifies a group of customers who are not willing to pay the regular price and then offers a discount to people in the group. Here are some examples of price discrimination with group discounts:

- **Discounts on airline tickets.** Airlines offer discount tickets to travelers who spend Saturday night away from home because they are likely to be tourists, not business travelers. The typical tourist is not willing to pay as much for air travel as the typical business traveler. Airlines also offer discount tickets to people who plan weeks ahead, because tourists plan longer ahead than business travelers.
- **Discount coupons for groceries and restaurant food**. The typical coupon-clipper is not willing to pay as much as the typical consumer.
- **Manufacturers' rebates for appliances**. A person who takes the trouble to mail a rebate form to the manufacturer is not willing to pay as much as the typical consumer.
- **Senior-citizen discounts on airline tickets, restaurant food, drugs, and entertainment.**
- **Student discounts on movies and concerts.**

The only legal restriction on price discrimination is that a firm cannot use it to drive rival firms out of business.

The challenge for a firm is to figure out which groups of consumers should get discounts. Firms can experiment with different prices and identify groups of consumers that are most sensitive to price. In September 2000, Amazon.com started charging different prices for different types of consumers. For example, consumers who used Netscape's browser paid $65 for the *Planet of the Apes* DVD, while Internet

Explorer users paid $75 for the same DVD. Prices also varied with the consumer's Internet service provider and the number of previous purchases from Amazon. An Amazon spokeswoman said that the company varied prices in a random fashion, as part of ongoing tests to see how consumers respond to price changes. In other words, it appears that Amazon was assessing the willingness to pay of different types of consumers. In principle, Amazon could use the data collected to develop systems of price discrimination, giving discounts to the most price-sensitive consumers. After widespread protests of the Amazon pricing experiments, the company stopped the practice and issued refunds to about 7,000 consumers who paid relatively high prices.

### Senior Discounts in Restaurants

Consider a restaurant whose patrons can be divided into two groups, senior citizens and others. In Figure 7.4, the demand curve for senior citizens is lower than the demand curve for other groups, reflecting the assumption that the typical senior is willing to pay less than the typical nonsenior. The lower willingness to pay could result from lower income or more time to shop for low prices.

Under a price-discrimination plan, the restaurant will simply apply the marginal principle twice, once for seniors and a second time for nonseniors. This approach is sensible, because the two groups have different demands for restaurant meals, so the restaurant should treat them differently. Panel A of Figure 7.4 shows how to pick a price for senior citizens. The marginal principle—marginal revenue equals marginal cost—is satisfied at point *a*, with 280 senior meals per day. Therefore, the appropriate price for seniors is $3, as shown by point *b* on the senior demand curve. In Panel B of Figure 7.4, the marginal principle is satisfied at point *c* for nonseniors, with 260 meals per day and a price of $6 per meal.

We know that the application of the marginal principle maximizes profit in each segment of the market. Therefore, price discrimination—with a price of $3 for seniors and a price of $6 for everyone else—maximizes the restaurant's total profit. If the restaurant were instead to charge a single price of $5 for both groups, the profit from each group would be lower, so the restaurant's total profit would be lower too.

### Price Discrimination and the Elasticity of Demand

We can use the concept of price elasticity of demand to explain why price discrimination increases the restaurant's profit. From the chapter on elasticity, we know that when demand is elastic ($E_d > 1$), there is a negative relationship between price and total revenue: When the price decreases, total revenue (price times quantity sold) increases because the percentage increase in the quantity demanded exceeds the percentage decrease in price.

Suppose the restaurant initially has a single price of $5 for both seniors and nonseniors. Compared to other consumers, senior citizens have more elastic demand for

▶ **FIGURE 7.4**

**The Marginal Principle and Price Discrimination**

To engage in price discrimination, the firm divides potential customers into two groups and applies the marginal principle twice—once for each group. Using the marginal principle, the profit-maximizing prices are $3 for seniors (point *b*) and $6 for nonseniors (point *d*).

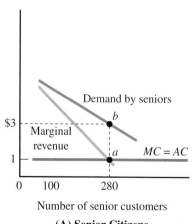

**(A) Senior Citizens**

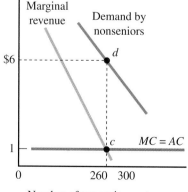

**(B) Nonseniors**

# APPLICATION

## 3

### PAYING FOR A COLD SOFT DRINK ON A HOT DAY

**APPLYING THE CONCEPTS #3:** When does a firm have an opportunity to charge different prices to different consumers?

On a hot day, are you willing to pay more than you normally would for an ice-cold can of Coke? If so, you're the type of consumer Coca-Cola Company had in mind when it developed a high-tech vending machine, complete with heat sensors and microchips, that charges a higher price when the weather is hot. According to Douglas Ivester, the head of Coca-Cola, the desire for a cold drink increases when it is hot, so "it is fair that it should be more expensive. The machine will simply make the process more automatic."

The announcement of the new vending machine led to howls of protest from consumers. In response, Coca-Cola Company said that it would not actually use the new machine, but was "exploring innovative technology and communication systems that can actually improve product availability, promotional activity, and even offer consumers an interactive experience when they purchase a soft drink from a vending machine." Based on the reaction to the news of the heat-sensing vending machine, you can imagine the "interactive experience" when a hot and thirsty consumer discovers the higher price for a cold drink on a hot day. By the beginning of 2006, Coca-Cola had not used the new vending machines.
*Related to Exercises 4.3 and 4.6.*

SOURCE: Rance Crain, "Is Thirst for Alpha Status Behind Coke's High-Tech Talk?" *Advertising Age*, vol. 70, November 22, 1999, p. 26.

restaurant meals, in part because they have lower income and more time to shop for low prices. A price cut for senior citizens brings good news and bad news for the restaurant:

- **Good news:** Demand is highly elastic, so total revenue increases by a large amount.
- **Bad news:** More meals are served, so total cost increases.

If the senior demand for meals is highly elastic, that is, $E_d$ is well above 1.0, the good news will dominate the bad news: The increase in revenue will more than offset the increase in cost. Consequently, a price cut will increase the firm's profit.

For nonseniors, the firm will have an incentive to increase the price above the initial common price of $5. Suppose nonseniors have a mildly elastic demand for meals, with $E_d$ just above 1.0. A price hike for nonseniors brings bad news on the revenue side and good news on the cost side:

- **Bad news:** Demand is mildly elastic, so total revenue decreases by a small amount.
- **Good news:** Fewer meals are served, so total cost decreases.

If the demand by nonseniors is mildly elastic, the good news will dominate the bad news: The savings in production costs will exceed the revenue loss. Consequently, the price hike for nonseniors will increase the firm's profit.

# APPLICATION

## THE PRICING OF MOVIE ADMISSION AND POPCORN

**APPLYING THE CONCEPTS #4:** When does price discrimination work?

Why do senior citizens pay less than everyone else for admission to a movie, but pay the same as everyone else for popcorn? As we've seen, a senior discount is not an act of generosity by a firm, but an act of profit maximization. Senior citizens are typically willing to pay less than other citizens for movies, so a theater divides its consumers into two groups—seniors and others—and offers a discount to seniors. This price discrimination in favor of senior citizens increases the theater's profit. Why don't theaters offer a senior discount for popcorn? Unlike admission to the theater, popcorn can be easily transferred from one customer to another. If senior citizens could buy popcorn at half the regular price, many nonseniors would get seniors to buy popcorn for them, so the theater wouldn't sell as much popcorn at the regular price, and the theater's profit would decrease. In contrast, as long as ticket takers check consumers' admissions tickets, admission to the movie is not transferable.  *Related to Exercises 4.4 and 4.7.*

# APPLICATION

## HARDBACK BOOKS ARE RELATIVELY EXPENSIVE

**APPLYING THE CONCEPTS #5:** What types of consumers pay relatively high prices?

Why is the price of the hardback edition of *The Da Vinci Code* three times the price of the paperback edition? Most books are published in two forms—hardback and paperback. Although the cost of producing a hardback book is only about 20 percent higher than producing a paperback, the hardback price is typically three times the paperback price. The hardback edition comes first, and the paperback edition is published months, or even years, later. For example, *The Da Vinci Code* by Dan Brown sold as a hardback in 2003 at a price of $25 and then three years later sold as a paperback at a price of $8. Why are hardbacks so expensive compared to paperbacks?

The key to solving this puzzle is the fact that hardback books are published first, followed by the paperback edition. Booksellers use hardbacks and paperbacks to distinguish between two types of consumers: those who are willing to pay a lot and those who are willing to pay a little. Some people are eager to read a book when it first comes out, and publishers provide them with high-price hardbacks. The more casual readers are willing to wait for the lower-priced paperback. The pricing of hardback and paperback books is another example of price discrimination, with consumers with less elastic demand paying a higher price. *Related to Exercises 4.5 and 4.8.*

# SUMMARY

In this chapter, we've seen some of the subtleties of monopolies and their pricing policies. Compared to a perfectly competitive market, a monopoly charges a higher price, produces a smaller quantity, and wastes resources in the pursuit of monopoly power. On the positive side, some of the products we use today might never have been invented without the patent system and the monopoly power it grants. Firms with market power often use price discrimination to increase their profits. Here are the main points of the chapter:

1 Compared to a perfectly competitive market, a market served by a monopolist will charge a higher price and produce a smaller quantity of output.

2 Some firms use resources to acquire monopoly power, a process known as *rent seeking*.

3 *Patents* protect innovators from competition, leading to higher prices for new products but greater incentives to develop new products.

4 To engage in *price discrimination*, a firm divides its customers into two or more groups and charges lower prices to groups with more elastic demand.

5 Price discrimination is not an act of generosity; it's an act of profit maximization.

# KEY TERMS

barrier to entry, p. 158

market power, p. 158

monopoly, p. 158

natural monopoly, p. 158

network externalities, p. 158

patent, p. 158

price discrimination, p. 167

rent seeking, p. 164

# EXERCISES

Get Ahead of the Curve

Visit www.myeconlab.com to complete these exercises online and get instant feedback.

## 7.1 | The Monopolist's Output Decision

1.1 Arrows up or down: A monopolist's marginal revenue is less than its price because to increase the quantity sold, the monopolist must _____ the price, and so the revenue from consumers who purchased the product at the higher price _____.

1.2 At a price of $18 per CD, a firm sells 60 CDs. If the slope of the demand curve is –$0.10, marginal revenue for the 61st CD is $_____. The firm should cut the price to sell one more CD if the marginal cost is less than $_____.

1.3 Arrow up or down: As the quantity produced by a monopolist increases, the gap between the marginal-revenue curve and demand curve _____.

1.4 To maximize profit, a monopolist picks the quantity at which _____ equals _____.

1.5 Arrows up or down: At a price of $18 per CD, the marginal revenue of a CD seller is $12. If the marginal cost of CDs is $9, the firm should _____ its price to _____ the quantity.

1.6 You want to determine the profit-maximizing quantity for a monopolist. You can ask the firm's accountant to draw the firm's revenue and costs curves, but each curve will cost you $1,000. From the following list, indicate which curves you will request: average total cost, average fixed cost, average variable cost, marginal cost, demand, marginal revenue.

**1.7 Textbook Pricing: Publishers Versus Authors.** Consider the problem of setting a price for a book. The marginal cost of production is constant at $20 per book. The publisher knows from experience that the slope of the demand curve is −$0.20 per textbook: Starting with a price of $44, a price cut of $0.20 will increase the quantity demanded by one textbook. For example, here are some combinations of price and quantity:

| Price per textbook | $44 | $40 | $36 | $32 | $30 |
|---|---|---|---|---|---|
| Quantity of textbooks | 80 | 100 | 120 | 140 | 150 |

    **a.** What price will the publisher choose?
    **b.** Suppose that the author receives a royalty payment equal to 10 percent of the total sales revenue from the book. If the author could choose a price, what would it be?
    **c.** Why would the publisher and the author disagree about the price for the book?
    **d.** Design an alternative author-compensation scheme under which the author and the publisher would choose the same price.

**1.8 Restaurant Pricing.** Consider a restaurant that charges $10 for all you can eat and has 30 customers at this price. The slope of the demand curve is −$0.10 per meal, and the marginal cost of providing a meal is $3. Compute the profit-maximizing price and quantity, and illustrate with a complete graph.

**1.9 Empty Seats.** Consider the Slappers, a hockey team that plays in an arena with 8,000 seats. The only cost associated with staging a hockey game is a fixed cost of $6,000: The team incurs this cost regardless of how many people attend a game. The demand curve for hockey tickets has a slope of −$0.001 per ticket ($1 divided by 1,000 tickets): Each $1 increase in price decreases the number of tickets sold by 1,000. For example, here are some combinations of price and quantity:

| Price per ticket | $4 | $5 | $6 | $7 |
|---|---|---|---|---|
| Quantity of tickets | 8,000 | 7,000 | 6,000 | 5,000 |

The owner's objective is to maximize the profit per hockey game (total revenue minus the $6,000 fixed cost).
    **a.** What single price will maximize profit?
    **b.** If the owner picks the price that maximizes profit, how many seats in the arena will be empty? Why is it rational to leave some seats empty?
    **c.** Suppose the owner could engage in price discrimination. Would you expect the number of filled seats to increase or decrease? Explain.

## 7.2 | The Consequences of Monopoly

**2.1** A monopoly is inefficient solely because the monopolist gets a profit at the expense of consumers. _____ (True/False)

**2.2** Consider the scoreboard story at the beginning of the chapter. The cost of the scoreboard built by Coca-Cola is borne by _____ because getting the monopoly causes Coca-Cola to _____.

**2.3** The average cost for providing off-street parking is $30 per space per day, and as a monopolist you could charge $35 per space per day for 200 spaces. The maximum amount that you are willing to pay for a monopoly is $_____.

**2.4** Arrows up or down: When the government ended the monopoly on registering Internet addresses, the number of firms _____, the price _____, and the number of service options _____. (Related to Application 1 on page 164.)

**2.5 Ending a Casino Monopoly.** Consider a state that initially has a single casino for gambling. Suppose the state allows a second casino to enter the market. How would you expect the entry of the second casino to affect (a) the variety of games offered in the casinos and (b) the payout (winnings) per dollar spent? (Related to Application 1 on page 164.)

**2.6 Payoff for Casino Approval.** In 1996, developers interested in building a casino in Creswell, Oregon, placed a curious announcement in the local newspaper. If local voters approved the casino, the developers promised to give citizens $2 million per year. Given an adult population of about 1,600, each adult in Creswell would receive a cash payment of $1,250 per year. Why did the developers propose this deal? Why aren't similar deals proposed for new clothing stores, music stores, or auto repair shops?

**2.7 Rules of Monopoly.** In the board game *Monopoly*, when a player gets the third deed for a group of properties (for example, the third orange property), the player doubles the rent charged on each property in the group. Similarly, a player who has a single railroad charges a rent of $25, while a player who has all four railroads charges a rent of $200 for each railroad. Are these pricing rules consistent with the analysis of monopoly in this chapter

## 7.3 | Patents and Monopoly Power

**3.1** Arrows up or down: A patent _____ the incentives to develop new products and _____ the price of the products.

**3.2** Consider the arthritis drug example on page 165. If the research and development costs are $20 million, Flexjoint will develop the drug if it gets a patent that lasts at least _____ years.

**3.3** To prolong their monopoly power, the producers of branded drugs pay millions of dollars to _____. (Related to Application 2 on page 166.)

**3.4** **Paying to Keep a Generic Out.** Suppose your firm produces a branded drug at an average cost of $2 per dose and a price of $5 per dose. You sell 1,000 doses per day. If a generic version of the drug were introduced, your daily sales would decrease to 400 doses. How much are you willing to pay each day to prevent the entry of the generic version? (Related to Application 2 on page 166.)

**3.5** **Patent for NoSmak.** A potential new drug, No-Smak, cures lip-smacking with one dose, but research and development would cost $80 million. The monopoly profit (earned while a single firm produces the product) will be $10 million per year. After a patent expires, the original developer of the drug will have sufficient brand loyalty to earn $3 million per year for another 10 years.
**a.** What is the shortest patent length required to induce a firm to develop the drug?
**b.** How would your answer to part (a) change if we ignore the profit earned after the patent expires?

## 7.4 | Price Discrimination

**4.1** Arrows up or down: Suppose a firm starts with a single price and then switches to a price-discrimination scheme. The firm will _____ the price for the group of consumers with the less elastic demand and _____ the group with the more elastic demand.

**4.2** The aspirin sold in airports is more expensive than aspirin sold in grocery stores because the demand for aspirin in airports is relatively _____.

**4.3** The rationale for charging a higher price for a soft drink on a hot day is that demand is _____ (more/less) elastic on hot days. (Related to Application 3 on page 169.)

**4.4** Senior citizens pay less than everyone else for admission to a movie, but pay the same as everyone else for popcorn because popcorn is _____, but admission is not. (Related to Application 4 on page 170.)

**4.5** The price of the hardback edition of *The Da Vinci Code* is three times the price of the paperback edition because the eager consumers who buy hardbacks have _____ (more/less) elastic demand for the book. (Related to Application 5 on page 170.)

**4.6** **Trade-Offs from a Heat-Sensing Vending Machine.** Suppose a soft-drink vending machine has a capacity of 180 cans and is filled every 10 days. The following table shows the quantities demanded on hot and cold days with different prices. The first row shows what happens with a single price of $2, and the second row shows what happens with heat-based pricing. (Related to Application 3 on page 169.)

| Price on Hot Days | Price on Cold Days | Quantity of Cans Sold on Hot Days | Quantity of Cans Sold on Cold Days | Total Quantity of Cans Demanded: 5 Hot Days, 5 Cold Days | Total Quantity of Cans Demanded: 10 Hot Days |
| --- | --- | --- | --- | --- | --- |
| $2 | $2 | 20 | 10 | 150 | 200 |
| 3 | 1 | 15 | 20 | 175 | 150 |

**a.** How does the switch to heat-based pricing affect the total quantity sold when there are 5 hot days and 5 cold days?
**b.** This occurs because the cold-weather consumers, who experience a lower price, have a _____ (more/less) elastic demand than hot-weather consumers, who experience a higher price.

**4.7** **Senior Discounts for Movies.** Your movie theater charges a single price of $6. The marginal cost of each patron is $1. A recent marketing survey revealed the following information about senior citizens and nonseniors. (Related to Application 4 on page 170.)

| | Price | Number of Patrons | Slope of Demand Curve |
| --- | --- | --- | --- |
| **Seniors** | $6 | 100 | –$0.01 per patron |
| **Nonseniors** | 6 | 80 | –0.10 per patron |

**a.** The marginal revenue for senior citizens is $_____, while the marginal revenue for nonseniors is $_____.
**b.** If your objective is to maximize profit, the marginal principle tells you to _____ the price for seniors and _____ the price for nonseniors.

**4.8** **Book Pricing and Elasticity of Demand.** A publisher initially prices both hardback books and paperback books at $20 per book. The hardback version comes out first, followed two months later by the paperback version. The publisher initially sells the same number of hardbacks and paperbacks (100 each). Each book costs $2 to produce. (Related to Application 5 on page 170.)

**a.** Complete the following table.

| | Price | Quantity | Total Revenue | Total Cost | Profit |
|---|---|---|---|---|---|
| Hardback | $20 | 100 | _____ | _____ | _____ |
| Paperback | 20 | 100 | _____ | _____ | _____ |
| Total | _____ | 200 | _____ | _____ | _____ |

**b.** The price elasticity of demand for hardback (eager) buyers is 0.50, and the price elasticity of demand for paperback (patient) buyers is 2.00. Suppose the publisher increases the price for hardbacks by 10 percent and decreases the price of paperbacks by 10 percent. Complete the following table.

| | Price | Quantity | Total Revenue | Total Cost | Profit |
|---|---|---|---|---|---|
| Hardback | $22 | _____ | _____ | _____ | _____ |
| Paperback | 18 | _____ | _____ | _____ | _____ |
| Total | _____ | | _____ | _____ | _____ |

**c.** Does price discrimination increase or decrease the publisher's profit?

**4.9 Haircuts in Mulletville.** The town of Mulletville has a single hairstylist. The marginal cost of a haircut is the same for men and women ($10). The quantity of haircuts is 100 for men and 100 for women. The profit-maximizing price for women is $35, compared to $15 for men.

**a.** What explains the price difference?

**b.** Illustrate with a complete graph.

**4.10 Tax Cuts for Discounters?** Consider the following statement from a member of a city council: "Several of the merchants in our city offer discounts to our senior citizens. These discounts obviously decrease the merchants' profits, so we should decrease the merchants' taxes to offset their losses on senior-citizen discounts." Do you agree or disagree? Explain.

**4.11 Airline Pricing.** Consider an airline that initially has a single price of $300 for all consumers. At this price, it has 120 business travelers and 80 tourists. The airline's marginal cost is $100. The slope of the business demand curve is −$2 per traveler, and the slope of the tourist demand curve is −$1 per traveler. Does the single-price policy maximize the airline's profit? If not, how should it change its prices?

# ECONOMIC EXPERIMENT

## Price Discrimination

Here is an experiment that shows how a monopolist—a museum—picks different prices for different consumer groups. Some students play the roles of consumers, and others play the roles of museum managers. Here is how the experiment works:

- The instructor picks a small group of 3 to 5 students to represent the museum. There is a fixed marginal cost of each museum patron for ticket-takers, guides, cleanup, and other tasks.

- Of the 40 consumers—potential museum patrons—half are senior citizens with senior-citizen cards. Each consumer receives a number indicating how much he or she is willing to pay for a trip to a museum.

- In each round of the experiment, each museum posts two prices: one for senior citizens and one for nonseniors. Consumers then decide whether to buy a ticket at the relevant posted price.

- A consumer's score in a particular round equals the difference between his or her willingness to pay and the amount actually paid for a museum admission.

- A museum's score equals its profit, equal to its total revenue minus its total cost. The total cost is equal to $2 times the number of patrons.

- The experiment is run for 5 rounds. At the end of the experiment, each consumer computes his or her score by adding up the consumer surpluses. The museum's score equals the sum of the profits from the 5 rounds.

## NOTES

1. Jeannie Donnelly, "OSU Beverages Will Be Provided Exclusively by Coca-Cola," *The Daily Barometer*, May 27, 1994, p. 1.

2. Richard A. Posner, "The Social Costs of Monopoly and Regulation," *Journal of Political Economy*, vol. 83, 1975, pp. 807–827.

3. Linda Rosencrance, "Amazon Charging Different Prices on Some DVDs," *Computerworld*, September 5, 2000, p. 23.

# 8

# Market Entry, Monopolistic Competition and Oligopoly

Tweeter just inherited a lot of money, enough to start her own car-stereo business. Woofer owns the only store in town selling car stereos, and he prices each stereo at $230. Woofer's average cost per stereo is $200, so he earns a profit of $30 on each one he sells. Should Tweeter use her inheritance to open her own car-stereo store? If she does, will she make a profit of $30 per stereo, just like Woofer?

Like entrepreneurs around the world, Tweeter has a difficult decision to make. Before she decides

## APPLYING THE CONCEPTS

1 How does market entry affect prices and profits?
  *Deregulation and Entry in Trucking*

2 How does brand competition within stores affect prices?
  *Name Brands Versus Store Brands*

3 What does it take to enter a market with a franchise?
  *Opening a Dunkin' Donuts Shop*

4 What signal does an expensive advertising campaign send to consumers?
  *Advertising and Movie Buzz*

5 How do firms conspire to fix prices?
  *Vitamin Inc. Gets Busted*

6 Does a low-price guarantee lead to higher or lower prices?
  *Low-Price Guarantees and Empty Promises*

7 What means—legal and illegal—do firms use to prevent other firms from entering a market?
  *Legal and Illegal Entry Deterrence*

8 When does a natural monopoly occur?
  *XM and Sirius Satellite Radio*

9 Does competition between the second- and third-largest firms matter?
  *Heinz and Beech-Nut Battle for Second Place*

10 How does a merger affect prices?
  *Xidex Recovers Its Acquisition Cost in Two Years*

whether to enter the car-stereo market, she must predict how much she would be able to charge for her car stereos and how much it would cost her to supply them. Before she enters the market, there is a $30 gap between price and average cost per stereo, but the price is likely to drop when she enters the market and begins competing with Woofer for customers. In addition, Tweeter may have a higher average cost per stereo than Woofer. If the price she can get for her stereos drops below her average cost, Tweeter will lose money and would be better off using her inheritance some other way.

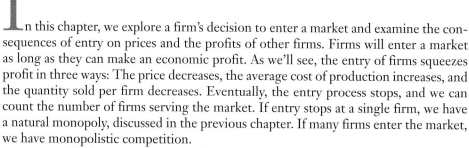

I n this chapter, we explore a firm's decision to enter a market and examine the consequences of entry on prices and the profits of other firms. Firms will enter a market as long as they can make an economic profit. As we'll see, the entry of firms squeezes profit in three ways: The price decreases, the average cost of production increases, and the quantity sold per firm decreases. Eventually, the entry process stops, and we can count the number of firms serving the market. If entry stops at a single firm, we have a natural monopoly, discussed in the previous chapter. If many firms enter the market, we have monopolistic competition.

**Monopolistic competition** is a hybrid market structure, with features of both monopoly and perfect competition. The term may seem like an oxymoron—a pair of contradictory words—similar to "virtual reality" and "books on tape." However, the term actually conveys the two key features of the market.

- **monopolistic competition**
  A market served by many firms that sell slightly different products.

- Each firm in the market produces a good that is slightly different from the goods of other firms, so each firm has a narrowly defined *monopoly*.

- The products sold by different firms in the market are close substitutes for one another, so there is intense *competition* between firms for consumers. For example, your local grocery store may stock several brands of toothbrushes with different design features. If the price of one brand increases, some loyal customers will continue to buy the brand, but others will switch to different brands that are close substitutes.

Some other examples of monopolistic competition are the markets for bread, clothing, restaurant meals, and gasoline. In each case, firms in the market sell products that are close, but not perfect, substitutes.

Later in the chapter, we look at an **oligopoly**, a market with just a few firms. Given the small number of firms in an oligopoly, the actions of one firm have a large effect on the other firms. Therefore, firms in an oligopoly act strategically. Before a firm takes a particular action, it considers the possible reactions of its rivals. We'll use **game theory**, the study of behavior in strategic situations, to discuss price fixing (conspiring to fix prices) and entry deterrence (preventing another firm from entering a market).

- **oligopoly**
  A market served by a few firms.

- **game theory**
  The study of decision making in strategic situations.

The final two parts of the chapter look at various public policies dealing with markets that are dominated by a small number of firms. We'll start with the case of natural monopoly, which occurs when the scale economies in production are so large that only a single large firm can survive. In this case, the government can intervene by regulating the price charged by the natural monopolist. Then we'll look at markets in which the government can affect the number of firms in the market by using various policies to promote competition. The government uses antitrust policies to break monopolies into several smaller companies, prevent corporate mergers that would reduce competition, and regulate business practices that tend to reduce competition.

# 8.1 | THE EFFECTS OF MARKET ENTRY

Consider a market served by a single profitable firm, a monopolist. As we saw earlier in the book, a firm in any market can use the marginal principle to decide how much output to produce.

## MARGINAL PRINCIPLE

Increase the level of an activity as long as its marginal benefit exceeds its marginal cost. Choose the level at which the marginal benefit equals the marginal cost.

Consider a firm whose activity is producing toothbrushes. On the cost side, the firm has the conventional cost curves: For small quantities produced, the average-cost

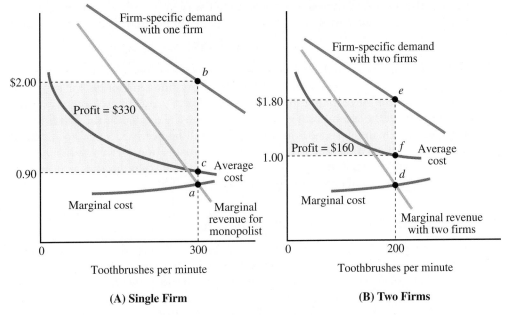

**(A) Single Firm**

**(B) Two Firms**

◄ **FIGURE 8.1**

**Market Entry Decreases Price and Squeezes Profit**

**(A)** A monopolist maximizes profit at point *a*, where marginal revenue equals marginal cost. The firm sells 300 toothbrushes at a price of $2.00 (point *b*) and an average cost of $0.90 (point *c*). The profit of $330 is shown by the shaded rectangle.

**(B)** The entry of a second firm shifts the firm-specific demand curve for the original firm to the left. The firm produces only 200 toothbrushes (point *d*) at a lower price ($1.80, shown by point *e*) and a higher average cost ($1.00, shown by point *f*). The firm's profit, shown by the shaded rectangle, shrinks to $160.

curve is negatively sloped and marginal cost is less than average cost. On the benefit side, the marginal benefit of producing toothbrushes is the marginal revenue from selling one more brush. In Panel A of Figure 8.1, if a single firm produces toothbrushes, the firm-specific demand curve (the demand curve applicable to a specific firm) is the same as the market demand curve. As we saw in the chapter on monopoly, the firm's marginal-revenue curve lies below the demand curve because a monopolist must cut its price to sell more output.

As we saw in the previous chapter, a monopolist maximizes profit by picking the quantity at which marginal revenue equals marginal cost. In Figure 8.1, this happens at point *a*, with a quantity of 300 toothbrushes. From point *b* on the demand curve, the price associated with this quantity is $2.00. From point *c* on the average-cost curve, we see that the average cost of this quantity is $0.90. The firm's profit, shown by the shaded rectangle, is $330:

$$\text{profit} = (\text{price} - \text{average cost}) \times \text{quantity} = (\$2.00 - \$0.90) \times 300 = \$330$$

Given the large profits in the toothbrush market, will a second firm enter the market?

## Entry Squeezes Profits from Three Sides

Suppose a second firm, producing a slightly different toothbrush, enters the market. When the second firm enters, the firm-specific demand curve for the original firm will shift to the left. At any particular price, some consumers will patronize the new firm, so there will be fewer consumers for the original firm: The original firm will sell fewer brushes at each price. In Panel B of Figure 8.1, the firm-specific demand curve for the original monopolist shifts to the left, and profit decreases for three reasons:

1 *The market price drops.* The marginal principle is satisfied at point *d*, so the original firm now produces 200 toothbrushes at a price of $1.80 (point *e*). The competition between the two firms causes the price to drop, from $2.00 to $1.80.

2 *The quantity produced by the first firm decreases.* The original firm produces only 200 toothbrushes, down from the 300 it produced as a monopolist.

3 *The first firm's average cost of production increases.* The decrease in the quantity produced causes the firm to move upward along its negatively sloped average-cost curve to a higher average cost per toothbrush, from $0.90 to $1.00 (point *f*).

The effects of entry are shown by comparing the profit rectangles in Panels A and B of Figure 8.1. Entry shrinks the firm's profit rectangle because it is squeezed from three directions. The top of the rectangle drops because the price decreases. The bottom of the

179

rectangle rises because the average cost increases. The right side of the rectangle moves to the left because the quantity decreases. In this example, profit drops from $330 to $160:

$$\text{profit} = (\text{price} - \text{average cost}) \times \text{quantity} = (\$1.80 - \$1.00) \times 200 = \$160$$

What about the second firm? If we assume that the second firm has access to the same production technology as the first firm and pays the same prices for its inputs, the cost curves for the second firm will be the same as the cost curves for the first firm. If the product of the second firm is nearly identical to the product as the first firm, the firm-specific demand curve for the second firm will be nearly identical to the firm-specific demand curve for the first firm. As an approximation, we can use Panel B of Figure 8.1 to represent both firms. Each firm produces 200 toothbrushes at an average cost of $1.00 per toothbrush and sells them at a price of $1.80.

## Woofer, Tweeter, and the Stereo Business

For an example of the effects of entry on price, cost, and profit, recall Tweeter's hypothetical entry decision described at the beginning of the chapter. Woofer the monopolist initially sells 10 stereos per day at a price of $230 and an average cost of $200 per stereo. Suppose that if Tweeter enters the market, the price will drop to $225 and her average cost will be $205, so she could earn a profit of $20 per stereo. Although Tweeter's entry squeezes profit from both sides—decreasing the market price and increasing the average cost—there is still some profit to be made, so she will enter the market. Of course, other firms may enter the market, so Tweeter should not count on making a $20 profit per stereo for very long.

# APPLICATION

## DEREGULATION AND ENTRY IN TRUCKING

**APPLYING THE CONCEPTS #1:** How does market entry affect prices and profits?

What happens when the government eliminates artificial barriers to entry? The Motor Carrier Act of 1980 eliminated the government's entry restrictions on the trucking industry, most of which had been in place since the 1930s. New firms entered the trucking market, and freight prices dropped by about 22 percent. The market value of a firm's trucking license indicates how much profit the firm can earn in the market. Deregulation increased competition and decreased prices and profits, and the average value of a trucking license dropped from $579,000 in 1977 to less than $15,000 in 1982.

Empirical studies of other markets provide ample evidence that entry decreases market prices and firms' profits. In other words, consumers pay less for goods and services, and firms earn lower profits. In one study of the retail pricing of tires, a market with only two tire stores had a price of $55 per tire, compared to a price of $53 in a market with three stores, $51 with four stores, and $50 with five stores. In other words, the larger the number of stores, the lower the price of tires. *Related to Exercises 1.3 and 1.5.*

SOURCES: Theodore E. Keeler, "Deregulation and Scale Economies in the U.S. Trucking Industry: An Econometric Extension of the Survivor Principle," *Journal of Law and Economics*, vol. 32, October 1989, pp. 229–253; Thomas Gale Moore, "Rail and Truck Reform—The Record So Far," *Regulation*, November–December 1988, pp. 57–62; Leonard W. Weiss, ed., *Concentration and Price* (Cambridge, MA: MIT Press, 1989); Timothy F. Bresnahan and Peter C. Reiss, "Entry and Competition in Concentrated Markets," *Journal of Political Economy*, vol. 99, October 1991, pp. 977–1009.

# APPLICATION

## NAME BRANDS VERSUS STORE BRANDS

**APPLYING THE CONCEPTS #2:** How does brand competition within stores affect prices?

In many stores, nationally advertised brands share the shelves with store brands. For example, you can buy Kellogg's Frosted Flakes or Safeway's Frosted Flakes. Similarly, Bayer Aspirin shares a shelf with Safeway Aspirin. The introduction of a store brand is a form of market entry—a new competitor for a national brand—and usually decreases the price of the national brand.

The classic example of the price effects of store brands occurred in the market for lightbulbs. In the early 1980s, the price of a four-pack of General Electric bulbs was about $3.50. The introduction of store brands at a price of $1.50 caused General Electric to cut its price to $2.00. In markets without store brands, the General Electric price remained at $3.50. Similarly, in the market for disposable diapers, increased competition from store brands caused Procter & Gamble to cut its prices by 16 percent. For a wide variety of products—laundry detergent, ready-to-eat breakfast cereals, motor oil, and aluminum foil—the entry of store brands decreased the price of national brands. *Related to Exercises 1.4 and 1.6.*

SOURCE: Robert L. Steiner, "The Nature and Benefits of National Brand/Private Label Competition," *Review of Industrial Organization*, vol. 24, no. 2 (2004), pp. 105–127.

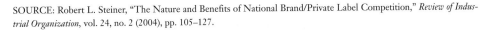

# 8.2 | MONOPOLISTIC COMPETITION

We've seen that the entry of a firm in a profitable market decreases the price and the profit per firm. Under a market structure called *monopolistic competition*, firms will continue to enter the market until economic profit is zero. Here are the features of monopolistic competition:

- *Many firms.* Because there are relatively small economies of scale, a small firm can produce its product at about the same average cost as a large firm. For example, a small donut shop can produce donuts and coffee at about the same average cost as a large shop. Because even a small firm can cover its costs, the market can support many firms.

- *A differentiated product.* Firms engage in **product differentiation**, the process used by firms to distinguish their products from the products of competing firms. A firm can distinguish its products from the products of other firms by offering a different performance level or appearance. For example, automobiles differ in horsepower and fuel efficiency, and toothpastes differ in flavor and their ability to clean teeth. Some products are differentiated by the services that come with them. For example, some stores provide informative and helpful salespeople, whereas others require consumers to make decisions on their own. Some pizza firms offer home delivery, and some software producers offer free technical assistance. As we'll see later in the chapter, some products are differentiated by where they are sold.

- *No artificial barriers to entry.* There are no patents or regulations that could prevent firms from entering the market.

These characteristics explain the logic behind the label "monopolistic competition." Product differentiation means that each firm is the sole seller of a narrowly

- **product differentiation**
  The process used by firms to distinguish their products from the products of competing firms.

defined good. For example, each firm in the toothbrush market has a unique design for its toothbrushes, so each is a monopolist in the narrowly defined market for that design. Because the products from different firms are close substitutes, there is keen competition for consumers. When one toothbrush maker increases its price, many of its consumers will switch to the similar toothbrushes produced by other firms. In other words, the demand for the product of a monopolistically competitive firm is very price elastic: An increase in price decreases the quantity demanded by a relatively large amount because consumers can easily switch to another firm selling a similar product.

## When Entry Stops: Long-Run Equilibrium

We'll use the toothbrush example to illustrate the features of monopolistic competition. The producers of toothbrushes differentiate their products with respect to color, bristle design, handle size and shape, and durability. As we saw earlier, after a second firm enters the toothbrush market, both firms still make a profit. Will a third firm enter this lucrative market? The entry of a third firm will shift the firm-specific demand curve for each firm farther to the left. As we saw earlier, a leftward shift of a firm's demand curve decreases the market price, decreases the quantity produced per firm, and increases the average cost per toothbrush. If after the third firm enters the market profit is still positive for all three firms, a fourth firm will enter.

Because there are no barriers to entering the toothbrush market, firms will continue to enter the market until each firm makes zero economic profit. Figure 8.2 shows the long-run equilibrium from the perspective of the typical firm. Suppose a total of six firms are in the toothbrush market. Given the firm-specific demand curve in a market with six firms, the typical firm satisfies the marginal principle at point *a* by selling 80 brushes per minute at a price of $1.40 (point *b*) and an average cost of $1.40. Because the price equals the average cost, the typical firm makes zero economic profit. Each firm's revenue is high enough to cover all its costs—including the opportunity cost of all its inputs—but not enough to cause additional firms to enter the market. In other words, each firm makes just enough money to stay in business.

What are the implications of market entry for the market as a whole? In Figure 8.2, each of the six firms in the market produces 80 toothbrushes at a price of $1.40, so the total quantity produced is 480. In contrast, we started with a monopoly that had a price of $2.00 and a quantity of 300 toothbrushes. In other words, market entry decreased the price from $2.00 to $1.40 and increased the total quantity demanded from 300 to 480, consistent with the law of demand.

▶ **FIGURE 8.2**
**Long-Run Equilibrium with Monopolistic Competition**
Under monopolistic competition, firms continue to enter the market until economic profit is zero. Entry shifts the firm-specific demand curve to the left. The typical firm maximizes profit at point *a*, where marginal revenue equals marginal cost. At a quantity of 80 toothbrushes, price equals average cost (shown by point *b*), so economic profit is zero.

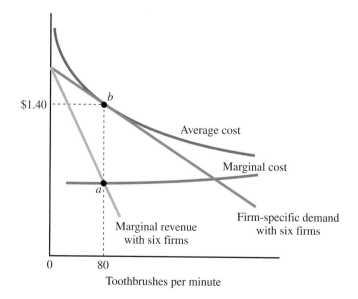

## Differentiation by Location

In some monopolistically competitive markets, differentiation is simply a matter of location. Some examples are gas stations, music stores, video stores, grocery stores, movie theaters, and ice-cream parlors. In each case, many firms sell the same product at different locations. Your city probably has several video stores, each of which sells a particular DVD at about the same price. Everything else being equal, you are likely to purchase DVDs from the most convenient store, but if a store across town offers lower prices, you might purchase your DVDs there instead. In other words, each store has a monopoly in its own neighborhood, but competes with video stores in the rest of the city.

Figure 8.3 shows the long-run equilibrium in the market for DVDs. Because there are no barriers to entering the market, new video stores will enter the market until each store makes zero economic profit. The typical video store satisfies the marginal principle at point *a*, selling 70 DVDs per hour at a price of $14 per DVD (point *b*) and an average cost of $14 per DVD. The price equals the store's average cost, so the typical store makes zero economic profit. Each store's revenue is high enough to cover all its costs—including the opportunity cost of all its inputs—but not enough to cause additional stores to enter the market. In other words, the firm makes just enough money to stay in business.

## 8.3 | TRADE-OFFS WITH ENTRY AND MONOPOLISTIC COMPETITION

We've seen that market entry leads to lower prices and a larger total quantity in the market. At the same time, entry decreases the output per firm and increases the average cost of production. As shown in Figures 8.2 and 8.3, monopolistically competitive firms operate on the negatively sloped portion of their average-cost curves, so average cost is higher than the minimum. In other words, the average cost of production would be lower if a single toothbrush firm served the entire market by providing a single type of toothbrush. What are the other consequences of entry and monopolistic competition?

## Average Cost and Variety

There are some trade-offs associated with monopolistic competition. Although the average cost of production is higher than the minimum, there is also more product variety. In a market with many toothbrush firms, consumers can choose from a wide variety

# APPLICATION

## OPENING A DUNKIN' DONUTS SHOP

**APPLYING THE CONCEPTS #3:** What does it take to enter a market with a franchise?

One way to get into a monopolistically competitive market is to get a franchise for a nationally advertised product. If you want to get into the donut market, you could pay a franchise fee of $40,000 to Allied Domecq, the parent company of Dunkin' Donuts. That gives you the right to sell donuts under the Dunkin' Donuts brand. You'll also get a few weeks training at the corporate headquarters in Massachusetts and some help in organizing a grand opening. Once you start making money, you'll pay a royalty to the parent company equal to 5.9 percent of your sales.

How much money are you likely to make in your donut shop? You will compete for donut consumers with other donut shops, bakeries, grocery stores, and coffee shops. Given the small barriers to entering the donut business, you should expect keen competition for consumers. Although your brand-name donuts will give you an edge over your competitors, remember that you must pay the franchise fee and royalties. In the monopolistically competitive donut market, you should expect to make zero economic profit, with total revenue equal to total cost. Your total cost includes the franchise fee and royalties, as well as the opportunity cost of your time and the opportunity cost of any funds you invest in the business.

Table 8.1 shows the franchise fees and royalty rates for several franchising opportunities. The fees indicate how much entrepreneurs are willing to pay for the right to sell a brand-name product. *Related to Exercises 2.4 and 2.5.*

**Table 8.1** FRANCHISING FEES AND ROYALTIES

| Brand and Product | Franchising Fee | Royalty Rate |
|---|---|---|
| Dunkin' Donuts: Coffee and donuts | $40,000 | 5.9% |
| Great Clips: Haircuts | 25,000 | 6 |
| Glass Doctor: Mobile windshield repair | 20,000 | 4 |
| Kabloom: Cut flowers | 30,000 | 4.5 |

SOURCE: entrepreneur.com, accessed May 13, 2006.

of designs, so the higher average cost is at least partly offset by greater product variety. Here are two other examples of the benefits of product variety:

- *Restaurant meals.* The typical large city has dozens of Italian restaurants, each of which has a different menu and prepares its food in different ways. Consumers can pick from restaurants offering a wide variety of menus and preparation techniques. Although a city with a single Italian restaurant would have a lower average cost of preparing Italian meals, consumers would get less variety.

- *Shoes and clothing.* Shoes are differentiated according to their style and performance. If we all wore the same type of shoes, the average cost of producing shoes would be lower, but consumers would be unable to match their shoe preferences with suitable shoes. Similarly, if we all wore uniforms, the average cost of clothing would be lower, but that would eliminate clothing choice.

What are the trade-offs when products are differentiated by location? When firms sell the same product at different locations, the larger the number of firms, the higher the average cost of production. But when firms are numerous, consumers travel shorter distances to get the product. Therefore, higher production costs are at least partly offset by lower travel costs. If a large metropolitan area had only one video store, the average cost of DVDs would be lower, but consumers would spend more time traveling to get the DVDs.

## Monopolistic Competition Versus Perfect Competition

Product differentiation is what makes monopolistic competition different from perfect competition. Perfectly competitive firms produce homogeneous products, while monopolistically competitive firms produce differentiated products. Panel A of Figure 8.4 shows the equilibrium for a perfectly competitive firm. Each price-taking firm has a horizontal demand curve. Point *a* shows the long-run equilibrium because the typical firm (1) satisfies the marginal principle, choosing the quantity where marginal revenue equals marginal cost and (2) earns zero economic profit because price equals average cost:

$$\text{price} = \text{marginal cost} = \text{average cost}$$

The only place where price equals both marginal cost *and* average cost is the minimum point of the average-cost curve, shown by point *a*.

Panel B shows the equilibrium for a monopolistically competitive firm. The firm has a differentiated product, so its demand curve is negatively sloped and marginal revenue is less than the price. With a negatively sloped demand curve, the zero-profit condition—price equals average cost—will be satisfied along the negatively sloped portion of the average-cost curve. In other words, the only place where a tangency can occur is along the negatively sloped portion of the average-cost curve. Compared to a perfectly competitive firm, a monopolistically competitive firm produces less output at a higher average cost. In Figure 8.4, the average cost for the monopolistically competitive firm is $P_2$, compared to $P_1$ for a perfectly competitive firm.

To illustrate the difference between the two market structures, imagine that product differentiation diminishes. Suppose for example that consumers decide that the distinguishing features of toothbrushes—color, shape, and bristle design—don't matter. As a result, the products of competing firms will become better substitutes, so the demand for a particular firm's product will becomes more elastic. In Panel B of Figure 8.4, the

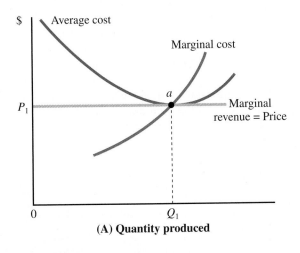

**(A) Quantity produced**

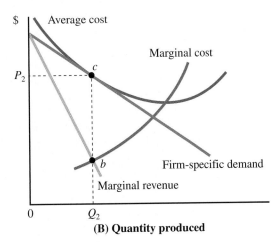

**(B) Quantity produced**

## ▲ FIGURE 8.4

**Monopolistic Competition Versus Perfect Competition**

**(A)** In a perfectly competitive market, the firm-specific demand curve is horizontal at the market price, and marginal revenue equals price. In equilibrium, price = marginal cost = average cost. The equilibrium occurs at the minimum of the average-cost curve.

**(B)** In a monopolistically competitive market, the firm-specific demand curve is negatively sloped and marginal revenue is less than price. In equilibrium, marginal revenue equals marginal cost (point *b*) and price equals average cost (point *c*).

firm-specific demand curve will become flatter and will be tangent to the average-cost curve at a larger quantity, closer to the perfectly competitive quantity $Q_1$. As differentiation continues to diminish, the firm's demand curve will become flatter and flatter, and we will get closer and closer to the perfectly competitive outcome, where the average cost reaches its minimum.

# 8.4 | ADVERTISING FOR PRODUCT DIFFERENTIATION

We've seen that product differentiation is a key feature of monopolistic competition. A firm can use advertising to inform consumers about the features of its product and thus distinguish its product from the products of other firms. In addition, advertisements can inform consumers about prices. A famous study of the eyeglass market found that advertising promoted price competition between firms and reduced eyeglass prices by about 20 percent.[1]

Some advertisements don't provide any real information about a product or its price. You've seen the advertisements of beer drinkers frolicking on the beach with attractive people, cigarette smokers riding horseback, drivers of sports cars impressing classmates at high-school reunions, and sports-drink consumers performing amazing athletic feats. These sorts of advertisements are designed to promote an image for a product, not to provide information about the product's features.

## Celebrity Endorsements and Signaling

An advertisement that doesn't provide any product information may actually help consumers make decisions. Firms spend millions of dollars to get celebrities like Tiger Woods and Paula Abdul to endorse their products. When a famous athlete or actor appears in an advertisement for a product, everyone realizes that the celebrity is doing the advertisement for money, not to share his or her enthusiasm for the advertised product. Nonetheless, these advertisements are effective in increasing sales. Why do they work?

By paying millions of dollars to run an advertisement, a firm sends a signal to consumers that the advertised product is appealing and likely to be popular. To illustrate this signaling effect, consider a firm that develops a new energy bar and picks a celebrity to endorse it. The purpose of a celebrity advertisement is to get people to try the product for the first time. After that, a consumer will base any repeat purchases on the taste and nutritional value of the energy bar. Suppose an advertisement with a cost of $10 million would cause 10 million consumers to try the energy bar. As shown in the first row of Table 8.2, energy bar A is an appealing product, and half of the consumers who try it will become repeat consumers. If the firm makes a profit of $4 on each repeat customer, the firm's profit of $20 million exceeds the $10 million cost of the advertisement, so the firm will run the advertisement.

**Table 8.2** | ADVERTISING PROFITABILITY AND SIGNALING

| Product | Number of Consumers Who Try the Product | Number of Repeat Customers | Profit per Repeat Customer | Profit from Repeat Customers | Cost of Advertisement |
|---|---|---|---|---|---|
| Energy bar A | 10 million | 5 million | $4 | $20 million | $10 million |
| Energy bar B | 10 million | 1 million | 4 | 4 million | 10 million |

# 4

# APPLICATION

## ADVERTISING AND MOVIE BUZZ

**APPLYING THE CONCEPTS #4:** What signal does an expensive advertising campaign send to consumers?

For another example of the signaling from advertising, consider movies. A movie distributor may produce several movies each year, but may advertise just a few of them. Although there are few repeat consumers for a particular movie, there is word-of-mouth advertising, also known as "buzz": People who enjoy a movie talk about it and persuade their friends and family members to see the movie. If a distributor believes that a movie will be appealing and thus generate a lot of buzz, an advertisement that gets the buzz started could pay for itself. In contrast, a distributor won't expect much buzz from a less-appealing movie, so advertising won't be sensible. In general, an expensive advertisement sends a signal that the movie will generate enough word-of-mouth advertising to cover the cost of the advertisement. *Related to Exercise 4.4.*

What about a product that is less appealing? The second row of Table 8.2 shows the effects of an advertisement for energy bar B. Only one in 10 people who try energy bar B will become a repeat customer, so the firm's profit from an advertisement is only $4 million. That is not enough to cover the $10 million cost, so the firm won't advertise the less-appealing product. Notice that celebrity endorsements for the two products are equally effective in getting people to try the products, but what matters is repeat customers. The less-appealing product gets fewer repeat customers because it's an inferior product, and that's why it's not worthwhile to pay for an advertisement.

Celebrity endorsements and other expensive advertising send a signal to consumers that the producer expects many repeat customers. Firms undertake extensive marketing research to project the sales of their products, and when their research suggests that the product will be popular, they have an incentive to spend money on advertising to send the signal to consumers. The signal tells consumers which new products are expected to have the greatest general appeal.

# 8.5 | WHAT IS AN OLIGOPOLY?

In an oligopoly, defined as a market served by a few firms, producers have market power—the power to control prices. Economists use **concentration ratios** to measure the degree of concentration in a market, computed as the percentage of the market output produced by the largest firms. For example, a four-firm concentration ratio is the percentage of total output in a market produced by the four largest firms. In Table 8.3, the four-firm concentration ratio for cigarettes is 95 percent, indicating that the largest four firms produce 95 percent of the cigarettes in the United States.

An alternative measure of market concentration is the *Herfindahl-Hirschman Index (HHI)*. It is calculated by squaring the market share of each firm in the market and then summing the resulting numbers. For example, consider a market with two firms,

• **concentration ratio**
The percentage of the market output produced by the largest firms.

| Table 8.3 | CONCENTRATION RATIOS IN SELECTED MANUFACTURING INDUSTRIES |  |  |
|---|---|---|---|

| Industry | Four-Firm Concentration Ratio (%) | Eight-Firm Concentration Ratio (%) |
|---|---|---|
| Primary copper smelting | 99 | Not available |
| House slippers | 97 | 99 |
| Guided missiles and space vehicles | 96 | 99 |
| Cigarettes | 95 | 99 |
| Soybean processing | 95 | 99 |
| Household laundry equipment | 93 | Not available |
| Breweries | 91 | 94 |
| Electric lamp bulbs | 89 | 90 |
| Military vehicles | 88 | 93 |
| Primary battery manufacturing | 87 | 99 |
| Beet sugar processing | 85 | 98 |
| Household refrigerators and freezers | 85 | 95 |
| Small arms (weapons) | 84 | 90 |
| Breakfast cereals | 82 | 93 |
| Motor vehicles and car bodies | 81 | 91 |
| Flavoring syrup | Not available | 89 |

*SOURCE:* U.S. Bureau of the Census, 2002 Economic Census, Manufacturing, *Concentration Ratios: 2002* (Washington, D.C.: U.S. Government Printing Office, 2006).

one with a 60-percent market share and a second with a 40-percent share. The HHI for the market is 5,200:

$$\text{HHI} = 60^2 + 40^2 = 3,600 + 1,600 = 5,200$$

In contrast, for a market with 10 firms, each with a 10-percent market share, the HHI is 1,000:

$$\text{HHI} = 10^2 \times 10 = 100 \times 10 = 1,000$$

According to the guidelines established by the U.S. Department of Justice in 1992, a market is "unconcentrated" if the HHI is below 1,000 and "highly concentrated" if it is above 1,800. For example, a market with five firms, each with a 20-percent market share, has a HHI of 2,000 and would be considered highly concentrated:

$$\text{HHI} = 20^2 \times 5 = 400 \times 5 = 2,000$$

An oligopoly—a market with just a few firms—occurs for three reasons:

1 *Government barriers to entry.* As we saw in Chapter 7, the government may limit the number of firms in a market by issuing patents or controlling the number of business licenses.

2 *Economies of scale in production.* A natural monopoly occurs when there are relatively large economies of scale in production, so a single firm produces for the entire market. In some cases, scale economies are not large enough to generate a natural monopoly, but are large enough to generate a natural oligopoly, with a few firms serving the entire market.

3 *Advertising campaigns.* In some markets, a firm cannot enter a market without a substantial investment in an advertising campaign. For example, the breakfast-cereal oligopoly results from the huge advertising campaigns required to get a foothold in the market. As in the case of economies of scale in production, just a few firms will enter the market.

# 8.6 | CARTEL PRICING AND THE DUOPOLISTS' DILEMMA

One of the virtues of a market economy is that firms compete with one another for customers, and this leads to lower prices and larger quantities. But in some markets, firms cooperate instead of competing with one another. Eighteenth-century economist Adam Smith recognized the possibility that firms would conspire to raise prices: "People of the same trade seldom meet together, even for merriment and diversion, but the conversation ends in a conspiracy against the public, or in some contrivance to raise prices."[2] We'll see that raising prices is not simply a matter of firms getting together and agreeing on higher prices. An agreement to raise prices is likely to break down unless the firms find some way to punish a firm that violates the agreement.

We'll use a market with two firms—a **duopoly**—to explain the key features of an oligopoly. The basic insights from a duopoly apply to oligopolies with more than two firms. Consider a duopoly in the market for air travel between two hypothetical cities. The two airlines can use prices to compete for customers, or they can cooperate and conspire to raise prices. To simplify matters—and to keep the numbers manageable— let's assume that the average cost of providing air travel is constant at $100 per passenger. As shown in Figure 8.5, the average cost is constant, which means that marginal cost equals average cost.

A **cartel** is a group of firms that act in unison, coordinating their price and quantity decisions. In our airline example, the two airlines could form a cartel and choose the monopoly price. In Figure 8.5, the firm-specific demand curve for a monopolist is the market-demand curve, and the marginal-revenue curve intersects the marginal-cost curve at a quantity of 60 passengers per day (point *a*). If the two airlines act as one, they will pick the monopoly price of $400 and split the monopoly output, so each will have 30 passengers per day. The average cost per passenger is $100, so each airline earns a daily profit of $9,000:

profit = (price – average cost) × quantity per firm = ($400 – $100) × 30 = $9,000

This is an example of **price-fixing**, an arrangement in which firms conspire to fix prices. As we'll see later in the chapter, cartels and price-fixing are illegal under U.S. antitrust laws.

• **duopoly**
A market with two firms.

• **cartel**
A group of firms that act in unison, coordinating their price and quantity decisions.

• **price-fixing**
An arrangement in which firms conspire to fix prices.

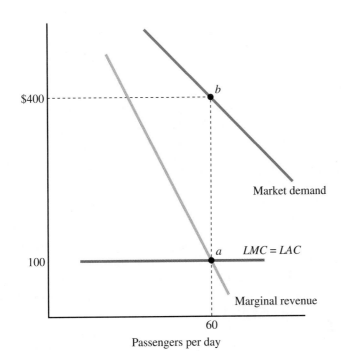

◄ **FIGURE 8.5**
**A Cartel Picks the Monopoly Quantity and Price**
The monopoly outcome is shown by point *a*, where marginal revenue equals marginal cost. The monopoly quantity is 60 passengers and the price is $400. If the firms form a cartel, the price is $400 and each firm has 30 passengers (half the monopoly quantity). The profit per passenger is $300 (equal to the $400 price minus the $100 average cost), so the profit per firm is $9,000.

► **FIGURE 8.6**
**Competing Duopolists Pick a
Lower Price**
**(A)** The typical firm maximizes profit at
point *a*, where marginal revenue equals
marginal cost. The firm has 40 passengers.
**(B)** At the market level, the duopoly outcome is shown by point *d*, with a price of
$300 and 80 passengers. The cartel out-
come, shown by point *c*, has a higher price
and a smaller total quantity.

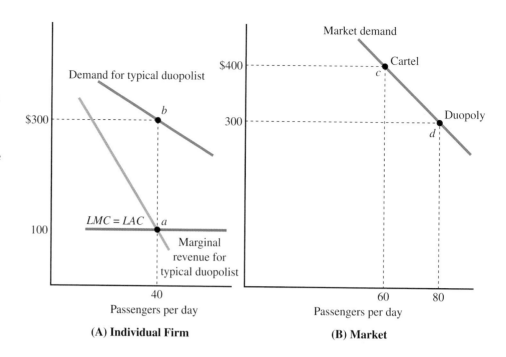

**(A) Individual Firm**    **(B) Market**

What would happen if the two firms competed rather than conspiring to fix the price? If they do, each firm will have its own demand curve. As we saw in the previous chapter, the firm-specific demand curve for the typical firm lies to the left of the market demand curve because consumers can choose from two firms. At a particular price, consumers will be divided between the two firms, so each firm will serve only part of the market. In Figure 8.6, the demand curve for the typical duopolist is below the market demand curve. For example, at a price of $300, point *d* shows that the market quantity is 80 passengers, while point *b* shows that each firm has 40 passengers.

Panel A in Figure 8.6 shows the quantity and price choice of an individual firm. Given the firm-specific demand curve and marginal-revenue curve, the marginal principle is satisfied at point *a*, where marginal revenue equals marginal cost. The firm has 40 passengers at a price of $300 (point *b*). The two firms are identical, so each has 40 passengers at a price of $300. Given an average cost of $100, each firm earns a profit of $8,000:

$$\text{profit} = (\text{price} - \text{average cost}) \times \text{quantity per firm} = (\$300 - \$100) \times 40 = \$8,000$$

## Price-Fixing and the Game Tree

Clearly, each firm will earn more profit under a price-fixing cartel, but will a cartel succeed, or will firms cheat on a cartel agreement? Game theory is the study of decision making in strategic situations. A **game tree** is a graphical representation of the consequences of different actions in a strategic setting. Each firm must choose a price for airline tickets, either the high price (the $400 cartel price) or the low price (the duopoly price of $300). Each firm can use the game tree to pick a price, knowing that the other firm is picking a price too.

Figure 8.7 shows the game tree for the price-fixing game. Let's call the managers of the airlines Jack and Jill. The game tree has three components:

- • The squares are decision nodes. Each square has a player (Jack or Jill) and a list of the player's possible actions. For example, the game starts at square *A*, where Jill has two options: high price or low price.
- • The arrows show the possible paths of the game from left to right. Jill chooses her price first, so we move from square *A* to one of Jack's decision nodes, either square *B* or square *C*. If Jill chooses the high price, we move from square *A* to square *B*. Once we reach one of Jack's decision nodes, he chooses a price—high

• **game tree**
A graphical representation of the
consequences of different actions in a
strategic setting.

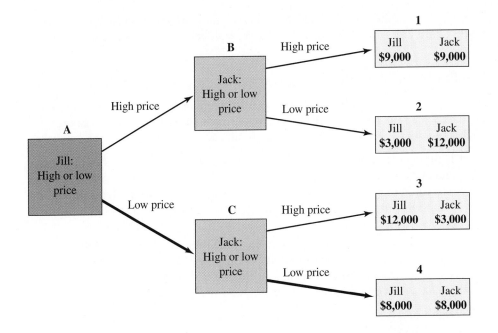

◄ FIGURE 8.7
**Game Tree for the Price-Fixing Game**
The equilibrium path of the game is square *A* to square *C* to rectangle *4*: Each firm picks the low price and earns a profit of $8,000. The duopolists' dilemma is that each firm would make more profit if both picked the high price, but both firms pick the low price.

or low—and then we move to one of the rectangles. For example, if Jack chooses the high price too, we move from square *B* to rectangle 1.

• The rectangles show the profits for the two firms. When we reach a rectangle, the game is over, and the players receive the profits shown in the rectangle. There is a profit rectangle for each of the four possible outcomes of the price-fixing game.

We've already computed the profits for two payoff rectangles. Rectangle 1 shows what happens when each firm chooses the high price. This is the cartel or price-fixing outcome, with each firm earning $9,000. Rectangle 4 shows what happens when each firm chooses the low price. This is the duopoly outcome, when firms compete and each firm earns a profit of $8,000.

What would happen if the two firms chose different prices? If Jill chooses the high price and Jack chooses the low price, Jack will capture a large share of the market and gain at Jill's expense. In the first column of Table 8.4, Jill charges the high price and has only 10 passengers at a price of $400, so her profit is $3,000:

$$\text{profit} = (\text{price} - \text{average cost}) \times \text{quantity per firm} = (\$400 - \$100) \times 10 = \$3,000$$

In the second column, Jack charges the low price and has 60 passengers at a price of $300 so his profit is $12,000:

$$\text{profit} = (\text{price} - \text{average cost}) \times \text{quantity per firm} = (\$300 - \$100) \times 60 = \$12,000$$

This is shown by rectangle 2 in Figure 8.7: The path of the game is square *A* to square *B* to rectangle 2. The other underpricing outcome is shown by rectangle 3. In this

**Table 8.4** DUOPOLISTS' PROFITS WHEN THEY CHOOSE DIFFERENT PRICES

|  | Jill: High Price | Jack: Low Price |
| --- | --- | --- |
| Price | $400 | $300 |
| Average cost | $100 | $100 |
| Profit per passenger | $300 | $200 |
| Number of passengers | 10 | 60 |
| Profit | $3,000 | $12,000 |

case, Jill chooses the low price and Jack chooses the high price, so Jill gains at Jack's expense. The roles are reversed, and so are the numbers in the profit rectangle.

## Equilibrium of the Price-Fixing Game

We can predict the equilibrium of the price-fixing game by a process of elimination. We'll eliminate the rectangles that would require one or both firms to act irrationally, leaving us with the rectangle showing the equilibrium of the game:

- If Jill chooses the high price, we'll move along the upper branches of the tree and eventually reach rectangle 1 or 2, depending on what Jack does. Although Jill would like Jack to choose the high price, too, this would be irrational for Jack. He can earn $12,000 profit by choosing the low price, compared to $9,000 with the high price. Therefore, we can eliminate rectangle 1.

- If Jill chooses the low price, we'll move along the lower branches of the tree and eventually reach rectangle 3 or 4, depending on Jack's choice. Jack won't choose the high price because he can earn $8,000 with the low price, compared to $3,000 with the high price. Therefore, we can eliminate rectangle 3.

We've eliminated the two profit rectangles that involve a high price for Jack—rectangles 1 and 3. That means that the low price is a **dominant strategy** for Jack: Regardless of what Jill does, Jack's best choice is the low price.

Two profit rectangles are left—2 and 4—and Jill's action will determine which rectangle is the equilibrium. Jill knows that Jack will choose the low price regardless of what she does. She could choose the high price and allow Jack to capture most of the market, leaving her with a profit of only $3,000 in rectangle 2. A better choice is to pick the low price and get a profit of $8,000 in rectangle 4. In other words, it would be irrational for Jill to allow herself to be underpriced, so the outcome of the game is shown by profit rectangle 4: Each player chooses the low price. The thick arrows show the equilibrium path of the game, from square *A* to square *C* to rectangle 4.

Both firms will be unhappy with this equilibrium because each could earn a higher profit with rectangle 1. To get there, however, each firm must choose the high price. The **duopolists' dilemma** is that although both firms would be better off if they both chose the high price, each firm chooses the low price. The dilemma occurs because there is a big payoff from underpricing the other firm and a big penalty from being underpriced, so both firms pick the low price. As we'll see later in the chapter, to avoid the dilemma the firms must find some way to prevent underpricing.

## Nash Equilibrium

We have used a game tree to find the equilibrium in a price-fixing game. It is an equilibrium in the sense that each player (firm) is doing the best he or she can, given the actions of another player. The label for such an equilibrium is **Nash equilibrium**. This concept is named after John Nash, the recipient of the 1994 Nobel Prize in economics, who developed his equilibrium concept as a 21-year-old graduate student at Princeton University. His life story, which includes a 25-year bout with schizophrenia and a dramatic recovery, is chronicled in the book *A Beautiful Mind*, later made into a movie starring Russell Crowe as John Nash.[3]

In the price-fixing game, the Nash equilibrium is for both firms to pick the low price. Each firm is doing the best it can, given the action of the other firm:

- If Jill picks the low price, Jack's best action is to pick the low price.
- If Jack picks the low price, Jill's best action is to pick the low price.

What about the other potential outcomes? Consider first the possibility that both firms pick the high price. This is not a Nash equilibrium because neither firm is doing the best it can, given the action of the other firm:

---

**• dominant strategy**
An action that is the best choice for a player, no matter what the other player does.

**• duopolists' dilemma**
A situation in which both firms in a market would be better off if both chose the high price, but each chooses the low price.

**• Nash equilibrium**
An outcome of a game in which each player is doing the best he or she can, given the action of the other players.

- If Jill picks the high price, Jack's best action is to pick the low price.
- If Jack picks the high price, Jill's best action is to pick the low price.

Consider next the possibility that Jill picks the low price and Jack picks the high price. This is not a Nash equilibrium because Jack is not doing the best he can, given Jill's choice:

- If Jill picks the low price, Jack's best action is to pick the low price.

The concept of the Nash equilibrium has been applied to a wide variety of decisions. Later in the chapter, we will use it to predict the outcome of games involving entry deterrence and advertising. In addition to strategic decisions for firms, it has been used to analyze the nuclear arms race, terrorism, evolutionary biology, art auctions, environmental policy, and urban development.

5

# APPLICATION

## VITAMIN INC. GETS BUSTED

**APPLYING THE CONCEPTS #5:** How do firms conspire to fix prices?

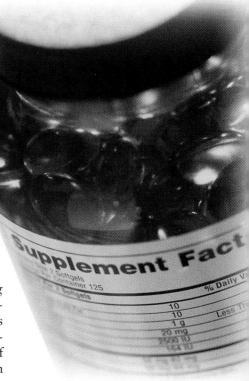

In April 2000, four former executives of drug companies pled guilty to conspiring to fix the prices of bulk vitamins worldwide. It was the largest price-fixing case in U.S. history. The leading companies involved in the illegal cartel were Hoffman-La Roche (with 60 percent of the U.S. vitamin market), BASF AG (28 percent), and Rhone-Poulenc (7 percent). They were joined by other vitamin producers from Japan, Switzerland, and Canada. The announcement brought the number of Swiss and German executives imprisoned for the case to six, with fines for the individual executives and their companies totaling $1 billion.

For almost a decade, these executives conspired to stifle competition around the globe by fixing prices on vitamins A, B2, B5, C, E, and beta carotene. The executives called their group "Vitamin Inc." and met regularly in hotel rooms to carve up the market. Market shares for each region were specified down to a half percentage point, and prices for each vitamin were agreed upon down to the penny. For vitamin "premixes" (used for livestock feed and human food such as breakfast cereals), the executives rigged the bidding process for contracts, specifying a price and designating a "winner" for each contract. To help prevent cheating, they had "budget meetings" to check each other's data on sales and market shares. The cartel managed to boost the prices of vitamins, with markups averaging about 20 percent, or even more at the high-end of the vitamin price range. For example, the price of vitamin A nearly doubled, from about $12 per pound to $20.

Hoffman-La Roche ultimately paid a fine of $500 million, about half of its annual revenue from its vitamin business in the United States. BASF AG paid a fine of $225 million. Rhone-Poulenc broke ranks early in the investigation, and by cooperating with U.S. Justice Department investigators the firm avoided any fines. A group of Japanese companies paid a total of $137 million.

*Related to Exercises 6.8 and 6.9.*

SOURCE: David Barboza, "Tearing Down the Facade of 'Vitamin Inc.'" *New York Times*, October 10, 1999, Section 3, p. 1; Department of Justice, "Four Foreign Executives of Leading European Vitamin Firms Agree to Plead Guilty to Participating in International Vitamin Cartel," Press Release, April 6, 2000.

# $8.7$ | OVERCOMING THE DUOPOLISTS' DILEMMA

The duopolists' dilemma occurs because the two firms are unable to coordinate their pricing decisions and act as one. Each firm has an incentive to underprice the other firm because the low-price firm will capture a larger share of the market and earn a larger profit. The dilemma can be avoided in two ways: low-price guarantees, and repetition of the pricing game, with retaliation for underpricing.

## Low-Price Guarantees

The duopolists' dilemma occurs because the payoff from underpricing the other firm is too lucrative to miss. To eliminate the possibility for underpricing, one firm can guarantee that it will match a lower price of a competitor. Suppose Jill places the following advertisement in the local newspaper:

> If you buy an airline ticket from me and then discover that Jack offers the same trip at a lower price, I will pay you the price difference. If I charge you $400 and Jack's price is only $300, I will pay you $100.

• **low-price guarantee**
A promise to match a lower price of a competitor.

Jill's **low-price guarantee** is a credible promise because she announces it in the newspaper. Suppose Jack makes a similar commitment to match a lower price from Jill.

Figure 8.8 shows the effect of low-price guarantees on the game tree. Jill now has two decision nodes. As before, she starts the game in square *A*. If Jill picks the high price and then Jack picks the high price, we end up at rectangle 1, as before. But if Jill picks the high price and Jack picks the low price, we get to square *D*. Jill will issue a refund of $100 to each of her consumers. In effect, she has retroactively chosen the low price, and payoff rectangle 2 is the duopoly outcome, with both firms picking the low price. For the lower half of the game tree, recall that Jack has committed to match a lower price by Jill, so the old payoff rectangle 3 disappears, leaving us with rectangle 4, where both firms choose the low price and get the duopoly profit.

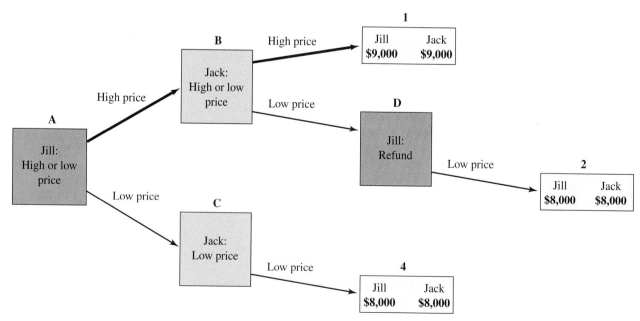

▲ **FIGURE 8.8**

**Low-Price Guarantees Increase Prices**

When both firms have a low-price guarantee, it is impossible for one firm to underprice the other. The only possible outcomes are a pair of high prices (rectangle 1) or a pair of low prices (rectangles 2 or 4). The equilibrium path of the game is square A to square B to rectangle 1. Each firm picks the high price and earns a profit of $9,000.

# APPLICATION

## LOW-PRICE GUARANTEES AND EMPTY PROMISES

**APPLYING THE CONCEPTS #6:** Does a low-price guarantee lead to higher or lower prices?

If you shop around for a new car stereo, you'll notice that most sellers have a low-price guarantee. If you buy a stereo from firm A and later discover that firm B sells the same stereo at a lower price, firm A will pay you the difference in price. The guarantee typically excludes discontinued and closeout products, and the other store must be an authorized dealer of the product you bought. Will the low-price guarantee lead to lower prices? As we've seen, a low-price guarantee eliminates the possibility that one firm will underprice the other and, thus leads to high prices.

To most people, the notion that a low-price guarantee leads to higher prices is surprising. After all, if firm A promises to give refunds if its price exceeds firm B's price, we might expect firm A to keep its price low to avoid handing out a lot of refunds. In fact, firm A doesn't have to worry about giving refunds because firm B will also choose the high price. In other words, the promise to issue refunds is an *empty* promise. Although consumers might think that a low-price guarantee will protect them from high prices, it means that consumers are more likely to pay the high price. *Related to Exercises 7.5 and 7.6.*

The thick arrows show the path of the game with low-price guarantees. Consider Jack's decision first:

- If Jill picks the high price, Jack chooses between payoff rectangles 1 and 2, a pair of high prices or a pair of low prices. His profit is higher at $9,000 with a pair of high prices (rectangle 1), so if Jill picks the high price, he will, too.
- If Jill picks the low price, Jack is committed to the low price, too.

Consider Jill's decision. She knows that Jack will match her price—either high or low—meaning that she chooses between profit rectangles 1 and 4. Profit is higher with rectangle 1, so she will pick the high price.

The low-price guarantee eliminates the possibility of underpricing, so it eliminates the duopolists' dilemma and promotes cartel pricing. The firms don't have to create a formal cartel to get the benefits from cartel pricing. The motto of a low-price guarantee is "Low for one means low for all," so both firms charge the high price. Once the possibility of underpricing has been eliminated, the duopoly will be replaced by an informal cartel, with each firm picking the price that would be picked by a monopolist.

## Repeated Pricing Games with Retaliation for Underpricing

Up to this point, we've assumed that the price-fixing game is played only once. Each firm chooses a price and keeps that price for the lifetime of the firm. What happens when two firms play the game repeatedly, picking prices over an extended period of

● **grim-trigger strategy**
A strategy where a firm responds to underpricing by choosing a price so low that each firm makes zero economic profit.

● **tit-for-tat**
A strategy where one firm chooses whatever price the other firm chose in the preceding period.

time? We'll see that repetition makes price-fixing more likely because firms can punish a firm that cheats on a price-fixing agreement, whether it's formal or informal.

Firms use several strategies to maintain a price-fixing agreement. Continuing our airline example, suppose Jack and Jill pick their prices at the beginning of each month. Jill chooses the cartel price for the first month and will continue to choose the cartel price as long as Jack does too. Jill could use one of the following strategies to punish Jack if he underprices her:

**1** *A duopoly pricing strategy.* Jill chooses the lower duopoly price for the remaining lifetime of her firm. Once Jill is underpriced, she abandons the idea of cartel pricing and accepts the duopoly outcome, which is less profitable than the cartel outcome but more profitable than being underpriced by the other firm.

**2** *A grim-trigger strategy.* When Jack underprices Jill, she responds by dropping her price to a level at which each firm will make zero economic profit. This is called the **grim-trigger strategy**, because grim consequences are triggered by Jack's underpricing.

**3** *A tit-for-tat strategy.* Starting in the second month, Jill chooses whatever price Jack chose the preceding month. This is the **tit-for-tat** strategy—one firm chooses whatever price the other firm chose in the preceding period. As long as Jack chooses the cartel price, the cartel arrangement will persist. But if Jack underprices Jill, the cartel will break down.

Figure 8.9 shows how a tit-for-tat system works. Jack underprices Jill in the second month, so Jill chooses the low price for the third month, resulting in the duopoly outcome. To restore the cartel outcome, Jack must eventually choose the high price, allowing Jill to underprice him for one month. This happens in the fourth month, and the cartel is restored in the fifth month. Although Jack can gain at Jill's expense in the second month, if he wants to restore cartel pricing, he must allow her to gain at his expense during some other month. Under a tit-for-tat strategy, a duopolist does exactly what his or her rival did the last round. This encourages firms to cooperate rather than compete. Several studies have shown that a tit-for-tat strategy is the most effective strategy to promote cooperation.[4]

These three pricing schemes promote cartel pricing by penalizing the firm that underprices the other firm. To decide whether to underprice Jill, Jack must weigh the short-term benefit against the long-term cost:

- The short-term benefit is the increase in profit in the current period. If Jack underprices Jill, he can increase his profit from the cartel profit of $9,000 to the $12,000 earned by a firm that underprices the other firm. Therefore, the short-term benefit of underpricing is $3,000.

- The long-term cost is the loss of profit in later periods. Jill will respond to Jack's underpricing by cutting her price, and this decreases Jack's profit. For example, if Jill retaliates with the duopoly price, Jack's future profit will be $8,000 per day

▶ **FIGURE 8.9**
**A Tit-for-Tat Pricing Strategy**
Under tit-for-tat retaliation, the first firm (Jill, the square) chooses whatever price the second firm (Jack, the circle) chose the preceding month.

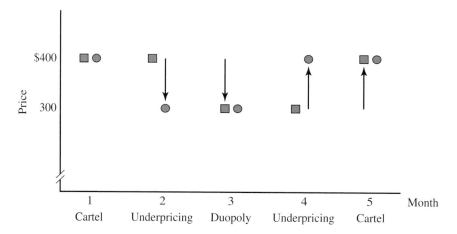

instead of the $9,000 he could have earned by going along with the cartel price. The cost of underpricing is the daily loss of $1,000 in profit.

If the two firms expect to share the market for a long time, the long-term cost of underpricing will exceed the short-term benefit, so underpricing is less likely. The threat of punishment makes it easier to resist the temptation to cheat on the cartel.

## Price-Fixing and the Law

Under the Sherman Antitrust Act of 1890 and subsequent legislation, explicit price-fixing is illegal. It is illegal for firms to discuss pricing strategies or methods of punishing a firm that underprices other firms. In one of the early price-fixing cases (*Addyston Pipe*, 1899), six manufacturers of cast-iron pipe met to fix prices. Several months after the Supreme Court ruled that their cartel pricing was illegal, the firms merged into a single firm, so instead of acting like a monopolist, they became a monopolist. Here are some other examples of price-fixing:

1 *Electric generators (1961).* Executives from General Electric and Westinghouse were convicted of fixing prices for electrical generators, resulting in fines of over $2 million and imprisonment or probation for 30 corporate executives.

2 *Infant formula (1993).* The three major U.S. producers of infant formula—Abbott Labs, Mead Johnson, and American Home Products—which together served 95 percent of the market, paid a total of $200 million to wholesalers and retailers to settle lawsuits claiming that they had conspired to fix prices.

3 *Carton-board pricing in Europe (1994).* The European Union Commission fined 19 manufacturers of carton board a total of 132 million euros ($165 million) for operating a cartel that fixed prices at secret meetings in luxury Zurich hotels.

4 *Food additives (1996).* An employee of Archer Daniels Midland (ADM), a huge food company, provided audio and videotapes of ADM executives conspiring to fix prices. ADM pleaded guilty to the charges of price-fixing and was fined $100 million.

5 *Music distribution (2000).* In exchange for advertising subsidies, music retailers agreed to adhere to the minimum advertised prices (MAP) specified by distributors. Any retailer that advertised a CD for less than the MAP would lose all of its "cooperative advertising" funds from the distributor. In May 2000, the Federal Trade Commission reached an agreement with music distributors to end the MAP scheme. The FTC estimated that the MAP scheme imposed an annual cost of $160 million on U.S. music consumers.[5]

## 8.8 | THE INSECURE MONOPOLIST AND ENTRY DETERRENCE

We've seen what happens when two duopolists try to act as one, fixing the price at the monopoly level. Consider next how a monopolist might try to prevent a second firm from entering its market. We will use some of the numbers from our airline example, although we will look at a different city with a different cast of characters.

Suppose that Mona initially has a secure monopoly in the market for air travel between two cities. When there is no threat of entry, Mona uses the marginal principle (marginal revenue equals marginal cost) to pick a quantity and a price. In Figure 8.10, we start at point *c* on the market demand curve, with a quantity of 60 passengers per day and a price of $400 per passenger. Her profit is $18,000:

profit = (price − average cost) × quantity per firm = ($400 − $100) × 60 = $18,000

If Mona discovers that a second airline is thinking about entering the market, what will she do? Now that her monopoly is insecure, she has two options: She can be passive and allow the second airline to enter the market, or she can try to prevent the other firm from entering the market.

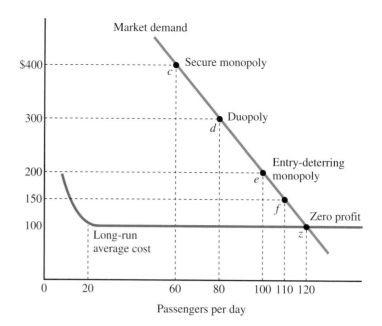

## The Passive Approach

The passive approach will lead to the duopoly outcome we saw earlier in the chapter. In Figure 8.10, if the second firm enters the market, we move downward along the market demand curve from point *c* to point *d*. In a duopoly, each firm charges a price of $300 and serves 40 passengers, half the total quantity demanded at a price of $300. For each duopolist, the daily profit is $8,000:

$$\text{profit} = (\text{price} - \text{average cost}) \times \text{quantity per firm} = (\$300 - \$100) \times 40 = \$8,000$$

## Entry Deterrence and Limit Pricing

The second option is to take actions to prevent the second firm from entering the market. To decide whether to deter the entry of the other firm, Mona must answer two questions:

- What must she do to deter entry?
- Given what she must do to deter entry, is deterrence more profitable than being passive and sharing the market with the second firm?

To prevent the second firm from entering the market, Mona must commit herself to serving a large number of passengers. If she commits to a large passenger load, there won't be enough passengers left for a potential entrant to make a profit. Suppose there are economies of scale in providing air travel, and the minimum entry quantity is 20 passengers per day: That is, it would be impractical for a firm to serve fewer than 20 passengers. In Figure 8.10, the long-run average cost curve is negatively sloped for relatively low levels of output, and the average cost for the minimum entry quantity of 20 passengers is just over $100, say $101.

Mona must compute the quantity of output that is just large enough to prevent the second firm from entering the market. In Figure 8.10, point *z* shows the point of zero economic profit in the market: If the two firms serve a total of 120 passengers per day and split the market equally, with 60 passengers each, the price ($100) equals average cost, so each firm would earn zero economic profit. The quantity required to prevent the entry of the second firm is computed as follows:

$$\text{deterring quantity} = \text{zero profit quantity} - \text{minimum entry quantity}$$
$$100 = 120 - 20$$

If Mona commits to serve 100 passengers and a second firm were to enter with the minimum quantity of 20 passengers, the price would drop to $100. Mona, with an average cost of $100 to serve 100 passengers, would break even. The second firm, with an average cost just above $100, would lose money. Specifically, if the average cost of 20 passengers is $101, the second firm would lose $1 per passenger, or $20 in total.

It's important to note that Mona cannot simply announce that she will serve 100 passengers. She must take actions that ensure that her most profitable output is in fact 100 passengers. In other words, she must commit to 100 passengers. She could commit to the larger passenger load by purchasing a large fleet of airplanes and signing labor contracts that require her to hire a large workforce.

Which is more profitable, entry deterrence or the passive duopoly outcome? The deterrence strategy, shown by point $e$ in Figure 8.10, generates a price of $200 and a profit of $10,000:

$$\text{profit} = (\text{price} - \text{average cost}) \times \text{quantity per firm} = (\$200 - \$100) \times 100 = \$10,000$$

This is larger than the $8,000 profit under the passive approach, so deterrence is the best strategy.

Figure 8.11 uses a game tree to represent the entry-deterrence game. Mona makes the first move, and she considers the consequences of her two options:

- If Mona is passive and commits to serve only 40 passengers, we reach the upper branch of the game tree. The best response for Doug, the manager of the second firm, is to enter to earn a profit of $8,000, as shown by rectangle 1.

- If Mona commits to serve 100 passengers, we reach the lower branch of the game tree. If Doug enters with the minimum entry quantity of 20 passengers, his average cost will be $101, which exceeds the market price of $100. Therefore, the best response is to stay out of the market and avoid losing money.

Mona can choose between rectangles 1 and 4. Mona's profit is higher in rectangle 4, so that's the equilibrium. The equilibrium path of the game is square $A$ to square $C$ to rectangle 4.

Mona's entry-deterrence strategy generates a market price of $200, which is less than the $400 price charged by a secure monopolist and less than the $300 price with two competing firms. Mona can keep the second firm out of the market, but only by producing a large quantity and charging a relatively low price. This is known as **limit pricing**: To prevent a firm from entering the market, the firm reduces its price.

• **limit pricing**
The strategy of reducing the price to deter entry.

◄ **FIGURE 8.11**
**Game Tree for the Entry-Deterrence Game**
The path of the game is square $A$ to square $C$ to rectangle 4. Mona commits to the entry-deterring quantity of 100, so Doug stays out of the market. Mona' profit of $10,000 is less than the monopoly profit but more than the duopoly profit of $8,000.

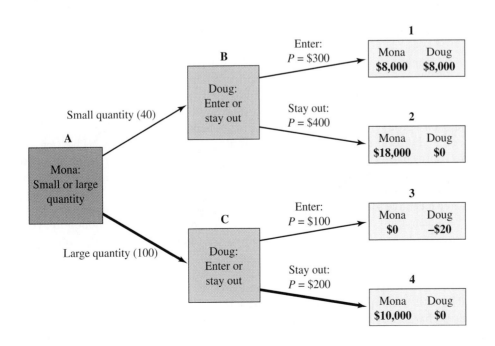

# APPLICATION

## LEGAL AND ILLEGAL ENTRY DETERRENCE

**APPLYING THE CONCEPTS #7:** What means—legal and illegal—do firms use to prevent other firms from entering a market?

When firms use limit pricing to prevent other firms from entering the market, entry deterrence is legal. For example, between 1893 and 1940, the Aluminum Company of America (Alcoa) had a monopoly on aluminum production in the United States. During this period, Alcoa kept other firms out of the market by producing a large quantity and keeping its price relatively low. Although a higher price would have generated more profit in the short run, the entry of other firms would have eventually reduced Alcoa's profit.

In recent years, the European Commission has uncovered many examples of entry deterrence that are illegal under the rules of the European Union. Van den Bergh Foods, a subsidiary of Unilever, held a dominant position in the market for ice cream in Ireland in 1998. The company provided "free" freezer cabinets to retailers, under the condition that the cabinets were to be used exclusively for the storage of Unilever's products. Irish retailers were reluctant to replace Unilever cabinets, so 40 percent of retailers sold only Unilever ice-cream products. The Commission concluded that this practice constituted an abuse of Unilever's dominant position. In 2003, the European Court of First Instance ordered Unilever to share the freezer cabinets with its competitors, including the Mars Company, which had argued that it was unable to sell its ice cream in many retail outlets in Ireland. *Related to Exercise 8.7.*

SOURCES: Leonard W. Weiss, *Economics and American Industry* (New York: Wiley, 1963), pp. 189–204; European Commission, *Report on Competition Policy 1998*, pp. 35–39.

## Examples: Microsoft Windows and Campus Bookstores

For an example of limit pricing, consider the pricing of the Windows operating system by Microsoft. The Windows operating system runs about 90 percent of the world's personal computers, so it is natural to think that Microsoft has a monopoly in the market for operating systems. According to economist Richard Schmalensee, Microsoft's profit-maximizing monopoly price is between $900 and $2,000. That's the amount Microsoft would charge if it acted like a secure monopolist.[6] The fact that Microsoft charges only $99 for Windows suggests that Microsoft is an insecure monopolist, and that it picks a lower price to discourage entry and preserve its monopoly. If Microsoft charged $2,000 for its operating system, there would be a greater incentive for other firms to develop competing operating systems.

We can apply the notion of entry deterrence to your favorite monopoly: your campus bookstore. On most college campuses, the campus bookstore has a monopoly on the sale of textbooks. Other organizations are prohibited, usually by the state government or the college, from selling textbooks on campus. The recent growth of Internet commerce has given students another option: Order textbooks over the Web and have them shipped by mail, UPS, FedEx, or Airborne Express. Several Web booksellers charge less than the campus bookstore, and the growth of Web book sales threatens the campus bookstore monopoly. If your campus bookstore suddenly feels insecure about its monopoly position, it could cut its prices to prevent Web booksellers from capturing too many of its customers. If it does this, you will pay lower prices even if you don't patronize the Web seller.

## Entry Deterrence and Contestable Markets

We've seen that an insecure monopolist may cut its price to prevent a second firm from entering the market. The same logic applies to a market that has a few firms and could potentially have many firms. The mere existence of a monopoly or oligopoly does not necessarily generate high prices and large profits. To protect its market share, an oligopolist may act like a firm in a market with many firms, leading to relatively low prices.

The threat of entry faced by an insecure monopolist underlies the theory of market contestability. A **contestable market** is a market with low entry and exit costs. The few firms in a contestable market will be threatened constantly by the entry of new firms, so prices and profits will be relatively low. In the extreme case of perfect contestability, firms can enter and exit a market at zero cost. In this case, the price will be the same as the price that would occur in a competitive market. Although few markets are perfectly contestable, many markets are contestable to a certain degree, and the threat of entry tends to decrease prices and profits.

• **contestable market**
A market with low entry and exit costs.

## When Is the Passive Approach Better?

Although our example shows that entry deterrence is the best strategy for Mona, it won't be the best strategy for all insecure monopolists. The key variable is the minimum entry quantity. Suppose that the scale economies in air travel were relatively small, so a second firm could enter the market with as few as 10 passengers. In this case, if Mona commits to serving only 100 passengers, that won't be enough to deter entry: A firm entering with 10 passengers will still make a profit. If the minimum entry quantity is 10 passengers, the entry-deterring quantity rises to 110 passengers:

deterring quantity = zero profit quantity – minimum entry quantity

$$110 = 120 - 10$$

Mona can commit to serving 110 passengers and thus prevent the second firm from entering the market, but is this the most profitable strategy? As shown by point $f$ in Figure 8.10, the limit price associated with an entry-deterring quantity is $150. Mona's profit from entry deterrence would be $5,500:

profit = (price – average cost) × quantity per firm = ($150 – $100) × 110 = $5,500

This is less than the $8,000 profit she could earn by being passive and letting the second firm enter the market. In this case, the minimum entry quantity is relatively small, so the entry-deterring quantity is large and the limit price is low. As a result, sharing a duopoly is more profitable than increasing output and cutting the price to keep the other firm out.

# 8.9 | NATURAL MONOPOLY

In Chapter 7, we considered monopolies that resulted from artificial barriers to entry, such as patents and government licenses. In this chapter, we'll look at natural monopolies, which occur when the economies of scale for producing a product are so large that only a single firm can survive. Some examples of natural monopolies are water systems,

**A Natural Monopoly Uses the Marginal Principle to Pick Quantity and Price**

Because of the indivisible input of cable TV service (the cable TV system), the long-run average-cost curve is negatively sloped. The monopolist chooses point *a*, where marginal revenue equals marginal cost. The firm serves 70,000 subscribers at a price of $27 each (point *b*) and an average cost of $21 (point *c*). The profit per subscriber is $6 ($27 − $21).

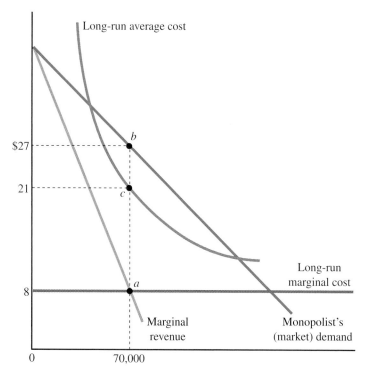

electricity transmission, and cable TV service. It is efficient for a city to have a single supplier of water service because a second supplier would install a second set of water pipes when a single set of pipes would suffice. Similarly, it is efficient to have a single set of transmission lines for electricity and a single set of cables for TV service.

### Picking an Output Level

Figure 8.12 shows the long-run average-cost curve for cable TV service in a particular city. The curve is negatively sloped and steep, reflecting the large economies of scale that occur because cable service requires a costly cable system, and the cost is the same whether the firm serves 70 subscribers or 70,000 subscribers. As the number of subscribers increases, the average cost of cable service decreases because the cost of the cable system is spread over more people.

What about the long-run marginal cost—the cost to add one subscriber—once the system is built? For each additional subscriber, a cable company incurs the cost of hooking the house into the system and the administrative cost associated with billing the subscriber. To simplify matters, we'll assume that each additional subscriber increases costs by $8 per month, so the marginal-cost curve is horizontal at $8 per subscriber.

Figure 8.12 shows how to use the cost curves and revenue curves to pick the output level that maximizes profit. Like other firms, the provider of cable TV can use the marginal principle.

## MARGINAL PRINCIPLE

Increase the level of an activity as long as its marginal benefit exceeds its marginal cost. Choose the level at which the marginal benefit equals the marginal cost.

If a single firm—a monopolist—provides cable service, the firm-specific demand curve is the same as the market demand curve: The market demand curve shows, for each price, the number of subscribers for the monopolist. From the firm's perspective,

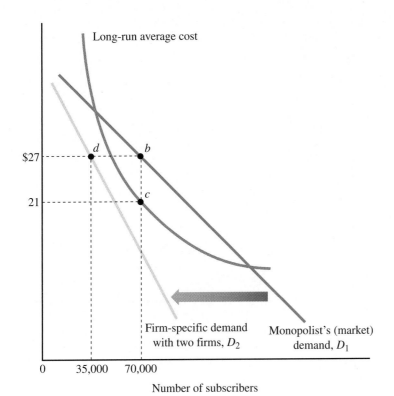

◄ **FIGURE 8.13**
**Will a Second Cable Firm Enter the Market?**
The entry of a second cable firm would shift the demand curve of the typical firm to the left. After entry, the firm's demand curve lies entirely below the long-run average-cost curve. No matter what price the firm charges, it will lose money. Therefore, a second firm will not enter the market.

the marginal benefit of a subscriber is the increase in revenue from the subscriber—the marginal revenue. The marginal principle is satisfied at point $a$, with 70,000 subscribers. The price associated with this quantity is $27 per subscriber (shown by point $b$), and the average cost is $21 per unit (shown by point $c$), so the profit per subscriber is $6. The price exceeds the average cost, so the cable company will earn a profit.

## Will a Second Firm Enter?

If there are no artificial barriers to entry, a second firm could enter the cable TV market. What would happen if a second firm entered the market? In Figure 8.13, the entry of a second firm would shift the demand curve of the first firm—the former monopolist—to the left, from $D_1$ to $D_2$: At each price, the first firm will have fewer subscribers because it now shares the market with another firm. For example, at a price of $27, there are 70,000 subscribers, or 35,000 for each firm (point $d$). In general, the larger the number of firms, the lower the demand curve for the typical firm.

Will a second firm enter the market? Notice that the demand curve of the typical firm in a two-firm market lies entirely below the long-run average-cost curve, so there is no quantity at which the price exceeds the average cost of production. No matter what price the typical firm charges, it will lose money. The firm's demand curve lies below the average-cost curve because the average-cost curve is steep, reflecting the large economies of scale for cable service. A second firm—with half the market—would have a very high average cost and wouldn't be able to charge a price high enough to cover the cost of building the system in the first place. Therefore, the second firm will not enter the market, so there will be a single firm, a natural monopoly.

## Price Controls for a Natural Monopoly

When a natural monopoly is inevitable, the government often sets a maximum price that the monopolist can charge consumers. There are many examples of natural monopolies that are subject to maximum prices. Local governments regulate utilities and firms that provide water, electricity, cable service, and local telephone service.

**Regulators Use Average-Cost Pricing to Pick a Monopoly's Quantity and Price**

Under an average-cost pricing policy, the government chooses the price at which the demand curve intersects the long-run average-cost curve—$12 per subscriber. Regulation decreases the price and increases the quantity.

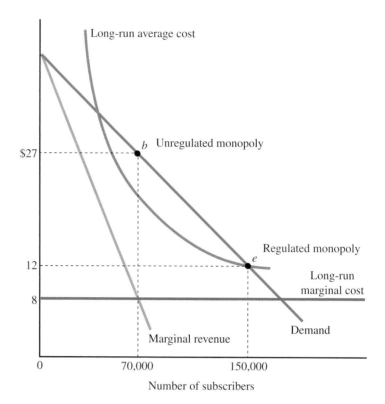

Many state governments use public utility commissions (PUCs) to regulate the electric power industry.

We can use the cable TV market to explain the effects of government regulation on a natural monopoly. Suppose the government sets a maximum price for cable service and forces the cable company to serve all consumers who are willing to pay the maximum price. In other words, the government—not the firm—picks a point on the market demand curve. Under an *average-cost pricing policy*, the government picks the price at which the market demand curve intersects the monopolist's long-run average-cost curve. In Figure 8.14, the average-cost curve intersects the demand curve at point *e*, with a price of $12 per subscriber. This is much lower than the profit-maximizing price of $27. As a result, the number of subscribers is much larger—150,000 compared to 70,000. The purpose of the average-cost pricing policy is to get the lowest feasible price. The cable company would lose money at any price less than $12, so a lower price isn't feasible.

How will this regulatory policy affect the monopolist's production costs? Under average-cost pricing, a change in the monopolist's production cost will have little effect on its profit, because the government will soon adjust the regulated price to keep the price equal to the average cost. The government will increase the regulated price when the monopolist's cost increases and decrease the price when the monopolist's cost decreases. Because the monopolist has no incentive to cut costs and faces no penalty for higher costs, its costs are likely to creep upward. As average cost increases, the regulated price will, too.

# 8.10 | ANTITRUST POLICY

• **trust**

An arrangement under which the owners of several companies transfer their decision-making powers to a small group of trustees.

A **trust** is an arrangement under which the owners of several companies transfer their decision-making powers to a small group of trustees. The purpose of antitrust policy is to promote competition among firms, which leads to lower prices for consumers.

Two government organizations, the Antitrust Division of the Department of Justice and the Federal Trade Commission, are responsible for initiating actions against individuals or firms that may be violating antitrust laws. The courts have the power to

# APPLICATION

## XM AND SIRIUS SATELLITE RADIO

**APPLYING THE CONCEPTS #8:** When does a natural monopoly occur?

The biggest development in radio since the emergence of the FM band is satellite radio. Two firms—Sirius Satellite Radio and XM Satellite Radio—provide dozens of national radio channels that can be accessed by special radio receivers for cars and homes. The quality of the reception is on par with compact discs and is the same throughout the continental United States. Both firms provide dozens of channels, including music channels with rock and roll, punk, pop, country/western, R&B, and classical music. The information channels include the Bloomberg News Radio, CNBC, C-SPAN, BBC WorldService, NPR Talk, and Public Radio International.

The advantage of satellite radio is that most stations are free of annoying commercials that clutter most broadcast radio stations. The music channels on the Sirius system are commercial-free, and the information channels air just a few minutes of commercials every hour. About half the XM channels are commercial-free, and the others have no more than six minutes of commercials every hour (compared to 20 minutes at the typical broadcast radio station). The monthly charge for Sirius is $13. XM radio has a lower price—$10 per month—because it has more commercials.

How many satellite radio systems can the market support? The cost of the infrastructure to set up a single system—satellites and ground stations—is about $2 billion. In addition, both systems added to their setup costs by signing contracts with radio personalities, news organizations, and sports information sources. For example, Sirius agreed to pay Howard Stern $679 million over a five-year period. To cover the cost of the Stern contract, Sirius needs an additional 2.4 million subscribers. In early 2006, both firms were gaining subscribers but still losing money. If subscriptions continue to grow rapidly, both firms will become profitable in the next few years. But if subscription growth slows, there will be enough demand to support one satellite radio firm, but not two. *Related to Exercises 9.4 and 9.5.*

SOURCES: Associated Press Wire News, "Satellite Radio Takes Off in U.S.," June 1, 2003; David Ng, "Stern Compensation at Sirius Higher Than Estimated." Forbes.com, January 27, 2006 (http://www.forbes.com/markets/2006/01/27/sirius-howard-stern-0127markets03.html; accessed June 28, 2006); Ed Lin. "Sirius Seen Reaching Breakeven Before XM," Forbes.com, December 20, 2005. (http://www.forbes.com/markets/2005/12/20/sirius-xm-satellite-radio-1220markets10.html; accessed June 28, 2006).

impose penalties on the executives found to be in violation of the laws, including fines and prison sentences. In some cases, the government seeks no penalties but directs the firm to discontinue illegal practices and take other measures to promote competition. We'll explore three types of antitrust policies: breaking up monopolies, blocking mergers, and regulating business practices.

## Breaking Up Monopolies

One form of antitrust policy is to break up a monopoly into several smaller firms. The label "antitrust" comes from the names of the early conglomerates that the government broke up. The classic example is John D. Rockefeller's Standard Oil Trust, which was formed in 1882 when the owners of 40 oil companies empowered nine trustees to make the decisions for all 40 companies. The trust controlled over 90 percent of the market for refined petroleum products, and the trustees ran it like a monopoly. In 1911, the government ordered its breakup. The Supreme Court found that Rockefeller had used "unnatural methods" to maintain his monopoly power and drive his rivals out of business. In addition to forming the trust, he coerced railroads to give him special rates for shipping, and he spied on his competitors. The government broke up Standard Oil into 34 separate companies, including the corporate ancestors of Exxon, Mobil, Chevron, and Amoco.

The American Tobacco Company started in 1890 as a merger of several tobacco firms. By 1907, the company had acquired over 200 rival firms and controlled 95 percent of the U.S. cigarette market. The U.S. Supreme Court found that American Tobacco maintained its monopoly power by driving rivals out of business and agreeing to exclusive contracts with wholesalers that prevented them from purchasing cigarettes from other companies. The court-ordered breakup in 1911 led to several new companies, including several of today's big cigarette companies: Reynolds, Liggett and Meyers, and P. Lorillard.

In 1982, the government broke up American Telephone and Telegraph (AT&T) into seven regional phone companies. AT&T had used its legal monopoly in local telephone service to prevent competition in the markets for long-distance service and communications equipment. After an eight-year legal battle, AT&T agreed to form seven Regional Bell Operating Companies, transforming "Ma Bell" into seven "Baby Bells." The new AT&T was allowed to compete in the market for long-distance service, where it faced competition from newcomers MCI and Sprint. AT&T was also allowed to operate in the market for communications equipment, where it faced competition from newcomers Mitel and Northern Telecom.

### Blocking Mergers

• **merger**
A process in which two or more firms combine their operations.

A **merger** occurs when two or more firms combine their operations. A *horizontal merger* involves two firms producing a similar product, for example, two producers of pet food. A *vertical merger* involves two firms at different stages of the production process, for example, a sugar refiner and a candy producer. A second type of antitrust policy is to block corporate mergers that would reduce competition and lead to higher prices. We saw in an earlier chapter that as the number of firms in a market increases, competition among firms drives down prices. Because a merger decreases the number of firms in a market, it is likely to lead to higher prices. In 1994, Microsoft tried to purchase Intuit, the maker of Quicken, a personal-finance software package that was a substitute for a similar Microsoft product. The merger would have reduced competition in the personal-finance software market, so the government blocked it.

Of course, the government does not oppose all corporate mergers. One possible benefit from a merger is that the new firm could combine production, marketing, and administrative operations, producing products at a lower average cost. Consumers might reap the rewards in the form of lower prices. In 1997, the Justice Department and the Federal Trade Commission (FTC) released new guidelines for proposed mergers. The new guidelines allow companies involved in a proposed merger to present evidence that the merger would reduce costs and lead to lower prices, better products, or better service. If the evidence for greater efficiency is convincing, the government might allow a merger that reduces the number of firms in a market. The chairman of the FTC assessed the effects of the new guidelines as follows[7]:

> There may be some deals that go through which otherwise would not have. But it won't change the result in a large number of cases [rather it will have] the greatest impact in a transaction where the potential anticompetitive problem is modest and efficiencies that would be created are great.

The new guidelines will bring the U.S. antitrust rules closer in line with those of Europe and Canada and could help U.S. companies compete in those markets.

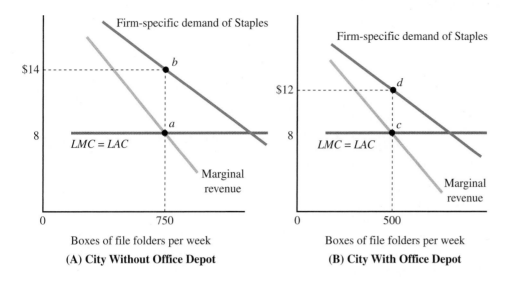

◄ **FIGURE 8.15**

**Pricing by Staples in Cities With and Without Competition**
Using the marginal principle, Staples picks the quantity at which its marginal revenue equals its marginal cost. In a city without a competing firm, Staples picks the monopoly price of $14. In a city where Staples competes with Office Depot, the demand facing Staples is lower, so the profit-maximizing price is only $12.

In recent years, the analysis of proposed mergers has shifted from counting the number of firms in a market to predicting how a particular merger would affect prices. The data generated by retail checkout scanners provide an enormous amount of information about prices and quantities sold. Using these data, economists can determine how one firm's pricing policies affect the sales of that firm and its competitors. Economists can use this information to predict whether a merger would lead to higher prices.

The FTC used pricing data to support its decision to block a proposed merger between Staples and Office Depot.[8] The data showed that Staples charged lower prices in cities where Office Depot also had stores. Figure 8.15 shows Staples' revenue and cost curves for one specific product: file folders. Panel A shows what happens when Staples faces no competition from an Office Depot, and Panel B shows what happens when it does. The demand curve of Staples is lower in the city where it faces competition with Office Depot because the two firms share the market. Using the marginal principle, Staples picks the quantity and price where its marginal revenue equals its marginal cost. The profit-maximizing price is $14 in a city without an Office Depot and $12 in a city with one.

The FTC used this logic to convince the court that the proposed merger of Staples and Office Depot would lead to higher prices. The judge in the case observed that,

> direct evidence shows that by eliminating Staples' most significant, and in many markets, only, rival, the merger would allow Staples to increase prices or otherwise maintain prices at an anticompetitive level.

Evidence from the companies' pricing data showed that the merger would have allowed Staples to increase its prices by about 13 percent. According to an FTC study, blocking the merger saved consumers an estimated $1.1 billion over five years.

## Merger Remedy for Wonder Bread

In some cases, the government allows a merger to happen but imposes restrictions on the new company. In 1995, Interstate Bakeries, the nation's third-largest wholesale baker, tried to buy Continental Baking, the maker of Wonder Bread. Based on grocery store scanner data, the government concluded that Wonder Bread is a close substitute for Interstate's bread: The demand for Wonder Bread increases when the price of Interstate's bread increases, and vice versa.[9] The scanner data showed that when Interstate increased its price, many consumers switched to Wonder Bread, so their bread money went to Continental instead of Interstate. The substitutability of the two brands discouraged Interstate from increasing its prices.

# APPLICATION

## HEINZ AND BEECH-NUT BATTLE FOR SECOND PLACE

APPLYING THE CONCEPTS #9: Does competition between the second- and third-largest firms matter?

In 2001, H.J. Heinz Company announced plans to buy Milnot Holding Company's Beech-Nut for $185 million. The merger would combine the nation's second- and third-largest sellers of baby food, with a combined market share of 28 percent. The combined company would still be less than half the size of the market leader, Gerber, with its 70-percent market share. The FTC successfully blocked the merger, based on two observations:

• Most retailers stock only two brands of baby food, Gerber and either Heinz or Beech-Nut. The two smaller companies compete vigorously for shelf space, with discounts, coupons, and other programs that lead to lower prices for consumers. After the merger, the Heinz brand would disappear, leaving Beech-Nut as a secure second brand on the shelves next to Gerber. The elimination of competition for second place would lead to higher prices.

• The smaller the number of firms in an oligopoly, the easier it is to coordinate pricing. The FTC argued that "significant market concentration makes it easier for firms in the market to collude, expressly or tacitly, and thereby force price above or farther above the competitive level." In other words, in a market with two firms instead of three, it would be easier for the baby-food manufacturers to fix prices. *Related to Exercises 10.5 and 10.7.*

SOURCES: "Baby-Food Makers Heinz, Beech-Nut Call Off Merger Following Court Ruling," *Wall Street Journal*, April 27, 2001, p. A13; United State District Court for the District of Columbia, "*Federal Trade Commission v. H. J. Heinz Company*: Memorandum in Support of Plaintiff's Motion for Preliminary Injunction," July 24, 2000.

Table 8.5 shows an example of a merger leading to higher prices and smaller quantities. Let's assume that the average cost per loaf of bread is $1.50, and this doesn't change with a merger. The situation before the merger is shown in columns 1 and 3: For each brand, the price per loaf of bread is $2.00, the quantity is 100 loaves, and the profit is $50 (the profit $0.50 per loaf times 100 loaves).

How would a merger affect the incentives to raise prices? After a merger, a single company would earn the profits from both brands (Wonder and Interstate) and pick both prices. Suppose the new company increased the price of Interstate bread to $2.20 but kept the price of Wonder Bread at $2.00. The price hike would bring bad news and good news for the new company:

• **Bad news:** Less profit on Interstate Bread. As shown in columns 3 and 4, the price hike decreases the quantity of Interstate bread from 100 to 70 loaves. Although the profit per loaf increases to $0.70 (the new price of $2.20 minus the average cost of $1.50), only 70 loaves are sold, so the profit from the brand drops to $49, down from $50. The bad news is the $1 loss of profit on Interstate Bread.

**Table 8.5** | A MERGER INCREASES PRICES

| | Wonder Brand | | Interstate Brand | | Total | |
|---|---|---|---|---|---|---|
| | 1 Before Merger | 2 After Merger | 3 Before Merger | 4 After Merger | 5 Before Merger | 6 After Merger |
| **Average cost** | $1.50 | $1.50 | $1.50 | $1.50 | | |
| **Price** | $2.00 | $2.00 | $2.00 | $2.20 | | |
| **Quantity** | 100 | 110 | 100 | 70 | 200 | 180 |
| **Profit** | $50 | $55 | $50 | $49 | $100 | $104 |

- **Good news:** More profit on Wonder Bread. As shown in columns 1 and 2, the increase in the price of Interstate Bread increases the quantity of Wonder Bread sold from 100 to 110 loaves. The profit per loaf is still $0.50 per bread, so the profit on Wonder Bread increases to $55, up from $50. The good news is the extra $5 of profit on Wonder Bread.

In this case, the good news ($5 more profit from Wonder) exceeds the bad news ($1 less profit from Interstate), so the price hike increases the total profit of the merged company. This is shown in columns 5 and 6. Although the total quantity drops, total profit increases by $4. A merger means that the good news from a price hike stays within the larger firm, encouraging that firm to increase prices.

The lesson from this example is that a merger of two firms selling close substitutes may lead to higher prices. That's what the Department of Justice concluded in the case of Interstate Bakeries and Continental Bakery. The government allowed the merger between the two companies but forced Interstate to sell some of its brands and bakeries. For example, Interstate sold the rights to sell its Weber brand bread to Four-S Baking Company. The idea was to ensure that other companies would be able to compete with the newly merged company.

## Regulating Business Practices: Price-Fixing, Tying, and Cooperative Agreements

The third type of antitrust policy involves the regulation of business practices. The government may intervene when a specific business practice increases market concentration in an already concentrated market. A **tie-in sale** occurs when a business forces the buyer of one product to purchase another product. The FTC recently charged a pharmaceutical company with tying the sale of clozapine, an antipsychotic drug, to a blood testing and monitoring system. Another illegal business practice is a cooperative agreement to limit advertising. The FTC recently charged a group of auto dealers with restricting comparative and discount advertising.

The Robinson–Patman Act prohibits the selling of products at "unreasonably low prices" with the intent of reducing competition, a practice known as **predatory pricing**. A firm engages in predatory pricing when it sells a product at a price below its production costs, with the objective of driving a rival out of business. Once the predator's rivals drop out of the market, the firm then charges a monopoly price, well above its production cost. This strategy will be profitable if the firm can charge the monopoly price for a long enough period to offset the losses it experienced while driving its rivals out of business.

But is predatory pricing really practical? Consider a market with two firms, one of which is determined to have the market to itself. By cutting its price below its cost, the firm can drive its competitor out of business, losing perhaps $10 million in the process. If it increases its price next year, there may be nothing to prevent a new firm from entering the market. If so, it would have to cut its price below its cost again to drive the new firm out. The problem with predatory pricing is that it never ends. The firm must repeatedly lose money to drive out an endless series of competitors.

- **tie-in sales**
  A business practice under which a business requires a consumer of one product to purchase another product.

- **predatory pricing**
  A firm sells a product at a price below its production cost to drive a rival out of business and then increases the price.

# APPLICATION

## XIDEX RECOVERS ITS ACQUISITION COST IN TWO YEARS

**APPLYING THE CONCEPTS #10:** How does a merger affect prices?

In 1981, the FTC brought an antitrust suit against Xidex Corporation for its earlier acquisition of two rivals in the microfilm market. By acquiring Scott Graphics, Inc., in 1976 and Kalvar Corporation in 1979, Xidex increased its market share of the U.S. microfilm market from 46 to 71 percent. As a result, the price of microfilm increased: The price of one type of microfilm (diazo) increased by 11 percent, and the price of a second type (vesicular) increased by 23 percent. These price hikes were large enough that Xidex recovered the cost of acquiring its two rivals ($4.2 million for Scott Graphics and $6 million for Kalvar) in less than two years. To settle the antitrust lawsuit, Xidex agreed to license its microfilm technology—at bargain prices—to other firms. The idea was that if other firms have access to the microfilm technology, the competition between Xidex and the competing firms would decrease the price of microfilm. *Related to Exercises 10.6 and 10.8.*

SOURCE: David M. Barton and Roger Sherman, "The Price and Profit Effects of Horizontal Merger: A Case Study," *Journal of Industrial Economics*, vol. 33, December 1984, pp. 165–177.

## The Microsoft Cases

In recent years, the most widely reported antitrust actions have involved Microsoft Corporation, the software giant. Microsoft receives royalties from computer makers that install the Microsoft operating software on their computers. The curious—and illegal—feature of the original arrangement was that Microsoft received a royalty for every computer made by the firm, even if the firm installed other operating systems on some of its computers. This scheme discouraged computer makers from using software from Microsoft's rivals, and the courts declared the practice illegal in 1994.

In the case of *United States v. Microsoft Corporation*, the judge concluded that Microsoft stifled competition in the software industry. Specifically, Microsoft tried to use its monopoly in the market for operating systems to get a monopoly in the browser market. Under an initial ruling, the judge's remedy was to break up the corporation into two companies, one producing the Windows operating system and a second producing application software. On appeal, the U.S. Justice Department rejected this remedy, and in 2002 directed Microsoft to accommodate rival browsers on the Windows desktop and release more technical information about its operating system.

## A Brief History of U.S. Antitrust Policy

Table 8.6 provides a brief summary of the history of antitrust policy. The first legislation was the Sherman Antitrust Act of 1890, which made it illegal to monopolize a market or to engage in practices that result in a restraint of trade. Because the act did not specify which practices were illegal, it led to conflicting court rulings.

Many of the ambiguities of the Sherman Act were resolved by the Clayton Act of 1914. The Clayton Act outlawed specific practices that discourage competition, including tie-in sales contracts and price discrimination that reduces competition.

| Law | Date Enacted | Regulation Enacted |
|---|---|---|
| Sherman Act | 1890 | Made it illegal to monopolize a market or to engage in practices that result in a restraint of trade. |
| Clayton Act | 1914 | Outlawed specific practices that discourage competition, including tie-in sales contracts, price discrimination for the purpose of reducing competition, and stock-purchase mergers that would substantially reduce competition. |
| Federal Trade Commission Act | 1914 | Created a mechanism to enforce antitrust laws. |
| Robinson–Patman Act | 1936 | Prohibited selling products at "unreasonably low prices" with the intent of reducing competition. |
| Celler–Kefauver Act | 1950 | Outlawed asset-purchase mergers that would substantially reduce competition. |
| Hart–Scott–Rodino Act | 1980 | Extended antitrust legislation to proprietorships and partnerships. |

The act also outlawed mergers resulting from the purchase of a competitor's stock when such a merger would substantially reduce competition.

More recent legislation clarified and extended antitrust laws. The Robinson–Patman Act of 1936 prohibited predatory pricing. The Celler–Kefauver Act of 1950 closed a loophole in the Clayton Act by prohibiting one firm from purchasing another firm's physical assets, such as buildings and equipment, when the acquisition would reduce competition substantially. The Hart–Scott–Rodino Act of 1980 extended antitrust legislation to proprietorships and partnerships. Before this act, antitrust legislation applied only to corporations.

# SUMMARY

This chapter is about market entry, monopolistic competition, and oligopoly. In a monopolistically competitive market, firms differentiate their products, and entry continues until each firms in the market makes zero economic profit. In an oligopoly, a few firms serve a market, and firms have an incentive to act strategically: They may cooperate to fix prices, and may price their products strategically to keep other firms out of the market. In markets with a small number of firms, the role of public policy is to regulate monopolists and promote competition. Here are the main points of the chapter:

1 The entry of a firm into a market decreases the market price, decreases output per firm, and increases the average cost of production.

2 In the long-run equilibrium with monopolistic competition, marginal revenue equals marginal cost, price equals average cost, and economic profit is zero.

3 A firm can use celebrity endorsements and other costly advertisements to signal its belief that a product will be appealing.

4 Each firm in an oligopoly has an incentive to underprice the other firms, so price-fixing will be unsuccessful unless firms have some way of enforcing a price-fixing agreement.

5 To prevent a second firm from entering a market, an insecure monopolist may commit to produce a relatively large quantity and accept a relatively low price.

6 Under an average-cost pricing policy, the regulated price for a natural monopoly equals the average cost of production.

7 The government uses antitrust policy to break up some dominant firms, prevent some corporate mergers, and regulate business practices that reduce competition.

## KEY TERMS

## EXERCISES

Visit www.myeconlab.com to complete
*Get Ahead of the Curve*    these exercises online and get instant feedback.

### 8.1 | The Effects of Market Entry

**1.1** A profit-maximizing firm picks the quantity of output at which _____ equals _____.

**1.2** Arrows up or down: The entry of a third firm into a market with two original firms _____ the market price, _____ the average production cost, _____ the quantity produced per firm, and _____ profit of each original firm.

**1.3** Arrows up or down: Changes in regulatory policy in the 1980s _____ the price of trucking services and _____ the profits of trucking firms. (Related to Application 1 on page 180.)

**1.4** When grocery stores introduced their own light-bulb brands, the price of General Electric light-bulbs _____ (increased/decreased). (Related to Application 2 on page 181.)

**1.5** **Bidding for Bookstore Licenses.** Paige initially has the only license to operate a bookstore in Bookville. She charges a price of $9 per book, has an average cost of $4 per book, and sells 1,001 books per year. When Paige's licenses expires, the city decides to auction two bookstore licenses to the highest bidders. Suppose the relevant variables (price, average cost, and output per firm) take on only integer values—no fraction or decimals. (Related to Application 1 on page 180.)

**a.** Suppose Paige is optimistic and imagines the best possible outcome with a two-firm market. What is the maximum amount she is willing to pay for one of the two licenses?

**b.** Suppose Paige is pessimistic and imagines the worst possible outcome with a two-firm market. What is the maximum amount she is willing to pay for one of the two licenses?

**1.6** **Draw the Lightbulb Graph.** Consider the "Name Brands Versus Store Brands" application. Use a graph to show that the entry of store-brand lightbulbs

decreased the profit-maximizing price of General Electric lightbulbs from $3.50 to $2.00. (Related to Application 2 on page 181.)

**1.7** **Beware the Too-Easy Answer.** Your city initially restricts the number of pizzerias to one. The existing monopolist sells 3,000 pizzas per day. A pizzeria reaches the horizontal portion of its long-run average cost curve at an output of about 1,000 pizzas per day. Suppose the city eliminates the entry restrictions. Predict the equilibrium number of pizzerias. Beware of the TEC (too easy to be correct) answer.

### 8.2 | Monopolistic Competition

**2.1** *Monopolistic competition* refers to a market in which old boys act naturally as they transport tight slacks in the back of Dodge Ram pickup trucks. _____ (True /False)

**2.2** There are _____ oxymorons in question 2.1.

**2.3** There are two conditions for a long-run equilibrium in a monopolistically competitive market:

(1) _____ equals _____ and (2) _____ equals _____.

**2.4** To enter the donut market as a seller of Dunkin' Donuts, you'll pay a one-time franchise fee of $_____ and then pay _____ percent of your sales. (Related to Application 3 on page 184.)

**2.5** **Willingness to Pay for a Dunkin' Donuts Franchise.** You operate a Dunkin' Donuts shop under a franchise agreement. You pay a royalty of 6 percent of your sales revenue to the parent company. Your profit-maximizing quantity is 10,000 donuts per year, and at this quantity, your price is $1.00 and your average cost per donut (including all the opportunity cost of production but not the 6% royalty) is $0.44. (Related to Application 3 on page 184.)

**a.** Draw a graph with revenue and costs curves to show your profit-maximizing choice.

**b.** What is the maximum amount you are willing to pay per year for the franchise?

**2.6 How Many Video Stores?** The city of Discville initially allows only one video store, which sells DVDs at a price of $20 and an average cost of $11. Suppose the city eliminates its restrictions on video stores, allowing additional stores to enter the market. According to an expert in the music market, "Each additional music store will decrease the price of DVDs by $2 per DVD and increase the average cost of selling DVDs by $1 per DVD." Predict the equilibrium number of video stores.

**2.7 Lawn-Cutting Equilibrium.** Consider the market for cutting laws. Each firm has a fixed daily cost of $18 for equipment, and the marginal cost of cutting a lawn is $4. Suppose each firm can cut up to three lawns per day. The market demand curve for lawn cuts is linear, with a vertical intercept of $70 and a slope of –$1 per lawn.
**a.** If each firm in the market cuts three lawns, what is the average cost per lawn?
**b.** What is the equilibrium price under monopolistic competition?
**c.** How many lawns will be cut in total, and how many firms will be in the market?

**2.8 Zero Price for a Permit.** Consider a city that initially issues five licenses to pet groomers and does not allow the licenses to be bought and sold. Shortly after an economist joins the city licensing authority, the city decides to allow the licenses to be bought and sold on the open market. Much to the surprise of the licensers, the price of the licenses was zero: No one was willing to pay a positive amount for a pet grooming license.
**a.** Explain why the price of grooming licenses was zero.
**b.** Illustrate your answer with a complete graph.

**2.9 Auctioning Business Licenses.** The following table shows the relationships between the number of firms in the market, the market price, the quantity per firm, and the average cost of production.

| Number of Firms | Price | Quantity per Firm | Average Cost |
|---|---|---|---|
| 1 | $20 | 38 | $9 |
| 2 | 18 | 35 | 10 |
| 3 | 16 | 32 | 11 |
| 4 | 14 | 29 | 12 |
| 5 | 12 | 26 | 13 |
| 6 | 10 | 23 | 14 |
| 7 | 8 | 20 | 15 |

A business license allows a firm to operate the business for one day. The city will auction up to seven business licenses to the highest bidders, and the auctioning of licenses will continue as long as someone bids a posi-

tive amount for one of the licenses. Assume that each firm can buy only one license. What is the maximum amount you would be willing to pay for a license?

## 8.3 | Trade-Offs with Entry and Monopolistic Competition

**3.1** The trade-off with entry is that an increase in the number of firms leads to higher _____ but greater _____.

**3.2** When products are differentiated by location, the entry of firms generates benefits for consumers in the form of _____.

**3.3** A perfectly competitive firm has a _____ demand curve, whereas a monopolistic competitive firm has a _____ demand curve.

**3.4** In the long-run equilibrium in a perfectly competitive market, price is equal to both _____ and _____.

**3.5** Arrows up or down: As product differentiation diminishes, the price elasticity of demand for the product of a monopolistically competitive firm _____ and the average cost of production _____.

**3.6 Uniform Trade-Offs.** A prominent feature of Mao's Communist China in the 1940s through the 1970s was the blue uniform worn by all citizens.
**a.** Explain the trade-offs associated with the use of uniforms. What were the benefits? What were the costs?
**b.** Suppose people had a choice among five uniform colors rather than being required to wear blue uniforms. Would you expect the benefits of requiring uniforms to decrease by a little or a lot?

## 8.4 | Advertising for Product Differentiation

**4.1** Advertising for eyeglasses _____ (increases/decreases) the price of eyeglasses.

**4.2** An advertisement that succeeds in getting consumers to try the product will be sensible only if the number of _____ customers is large.

**4.3** In Table 8.2 on page 186, the profit from repeat customers will equal the cost of the advertisement if there are _____ repeat customers.

**4.4 Movie-Buzz Numbers.** Consider a theater that earns a profit of $2 per movie ticket sold. An advertisement that costs $3,400 would have the direct effect of getting 1,000 people to buy tickets. To make the advertisement worthwhile, how many of the original ticket buyers must each persuade just one other person to buy a ticket? (Related to Application 4 on page 187.)

**4.5 The Cost of Celebrities.** Consider a firm that hires an expensive celebrity to advertise its products. Does the firm have an incentive to prevent its customers from discovering how much it pays the celebrity?

**4.6** **Word-of-Mouth Book Sales.** Consider a publisher who earns a profit of $2 per book sold. An advertisement that costs $320,000 would sell 100,000 books directly. To make the advertisement worthwhile, how many of the original buyers must each persuade just one other person to buy the book?

# 8.5 | What Is an Oligopoly?

**5.1** A market is considered "unconcentrated" if the Heerfindahl-Hirschman Index (HHI) is below _____; it is considered highly concentrated if the HHI is at least _____.

**5.2** For a market with four firms, each with a 25-percent market share, the Herfindahl-Hirschman Index (HHI) is equal to _____.

**5.3** Oligopolies occur for three reasons: (1) the government may limit the number of firms in a market by granting _____ or limiting the number of _____; (2) large economies of _____; (3) to get a foothold in the market, large expenditures on _____ are required.

**5.4** The production of breakfast cereals is not subject to large-scale economies, but the market is an oligopoly because of the barriers to entry from _____.

# 8.6 | Cartel Pricing and the Duopolists' Dilemma

**6.1** Arrows up or down: If we move from the cartel outcome to the duopoly outcome, the price _____, the quantity per firm _____, and the profit per firm _____.

**6.2** A dominant strategy is the strategy that allows one firm to dominate the market. _____ (True/False)

**6.3** The duopolists' dilemma is that each firm would make more profit if both picked the _____ price, but both firms pick the _____ price.

**6.4** In a Nash equilibrium, each player is doing the best he or she can, given _____.

**6.5** In Figure 8.7 on page 191, rectangle 3 is not a Nash equilibrium because if _____ picks a(n) _____ price, the best response of _____ is to pick the _____ price.

**6.6** In Figure 8.7 on page 191, suppose Jack promises Jill that if she picks the high price, he will, too. Is this promise credible? Explain.

**6.7** Buzz and Moe are duopolists in the lawn-care market. The game tree below shows the possible pricing outcomes and their payoffs. The outcome of the pricing game is that Buzz will pick the _____ price and Moe will pick the _____ price.

**6.8** The executives from the world's largest vitamin producers conspired to fix vitamin prices, increasing the prices of vitamins by an average of _____ percent. (Related to Application 5 on page 193.)

**6.9** **Vitamin Market Areas.** Beta and Gamma produce vitamin A at a constant average cost of $5 per unit. Assume that low-price guarantees are illegal. Here are the possible outcomes:
- Price-fixing (cartel). Each firm sells 30 units at a price of $20 per unit.
- Duopoly (no price-fixing). Each firm sells 40 units at a price of $12 per unit.
- Underpricing (one firm charges $20 and the other charges $12). The low-price firm sells 70 units and the high-price firm sells five units.

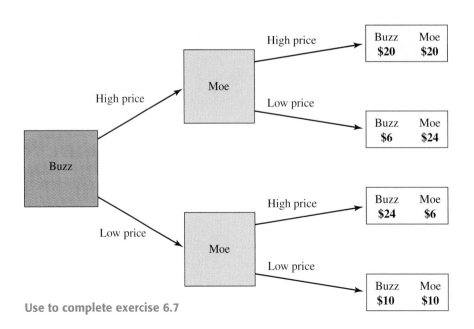

**Use to complete exercise 6.7**

**a.** Suppose Beta chooses a price first, followed by Gamma. Draw a game tree for the price-fixing game and predict the outcome. (Related to Application 5 on page 193.)

**b.** Suppose the firms agree to pick the high price. Once Beta picks the high price, how much more could Gamma earn if it cheated on the price-fixing agreement?

**c.** Suppose the firms divide the market into two areas of equal size. and assign each firm one of the areas. Each firm agrees to sell only in its assigned areas. Will this arrangement generate a successful cartel?

**6.10 Airporter Price Fixing?** Hustle and Speedy provide transportation service from downtown to the city airport. Assume that low-price guarantees are illegal. The average cost per passenger is constant at $10. Here are the possible outcomes:
- Price-fixing (cartel). Each firm has 15 passengers at a price of $25.
- Duopoly (no price-fixing). Each firm has 20 passengers at a price of $20.
- Underpricing (one firm charges $20 and the other charges $25). The low-price firm has 28 passengers and the high-price firm has five passengers.

Hustle chooses a price first, followed by Speedy. Draw a game tree for the price-fixing game and predict the outcome.

**6.11 Hotel Price Fixing?** Waikiki Beach has two hotels, one run by Juan and a second run by Tulah. The average cost of providing rooms is constant at $30 per day. Assume that low-price guarantees are illegal. Here are the possible outcomes:
- Price-fixing (cartel). Each firm has 30 customers at a price of $40.
- Duopoly (no price-fixing). Each firm has 40 customers per day at a price of $37.
- Underpricing (one firm charges $40 and the other charges $37). The low-price firm has 50 customers and the high-price firm has 10 customers.

Juan chooses a price first, followed by Tulah. Draw a game tree for the price-fixing game and predict the outcome.

## 8.7 | Overcoming the Duopolists' Dilemma

**7.1** For firms with a low-price guarantee, the promise of matching a lower price is a(n) _____ promise, because all firms will charge the same _____ price.

**7.2** Suppose that Jack and Jill use a tit-for-tat scheme to encourage cartel pricing. Jill chooses the low price for two successive months, and then switches to the high price. The two firms will deviate from cartel pricing for a total of _____ months.

**7.3** If two firms expect to be in the market together for a long time, the _____ (cost/benefit) of underpricing will be large relative to the _____ (cost/benefit).

**7.4** At the beginning of this chapter, we saw that Jason paid more for his plane ticket than Melissa did for hers, even though both people live in cities that are served by two airlines. Two cities with the same number of airlines could have different prices if in one city firms use a _____ guarantee to keep prices high.

**7.5** If a seller promises to refund any difference between its price and the price of its competitors, this practice will lead to _____ (higher/lower) prices. (Related to Application 6 on page 195.)

**7.6 Low-Price Guarantees for a Canopy Tour.** Dip and Zip provide canopy tours in a rain forest. The average cost per rider is constant at $10. Here are the possible outcomes:
- Price-fixing (cartel). Each firm has six passengers at a price of $20.
- Duopoly (no price-fixing). Each firm has eight passengers at a price of $15.
- Underpricing (one firm charges $20 and the other charges $15). The low-price firm has 13 passengers and the high-price firm has two passengers.

Dip chooses a price first, followed by Zip. (Related to Application 6 on page 195.)

**a.** Assume that the firms do not provide low-price guarantees. Draw a game tree and predict the outcome of the price-fixing game.

**b.** Suppose both firms provide low-price guarantees. Draw a new game tree and predict the outcome of the price-fixing game.

**c.** Is the promise to match any lower price a substantive promise or an empty promise?

**7.7 Going Out of Business Sales?** Many firms have going-out-of-business sales with remarkable bargains. What insights does the material in this chapter provide about such sales?

## 8.8 | The Insecure Monopolist and Entry Deterrence

**8.1** Otto has a monopoly on limousine service, and Carla is thinking about entering the market. The outcome of the entry-deterrence game represented by the game tree on page 216 is that Otto picks the _____ quantity and Carla _____ the market.

**8.2** Use the game tree in the previous exercise as a starting point. If the minimum entry quantity increases, a single number in one of the profit rectangles changes from $_____ to a smaller number. If the relevant number is reduced by half, the new outcome of the entry-deterrence game is that Otto picks the _____ quantity and Carla _____ the market.

**8.3** Consider a market with an insecure monopolist. The zero-profit quantity is 60 units and the minimum entry quantity is 5 units. The entry-deterring quantity is _____ units. The zero-profit price is $80. The slope of the market demand curve is –$2 per unit of output. The limit price is $_____.

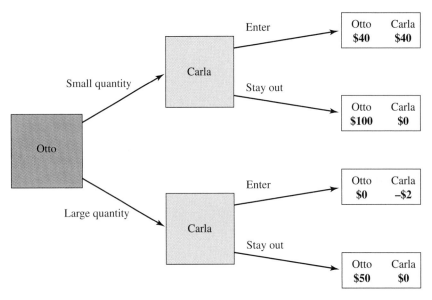

**Use to complete exercise 8.1**

**8.4** To deter entry, a monopolist can simply threaten that if a second firm enters, the monopolist will cut his price to the average cost. _____ (True/False)

**8.5** Arrows up or down: As the minimum entry quantity decreases, the entry-deterring quantity _____, the limit price _____, and the profit from the entry-deterrence strategy _____.

**8.6** In Figure 8.11 on page 199, rectangle 2 is not a Nash equilibrium because if _____ picks a small quantity, the best response for _____ is to _____.

**8.7** To prevent other firms from entering the Irish ice-cream market, Van den Bergh Foods provided free _____ to retailers on the condition that _____. (Related to Application 7 on page 200.)

**8.8** **Ninja Turtles Versus Tai Chi Frogs.** The demand for fantasy amphibians is linear, with a slope of –$0.01 per amphibian. The average cost of production is constant at $7. The demand curve intersects the horizontal average-cost curve at a quantity of 600 amphibians. A firm selling ninja turtles currently has a monopoly, selling 300 turtles at a price of $6. A second firm is considering entering the market with tai-chi frogs, and the minimum entry quantity is 100 amphibians. If the turtle firm is passive and lets the frog firm enter, each firm will sell 200 amphibians at a price of $5.
  **a.** Draw a graph like the one shown in Figure 8.10 on page 198 with all the relevant numbers.
  **b.** Draw a game tree like the one shown in Figure 8.11 on page 199 and predict the outcome of the game. How will the turtle firm respond to the threat of entry? Will the frog firm enter the market?
  **c.** How would your response to part (a) change if the minimum entry quantity dropped to 50 amphibians?

**8.9** **Shuttle Deterrence?** Consider the market for air travel between Boston and New York. The long-run average cost is constant at $100 per passenger, and the demand curve is linear, with a slope of –$2 per passenger. The demand curve intersects the horizontal average-cost curve at a quantity of 120 passengers. The minimum entry quantity is 20 passengers. FirstShuttle currently has a monopoly, with 60 passengers at a price of $220. Another firm, SecondShuttle, is considering the market, and the minimum entry quantity is 20 passengers. If FirstShuttle is passive and lets the other firm enter, each firm will have 40 passengers at a price of $180.
  **a.** Draw a graph like the one shown in Figure 8.10 with all the relevant numbers.
  **b.** Draw a game tree like the one shown in Figure 8.11 and predict the outcome of the game. How will FirstShuttle respond to the threat of entry? Will SecondShuttle enter the market?
  **c.** How would your response to part (a) change if the minimum entry quantity dropped to 10 passengers?

## 8.9 | Natural Monopoly

**9.1** A natural monopolist picks the quantity of output at which _____ equals _____.

**9.2** The entry of a second firm shifts the demand curve of the original firm to the _____, so that at each price the original firm will sell a(n) _____ quantity.

**9.3** A natural monopoly occurs when the long-run cost curve lies entirely _____ (above/below) the demand curve of the typical firm in a two-firm market.

**9.4** If subscriptions to satellite radio continue to grow rapidly, the market will support _____ satellite radio systems. (Related to Application 8 on page 205.)

**9.5** **Duopoly Versus Monopoly Satellite Radio.** Suppose the demand for satellite radio levels off at the number of subscribers reached in early 2006. (Related to Application 8 on page 205.)

    **a.** Use a graph to show the average-cost curve and firm-specific demand curve for one of the two satellite radio firms.

    **b.** Suppose the two firms merge into a single profitable firm. Draw the average-cost curve and firm-specific demand curve for the monopolist. Then use the marginal principle to show the profit-maximizing quantity and price. Would you expect the price to be higher or lower than the prices charged in 2006 by XM ($10) and Sirius ($13)?

**9.6** **Decrease in Cable Demand.** Consider a cable TV company that has a fixed cost of $48 million and a marginal cost of $5 per subscriber. The company is regulated with average-cost pricing policy.

    **a.** The first two columns of the following table show three points on the initial demand curve. For example, at a price of $15 the quantity demanded is 6 million subscribers. For each $2 reduction in price, the number of subscribers increases by 1 million. Fill the blanks in the following table. The regulated price is _____.

| Price | Subscribers (millions) | Average Cost |
|---|---|---|
| $15 | 6 | _____ |
| 13 | 7 | _____ |
| 11 | 8 | _____ |

    **b.** Suppose the demand for the product decreases, with the demand curve shifting to the left by 1 million subscribers. Fill the blanks in the following table. The new regulated price is $_____.

| Price | Subscribers (millions) | Average Cost |
|---|---|---|
| $15 | _____ | _____ |
| 13 | _____ | _____ |
| 11 | _____ | _____ |

**9.7** **Environmental Costs for Regulated Monopoly.** The Bonneville Power Administration (BPA) is a regulated monopoly in the Northwest that uses dozens of hydroelectric dams to generate electricity. Unfortunately, the BPA's dams block the paths of migrating fish, contributing to the decline of several species. Suppose that BPA spends $100 million to make its hydroelectric dams less hazardous for migrating fish. Who will bear the cost of this program?

## 8.10 | Antitrust Policy

**10.1** The purpose of antitrust policy is to promote _____, which leads to lower _____.

**10.2** In the Staples case discussed in this chapter, the data showed that competition with Office Depot led to _____ prices, suggesting that a merger would harm _____.

**10.3** In the Interstate Baking case discussed in this chapter, scanner data showed that the products of Interstate and Continental Baking were _____, so a merger would lead to higher _____.

**10.4** Predatory pricing provides a practical and effective means of getting and keeping a monopoly. _____ (True/False)

**10.5** The government blocked the proposed merger between Heinz and Beech-Nut because a merger would eliminate competition for _____ (first/second/third) place in the baby-food market. (Related to Application 9 on page 208.)

**10.6** After Xidex Corporation acquired two of its rivals for $10 million, it _____ (increased/decreased) prices and recovered the acquisition cost in _____ years. (Related to Application 10 on page 210.)

**10.7** **Incentive to Raise Prices After a Merger.** Consider the Application 9 "Heinz and Beech-Nut Battle for Second Place." Suppose the merger of two firms will reduce the price elasticity of demand for each firm's product from 3.0 to 1.50. For each firm, the average cost of production is constant at $5 per unit. Suppose Heinz initially has a price of $10 and is considering raising the price to $11. (Related to Application 9 on page 208.)

    **a.** Fill the blanks in the following table, showing the payoffs from raising the price before the merger (elasticity = 3.0) and after the merger (elasticity = 1.50).

| Price | Quantity | Total Revenue | Total Cost | Profit |
|---|---|---|---|---|
| Initial: $10 | 100 | $1,000 | $500 | $500 |
| New: $11 Before merger: Elasticity of demand = 3.0 | | | | |
| _____ | _____ | _____ | _____ | _____ |
| New: $11 After merger: Elasticity of demand = 1.50 | | | | |
| _____ | _____ | _____ | _____ | _____ |

    **b.** Before the merger, raising the price would _____ the firm's profit. After the merger, raising the price would _____ the firm's profit.

    **c.** Why is it reasonable to assume that the merger will decrease the elasticity of demand for each firm's products?

**10.8** **Recovering the Acquisition Cost.** The long-run average cost of production is constant at $6 per unit. Suppose firm X acquires Y at a cost of $24 million and increases the price to $14. At the new price, X sells 1.5 million units per year.

    **a.** How does the acquisition affect X's annual profit?

    **b.** How many years will it take for X to recover the cost of acquiring Y? (Related to Application 10 on page 210.)

**10.9 Check the Yellow Pages?** On Yellin's first day on the job as an economist with the FTC, she was put on a team examining a proposed merger between the country's second- and fourth-largest hardware store chains. Her job was to predict whether a merger would increase hardware prices. Her boss handed her some CDs with checkout scanner data from the second-largest chain. Each CD contained scanner data from one small town, listing the prices and quantities of hammers, wrenches, nuts, bolts, rakes, glue, drills, and hundreds of other hardware products. Her boss also gave her the telephone Yellow Pages for each small town. How can she use the information in the disks and the Yellow Pages to make a prediction?

**10.10 Cost Savings from a Merger.** Consider the following statement from a firm that has proposed a merger between two companies: "The two companies could save about $50 million per year by combining our production, marketing, and administrative operations. In other words, we could realize substantial economies of scale. Therefore, the government should allow the merger." In light of the new guidelines concerning mergers, how would you react to this statement?

# ECONOMIC EXPERIMENT

## Fixed Costs and Entry

Here is an experiment that shows the implications of entry for prices and profits. Students play the role of entrepreneurs who must decide whether to enter the market for lawn cutting. If they decide to enter the market, they must then decide how much to charge for cutting lawns.

- There are 8 potential lawn-cutting firms, each represented by 1 to 3 students. The firms have two sorts of costs: a fixed cost per day and a marginal cost of cutting each lawn. Each firm can cut up to 2 lawns per day.

- There are 16 potential consumers. Each potential consumer is willing to pay a different amount to have his or her lawn cut.

- The experiment has two stages. In the first stage, each potential firm decides whether to enter the market. The entry decision is sequential: The instructor will go down

the list of potential firms, one at a time, and give each firm the option of entering the market. The entry decisions are public knowledge. When a firm enters the market, it incurs a fixed cost of $14.

- Each firm in the market posts a price for lawn cutting, and consumers shop around and decide whether to purchase lawn care at the posted prices.

- Each trading period lasts several minutes, and each firm can change its posted price up to three times each period.

- A consumer's score in a trading period equals the difference between the amount that the consumer is willing to pay for lawn care and the price actually paid.

- A firm's score equals its profit, which is its total revenue minus its total cost (the fixed cost of $14 plus the variable cost, equal to $3 per lawn times the number of lawns cut).

# ECONOMIC EXPERIMENT

## Price-Fixing

Here is a price-fixing or cartel game for the classroom. You'll have an opportunity to conspire to fix prices in a hypothetical market with five firms. The instructor divides the class into five groups. Each group represents one of five firms that produce a particular good.

Each group must develop a pricing strategy for its firm, recognizing that the other groups are choosing prices for their firms at the same time. Only two choices are possible: a high price (the cartel price) or a low price.

The profit of a particular firm depends on the price chosen by the firm and the prices chosen by the four other firms. Here is the profit matrix:

| Number of High-Price Firms | Number of Low-Price Firms | Profit for Each High-Price Firm | Profit for Each Low-Price |
|:---:|:---:|:---:|:---:|
| 0 | 5 | — | $5 |
| 1 | 4 | $2 | 7 |
| 2 | 3 | 4 | 9 |
| 3 | 2 | 6 | 11 |
| 4 | 1 | 8 | 13 |
| 5 | 0 | 10 | — |

From the second row, if one of the five firms chooses the high price, and the other four firms choose the low price, the high-price firm earns a profit of $2, and each low-price firm earns a profit of $7. The game is played for several rounds. In the first three rounds, the firms make their choices without talking to each other in advance. In the fourth and fifth rounds, the firms discuss their strategies, disperse, and then make their choices. The group's score equals the profit earned by the firm.

## NOTES

1. Lee Benham, "The Effect of Advertising on the Price of Glasses," *Journal of Law and Economics*, vol. 15, no. 2 (1972), pp. 337–352.

2. Adam Smith, *The Wealth of Nations* (New York: Modern Library, 1994).

3. Sylvia Nassar, *A Beautiful Mind* (New York: Simon & Schuster, 1998).

4. Robert Axelrod, *The Evolution of Cooperation*, (New York: Basic Books, 1984).

5. Federal Trade Commission, "Record Companies Settle FTC Charges of Restraining Competition in CD Music Market," Press Release, May 10, 2000.

6. "Big Friendly Giant," *The Economist*, January 30, 1999, p. 72.

7. John R. Wilke, "New Antitrust Rules May Ease Path to Mergers," *Wall Street Journal*, April 9, 1997, pp. A3–A4.

8. "The Economics of Antitrust: The Trustbuster's New Tools," *The Economist*, May 2, 1998, pp. 62–64; Federal Trade Commission v. Staples, Inc., 970 F. Supp. 1066 (D.D.C. 1997, Hogan, J); U.S. Federal Trade Commission, Promoting Competition, Protecting Consumers: A Plain English Guide to Antitrust Laws, available online at www.ftc.gov/bc/compguide/index.htm, accessed 06/28/2006.

9. "The Economics of Antitrust: The Trustbuster's New Tools," *The Economist*, May 2, 1998, pp. 62–64.

# 9

# Market Failure: Imperfect Information, External Benefits, and External Cost

"So, why are you selling this used car?"

The buyers of used cars ask this question frequently and then listen carefully to the answer. Assuming the car seller is honest, the answer the buyer hopes for is, "Because I need a different car for my new job," or

1 Why does a new car lose about 20 percent of its value in the first week?
   *The Resale Value of a Week-Old Car*

2 How can government solve the adverse-selection problem?
   *Regulation of the California Kiwifruit Market*

3 Does the market for baseball pitchers suffer from the adverse-selection problem?
   *Baseball Pitchers Are Like Used Cars*

4 What is the free-rider problem?
   *Free Riders and the Three-Clock Tower*

5 How can we pay for public goods?
   *Paying Landowners to Host Wolves*

6 How do we determine the optimum level of pollution?
   *The Optimal Level of Sulfur Dioxide Emissions*

7 What is the economic approach to global warming?
   *The Effects of a Carbon Tax*

8 Are there different ways to reduce pollution or mitigate its effects?
   *Dear Abby and Environmental Policy*

9 What determines the price of a marketable pollution permit?
   *Marketable Permits for Sulfur Dioxide*

10 What are the benefits of giving firms options for reducing greenhouse gases?
   *Chicago Climate Exchange*

"I buy a new car every three years." The buyer is trying to avoid sellers who are trying to get rid of a "lemon"—a car that breaks down frequently and generates large repair bills. People don't ask this sort of question in other markets. For example, no one ever asks, "So, why are you selling this pizza?"

**"Does my insurance policy cover accidental death from bungee jumping?"**

Life is risky, and people buy insurance to decrease the financial losses from events such as theft, sickness, injury, and death. This question above from the potential bungee jumper reveals an important fact about insurance: It causes people to take greater risks because they know insurance will cover part of the cost of an accident.

• **asymmetric information**
A situation in which one side of the market—either buyers or sellers—has better information than the other.

• **mixed market**
A market in which goods of different qualities are sold for the same price.

Earlier in the book we used the model of demand and supply to show how individual decisions in markets generate equilibrium prices and quantities. Adam Smith used the metaphor of the invisible hand to explain how individuals in markets, each acting in his or her own self-interest may actually promote the interest of society as a whole[1]: "It is not from the benevolence of the butcher, the brewer, or the baker that we expect our dinner, but from their regard to their own interest. We address ourselves, not to their humanity but to their self-love, and never talk to them of our own necessities but of their advantages. . . . [Man is] led by an invisible hand to promote an end which was no part of this intention. . . . By pursuing his own interest he frequently promotes that of the society more effectually than when he really intends to promote it. . . . Nobody but a beggar chooses to depend chiefly upon which the benevolence of his fellow citizens."

In this chapter we will explore the circumstances under which the decisions of individuals do not promote the social interest.

- **Imperfect information:** One side of the market, either buyers or sellers, does not know enough about the product to make informed decisions about whether to buy or sell it. In a world of fully informed buyers and sellers, markets operate smoothly, generating an equilibrium price and an equilibrium quantity for each good. In a world with imperfect information, some goods will be sold in very small numbers, or not sold at all. In addition, buyers and sellers will use resources to acquire information to help make better decisions.

- **External benefits:** The benefits of a product are not confined to the person who pays for it. For example, if a farmer builds a levee for flood protection, other farmers in the flood plain will benefit from the levee. When there are external benefits, collective decision making will improve efficiency.

- **External costs:** The cost of producing a product is not confined to the person who sells it. For example, producing electricity from coal fouls the air and imposes costs on people who suffer from asthma. The economic approach to external costs, is to internalize the costs, forcing polluters to pay for pollution in the same way that they pay for raw materials and labor.

# 9.1 | THE LEMONS PROBLEM

The classic example of a market with imperfect information is the market for used cars.[2] Suppose there are two types of cars, low quality and high quality. A low-quality car, also known as a "lemon," breaks down frequently and has relatively high repair costs. A high-quality car, also known as a "plum," is reliable and has relatively low repair costs. Suppose buyers cannot distinguish between lemons and plums. Although a buyer can get some information about a particular car by looking at the car and taking it for a test drive, the information gleaned from this kind of inspection is not enough to determine the quality of the car. In contrast, a person selling a car after owning it for a while knows from experience whether the car is a lemon or a plum. We say that there is **asymmetric information** in a market if one side of the market—either buyers or sellers—has better information than the other side. Because buyers cannot distinguish between lemons and plums, there will be a single market for used automobiles: Both types of cars will be sold together in a **mixed market** for the same price.

## Uninformed Buyers and Knowledgeable Sellers

How much is a consumer willing to pay for a used car that could be either a lemon or a plum? To determine a consumer's willingness to pay in a mixed market with both lemons and plums, we must answer three questions:

**1** How much is the consumer willing to pay for a plum?

**2** How much is the consumer willing to pay for a lemon?

**3** What is the chance that a used car purchased in the mixed market will be of low quality?

Suppose the typical buyer is willing to pay $4,000 for a plum and $2,000 for a lemon. The buyer is willing to pay less for a lemon because it is less reliable and has higher repair costs. For someone who is willing to put up with the hassle and repair expense, a lemon is a reasonable car. That's why the typical buyer is willing to pay $2,000, not zero, for a low-quality car that we tag with the label "lemon." Someone who pays $2,000 and gets a lemon is just as happy as someone who pays $4,000 and gets a plum.

Consumer expectations play a key role in determining the market outcome when there is imperfect information. Suppose that half the used cars *on the road* are lemons, and consumers know this. A reasonable expectation for consumers is that half the cars *on the used-car market* will be lemons, too. In other words, buyers initially expect a 50–50 split between the two types of cars. A reasonable assumption is that a buyer in the mixed market is willing to pay the average value of the two types of cars, or $3,000. In other words, a buyer is willing to pay $3,000 for a 50–50 chance of getting either a plum or a lemon.

The current owner of a used car knows from everyday experience whether the car is a lemon or a plum. For each owner, the question is, given the single market price for all used cars, lemons and plums alike, should I sell my car? The answers to this question are shown by the two supply curves in Figure 9.1, one for lemons and one for plums:

- **Lemon supply.** As shown by the lower curve, the minimum supply price for lemons is $500: At any price less than $500, no lemons will be supplied. Lemons have a lower minimum price because they are worth less to their current owners. The number of lemons supplied increases with price. For example, 80 cars will be supplied at a price of $3,000 (point *b*).

- **Plum supply.** As shown by the upper curve, the minimum supply price for plums is $2,500: At any price less than $2,500, no plums will be supplied. Consistent with the law of supply, the higher the price of used cars, the larger the number of plums supplied. For example, 20 plums will be supplied at a price of $3,000 (point *a*).

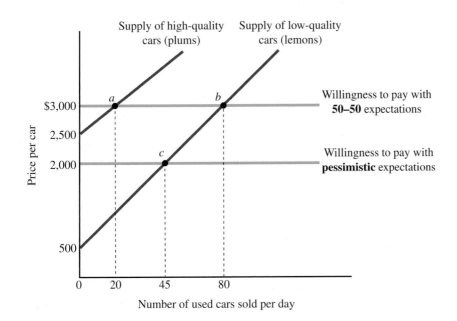

**◄ FIGURE 9.1**

**All Used Cars on the Market Are Lemons**

If buyers assume that there is a 50–50 chance of getting a lemon or a plum, they are willing to pay $3,000 for a used car. At this price, 20 plums are supplied (point *a*) along with 80 lemons (point *b*). This is not an equilibrium because consumers' expectation of a 50–50 split are not realized. If consumers become pessimistic and assume that all cars on the market will be lemons, they are willing to pay $2,000 for a used car. At this price, only lemons will be supplied (point *c*). Consumer expectations are realized, so the equilibrium is shown by point *c*, with an equilibrium price of $2,000.

**Table 9.1** | EQUILIBRIUM WITH ALL LOW-QUALITY GOODS

|  | Buyers Initially Have 50–50 Expectations | Equilibrium: Pessimistic Expectations |
|---|---|---|
| **Demand Side of Market** | | |
| Amount buyer is willing to pay for a lemon | $2,000 | $2,000 |
| Amount buyer is willing to pay for a plum | $4,000 | $4,000 |
| Assumed chance of getting a lemon | 50% | 100% |
| Assumed chance of getting a plum | 50% | 0% |
| Amount buyer is willing to pay for a used car in mixed market | $3,000 | $2,000 |
| **Supply Side of Market** | | |
| Number of lemons supplied | 80 | 45 |
| Number of plums supplied | 20 | 0 |
| Total number of used cars supplied | 100 | 45 |
| Actual chance of getting a lemon | 80% | 100% |

## Equilibrium with All Low-Quality Goods

Table 9.1 shows two scenarios for our hypothetical used-car market, based on the supply curves shown in Figure 9.1. In the first column, we assume that buyers have 50–50 expectations about the quality of used cars. As we saw earlier, if buyers expect a 50–50 split between lemons and plums, the typical buyer will be willing to pay $3,000 for a used car. From the supply curves in Figure 9.1, we know that at this price 20 plums and 80 lemons will be supplied, so 80 percent of the used cars (80 of 100) will be lemons. In this case, consumers are too optimistic and underestimate the chance of getting a lemon.

The experiences of these 100 consumers show that the actual chance of getting a lemon is 80 percent, not 50 percent as initially assumed. Once future buyers realize this, they will of course become more pessimistic about the used-car market. Suppose they assume that all the used cars on the market will be lemons. Under this assumption, the typical buyer will be willing to pay only $2,000 (the value of a lemon) for a used car. As shown in Figure 9.1, this price is less than the $2,500 minimum price for supplying plums, so plums will disappear from the used-car market. At a price of $2,000, the quantity of plums supplied is zero, but the quantity of lemons supplied is 45 (point *c*). In other words, all the used cars will be lemons, so consumers' pessimism is justified. Because consumers' expectations are consistent with their actual experiences in the market, the equilibrium price of used cars is $2,000. The equilibrium in the used-car market is shown in the second column of Table 9.1.

In this equilibrium, no plums are bought or sold, so every buyer will get a lemon. People get exactly what they pay for: They are willing to pay $2,000 for a serviceable but low-quality car, and that's what each consumer gets. The domination of the used-car market by lemons is an example of the **adverse-selection problem**. The uninformed side of the market (buyers in this case) must choose from an undesirable or adverse selection of used cars. The asymmetric information in the market generates a downward spiral of price and quality:

- The presence of low-quality goods on the market pulls down the price that consumers are willing to pay.

- A decrease in price decreases the number of high-quality goods supplied, decreasing the average quality of goods on the market.

- The decrease in the average quality of goods on the market pulls down the price that consumers are willing to pay again.

• **adverse-selection problem**
A situation in which the uninformed side of the market must choose from an undesirable or adverse selection of goods.

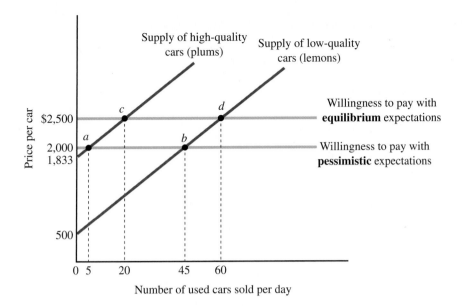

If buyers are pessimistic and assume that only lemons will be sold, they are willing to pay $2,000 for a used car. At this price, 5 plums are supplied (point *a*), along with 45 lemons (point *b*). This is not an equilibrium because 10% of consumers get plums, contrary to their expectations. If consumers assume that there is a 25% change of getting a plum, they are willing to pay $2,500 for a used car. At this price, 20 plums are supplied (point *c*), along with 60 lemons (point *d*). This is an equilibrium because 25% of consumers get plums, consistent with their expectations. Consumer expectations are realized, so the equilibrium is shown by points *c* and *d*.

In the extreme case, this downward spiral continues until all the cars on the market are lemons.

## A Thin Market: Equilibrium with Some High-Quality Goods

The disappearance of plums from our hypothetical used-car market is an extreme case. The plums disappeared from the market because informed plum owners decided to keep their cars rather than selling them at a relatively low price in the used-car market. This outcome would change if the minimum supply price of plums were lower, specifically if it is below $2,000. In this case, most but not all the used cars on the market will be lemons, and some lucky buyers will get plums. In this case, we say that asymmetric information generates a **thin market**: Some high-quality goods are sold, but fewer than would be sold in a market with perfect information.

Figure 9.2 shows the situation that leads to a thin market. The minimum supply price for plums is $1,833, and the quantity of plums supplied increases with the price of used cars. Suppose that consumers are initially pessimistic, assuming that all cars for sale will be lemons. This means that consumers are willing to pay only $2,000 for a used car. Because the minimum supply price for plums ($1,833) is now less than the willingness to pay for a lemon, some plums will be supplied at a price of $2,000. In Figure 9.2, 5 plums and 45 lemons are supplied at this price, so 1 out of every 10 buyers will get a plum. In this case, pessimism is not an equilibrium, because some buyers will get plums when they expect lemons. This is also shown in the first column of Table 9.2.

In equilibrium, consumer expectations about the chances of getting the two types of cars are realized. Suppose that consumers expect 1 of every 4 cars to be a plum. Let's assume that each consumer is willing to pay $2,500 for a used car under these circumstances. Consumers are willing to pay a bit more than the value of a lemon because there is a small chance of getting a plum. In Figure 9.2, at this price 20 plums are supplied (point *c*) and 60 lemons are supplied (point *d*), so in fact 1 in 4 consumers actually gets a plum. This is an equilibrium because 25 percent of the cars sold are plums and 75 percent are lemons, consistent with consumers' expectations. This is also shown in the second column of Table 9.2.

• **thin market**
A market in which some high-quality goods are sold but fewer than would be sold in a market with perfect information.

Table 9.2 | A THIN MARKET FOR HIGH-QUALITY GOODS

| | Initial Pessimistic Expectations | Equilibrium: 75–25 Expectations |
|---|---|---|
| **Demand Side of Market** | | |
| Amount buyer is willing to pay for a lemon | $2,000 | $2,000 |
| Amount buyer is willing to pay for a plum | $4,000 | $4,000 |
| Assumed chance of getting a lemon | 100% | 75% |
| Assumed chance of getting a plum | 0% | 25% |
| Amount buyer is willing to pay for a used car in mixed market | $2,000 | $2,500 |
| **Supply Side of Market** | | |
| Number of lemons supplied | 45 | 60 |
| Number of plums supplied | 5 | 20 |
| Total number of used cars supplied | 50 | 80 |
| Actual chance of getting a lemon | 90% | 75% |

# 9.2 | RESPONDING TO THE LEMONS PROBLEM

In a market with asymmetric information, there are strong incentives for buyers and sellers to solve the lemons problem. In our example of a thin market, the price of a used car is $2,500, but consumers are willing to pay $4,000 for a plum. This $1,500 gap between the willingness to pay for a plum and the price in the mixed market provides an incentive for buyers to acquire information to help identify plums. It also provides an incentive for plum owners to prove that they are selling high-quality cars.

## Buyers Invest in Information

In our model of the thin market, 1 of 4 buyers pays $2,500 to get a plum worth $4,000. The more information a buyer has, the greater the chance of picking a plum from the cars in the mixed market. Suppose a buyer gets enough information to identify the plums in a market. The buyer could purchase a plum worth $4,000 at the prevailing price of $2,500, generating a gain of $1,500. A buyer can get information about individual cars by taking the car to a mechanic for a careful inspection. In addition, a buyer can get general information about the reliability of different models from magazines and the Internet. *Consumer Reports* publishes information on repair histories of different models and even computes a "Trouble" index, scoring each model on a scale of 1 to 5. By consulting these information sources, a buyer improves the chances of getting a high-quality car.

## Consumer Satisfaction Scores from ValueStar and eBay

The problem of asymmetric information in consumer goods such as cars also occurs for some types of consumer services. Most consumers can't easily determine the quality of service they will receive from an auto repair shop, a landscaper, or a plumber. How can a high-quality service provider distinguish itself from low-quality providers?

If you live in the San Francisco Bay area, you can get information about the performance of firms providing consumer services such as medical and dental care, gardening and landscaping, pet grooming, auto repair, and home improvement. ValueStar is a consumer guide and business directory that uses customer satisfaction surveys to determine how well a firm does relative to its competitors in providing quality service. To earn the right to display a Customer-Rated seal from ValueStar, a firm must prove that it has all the required licenses and insurance and must agree to pay for a survey of its past customers. ValueStar uses consumer surveys to compute a consumer-satisfaction score for each company. Any company receiving a score of at least 85 out of 100 has the right to display a Customer-Rated Gold seal for a one-year period.

Another example of consumer satisfaction scores is evident on eBay, the Internet auction site. On eBay, buyers must rely on sellers to honestly disclose the quality of the goods they are auctioning and to promptly ship them once a consumer pays. Buyers help other purchasers distinguish "good" from "bad" sellers on eBay by rating them online with "stars," indicating their satisfaction with their transactions.

## Guarantees and Lemons Laws

Used-car sellers also have an incentive to solve the lemons problem. If a plum owner persuades a buyer that her car is a plum and then sells the car for $4,000 rather than $2,500, the seller's gain is $1,500. Sellers can identify a car as a plum in a sea of lemons by offering one of the following guarantees:

- *Money-back guarantees.* The seller could promise to refund the $4,000 price if the car turned out to be a lemon. Because the car is in fact a plum—a fact known by the seller—the buyer will not ask for a refund, so both the buyer and the seller will be happy with the transaction.
- *Warranties and repair guarantees.* The seller could promise to cover any extraordinary repair costs for one year. Because the car is a plum, there won't be any extraordinary costs, so both the buyer and the seller will be happy with the transaction.

Many states have laws that require automakers to buy back cars that experience frequent problems in the first year of use. For example, under California's Song–Beverly Consumer Warranty Act, also known as the "Lemons Law," auto dealers are required to repurchase vehicles that have been brought back for repair at least four times for the same problem or have been in the mechanic's shop for at least 30 calendar days in the first year following purchase. A vehicle repurchased under the lemons law

# APPLICATION

## THE RESALE VALUE OF A WEEK-OLD CAR

**APPLYING THE CONCEPTS #1:** Why does a new car lose about 20 percent of its value in the first week?

If you buy a new car for $20,000 today and then try to sell it a week later, you probably won't get more than $16,000 for it. Even if you drove it just a couple hundred miles, cleaned it up, and returned it to the dealer with that new-car smell, the car will lose about 20 percent of its value in the first week. You won't fare any better by putting an advertisement in the newspaper or trying to sell the car on eBay. Why does the typical new car lose so much of its value in the first week?

A potential buyer of a week-old car might believe that a person who returns a car after only one week could have discovered it was a lemon and may be trying to get rid of it. Alternatively, the seller could have simply changed his or her mind about the car. The problem is that buyers don't know why the car is being sold, and as long as there is a chance that the car is a lemon they won't be willing to pay the full "new" price for it. In general, buyers are willing to pay a lot less for a week-old car, and so the owners of high-quality, week-old cars are less likely to put them on the market. This downward spiral ultimately reduces the price of week-old cars by about 20 percent.
*Related to Exercises 2.4 and 2.10.*

must be fixed before it is sold to another customer and must be identified as a lemon with a stamp on the title and a sticker on the car that says "lemons law buyback." One problem with enforcing these laws is that lemons can cross state lines without a paper trail. The interstate commerce in lemons has led to new laws in some states requiring the branding of lemons on vehicle titles to follow the car when it crosses state lines.

### Evidence for the Lemons Effect

The lemons model makes two predictions about markets with asymmetric information. First, the presence of low-quality goods in a market will at least reduce the number of high-quality goods in the market and may even eliminate them. Second, buyers and sellers will respond to the lemons problem by investing in information and other means of distinguishing between low-quality and high-quality goods. What's the evidence for the lemons model?

## APPLICATION

### REGULATION OF THE CALIFORNIA KIWIFRUIT MARKET

APPLYING THE CONCEPTS #2: How can government solve the adverse-selection problem?

Kiwifruit is subject to imperfect information because buyers cannot determine its sweetness—its quality level—by simple inspection. The sweetness level at the time of consumption is determined by the fruit's "maturity"—its sugar content at the time of harvest. Kiwifruit continues to convert starch into sugar after it is picked, so a harvest-time sugar content of 6.5 percent leads to a sugar content of about 14 percent at the time of consumption. Fruit that is picked early has a low sugar content at harvest time and never tastes sweet. There is asymmetric information because producers know the maturity of the fruit, but fruit wholesalers and grocery stores, who buy fruit at the time of harvest, cannot determine whether a piece of fruit will ultimately be sweet or sour.

Before 1987, kiwifruit from California suffered from the "lemons" problem. Maturity levels of the fruit varied across producers. On average, the sugar content at the time of harvest was below the industry standard, established by kiwifruit from New Zealand. Given the large number of "lemons" among California kiwifruit, grocery stores were not willing to pay as much for California fruit. In other words, the presence of low-quality (immature) fruit in the mixed market pulled down the price of California fruit. Mature kiwifruit is more costly to produce than immature fruit, and the low price decreased the production of mature fruit. This is similar to low used-car prices decreasing the number of high-quality used cars on the market. In general, adverse selection led to low prices and a relatively large volume of low-quality kiwifruit from California.

In 1987, California producers implemented a federal marketing order to address the lemon–kiwi problem. The federal order specified a minimum maturity standard (6.5 percent sugar content at the time of harvest), and as the average quality of California fruit increased, so did the price. Within a few years, the gap between California and New Zealand prices had decreased significantly.

*Related to Exercises 2.6 and 2.11.*

SOURCE: Christopher Ferguson and Hoy Carman, "Kiwifruit and the 'Lemon' Problem: Do Minimum Quality Standards Work?" Working Paper, 1999. International Food and Agribusiness Management Association.

# APPLICATION

## BASEBALL PITCHERS ARE LIKE USED CARS

**APPLYING THE CONCEPTS #3:** Does the market for baseball pitchers suffer from the adverse-selection problem?

Professional baseball teams compete with each other for players. After six years of play in the major leagues, a player has the option of becoming a free agent and offering his services to the highest bidder. A player is likely to switch teams if the new team offers him a higher salary than his original team. One of the puzzling features of the free-agent market is that pitchers who switch teams are more prone to injuries than pitchers who don't. On average, pitchers who switch teams spend 28 days per season on the disabled list, compared to only 5 days for pitchers who do not switch teams. This doesn't mean that all the switching pitchers are lemons; many of them are injury-free and are valuable additions to their new teams. But on average, the switching pitchers spend five times longer recovering from injuries.

This puzzling feature of the free-agent market for baseball players is explained by asymmetric information and adverse selection. Because the coaches, physicians, and trainers from the player's original team have interacted with the player on a daily basis for several years, they know from experience whether he is likely to suffer from injuries that prevent him from playing. In contrast, the new team has much less information. Its physicians can examine the pitcher, and the team can check league records to see how long the pitcher has spent on the disabled list, but these measures do not eliminate the asymmetric information. The original team has several years of daily experience with the pitcher and has better information about the pitcher's physical health.

To illustrate the lemons problem for pitchers, consider the incentives for a team to outbid another team for a pitcher. Suppose the market price for pitchers is $1 million per year, and a pitcher who is currently with the Detroit Tigers is offered this salary by another team. If the Tigers think the pitcher is likely to spend a lot of time next season recovering from injuries, they won't try to outbid the other team for the pitcher: They will let the pitcher switch teams. But if the Tigers think the pitcher will be injury-free and productive, he will be worth more than $1 million to the Tigers, so they will outbid other teams and keep him. In general, an injury-prone pitcher is more likely to switch teams. As in the used-car market, there are many "lemons" on the used-pitcher market. The market for baseball players playing other positions does not suffer from the adverse selection, perhaps because the injuries that affect their performance are easier for other teams to detect.

Although you may think it's bizarre to compare baseball pitchers to used cars, people in baseball don't think so. They recognize the similarity between the two markets. Jackie Moore, who managed a free-agent camp where teams looking for players can see free agents in action, sounds like a used-car salesman: "We want to get players off the lot. We want to cut a deal. How many camps can you go into where you can look at a player and take him home with you?" *Related to Exercises 2.7 and 2.12.*

SOURCES: Kenneth Lehn, "Information Asymmetries in Baseball's Free Agent Market," *Economic Inquiry*, vol. 22, January 1984, pp. 37–44; Chris Sheridan, "Free Agents at End of Baseball's Earth," Associated Press, printed in *Corvallis Gazette-Times*, April 15, 1995, p. B1.

Studies of the market for used pickup trucks have provided mixed results concerning the lemons problem.[3] It appears that for trucks less than 10 years old, those sold on the market are just as reliable, on average, as those that remain with their current owners. These studies provide support for the second implication of the theory of lemons, that people acquire information and develop effective means to deal with the problem of asymmetric information. In contrast, there does seem to be a lemons problem for trucks at least 10 years old, which represent about one-third of transactions. Compared to old trucks that remain with their current owners, old trucks that are sold have significantly higher repair costs, with a difference in cost of about 45 percent. Old trucks that are sold have a much higher probability of requiring engine and transmission repairs.

# $9.3$ | INSURANCE AND MORAL HAZARD

Does insurance affect people's risk-taking behavior? The answer is yes. Insurance causes people to take greater risks because they know part of the cost of an undesirable outcome will be borne by their insurance companies. Here are some examples of people taking greater risks because they have insurance:

- Will Irma buy a fire extinguisher for her kitchen? If she had to pay for any property damage caused by a fire, she would definitely buy a fire extinguisher. But because her homeowner's insurance covers property damage from fires, she doesn't buy a fire extinguisher.
- Will Harry drive his car carefully? If he had to pay for all repairs resulting from a collision out of his own pocket, he would drive very carefully. But because his auto insurance covers some of the repair costs, he drives fast and recklessly.
- Will Flo fly on a commercial airline or hitch a ride with her pilot friend in a four-seat airplane? Traveling in small airplanes is much riskier. If Flo dies in an airplane crash, her family will lose the income she would otherwise earn. If she didn't have life insurance to offset these income losses, she would be less likely to risk harming her family by flying on the small plane instead of the commercial airline. But because she knows her family will collect $1 million in life insurance, she is willing to take the risk.

- **moral hazard**
  A situation in which one side of an economic relationship takes undesirable or costly actions that the other side of the relationship cannot observe.

The risky behavior triggered by insurance is an example of the moral-hazard problem. **Moral hazard** occurs when one side of an economic relationship takes undesirable or costly actions that the other side of the relationship cannot observe. For example, Irma's insurance company doesn't know whether she has a fire extinguisher. She doesn't buy an extinguisher because her insurance will cover the cost of a kitchen fire. If there is a fire, Irma's hidden action—going without an extinguisher—is costly for the insurance company. Similarly, Harry's insurance company doesn't know how fast and recklessly he drives, and insurance encourages him to drive recklessly. His hidden action of reckless driving increases the likelihood of a costly accident. Just as collision insurance encourages risky driving, life insurance encourages risky activities such as flying small airplanes, parachuting, and bungee jumping. Similarly, health insurance encourages risky behavior such as smoking, drinking, and unhealthy diets.

Insurance companies use various measures to decrease the moral-hazard problem. Many insurance policies have a deductible—a dollar amount that a policy holder must pay before getting compensation from the insurance company. For example, if your car insurance policy has a $500 deductible and the damage from a collision is $900, the insurance company will pay you only $400. To compute its payment, the insurance company deducts your $500 deductible from the $900 damage figure, and then pays you $400. Deductibles reduces the moral-hazard problem because they shift part of the cost of a collision to the policy holder. Like a deductible, an insurance copayment shifts part of the cost of risky behavior to policy holders and thus reduces the moral-hazard problem.

## Deposit Insurance for Savings & Loans

For another example of moral hazard, consider the insurance provided for bank deposits. When you deposit money in a Savings and Loan (S&L), the money doesn't just sit in a vault. The S&L will invest the money, loaning it out and expecting to make a profit when loans are repaid with interest. Unfortunately, some loans are not repaid, and the S&L could lose money and be unable to return your money. To protect people who put their money in S&Ls and other banks, the Federal Deposit Insurance Corporation (FDIC) insures the first $100,000 of your deposit, so if the S&L goes bankrupt, you'll still get your money back. The government enacted the federal deposit insurance law in 1933 in response to the bank failures of the Great Depression.

How does deposit insurance affect you and the people who manage the S&L? If you know you'll get your money back no matter what happens to the S&L, you may deposit your money there without evaluating the performance of the S&L and the riskiness of its loans to borrowers and investments in the stock market. The manager of an S&L will also be more likely to make risky investments knowing that if it doesn't pay off and the S&L goes bankrupt, the federal government will reimburse depositors. Recognizing this moral hazard problem, the federal government has historically limited S&Ls to relatively safe investments.

In the 1980s, the federal government loosened some of the investment restrictions on S&Ls, and S&L managers began investing in volatile securities, including high-risk commercial mortgages and junk bonds. When these risky investments failed, many of the S&Ls went into bankruptcy. The government then bailed out the failed S&Ls, at a total cost to taxpayers of about $200 billion.

## 9.4 | EXTERNAL BENEFITS AND PUBLIC GOODS

For most goods, the benefits of consumption are confined to the person who buys the good. The benefit experienced by a buyer is called a *private benefit*. In contrast, when someone else benefits from a good, the good generates an **external benefit**. To illustrate the idea of external benefits and inefficiency, consider a dam built for flood-control purposes. One thousand people would be protected by the dam, and each person gets a $50 benefit. If one person builds a dam, the private benefit is $50 and the external benefit is $49,950, or $50 for each of the 999 other people who benefit from the dam. If the cost of building the dam is $20,000, no single person will build it because the cost exceeds the $50 private benefit. In other words, if we rely on the forces of supply and demand, with each person considering only private benefits and the costs of the dam, it won't be built.

When there are external benefits from a good, collective decision making generates more-efficient choices. In the case of the dam, the total benefit of $50,000 exceeds the $20,000 cost, so the dam is efficient and society as a whole will be better off if it is built. The government can solve this problem by collecting enough tax revenue to pay for the dam. Suppose the government proposes to collect $20 per person to pay for the dam. The tax raises $20,000 in tax revenue ($20 per person times 1,000 people), which is just high enough to pay the $20,000 cost of the dam. Most people will support this proposal because the $20 tax per person is less than the $50 benefit per person. The government can use its taxing power to provide a good that would otherwise not be provided.

• **external benefit**
A benefit from a good experienced by someone other than the person who buys the good.

## Public Goods and the Free-Rider Problem

The dam is an example of a *public good*. A **public good** is available for everyone to utilize, regardless of who pays for it and who doesn't. More precisely, a public good is *nonrival* in consumption: The fact that one person benefits from a good does not prevent another person from benefiting. For example, the fact that I

• **public good**
A good that is available for everyone to consume, regardless of who pays and who doesn't; a good that is nonrival in consumption and nonexcludable.

# APPLICATION

## FREE RIDERS AND THE THREE-CLOCK TOWER

What is the free-rider problem?

Back in the days before inexpensive wristwatches, most people did not carry their own timepieces. Many towns built clock towers to help their citizens keep track of time. The towns paid for the clock towers with voluntary contributions from citizens. One town in the northeastern United States built a four-sided tower but put clock faces on only three sides of the tower. To most people, this seems bizarre. If you build a clock tower, why not put clock faces on all four sides? It turns out that one of the town's wealthy citizens refused to contribute money to help build the clock tower. The town officials decided not to put a clock face on the side of the tower facing the wealthy citizen's house. In other words, the citizen tried—unsuccessfully—to get a free ride. The problem is that other citizens on the same side of town also suffered from not seeing the clock. In this case, preventing a free ride by one citizen caused problems for other citizens. *Related to Exercise 4.5.*

benefit from a flood-control dam doesn't reduce your benefit from the dam. Public goods are also *nonexcludable*: It is impractical to exclude people who don't pay. Some examples of public goods are national defense, law enforcement, space exploration, the preservation of endangered species, the protection of the earth's ozone layer, and fireworks shows. If someone refuses to pay for one of these public goods, it would be impractical to prevent that person from consuming or benefiting from the good.

In contrast with public goods, each unit of a **private good** is consumed by a single person or household. For example, only one person can eat a hot dog, so it is a private good. If a government hands out free cheese to the poor, is the free cheese a public good or a private good? Although anyone can get in line for the cheese, only one person can actually consume a particular piece of cheese, so the free cheese is a private good that happens to be available free of charge from the government. Similarly, an apartment in a public housing project can be occupied by a single household, so it is a private good provided by the government.

Most public goods are supported by taxes. What would happen if we eliminated taxes and asked people to contribute money to pay for national defense, dams, city streets, and the police? Would people contribute enough money to support these programs at the efficient level? The problem with using voluntary contributions to support public goods is known as the *free-rider problem*. A **free rider** is a person who gets the benefit from a good but does not pay for it. Each person has a financial incentive to try

- **private good**
  A good that is consumed by a single person or household; a good that is rival in consumption and excludable.

- **free rider**
  A person who gets the benefit from a good but does not pay for it.

to get the benefits of a public good without paying for it. That is, some people will try to get a "free ride" at the expense of others who do pay. Of course, if everyone tries to get a free ride there will be no money to support the public good, so it won't be provided.

The flip side of the free-rider problem is the chump problem: No one wants to be the chump—the person who gives free rides to other people—so no one contributes any money. The free-rider problem suggests that if taxes were replaced with voluntary contributions, the government would be forced to cut back or eliminate many programs.

## Overcoming the Free-Rider Problem

Many organizations, including public radio and television, religious organizations, and charitable organizations, raise money through voluntary contributions. So it appears that some people overcome their inclination to be free riders and contribute voluntarily to organizations that provide public goods. The successful organizations use a number of techniques to encourage people to contribute:

- *Giving contributors private goods such as coffee mugs, books, musical recordings, and magazine subscriptions.* People are more likely to contribute if they get something for it.
- *Arranging matching contributions.* You are more likely to contribute if you know that your $30 contribution will be matched with a contribution from another person or your employer.
- Appealing to a person's sense of civic or moral responsibility.

It's important to note, however, that these organizations are only partly successful in mitigating the free-rider problem. Public radio is one of the success stories, even though the typical public-radio station gets contributions from less than a quarter of its listeners.

## Asteroid Diversion as a Public Good

Consider the issue of protecting the earth from catastrophic collisions with asteroids. On average, the earth is hit by a 200-meter asteroid every 10,000 years, by a 2-kilometer asteroid every million years, and by a 10-kilometer asteroid every 100 million years.[4]

A collision will generate a stratospheric dust cloud that will inhibit photosynthesis and retard plant growth, resulting in lower agricultural yields and higher food prices throughout the world. According to scientists at the National Aeronautics and Space Administration (NASA), we have the technology to divert approaching asteroids. Large optical telescopes would detect an asteroid on a collision course with the earth, and an orbiting gossamer mirror of coated polyester would focus a tight beam of sunlight on the asteroid, vaporizing enough of its surface to change its path.

The diversion of asteroids is a public good in the sense that it is available for everyone's benefit, regardless of who pays and who doesn't. As with any public good, the key to developing an asteroid-diversion program is to collect money to pay for the program. According to NASA scientists, the program would require several new telescopes, which would cost about $50 million to install and about $10 million per year to operate.[5] The cost of the gossamer mirror or the nuclear weapons required to change the path of the asteroid would be $100 million to $200 million. Although it would be sensible to finance the program with contributions from all earthlings, it may be impossible to collect money from everyone. A more likely outcome is that one or more developed countries will finance their own diversion systems.

# APPLICATION

**PAYING LANDOWNERS TO HOST WOLVES**

**APPLYING THE CONCEPTS #5:** How can we pay for public goods?

We can apply the concepts of public goods and free riding to the issue of preserving wildlife. There are some trade-offs associated with preserving wolves and other wildlife in Yellowstone Park. To environmentalists, wolves are a part of the natural ecosystem. To ranchers, wolves are predators that eat livestock. In other words, there are costs as well as benefits associated with the preservation of wolves, just as there are costs and benefits associated with other public goods such as dams, fireworks, national defense, and space exploration.

One response to the wolf-preservation problem comes from Defenders of Wildlife, an environmental group in Montana. The organization collects money from its members and uses the money to reward landowners who allow wolves to live on their properties. The host landowner receives a payment of $5,000 for each litter of wolf pups reared on the property. In addition, the organization compensates ranchers for livestock killed by wolves. As a result of these programs, ranchers in the Yellowstone area are more likely to support efforts to maintain the wolves as part of Yellowstone Park's ecosystem. The programs treat preservation as a public good, one that is supported by money contributed by people who benefit from preservation. The organization has collected contributions from thousands of people despite the free-rider problem. The success of Defenders of Wildlife illustrates one of the key principles of economics. *Related to Exercise 4.6.*

# PRINCIPLE OF VOLUNTARY EXCHANGE

A voluntary exchange between two people makes both people better off.

SOURCE: Terry L. Anderson, "A Carrot to Save the Wolf," *The Margin,* Spring 1992, p. 28.

# 9.5 | THE OPTIMAL LEVEL OF POLLUTION

Should we eliminate all pollution? Although a pristine environment with pure water and air sounds appealing, there would be some very unappealing consequences. To reduce air pollution, we could eliminate trucks, but shipping goods by horse-drawn wagon would result in higher freight costs and higher prices for most products—and a different sort of pollution. We could reduce water pollution by shutting down all the paper mills, but reverting to parchment and slate boards would be unwieldy. Given the consequences of eliminating pollution, it is sensible to allow some pollution to occur. What's the optimal level of pollution?

## Using the Marginal Principle

The most convenient way to discuss pollution policies is in terms of pollution abatement, that is, reductions in pollution from some starting level. We can use the marginal principle to determine the optimal level of pollution abatement.

# APPLICATION

6

## THE OPTIMAL LEVEL OF SULFUR DIOXIDE EMISSIONS

**APPLYING THE CONCEPTS #6:** How do we determine the optimum level of pollution?

Sulfur dioxide ($SO_2$) emissions contribute to health problems such as upper respiratory illness, bronchitis, coughing episodes, and chest discomfort. $SO_2$ is a contributing factor—along with nitrogen oxide and other pollutants—in thousands of premature deaths each year. When sulfur dioxide is combined with nitrogen oxides and other chemicals in the atmosphere, the result is acid rain, which damages vegetation and buildings and kills aquatic life.

A recent study estimated the marginal benefits and marginal costs of reducing $SO_2$ emissions from electricity generation facilities, looking ahead to the year 2010. Figure 9.3 shows the marginal-benefit and marginal-cost curves for $SO_2$ abatement. Notice that along the horizontal axis, abatement increases as we move to the right, while the amount of $SO_2$ discharged decreases. The sum of abatement and discharges is 9.1 million tons:

- The marginal-benefit curve is horizontal at $3,500, because for each additional ton of $SO_2$ discharged into the atmosphere, the costs associated with premature deaths and health problems increase by about $3,500.

- The marginal-cost curve is positively sloped, because the more pollution we abate, the higher the marginal cost of abatement. The first 2 million tons can be abated at a relatively low cost—$500 per ton—by switching to coal with a lower sulfur content. The next several million tons can be abated at a higher cost by installing scrubbers that remove sulfur from coal smoke. Further abatement requires a switch from coal to natural gas, a more expensive fuel. For the last million tons abated, the marginal cost is about $6,000 per ton.

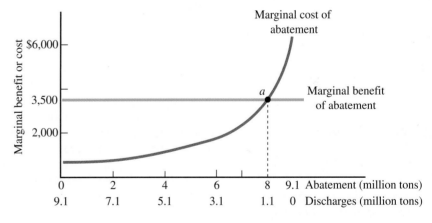

▲ **FIGURE 9.3**
**The Optimal Level of Sulfur Dioxide Emissions in 2010**
The optimum level of pollution abatement is shown by point *a*, where the marginal benefit of abatement equals its marginal cost.

The marginal-cost curve intersects the marginal-benefit curve at 8 million tons of abatement, leaving 1.1 million tons of $SO_2$ to be discharged in 2010. The current level of emissions is about 10 million tons per year. Under the provisions of the Clean Air Act passed by the U.S. government in 1990, emissions are scheduled to drop to 1.25 million tons by 2010, just above the optimal level shown in Figure 9.3.
*Related to Exercises 5.4 and 5.5.*

SOURCE: Spencer Banzhaf, Dallas Burtraw, and Karen Palmer, "Efficient Emission Fees in the U.S. Electricity Sector," Resources for the Future Discussion Paper 02-45, October 2002.

# MARGINAL PRINCIPLE

Increase the level of an activity as long as its marginal benefit exceeds its marginal cost. Choose the level at which the marginal benefit equals the marginal cost.

According to this principle, we should cut pollution to the level where the marginal benefit of abatement equals its marginal cost.

The marginal principle focuses our attention on the trade-offs from pollution—its costs and benefits. From society's perspective, there are many benefits from pollution abatement:

- *Better health.* Cleaner water means less sickness from waterborne pollutants, and cleaner air means fewer respiratory problems and thus lower health-care costs and fewer sick days taken by workers.
- *Increased enjoyment of the natural environment.* Improving the air quality increases visibility and improves the health of trees. Improving the water quality enhances recreational activities, such as swimming, boating, and fishing.
- *Lower production costs.* Some firms are dependent on clean water for survival: Farmers use water for irrigation, and some manufacturers use clean water as part of the production process. Cleaner water means lower production costs for these firms.

On the other hand, pollution abatement is costly because resources—labor, capital, and land—are used in the abatement process. Using the marginal principle, we look for the level of pollution abatement where the marginal benefit equals the marginal cost.

# 9.6 | TAXING POLLUTION

The economic approach to pollution is to get producers to pay for the waste they generate, just as they pay for labor, capital, and materials. The costs of labor, capital, and materials are the **private cost of production**, the cost borne by the producer of the product. The **external cost of production** is the cost incurred by someone other than the producer, for example, the cost associated with health problems and premature deaths from sulfur dioxide. The **social cost of production** is the sum of the private cost and the external cost. The idea of a **pollution tax** equal to the external cost per unit of pollution is to "internalize" the externality—to make the producer responsible for the external cost of production. When the tax equals the external cost imposed on others, the externality is internalized. In the example of sulfur dioxide pollution, the appropriate pollution tax is the external cost of $3,500 per ton.

## A Firm's Response to a Pollution Tax

A polluting firm will respond to a pollution tax in the same way as it responds to the prices of labor and materials. The firm will use the marginal principle to decide how much waste to generate and how much to abate. The firm will increase the level of abatement as long as the marginal benefit exceeds the marginal cost and stop when the marginal benefit equals the marginal cost.

Figure 9.4 shows an electricity producer's marginal benefits and costs of abating $SO_2$. The marginal cost is $2,200 for the first ton abated (point *a*), and the marginal cost increases with the level of abatement, to $3,500 for the sixth ton abated (point *c*) and $4,500 for the seventh ton (point *d*). The marginal cost increases with the amount abated

**private cost of production**
The production cost borne by a producer, which typically includes the costs of labor, capital, and materials.

**external cost of production**
A cost incurred by someone other than the producer.

**social cost of production**
Private cost plus external cost.

**pollution tax**
A tax or charge equal to the external cost per unit of pollution.

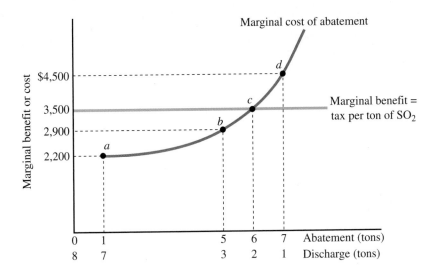

◄ **FIGURE 9.4**

**The Firm's Response to a SO₂ Tax**

From the perspective of a firm subject to a pollution tax, the marginal benefit of abatement is the $3,500 pollution tax that can be avoided by cutting pollution by 1 ton. The firm satisfies the marginal principle at point *c*, with 6 tons of abatement, leaving 2 tons of SO₂ discharged into the atmosphere.

because the firm must use progressively more costly means to cut emissions. From the firm's perspective, the benefit of abating pollution is that it can avoid paying the pollution tax. The marginal benefit of abatement is the $3,500 savings in pollution taxes from abating a ton of $SO_2$ rather than discharging it into the air. The firm satisfies the marginal principle at point *c*, with 6 tons of abatement. For the first 6 tons abated, the marginal benefit of abatement—avoiding the $3,500 tax—is greater than or equal to the marginal cost. The firm stops at 6 tons because the marginal cost of abating a seventh ton ($4,500, as shown by point *d*), exceeds the marginal benefit (the $3,500 tax avoided). Instead of paying $4,500 to abate one more ton, the firm will instead pay the $3,500 tax.

## The Market Effects of a Pollution Tax

Consider the effect of a pollution tax on the market for the product produced by polluting firms. For example, a tax on $SO_2$ increases the cost of producing electricity because firms pay for abatement and also pay pollution taxes on any remaining waste they generate. As we saw in an earlier chapter, a tax shifts the supply curve upward by the amount of the tax, decreasing the equilibrium quantity and increasing the equilibrium price.

Consider the effects of pollution taxes on the market for electricity. The production of electricity generates two major pollutants:

- **Sulfur dioxide.** Electric power plants are responsible for about two-thirds of $SO_2$ emissions. As we saw earlier in the chapter, the marginal damage from $SO_2$ is $3,500 per ton, so that's the appropriate pollution tax.

- **Nitrogen oxides (NO_x).** Power plants are also responsible for about one-quarter of the nation's $NO_x$ emissions, a contributing factor in acid rain and the most important factor in urban smog. The study cited earlier in the chapter estimated that the appropriate tax for $NO_x$ is about $1,100 per ton.

Figure 9.5 shows the effects of pollution taxes in the market for electricity. The taxes increase the cost of producing electricity, shifting the supply curve upward. The equilibrium moves from point *a* to point *b*, where the demand curve intersects the new supply curve. According to the electricity study, the pollution taxes would increase the price of electricity from $64.90 to $67.60 per megawatt-hour, an increase of 4 percent. The price elasticity of demand for electricity is 0.28, so the 4-percent increase in price decreases the quantity of electricity demanded by 1.1 percent, from 4,294 to 4,247 megawatt hours. Like other taxes, the pollution tax is shifted forward to consumers in the form of a higher price, and they respond by consuming less of the polluting good. When consumers face the full cost of producing electricity, they buy less of it.

**The Effects of SO₂ and NOₓ Taxes on the Electricity Market**

The pollution tax increases the cost of producing electricity, shifting the market supply curve up. The equilibrium moves from point *a* to point *b*. The tax increases the equilibrium price from $64.90 to $67.60 per megawatt -hour and decreases the equilibrium quantity.

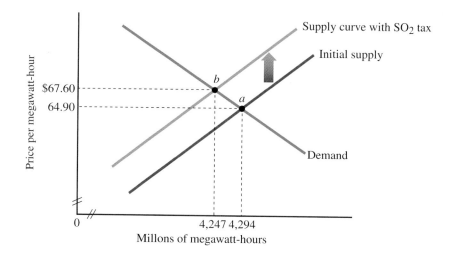

A pollution tax also changes the production process as firms switch to cleaner technology. Figure 9.6 shows the effects of pollution taxes on the energy sources used to generate electricity. Producers respond to the taxes by switching to low-sulfur coal, which is more expensive but reduces their SO₂ taxes. The share of power generated with low-sulfur coal increases from 0.43 to 0.53. The taxes increase the cost of using coal relative to the cost of using natural gas and nuclear power, so the share of electricity from these other sources increases while the share of power from coal decreases. As firms shift to cleaner energy sources, the amount of SO₂ and NOₓ emissions per unit of electricity generated decreases.

These pollution taxes decrease the total amount of air pollution for two reasons. First, as shown in Figure 9.5, the increase in the price of electricity decreases the quantity of electricity demanded by 1 percent. Second, as shown in Figure 9.6, the shift to cleaner energy sources means that each unit of electricity generates less pollution. The combined effect of these two changes is a substantial reduction in pollution: SO₂ decreases to 11 percent of its initial volume, and NOₓ decreases to 30 percent of its initial volume. An added bonus of the pollution tax is that the government could use the revenue from the tax to cut other taxes, for example, the payroll tax or the income tax.

► FIGURE 9.6

**Responses to SO₂ and NOₓ Taxes on Electricity Generation**

Taxes on SO₂ and NOₓ cause eletricity generators to switch to low-sulfur coal and to alternative energy sources that generate less SO₂ and NOₓ.

SOURCE: Based on Spencer Banzhaf, Dallas Burtraw, and Karen Palmer, "Efficient Emission Fees in the U.S. Eletricity Sector," Resource and Energy Economics, vol. 26 (2004), pp. 317–341.

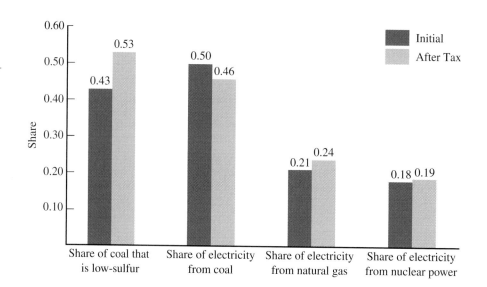

# APPLICATION

## THE EFFECTS OF A CARBON TAX

**APPLYING THE CONCEPTS #7:** What is the economic approach to global warming?

A report from the National Academy of Sciences, the nation's most prestigious scientific body, concluded that "greenhouse gases are accumulating in the Earth's atmosphere as a result of human activities" and that the "human-induced warming and associated sea level changes are expected to continue through the twenty-first century." The most important greenhouse gas is carbon dioxide, which is generated when we burn carbon-based fuels such as oil, coal, and gas. The report notes that there is considerable uncertainty about how our ecosystems will respond to a rapid increase in carbon dioxide and temperatures.

One approach to dealing with the problem of greenhouse gases is to tax carbon-based fuels. A carbon tax of $100 per ton of carbon content would translate into taxes of $0.28 per gallon of gasoline, $12 per barrel of oil, and $70 per ton of coal. The tax on coal would be relatively high because of its higher carbon content. A carbon tax would reduce greenhouse emissions in several ways:

- The price of gasoline would increase, causing people to drive less and buy more energy-efficient vehicles.

- The tax would increase the price of electricity, decreasing the quantity of electricity demanded and the quantity of fossil fuels burned.

- The higher price of home heating would cause people to turn down their thermostats and improve the heating efficiency of their homes, perhaps by installing energy-efficient windows or more insulation.

- Some electricity producers would switch from coal to natural gas, which has a lower carbon content, and thus a lower carbon tax. Others would switch to noncarbon energy sources such as the wind, the sun, and geothermal sources.

In 2002, New Zealand announced plans to implement a tax of $12 per ton of carbon, starting in 2007. New Zealand ranks fourth (behind the United States, Australia, and Canada) in per capita carbon emissions. About half of the greenhouse gases come from the methane emitted from the country's 50 million sheep and cattle during digestion. However, New Zealand farmers and ranchers will be exempt from the tax, over the strenuous objection of coal producers, who will pay a 20-percent tax. *Related to Exercise 6.6.*

SOURCES: National Academy of Sciences, *Climate Change Science: An Analysis of Some Key Questions* (Washington, D.C.: National Academy Press, 2001); William D. Nordhaus, "Economic Approaches to Global Warming," in *Global Warming: Economic Policy Responses*, edited by Rudiger Dornbush and James M. Poterba (Cambridge, MA: MIT Press, 1991); Graeme Peters, "New Zealand Plans Carbon Tax to Meet Kyoto Targets," Reuters News Service, October 18, 2002.

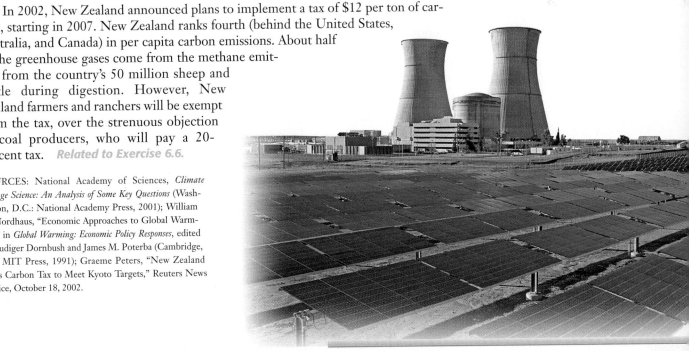

# $9.7$ | TRADITIONAL REGULATION

Although the economic approach to pollution is to get polluters to pay for the waste they generate, governments often take a different approach. Under a traditional regulation policy, the government tells each firm how much pollution to abate and what abatement techniques to use.

## Uniform Abatement with Permits

To illustrate the effects of regulation, consider an area with two electricity generators, firm L (for low cost) and firm H (for high cost). Suppose that in the absence of pollution-abatement efforts, each firm would discharge 5 tons of pollution per hour. Suppose the government sets a target abatement level of 2 tons of $SO_2$ per hour, divided equally between the two firms. Under this *uniform abatement policy*, the government will issue 4 pollution permits to each firm, forcing each firm to cut pollution from 5 tons to 4 tons. Suppose the marginal abatement cost of firm L is $2,000 and the marginal abatement cost for firm H is $5,000.

A uniform abatement policy is likely to be inefficient because it does not take advantage of the differences in abatement costs between the two firms. The cost of abating 2 tons is $7,000, including $2,000 for firm L and $5,000 for firm H. To show the inefficiency of the uniform abatement policy, imagine that the low-cost firm did all the abating, incurring a cost of $4,000 to abate 2 tons ($2,000 per ton times 2 tons). The total cost of abating 2 tons has dropped from $7,000 to $4,000. It's not a coincidence that the savings in abatement cost equals the difference in the abatement costs of the two firms. By shifting abatement responsibility to the low-cost firm, the savings in abatement cost equals the gap between the marginal abatement costs of the two firms. The basic problem with the uniform abatement policy is that it treats firms equally with respect to pollution abatement, even though the firms are unequal in terms of their abatement costs.

In contrast, a pollution tax would exploit the differences in abatement costs. Suppose the pollution tax is $3,500 per ton. Firm L, with a marginal abatement cost of only $2,000, will abate pollution rather than paying the tax. In contrast, firm H, with a marginal abatement cost of $5,000 will pollute and pay the tax. The tax is superior to the uniform abatement policy because it gets the low-cost firm to do more abating. The low-cost firm abates more but also pays less in pollution taxes.

## Command and Control

Traditional regulation policies have another dimension that contributes to higher compliance costs. Under a command-and-control policy, the government requires each firm to produce no more than a certain volume of pollution and requires the abatement be done with a particular technology. The problem with this approach is that the mandated abatement technology—the control part of the policy—is unlikely to be the most efficient technology for two reasons:

- The regulatory policy specifies a single abatement technology for all firms. Because the producers of a polluting good often use different materials and production techniques, an abatement technology that is efficient for one firm may be inefficient for others.

- The regulatory policy decreases the incentives to develop more efficient abatement technologies. The command part of the policy specifies a maximum volume of waste for each firm, so there is no incentive to cut the volume of waste below the maximum allowed. In other words, the benefit of developing new technologies is relatively small because there is no payoff from using them.

In contrast, a pollution tax provides the right incentives: If the firm develops a new technology that cuts pollution, it will pay less in pollution taxes.

A command-and-control policy causes firms to use inefficient abatement technologies, so production costs will be higher than they would be under a pollution tax.

## Market Effects of Pollution Regulations

How do the market effects of pollution regulation compare to the effects of a pollution tax? Recall that the uniform abatement policy achieves the same reduction in pollution at a higher cost because it doesn't exploit differences in abatement costs across firms. In addition, the control part of command and control may lead to relatively costly abatement techniques because there's no incentive to develop better ones. This will cause the supply curve for the polluting good to shift upward by a larger amount than it would with a tax. A larger supply shift causes a larger increase in the equilibrium price and a larger reduction in quantity. The inefficiency of regulations is passed on to consumers, who pay higher prices.

One advantage of the command-and-control policy is its predictability. The policy specifies how much waste each firm can produce, so we can predict the total volume of waste. In contrast, we don't know exactly how firms will respond to the pollution tax—they could pollute a little or a lot, depending on the tax and the cost of abating pollution—so it is difficult to predict the total volume of waste that will be emitted.

# 9.8 | MARKETABLE POLLUTION PERMITS

In recent years, policy makers have developed a new approach to environmental policy. The approach uses **marketable pollution permits**, sometimes called *pollution allowances*. Here is how a government runs a system of marketable pollution permits:

- Pick a target pollution level for a particular area.
- Issue just enough permits to meet the pollution target.
- Allow firms to buy and sell the permits.

In the policy world, this is known as a *cap-and-trade system*: The government "caps" the total emissions by issuing a fixed number of permits, and then allows firms to trade the permits.

• **marketable pollution permits**
A system under which the government picks a target pollution level for a particular area, issues just enough pollution permits to meet the pollution target, and allows firms to buy and sell the permits; also known as a *cap-and-trade system*.

## Voluntary Exchange and Marketable Permits

Making pollution permits marketable is sensible because it allows mutually beneficial exchanges between firms with different abatement costs. This is another illustration of the principle of voluntary exchange.

## THE PRINCIPLE OF VOLUNTARY EXCHANGE

A voluntary exchange between two people makes both people better off.

Firms will buy and sell pollution permits only when an exchange will make both firms better off. This happens when the firms have different abatement costs.

To illustrate the effects of marketable permits, let's return to the example of the two electricity generators with different abatement costs. Suppose the government issues each firm several pollution permits, one less than the initial level of pollution. In

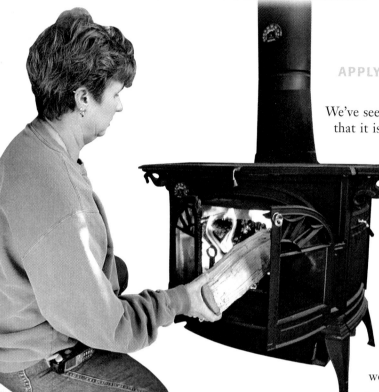

# APPLICATION

## DEAR ABBY AND ENVIRONMENTAL POLICY

**APPLYING THE CONCEPTS #8:** Are there different ways to reduce pollution or mitigate its effects?

We've seen that one problem with traditional environmental policy is that it is inflexible. It doesn't allow firms to use the most efficient abatement methods available. An example of different abatement strategies comes from the column of advice columnist Abigail Van Buren. A person with the moniker "Dreading Winter" sought advice about how to deal with a pollution problem. Her neighbors heated their home with a wood-burning stove, and the smell and smoke from the wood fire gave Dreading Winter burning eyes, a stuffy nose, and painful sinuses. She offered the neighbors $500 to stop burning wood, but they declined the offer. The readers of "Dear Abby" offered the following suggestions to Dreading Winter:

- Buy the neighbors a catalytic add-on for the wood stove or a wood-chip gasifier for an oil furnace. In either case, there would be much less air pollution from burning wood.
- Soak a towel in water, swish it around the room, and watch the smoke disappear.
- Leave a saucer of vinegar in each room to eliminate the smoke odor.
- Pay your neighbors to hire a chimney sweep to clean their flue.
- Seal and caulk your windows to keep the smoke outside at a cost of less than $500.
- Use the $500 to purchase an air purifier for your home.

These suggestions demonstrate a fundamental idea behind environmental economics: There is usually more than one way to deal with a pollution problem. The economic question is: What is the most efficient and least costly way to reduce the problem? In some cases, it may be more efficient to prevent the pollution by switching to an alternative fuel or installing a catalytic add-on to the stove than to clean up the environment after it has been polluted by installing an air purifier. In other cases, cleanup will be more efficient than prevention.
*Related to Exercises 7.4 and 7.5.*

SOURCE: Abigail Van Buren, "Aid for Reader's Winter Woe," *Sacramento Bee*, February 15, 1984, p. XX.

other words, the government will reduce pollution by two tons. Can the two firms make a deal for a permit?

- Firm H is willing to pay a maximum of $5,000 for a permit because that's how much it costs to abate a ton of pollution.
- Firm L is willing to accept a minimum of $2,000 for a permit because that's how much it costs to abate a ton of pollution.

Firm H is willing to pay up to $5,000 and firm L is willing to accept as little as $2,000, so there is an opportunity for mutually beneficial exchange. If the two firms split the difference, the price of a permit is $3,500, and each firm gains $1,500 from the transaction. Firm H pays $3,500 to save $5,000 on abatement cost, for a savings of $1,500. Firm L gets $3,500 but pays an additional $2,000 in abatement cost, for a benefit of $1,500.

How does the marketability of permits affect the total cost of abatement? In our example, the total cost with nonmarketable permits is $7,000, including $2,000 for firm L and $5,000 for firm H. In contrast, when a single firm does all the abating, the cost for 2 tons of abatement is $4,000 (2 tons times $2,000 per ton). The savings of $3,000 equals the gap between the abatement cost of the high-cost and low-cost firm. Making the permits marketable exploits differences in abatement costs across firms, so we as a society can achieve the same level of abatement at a lower total cost.

The first program of marketable pollution permits, started in 1976 by the U.S. Environmental Protection Agency, allowed limited trading of permits for several airborne pollutants. Trading was later extended to lead in gasoline (in 1985) and then to the chemicals responsible for the depletion of the ozone layer (in 1988). As we'll see later in the chapter, there are now active markets for permits to discharge sulfur dioxide, carbon dioxide, and nitrogen oxides.

## Supply, Demand, and the Price of Marketable Permits

We can use a model of supply and demand to represent the market for pollution permits. Figure 9.7 depicts a trading system introduced in the Los Angeles basin for smog pollutants such as $NO_x$. The supply curve for permits is vertical at the fixed number of permits provided by the government. The demand for permits comes from firms that can use a permit to avoid paying for pollution abatement, and the willingness to pay for a permit equals the savings in abatement costs. In Figure 9.7, the demand curve for permits is negatively sloped, meaning that the larger the number of permits available, the lower the willingness to pay for a permit. This is sensible because with more permits and pollution, the marginal cost of abatement will be relatively low. With a fixed supply of 100 permits in 1994, the equilibrium price, shown by the intersection of the demand curve and the 1994 supply curve at point *a*, is $7.

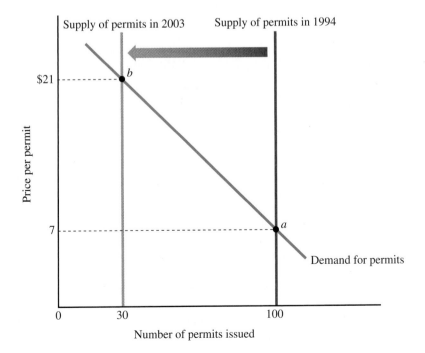

◀ **FIGURE 9.7**
**The Market for Pollution Permits**
The equilibrium price of permits is shown by the intersection of the demand curve and the vertical supply curve. The supply curve is vertical because each year the government specifies a fixed number of permits. A decrease in the number of permits shifts the supply curve to the left, increasing the equilibrium price.

# APPLICATION

## MARKETABLE PERMITS FOR SULFUR DIOXIDE

**APPLYING THE CONCEPTS #9:** What determines the price of a marketable pollution permit?

The Clean Air Act of 1990 established a system of marketable pollution permits (also know as *allowances*) for $SO_2$. Under the cap-and-trade program, in 1990 the government issued permits for $SO_2$ emissions based on a firm's emission levels 10 years earlier. Each company initially received enough permits to discharge between 50 and 70 percent of the volume it had discharged a decade earlier, and, over time, the number of permits decreases. Firms can also buy or sell the permits. For example, if one firm has an abatement cost of $140 and a second firm has an abatement cost of $180, the low-cost firm could sell a permit to the high-cost firm at a price of $160, giving each firm a benefit of $20: The low-cost firm gets $160 for a permit and incurs an abatement cost of $140; the high-cost firm pays $160 for a permit but saves $180 in abatement cost. A report from the National Acid Precipitation Assessment Program (NAPAP) showed that being able to buy and sell permits lowered the total cost of abatement by 15 to 20 percent. By 2002, total $SO_2$ emissions dropped to about half of what they were in 1970.

The permits for $SO_2$ pollution are now bought and sold on the Chicago Board of Trade. Each year the Environmental Protection Agency issues permits to existing $SO_2$ sources but withholds some permits for auction. Utilities can also put their permits up for bid on the Chicago Board of Trade. In 2002, a total of 127,388 permits were auctioned at an average price of $167 per ton. Individuals and environmental groups are allowed to buy the permits and, if they wish, reduce pollution by withdrawing them from the market. In 2001, a total of 31 permits went to schools and environmental groups, including a group of students at Hobart and William Smith Colleges, who paid $181 for a permit. *Related to Exercise 8.5.*

SOURCES: http://www.epa.gov/airmarkets/auctions/; accessed July 9, 2006.

Under Los Angeles's smog program, the number of $NO_x$ permits decreased each year, and in 2003 reached its goal of cutting $NO_x$ discharges to 30 percent of the level attained nine years earlier.[6] In Figure 9.7, the decrease in the number of permits from 100 to 30 shifts the supply curve to the left, increasing the equilibrium price of permits from $7 at point *a* to $21 at point *b*. Polluters in Los Angeles responded to the higher permit prices by abating more. The Los Angeles Department of Water and Power installed abatement equipment—at a cost of $40 million—because abatement was cheaper than buying pollution permits. Libbey Glass Company installed low-pollution burners in its plant, dropping its emissions below the volume allowed by its permits. The company sold its extra permits to other firms, generating income for Libbey. The firms that bought the permits from Libbey were able to continue production using their existing abatement equipment.

How do technological advances in abatement technology affect the price of pollution permits? A pollution permit allows a firm to avoid paying for abatement, and the higher the abatement cost that can be avoided, the larger the amount a firm is willing to pay for a permit. A technological innovation that decreases abatement costs will encourage firms to use the new technology to abate pollution rather than buying permits that allow pollution. As a result, the demand curve for permits shifts downward and to the left, and the equilibrium price of permits will decrease.

# APPLICATION

## CHICAGO CLIMATE EXCHANGE

**APPLYING THE CONCEPTS #10:** What are the benefits of giving firms options for reducing greenhouse gases?

The Chicago Climate Exchange (CCX) allows firms to cut their emissions of greenhouse gases in different ways. When a firm joins CCX, it agrees to reduce its contribution to greenhouse gases by 4 percent within four years by (1) cutting its own emissions, (2) paying for extra reductions by other firms, or (3) paying for projects such as reforestation that offset the firm's emissions. Among the members of CCX are Ford Motor Company, DuPont, Motorola, IBM, American Electric Power, the City of Chicago, and Tufts University. In the first auctions in 2003, the price for carbon dioxide emissions was about $1 per ton.

The experience of American Electric Power (AEP), the nation's largest electricity producer, illustrates how CCX works. AEP bought 10,000 acres of fallow land and planted walnut trees, which each year will withdraw about 71,000 tons of carbon dioxide from the air and convert it into solid wood. As long as the wood doesn't burn or decompose, AEP can use the trees to offset some of its carbon emissions. The cost of tree farming is $1.25 per ton of carbon absorbed, or "sequestered," which is small relative to the alternative—converting the company's generators from coal to natural gas at a cost of about $50 per ton of carbon abated. *Related to Exercise 8.6.*

SOURCE: Thomas Kellner, "Got Gas?" *Forbes*, March 17, 2003, p. 56.

# SUMMARY

In this chapter, we've explored the implications of market failure from imperfect information, external benefits, and external costs. Here are the main points of the chapter:

1 The *adverse-selection problem* occurs when one side of the market cannot distinguish between high-quality and low-quality goods. The presence of low-quality goods pulls down the price that buyers are willing to pay, which decreases the quantity of high-quality goods supplied, which further decreases the average quality and the price. In the extreme case, only low-quality goods are sold.

2 Insurance encourages risky behavior because part of the cost of an unfavorable outcome is paid by an insurance company.

3 A public good is available for everyone to consume (nonrival in consumption), regardless of who pays and who doesn't (nonexcludable).

4 A system of voluntary contributions suffers from the free-rider problem: People do not have an incentive to support public goods.

5 The optimum level of pollution abatement is where the marginal benefit equals the marginal cost.

6 A tax on the emissions of electricity generators decreases total emissions as firms switch to cleaner fuels and consumers buy less electricity at the higher price.

7 Compared to a pollution tax, traditional pollution regulations lead to higher production costs and higher product prices.

EXERCISES  Visit www.myeconlab.com to complete
*Get Ahead of the Curve* these exercises online and get instant feedback.

## 9.1 | The Lemons Problem

**1.1** There is asymmetric information in the used-car market because _____ (buyers/sellers) cannot distinguish between lemons and plums but _____ (buyers/sellers) can.

**1.2** In the used-car market, suppose the typical consumer is willing to pay $4,000 for a plum and $1,000 for a lemon. If there is a 50-percent chance of getting a lemon, the consumer is willing to pay $ _____ for a used car.

**1.3** The following table shows the prices and quantities in three different used-car markets. Complete the table by filling in the last two rows.

| | Market A | Market B | Market C |
|---|---|---|---|
| Assumed chance of getting a lemon | 60% | 80% | 95% |
| Willingness to pay for a used car | $6,000 | $5,000 | $4,500 |
| Number of lemons supplied | 70 | 40 | 90 |
| Number of plums supplied | 30 | 10 | 10 |
| Total number of used cars supplied | 100 | 50 | 100 |
| Equilibrium: Yes or No? | _____ | _____ | _____ |
| If disequilibrium, will price then rise or drop? | _____ | _____ | _____ |

**1.4** We will have a thin market for used cars if the minimum supply price for plums (high quality) is _____ (greater than/less than) the willingness to pay for a lemon.

**1.5** Arrows up or down: As the minimum supply price of plums (high quality) decreases, the number of plums supplied at each price will _____, so the likelihood of getting a plum will _____.

**1.6** The typical consumer is willing to pay $1,000 for a low-quality 1995 Z13 car and $5,000 for a high-quality 1995 Z13 car. If equilibrium price for such a car is $1,800, the likelihood of getting a lemon is _____ chances in 5, and the likelihood of getting a plum is _____ chances in 5.

**1.7** *Consumer Reports*. You want to buy a used car, specifically a 1999 Zephyr. According to *Consumer Reports*, half of the 1999 Zephyrs now on the road are lemons, meaning that they break down frequently and generate large repair bills. Consumers are willing to pay $2,000 for a lemon, but $5,000 for a plum. According to Ms. Wizard, "The equilibrium price of used 1999 Zephyrs will be $2,000 in Sourland but $2,600 in Sweetland."
**a.** Illustrate with a complete graph for each market.
**b.** What is the fundamental difference between the two markets?

**1.8** **Fashion and Prices.** You are in the market for a used car and have narrowed your options to two types of cars, type F and type P. According to *Consumer Reports*, the two types of cars have roughly the same frequency of lemons (50 percent). Like other consumers, you are willing to pay $1,000 for a lemon and $7,000 for a plum. The people who buy new F cars are fashion-conscious and purchase a new car every three years. The people who buy new P cars are insensitive to the whims of fashion. Predict the equilibrium prices of the two types of cars and defend your answer with two graphs, one for each type of car.

**1.9** **Double Ignorance.** Suppose both buyers and sellers of used cars are ignorant: No one can distinguish between lemons and plums. Would you expect the market to be dominated by lemons? Illustrate with a completely labeled graph.

**1.10** **Groucho Club.** Consider a classic quip from Groucho Marx: "I won't join any club that is willing to accept me as a member." Suppose Groucho wants to associate with high-income people (the higher the income the better) and everyone else has the same preferences as Groucho.
**a.** Use the notion of adverse selection to explain this quip.
**b.** Relate the quip to the adverse-selection problem.

**1.11** **Purchasing a Fleet of Used Cars.** You are responsible for buying a fleet of 10 used cars for your employees and must pick either brand B or brand C. For your purposes, the two brands are identical except for one difference: Based on your experience with the two brands, you figure that 50 percent of B cars in the market are lemons and only 20 percent of C cars in the market are lemons. You are willing to pay $1,000 for a known lemon and $3,000 for a known plum. If the price of B cars is $1,800 and the price of C cars is $2,200, which brand of car should you pick?

1.12 **Adverse Selection of Furbies.** Consider the market for used Furbies, with knowledgeable sellers and ignorant buyers. Half of the Furbies in existence are plums and half are lemons. Each buyer is willing to pay $50 for a plum or $20 for a lemon. The minimum supply price for a plum is $10 and the minimum supply price for a lemon is $2.

   a. In equilibrium, will the market be "thin" or will all the used Furbies in the market be lemons? Explain and illustrate your answer with a complete graph.

   b. Suppose that at a price of $26, the quantity of plums is 20 and the quantity of lemons is 80. Is this an equilibrium? Explain and illustrate your answer with a complete graph.

# 9.2 | Responding to the Lemons Problem

2.1 Suppose the price of a used car in a thin market is $2,800 and you are willing to pay $5,000 for a plum. You would be willing to pay up to $ _____ for information that identifies a true plum.

2.2 Consider a thin used-car market. Someone just developed a device that can instantly identify the nearest plum in a used-car lot. The device works only once. The maximum amount that a consumer would be willing to pay for the device equals _____ minus _____.

2.3 The price of a used car in a thin market is $2,800, and consumers are willing to pay $2,000 for a lemon and $5,000 for a plum. Suppose two sellers, a lemon owner and a plum owner, each provide a money-back guarantee when they sell their cars for $5,000.

   a. If the lemon owner sells the car with the guarantee, the net gain for the seller will be $ _____.

   b. If the plum owner sells the car with the guarantee, the net gain for the seller will be $ _____.

2.4 A new car loses about _____ percent of its value in the first week because recent buyers are more likely to want to sell a _____ (lemon/plum). (Related to Application 1 on page 227.)

2.5 Recall the discussion of the market for used pickup trucks. There is an adverse-selection problem for _____ trucks.

2.6 Arrows up or down: Government regulations for kiwifruit _____ the average quality and _____ the price of kiwifruit. (Related to Application 2 on page 228.)

2.7 Professional baseball pitchers are like used _____ because there is _____ information: A player's _____ has better information about the pitcher's

health and likelihood of injury. (Related to Application 3 on page 229.)

2.8 Your favorite baseball team just announced that it signed a new pitcher from the free-agent market. We expect the new pitcher to be injured _____ (more/less) often than free-agent pitchers who returned to their old teams.

2.9 **Paying for Information.** You are willing to pay $7,000 for a high-quality car—a plum. The current price of used cars is $4,000, and 4 of 5 cars in the market are lemons, meaning that 1 in 5 is a plum.

   a. Suppose you could pay a finder's fee to a personal shopper/mechanic who will find you a plum at a price of $4,000. What is the maximum you are willing to pay as a finder's fee?

   b. As you shop for a used car, you will bring each car you consider to your mechanic, who will thoroughly inspect the car and tell you for certain whether it is a plum or a lemon. If the price per inspection is $400, is it worth the money?

   c. How would your answer to part (b) change if only 1 out of 10 used cars was a plum?

2.10 **Mix of Lemons and Plums in the Week-Old Car Market.** Recall the application, "Resale Value of a Week-Old Car." Suppose the value of a high-quality week-old car (a plum) is $20,000 (the same as the purchase price of a new car), while the value of a low-quality week-old car (a lemon) is $10,000. Suppose that at a price of $16,000 per car, 6 of 10 cars on the used market are plums and 4 of 10 are lemons. (Related to Application 1 on page 227.)

   a. How much is the typical buyer willing to pay for a used car in the mixed market?

   b. Is the $16,000 price an equilibrium price? Why or why not?

   c. Suppose that for every 10 new cars sold by new-car dealer, 9 are plums and only 1 is a lemon. Why is the equilibrium mix in the used car market different from the mix of new cars sold?

2.11 **Equilibrium in the Kiwifruit Market.** Consumers are willing to pay 10 cents for a sour kiwifruit and 30 cents for a sweet kiwifruit. The minimum supply price for sour kiwifruit is 6 cents and the minimum supply price for sweet kiwifruit is 18 cents. The slope of each supply curve is 1 cent per thousand kiwifruit. (Related to Application 2 on page 228.)

   a. Suppose consumers initially expect a 50–50 mix of sweet and sour kiwifruits. Is this an equilibrium? Illustrate with a graph.

   b. Suppose consumers are pessimistic, expecting all sour kiwifruit. Is this an equilibrium? Illustrate with a graph. What is the price of kiwifruit?

   c. Suppose the state outlaws sour kiwifruit, and they disappear from the market. What happens to the equilibrium price of kiwifruit? What is the equilibrium quantity of sweet kiwifruit?

**2.12 Willingness to Pay for Used Baseball Pitchers.** Suppose a healthy baseball pitcher is worth $5 million per year to his team, compared to only $1 million per year for an unhealthy pitcher. Suppose that half the pitchers in the league are healthy, and half are unhealthy. According to an executive of a baseball team, "If my assumptions are correct, our team is willing to pay a maximum of $3 million for a pitcher in the free-agent market." (Related to Application 3 on page 229.)

a. What are the executive's assumptions?

b. Are these assumptions realistic?

## 9.3 | Insurance and Moral Hazard

**3.1** In the market for insurance, the moral-hazard problem is that insurance encourages _____.

**3.2** While shopping for office equipment, an office manager sees a display of fire extinguishers. After making a single phone call, the manager decides not to buy a fire extinguisher. The manager called her _____ and asked, "_____?"

**3.3** Many professional athletes purchase insurance against career-ending injuries. We expect the insured players to experience _____ (more/fewer) injuries than uninsured players.

**3.4** If you offer insurance against bicycle theft and base your price on last year's theft rate, you are likely to lose money because insurance _____ theft rates.

**3.5 Selling iPod Insurance.** On the campus of Klepto College, half the iPods are expensive (replacement value is $400) and half are cheap (replacement value is $100). There is a 20-percent chance that any particular iPod—expensive or cheap—will be stolen in the next year. Suppose a firm offers iPod-theft insurance for $50 per year: The firm will replace any insured iPod that is stolen. Suppose the firm sells 20 insurance policies.

a. Assume for the moment that the theft rate remains at 20 percent for both types of iPods. The firm's total revenue equals _____. The firm's cost—the money paid out to replace stolen iPods—will be $ _____ to replace expensive iPods and $ _____ to replace cheap iPods, for a total of $ _____. The insurance firm will make zero economic profit with a price of $ _____.

b. Is it realistic to assume that the introduction of insurance will not affect the theft rate? Which is a more plausible assumption, that the theft rate will decrease to 10 percent or that it will increase to 30 percent? For the more plausible theft rate, compute the zero-profit insurance price when insurance is purchased exclusively by the owners of expensive iPods.

**3.6 Skydiver Question.** Several of your friends have offered to take you on a tandem skydiving adventure: Strapped together with a single set of parachutes (main and emergency), you jump out of an airplane and then either float to earth or crash. All your skydiving friends are equally skillful, and none of them has the thrill-seeker gene. You can ask each of them a single question.

a. What's your question?

b. Provide the answer you're looking for in a skydiving mate.

**3.7 Insurance and Fire Prevention.** In a given year, there is a 10-percent chance that a fire in Ira's warehouse will cause $100,000 in property damage. If Ira spends $4,000 on a fire-prevention program, the probability of a fire would drop to zero.

a. If Ira doesn't have fire insurance, will he spend the money on the prevention program?

b. If Ira has an insurance policy that covers 80 percent of the property damage from a fire (covering $80,000 of the $100,000 worth of damage), will he spend the money on the prevention program?

## 9.4 | External Benefits and Public Goods

**4.1** Suppose 1,000 people would each get a benefit of $40 from a levee. Building the levee is socially efficient if its cost is less than $ _____. If the cost is $30,000, a tax of $ _____ per person would generate unanimous support for the levee.

**4.2** An external benefit is experienced by _____.

**4.3** A public good is _____ (rival/nonrival) in consumption and _____ (excludable/nonexcludable).

**4.4** A free rider is someone who _____.

**4.5 Paying for a WiFi Network.** Consider a small town with 1,000 households. The town could install a wireless WiFi network that would give everyone in town access to the Internet. Each household is willing to pay a maximum of $50 per year for the network, and the cost of the system is $20,000 per year. (Related to Application 4 on page 232.)

a. Is the WiFi system efficient?

b. Suppose the town asks for voluntary contributions to support the network. Would you expect the total contributions to cover the $20,000 cost?

c. Suppose the town keeps track of the contributions and issues passwords to people who contributed at least $20. Would you expect the total contributions to cover the $20,000 cost?

**4.6** **Defenders of Wildlife.** Each of the 80,000 citizens in a particular county is willing to pay $0.10 to increase the number of wolf litters by one. Each litter of wolves imposes a cost of $5,000 in livestock losses to ranchers. (Related to Application 5 on page 234.)

  **a.** Is the provision of an additional litter of wolves efficient from the social perspective?

  **b.** Design a system that will generate the socially efficient outcome.

**4.7** **Class Participation.** Consider a course with 40 students, some of whom are confused after the professor explains a concept. The professor doesn't know whether students are confused, but will clarify the concept if one student asks a question. A student who asks a question—and reveals his or her confusion—loses 10 utils. When the professor clarifies the concept in response to a question, each confused student gets a benefit of 2 utils.

  **a.** At what level of confusion (measured by the number of confused students) is a question from a confused student socially efficient?

  **b.** In the absence of participation incentives, will a confused student ask a question when it would be socially efficient to do so?

  **c.** Design an incentive system to generate efficient questioning.

**4.8** **Fireworks as Public Goods.** A three-person city is considering a fireworks display. Bertha is willing to pay $100 for the proposed fireworks display, Marian is willing to pay $30, and Sam is willing to pay $20. The cost of the fireworks display is $120.

  **a.** Will any single citizen provide the display on his or her own?

  **b.** If the cost of the fireworks display is divided equally among the citizens, will a majority vote in favor of the display?

  **c.** Describe a transaction that would benefit all three citizens.

**4.9** **Stream Preservation.** Consider a trout stream that is threatened with destruction by a nearby logging operation. Each of the 10,000 local fishers would be willing to pay $5 to preserve the stream. The owner of the land would incur a cost of $20,000 to change the logging operation to protect the stream.

  **a.** Is the preservation of the stream efficient from the social perspective?

  **b.** If the landowner has the right to log the land any way he wants, will the stream be preserved?

  **c.** Propose a solution to this problem. Describe a transaction that would benefit the fishers and the landowner.

## 9.5 | The Optimal Level of Pollution

**5.1** The optimal level of pollution abatement is the level at which the _____ of abatement equals the _____ of abatement.

**5.2** The marginal cost of abatement typically _____ (increases/decreases) with the level of abatement.

**5.3** In the case of sulfur dioxide pollution, the marginal benefit curve is _____ (positively sloped/negatively sloped/horizontal/vertical).

**5.4** The estimated optimal level of sulfur dioxide emissions for 2010 is roughly _____ million tons. (Related to Application 6 on page 235.)

**5.5** **Optimal Pollution Abatement.** Suppose the marginal benefit of pollution abatement is constant at $12 per unit. The marginal cost of abatement is $2 for the first unit abated and increases by $2 for each additional unit, to $4 for the second unit, $6 for the third unit, and so on. (Related to Application 6 on page 235.)

  **a.** What is the optimal level of pollution abatement?

  **b.** What is the appropriate pollution tax?

**5.6** **Optimal Noise Pollution.** Vivian is trying to learn to play the violin, much to the dismay of her housemates. Her marginal benefit from the first hour of practice is $8, and the marginal benefit decreases by $1 per hour, to $7 for the second hour, $6 for the third hour, and so on. For her housemates, the external cost from the noise pollution is $4 per hour.

  **a.** In the market equilibrium (no restrictions), how many hours will Vivian play? Illustrate with a graph.

  **b.** What is the socially efficient practice time?

  **c.** What is the economic approach to noise pollution, and how would it be applied in this case?

## 9.6 | Taxing Pollution

**6.1** The social cost of production equals the _____ cost plus the _____ cost.

**6.2** In the presence of a pollution tax, the marginal benefit of abating pollution equals _____. A firm will respond to a pollution tax by picking the level of abatement where the pollution tax equals _____.

**6.3** Arrows up or down: A pollution tax shifts the supply curve _____, which _____ the equilibrium price and _____ the equilibrium quantity of the polluting product.

**6.4** A pollution tax decreases the volume of pollution in two ways, by decreasing _____ and decreasing _____.

**6.5** Arrows up or down: A carbon tax will shift the supply curve for home heating oil _____, causing the equilibrium price to _____ and the equilibrium quantity to _____.

**6.6** **The Market Effects of a Carbon Tax.** Consider the market for gasoline. In the initial equilibrium, the price is $2.00 per gallon and the quantity is 100 million gallons. The price elasticity of demand is 0.70, and the price elasticity of supply is 1.0. Suppose a carbon tax shifts the supply curve upward by $0.34 and to the left by 17 percent. (Related to Application 7 on page 239.)
   a. Use a graph to show the effects of the tax on the equilibrium price and quantity of gasoline.
   b. After reviewing the price-change formula in the earlier chapter on elasticity, compute the new price and quantity. The new price is $ _____ per gallon and the new quantity is _____ million gallons.
   c. Consumers pay $ _____ of the $0.34 tax and producers pay the remaining $ _____ of the tax.

**6.7** **Shifting a Tax on Home Heating Oil.** You are an economic consultant to a member of Congress. Someone just introduced a bill that would impose a carbon tax of $100 per ton, which would shift the supply curve for heating oil upward by $0.30 per gallon and to the left by 15 percent. The initial (pretax) price of heating oil is $2.00.
   a. Use a graph to show the effects of the tax on the price and quantity of heating oil. Will the entire tax to be paid by consumers? If not, who else will bear part of the tax?
   b. Suppose the price elasticity of supply of heating oil is 1.0 and the price elasticity of demand is 0.50. Use the price-change formula developed in the chapter on elasticity to predict the new equilibrium price. What fraction of the tax is passed forward to consumers?

## 9.7 | Traditional Regulation

**7.1** Compared to a pollution tax, a uniform-abatement policy is _____ (more/less) efficient because it does not exploit differences in _____ across firms.

**7.2** A command-and-control policy is likely to be inefficient because it causes firms to use _____.

**7.3** Arrows up or down: A switch from a pollution-tax policy to a uniform-reduction policy will shift the supply curve of the polluting product _____ and _____ the equilibrium price.

**7.4** The lesson from the application, "Dear Abby and Environmental Policy" is that sometimes _____ is less costly than _____, and sometimes the reverse is true. (Related to Application 8 on page 242.)

**7.5** **Options for Abating Noise Pollution.** Radiohead enjoys loud music and is willing to pay $9 for the first song and $1 less for each succeeding song ($8 for the second, $7 for the third, and so on). For her dorm mates, the external cost from the noise pollution is $4 per song. (Related to Application 8 on page 242.)
   a. Suppose initially the price of songs is zero. How many songs will Radiohead play? Illustrate with a graph.
   b. Suppose the government imposes a pollution tax of $4 per song. How many songs will Radiohead play? Compute the loss in consumer surplus from the tax, which increases the price of songs from zero to $4.
   c. Radiohead could soundproof her room, eliminating the noise pollution and her responsibility to pay the pollution tax. If the soundproofing costs $30, is it worthwhile?
   d. Radiohead could compensate her dorm mates for each unit of noise pollution—each song played. How much compensation would be required? From Radiohead's perspective, is paying compensation better than paying the tax, worse, or the same?

**7.6** **Regulations Eliminate a Market?** Consider a market in which the initial equilibrium quantity of a polluting good is 20 tons.
   a. Use a graph to show the effects of a pollution tax that decreases the equilibrium quantity to 12 tons.
   b. Consider a command-and-control policy that generates the same volume of pollution as the pollution tax but decreases the equilibrium quantity of the polluting good to zero. Use a graph to show the effects of the command-and-control policy.

## 9.8 | Marketable Pollution Permits

**8.1** Under a system of marketable pollution permits, a firm with _____ (low/high) abatement costs will buy permits from a firm with _____ (low/high) abatement costs.

**8.2** Arrows up or down: A switch from regular pollution permits to marketable permits _____ the total cost of abatement.

**8.3** A decrease in the supply of marketable pollution permits will shift the supply curve for permits to the _____ and _____ the equilibrium price of permits.

**8.4** Arrows up or down: A technological advance that decreases abatement costs will _____ the demand for marketable pollution permits and _____ the equilibrium price.

**8.5 Split the Difference for a Pollution Permit.** Consider two firms, each of which is issued 3 marketable pollution permits. For firm H, the marginal cost of abatement is $190. For firm L, the marginal cost of abatement is $130. (Related to Application 9 on page 244.)

   **a.** Is there room for a mutually beneficial exchange of one permit? If so, which firm will buy a permit and which firm will sell a permit?

   **b.** If the two firms split the difference, what's the price of a permit?

   **c.** Suppose that after the exchange of one permit, the marginal cost of abatement for the firm that sold the permit is $170 and the marginal cost of the firm that bought the permit is $150. Will the firms exchange another permit, or are they done trading?

   **d.** What is the savings in abatement cost from allowing firms to buy and sell a permit?

**8.6 Reforestation Versus Abatement.** Suppose your firm joins the Chicago Climate Exchange and commits to reducing greenhouse gases by 11 tons per year. You can pay for a reforestation project that offsets your emissions at a cost of $7 per ton of carbon offset. Or you can modify your production cost to abate pollution. Your marginal cost of abating the first ton is $3; the marginal cost increases by $1 for each additional ton, to $4 for the second ton, $5 for the third ton, and so on. (Related to Application 10 on page 245.)

   **a.** What's the best combination of reforestation offsets and abatement?

   **b.** How much money does your firm save by using the offsets?

**8.7 No Permits Exchanged?** A state issued marketable permits for sulfur dioxide emissions to several electricity generators. Most of the permits were given to the utilities with the oldest generating facilities. One year later, none of the permits had been bought or sold. What could explain the absence of permit exchanges?

**8.8 Lower Abatement Cost and Permit Prices.** Suppose new technology decreases the cost of abating pollution by half. Depict graphically the implications of the decrease in abatement cost on the equilibrium price of marketable permits. Use Figure 9.7 on page 243 as a starting point, with an initial permit price of $21 (point *b*). What's the new equilibrium price?

# ECONOMIC EXPERIMENT

## Rolling for Lemons

In this experiment, students play the role of consumers purchasing used cars. Over half the used cars on the road (57 percent) are plums, and the remaining cars (43 percent) are lemons. Each consumer offers a price for a used car and then rolls a pair of dice to find out whether he or she gets a lemon or a plum. In general, rolling a big number is good news: To get a plum, you need to roll a big number. The higher the price you offer, the smaller the number you must roll to get a plum. Here is how the experiment works:

- Each consumer tells the instructor how much he or she is offering for a used car and then rolls the dice.

- The instructor tells the consumer whether the number rolled is large enough to get a plum. If the number is not large enough, the consumer gets a lemon.

- The consumers' scores equal the difference between the maximum amount they are willing to pay for the type of car they got ($1,200 for a plum and $400 for a lemon) and the price they actually paid. For example, if Otto offers $500 and gets a plum, his score is $700. If Carla offers $600 and gets a lemon, her score is –$200.

- The instructor announces the result of each transaction to the class.

- There are three to five buying periods. At the end of the last trading period, each consumer adds up his or her score.

# ECONOMIC EXPERIMENT

## Voluntary Contributions

Do people really try to get free rides? Or would most people contribute at least some money to support a public good? Here is a classroom experiment that helps to answer this question:

- The instructor selects 10 students and gives each student 10 dimes.

- Each student can contribute money to support a public good by dropping 1, 2, or 3 dimes into a public-good pot. Each student has the option of keeping all the dimes and not contributing anything. The contributions are anonymous: No one knows how much a particular student contributes.

- For each dime in the pot, the instructor adds 2 dimes. For example, if the students contribute a total of 40 dimes, the instructor adds 80 dimes, for a total of 120 dimes in the pot. The two-for-one match represents the idea that the benefits of public goods exceed the costs. In this case, the benefit–cost ratio is three to one.

- The instructor divides the money in the public-good pot equally among the 10 students. For example, if there are 120 dimes in the pot, each student receives 12 dimes.

- Steps 2 through 4 can be repeated four or five times.

We can change the experiment to mimic the compulsory tax system. The instructor could require each student to contribute 3 dimes, the maximum amount, each. Would a switch to a compulsory tax system make the students better or worse off?

### Experiment Debriefing

After completing the experiment, do the following exercise:

Consider the contribution incentives for Margie, one of the 10 students in the experiment. She thinks in marginal terms, and asks herself, "If I contribute one more dime, how would that affect my payoff from the experiment?

a. Answer Margie's question, assuming that her contribution does not affect the contribution of other students.

b. If Margie uses the marginal principle to make all her decisions, will she contribute the extra dime?

# ECONOMIC EXPERIMENT

## Pollution Permits

In this pollution-permit experiment, students play the role of paper firms that buy or sell pollution permits. The class is divided into groups of three to five students, with each group representing a firm that produces one ton of paper per period. The instructor provides each firm with data about its cost of production. The cost depends on how much waste the firm generates: The smaller the volume of waste, the higher the production cost. Here is an example:

| Gallons of waste generated | 2 | 3 | 4 |
|---|---|---|---|
| Production cost per ton | $36 | $26 | $20 |

Each firm receives 3 pollution permits for each of the five trading periods. A firm that does not sell any of its permits to other firms has the right to generate 3 gallons of waste in that period. A firm that sells one of its 3 permits can generate only 2 gallons of waste, and a firm that buys a permit from another firm can generate 4 gallons of waste.

At the beginning of each of the five trading periods, firms meet in the trading area to buy or sell pollution permits for that day. Each firm can buy or sell one permit per day. Once a transaction has been arranged, the buyer and the seller inform the instructor of the transaction, record the transaction on their report cards, and then leave the

trading area. The firm's objective is to maximize profit, and in each trading period we compute the firm's profit with the following equation:

profit = price of paper − production cost + revenue from permit sold − cost of permit purchased

In each period, a firm will either buy or sell a permit, so we compute the firm's profit with just three numbers. For example, using the production cost numbers shown in the table, if the price of paper is $50 per ton and a firm buys a permit for $5 and generates 4 gallons of waste, the firm's profit is:

$$\text{profit} = \$50 - \$20 + 0 - \$5 = \$25$$

If another firm sells a permit for $5 and generates 2 gallons of waste, the firm's profit is:

$$\text{profit} = \$50 - \$36 + \$5 - 0 = \$19$$

For the fourth and fifth trading periods, several environmental groups have the option of buying pollution permits. Each environmental group is given a fixed sum of money to spend on permits, and its objective is to get as many permits as possible, reducing the total volume of pollution in the process.

# NOTES

1. Adam Smith, *An Inquiry into the Nature and Causes of the Wealth of Nations* (First published in 1776; New York: Random House, 1973), Book 4, Chapter 2.

2. George Akerlof, "The Market for 'Lemons': Quality Uncertainty and the Market Mechanism," *Quarterly Journal of Economics*, August 1970, pp. 488–500.

3. Eric Bond, "A Direct Test of the 'Lemons' Model: The Market for Used Pickup Trucks," *American Economic Review*, September 1982, 72, pp. 836–840; Michael Pratt and George Hoffer, "Test of the 'Lemons' Model: Comment," *American Economic Review*, September 1984, 74, pp. 798–800; Eric Bond, "Test of the 'Lemons' Model: A Reply," *American Economic Review*, September 1984, 74, pp. 801–804.

4. Carl Sagan, "A Warning for Us?" Parade, June 5, 1994, p. 8; John Boudreau, "Collision Course: Scientists Say There's a Big Asteroid Bang in Our Future," *Parade* and *Washington Post*, April 6, 1994, p. C1.

5. "Mirror Beam Could Deflect Killer Asteroid, Theory Says," *New York Times*, November 9, 1994, p. C6.

6. Gary Polaroid, "Cost of Clean Air Credits Soars in Southland," *Los Angeles Times*, September 5, 2000, page B.

# The Labor Market, Income, and Poverty

Recent reports on the earnings of college graduates have made the jobs of college recruiters easier[1]:

- In 1972, the typical college graduate earned 43 percent more than a high-school graduate.

- In 2002, the typical college graduate earned roughly twice as much as a high-school graduate.

These facts raise two questions: First, why do college graduates earn so much more than high-school graduates? Second, why did the earnings gap almost double during the last three decades?

U p to this point in the book, we have discussed the markets for final goods and services. In this chapter, we switch to the market for one of the factors of production—labor. Labor costs are responsible for about three-fourths of production costs, and for most people labor income is by far the most important source of income. We'll use a model of demand and supply to see how wages are determined and why wages differ between college graduates and high-school graduates, men and women, and people in different occupations. We'll also take a look at the distribution of income and the problem of poverty.

# 10.1 | THE DEMAND FOR LABOR

We can use demand and supply curves to show how wages are determined and examine how changes in the labor market affect wages and employment. We'll start with the demand side of the labor market, looking first at how an individual firm can use the key principles of economics to decide how many workers to hire.

The demand for labor and other productive inputs is different from the demand for consumer products such as iPods, books, haircuts, and pizza. Firms use workers to produce the products demanded by consumers, and so economists say that labor demand is a "derived demand." That is, it is determined by, or derived from, the demand for the products produced by workers. As we'll see in this chapter, the demand for labor is determined by the demand for consumer products and the price of those products.

### Labor Demand by an Individual Firm in the Short Run

Consider a perfectly competitive firm that produces rubber balls. Because this firm is perfectly competitive, it takes the price of its output and the prices of its inputs as given. Because it hires a tiny fraction of the workers in the labor market, it takes the market wage as given and can hire as many workers as it wants at that wage. In addition, the firm produces a tiny fraction of the rubber balls sold in the market, so it takes the price of its output as given. Let's say the price of rubber balls is $0.50.

Consider the firm's hiring decision in the short run, defined as the period during which at least one input—for example, its factory—cannot be changed. We can use two of the key principles of economics to explain the firm's hiring decision. Recall the marginal principle.

## MARGINAL PRINCIPLE

Increase the level of an activity as long as its marginal benefit exceeds its marginal cost. Choose the level at which the marginal benefit equals the marginal cost.

The firm will pick the quantity of labor at which the marginal benefit of labor equals the marginal cost of labor. It can hire as many workers as it wants at the market wage, so the marginal cost of labor equals the hourly wage. If the wage is $8 per hour, the extra cost associated with one more hour of labor—the marginal cost—is $8, regardless of how many workers the firm hires.

What is the marginal benefit of labor? The firm hires labor to produce balls, so the marginal benefit equals the monetary value of the balls produced with an additional hour of labor. Table 10.1 shows how to compute the marginal benefit associated

## Table 10.1 | USING THE MARGINAL PRINCIPLE TO MAKE A LABOR DECISION

| (1) Workers | (2) Balls | (3) Marginal Product of Labor | (4) Price | (5) Marginal Revenue Product of Labor (*MRP*) | (6) Marginal Cost When Wage = $8 |
|---|---|---|---|---|---|
| 1 | 26 | 26 | $0.50 | $13 | $8 |
| 2 | 50 | 24 | 0.50 | 12 | 8 |
| 3 | 72 | 22 | 0.50 | 11 | 8 |
| 4 | 92 | 20 | 0.50 | 10 | 8 |
| 5 | 108 | 16 | 0.50 | 8 | 8 |
| 6 | 120 | 12 | 0.50 | 6 | 8 |
| 7 | 128 | 8 | 0.50 | 4 | 8 |
| 8 | 130 | 2 | 0.50 | 1 | 8 |

with different quantities of labor. The first two columns show the relationship between the number of workers and the quantity of balls produced. Recall the principle of diminishing returns.

## PRINCIPLE OF DIMINISHING RETURNS

Suppose that output is produced with two or more inputs and we increase one input while holding the other inputs fixed. Beyond some point–called the *point of diminishing returns*–output will increase at a decreasing rate.

As we saw earlier in the book, the **marginal product of labor**, the change in output from one additional unit of labor, typically rises for the first few workers and then eventually decreases. To simplify matters, we'll assume diminishing returns start to occur with the second worker. As shown in the third column of Table 10.1, the marginal product of labor decreases as the number of workers increases, from 26 for the first worker, to 24 for the second worker, and so on.

The marginal benefit of labor equals the **marginal-revenue product of labor** (**MRP**), which is defined as the extra revenue generated by one additional unit of labor. To compute the *MRP*, we multiply the marginal product of labor by the price of output ($0.50 per ball in this example):

$$MRP = \text{marginal product} \times \text{price of output}$$

Figure 10.1 shows the marginal-revenue product curve. Because the marginal product drops as the number of workers increases, the *MRP* curve is negatively sloped, falling from $11 for the third worker (point *a*) to $8 for the fifth worker (point *b*), and so on.

A firm can use its *MRP* curve to decide how much labor to hire at a particular wage. In Figure 10.1, the marginal-cost curve is horizontal at the market wage ($8). The perfectly competitive firm takes the wage as given, so the marginal-cost curve is also the labor-supply curve faced by the firm. The marginal principle is satisfied at point *b*, where the marginal cost equals the marginal-revenue product. The firm will hire 5 workers because for the first 5 workers, the marginal benefit (the *MRP*) is greater than or equal to the marginal cost (the $8 wage). It would not be sensible to hire another worker, because the additional revenue from the sixth worker ($6) would be less than the $8 additional cost of that worker. If the wage increases to $11, the firm will satisfy the marginal principle at point *a*, hiring only 3 workers.

The *MRP* curve is also the firm's **short-run demand curve for labor**, which shows the relationship between the wage and the quantity of labor demanded in the short run, when the firm cannot change its production facility. The demand curve answers

• **marginal product of labor**
The change in output from one additional unit of labor.

• **marginal-revenue product of labor** (*MRP*)
The extra revenue generated from one additional unit of labor; *MRP* is equal to the price of output times the marginal product of labor.

• **short-run demand curve for labor**
A curve showing the relationship between the wage and the quantity of labor demanded over the short run, when the firm cannot change its production facility.

**The Marginal Principle and the Firm's Demand for Labor**

Using the marginal principle, the firm picks the quantity of workers at which the marginal benefit (the marginal revenue product of labor) equals the marginal cost (the wage). The firm's short-run demand curve for labor is the marginal revenue product curve.

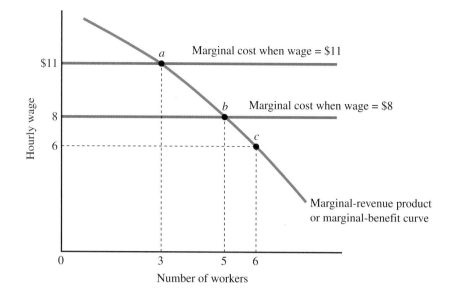

the following question: At each wage, how many workers does the firm want to hire? We've already used the *MRP* curve to answer this question for two different wages ($11 and $8), and we can do the same for any other wage. Because the *MRP* curve is a marginal-benefit curve, and the firm uses the marginal principle to decide how much labor to hire, the *MRP* curve is the same as the firm's demand curve for labor. If you pick a wage, the *MRP* curve tells you exactly how much labor the firm will demand at that wage.

What sorts of changes would cause the demand curve to shift? To draw the labor-demand curve, we fix the price of the output and the productivity of workers. Therefore, an increase in the price of the output will increase the *MRP* of workers, shifting the entire demand curve for labor to the right: At each wage, the firm will hire more workers. This is shown in Figure 10.2. An increase in the price of balls shifts the labor-demand curve to the right. At a wage of $8, the firm hires 7 workers instead of 5. Similarly, if workers become more productive, the increase in the marginal product of labor will increase the *MRP* and shift the demand curve to the right. Conversely, a decrease in price or labor productivity would shift the demand curve to the left.

► FIGURE 10.2

**An Increase in the Price of Output Shifts the Labor-Demand Curve**

An increase in the price of the good produced by workers increases the marginal revenue product at each quantity of workers, shifting the demand curve to the right. At each wage, the firm will demand more workers. For example, at a wage of $8, the demand for labor increases from 5 workers (point *b*) to 7 workers (point *d*).

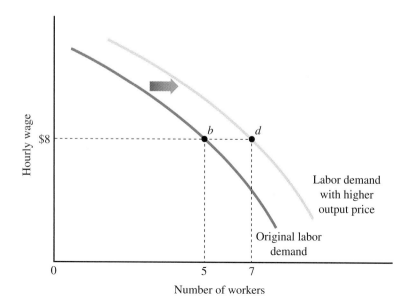

## Market Demand for Labor in the Short Run

To draw the short-run market demand curve for labor, we add the labor demands of all the firms that use a particular type of labor. In the simplest case, all firms are identical, and we simply multiply the number of firms by the quantity of labor demanded by the typical firm. If there were 100 firms and each hired 5 workers at a wage of $8, the market demand for labor would be 500 workers. Similarly, if the typical firm hired 3 workers at a wage of $11, the market demand would be 300 workers.

## Labor Demand in the Long Run

Recall that in the long run, firms can enter or leave the market and firms already in the market can change all of their inputs, including their production facilities. The **long-run demand curve for labor** shows the relationship between the wage and the quantity of labor demanded over the long run, when the number of firms in the market can change and firms in the market can modify their production facilities.

Although there are no diminishing returns in the long run, the market demand curve is still negatively sloped. As the wage increases, the quantity of labor demanded decreases for two reasons:

- The **output effect.** An increase in the wage will increase the cost of producing balls, and firms will pass on at least part of the higher labor cost to their consumers: Prices will increase. According to the law of demand, firms will sell fewer balls at the higher price, so they will need less of all inputs, including labor.

- The **input-substitution effect.** An increase in the wage will cause the firm to substitute other inputs for labor. At a wage of $4, it may not be sensible to use much machinery in the ball factory, but at a wage of $20 it may be sensible to mechanize the factory, using more machinery and fewer workers. This substitution of other inputs for labor decreases the labor input per unit of output.

The input-substitution effect decreases the labor input per unit of output while the output effect decreases total output. The two effects operate in the same direction, so the market demand curve is negatively sloped.

The notion of input substitution applies to other labor markets as well. For the most graphic examples of factor substitution, we can travel from a developed country, such as the United States, Canada, France, Germany, or Japan, to a less-developed country in South America, Africa, or Asia. Wages are much lower in the less-developed countries, so production tends to be more labor intensive. In other words, labor is less costly relative to machinery and equipment, so labor is substituted for these other inputs. Here are some examples:

- *Mining.* U.S. firms use huge earthmoving equipment to mine for minerals; firms in some less-developed countries use thousands of workers, digging by hand.

- *Furniture.* Firms in developed countries manufacture furniture with sophisticated machinery and equipment; firms in some less-developed countries make furniture by hand.

- *Accounting.* Accountants in developed countries use computers and sophisticated software programs; some accountants in less-developed countries use simple calculators and ledger paper.

## Short-Run Versus Long-Run Demand

How does the short-run demand curve for labor compare to the long-run demand curve? There is less flexibility in the short run because firms cannot enter or leave the

- **long-run demand curve for labor**
A curve showing the relationship between the wage and the quantity of labor demanded over the long run, when the number of firms in the market can change and firms can modify their production facilities.

- **output effect**
The change in the quantity of labor demanded resulting from a change in the quantity of output produced.

- **input-substitution effect**
The change in the quantity of labor demanded resulting from an increase in the price of labor relative to the price of other inputs.

market and they cannot modify their production facilities. As a result, the demand for labor is less elastic in the short run. That means the short-run demand curve is steeper than the long-run demand curve. You may recall that we used the same logic to explain why the short-run supply curve for a product (plain cotton T-shirts) was steeper than the long-run supply curve for the product.

# $10.2$ | THE SUPPLY OF LABOR

The labor-supply curve answers the following question: How many hours of labor will be supplied at each wage? When we speak of a labor market, we are referring to the market for a specific occupation in a specific geographical area. Consider the supply for nurses in the hypothetical city of Florence. The supply question is: How many hours of nursing services will be supplied at each wage? To answer that question, we must think about how many nurses are in the city and how many hours each nurse works.

### The Individual Labor-Supply Decision: How Many Hours?

Let's start with an individual's decision about how many hours to work. The decision to work is a decision to sacrifice some leisure time for money: Each hour of work reduces leisure time by one hour. Therefore, the demand for leisure is the flip side of the supply of labor. The price of leisure time is the income sacrificed for each hour of leisure, that is, the hourly wage. An increase in the wage—the price of leisure—has two effects on the demand for leisure.

• **substitution effect for leisure demand**
The change in leisure time resulting from a change in the wage (the price of leisure) relative to the price of other goods.

Consider first the **substitution effect for leisure demand**. The worker faces a trade-off between leisure time and consumer goods such as music, books, food, and entertainment. For each hour of leisure time Leah takes, she loses one hour of work time, and her income drops by an amount equal to the wage. Therefore, she has less money to spend on consumer goods. For example, if the wage is $8 per hour, each hour of leisure decreases the amount of income available to spend on consumer goods by $8. When the wage increases to, say, $10, Leah will sacrifice more income—and consumer goods—for each hour of leisure she takes. Given the larger sacrifice of consumer goods per hour of leisure time, she will demand less leisure. That means that she will work more hours and earn more money for consumer goods. In other words, as the wage increases, she will substitute income—and the consumer goods it buys—for leisure time.

• **income effect for leisure demand**
The change in leisure time resulting from a change in real income caused by a change in the wage.

Consider next the **income effect** of an increase in the wage. For most people, leisure is a normal good in the sense that the demand for leisure increases as real income increases. An increase in the wage increases Leah's real income in the sense that she can afford more of all goods, including leisure time. Suppose Leah has a total of 100 hours per week to divide between leisure and work. At a wage of $10, she works 36 hours and has 64 hours of leisure. She also earns $360 ($10 per hour times 36 hours of work) and spends that amount on consumer goods. If her wage increases to $15, her real income increases because she can have more consumer goods and more leisure time. For example, if she worked only 30 hours, she could buy $450 worth of consumer goods ($15 per hour times 30 hours) and have 70 hours of leisure (100 hours per week minus 30 hours of work). The increase in real income causes Leah to consume more of all normal goods, including leisure time. The increase in real income causes her to demand more leisure and supply less labor.

In the labor market, the income and substitution effects of an increase in wages operate in opposite directions. The substitution effect decreases the desired leisure time, while the income effect increases the desired leisure time. Therefore, we can't predict whether an increase in the wage will cause a worker to demand more leisure time (supply less labor) or less leisure (supply more labor).

# APPLICATION

## DIFFERENT RESPONSES TO A HIGHER WAGE

**APPLYING THE CONCEPTS #1:** When the wage increases, will the typical person work more hours or fewer hours?

A simple example will show why we can't predict a worker's response to an increase in the wage. Suppose each nurse in Florence initially works 36 hours per week at an hourly wage of $10 and the wage increases to $12. The following are three reasonable responses to the higher wage:

1 *Lester works fewer hours.* If Lester works 30 hours instead of 36 hours, he gets 6 hours of extra leisure time and still earns the same income per week ($360 = 30 hours × $12 per hour).

2 *Sam works the same number of hours.* If Sam continues to work 36 hours per week, he gets an additional $72 of income ($2 per hour × 36 hours) and the same amount of leisure time.

3 *Maureen works more hours.* If Maureen works 43 hours instead of 36 hours, she sacrifices 7 hours of leisure time but earns a total of $516, compared to only $360 at a wage of $10 per hour.

Empirical studies of the labor market confirm that each of these responses is reasonable. When the wage increases, some people work more, others work less, and others work about the same amount. In most labor markets, the average number of hours per worker doesn't change very much as the wage changes because the increases in work hours from people like Maureen are nearly offset by decreases in work hours from people like Lester. *Related to Exercise 2.6.*

SOURCE: Ronald Ehrenberg and Robert Smith, *Modern Labor Economics* (Boston: Addison-Wesley, 2005).

## The Market Supply Curve for Labor

Now that we know how individual workers respond to changes in wages, we're ready to consider the supply side of the labor market. The **market supply curve for labor** shows the relationship between the wage and the quantity of labor supplied. In Figure 10.3, the market supply curve for labor is positively sloped, consistent with the law of supply: There is a positive relationship between the wage (the price of labor) and the quantity of labor supplied, *ceteris paribus.* An increase in the wage affects the quantity of nursing supplied in three ways:

- **market supply curve for labor**
  A curve showing the relationship between the wage and the quantity of labor supplied.

1 *Hours worked per employee.* When the wage increases, some nurses will work more hours, some will work fewer hours, and some will work the same number of hours. We don't know for certain whether the average number of work hours will increase, decrease, or stay the same, but the change in the average number of hours worked is likely to be relatively small.

2 *Occupational choice.* An increase in the nursing wage will cause some workers to switch from other occupations to nursing and motivate more new workers to pick nursing over other occupations.

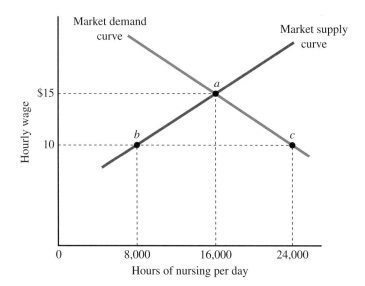

**3** *Migration.* Some nurses in other cities will move to Florence to earn the higher wages offered there.

The second and third effects reinforce one another, so an increase in the wage causes movement upward along the market supply curve. If the wage of Florence nurses increases from $10 to $15 per hour, the quantity of nurses supplied increases from 8,000 hours per day (point *b*) to 16,000 hours per day (point *a*). Although individual workers may not work more hours as the wage increases, the supply curve is positively sloped because an increase in the wage changes workers' occupational choices and causes migration.

# 10.3 | LABOR MARKET EQUILIBRIUM

We're ready to put demand and supply together to think about equilibrium in the labor market. A market equilibrium is a situation in which there is no pressure to change the price of a good or service. Figure 10.3 shows the equilibrium in the market for nurses. The supply curve intersects the demand curve at point *a*, so the equilibrium wage is $15 per hour and the equilibrium quantity is 16,000 hours of nursing per day. At this wage, there is neither an excess demand for labor nor an excess supply of labor, so the market has reached an equilibrium.

## Changes in Demand and Supply

How would a change in the demand for nurses affect the equilibrium wage of nurses? We know from Chapter 3 that a change in demand causes the equilibrium price and the equilibrium quantity to move in the same direction: An increase in demand increases the equilibrium price and quantity, whereas a decrease in demand decreases the equilibrium price and quantity. For example, suppose that the demand for medical care increases. Nurses help to provide medical care, so an increase in the quantity of medical care demanded will shift the demand curve for nurses to the right: At each wage, firms will demand more hours of nursing services. As shown in Figure 10.4, an increase in demand increases the equilibrium wage and the equilibrium quantity of nursing services.

How would a change in supply of nurses affect the equilibrium wage of nurses? We know from Chapter 3 that a change in supply causes price and quantity to move in opposite directions: An increase in supply decreases the equilibrium price but increases the equilibrium quantity, whereas a decrease in supply

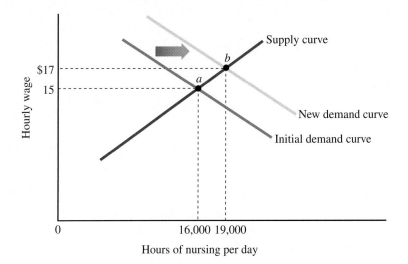

◄ **FIGURE 10.4**

**The Market Effect of an Increase in Demand for Labor**

An increase in the demand for nursing services shifts the demand curve to the right, moving the equilibrium from point *a* to point *b*. The equilibrium wage increases from $15 to $17 per hour, and the equilibrium quantity increases from 16,000 hours to 19,000 hours.

increases the equilibrium price but decreases the equilibrium quantity. Suppose a new television program makes nursing look like an attractive occupation, causing a large number of young people to become nurses rather than accountants, lawyers, or doctors. The supply curve for nurses will shift to the right: At each wage, more nursing hours will be supplied. The equilibrium wage will decrease, and the equilibrium quantity will increase.

## The Market Effects of the Minimum Wage

We can use the model of the labor market to show how various public policies, such as the federally mandated minimum wage, affect total employment. In 2006, the federal minimum wage was $5.15 per hour. Figure 10.5 shows the effects of a minimum wage on the market for restaurant workers. The market equilibrium is shown by point *a*: The supply of restaurant workers equals demand at a wage of $4.70 and a quantity of 50,000 worker hours per day. Suppose a minimum wage is established at $5.15 per hour. At this wage, the quantity of labor demanded is only 49,000 hours (point *b* on the demand curve). In other words, the minimum wage decreases the quantity of labor restaurants use by 1,000 hours per day.

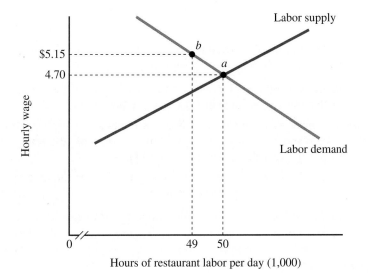

◄ **FIGURE 10.5**

**The Market Effects of a Minimum Wage**

The market equilibrium is shown by point *a*: The wage is $4.70 per hour, and the quantity of labor is 50,000 hours. A minimum wage of $5.15 decreases the quantity of labor demanded to 49,000 hours per day (point *b*). Although some workers receive a higher wage, others lose their jobs or work fewer hours.

# APPLICATION

## CODES OF CONDUCT AND LIVING WAGES

**APPLYING THE CONCEPTS #2:** Does a living wage have the same effects as a minimum wage?

In recent years, several widely publicized reports have documented poor working conditions and low wages in foreign factories that produce shoes, soccer balls, clothing, and toys for U.S. corporations. On college campuses, the United Students Against Sweatshops developed a code of conduct for companies that produce products bearing university logos. The code requires the companies to follow local laws concerning child labor, workplace safety, and minimum wages. The code also calls for producers to pay a "living wage," defined as a wage high enough to support a family.

How will a "living wage" affect overseas workers who produce T-shirts with a university logo? An increase in the wage will increase the cost of producing T-shirts, so the price of T-shirts will increase. Consumers will respond to the higher price by purchasing fewer T-shirts, consistent with the law of demand. Firms will produce fewer T-shirts, so they will employ fewer workers. In other words, a living wage is similar to a minimum wage in its effects on labor income: Some workers will earn higher wages, but others will lose their jobs.

Is there any way to avoid job losses when the wage increases? One possibility is that consumers are willing to pay a higher price for goods that are produced by living-wage workers. In this case, the increase in the price of shirts would cause a smaller decrease in the quantity of T-shirts demanded, so fewer workers would lose their jobs. Given the uncertainty about how much more consumers are willing to pay for living-wage products, it is difficult to predict the actual effects of living wages on overseas workers.

*Related to Exercises 3.5 and 3.7.*

What are the trade-offs associated with the minimum wage? For restaurant workers and restaurant diners, there is good news and bad news:

- *Good news for some restaurant workers.* Some workers keep their jobs and receive a higher wage ($5.15 per hour instead of $4.70 per hour).

- *Bad news for some restaurant workers.* Some workers lose their jobs. If the typical workday for restaurant workers is five hours, the loss of 1,000 hours of restaurant work per day translates into a loss of 200 jobs.

- *Bad news for diners.* The increase in the wage increases the cost of producing restaurant meals, increasing the price of meals.

There are winners and losers from the minimum wage. Workers who keep their jobs gain at the expense of other workers and at the expense of diners. A recent study suggests that a 10-percent increase in the minimum wage decreases the number of minimum wage jobs by about 1 percent.[2]

# APPLICATION

**3**

## TRADE-OFFS FROM IMMIGRATION

**APPLYING THE CONCEPTS #3:** Who benefits from the immigration of low-skilled workers?

Since about 1850, international migration has played an important role in labor markets. In the first wave of immigration, from 1850 to 1913, over a million people migrated to the Americas each year. Most of the immigrants were from European countries. After several decades of war and economic depressions, massive immigration resumed in 1945, and most of the immigrants were from less-developed countries. The most recent wave of immigration started in 1990 and has increased the supply of labor to the U.S. economy by about 10 percent per decade.

Immigration creates winners and losers within the economy. The increase in the supply of labor decreases wages for the native workers who have the same skill level as the immigrants. Because the average U.S. immigrant has less education and earns less income than the average native, immigrants compete with low-skill natives, decreasing their wages. On the benefit side, the decrease in the wages of low-skill labor decreases production costs and product prices, so consumers benefit. In general, we expect low-skill workers to lose as a result of immigration because the lower wages will dominate the benefits of lower consumer prices. In contrast, we expect high-skill workers to benefit from lower prices.

Economists have estimated the net effect of immigration on the U.S. economy. George Borjas shows that immigration to the United States has a small positive effect, with the losses in wages of low-skilled workers more than offset by gains to consumers and firms. This conclusion is consistent with the idea that exchange increases efficiency and the size of the overall economic pie. Studies of the most recent wave of immigration suggest that immigration decreases the wages of high-school dropouts and other low-skilled workers. *Related to Exercises 3.6 and 3.8.*

SOURCES: George Borjas, "The Economics of Immigration," *Journal of Economic Literature*, vol. 32 (1994), pp. 1667–1717; George Borjas, "The Labor Demand Curve Is Downward Sloping: Reexamining the Impact of Immigration on the Labor Market," *Quarterly Journal of Economics*, vol. 108 (2003), pp. 1335–1374; Gianmarco Ottaviano and Giovanni Peri, "Rethinking the Gains from Immigration: Theory and Evidence from the U.S.," NBER Working Paper 11672 (2005).

## 10.4 | EXPLAINING DIFFERENCES IN WAGES AND INCOME

Now that we know how the equilibrium wage for a particular occupation is determined, we're ready to explain why wages vary from one job to another. Let's think about why some occupations pay more than others, why women earn less than men, and why college graduates earn more than high-school graduates.

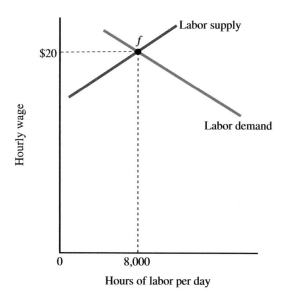

► **FIGURE 10.6**
**The Equilibrium Wage When Labor Supply Is Low Relative to Demand**
If supply is low relative to demand—because few people have the skills, training costs are high, or the job is undesirable—the equilibrium wage will be high.

## Why Do Wages Differ Across Occupations?

There is substantial variation in wages across occupations. Most professional athletes earn more than medical doctors, who earn more than college professors, who earn more than janitors. We'll see that the wage for a particular occupation will be high if the supply of workers in that occupation is small relative to the demand for those workers. This is shown in Figure 10.6, where the supply curve intersects the demand curve at a high wage. The supply of workers in a particular occupation could be small for four reasons:

1 *Few people with the required skills.* To play professional baseball, people must be able to hit balls thrown at them at about 90 miles per hour. The few people who have this skill are paid a lot of money, because baseball owners compete with one another for skillful players, bidding up the wage. The same logic applies to other professional athletes, musicians, and actors. The few people who have the skills required for these occupations are paid high wages.

2 *High training costs.* The skills required for some occupations can only be acquired through education and training. For example, the skills that are required of a medical doctor can only be acquired in medical school, and legal skills can only be acquired in law school. If it is costly to acquire these skills, a relatively small number of people will become skilled, and they will receive high wages. The higher wage compensates workers for their training costs.

3 *Undesirable working conditions.* Some occupations have undesirable working conditions, and workers demand higher wages as compensation. Wages are higher for jobs that are dangerous, dirty, stressful, or require people to work at odd hours.

4 *Artificial barriers to entry.* Government and professional licensing boards restrict the number of people in certain occupations, and labor unions restrict their membership. These supply restrictions increase wages.

## The Gender Pay Gap

Why do women, on average, earn less than men? In the United States, the typical woman earns about 75 percent as much as the typical man. The gender gap is smaller in European nations but much larger in Japan. An important factor in the gender gap is the concentration of women in occupations that pay low wages. Given the distribution of men and women in different occupations, about half of female workers would have to change occupations to achieve equal gender representation in all occupations.[3] A recent study explored several factors that contribute to the gender pay gap.[4] The

# APPLICATION

## WAGE PREMIUMS FOR DANGEROUS JOBS

**APPLYING THE CONCEPTS #4:** Do dangerous occupations pay higher wages?

Workers who choose dangerous occupations receive high wages, so they are compensated for the danger associated with their jobs. The workers with the greatest risk of losing their lives on the job are lumberjacks, boiler-makers, taxicab drivers, and mine workers. To compensate for the higher risk of getting killed on the job, steelworkers receive a wage premium of 3.7 percent. In the United States, the average job fatality rate is 1 in 25,000 workers per year. For a worker who faces twice the average fatality rate, the wage is about 1 percent higher.

The same logic applies to occupations with other undesirable features. The wage premium for jobs with an annual injury rate of 2 percent is 1.15 percent for men and 3.68 percent for women. Workers receive higher wages for night shifts, jobs in noisy environments, and jobs that cause mental stress, in part because stress contributes to health problems such as heart disease and stroke. *Related to Exercise 4.5.*

SOURCES: Craig Olson, "An Analysis of Wage Differentials Received by Workers on Dangerous Jobs," *Journal of Human Resources*, vol. 16, Spring 1981, pp. 167–185; John Leeth and John Ruser, "Compensating Wage Differentials for Fatal and Nonfatal Injury Risk by Gender and Race," *Journal of Risk and Uncertainty*, vol. 27 (2003), pp. 257–277; Michael French and Laura Dunlap, "Compensating Wage Differentials for Job Stress," *Applied Economics*, vol. 30 (1998), pp. 1067–1075; Ronald Ehrenberg and Robert Smith, *Modern Labor Economics* (Boston: Addison-Wesley, 2005).

study observed a gap of about 20 percent among workers aged 26 to 34. The study identified four factors that contribute to the gender gap:

- *Difference in worker skills and productivity.* On average, women have less education and work experience, so they are less productive and thus receive lower wages. An important factor in the lower-than-men-level of work experience among women is that many women interrupt their careers to raise children. The study concluded that lower productivity is the most important factor in the gender gap.

- *Differences in occupational preferences.* Wages vary across occupations: Clerical and service occupations receive lower wages than craft and professional occupations. Compared to men, women express stronger preferences for low-wage occupations, such as clerical and service occupations, and weaker preferences for some high-wage occupations, such as craft and operator occupations. In contrast, women have slightly stronger preferences for high-wage professional and technical occupations. On balance, the general orientation of women toward low-wage occupations contributes to the gender gap.

- *Occupational discrimination.* Given the variation in wages across occupations, if employers have a bias against hiring women for high-paying occupations, women will receive lower wages. The study shows that on average, women are less successful than men in attaining their desired occupations, and this occupational discrimination by employers explains between 7 and 25 percent of the gender gap.

• *Wage discrimination.* If employers pay women less than their equally productive male counterparts, women's wages will be lower. The results of the study on this issue are mixed, with some evidence that wage discrimination is a significant factor in the gender pay gap.

The general conclusion of the study is that differences in productivity and occupational status are the most important factors in the gender pay gap. It appears that the relatively large number of women in low-paying occupations results both from the occupational preferences of women and employer discrimination that inhibits occupational attainment for women.

## Racial Discrimination

What about differences in earnings by race? In 1995, African American males who worked full time earned 73 percent as much as their white counterparts earned, while African American females earned 86 percent as much as their white counterparts. Hispanic males earned 62 percent as much as white males, while Hispanic females earned 73 percent as much as white females.[5] For both males and females, part of the earnings gap is caused by differences in productivity: On average, whites have more education and work experience, so they are paid higher wages. Part of the wage gap is caused by racial discrimination. Some African American and Hispanic workers are paid lower wages for similar jobs, and others are denied opportunities to work in some high-paying jobs.

How much of the earnings gap is caused by discrimination? A recent study suggests that racial discrimination decreases the wages of African American men by about 13 percent.[6] Another study shows that these earnings differences have decreased over the last few decades and that the differences are now small enough that "most of the disparity in earnings between blacks and whites in the labor market of the 1990s is due to the differences in skills they bring to the market, and not to discrimination within the labor market."[7] The differences in skills brought to the labor market are caused by a number of factors, including past discrimination that has inhibited the acquisition of job skills and differences in educational opportunities. For example, in urban areas about one-third of African American high-school students have above-average scores on reading and math exams, compared to about two-thirds of white students.

## Why Do College Graduates Earn Higher Wages?

In 2002, the typical college graduate earned roughly twice as much as the typical high-school graduate. There are two explanations for the college premium.

The first explanation is based on supply and demand analysis. A college education provides the skills necessary to enter certain occupations, so a college graduate has more job options than a high-school graduate. Both high-school grads and college grads can fill jobs that require only a high-school education, so the supply of workers for these low-skill jobs is plentiful, and the equilibrium wage for these jobs is low. In contrast, there is a smaller supply of workers for jobs that require a college education, so the wages in these high-skill jobs are higher than the wages for low-skill jobs. This is the **learning effect** of a college education: College students learn the skills required for certain occupations, increasing their human capital.

The second explanation of the college premium requires a different perspective on college and its role in the labor market. Suppose certain skills are required for a particular job, but an employer cannot determine whether a prospective employee has these skills. For example, most managerial jobs require the employee to manage time efficiently, but it is impossible for an employer to determine whether a prospective employee is a good manager of time. Suppose that these skills are also required to complete a college degree. For example, to get passing grades in all your classes, you must be able to use your time efficiently. When you

• **learning effect**
The increase in a person's wage resulting from the learning of skills required for certain occupations.

# APPLICATION

**LAKISHA WASHINGTON VERSUS EMILY WALSH**

**APPLYING THE CONCEPTS #5:** How does racial discrimination affect the labor market?

Imagine that two recent high-school graduates apply for low-skill jobs advertised in the newspaper. The jobs include waiting tables, dishwashing, and working in warehouses. One man is white and admits to serving 18 months in prison for selling cocaine. The other applicant is an African American man without a criminal record. Which applicant has a greater chance of being called back for a second interview? In a carefully designed experiment with college students posing as job applicants, the white applicant with a criminal record was called back 17 percent of the time, while the crime-free African American applicant was called back only 14 percent of the time. In other words, the study implies that the disadvantage of being African American is roughly equivalent to the disadvantage of spending 18 months in prison.

This experiment in Milwaukee revealed substantial racial discrimination in hiring for low-skill jobs. According to Devah Pager, the researcher who conducted the experiment,

> *In these low-wage, entry-level markets, race remains a huge barrier. Affirmative-action pressures aren't operating here. Employers don't spend a lot of time screening applicants. They want a quick signal whether the applicant seems suitable. Stereotypes among young black men remain so prevalent and so strong that race continues to serve as a major signal of characteristics of which employers are wary.*

In another experiment, economists responded in writing to help-wanted ads in Chicago and in Boston, using hypothetical names that were likely to be identified by employers as either white or African American. Applicants named Greg Kelly or Emily Walsh were 50 percent more likely to be called for interviews than those named Jamal Jackson or Lakisha Washington. Having a white-sounding name on an application was equivalent to about eight additional years of work experience. The researchers experimented with different resumes for both types of applicants. Adding work experience and computer skills increased the likelihood of interviews by 30 percent for white-sounding applicants but only 9 percent for those whose names suggested an African American background. *Related to Exercise 4.6.*

SOURCE: David Wessel, "Racial Discrimination Is Still at Work in U.S.," *Wall Street Journal*, September 4, 2003, p. A2.

jobs.kaiserpermanente.org

get a college degree, firms will conclude that you have some of the skills they require, so they may hire you instead of a high-school graduate. This is the **signaling effect** of a college education: People who complete college provide a signal to employers about their skills. This second explanation suggests that colleges simply provide a testing ground where students can reveal their skills to potential employers.

- **signaling effect**
  The information about a person's work skills conveyed by completing college.

Over the last three decades, this wage gap, or "college premium," has almost doubled. The most important factor in doubling the college premium is technological change. Changes in technology have increased the demand for college graduates relative to the demand for other workers. In all sectors of the economy, firms are switching to sophisticated machinery and equipment that require highly skilled workers. Consequently, the share of jobs that require a college education has increased steadily, increasing the demand for college graduates. Of course, the supply of college graduates has increased, too, but not by as much as demand. Because the increase in demand is large relative to the increase in supply, the wages of college graduates have increased. Another factor in the growing college premium is the pace of technological change. Workers with more education can more easily learn new skills and new jobs, so firms are willing to pay more for college graduates.

# 10.5 | THE DISTRIBUTION OF INCOME

In 2004, the median household income in the United States was $44,389—half of households earned more income and half earned less. There is substantial variation in household income, with some households earning much more and others earning much less. In this part of the chapter, we'll discuss the extent of income inequality in the United States and explore some of the reasons why the households with the highest income are receiving a larger share of total income.

## Income Distribution Facts

Income can be measured in different ways, and two income measures are relevant for our discussion. *Market income* is defined as all earnings received from labor and capital markets. It includes wages and salaries, as well as earnings from bonds, stocks, and real estate. *Disposable income* equals market income, plus government transfers, minus taxes paid. The transfers include income supplements, Social Security payments, food stamps, and housing assistance. The taxes include state and federal income and payroll taxes, as well as local property taxes.

Table 10.2 shows the distributions of income before and after the effects of government transfer programs and taxes. To compute the numbers in the second column of the table (Percent of Market Income), we take four steps:

1 Rank the nation's households according to market income: The household with the highest income is at the top of the list, and the household with the lowest income is at the bottom of the list.

2 Divide the households into five groups, or "quintiles": The lowest fifth includes the poorest 20 percent of households (the lowest 20% of the list), the second fifth is the next poorest 20 percent, and so on.

3 Compute each group's income by adding up the income received by all the households in the group.

4 Compute each group's percentage of total income (the number in the third column of the table) by dividing the group's income by the nation's total income.

**Table 10.2 | SHARES OF INCOME EARNED BY DIFFERENT U.S. GROUPS, 2004**

| Income Group | Percent of Market Income | Percent of Disposable Income |
|---|---|---|
| Lowest fifth | 1.48% | 4.68% |
| Second fifth | 7.36 | 10.34 |
| Middle fifth | 14.10 | 16.08 |
| Fourth fifth | 23.63 | 24.02 |
| Highest fifth | 53.44 | 44.88 |

SOURCE: U.S. Census Bureau, *The Effects of Government Taxes and Transfers on Income and Poverty: 2004.*

By repeating this process for disposable income, we can compute the numbers in the third column of the table.

Consider first the distribution of market income, shown in the second column of Table 10.2. The lowest fifth earns only 1.48 percent of the total market income, while the highest fifth earns over half the total market income. If we combine the lowest two fifths, the lowest 40 percent of households earn only 8.84 percent of total market income. Three key factors explain these substantial differences in market income:

1 *Differences in labor skills and effort.* Some people have better labor skills—more human capital—than others, so they earn higher wages. Labor skills are determined by innate ability and education. In addition, some people work longer hours or at more demanding jobs, so they earn more income.

2 *Luck and misfortune.* Some people are luckier than others in investing their money, starting a business, or picking an occupation. Among the unlucky people are those who develop health problems that make it difficult to earn income. Among the lucky people are those who inherit wealth and earn income by investing the inherited wealth.

3 *Discrimination.* Some people are paid lower wages or have limited opportunities for education and work because of their race or gender.

Consider next the distribution of disposable income, which includes the effects of government redistribution and tax polices. Going from market income to disposable income, the largest changes occur at the top and the bottom of the income distribution. The share of the lowest fifth increases by just over 3 percentage points, while the share of the highest fifth decreases by almost 9 percentage points. In other words, government transfer and tax policies reduce income inequality.

## Recent Changes in the Distribution of Income

Table 10.3 shows the changes in the distribution of money income (total pretax cash income) between 1970 and 2004. The share of the top fifth rose from 43.3 to 50.0 percent, while the share of every other group dropped. By historical standards, these changes in the distribution of income were very rapid. What caused these changes in the distribution in money income?

It appears that the most important reason for growing inequality is what labor economists call an "increase in the demand for skill."[8] In the labor market, the demand for highly skilled (highly educated) workers has increased relative to the demand for less-skilled (less-educated) workers. As a result, the wage gap between the two groups has widened. As we saw at the beginning of the chapter, in the last three decades the college premium has increased significantly. At the same time, the premium for advanced degrees increased. Finally, the dropout penalty (the wage gap between high-school graduates and dropouts) has nearly doubled.

**Table 10.3** CHANGES IN U.S. INCOME SHARES, 1970–2001

| Year | Lowest Fifth | Second Fifth | Third Fifth | Fourth Fifth | Highest Fifth |
|------|------|------|------|------|------|
| 2004 | 3.4% | 8.7% | 14.8% | 23.0% | 50.0% |
| 2000 | 3.6 | 8.9 | 14.8 | 23.0 | 49.8 |
| 1995 | 3.7 | 9.1 | 15.2 | 23.3 | 48.7 |
| 1990 | 3.9 | 9.6 | 15.9 | 24.0 | 46.6 |
| 1985 | 4.0 | 9.7 | 16.3 | 24.6 | 45.3 |
| 1980 | 4.3 | 10.3 | 16.9 | 24.9 | 43.7 |
| 1975 | 4.4 | 10.5 | 17.1 | 24.8 | 43.2 |
| 1970 | 4.1 | 10.8 | 17.4 | 24.5 | 43.3 |

SOURCE: U.S. Bureau of the Census, *Current Population Reports, Selected years.*

Why did the demand for skill increase over the last three decades? There are two main reasons:

- ***Technological change.*** Advances in technology have simultaneously decreased the demand for less-educated workers and increased the demand for college graduates and people with advanced degrees. While the new technology has made it possible to replace many low-skilled workers with "smart" machines and computers, it has increased the demand for workers who have the education and skills required to produce the new technology and use it.

- ***Increased international trade.*** An increase in international trade means more exports and imports. Trade allows developed countries like the United States to easily export goods produced with high-skilled labor and import goods produced with low-skilled labor. As a result, the expansion of international trade in the last three decades has increased the demand for high-skilled workers and decreased the demand for low-skilled workers in the United States.

Economists have not yet reached a consensus on the relative importance of these two factors.

## Changes in the Top End of Income Distribution: 1920–1998

Figure 10.7 shows the trends in the income shares of the several groups at the top of the income distribution. The upper line shows the share for the top decile (top 10 percent) of income earners. The income share was just over 40 percent in 1917 and just under 45 percent at the start of World War II. The share plunged during the war and leveled out in the postwar period at about 33 percent. The share started increasing in 1970, rising from 32 to 42 percent by 1998. The middle line shows the income share for the top 5 percent of earners. It follows a similar pattern, with lower shares after the war, a long period of relative stability, and then increases starting in 1970. The lower line, showing the income share for the top 1 percent of the distribution, shows a similar pattern.

What caused these patterns? Recent studies of the trends for the top decile generated the following observations[9]:

1 During World War II, the income share of the top decile decreased because government wage controls compressed wages. In addition, the government increased tax rates on invested money (stock dividends, interest earnings, and entrepreneurial income) to support the war effort, and these rates remained relatively high until the 1980s. The higher tax rates decreased the return that could be earned on investments and slowed the rate at which fortunes were amassed.

▶ **FIGURE 10.7**
**Top Income Distribution Shares, 1920–1998**
*SOURCE: Author's computation based on Thomas Piketly and Emmanuel Sace, "Income Inequality in the United States, 1913–1998," Quarterly Journal of Economics, 118 (2003), pp. 1–39.*

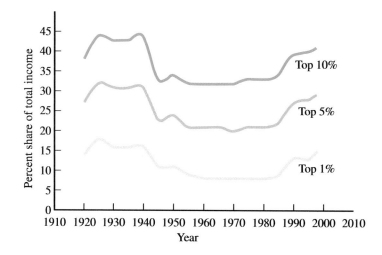

**2** The stability of the income share in the period 1945–1970 is puzzling because one would expect wages to rebound after wage controls ended following World War II. During this time period, there *was* a postwar rebound in top-decile wages in France and other countries, but not in the United States.

**3** Between 1920 and 1998, the share of income from wages increased at the expense of income from investments. For the top decile, the share of income from wages rose from 58 to 84 percent. For the top 1 percent, the wage share rose from 42 to 70 percent.

**4** The increase in the income shares since 1970 has been caused by rapid increases in the compensation of the highest-wage workers—the executives of large corporations and other organizations. Most of the action in the top decile is in the top 1 percent of earners, and most of the action at the top is in rising wages, not increases in investment income. After adjusting for inflation, the salaries of top executives increased by about 6 percent per year in the 1990s, much more rapidly than average salaries.

**5** Chief executives in the United States are paid much more than their counterparts in other developed nations. For example, U.S. executives receive three to four times more than their counterparts in Britain, Germany, and France. In the United States, the average pay for a chief executive is 24 times the pay of the average production worker. In Germany, the average executive is paid only eight times as much as the average production worker.

**6** The U.S. experience in the last 30 years contrasts sharply with that of France, where the income share of the top decile actually decreased between 1970 and 1998, from 33 to 32 percent.

# 10.6 | POVERTY AND PUBLIC POLICY

The U.S. government defines a poor household as one with a total income less than the amount required to satisfy the "minimum needs" of the household. The government estimates a minimum food budget for each type of household and multiplies the food budget by three to get the official poverty budget. A household with income lower than the official poverty budget is considered poor. In 2004, the poverty budget was $15,067 for a three-person household and $19,307 for a four-person household, compared to a median income of $44,389. In 2004, almost 37 million people were below the poverty line, or 12.7 percent of the population.

## Poverty Rates for Different Groups

Table 10.4 shows the incidence of poverty among different groups of people. For each group, the poverty rate equals the percentage of people in that group who live in households with incomes lower than the official poverty budget. In 2004, the overall poverty rate was 12.7 percent, and there was substantial variation in poverty rates among the listed groups:

**1** *Race.* The poverty rates for both blacks and Hispanics are more than twice the poverty rates for whites.

**2** *Type of family.* The poverty rate for female-headed households is about five times the poverty rate for households headed by a married couple.

**3** *Age.* One of the successes in the war on poverty has been the decrease in poverty among the aged; their poverty rate dropped from 35 percent in 1959 to 9.8 percent in 2004, largely as a result of increased Social Security benefits. About one-sixth of children lived in poverty in 2004, with much higher poverty rates for racial minorities.

**Table 10.4** | POVERTY RATES FOR DIFFERENT GROUPS, 2004

| Characteristic | Poverty Rate in 2004 |
| --- | --- |
| **All** | 12.7% |
| **Race** | |
| White | 10.8 |
| Black | 24.7 |
| Hispanic | 21.9 |
| Asian | 9.8 |
| **Type of Family** | |
| Married couple | 5.5 |
| Female-headed household | 28.4 |
| **Age** | |
| Under 18 years | 17.8 |
| 65 years and older | 9.8 |

SOURCE: U.S. Census Bureau, *Poverty in the United States* (2004).

Education is a key factor in determining wages, and poverty rates are lower for more-educated workers. As we saw earlier in the chapter, college graduates earn roughly twice as much as high-school graduates. The poverty rate for college graduates is 3 percent, compared to 9 percent for high-school graduates. For high-school dropouts, the poverty rate is 22 percent.

### Redistribution Programs for the Poor

• **means-tested program**
A government spending program that provides assistance to those whose income falls below a certain level.

The government uses a number of programs to provide assistance to the poor. These programs, broadly defined as "welfare programs," are **means-tested programs**, meaning that only people whose incomes fall below a certain level receive assistance. These programs reduce the poverty rate by a substantial margin. In 2004, the poverty rate based on market income—before accounting for government tax and spending programs—was 19.4 percent. The poverty rates shown in Table 10.4 incorporate the effects of cash transfers to poor households, indicating that cash transfers decreased the overall poverty rate from 19.4 to 12.7 percent. As a final calculation, we can compute poverty rates for disposable income, which includes taxes as well as the value of noncash programs, such as food stamps. With this definition of income, the poverty rate is 10.6 percent. To summarize, government tax and spending programs reduced the 2004 poverty rate from 19.4 to 10.6 percent.

Table 10.5 shows the government expenditures on means-tested programs in 2002. As shown in the second row, cash assistance is responsible for only about one-fifth of total spending, while medical care makes up over half of total spending.

### Welfare Reform and TANF

In 1996, the overhaul of federal antipoverty programs ended decades of policy based on the notion that poor families are entitled to cash and in-kind assistance. The Personal Responsibility and Work Opportunity Reconciliation Act of 1996 eliminated the entitlement of poor families to receive cash assistance. The federal government now provides block grants to states to provide Temporary Aid to Needy Families (TANF), with restrictions on what recipients must do to qualify for assistance and limits on how long they can receive assistance:

• A recipient must participate in work activities, defined as employment, on-the-job training, work experience, community service, or vocational training.
• After a total of 60 months of cash assistance (consecutive or nonconsecutive), assistance stops. States can allow exceptions to the 60-month rule for up to 20 percent of recipients.

**Table 10.5 | EXPENDITURES ON MEANS-TESTED PROGRAMS, 2002**

| | Spending ($ billion) | | |
| --- | --- | --- | --- |
| | Federal | State and Local | Total |
| Medical care | $164 | $119 | $282 |
| Cash aid | 82 | 20 | 102 |
| Food benefits | 37 | 2 | 39 |
| Housing aid | 35 | 1 | 36 |
| Education | 29 | 2 | 30 |
| Services | 18 | 5 | 22 |
| Jobs/training | 7 | 1 | 8 |
| Energy aid | 2 | 0 | 2 |
| **Total** | **373** | **149** | **522** |

SOURCE: Vee Burke, *Cash and Noncash Benefits for Persons with Limited Income,* Congressional Research Service (2003).

The general thrust of welfare reform was to change an entitlement program into a program that requires work in exchange for time-limited assistance.

In the years since welfare reform was implemented, the number of people receiving assistance has decreased dramatically. Between 1994 and 2002, the national welfare caseload dropped by over 50 percent, and the employment of single mothers increased. During this period, the economy grew rapidly, increasing employment opportunities for all households. Although the rapidly growing economy was partly responsible for the reduction in welfare caseloads, the implementation of TANF certainly played a role in reducing the number of people on welfare. It also was an important factor in reducing poverty among children, from 23 percent in 1993 to 18 percent in 2004.[10]

## Welfare and Work Incentives

How does cash assistance to the poor affect their incentives to work? Two features of an assistance program affect work incentives. The first feature is the base cash payment. The larger the amount provided as a base—the payment to someone who earns no market income—the lower the incentive to work to supplement the base income. There is considerable variation across states in the base payment. In Alabama, the monthly payment for a single-parent family of three is $164, compared to $801 in Minnesota.[11]

The second feature that affects work incentives is the benefit reduction rate for market income. When a recipient earns market income, the welfare payment decreases. For example, if the benefit reduction rate is 40 percent, each dollar of market income reduces the welfare payment by $0.40, so the net income from a dollar of market income is $0.60. There is considerable variation across states in benefit reduction rates. In about a third of states, the benefit reduction rate is 100 percent: Each dollar of market income reduces the welfare payment by a dollar. California allows recipients to earn $225 without any benefit reduction, and each additional dollar reduces the welfare payment by 50 cents. About one-third of states have reduction rates of 50 percent or less. The larger the reduction rate, the lower the payoff for each hour of market income, and the lower the incentive to earn additional income. There is evidence that in states with relatively large work incentives, welfare recipients work more hours and earn more market income.[12]

# SUMMARY

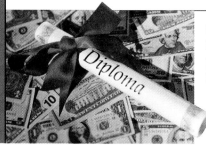

In this chapter, we've seen how wages are determined in perfectly competitive labor markets and why wages differ from one occupation to another. We've also looked at the distribution of income in the United States and explored possible reasons for growing inequality. Here are the main points of the chapter:

1 The *long-run demand curve for labor* is negatively sloped because the output and input-substitution effects operate in the same direction: An increase in the wage decreases labor per unit of output and decreases the total output produced.

2 An increase in the wage triggers *income* and *substitution effects* that operate in opposite directions, so an increase in the wage has an ambiguous effect on the quantity of labor supplied.

3 The wage in a particular occupation will be relatively high if supply is small relative to demand. This will occur if (1) few people have the skills required for the occupation, (2) training costs are high, or (3) the job is dangerous or stressful.

4 College graduates earn more than high-school graduates because a college education provides new skills and allows people to reveal their skills to employers.

5 The trade-off with a minimum wage is that some workers earn higher income, but others lose their jobs.

6 The wealthiest 20 percent of families in the United States earn about half of total income, while the wealthiest 10 percent earn 42 percent of total income. At the other end of the income distribution, the poorest 20 percent earn only 3.5 percent of total income.

7 Poverty rates are relatively high among African Americans, Hispanics, high-school dropouts, and female-headed households.

## KEY TERMS

income effect for leisure
   demand, p. 260

input-substitution effect, p. 259

learning effect, p. 268

long-run demand curve for
   labor, p. 259

marginal product of labor, p. 257

marginal-revenue product of labor
   (*MRP*), p. 257

market supply curve for labor, p. 261

means-tested programs, p. 274

output effect, p. 259

short-run demand curve for
   labor, p. 257.

signaling effect, p. 269

substitution effect for leisure
   demand, p. 260

## EXERCISES  *Get Ahead of the Curve*

Visit www.myeconlab.com to complete these exercises online and get instant feedback.

### 10.1 | The Demand for Labor

**1.1** The marginal revenue product of labor equals _____ times _____.

**1.2** A profit-maximizing firm will hire the number of workers where _____ equals _____.

**1.3** Your favorite professional team is considering hiring a new player for $3 million per year. It will be sensible (profitable) to hire the player if his _____ is greater than the $3 million cost.

**1.4** Arrows up or down: The logic of the output effect is that a decrease in the wage will _____ production costs, so the price of output will _____ and the quantity of output demanded will _____. As a result, the quantity of labor demanded will _____.

**1.5** The logic of the input-substitution effect is that a decrease in the wage causes the firm to _____.

**1.6** The long-run market demand curve for labor is _____ (steeper/flatter) than the short-run market demand curve for labor.

**1.7** **Demand for News Kids.** Consider the market for newspaper delivery kids in Kidsville. Each news kid receives a piece rate of $2 per subscriber per month and has a fixed territory that initially has 100 subscribers. The price elasticity of demand for subscriptions is 2.0. Suppose the new city council of Kidsville passes a law that establishes a minimum piece rate of $3 per subscriber per month. As a result, the publisher increases the monthly price of a subscription by 20 percent. How will the new law affect the monthly income of the typical news kid?

**1.8** **Demand for Airline Pilots.** Comment on the following: "There is no substitute for an airline pilot: Someone has to fly the plane. Therefore, an increase in the wage of airline pilots will not change the number of pilots used by the airlines."

## 10.2 | The Supply of Labor

**2.1** Arrows up or down: The logic of the substitution effect for leisure is that an increase in the wage _____ the opportunity cost of leisure time, which tends to _____ leisure time and _____ labor time.

**2.2** Arrows up or down: The logic of the income effect for leisure is that an increase in the wage _____ real income, and if leisure is a normal good this tends to _____ leisure time and _____ labor time.

**2.3** We cannot predict a worker's response to an increase in the wage because the _____ effect and the _____ effect work in _____ direction(s).

**2.4** Your objective is to earn exactly $120 per week. If your wage decreases from $6 to $4 per hour, you will respond by working _____ hours instead of _____ hours. In other words, your labor-supply curve is _____ sloped.

**2.5** If every worker in a particular occupation works exactly 40 hours per week, regardless of the wage, the individual supply curve is vertical. _____ (True/False)

**2.6** **Income and Substitution Effects.** Sabrina works for a workers' cooperative that initially pays her a lump sum of $200 per week (as long as she works at least 15 hours per week) and a wage of $20 per hour of work. She initially works 40 hours per week. Suppose the cooperative changes its pay plan by increasing the lump-sum payment to $280 and decreasing the hourly wage to $18. (Related to Application 1 on page 261.)
   **a.** If Sabrina continues to work 40 hours per week, how does the change in the pay plan affect her total income?
   **b.** Use the concepts of the income and substitution effects to predict whether Sabrina will work more hours, fewer hours, or the same number of hours. (*Hint:* Is there an income effect to consider?)

**2.7** **City Versus National Carpenter Supply.** Consider two markets for carpenters: the city of Portland and the United States. Draw two supply curves for carpenters: one for the city of Portland and one for the United States. In which market would you expect a more elastic supply of carpenters?

**2.8** **Tax Rate and Tax Revenue.** Critically appraise the following statement: "The law of supply says that an increase in price increases the quantity supplied. A decrease in the income tax rate will increase the worker's net wage, so each worker will work more hours. As a result, the revenue from the income tax will increase."

**2.9** **Personal Labor Supply.** We discussed the responses of Lester, Sam, and Maureen to a wage increase. Which person's response is closest to your own? If your wage increased, would you work more hours, fewer hours, or about the same number of hours?

## 10.3 | Labor Market Equilibrium

**3.1** Arrows up or down: A decrease in the supply of nurses will _____ the equilibrium wage and _____ the equilibrium quantity of nursing services.

**3.2** Arrows up or down: An increase in the demand for nursing services will _____ the equilibrium wage and _____ the equilibrium quantity of nursing services.

**3.3** A minimum wage for restaurant workers brings good news to _____, but bad news to _____ and _____.

**3.4** Arrows up or down: The immigration of low-skill workers _____ the supply of low-skill labor, which _____ the wages of low-skill natives and _____ consumer prices.

**3.5** Arrows up or down: Suppose that a code of conduct for firms producing apparel overseas increases the wage paid to workers. The code will _____ the firms' cost of production, _____ the price of apparel products, _____ the quantity of apparel products demanded, and _____ the quantity of labor demanded. (Related to Application 2 on page 264.)

**3.6** The immigration of low-skill workers generates net benefits for _____ workers because they benefit from lower _____ without bearing the cost associated with lower _____. (Related to Application 3 on page 265.)

**3.7** **Living Wage and Labor Income.** Consider a university that has sweatshirts bearing its logo produced overseas by a contractor who initially pays a wage of $8 per sweatshirt and has other costs of $12 per sweatshirt, resulting in a price of $20 per sweatshirt. At this price, the university sells 100 sweatshirts per week. Suppose a student group succeeds in getting the contractor to increase the wage to $10 per shirt and the other costs of production don't change. (Related to Application 2 on page 264.)
   **a.** The price per sweatshirt will increase from _____ to _____, an increase of _____ percent.
   **b.** Suppose the price elasticity of demand for the university's sweatshirts is 3.0. At the higher price, a total of _____ sweatshirts will be purchased and the total spending on sweatshirt labor (total labor income) will change from $_____ to $_____.

**c.** Suppose consumers are willing to pay a higher price for sweatshirts made by workers receiving a higher wage. How would this change the numbers in part (b)? Provide an example in which the higher wage actually increases the total spending on sweatshirt labor.

**3.8 Wage and Price Effects of Immigration.** In the initial equilibrium in the market for farm workers, the wage is $10 per hour. The elasticity of supply of farm workers is 2.0, and the elasticity of demand for farm workers is 1.0. Suppose that immigration increases the supply of farm workers by 12 percent: The supply curve shifts to the right by 12 percent. (Related to Application 3 on page 265.)

**a.** Use the price-change formula discussed in Chapter 4 to compute the change in the equilibrium wage.

**b.** Suppose that farm workers are responsible for one-fourth of the production cost of food. What are the implications of immigration for the cost of producing food and its price?

**3.9 Payroll Tax.** You are an economic consultant to a city that just imposed a payroll tax of $1 per hour of work. This payroll tax is paid by workers through a payroll deduction: For each hour of work, the employer deducts $1 and sends the money to the city government. The initial wage (before the tax) is $10, and total employment is 20,000 hours per day. Use a graph to show the effect of the tax on the equilibrium wage and employment.

**3.10 Higher Teacher Salaries.** Advocates of higher salaries for teachers point out that most teachers have college degrees and that teaching children is an important job.

**a.** Why aren't teachers' salaries higher, given the importance of the job and the education required?

**b.** Suppose a new law establishes a minimum teacher salary that is 20 percent higher than the prevailing salary. How would expect this law to affect the average quality of teachers and the taxes paid by the typical household?

# 10.4 | Explaining Differences in Wages and Income

**4.1** The wage for a particular occupation will be relatively low if labor _____ (demand/supply) is small relative to labor _____ (demand/supply).

**4.2** If a city has a relatively high crime rate, we would expect the wage for taxi drivers to be relatively _____ (high/low).

**4.3** In some countries, it is not customary to tip restaurant waiters. We would expect the wages paid to waiters to be _____ (higher/lower/the same) in countries where tips are customary.

**4.4** If a worker switches from a relatively safe factory job to a job in a steel mill, the wage will increase by roughly _____ (2/4/10/30) percent.

**4.5 Improved Safety and Wages.** Consider an occupation that initially has a relatively high rate of nonfatal injuries. The equilibrium wage is $20 per hour, and the equilibrium quantity is 100,000 hours. Suppose a new safety device cuts the injury rate in half, and the supply of labor increases by 12 percent: The labor supply curve shifts to the right by 12 percent. (Related to Application 4 on page 267.)

**a.** Use a graph to show the effects of the safety device on the equilibrium wage and employment.

**b.** Suppose the elasticity of supply of labor is 3.0 and the elasticity of demand is 1.0. Use the price-change formula discussed in Chapter 4 to compute the change in the equilibrium wage.

**c.** Suppose the demand curve you've drawn is a long-run demand curve. Explain the roles of the output effect and substitution effect on the change in the quantity of labor demanded.

**4.6 Quick Signals from High School.** Consider the application, "Lakisha Washington Versus Emily Walsh." According to the researcher, "They (employers) want a quick signal whether the applicant seems suitable." Suppose a firm hiring workers cannot distinguish between high-productivity and low-productivity applicants. But the firm knows whether an applicant graduated from high-school H, where the average achievement level is relatively high, or high-school L, where the average achievement level is relatively low (Related to Application 5 on page 269.).

**a.** If the firm will hire one of two applicants, one from high-school H and a second from high-school L, which is the better choice?

**b.** What insights does this exercise provide about why firms are more likely to interview and hire applicants with white-sounding names?

**4.7 Waiter Tips and Income.** Consider a city where the typical waiter has a five-hour shift and daily "sales" (total bills presented to customers) of $400. The customary tip is 15 percent, so tips add up to $60 per day (15% of $400). The initial wage is $10 per hour, so the typical waiter initially earns $50 in wages paid directly by the restaurant. Suppose a local waiter association runs a successful campaign to get the city's restaurant patrons to increase the average tip from 15 to 20 percent.

**a.** Use a supply and demand graph with wage (excluding tips) on the vertical axis to show the effects of the new tip rate on the labor market.

**b.** How will the new tip rate affect the daily income (wages plus tips) of the typical waiter?

## 10.5 | The Distribution of Income

**5.1** Government transfer and tax policies increase the income share of the lowest quintile of the income distribution from about _____ percent to about _____ percent.

**5.2** The college premium is defined as the percentage difference between the incomes of _____ and _____. It is currently about _____ percent.

**5.3** Arrows up or down: Since 1970, the income share of the top fifth of the income distribution has _____, while the shares of the lowest and middle fifths have _____.

**5.4** Arrows up or down: An important factor in growing inequality over the last 30 years is technological change that has _____ the demand for college graduates and _____ the demand for less-educated workers.

## 10.6 | Poverty and Public Policy

**6.1** For each of the following pairs of population groups, indicate which group has a higher poverty rate:

White, Hispanic _____

White, Asian _____

Married couple, Female-headed household _____

Under 18 years, 65 years and older _____

**6.2** Government spending and tax policies reduce the overall poverty rate from roughly _____ (25/20/15/10) percent to roughly _____ (15/10/5/2) percent.

**6.3** Cash aid to the poor makes up roughly _____ (90/50/30/20) percent of the total spending on means-tested programs.

**6.4** A low-income person receiving cash aid under TANF receives a fixed sum per month for an unlimited length of time. _____ (True/False)

## NOTES

1. W. Michael Fox and Beverly J. Fox, "What's Happening to Americans' Income?" *The Southwest Economy, Federal Reserve Bank of Dallas*, Issue 2, 1995, pp. 3–6; *U.S. Bureau of the Census, Statistical Abstract of the United States 2006* (Washington, D.C.: U.S. Government Printing Office, 2006).

2. Victor R. Fuchs, Alan B. Krueger, and James M. Poterba, "Why Do Economists Disagree About Policy? The Role of Beliefs About Parameters and Values," *Journal of Economic Literature*, vol. 36, no. 3 (1998), pp. 1387–1426.

3. Suzanne Bianchi and Daphne Spain, "Women, Work, and Family in America," *Population Bulletin*, vol. 51, no. 3 (1998), pp. 2–48.

4. Eric J. Solberg, "Occupational Assignment, Hiring Discrimination, and the Gender Pay Gap," *Atlantic Economic Journal*, vol. 32 (2004), pp. 11–27.

5. U.S. Department of Labor, *Employment and Earnings* (Washington, D.C.: U.S. Government Printing Office, 1996).

6. William Darity and Patrick Mason, "Evidence on Discrimination in Employment: Codes of Color, Codes of Gender," *Journal of Economic Perspectives*, vol. 12, no. 2 (1998), pp. 63–90.

7. James Heckman, "Detecting Discrimination," *Journal of Economic Perspectives*, vol. 12, no. 2 (1998), pp. 101–116.

8. Finis Welch, "In Defense of Inequality," *American Economic Review*, vol. 89, no. 2 (1999), pp. 1–17.

9. Thomas Piketty and Emmanuel Saez, "Income Inequality in the United States, 1913–1998," *Quarterly Journal of Economics*, vol. 118 (2003), pp. 1–39; Alan Krueger, "Attempting to Explain Income Inequality," *New York Times*, April 4, 2002, p. C2.

10. Rebecca Blank and Robert Schoeni, "Changes in the Distribution of Children's Family Income over the 1990s," *The American Economic Review*, vol. 93 (2003), pp. 304–308.

11. Robert Moffitt, "The Temporary Assistance to Needy Families Program," Working Paper No. 8749, National Bureau of Economic Research (2002).

12. Rebecca Blank and Robert Schoeni, "Changes in the Distribution of Children's Family Income over the 1990s," *The American Economic Review*, vol. 93 (2003), pp. 304–308.

# 11

# Measuring a Nation's Production and Income

On December 7, 1999, the United States Department of Commerce announced its "achievement of the century." What sort of achievement could rival other great U.S. accomplishments, such as providing electricity to homes and businesses throughout the country, completing the interstate highway system, or landing a man on the moon? The Department of Commerce chose, as its great achievement, the development of the National Income and Product Accounts.

When the Department of Commerce made its announcement, it noted that the National Income and Product Accounts had played a role in winning World War II by helping the government to understand the development of the U.S. economy, thus allowing policy makers to stabilize it to promote economic growth. Today, in our global economy, we face new data challenges. As corporations increasingly locate their operations throughout the globe, we need to be able to track the flows of goods and services across borders. The Department of Commerce is now refining its measures to better track the "outsourcing" of services abroad, such as skilled computer programmers in India providing services to companies located in the United States. Keeping up with the pace of globalization will be the challenge for the twenty-first century.

• **macroeconomics**
The study of the nation's economy as a whole; focuses on the issues of inflation, unemployment, and economic growth.

This chapter begins your study of **macroeconomics**: the branch of economics that deals with a nation's economy as a whole. Macroeconomics focuses on the economic issues—unemployment, inflation, growth, trade, and the gross domestic product—that are most often discussed in newspapers, on the radio, and on television.

Macroeconomic issues lie at the heart of political debates. All presidential candidates must first learn a quick lesson in macroeconomics. Once elected, a president learns that the prospects for reelection will depend on how well the economy performs during the term in office. If the voters believe that the economy has performed well, the president will be reelected. Otherwise, the president will not likely be reelected. Democrat Jimmy Carter as well as Republican George H. W. Bush failed in their bids for reelection in 1980 and 1992, respectively, because of voters' macroeconomic concerns. Both Republican Ronald Reagan in 1984 and Democrat Bill Clinton in 1996 easily won reelection because the voters believed that the economy was performing well in their first terms.

Macroeconomic events profoundly affect our everyday lives. For example, if the economy fails to create enough jobs, workers will become unemployed throughout the country, and millions of lives will be disrupted. Similarly, slow economic growth means that living standards will not increase rapidly. If prices for goods begin rising rapidly, some people will find it difficult to maintain their lifestyles.

This chapter and the next will introduce you to the concepts you need to understand what macroeconomics is all about. In this chapter, we'll focus on a nation's production and income. We'll learn how economists measure the income and production for an entire country and what these measures are used for. In the next chapter, we'll look carefully at unemployment and inflation. Both chapters will explain the terms that the media often uses when reporting economic information.

Macroeconomics focuses on two basic issues: long-run economic growth and economic fluctuations. We need to understand what happens during the long run to understand the factors behind the rise in living standards in modern economies. Today, living standards are much higher in the United States than they were for our grandparents. Living standards are also much higher than those of millions of people throughout the globe. Although living standards have improved over time, the economy has not always grown smoothly. Economic performance has fluctuated over time. During periods of slow economic growth, not enough jobs are created, and large numbers of workers become unemployed. Both the public and policy makers become concerned about the lack of jobs and the increase in unemployment.

At other times, unemployment may not be a problem, but we become concerned that the prices of everything that we buy seem to increase rapidly. Sustained increases in prices are called **inflation**. We'll explore inflation in the next chapter.

• **inflation**
Sustained increases in the average prices of all goods and services.

# 11.1 | THE "FLIP" SIDES OF MACROECONOMIC ACTIVITY: PRODUCTION AND INCOME

Before we can study growth and fluctuations, we need to have a basic vocabulary and understanding of some key concepts. We begin with the terms *production* and *income* because these are the "flip" sides of the macroeconomic "coin," so to speak. Every day, men and women go off to work, where they produce or sell merchandise or provide services. At the end of the week or month, they return home with their paychecks or "income." They spend some of that money on other products and services, which are produced by other people. In other words, production leads to income, and income leads to production.

But this chapter really isn't about production and income of individuals in markets. That's what a microeconomist studies. On the contrary, this chapter is about the production and income of the economy *as a whole*. From a "big picture" perspective, we will look at certain measures that will tell us how much the economy is producing and how well it is growing. We will also be able to measure the total income generated in the economy and how this income flows back to workers and investors. These two measures—a country's production and income—are critical to a nation's economic health. Macroeconomists collect and analyze production and income data to understand how many people will find jobs and whether their living standards are rising or falling. Government officials use the data and analysis to develop economic policies.

## The Circular Flow of Production and Income

Let's begin with a simple diagram known as the *circular flow*, shown in Figure 11.1. Let's start with a very simple economy that does not have a government or a foreign sector. Households and firms make transactions in two markets known as *factor markets* and *product markets*. In factor, or input, markets, households supply labor to firms. Households are also the ultimate owners of firms, as well as all the resources that firms use in their production, which we call *capital*. Consequently, we can think of households as providing capital to firms—land, buildings, and equipment—to produce output. Product, or output, markets are markets in which firms sell goods and services to consumers.

The point of the circular flow diagram is simple and fundamental: Production generates income. In factor markets, when households supply labor and capital to firms they are compensated by the firms. They earn wages for their work, and they earn interest, dividends, and rents on the capital that they supply to the firms. The households then use their income to purchase goods and services in the product markets. The firm uses the revenues it receives from the sale of its products to pay for the factors of production (land, labor, and capital).

When goods and services are produced, income flows throughout the economy. For example, consider a manufacturer of computers. At the same time the computer manufacturer produces and sells new computers, it also generates income through its production. The computer manufacturer pays wages to workers, perhaps pays rent on offices and factory buildings, and pays interest on money it borrowed from a bank. Whatever is left over after paying for the cost of production is the firm's profit, which is income to the owners of the firm. Wages, rents, interest, and profits are all different forms of income.

In another example, your taxes pay for a school district to hire principals, teachers, and other staff to provide educational services to the students in your community. These educational services are an important part of production in our modern economy that produces both goods and services. At the same time, the principals, teachers, and staff all earn income through their employment with the school district. The school district may also rent buildings where classes are held and pay interest on borrowed funds.

Our goal is to understand both sides of this macroeconomic "coin"—the production in the economy and the generation of income in the economy. In the United States, the National Income and Product Accounts, published by the Department of Commerce, are the source for the key data on production and income in the economy. As we will see, we can measure the value of output produced in the economy by looking at either the production or income side of the economy. Let's begin by learning how to measure the production for the entire economy.

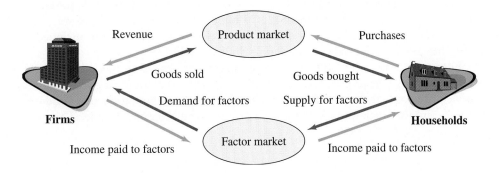

◄ **FIGURE 11.1**
**The Circular Flow of Production and Income**
The circular flow shows how the production of goods and services generates income for households and how households purchase goods and services produced by firms.

## 11.2 | THE PRODUCTION APPROACH: MEASURING A NATION'S MACROECONOMIC ACTIVITY USING GROSS DOMESTIC PRODUCT

• **gross domestic product (GDP)**
The total market value of final goods and services produced within an economy in a given year.

To measure the production of the entire economy, we need to combine an enormous array of goods and services—everything from new computers to NBA basketball games. We can actually add computers to basketball games, as we could add apples and oranges if we were trying to determine the total monetary value of a fruit harvest. Our goal is to summarize the total production of an entire economy into a single number, which we call the **gross domestic product (GDP)**. Gross domestic product is the total market value of all the final goods and services produced within an economy in a given year. GDP is also the most common measure of an economy's total output. All the words in the GDP definition are important, so let's analyze them.

"Total market value" means that we take the quantity of goods produced, multiply them by their respective prices, and then add up the totals. If an economy produced two cars at $25,000 per car and three computers at $2,000 per computer, the total value of these goods would be

$$
\begin{aligned}
2 \text{ cars} \times \$25{,}000 \text{ per car} &= \$50{,}000 \\
&+ \\
3 \text{ computers} \times \$2{,}000 \text{ per computer} &= \$\ 6{,}000 \\
&= \$56{,}000
\end{aligned}
$$

The reason we multiply the goods by their prices is that we cannot simply add together the number of cars and the number of computers. Using prices allows us to express the value of everything in a common unit of measurement—in this case, dollars. (In countries other than the United States, we would express the value in terms of the local currency.) We add apples and oranges together by finding out the value of both the apples and the oranges, as measured by what you would pay for them, and adding them up in terms of their prices.

"Final goods and services" in the definition of GDP means those goods and services that are sold to ultimate, or final, purchasers. For example, the two cars that were produced would be final goods if they were sold to households or to a business. However, to produce the cars the automobile manufacturer bought steel that went into the body of the cars. This steel would not be counted as a final good or service in GDP. Steel is an example of an **intermediate good**, a good that is used in the production process. An intermediate good is not considered a final good or service.

• **intermediate goods**
Goods used in the production process that are not final goods and services.

The reason we do not count intermediate goods as final goods is to avoid double-counting. The price of the car already reflects the price of the steel that is contained in it. We do not want to count the steel twice. Similarly, the large volumes of paper an accounting firm uses also are intermediate goods because the paper becomes part of the final product delivered by the accounting firm to its clients.

The final words in our definition of GDP are "in a given year." GDP is expressed as a rate of production, that is, as "X" amount of dollars per year. In 2005, for example, GDP in the United States was $12,479 billion. Goods produced in prior years, such as cars or houses that one consumer later sells to another, are not included in GDP. Only newly produced products are included in GDP.

Because we measure GDP using the current prices for goods and services, GDP will increase if prices increase, even if the physical amount of goods that are produced remains the same. Suppose that next year the economy again produces two cars and three computers, but all the prices in the economy double: The price of cars is $50,000, and the price of computers is $4,000. GDP will also be twice as high, or $112,000, even though the quantity produced is the same as during the prior year:

$$2 \text{ cars} \times \$50,000 \text{ per car} \qquad\qquad = \$100,000$$
$$+$$
$$3 \text{ computers} \times \$4,000 \text{ per computer} \quad = \$\ 12,000$$
$$= \$112,000$$

But to say that GDP has doubled would be misleading. To avoid this problem, let's apply the real-nominal principle, one of our five basic principles of economics.

## REAL-NOMINAL PRINCIPLE

What matters to people is the real value of money or income—its purchasing power—not the face value of money or income.

What we need is another measure of total output that doesn't increase just because prices increase. For this reason, economists have developed the concept of **real GDP**, a measure of GDP that takes price changes into account. Later in this chapter, we explain how real GDP is calculated. The basic idea is simple. When we use current prices to measure GDP, we are using **nominal GDP**. Nominal GDP can increase for one of two reasons: Either the production of goods and services has increased or the prices of those goods and services have increased.

To explain the concept of real GDP, we need first to look at a simple example. Suppose an economy produces a single good: computers. In year 1, 10 computers were produced, and each sold for $2,000. In year 2, 12 computers were produced, and each sold for $2,100. Nominal GDP would be $20,000 in year 1 and $25,200 in year 2. Nominal GDP would have increased by a factor of 1.26. We can measure real GDP by calculating GDP using year 1 prices as a measure of what was produced in year 1 and also what was produced in year 2. In year 1, real GDP would be

$$10 \text{ computers} \times \$2,000 \text{ per computer} = \$20,000$$

In year 2, real GDP would be

$$12 \text{ computers} \times \$2,000 \text{ per computer} = \$24,000$$

Real GDP in year 2 is greater than real GDP in year 1 by a factor of 1.2, or 20 percent. The key idea is that we construct a measure using the same prices for both years and thereby take price changes into account.

Figure 11.2 plots real GDP for the U.S. economy for the years 1930 through 2005. The graph shows that real GDP has grown substantially over this period. This is what economists call **economic growth**—sustained increases in the real GDP of an economy over a long period of time. In Chapter 13, we'll study economic growth in detail. Later in this chapter, we'll look carefully at the behavior of real GDP over shorter periods, during which time it can rise and fall. Decreases in real GDP disrupt the economy greatly and lead to unemployment.

### The Components of GDP

Economists divide GDP into four broad categories, each corresponding to different types of purchases represented in GDP:

**1** *Consumption expenditures:* purchases by consumers

- **real GDP**
  A measure of GDP that controls for changes in prices.

- **nominal GDP**
  The value of GDP in current dollars.

- **economic growth**
  Sustained increases in the real GDP of an economy over a long period of time.

During the Great Depression in the 1930s, GDP initially fell and then was relatively flat. The economy was not growing much. However, the economy began growing rapidly in the 1940s during Word War II and has grown substantially since then.
*SOURCE: Department of Commerce.*

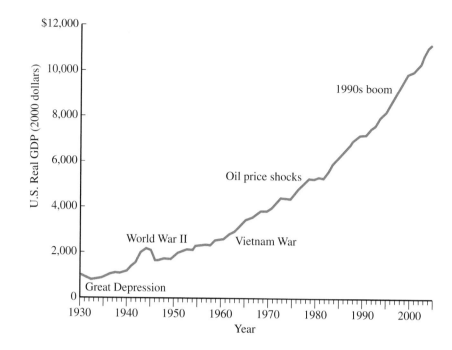

**2** *Private investment expenditures:* purchases by firms

**3** *Government purchases:* purchases by federal, state, and local governments

**4** *Net exports:* net purchases by the foreign sector (domestic exports minus domestic imports)

Before discussing these categories, let's look at some data for the U.S. economy to get a sense of the size of each of these four components. Table 11.1 shows the figures for GDP for the third quarter of 2005. (A quarter is a three-month period; the first quarter runs from January through March, and the third quarter runs from July through September.) In the third quarter of 2005, GDP was $12,605 billion, or approximately $12.6 trillion. To get a sense of the magnitude, consider that the U.S. population is approximately 300 million people, making GDP per person approximately $42,017. (This does not mean that every man, woman, and child actually spends $42,017, but it is a useful indicator of the productive strength of the economy.)

## CONSUMPTION EXPENDITURES

• **consumption expenditures**
Purchases of newly produced goods and services by households.

**Consumption expenditures** are purchases by consumers of currently produced goods and services, either domestic or foreign. These purchases include TV sets, MP3 players, automobiles, clothing, hair-styling services, jewelry, movie or basketball tickets, food, and all other consumer items. We can break down consumption into durable goods, nondurable goods, and services. *Durable goods*, such as automobiles or refrigerators, last for a long time. *Nondurable goods*, such as food, last for a short time. *Services* reflect work done in which people play a prominent role in delivery (such as a dentist

**Table 11.1** | COMPOSITION OF U.S. GDP, THIRD QUARTER 2005 (BILLIONS OF DOLLARS EXPRESSED AT ANNUAL RATES)

| GDP | Consumption Expenditures | Private Investment Expenditures | Government Purchases | Net Exports |
|---|---|---|---|---|
| $12,605 | $8,844 | $2,099 | $2,392 | –$730 |

*SOURCE: U.S. Department of Commerce.*

filling a cavity). Services range from haircutting to health care. Services are the fastest-growing component of consumption in the United States. Overall, consumption spending is the most important component of GDP, constituting about 70 percent of total purchases.

## PRIVATE INVESTMENT EXPENDITURES

**Private investment expenditures** in GDP consist of three components:

**1** First, there is spending on new plants and equipment during the year. If a firm builds a new factory or purchases a new machine, it is included in the year's GDP. Purchasing an existing building or buying a used machine does not count in GDP, because the goods were not produced during the current year.

**2** Second, newly produced housing is included in investment spending. The sale of an existing home to a new owner is not counted, because the house was not built in the current year.

**3** Finally, if firms add to their stock of inventories the increase in inventories during the current year is included in GDP. If a hardware store had $1,000 worth of nuts and bolts on its shelves at the beginning of the year and $1,100 at the year's end, its inventory investment would be $100 ($1,100 − $1,000). This $100 increase in inventory investment is included in GDP.

We call the total of new investment expenditures **gross investment**. During the year, some of the existing plant, equipment, and housing will deteriorate or wear out. This wear and tear is called **depreciation**, or sometimes a *capital consumption allowance*. If we subtract depreciation from gross investment, we obtain net investment. **Net investment** is the true addition to the stock of plant, equipment, and housing in a given year.

Make sure you understand this distinction between gross investment and net investment. Consider the $2,099 billion in total investment spending for the third quarter of 2005, a period in which there was $1,604 billion in depreciation. That means that there was only $495 billion ($2,099 − $1,604) in net investment by firms in that year; 76 percent of gross investment went to make up for depreciation of existing capital.

**WARNING:** When we discuss measuring production in the GDP accounts, we use *investment* in a different way than when we use the word in the sense we have come to understand it. For an economist, investment in the GDP accounts means purchases of new final goods and services by firms. In everyday conversation, we may talk about investing in the stock market or investing in gold. Buying stock for $1,800 on the stock market is a purchase of an existing financial asset; it is not the purchase of new goods and services by firms. That $1,800 does not appear anywhere in GDP. The same is true of purchasing a gold bar. In GDP accounting, *investment* denotes the purchase of new capital. Be careful not to confuse the common usage of *investment* with the definition of *investment* as we use it in the GDP accounts.

## GOVERNMENT PURCHASES

**Government purchases** are the purchases of newly produced goods and services by federal, state, and local governments. They include any goods that the government purchases plus the wages and benefits of all government workers (paid when the government purchases their services as employees). The majority of spending in this category comes from state and local governments: $1,500 billion of the total $2,392 billion in 2005. Government purchases affect our lives very directly. For example, all salaries of U.S. postal employees and federal airport security personnel are counted as government purchases.

> **private investment expenditures**
> Purchases of newly produced goods and services by firms.

> **gross investment**
> Total new investment expenditures.

> **depreciation**
> Reduction in the value of capital goods over a one-year period due to physical wear and tear and also to obsolescence; also called *capital consumption allowance*.

> **net investment**
> Gross investment minus depreciation.

> **government purchases**
> Purchases of newly produced goods and services by local, state, and federal governments.

- **transfer payments**
  Payments from governments to individuals that do not correspond to the production of goods and services.

- **import**
  A good produced in a foreign country and purchased by residents of the home country (for example, the United States).

- **export**
  A good produced in the home country (for example, the United States) and sold in another country.

- **net exports**
  Exports minus imports.

- **trade deficit**
  The excess of imports over exports.

- **trade surplus**
  The excess of exports over imports.

This category does not include all the spending by governments. It excludes **transfer payments**, funds paid to individuals that are not associated with the production of goods and services. For example, payments for Social Security, welfare, and interest on government debt are all considered transfer payments and are not included in government purchases in GDP. The reason they are excluded is that nothing is being produced by the recipients in return for money being paid, or "transferred," to them. But wage payments to the police, postal workers, and the staff of the Internal Revenue Service are all included, because these payments do correspond to services that are currently being produced.

Because transfer payments are excluded from GDP, a vast portion of the budget of the federal government is not part of GDP. In 2005, the federal government spent approximately $2,473 billion, of which only $962 billion (about 40 percent) was counted as federal government purchases. Transfer payments are important, however, because they affect both the income of individuals and their consumption and savings behavior. Transfer payments also affect the size of the federal budget deficit, which we will study in a later chapter. At this point, keep in mind the distinction between government purchases—which are included in GDP—and total government spending or expenditure—which may not be included.

### NET EXPORTS

To understand the role of the foreign sector, we first need to define three terms. **Imports** are goods we buy from other countries. **Exports** are goods made here and sold to other countries. **Net exports** are total exports minus total imports. In Table 11.1 on page 286, we see that net exports in the third quarter of 2005 were –$730 billion. Net exports were negative because our imports exceeded our exports.

Consumption, investment, and government purchases include all purchases by consumers, firms, and the government, whether or not the goods were produced in the United States. However, GDP is supposed to measure the goods produced in the United States. Consequently, purchases of foreign goods by consumers, firms, or the government are subtracted when we calculate GDP, because these goods were not produced in the United States. At the same time, we add to GDP any goods produced here and sold abroad. For example, airplanes made in the United States and sold in Europe should be added to GDP. By including net exports as a component of GDP, we correctly measure U.S. production by adding exports and subtracting imports.

For example, suppose someone in the United States buys a $25,000 car made in Japan. If we look at final purchases, we will see that consumption spending rose by $25,000 because a consumer made a purchase of a consumption good. Net exports fell by $25,000, however, because the value of the import (the car) was subtracted from total exports. Notice that total GDP did not change with the purchase of the car. This is exactly what we want in this case because the car wasn't produced in the United States.

Now suppose that the United States sells a car for $22,000 to a resident of Spain. In this case, net exports would increase by $22,000 because the car was a U.S. export. GDP would also be a corresponding $22,000 higher because this sale represents U.S. production.

Recall that for the United States in the third quarter of 2005 net exports were –$730 billion dollars. In other words, in that quarter the United States bought $730 billion more goods from abroad than it sold abroad. When we buy more goods from abroad than we sell, we have a **trade deficit**. A **trade surplus** occurs when our exports exceed our imports. Figure 11.3 shows the U.S. trade surplus as a share of GDP from 1960 to 2005. Although at times the United States has had a small trade surplus, the United States has generally run a trade deficit. In recent years, the trade deficit has increased and now exceeds 5 percent of GDP. In later chapters, we study how trade deficits can affect a country's GDP.

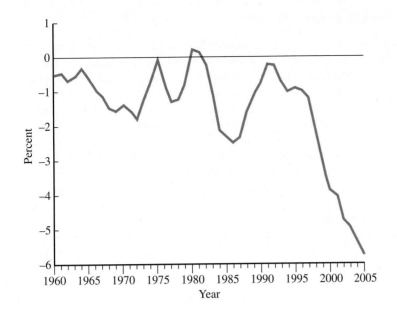

◄ **FIGURE 11.3**
**U.S. Trade Balance as a Share of GDP, 1960–2005**
In the 1980s, the United States ran a trade surplus (when the line on the graph is above zero, this indicates a surplus). However, in other years the United States has run a trade deficit. In 2005, the trade deficit exceeded 5 percent of GDP.
*SOURCE: Department of Commerce.*

## Putting It All Together: The GDP Equation

We can summarize our discussion of who purchases GDP with a simple equation that combines the four components of GDP:

$$Y = C + I + G + NX$$

where

$$Y = \text{GDP}$$
$$C = \text{Consumption}$$
$$I = \text{Investment}$$
$$G = \text{Government purchases}$$
$$NX = \text{net exports}$$

In other words,

GDP = consumption + investment + government purchases + net exports

This equation is an *identity*, which means that it is always true. In any economy, GDP consists of the sum of its four components. This equation can help you remember the components that constitute GDP.

# 11.3 | THE INCOME APPROACH: MEASURING A NATION'S MACROECONOMIC ACTIVITY USING NATIONAL INCOME

Recall from the circular flow that when GDP is produced, income is created. One person's production ends up being another person's income. Income is the flip side of our macroeconomic "coin." As a result, in addition to measuring a nation's activity by measuring production, we can also gauge it by measuring a nation's income. The total income generated earned by a nation's residents both in the United States domestically and abroad is called **national income**.

• **national income**
The total income earned by a nation's residents both domestically and abroad in the production of goods and services.

## Measuring National Income

To measure national income, economists first make two primary adjustments to GDP.

First, we add to GDP the net income earned by U.S. firms and residents abroad. To make this calculation, we add to GDP any income earned abroad by U.S. firms or residents and subtract any income earned in the United States by foreign firms or residents. For example, we add the profits earned by U.S. multinational corporations that are sent back to the United States but subtract the profits from multinational corporations operating in the United States that are sent back to their home countries. For example, the profits that Wal-Mart sends back to the United States from its stores in Mexico are added to GDP. The profits that Toyota earns in the United States that are sent back to Japan are subtracted from GDP. The result of these adjustments is the total income earned worldwide by U.S. firms and residents. This is called the **gross national product (GNP)**.

• **gross national product**
GDP plus net income earned abroad.

For most countries, the distinction between what they produce within their borders, GDP, and what their citizens earn, GNP, is not that important. For the United States, the difference between GDP and GNP is typically just 0.2 percent. In some countries, however, the differences are much larger. The country of Kuwait, for example, earned vast amounts of income from its oil riches, which it invested abroad in stocks, bonds, and other types of investments. Earnings from these investments are included in Kuwait's GNP. In 2004, those earnings from investments comprised approximately 15.1 percent of Kuwait's GNP. Australia has traditionally had large amounts of foreign investment into the country. Consequently, as profits from foreign investors were sent back to their home country, Australia's net income from abroad was negative in 2004, and Australian GDP in that year exceeded Australian GNP by 3.7 percent.

The second adjustment that we make when calculating national income is to subtract depreciation from GNP. Recall that depreciation is the wear and tear on plant and equipment that occurred during the year. In a sense, our income is reduced because our buildings and machines are wearing out. When we subtract depreciation from GNP, we reach *net national product (NNP)*, where *net* means "after depreciation."

After making these adjustments and taking into account statistical discrepancies, we reach national income. (Statistical discrepancies arise when government statisticians make their calculations using different sources of data.) Table 11.2 shows the effects of these adjustments for the third quarter of 2005.

In turn, national income is divided among six basic categories: compensation of employees (wages and benefits), corporate profits, rental income, proprietor's income (income of unincorporated business), net interest (interest payments received by households from business and from abroad), and other items.

Approximately 67 percent of all national income goes to workers in the form of wages and benefits. For most of the countries in the world, wages and benefits are the largest part of national income.

• **personal income**
Income, including transfer payments, received by households.

In addition to national income, which measures the income earned in a given year by the entire private sector, we are sometimes interested in determining the total payments that flow directly into households, a concept known as **personal income**. To calculate personal income, we begin with national income and subtract any corporate profits that are retained by the corporation and not paid out as dividends to households. We also subtract all taxes on production and imports and social insurance taxes, which are payments for Social Security and Medicare. We then add any personal

| Table 11.2 | FROM GDP TO NATIONAL INCOME, THIRD QUARTER 2005 (BILLIONS OF DOLLARS) |
|---|---|
| Gross domestic product | $12,605 |
| Gross national product | 12,650 |
| Net national product | 10,786 |
| National income | 10,719 |

interest income received from the government and consumers and all transfer payments. The result is the total income available to households, or personal income. The amount of personal income that households retain after paying income taxes is called **personal disposable income**.

## Measuring National Income Through Value Added

Another way to measure national income is to look at the **value added** of each firm in the economy. For a firm, we can measure its value added by the dollar value of the firm's sales minus the dollar value of the goods and services purchased from other firms. What remains is the sum of all the income—wages, profits, rents, and interest—that the firm generates. By adding up the value added for all the firms in the economy (plus nonprofit and governmental organizations), we can calculate national income. Let's consider a simple example that is illustrated in Table 11.3.

Suppose an economy consists of two firms: an automobile firm that sells its cars to consumers and a steel firm that sells only to the automobile firm. If the automobile company sells a car for $16,000 to consumers and purchases $6,000 worth of steel from the steel firm, the auto firm has $10,000 remaining—its value added—which can then be distributed as wages, rents, interest, and profits. If the steel firm sells $6,000 worth of steel but does not purchase any inputs from other firms, its value added is $6,000, which is paid out in the form of wages, rents, interest, and profits. Total value added in the economy from both firms is $16,000 ($10,000 + $6,000), which is the sum of wages, rents, interest, and profits for the entire economy (consisting of these two firms).

As this example illustrates, we measure the value added for a typical firm by starting with the value of its total sales and subtracting the value of any inputs it purchases from other firms. The amount of income that remains is the firm's value added, which is then distributed as wages, rents, interest, and profits. In calculating national income, it is important to include all the firms in the economy, even the firms that produce intermediate goods.

## An Expanded Circular Flow

Now that we have examined both production and income, including both the government and the foreign sector, let's take another look at a slightly more realistic circular flow. Figure 11.4 depicts a circular flow that includes both the government and the foreign sector. Both households and firms pay taxes to the government. The government, in turn, supplies goods and services in the product market and also purchases inputs—labor and capital—in the factor markets, just like private-sector firms do. Net exports, which can be positive or negative, are shown interacting with the product market.

In summary, we can look at GDP from two sides: We can ask who buys the output that is produced, or we can ask how the income that is created through the production process is divided between workers and investors. From the spending side, we saw that nearly 70 percent of GDP consists of consumer expenditures. From the income side, we saw that nearly 67 percent of national income is paid in wages and benefits. Macroeconomists may use data based either on the production that occurs in the economy or on its flip side, the income that is generated, depending on whether they are more focused on current production or on current income.

- **personal disposable income**
  Personal income that households retain after paying taxes.

- **value added**
  The sum of all the income—wages, interest, profits, and rent—generated by an organization. For a firm, we can measure value added by the dollar value of the firm's sales minus the dollar value of the goods and services purchased from other firms.

**Table 11.3** | CALCULATING VALUE ADDED IN A SIMPLE ECONOMY

|  | Automobile Firm | Steel Firm | Total Economy |
|---|---|---|---|
| Total sales | $16,000 | $6,000 | $22,000 |
| Less purchases from other firms | 6,000 | 0 | 6,000 |
| Equals value added: the sum of all wages, interest, profits, and rents | 10,000 | 6,000 | 16,000 |

# APPLICATION

## USING VALUE ADDED TO MEASURE THE TRUE SIZE OF WAL-MART

**APPLYING THE CONCEPTS #1:** How can we use economic analysis to compare the size of a major corporation to a country?

During 2004, Wal-Mart's sales were approximately $285 billion, nearly 2.4 percent of U.S. GDP. Some social commentators might want to measure the impact of Wal-Mart just through its sales. But to produce those sales, Wal-Mart had to buy goods from many other companies. Wal-Mart's value added was substantially less than its total sales. Based on Wal-Mart's annual reports, its cost of sales was $219 billion, leaving approximately $66 billion in value added. This is a very large number, as might be expected from the world's largest retailer, but it is much smaller than its total sales. If we used Wal-Mart's sales to compare it to a country, it would have a GDP similar to Indonesia, which is ranked 23rd in the world. However, using the more appropriate measure of value added, Wal-Mart's size is closer to the Ukraine, which is ranked 53rd in the world. *Related to Exercise 3.9.*

SOURCE: Wal-Mart Annual Report, 2004. http://www.walmartstores.com/Files/annualreport_2004.pdf. Accessed January, 2006

▶ **FIGURE 11.4**

**The Circular Flow with Government and the Foreign Sector**

The new linkages (in blue) demonstrate the roles that the government and the foreign sector (imports and exports) play in the circular flow.

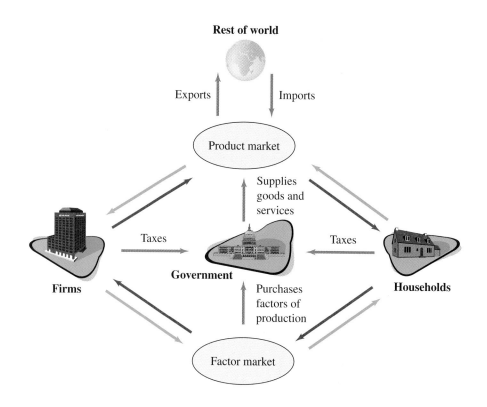

# 11.4 | A CLOSER EXAMINATION OF NOMINAL AND REAL GDP

We have discussed different ways to measure the production of an economy, looking at both who purchases goods and services and the income it generates. Of all the measures we have discussed, GDP is the most commonly used both by the public and by economists. Let's take a closer look at it.

## Measuring Real Versus Nominal GDP

Output in the economy can increase from one year to the next. And prices can rise from one year to the next. Recall that we defined nominal GDP as GDP measured in current prices, and we defined real GDP as GDP adjusted for price changes.

Now we take a closer look at how real GDP is measured in modern economies. Let's start with a simple economy in which there are only two goods—cars and computers—produced in the years 2009 and 2010. The data for this economy—the prices and quantities produced for each year—are shown in Table 11.4. The production of cars and the production of computers increased, but the production of computers increased more rapidly. The price of cars rose, while the price of computers remained the same.

Let's first calculate nominal GDP for this economy in each year. Nominal GDP is the total market value of goods and services produced in each year. Using the data in the table, we can see that nominal GDP for the year 2009 is

$$(4 \text{ cars} \times \$10,000) + (1 \text{ computer} \times \$5,000) = \$45,000$$

Similarly, nominal GDP for the year 2010 is

$$(5 \text{ cars} \times \$12,000) + (3 \text{ computers} \times \$5,000) = \$75,000$$

Now we'll find real GDP. To compute real GDP, we calculate GDP using constant prices. What prices should we use? For the moment, let's use the prices for the year 2009. Because we are using 2009 prices, real GDP and nominal GDP for 2009 are both equal to $45,000. But for 2010, they are different. In 2010, real GDP is

$$(5 \text{ cars} \times \$10,000) + (3 \text{ computers} \times \$5,000) = \$65,000$$

Note that real GDP for 2010, which is $65,000, is less than nominal GDP for 2010, which is $75,000. The reason real GDP is less than nominal GDP here is because prices of cars rose by $2,000 between 2009 and 2010, and we are measuring GDP using 2009 prices. We can measure real GDP for any other year simply by calculating GDP using constant prices.

We now calculate the growth in real GDP for this economy between 2009 and 2010. Because real GDP was $45,000 in 2009 and $65,000 in 2010, real GDP grew by $20,000. In percentage terms, this is a $20,000 increase from the initial level of $45,000 or

$$\text{Percentage growth in real GDP} = \frac{\$20,000}{\$45,000} = .444$$

which equals 44.4 percent. This percentage is an average of the growth rates for both goods, cars, and computers.

**Table 11.4** | GDP DATA FOR A SIMPLE ECONOMY

| Year | Quantity Produced | | Price | |
| | Cars | Computers | Cars | Computers |
|---|---|---|---|---|
| 2009 | 4 | 1 | $10,000 | $5,000 |
| 2010 | 5 | 3 | 12,000 | 5,000 |

► **FIGURE 11.5**
U.S. Nominal and Real GDP,
1950–2005
This figure plots both real and nominal
GDP for the United States in billions of
dollars. Real GDP is measured in 2000
dollars.

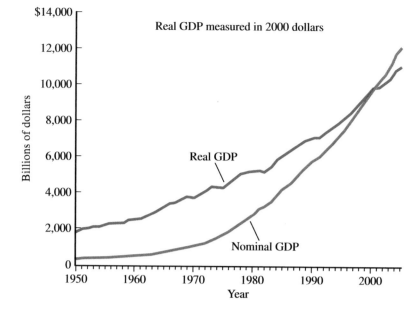

Figure 11.5 depicts real and nominal GDP for the United States from 1950 to 2005. Real GDP is measured in 2000 dollars, so the curves cross in 2000. Before 2000, nominal GDP is less than real GDP because prices in earlier years were lower than they were in 2000. After 2000, nominal GDP exceeds real GDP because prices in later years were higher than they were in 2000.

### How to Use the GDP Deflator

• **GDP deflator**
An index that measures how the
prices of goods and services included
in GDP change over time.

We can also use the data in Table 11.4 to measure the changes in prices for this economy of cars and computers. The basic idea is that the differences between nominal GDP and real GDP for any year arise only because of changes in prices. By comparing real GDP and nominal GDP, we can measure the changes in prices for the economy. In practice, we do this by creating an index, called the **GDP deflator**, that measures how prices of goods and services change over time. Because we are calculating real GDP using year 2009 prices, we will set the value of this index equal to 100 in the year 2009, which we call the base year. To find the value of the GDP deflator for the year 2010 (or other years), we use the following formula:

$$\text{GDP Deflator} = \frac{\text{Nominal GDP}}{\text{Real GDP}} \times 100$$

Using this formula, we find that the value of the GDP deflator for 2010 is

$$\frac{\$75,000}{\$65,000} \times 100 = 1.15 \times 100 = 115$$

Because the value of the GDP deflator is 115 in 2010 and was 100 in the base year of 2009, this means that prices rose by 15 percent between the two years:

$$\frac{115 - 100}{100} = \frac{15}{100} = 0.15$$

Note that this 15 percent is an average of the price changes for the two goods—cars and computers.

Up until 1996, the Commerce Department, which produces the GDP figures, used these formulas to calculate real GDP and measure changes in prices. Economists at the department chose a base year and measured real GDP by using the prices in that base year. They also calculated the GDP deflator, just as we did, by taking the ratio of nominal GDP to real GDP. Today, the Commerce Department calculates real GDP and the price index for real GDP using a more complicated method. In our example, we measured real GDP using 2009 prices. But we could have also measured real GDP using prices from 2010. If we did, we would have come up with slightly different numbers both for the increase in prices between the two years and for the increase in real GDP. To avoid this problem, the Commerce Department now uses a **chain-weighted index**, which is a method for calculating price changes that takes an average of price changes using base years from consecutive years (that is, 2009 and 2010 in our example). If you look in the newspapers today or at the data produced by the Commerce Department, you will see real GDP measured in chained dollars and a chain-type price index for GDP.

• **chain-weighted index**
A method for calculating changes in prices that uses an average of base years from neighboring years.

# 11.5 | FLUCTUATIONS IN GDP

As we have discussed, real GDP does not always grow smoothly—sometimes it collapses suddenly, and the result is an economic downturn. These fluctuations are often known as *business cycles*. Let's look at an example of a business cycle from the late 1980s and early 1990s. Figure 11.6 plots real GDP for the United States from 1988 to 1992. Notice that in mid-1990, real GDP begins to fall. A **recession** is a period when real GDP falls for six or more consecutive months. Economists talk more in terms of quarters of the year—consecutive three-month periods—than in terms of months. So they would say that when real GDP falls for two consecutive quarters, that's a recession. The date at which the recession starts—that is, when output starts to decline—is called the **peak**. The date at which the recession ends—that is, when output starts to increase again—is called the **trough**. In Figure 11.6, we see the peak and trough of the recession. After a trough, the economy enters a recovery period, or period of **expansion**.

• **recession**
Commonly defined as six consecutive months of declining real GDP.

• **peak**
The date at which a recession starts.

• **trough**
The date at which output stops falling in a recession.

• **expansion**
The period after a trough in the business cycle during which the economy recovers.

From World War II through 2001, the United States experienced 10 recessions. Table 11.5 contains the dates of the peaks and troughs of each recession, the percent decline in real GDP from each peak to each trough, and the length of the recessions in months. The sharpest decline in output occurred during the recession from 1973 to 1975, which started as a result of a sharp rise in world oil prices. This was also one of the longest recessions. In the last three decades, there have been three recessions, starting near the beginning of each of the decades: 1981, 1990, and 2001. In the most

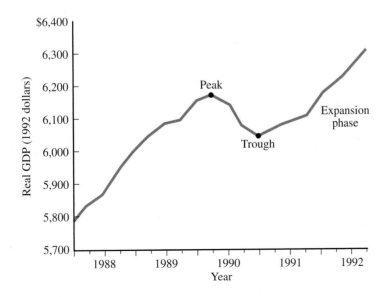

◄ **FIGURE 11.6**

**The 1990 Recession**

Recessions can be illustrated by peaks, troughs, and an expansion phase. The date at which the recession starts and output begins to fall is called the peak. The date at which the recession ends and output begins to rise is called the trough. The expansion phase begins after the trough.

*SOURCE: U.S. Department of Commerce.*

Table 11.5 | TEN POSTWAR RECESSIONS

| Peak | Trough | Percent Decline in Real GDP | Length of Recession (months) |
|---|---|---|---|
| November 1948 | October 1949 | −1.5 | 11 |
| July 1953 | May 1954 | −3.2 | 10 |
| August 1957 | April 1958 | −3.3 | 8 |
| April 1960 | February 1961 | −1.2 | 10 |
| December 1969 | November 1970 | −1.0 | 11 |
| November 1973 | March 1975 | −4.9 | 16 |
| January 1980 | July 1980 | −2.5 | 6 |
| July 1981 | November 1982 | −3.0 | 16 |
| July 1990 | March 1991 | −1.4 | 8 |
| March 2001 | November 2001 | −0.6 | 8 |

• **depression**
The common name for a severe recession.

recent recession, employment began to fall in March of 2001, before the terrorist attack on the United States on September 11, 2001. The attack further disrupted economic activity, damaged producer and consumer confidence, and the economy tumbled into a recession.

Throughout the broader sweep of U.S. history, other downturns have occurred—20 of them from 1860 up to World War II. Not all of these were particularly severe, and in some unemployment hardly changed. However, some economic downturns, such as those in 1893 and 1929, were severe.

Although we used the common definition of a recession as a period when real GDP falls for six months, in practice, a committee of economists at the National Bureau of Economics Research (NBER), a private research group in Cambridge, Massachusetts, of primarily academic economists, officially proclaims the beginning and end of recessions in the United States using a broader set of criteria than just GDP.

**Depression** is the common term for a severe recession. In the United States, the Great Depression refers to the years 1929 through 1933, the period when real GDP fell by over 33 percent. This drop in GDP created the most severe disruptions to ordinary economic life in the United States during the twentieth century. Throughout the country and in much of the world, banks closed, businesses failed, and many people lost their jobs and their life savings. Unemployment rose sharply. In 1933, over 25 percent of people who were looking for work failed to find jobs.

Although the United States has not experienced a depression since that time, other countries have. In the last 20 years, several Asian countries (for example, Thailand) and Latin American countries (for example, Argentina) suffered severe economic disruptions that were true depressions.

# 11.6 | GDP AS A MEASURE OF WELFARE

GDP is our best measure of the value of output produced by an economy. As we have seen, we can use GDP and related indicators to measure economic growth within a country. In a later chapter, we will use GDP to compare the value of output across countries as well. Economists use GDP and related measures to determine if an economy has fallen into a recession or has entered into a depression. But while GDP is a very valuable measure of the health of an economy, it is not a perfect measure.

## Shortcomings of GDP as a Measure of Welfare

You need to be wary of several recognized flaws in the construction of GDP. We should be cautious in interpreting GDP as a measure of our economic well-being, because it does not take into account housework and childcare, leisure, the underground economy, or pollution.

# APPLICATION

2

## THE NBER AND THE 2001 RECESSION

**APPLYING THE CONCEPTS #2:** How do we determine when a recession has occurred in the United States?

Although the level of GDP is an extremely important indicator, the NBER committee also examines a full range of other data, including data on retail and wholesale trade, personal income, and measures of employment. This examination takes time, which is why the NBER often announces the beginning and end of a recession many months later. For example, on November 26, 2001, the NBER announced that the peak of the 2001 recession occurred in March 2001. Nearly two years later, on July 17, 2003, they dated the trough as occurring in November 2001. In deciding on the timing of the recession, the committee followed its past practices of looking at a full range of economic data.

Although the common definition of a recession is a six-month consecutive period of negative economic growth, the NBER defines a recession as a "significant decline in activity spread across the economy, lasting more than a few months, visible in industrial production, employment, real income, and wholesale-retail trade." When the NBER first dated the peak of the recession, the quarterly GDP data from the U.S. Department of Commerce did *not* show a six-month fall in GDP. This created some confusion in the popular press, which was accustomed to the common definition. However, this is a useful reminder that the NBER looks carefully at a wide range of data on a monthly basis, not just quarterly data for GDP. *Related to Exercise 5.7.*

SOURCE: National Bureau of Economic Research, http://www.nber.org/cycles/main.html. Accessed. January, 2006

## HOUSEWORK AND CHILDCARE

First, GDP ignores transactions that do not take place in organized markets. The most important example is services, such as cleaning, cooking, and providing free childcare that people do for themselves in their own homes. Because these services are not transferred through markets, GDP statisticians cannot measure them. This has probably led us to overestimate GDP growth in recent years. For example, in the last four decades the percentage of women in the labor force has increased dramatically. Because more women are now working outside the home, demand for meals in restaurants, cleaning services, and paid childcare has increased. All this new demand shows up in GDP, but the services that were provided earlier—when they were provided free—did not show up in earlier GDP. This naturally overstates the true growth in GDP.

## LEISURE

Second, leisure time is not included in GDP, because GDP is designed to be a measure of the production that occurs in the economy. Leisure time, along with other nonmarket activities, is ignored in GDP accounting. To the extent that leisure is valued by households, increases in leisure time will lead to higher social welfare, but not higher GDP.

## UNDERGROUND ECONOMY

Third, GDP ignores the underground economy, where transactions are not reported to official authorities. These transactions can be legal, but people don't report the income they have generated because they want to evade paying taxes on it. For example, waiters and waitresses may not report all their tips, and owners of flea markets may make under-the-table cash transactions with their customers. Illegal transactions, such as profits from the illegal drug trade, also result in unreported income. In the United States, in 2005 the Internal Revenue Service estimated (based on the tax returns from 2001) that about $310 billion in federal income taxes from the underground economy were not collected each year. If the average federal income tax rate was about 20 percent, approximately $1.5 trillion ($310 billion ÷ 0.20) in income escaped the GDP accountants from the underground economy that year, or about 15 percent of GDP at the time.

A number of economists have used a variety of methods to estimate the extent of the underground economy throughout the world. They typically find that the size of the underground economy is much larger in developing countries than in developed countries. For example, in the highly developed countries, estimates of the underground economy are between 15 and 20 percent of reported or official GDP. However, in developing countries, estimates are closer to 40 percent of reported GDP. Table 11.6 contains estimates of the underground economy as a percent of reported GDP for different regions of the world.

## POLLUTION

Fourth, GDP does not value changes in the environment that occur in the production of output. Suppose a factory produces $1,000 of output but pollutes a river and lowers the river's value by $2,000. Instead of recording a loss to society of $1,000, GDP will show a $1,000 increase. This is an important limitation of GDP accounting as a measure of our economic well-being, because changes in the environment are important.

In principle, we can make adjustments to try to correct for this deficiency. In the early 1990s, the U.S. Department of Commerce, which collects the GDP data, undertook a study to account for environmental changes. In 1994, it released a report on the first phase of the study, which focused on the value of mineral resources such as oil, gas, and coal in the United States. The government first measured "proven" reserves of minerals from 1958 to 1991. Proven reserves are those that can be extracted, given current technology and current economic conditions. Proven reserves decrease when minerals are extracted and increase when new investments, such as oil wells or mines, are made.

The Commerce Department was trying to determine whether the stock of proven reserves had been depleted—that is, depreciated—over time. The stock of proven reserves had depreciated, but only by a very small amount—less than $1 billion per year. It is important to note that this calculation focuses only on proven reserves, not the total stock of minerals in the earth. The reason the Commerce Department counts only proven reserves is that some mineral deposits are simply too expensive to extract under current economic conditions. Changes in proven reserves alone correspond most closely to changes in our current economic well-being.

Because the depreciation of proven reserves turned out to be very small, the Commerce Department found that these adjustments had very little effect on mea-

**Table 11.6** | THE WORLD UNDERGROUND ECONOMY, 2002–2003

| Region of the World | Underground Economy as Percent of Reported GDP |
| --- | --- |
| Africa | 41% |
| Central and South America | 41 |
| Asia | 30 |
| Transition Economies | 38 |
| Europe, United States, and Japan | 17 |
| Unweighted Average over 145 Countries | 35 |

*SOURCE*: Estimates by Friedrich Schneider in "The Size of Shadow Economies in 145 Countries from 1999 to 2003," unpublished paper, 2005.

sures of national income. However, mineral stocks comprise only part of our environment. The same GDP adjustment methods could, in principle, be extended to include renewable resources, such as forests and fish, although the data may not be as accurate as the data for minerals. A much more challenging task would be to value changes in clean air and clean water. Has our environment improved or deteriorated as we experienced economic growth? Finding the answer to this question will pose a real challenge for the next generation of economic statisticians.

Most of us would prefer to live in a country with a high standard of living, and few of us would want to experience poverty up close. But does a higher level of GDP really lead to more satisfaction?

3

# APPLICATION

## THE LINKS BETWEEN SELF-REPORTED HAPPINESS AND GDP

**APPLYING THE CONCEPTS #3:** Do increases in gross domestic product necessarily translate into improvements in the welfare of citizens?

Two economists, David Blanchflower of Dartmouth College and Andrew Oswald of Warwick University in the United Kingdom, have systematically analyzed surveys over a nearly 30-year period that ask individuals to describe themselves as "happy, pretty happy, or not too happy." The results of their work are provocative. Over the last 30 years, reported levels of happiness have actually declined in the United States and remained relatively flat in the United Kingdom despite very large increases in per capita income in both countries. Could it be the increased stress of everyday life has taken its toll on our happiness despite the increase in income?

At any point in time, however, money does appear to buy happiness. Holding other factors constant, individuals with higher incomes do report higher levels of personal satisfaction. But these "other factors" are quite important. Unemployment and divorce lead to sharply lower levels of satisfaction. Blanchflower and Oswald calculate that a stable marriage is worth $100,000 in terms of equivalent reported satisfaction.

Perhaps most interesting are their findings about trends in the relative happiness of different groups in our society. While whites report higher levels of happiness than African Americans, the gap has decreased over the last 30 years, as the happiness of African Americans has risen faster than whites. Men's happiness has risen relative to that of women over the last 30 years.

Finally, reported happiness appears to peak at age 40. People younger than 40 report lesser levels of happiness than those at 40. Retired people also report much lower measures of satisfaction.

*Related to Exercises 6.2 and 6.9.*

SOURCE: David Blanchflower and Andrew Oswald, "Well-Being Over Time in Britain and the USA," National Bureau of Economic Research Working Paper 7847, January 2000.

# SUMMARY

In this chapter, we learned how economists and government statisticians measure the income and production for an entire country and what these measures are used for. Developing meaningful statistics for an entire economy is difficult. As we have seen, statistics can convey useful information—if they are used with care. Here are some of the main points to remember in this chapter:

1 The circular flow diagram shows how the production of goods and services generates income for households and how households purchase goods and services by firms. The expanded circular flow diagram includes government and the foreign sector.

2 *Gross domestic product* (GDP) is the market value of all final goods and services produced in a given year.

3 GDP consists of four components: consumption, investment, government purchases, and net exports. The following equation combines these components:

$$Y = C + I + G + NX$$

The *GDP deflator* is an index that measures how the prices of goods and services included in GDP change over time. The following equation helps us find the GDP deflator:

$$\text{GDP Deflator} = \frac{\text{Nominal GDP}}{\text{Real GDP}} \times 100$$

4 *National income* is obtained from GDP by adding the net income U.S. individuals and firms earn from abroad, then subtracting depreciation.

5 *Real GDP* is calculated by using constant prices. The Commerce Department now uses methods that take an average using base years from neighboring years.

6 *A recession* is commonly defined as a six-month consecutive period of negative growth. However, in the United States, the National Bureau of Economic Research uses a broader definition.

7 GDP does not include nonmarket transactions, leisure time, the underground economy, or changes to the environment.

## KEY TERMS

## EXERCISES

*Get Ahead of the Curve*   Visit www.myeconlab.com to complete these exercises online and get instant feedback.

### 11.1 | The "Flip" Sides of Macroeconomic Activity: Production and Income

1.1 The circular flow describes the process by which GDP generates _____, which is spent on goods and services.

1.2 In _____ markets, labor and capital are traded; in _____ markets, goods and services are traded.

1.3 Which government department produces the National Income and Product Accounts?
   a. The Department of Education
   b. The Department of Commerce
   c. The Congressional Budget Office
   d. The Council of Economic Advisors

1.4 Macroeconomists are primarily interested in the incomes of particular individuals and production from particular firms. _____ . (True/False)

1.5 **Understanding the Circular Flow Diagram.** In the circular flow diagram, why do the arrows corresponding to the flow of dollars and the arrows corresponding to the flow of goods go in the opposite direction?

1.6 **Making the Circular Flow Diagram More Realistic.** What is included in more complicated circular flow diagrams and not in the simple one?

## 11.2 | The Production Approach: Measuring a Nation's Macroeconomic Activity Using Gross Domestic Product

**2.1** Which of the following is not a component of GDP?
   **a.** Consumption
   **b.** Investment
   **c.** Consumer Price Index
   **d.** Government purchases
   **e.** Net exports

**2.2** What part of government spending is excluded from GDP because it does not correspond to goods and services currently being produced?
   **a.** National defense
   **b.** Transfer payments
   **c.** Education
   **d.** Purchases of police cars

**2.3** The difference between gross investment and net investment is _____.

**2.4** Net exports is the difference between _____ and _____.

**2.5** **GDP Statistics and Unemployed Workers.** In Economy A, the government puts workers on the payroll who cannot find jobs for long periods, but these "employees" do no work. In Economy B, the government does not hire any long-term unemployed workers but gives them cash grants. Comparing the GDP statistics between the two otherwise identical economies, what can you determine about measured GDP and the actual level of output in each economy?

**2.6** **What Does a Price Index Tell Us?** Suppose someone told you that the value of a price index in a country was 115. What can you determine from this information?

**2.7** **The Upside and Downside of Trade Deficits.** A student once said, "Trade deficits are good because we are buying more goods than we are producing." What is the downside to trade deficits?

**2.8** **Depreciation and Consumer Durables.** Consumer durables depreciate over time. In your household, which consumer goods have substantial depreciation? Can you estimate the value of depreciation in a given year for consumer goods in your household?

**2.9** **Investment Spending Versus Intermediate Goods.** A publisher buys paper, ink, and computers to produce textbooks. Which of these purchases is included in investment spending? Which of these are intermediate goods?

## 11.3 | The Income Approach: Measuring a Nation's Macroeconomic Activity Using National Income

**3.1** What do we add to GDP to reach GNP?
   **a.** Net income earned abroad by U.S. households
   **b.** Personal income

   **c.** Depreciation
   **d.** Net exports

**3.2** What is the largest component of national income?
   **a.** Compensation of employees (wages and benefits)
   **b.** Corporate profits
   **c.** Rental income
   **d.** Proprietor's income (income of unincorporated business)
   **e.** Net interest

**3.3** Personal income and personal disposable income refer to payments ultimately flowing to _____ (households/firms).

**3.4** Value added does not include profits of firms. _____. (True/False)

**3.5** **Value Added and Avoiding Double-Counting.** When we calculate value added, we add up the value created in all organizations, even those producing intermediate goods. Explain why a value-added calculation does not result in double-counting.

**3.6** **Understanding Why GNP and GDP May Differ.** If a country discovered vast amounts of oil, sold it abroad, and invested the proceeds throughout the world, how would its GDP and GNP compare?

**3.7** **Transfer Payments, National Income, and Personal Income.** Taking into account the role of transfer payments, explain why national income could fall more than personal income during a recession.

**3.8** **Immigration, GNP, and GDP.** In 2005, immigrants to the United States sent back an estimated $167 billion to their home countries. Does this affect the GNP or GDP of their home countries?

**3.9** **Why Use Value Added?** In comparing a small country's GDP to a major corporation, why is it best to use the value added of the corporation rather than its total sales? When we calculate GDP for a country, do we use the total sales of all goods and services? (Related to Application 1 on page 292.)

## 11.4 | A Closer Examination of Nominal and Real GDP

**4.1** The GDP deflator is calculated for any given year by dividing nominal GDP by _____ GDP and multiplying by 100.

**4.2** Today, the Department of Commerce uses a(n) _____ index to measure price changes for GDP accurately.

**4.3** Measured price changes do not depend on the particular base year chosen when calculating
   **a.** the traditional GDP deflator.
   **b.** the chain-weighted GDP deflator.
   **c.** real GDP.

**4.4** To compute real GDP, it is not necessary to hold prices constant. _____ (True/False)

**4.5. Calculating Real GDP, Price Indices, and Inflation.** Using data from the table below, answer the following questions:
  **a.** Calculate real GDP using prices from 2009. By what percent did real GDP grow?
  **b.** Calculate the value of the price index for GDP for 2010 using 2009 as the base year. By what percent did prices increase?

| | Quantities Produced | | Prices | |
| | CDs | Tennis Rackets | Price per CD | Price per Tennis Racket |
|---|---|---|---|---|
| 2009 | 100 | 200 | $20 | $110 |
| 2010 | 120 | 210 | 22 | 120 |

**4.6. Using a New Base Year to Calculate Real GDP and Inflation.** Repeat Exercise 4.5 but use prices from 2010.

**4.7 The Importance of the Base Year for Measuring Real GDP.** In the 1980s and 1990s, computers were rapidly introduced into the economy. The prices of computers fell rapidly over time during this period. Suppose that in calculating real GDP, the Commerce Department used a single base year, one in which computer prices were still at their earlier high levels. What distortions would using this base year cause to measures of real GDP and to changes in prices?

**4.8 Using Official U.S. Economic Data to Measure the Economy.** Go to the Web site for the Federal Reserve Bank of St. Louis (research.stlouisfed.org/fred2/). Find the data for nominal GDP, real GDP in chained dollars, and the chain price index for GDP.
  **a.** Calculate the percentage growth for nominal GDP since 1990 until the most recent year.
  **b.** Calculate the percentage growth in real GDP since 1990 until the most recent year.
  **c.** Finally, calculate the percentage growth in the chain price index for GDP over this same period and compare it to the difference between your answers to (a) and (b).

## 11.5 | Fluctuations in GDP

**5.1** The date that a recession starts is called the _____.

**5.2** Most recessions are also depressions. _____ (True/False)

**5.3** The _____ marks the date that ends a recession and output starts to increase again.

**5.4** The organization that officially dates recessions is the
  **a.** Congressional Budget Office.
  **b.** Department of Commerce.
  **c.** National Bureau of Economic Research.
  **d.** Council of Economic Advisors.

**5.5 Counting Recessions.** Consider the data for the fictitious economy of Euronet:

| Year and Quarter | 2003: 1 | 2003: 2 | 2003: 3 | 2003: 4 | 2004: 1 | 2004: 2 | 2004: 3 |
|---|---|---|---|---|---|---|---|
| Real GDP | 195 | 193 | 195 | 196 | 195 | 194 | 198 |

How many recessions occurred in the economy over the time indicated?

**5.6 Alternative Methods of Measuring Recessions.** To compare how deeply recessions affected the economies of two different countries, we might use the following measures:
  **a.** The number of recessions
  **b.** The proportion of time each economy was in a recession
  **c.** The magnitude of the worst recession

Here are data from three hypothetical economies. According to each of the measures listed, which economy was affected most deeply by recessions?

| Year and Quarter | Country 1 | Country 2 | Country 3 |
|---|---|---|---|
| 2010:1 | 100.0 | 100.0 | 100.0 |
| 2010:2 | 103.0 | 103.0 | 103.0 |
| 2010:3 | 100.9 | 106.1 | 106.1 |
| 2010:4 | 95.9 | 102.9 | 109.3 |
| 2011:1 | 91.1 | 99.8 | 87.4 |
| 2011:2 | 86.5 | 96.8 | 69.9 |
| 2011:3 | 90.9 | 93.9 | 72.0 |
| 2011:4 | 95.4 | 91.1 | 74.2 |
| 2012:1 | 100.2 | 88.4 | 76.4 |
| 2012:2 | 105.2 | 85.7 | 78.7 |
| 2012:3 | 99.9 | 83.1 | 81.1 |
| 2012:4 | 94.9 | 85.6 | 83.5 |
| 2013:1 | 90.2 | 88.2 | 86.0 |
| 2013:2 | 85.7 | 90.9 | 88.6 |
| 2013:3 | 90.0 | 93.6 | 91.2 |
| 2013:4 | 94.5 | 96.4 | 94.0 |

**5.7 Indicators of a Recession.** Is it possible for the National Bureau of Economic Research to declare a recession even if real GDP has not fallen for six consecutive months? Discuss. (Related to Application 2 on page 297.)

## 11.6 | GDP as a Measure of Welfare

**6.1** Which of the following are not included in GDP?
  **a.** Leisure time
  **b.** Sales of new cars
  **c.** Strawberries sold in a grocery store
  **d.** Economics textbooks sold in the bookstore

**6.2** At any point in time, reported happiness does increase with income. _____ (True/False) (Related to Application 3 on page 299.)

**6.3** The approximate percentage of GDP in the United States that goes unreported because of the underground economy is _____.

**6.4** Illegal activities are not computed as part of measured GDP because they are not
a. legal.
b. production.
c. reported.
d. big enough to worry about.

**6.5 Does Spending Measure Welfare?** Suppose a community spends $1 million on salaries and equipment for its police department. Because it believes that citizens are now more law abiding, the community decides to cut back on the number of police it employs. As a result, the community now spends $800,000 less on the police officers. The crime rate remains the same.
a. What happens to measured GDP?
b. Does GDP accurately reflect welfare in this case? Discuss the underlying issue that this example poses.

**6.6 Disappearing Fish and National Income.** Suppose you were worried that national income does not adequately take into account the depletion of the stock of fish in the economy. How would you advise the Commerce Department to take this into account in its calculations?

**6.7 Air Quality and Measured GDP.** Air quality in Los Angeles deteriorated in the 1950s through the 1970s and then improved in the 1980s and 1990s. Can a change in air quality such as this be incorporated into our measures of national income? Discuss.

**6.8 Finding Data on the Underground Economy.** Search the Web for articles on the underground economy. You might want to go to Yahoo! and start with the topic "IRS and Underground Economy." What are some of the different ways in which economists try to measure the size of the underground economy?

**6.9 Does Money Buy Happiness?** Although people with high incomes appear to be happier than those with low incomes, people in the United States in general have become less happy over the last 30 years even though real GDP has risen. What are some of the reasons why the increase in real GDP does not always imply greater happiness? (Related to Application 3 on page 299.)

# 12

# Unemployment and Inflation

In early March, the Bureau of Labor Statistics (BLS) announced that the unemployment rate for February 2006 was 4.8 percent. That meant that of all the people who had jobs or were actively looking for work, 4.8 percent did not have jobs.

But the official unemployment statistics did not include the following individuals:

1 What do the recent data show about trends in the percentage of women who are working?
   *After Growing Sharply, Women's Labor Force Participation Has Leveled Off*

2 Who are the new discouraged workers in Japan?
   *NEETs Are the New Discouraged Workers in Japan*

3 What are the costs of either too high or too low levels of unemployment insurance?
   *Finding the Optimal Level of Unemployment Insurance*

4 Are Social Security payments properly adjusted for changes in the cost of living?
   *Using the CPI to Adjust Social Security Benefits*

- A steelworker in Ohio who was laid off two years ago. He stopped looking for work because there were no steel mills remaining in his town, and he believed no jobs were available.

- A young woman living in the far suburbs of a city. She wanted to work, and had worked in the past, but she had no transportation to the places where jobs were available.

- A young computer programmer who was working 25 hours a week. He wanted to work 40 hours a week, but his employer did not have enough work for him, because most of the company's programming work had been contracted to India. Nor could he easily find another job.

The BLS now publishes alternative statistics that reflect these cases. How big of a difference does it make to include these cases in the unemployment statistics?

I n this chapter, we look at unemployment and inflation, two key phenomena in macroeconomics. Losing a job is one of the most stressful experiences a person can suffer. For the elderly, the fear that the purchasing power of their wealth will evaporate with inflation is also a source of deep concern.

In this chapter, we will examine how economists define unemployment and inflation and the problems in measuring them. We also will explore the various costs that unemployment and inflation impose on society. Once we have a basic understanding of what unemployment and inflation are, we will be able to investigate their causes further.

# 12.1 | EXAMINING UNEMPLOYMENT

When an economy performs poorly, it imposes costs on individuals and society. Recall from Chapter 11 that one of the key issues for macroeconomics is understanding fluctuations—the ups and downs of the economy. During periods of poor economic performance and slow economic growth, unemployment rises sharply and becomes a cause of public concern. During times of good economic performance and rapid economic growth, unemployment falls, but does not disappear. Our first task is to understand how economists and government statisticians measure unemployment and then learn to interpret what they measure.

## How Is Unemployment Defined and Measured?

**labor force**
The total number of workers, both the employed and the unemployed.

**unemployment rate**
The percentage of the labor force that is unemployed.

**labor force participation rate**
The percentage of the population over 16 years of age that is in the labor force.

Let's begin with some definitions. The *unemployed* are those individuals who do not currently have a job but who are actively looking for work. The phrase *actively looking* is critical. Individuals who looked for work in the past but who are not looking currently are not counted as unemployed. The *employed* are individuals who currently have jobs. Together, the unemployed and employed comprise the **labor force**:

$$\text{labor force} = \text{employed} + \text{unemployed}$$

The **unemployment rate** is the number of unemployed divided by the total labor force. This rate represents the percentage of the labor force unemployed and looking for work:

$$\text{unemployment rate} = \frac{\text{unemployed}}{\text{labor force}}$$

Finally, we need to understand what is meant by the **labor force participation rate**, which is defined as the labor force divided by the population 16 years of age and older. This rate represents the percentage of the population 16 years of age and older that is in the labor force:

$$\text{labor force participation rate} = \frac{\text{labor force}}{\text{population 16 years and older}}$$

To illustrate these concepts, suppose that an economy consists of 200,000 individuals 16 years of age and older. Of all these people, 122,000 are employed and 8,000 are unemployed. This means that 130,000 (122,000 + 8,000) people are in the labor force. The labor force participation rate is 0.65, or 65 percent (130,000/200,000), and the unemployment rate is 0.0615, or 6.15 percent (8,000/130,000).

Figure 12.1 helps to put these measurements into perspective for the U.S. economy. The total civilian population 16 years of age and older in February 2006 was comprised of 227,764,000 individuals. This population is divided into two groups: those in the labor force (the employed plus the unemployed, totaling 150,450,000) and those outside the labor force (77,314,000). For this year, the labor force participation rate was 66.1 percent (150,450,000/227,764,000). As you can see, over three-fifths of the U.S. population participates in the labor force. Within the labor force,

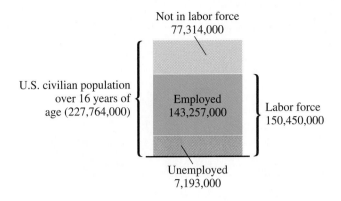

Not in labor force
77,314,000

U.S. civilian population
over 16 years of
age (227,764,000)

Employed
143,257,000

Labor force
150,450,000

Unemployed
7,193,000

◄ **FIGURE 12.1**
**Unemployment Data, February 2006**
Approximately 66.1 percent of the civilian population is in the labor force. The unemployment rate in February 2006 was 4.8 percent.
*SOURCE: Bureau of Labor Statistics, U.S. Department of Labor, 2006.*

143,257,000 were employed and 7,193,000 were unemployed. The unemployment rate was 4.8 percent (7,193,000/150,450,000). Military personnel are excluded from these measures.

One of the most important trends in the last 50 years has been the increase in the participation of women in the labor force. But it appears that increase has come to an end.

# APPLICATION

## AFTER GROWING SHARPLY, WOMEN'S LABOR FORCE PARTICIPATION HAS LEVELED OFF

**APPLYING THE CONCEPTS #1:** What do the recent data show about trends in the percentage of women who are working?

In 1948, the labor force participation rate for women 20 years and older was 32 percent. By 1970, it had grown to 43 percent, and by 1997 it had reached 60 percent. This trend reflected remarkable changes in our economy and society as women dramatically increased their presence in the workforce. But since 1997, the figure has remained virtually constant at 60 percent. It appears that women's labor force participation has reached a peak in the United States, somewhat short of the men's labor force participation rate of approximately 76 percent.

One explanation for this trend is that women may simply have run out of available time. From 1948 to the mid-1990s, women were able to increase their hours of work by cutting back on the time that they spent on housework and other home duties. With the advent of new technologies such as washing machines, dishwashers, and other labor-saving devices, women could increase their labor force participation yet still take primary care of their households. But even with new technology, housework and childcare do take time. Because women provide more household services than men, it is understandable why their labor force participation may have reached a peak.
*Related to Exercises 1.7 and 1.8.*

SOURCE: Bureau of Labor Statistics, 2006.

► **FIGURE 12.2**
**Unemployment Rates in Developed Countries**
Among the developed countries, unemployment rates vary substantially.
*SOURCE: The Economist, March 18, 2006.*

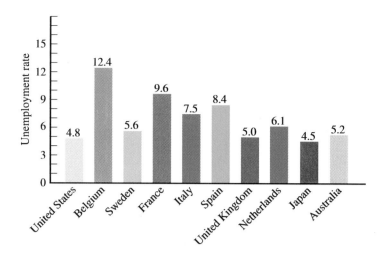

Figure 12.2 contains international data on unemployment for 2006 for developed countries. Despite the fact these countries all have modern, industrial economies, notice the sharp differences in unemployment. For example, Belgium had a 12.4 percent unemployment rate, whereas Japan had an unemployment rate of 4.5 percent. These sharp differences reflect a number of factors, including how much government support is provided to unemployed workers. In countries in which support is the most generous, there is less incentive to work and unemployment will tend to be higher.

## Alternative Measures of Unemployment and Why They're Important

We defined the unemployed as those people who are looking for work but who do not currently have jobs. With that in mind, let's take a closer look at our measures of unemployment.

It is relatively straightforward in principle to determine who is employed: Just count the people who are working. What is more difficult is to distinguish between those who are unemployed and those who are not in the labor force. How are these two groups distinguished? The Bureau of Labor Statistics (BLS), which is part of the Department of Labor, interviews a large sample of households each month. The BLS asks about the employment situation of all members of households 16 years of age and older. If someone in a household is not working, the interviewer asks whether the person is actively looking for work. If the answer is "yes," he or she is classified as unemployed. If the answer is "no,"—he or she is not actively looking for work—that person is classified as not being in the labor force.

The BLS measure of unemployment, however, does not capture all the employment experiences individuals face. In the chapter opener, we highlighted the cases of three individuals who wanted full-time jobs but did not have them: a steelworker who stopped looking for work because he felt there were no jobs, a young woman who did not seek work because she had no transportation, and a computer programmer who worked only part-time but sought full-time employment. None of them would be counted as unemployed in the official statistics—the first two were not in the labor force and the third was employed. Because of these limitations, in 1994 the BLS began to publish alternative statistics that reflect these circumstances.

Individuals who want to work, have searched for work in the prior year, but are not currently looking for work because they believe they won't be able to find a job are called **discouraged workers**. Note that these individuals are not included in the official statistics because they are not currently looking for work.

In addition to discouraged workers, there are individuals who would like to work, have searched for work in the recent past, but have stopped looking for work for a variety of reasons. These individuals are known as *marginally attached workers*. Marginally attached workers consist of two groups: discouraged workers (who left the labor force because they could not find jobs) and workers who are not looking for jobs for other reasons, including lack of transportation or childcare.

• **discouraged workers**
Workers who left the labor force because they could not find jobs.

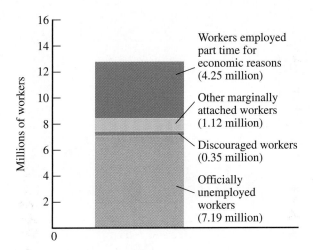

◄ **FIGURE 12.3**
**Alternative Measures of Unemployment, February 2006**
Including discouraged workers, marginally attached workers, and individuals working part time for economic reasons substantially increases measured unemployment in 2006 from 7.19 million to 12.91 million.
*SOURCE: Bureau of Labor Statistics, U.S. Department of Labor, 2006.*

Finally, there are those workers who would like to be employed full-time but hold part-time jobs. These individuals are counted as employed in the BLS statistics, because they have a job. However, they would like to be working more hours. They are known as *individuals working part time for economic reasons*. We do not include in this category individuals who prefer part-time employment.

How important are these alternative measures? Figure 12.3 puts these measures into perspective. In February 2006, 7.19 million individuals were officially classified as unemployed. The number of discouraged workers was relatively small—only 0.35 million. However, including the discouraged workers, there were 1.47 million marginally attached workers. If we add the marginally attached individuals to those who were involuntarily working part time, the total is 5.72 million. Thus, depending on the statistic you want to emphasize, there were anywhere between 7.19 million unemployed (the official number) and 12.91 million unemployed (the official number plus all those seeking full-time employment who did not have it). If we count those 12.91 million as unemployed, the unemployment rate in 2006 would be 8.6 percent—substantially higher than the official rate of 4.8 percent. As we have seen, the official statistics for unemployment do not include the full range of individuals who would like to participate fully in the labor market.

# APPLICATION

## NEETS ARE THE NEW DISCOURAGED WORKERS IN JAPAN

APPLYING THE CONCEPTS #2: Who are the new discouraged workers in Japan?

In Japan, there is growing concern about young people who are not joining the labor force. Young workers who have given up looking for work and often receive support from their parents are known as *NEETs*—"not in education, employment, or training." Because Japan has an aging population and does not encourage immigration, it is concerned about labor shortages and has focused attention on the NEETs. Many in Japan are concerned over this phenomenon because it potentially signals a change in the strong Japanese work ethic. However, the number of individuals in this category is quite small, only 2 percent of Japan's 33 million young people between the ages of 15 and 34. Nonetheless, the fact that the Japanese decided to name this group suggests that it is socially significant to them. In the United States, individuals not seeking work and supported by their parents would be out of the labor force and possibly marginally attached workers. *Related to Exercises 1.11 and 1.12.*

SOURCE: Ginny Parker Woods, "In Aging Japan, Young Slackers Stir Up Concerns," *Wall Street Journal*, December 29, 2005, p. A1.

**Selected U.S. Unemployment Statistics, Unemployment Rates for February 2006**

The incidence of unemployment differs sharply among demographic groups.
*SOURCE: Bureau of Labor Statistics, U.S. Department of Labor, 2006.*

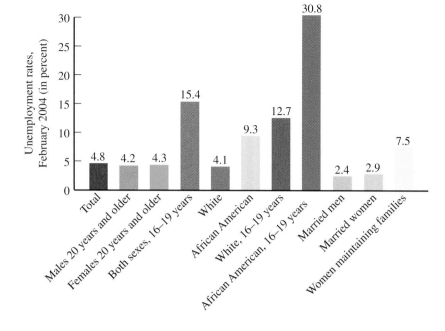

## Who Are the Unemployed?

Another fact about unemployment is that different groups of people suffer more unemployment than other groups. Figure 12.4 contains some unemployment statistics for selected groups for February 2006. Adults have substantially lower unemployment rates than teenagers. Minorities have higher unemployment rates. African American teenagers have extremely high unemployment rates. On average, men and women have roughly the same unemployment rates, but the unemployment rates for married men and married women are lower than unemployment rates of women who maintain families alone.

These relative differentials among unemployment rates do vary somewhat as GDP rises and falls. Teenage and minority unemployment rates often rise very sharply during poor economic times. In better times, a reduction of unemployment for all groups typically occurs. Nonetheless, teenage and minority unemployment remains relatively high at all times.

Many economic time series, including employment and unemployment, are substantially influenced by seasonal factors. These are recurring calendar-related effects caused by, for example, the weather, holidays, the opening and closing of schools, and related factors. Unemployment due to recurring calendar effects is called **seasonal unemployment**. Examples of seasonal unemployment include higher rates of unemployment for farm workers and construction workers in the winter and higher unemployment rates for teenagers in the early summer as they look for summer jobs.

The BLS uses statistical procedures to remove these seasonal factors—that is, it seasonally adjusts the statistics—so that users of the data can more accurately interpret underlying trends in the economy. The seasonally adjusted unemployment rates control for these predictable patterns, so those patterns aren't reflected in the overall unemployment numbers.

• **seasonal unemployment**
The component of unemployment attributed to seasonal factors.

# 12.2 | CATEGORIES OF UNEMPLOYMENT

To better understand the labor market, economists have found it very useful to break unemployment into a variety of categories. As we shall see, it is valuable to distinguish among the several different types of unemployment.

## Types of Unemployment: Cyclical, Frictional, and Structural

After seasonally adjusting the unemployment statistics, we can divide unemployment into three other basic types: cyclical, frictional, and structural. By studying each type separately, we can gain insight into some of the causes of each type of unemployment.

The unemployment rate is closely tied to the overall fortunes of the economy. Unemployment rises sharply during periods when real GDP falls and decreases when real GDP grows rapidly. During periods of falling GDP, firms will not want to employ as many workers as they do in good times because they are not producing as many goods and services. Firms will lay off or fire some current workers and will be more reluctant to add new workers to their payrolls. The result will be fewer workers with jobs and rising unemployment. Economists call the unemployment that occurs during fluctuations in real GDP **cyclical unemployment**. Cyclical unemployment rises during periods when real GDP falls or grows at a slower-than-normal rate and decreases when the economy improves.

However, unemployment still exists even when the economy is growing. For example, the unemployment rate in the United States has not fallen below 3.9 percent of the labor force since 1970. Unemployment that is not associated with economic fluctuations is either frictional unemployment or structural unemployment.

**Frictional unemployment** is the unemployment that occurs naturally during the normal workings of an economy. It occurs because it simply takes time for people to find the right jobs and for employers to find the right people to hire. This happens when people change jobs, move across the country, get laid off from their current jobs and search for new opportunities, or take their time after they enter the labor force to find an appropriate job. Suppose that when you graduate from college, you take six months to find a job that you like. During the six months in which you are looking for a good job, you are among those unemployed who make up frictional unemployment. Searching for a job, however, makes good sense. It would not be wise to take the first job you were offered if it had low wages, poor benefits, and no future. Likewise, employers are wise to interview multiple applicants for jobs to find the best employees, even if it takes some time.

Could we eliminate unemployment by posting all job vacancies on the Internet along with the résumés of job seekers and automatically match them up with one another? It's possible that such an automated system could shorten the duration of frictional unemployment, but it wouldn't eliminate it entirely. Some workers, for example, would prefer to continue searching for jobs in their own area rather than moving across country to take the jobs they had been automatically matched with. Firms would also still want to scrutinize employees very carefully, because hiring and training a worker is costly.

**Structural unemployment** occurs when the economy evolves. It occurs when different sectors give way to other sectors or certain jobs are eliminated while new types of jobs are created. For example, when the vinyl record industry gave way to the CD music industry in the 1980s, some workers found themselves structurally unemployed, which meant they had to take the time to train themselves for jobs in different industries. Structural unemployment is more of a "permanent condition" than frictional unemployment.

The line between frictional unemployment and structural unemployment is sometimes hard to draw. Suppose a highly skilled software engineer is laid off because his company shuts down its headquarters in his area and moves his job overseas. The worker would like to find a comparable job, but only lower-wage work is available in his immediate geographic location. Jobs are available, but not his kind of job, and this high-tech company will never return to the area. Is this person's unemployment frictional or structural? There really is no correct answer. You might think of the software engineer as experiencing either frictional or structural unemployment. For all practical purposes, however, it does not matter which it is. The former software engineer is still unemployed.

- **cyclical unemployment**
Unemployment that occurs during fluctuations in real GDP.

- **frictional unemployment**
Unemployment that occurs with the normal workings of the economy, such as workers taking time to search for suitable jobs and firms taking time to search for qualified employees.

- **structural unemployment**
Unemployment that occurs when there is a mismatch of skills and jobs.

- **natural rate of unemployment**
  The level of unemployment at which there is no cyclical unemployment. It consists of only frictional and structural unemployment.

- **full employment**
  The level of unemployment that occurs when the unemployment rate is at the natural rate.

### The Natural Rate of Unemployment

Total unemployment in an economy is composed of all three types of unemployment: cyclical, frictional, and structural. The level of unemployment at which there is no cyclical unemployment is called the **natural rate of unemployment**. The natural rate of unemployment consists of only frictional unemployment and structural unemployment. The natural rate of unemployment is the economist's notion of what the rate of unemployment should be when there is **full employment**. It may seem strange to think that workers can be unemployed when the economy is at full employment. However, the economy actually needs some frictional unemployment to operate efficiently: Frictional unemployment exists so that workers and firms find the right employment matches. An economy that lacks frictional unemployment will become stagnant.

In the United States today, economists estimate that the natural rate of unemployment is between 5.0 and 6.5 percent. The natural rate of unemployment varies over time and differs across countries. In Europe, for example, estimates of the natural rate of unemployment place it between 7 and 10 percent. In a later chapter, we explore why the natural rate of unemployment is higher in Europe than in the United States and why the natural rate of unemployment can vary over time in the same country.

The actual unemployment rate can be higher or lower than the natural rate of unemployment. During a period in which the real GDP fails to grow at its normal rate, there will be positive cyclical unemployment, and actual unemployment can far exceed the natural rate of unemployment. For example, in the United States in 1983 unemployment exceeded 10 percent of the labor force. As we pointed out in the previous chapter, a more extreme example occurred in 1933 during the Great Depression, when the unemployment rate reached 25 percent. When the economy grows very rapidly for a long period, actual unemployment can fall below the natural of unemployment. With sustained rapid economic growth, employers will be aggressive in hiring workers. During the late 1960s, unemployment rates fell below 4 percent, and the natural rate of unemployment was estimated to be over 5 percent. In this case, cyclical unemployment was negative.

Unemployment also fell to 4 percent in 2000. In this case, many economists believed that the natural rate of unemployment had fallen to close to 5 percent, so that cyclical unemployment in that year was negative.

Just as a car will overheat if the engine is overworked, so will the economy overheat if economic growth is too rapid. At low unemployment rates, firms will find it difficult to recruit workers, and competition among firms will lead to increases in wages. As wages increase, increases in prices soon follow. The sign of this overheating will be a general rise in prices for the entire economy, which we commonly call *inflation*. As we discuss in later chapters, when the actual unemployment rate falls below the natural rate of unemployment, inflation will increase.

# 12.3 | THE COSTS OF UNEMPLOYMENT

When there is excess unemployment—actual unemployment above the natural rate of unemployment—both society and individuals suffer economic loss. From a social point of view, excess unemployment means that the economy is no longer producing at its potential. The resulting loss of resources can be very large. For example, in 1983, when the unemployment rate averaged 9.6 percent, typical estimates of the shortfall of GDP from potential were near 6 percent. Simply put, this meant that society was wasting 6 percent of the total resources at its disposal.

To families with fixed obligations such as mortgage payments, the loss in income can bring immediate hardships. **Unemployment insurance**, payments received from the government upon becoming unemployed, can cushion the blow to some degree, but unemployment insurance is typically only temporary and does not replace a worker's full earnings.

The effects of unemployment can also linger into the future. Workers who suffer from a prolonged period of unemployment are likely to lose some of their skills. For

- **unemployment insurance**
  Payments unemployed people receive from the government.

example, an unemployed stockbroker might be unaware of the latest developments and trends in financial markets. This lack of knowledge will make it more difficult for that person to find a job in the future. Economists who have studied the high rates of unemployment among young people in Europe point to the loss of both skills and good work habits (such as coming to work on time) as key factors leading to long-term unemployment.

The costs of unemployment are not simply financial. In our society, a person's status and position are largely associated with the type of job the person holds. Losing a job can impose severe psychological costs. Some studies have found, for example, that increased crime, divorce, and suicide rates are associated with increased unemployment.

Not all unemployment lasts a long period of time for individuals. Some unemployment is very short term. Table 12.1 shows the percent of unemployed by the duration or length of unemployment. In February 2006, approximately 36 percent of unemployed workers had been out of work less than five weeks. At the other end, 19 percent were unemployed more than 27 weeks. Half of the unemployed had been out of work less than nine weeks. In the United States, unemployment is a mixture of both short- and long-term unemployment.

Although unemployment insurance can temporarily offset some of the financial costs of job loss, the presence of unemployment insurance also tends to increase the length of time that unemployed workers remain unemployed. The extra financial cushion that unemployment insurance provides allows workers to remain unemployed a bit longer before obtaining another job. In other words, unemployment insurance actually leads to additional time spent unemployed.

| Table 12.1 | THE DURATION OF UNEMPLOYMENT, FEBRUARY 2006 |
| --- | --- |
| **Weeks of Unemployment** | **Percent of the Unemployed** |
| Fewer than 5 weeks | 36.3 |
| 5 to 14 weeks | 29.0 |
| 15 to 26 weeks | 15.7 |
| Greater than 27 weeks | 19.0 |

*SOURCE*: Bureau of Labor Statistics, U.S. Department of Labor, 2006.

# APPLICATION

## FINDING THE OPTIMAL LEVEL OF UNEMPLOYMENT INSURANCE

**APPLYING THE CONCEPTS #3:** What are the costs of either too high or too low levels of unemployment insurance?

How do we balance the benefits and costs of unemployment insurance? Suppose that the government provided all unemployed workers a payment that was equal to their previous salary as long as they remained unemployed. While this would prevent unemployed workers from suffering any financial hardship, very few workers would return to work if the government were paying them their full salaries. This, of course, would lead to excessive unemployment. States recognize this and replace only a fraction of a worker's prior salary—typically about 40 percent.

Economist Jonathan Gruber of MIT explored both the benefits and costs of unemployment insurance and attempted to calculate the optimal amount of unemployment insurance. To measure the benefits, he used survey data to determine how much workers decreased their consumption after becoming unemployed. For example, without unemployment insurance, he estimated that food consumption would fall nearly 22 percent. Unemployment insurance can offset part of this sharp decrease in consumption. Looking at both the costs and the benefits of unemployment insurance, Gruber found that the optimal level of insurance was probably somewhat lower (closer to 30 percent) than the current 40 percent provided by the states. *Related to Exercise 3.5.*

SOURCE: Jonathan Gruber, "The Consumption Smoothing Benefits of Unemployment Insurance," *American Economic Review*, March 1997, pp. 192–205.

# 12.4 | THE CONSUMER PRICE INDEX AND THE COST OF LIVING

Suppose you were reading a book written in 1964 in which the main character received a starting salary of $5,000. Was that a high or low salary back then? To determine whether this was a high or low salary, we need to know what that $5,000 could purchase. Or, to put it another way, we need to know the value of the dollar—what a dollar would actually buy—in 1964. Only then could we begin to make sense of whether this was a high or low salary.

Or take another example. In 1976, a new starting professor in economics received a salary of $15,000. In 2006, at the same university, a new starting professor received $80,000. Prices, of course, had risen in these 30 years. Which starting professor had the better deal?

These examples are illustrations of one of our five principles of economics, the real-nominal principle.

## REAL-NOMINAL PRINCIPLE

What matters to people is the real value of money or income—its purchasing power—not the face value of money or income.

• **Consumer Price Index (CPI)**
A price index that measures the cost of a fixed basket of goods chosen to represent the consumption pattern of a typical consumer.

Economists have developed a number of different measures to track the cost of living over time. The best known of these measures is the **Consumer Price Index (CPI)**.

The CPI is widely used to measure changes in prices facing consumers. It measures changes in prices in a fixed *basket of goods*—a collection of items chosen to represent the purchasing pattern of a typical consumer. We first find out how much this basket of goods costs in a given year. This is called the *base year* (it serves a similar purpose as the base year we designated for the GDP deflator). We then ask how much it costs in other years and measure changes in the cost of living relative to this base year. The CPI index for a given year, say year $K$, is defined as

$$\text{CPI in year } K = \frac{\text{cost of basket in year } K}{\text{cost of basket in base year}} \times 100$$

Suppose a basket of goods costs $200 in 1992, which we'll define as the base year. In 2004, the same basket of goods is $250. First, the value for the CPI in 1992 (the base year) is

$$\text{CPI in 1992} = \frac{200}{200} \times 100 = 100$$

That is, the CPI for 1992 is 100. Note that the base year for the CPI will always equal 100. Now let's calculate the value of the CPI for 2004:

$$\text{CPI in 2004} = \frac{250}{200} \times 100 = 125$$

The CPI in 2004 is 125. The CPI rose from 100 in 1992 to 125 in 2004 in this example, a 25 percent increase in average prices over this 12-year period.

Here is how you would use this information. Suppose you had $300 in 1992. How much would you need to be able to have the same standard of living in 2004? The answer is given by multiplying the $300 by the ratio of the CPI in 2004 to the CPI in 1992:

$$\$300 \times \frac{125}{100} = \$375$$

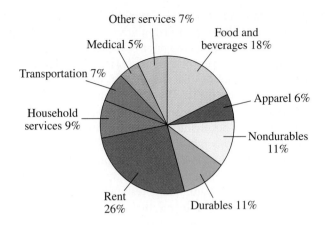

◄ **FIGURE 12.5**
**Components of the Consumer Price Index (CPI)**
Rent and food and beverages make up 44 percent of the CPI basket. The remainder consists of other goods and services.
*SOURCE: Bureau of Labor Statistics, U.S. Department of Labor, 2006.*

You need $375 in 2004 just to maintain what was your standard of living in 1992. This is the type of calculation that economists do to evaluate changes in living standards over time.

How do we actually calculate the CPI in practice? Each month, the BLS sends its employees out to sample prices for over 90,000 specific items around the entire country. Figure 12.5 shows the broad categories the BLS uses in the CPI and the importance of each category in household budgets. Rent and food and beverages account for 44 percent of total spending by households.

## The CPI Versus the Chain Index for GDP

In Chapter 11, we discussed measuring nominal GDP and real GDP. We also mentioned that since 1996 the Commerce Department has used a chain-weighted index (replacing the GDP deflator) to measure changes in prices for goods and services included in GDP. The chain-weighted index for GDP and the CPI are both measures of average prices for the economy, yet they differ in several ways.

First, the CPI measures the costs of a typical basket of goods for consumers. It includes goods produced in prior years (such as older cars) as well as imported goods. The chain-weighted price index for GDP does not measure price changes from either used goods or imports. The reason that the chain index for GDP does not include used or imported goods is that it is based on the calculation of GDP, which measures only goods and services produced in the United States in the current year.

Second, unlike the chain-weighted price index for GDP, the CPI asks how much a *fixed* basket of goods costs in the current year compared to the cost of those same goods in a base year. Because consumers will tend to buy less of goods whose prices rise, the CPI will tend to overstate true changes in the cost of living. For example, if the price of steak rises, consumers may switch to chicken and spend less on steak. But if the current basket of goods and services in the CPI includes steak, the CPI thinks the share of higher-priced steak in the basket is the same as the share of steak before its price increase. The CPI does not allow the share of steak in the index to decrease. Another measurement problem occurs when new products are introduced into the marketplace. Again, this is because the CPI measures a fixed basket of goods. The BLS will eventually adjust its "basket" to account for successful new products, but this will take some time.

## Problems in Measuring Changes in Prices

Most economists believe that in reality all the indexes, including the chain-weighted index for GDP and the CPI, overstate actual changes in prices. In other words, the increase in prices is probably less than the reported indexes tell us. The principal reason for this overstatement is that we have a difficult time measuring quality improvements. Suppose that the new computers sold to consumers become more powerful and more efficient each year. Further, suppose that the dollar price of a new computer remains the same each year.

Even though the prices remain the same, the computers in later years are of much higher quality. If we looked simply at the prices of computers and did not take into account the change in quality, we would say there was no price change for computers. But in later years we are getting more computer power for the same price. If we failed to take the quality change into account, we would not see that the price of computer power has fallen.

Government statisticians do try to adjust for quality when they can. But quality changes are so common in our economy and products evolve so rapidly that it is impossible to keep up with all that is occurring. As a result, most economists believe that we overestimate the inflation rate by between 0.5 and 1.5 percent each year. This overstatement has important consequences. Some government programs, such as Social Security, automatically increase payments when the CPI goes up. Some union contracts also have **cost-of-living adjustments (COLAs)**, automatic wage changes based on the CPI. If the CPI overstates increases in the cost of living, the government and employers might be overpaying Social Security recipients and workers for changes in the cost of living.

# 12.5 | INFLATION

We have now looked at two different price indexes: the chain-weighted price index used for calculating real GDP and the Consumer Price Index. Using either price index, we can calculate the percentage rate of change of the index. The percentage rate of change of a price index is the **inflation rate**:

inflation rate = percentage rate of change of a price index

Here is an example. Suppose that a price index in a country was 200 in 1998 and 210 in 1999. Then the inflation rate between 1998 and 1999 was

$$\text{inflation rate} = \frac{210 - 200}{200} = 0.05 = 5\%$$

In other words, the country experienced a 5 percent inflation rate.

It is important to distinguish between the price level and the inflation rate. In everyday language, people sometimes confuse the level of prices with inflation. You might hear someone say that inflation is high in San Francisco because rents for apartments are high, but this is not a correct use of the term *inflation*. Inflation refers not to the level of prices, whether they are high or low, but to their percentage change. If rents were high in San Francisco but remained constant between two years, there would be no inflation in rents there during that time.

**• cost-of-living adjustments (COLAs)**
Automatic increases in wages or other payments that are tied to the CPI.

**• inflation rate**
The percentage rate of change in the price level.

▶ **FIGURE 12.6**
**Price Index for U.S. GDP, 1875–2005**
After remaining relatively flat for 60 years, the price level began to steadily increase after World War II. The price of a postage stamp in 1940 and 2005 illustrates the change in the overall price level that occurred.
*SOURCES: R. J. Gordon, Macroeconomics (New York: Harper Collins, 1993) and U.S. Department of Commerce, 2006.*

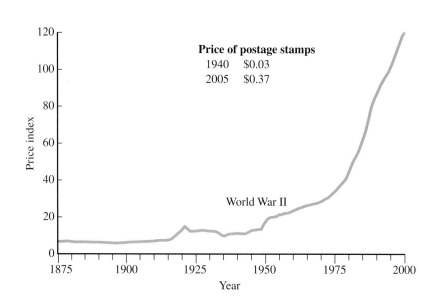

**Table 12.2** | PRICES OF SELECTED GOODS, 1940s AND 2005

| Item | 1940s Price | 2005 Price |
|---|---|---|
| Gallon of gasoline | $0.18 | $2.35 |
| Loaf of bread | 0.08 | 3.59 |
| Gallon of milk | 0.34 | 3.49 |
| Postage stamps | 0.03 | 0.39 |
| House | 6,550 | 350,000 |
| Car | 800 | 20,000 |
| Haircut in New York City | 0.50 | 50 |
| Movie tickets in New York City | 0.25 | 10.00 |
| Men's tweed sports jacket in New York City | 15 | 189 |
| Snake tattoo on arm | 0.25 | 60.00 |

*SOURCES:* Scott Derks, *The Value of a Dollar 1860–1989* (Farmington Hills, MI: Gale Group, 1993); and author's research.

## Historical U.S. Inflation Rates

To gain some historical perspective, Figure 12.6 plots a price index for GDP from 1875 to 2005 for the United States. As you can see from the figure, from 1875 to the period just before World War I, there was virtually no change in the price level. The price level rose during World War I, fell after the war ended, and also fell sharply during the early 1930s. However, the most pronounced feature of the figure is the sustained rise in prices beginning around the 1940s. Unlike the earlier periods, in which the price level did not have a trend, after 1940 the price level increased sharply. By 2005, the price level had increased by a factor of 14 over its value in 1940. Table 12.2 contains the prices of a few selected goods from the 1940s. Wouldn't you like to buy a postage stamp today for $0.03?

Taking a closer look at the period following World War II, Figure 12.7 plots the inflation rate, the percentage change in the price index, from 1950 to 2005. In the 1950s and 1960s, the inflation rate was frequently less than 2 percent a year. The inflation rate was a lot higher in the 1970s, reaching nearly 10 percent per year. In those years, the economy suffered from several increases in the world price of oil. In recent years, the inflation rate has subsided and has been between 2 and 3 percent.

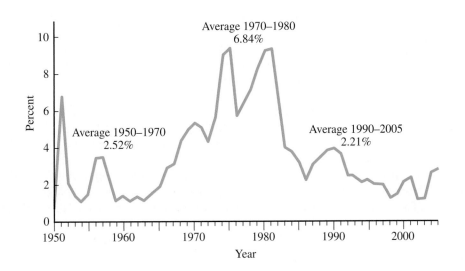

**◀ FIGURE 12.7**

**U.S. Inflation Rate, 1950–2005, Based on Chain-Weighted Price Index**

Inflation reached its highest peak in the postwar era during the mid-1970s when the economy was hit with several increases in oil prices. In recent years, the inflation rate has been relatively low.
*SOURCE: U.S. Department of Commerce, 2006.*

## USING THE CPI TO ADJUST SOCIAL SECURITY BENEFITS

**APPLYING THE CONCEPTS #4:** Are Social Security payments properly adjusted for changes in the cost of living?

Each year, the federal government increases Social Security payments to the elderly by the rate of increase of prices as measured by the Consumer Price Index. The reason for this adjustment is to make sure that the elderly, whose other income tends to be fixed, do not suffer from cost-of-living increases. But as we have seen, the CPI does not fully account for quality changes, so that the true increase in prices is less than the increase as measured by the CPI. Because Social Security payments are increased by the CPI, we actually overcompensate the elderly for price changes and thus increase their benefits in real terms.

How much extra are we paying the elderly because of the bias in the CPI? Economists believe that the CPI overstates actual price increases by between 0.5 and 1.5 percent a year. Assume that the figure is 1 percent. According to the Congressional Budget Office, if we reduced this adjustment for Social Security by 1 percent, it would save $42 billion over a five-year period! As you can tell, not accounting for technical change is a costly bias in our price indexes.

Defenders of the elderly claim that this is a misleading argument. Although the CPI may overstate price increases in general, it probably understates the rate of price increases facing the elderly. The elderly consume more medical care than do average citizens in the United States, and prices for medical care have increased faster than other prices in the economy. Regardless of which side of the debate we favor, it is evident that many tax dollars depend on precise calculation of the CPI. *Related to Exercise 5.6.*

## The Perils of Deflation

Prices rarely fall today, but they have actually fallen at times in world history. You might think it would be great if prices fell and we had what economists term a **deflation**. It may surprise you that we think you should hope that deflation never occurs.

During the Great Depression, the United States underwent a severe deflation. Prices fell 33 percent on average, and wages fell along with prices. The biggest problem caused by a deflation is that people cannot repay their debts. Imagine that you owe $40,000 for your education and expect to be able to pay it off over several years if you earn $27,000 a year. If a massive deflation caused your wages to fall to $18,000, you might not be able to pay your $40,000 debt, which does not fall with deflation. You would be forced to default on your loan, as millions of people did during the Great Depression.

In recent years, Japan experienced a deflation, although much milder than the Great Depression in the United States—only about 1 percent per year. Nonetheless, banks in Japan faced rocky economic times as borrowers, including large corporations, defaulted on their loans. With their banks in difficult shape, Japan's economy has suffered. Japan's experience today mirrors the experience of other countries throughout the world in the 1930s during the period of deflation.

**• deflation**
Negative inflation or falling prices of goods and services.

# 12.6 | THE COSTS OF INFLATION

Economists typically separate the costs of inflation into two categories. One includes costs associated with fully expected or **anticipated inflation**. The other includes the costs associated with unexpected or **unanticipated inflation**. Although inflation causes both types of costs, it is convenient to discuss each case separately.

## Anticipated Inflation

Let's consider the costs of anticipated inflation first. Suppose the economy had been experiencing 4 percent annual inflation for many years and everyone was fully adjusted to it.

Even in this case, inflation still has some costs. First, there are the actual physical costs of changing prices, which economists call **menu costs**. Restaurant owners, catalog producers, and any other business that must post prices will have to incur costs to physically change their prices because of inflation. For example, they will need to pay to reprint their menus or billboards. Economists believe that these costs are relatively small for the economy.

Second, people will want to hold less cash when there is inflation. Inflation will erode the value of the cash people hold. They will respond by holding less cash at any one time. If they hold less cash, they must visit the bank or their ATM more frequently because they will run out of cash sooner. Economists use the term **shoe-leather costs** to refer to the additional wear and tear necessary to hold less cash. Economists who have estimated these costs find that they can be large, as much as 1 percent of GDP.

In practice, our tax and financial systems do not fully adjust even to anticipated inflation. It is difficult for the government and businesses to change their normal rules of operation every time inflation changes. As an example, consider the tax system. Our tax system is typically based on nominal income, not real income. Suppose you own a stock in a corporation that increases by 5 percent during the year. If the inflation rate is also 5 percent a year, your stock did not increase in real terms—it just kept up with inflation. Nonetheless, if you sold your stock at the end of the year, you would be taxed on the full 5 percent gain, despite the fact that the real value of your stock did not increase. Inflation distorts the operation of our tax and financial system.

## Unanticipated Inflation

What if inflation is unexpected? The cost of unexpected inflation is arbitrary redistributions of income. Suppose you expected the inflation rate would be 5 percent and that you negotiated a salary based on that expectation. On the one hand, if you miscalculate and the inflation rate turns out to be higher, the purchasing power of your wages would be less than you anticipated. The firm would have gained at your expense. On the other hand, if the inflation rate turned out to be less than 5 percent, the purchasing power of your wage would be higher than you had anticipated. In this case, you would gain at the expense of the company. As long as the inflation rate differs from what is expected, there will be winners and losers.

These redistributions eventually impose real costs on the economy. Consider an analogy. Suppose you live in a very safe neighborhood where no one locks the doors. If a rash of burglaries (transfers between you and the crooks) starts to occur, people will invest in locks, alarms, and more police. You and your community will incur real costs to prevent these arbitrary redistributions.

The same is true for unanticipated inflation. If a society experiences unanticipated inflation, individuals and institutions will change their behavior. For example, potential homeowners will not be able to borrow from banks at fixed rates of interest, but will be required to accept loans whose rates can be adjusted as inflation rates change. Banks do not want to lend money at a fixed interest rate if there is a strong likelihood

- **anticipated inflation**
  Inflation that is expected.

- **unanticipated inflation**
  Inflation that is not expected.

- **menu costs**
  The costs associated with changing prices and printing new price lists when there is inflation.

- **shoe-leather costs**
  Costs of inflation that arise from trying to reduce holdings of cash.

that inflation will erode the real value of the income stream they expected. However, if banks become reluctant to make loans with fixed interest rates, this imposes more risk on homeowners.

What about the loans made prior to the unanticipated inflation? In this case, debtors will gain at the expense of creditors. Creditors, on the one hand, will lose because inflation will erode the amount of money they planned to earn on the loans. But since the loans have already been made, there's nothing they can do about it. Debtors, on the other hand, will get a deal. It will be easier for them to repay their loans with inflated dollars.

If unanticipated inflation becomes extreme, individuals will spend more of their time trying to profit from inflation rather than working at productive jobs. As inflation became more volatile in the late 1970s in the United States, many people devoted their time to speculation in real estate and commodity markets to try to beat inflation, and the economy became less efficient. Latin American countries that have experienced high and variable inflation rates know all too well these costs from inflation. Indeed, when inflation rates exceed 50 percent per month, we have what is called **hyperinflation**. Think about what an inflation rate of 50 percent a month means: If a can of soda costs $1.25 at the beginning of the year, it would cost $162.00 at the end of year! You can readily see that inflation of this magnitude would seriously disrupt normal commerce.

Even in less extreme cases, the costs of inflation are compounded as inflation rises. At high inflation rates, these costs grow rapidly, and at some point policy makers are forced to take actions to reduce inflation. As we mentioned earlier, when unemployment falls below the natural rate, inflation increases. Similarly, stopping inflation may require unemployment to exceed its natural rate and even plunge an economy into a recession. Although unemployment and recessions are quite costly to society, they sometimes become necessary in the face of high inflation.

• **hyperinflation**
An inflation rate exceeding 50 percent per month.

# SUMMARY

In this chapter, we continued our introduction to the basic concepts of macroeconomics and explored the nature of both unemployment and inflation. We also looked at the complex issues involved in measuring unemployment and inflation as well as the costs of both to society. Here are the key points to remember:

1 The unemployed are individuals who do not have jobs but who are actively seeking employment. The *labor force* comprises both the employed and the unemployed. The *unemployment rate* is the percentage of the labor force that is unemployed:

$$\text{unemployment rate} = \frac{\text{unemployed}}{\text{labor force}}$$

2 Economists distinguish among different types of unemployment. Seasonal patterns of economic activity lead to *seasonal unemployment*. There are three other types of unemployment. *Frictional unemployment* occurs through the normal dynamics of the economy as workers change jobs and industries expand and contract. *Structural unemploy-*

*ment* arises because of a mismatch of workers' skills with job opportunities. *Cyclical unemployment* occurs with the fluctuations in economic activity.

3 Unemployment rates vary across demographic groups. Alternative measures of unemployment take into account individuals who would like to work full time, but who are no longer in the labor force or are holding part-time jobs.

4 Economists measure changes in the cost of living through the *Consumer Price Index (CPI)*, which is based on the cost of purchasing a standard basket of goods and services. The CPI is used to measure changes in average prices over different periods of time. The CPI index for a given year, say year *K*, is defined as

$$\text{CPI in year } K = \frac{\text{cost of basket in year } K}{\text{cost of basket in base year}} \times 100$$

5 We measure *inflation* as the percentage change in the price level.

6 Economists believe that most price indexes, including the CPI and the chain-weighted index for GDP, overstate true inflation because they fail to capture quality improvements in goods and services.

7 Unemployment imposes both financial and psychological costs on workers.

8 Both *anticipated* and *unanticipated* inflation imposes costs on society.

# KEY TERMS

# EXERCISES

Visit www.myeconlab.com to complete
*Get Ahead of the Curve*  these exercises online and get instant feedback.

## 12.1 | Examining Unemployment

**1.1** Which of the following is not included in the labor force?
  **a.** People who are employed.
  **b.** People who do not have jobs, but who are actively searching for one.
  **c.** People who do not have jobs, and do not want one.
  **d.** The entire population is included in the labor force.

**1.2** Individuals who have stopped looking for work because they did not believe jobs were available are not counted as unemployed in the traditional unemployment statistics. _____ (True/False)

**1.3** The labor force participation rate shows
  **a.** the percentage of the labor force that has a job.
  **b.** the percentage of the labor force that is unemployed.
  **c.** the percentage of the relevant population that is employed.
  **d.** the percentage of the relevant population that is in the labor force.

**1.4** Besides discouraged workers, another example of a marginally attached worker is _____.

**1.5** **New Government Employment and True Unemployment.** Suppose the U.S. government hires workers who are currently unemployed but does not give them any work to do. What will happen to the measured U.S. unemployment rate? Under these circumstances, do changes in the measured U.S. unemployment rate accurately reflect changes in the underlying economic situation and production?

**1.6** **Suspicious Economic Statistics.** Is the interpretation of economic statistics always straightforward? Suppose that after a long period of high unemployment, government statisticians noticed that the labor force was smaller than it was before the spell of unemployment. One interpretation of this statistic is that fewer people are willing to work

and enter the labor force. Is there an alternative interpretation?

**1.7** **Calculating Data for the U.S. Economy.** Here are some data for the U.S. economy in February 2006:

227.7 million individuals 16 years of age and older
143.2 million employed
  7.2 million unemployed

Calculate the labor force, the labor force participation rate, and the unemployment rate for the U.S. economy. (Related to Application 1 on page 307.)

**1.8** **Women and Labor Force Participation.** What factors might limit women's labor force participation relative to men? Are these factors that could change as social customs change? (Related to Application 1 on page 307.)

**1.9** **Are Unemployment Measures Accurate in Inner Cities?** In inner cities, minority youths have high unemployment rates. Many economists believe that the unemployment picture is worse than the statistics portray. What could be the basis for this belief?

**1.10** **Housework and Labor Statistics.** Suppose the government decided that homemakers should be counted as employed because they perform important services. How do you think this change would affect our measure of the labor force, the labor force participation rate, and the unemployment rate?

**1.11** **Alternative Unemployment Measures.** An economy has 100,000,000 people employed, 8,000,000 unemployed, and 4,000,000 discouraged workers. What is the conventional measure of the unemployment rate? What would be the best alternative measure that takes into account discouraged workers? (Related to Application 2 on page 309.)

**1.12** **Discouraged Workers in Japan and the United States.** Japan was concerned about NEETs. In the United States, we also have young, discouraged workers. Discuss the types of young, discouraged workers you would most likely find in the United States. (Related to Application 2 on page 309.)

## 12.2 | Categories of Unemployment

**2.1** The three key types of unemployment are cyclical, frictional, and _____.

**2.2** The natural rate of unemployment consists solely of _____ and _____ unemployment.

**2.3** When the economy is at full employment, there is only cyclical unemployment. _____ (True/False)

**2.4** When MP3 players emerged and cassette players declined in popularity, what type, or types, of unemployment were created?
 a. Structural and frictional
 b. Structural and cyclical
 c. Frictional and cyclical
 d. Discouraged and cyclical

**2.5** **Understanding Unemployment Differences Across Countries.** A student looking at Figure 12.2 on page 308 argues that Belgium must have very high cyclical unemployment compared to Japan because the Belgian unemployment rate is so high. Explain why the student may be wrong.

**2.6** **Apartment Vacancies and Unemployment.** In a major city, the vacancy rate for apartments was approximately 5 percent, yet substantial numbers of individuals were searching for new apartments. Explain why this occurs. Relate this phenomenon to unemployment.

**2.7** **Should the Unemployment Rate Be Driven to Zero?** Should policy makers strive to drive the unemployment rate to zero? Explain.

**2.8** **Oil Price Changes and Frictional Unemployment.** When oil prices increased sharply in the 1970s, some businesses were affected more adversely than others. Explain why some economists believe that the rise in oil prices increased frictional unemployment.

## 12.3 | The Costs of Unemployment

**3.1** The costs of unemployment are solely financial. _____ (True/False)

**3.2** Most states do not replace the entire wages of individuals on unemployment insurance; instead, they replace about _____ percent.

**3.3** The effects of unemployment today may carry over into the future because:
 a. Discouraged workers are not measured in the unemployment rate.
 b. Those that experience prolonged unemployment lose job skills that are difficult to recover.

 c. A person must be actively seeking work to be counted as unemployed.
 d. None of the above.

**3.4** In 2006, approximately one-half of the unemployed had been unemployed less than _____ weeks.

**3.5** **Costs and Benefits of Unemployment Insurance.** Evaluate the following statement: "Paying people unemployment insurance just creates more unemployment. Therefore, we should abolish unemployment insurance." (Related to Application 3 on page 313.)

**3.6** **Long-Term Effects of Unemployment.** Why might you expect individuals who were unemployed in their 20s to have lower wages at the age of 40 than individuals with identical educational backgrounds but who were not unemployed?

## 12.4 | The Consumer Price Index and the Cost of Living

**4.1** The value of a price index in the base year is equal to _____.

**4.2** Economists believe that the CPI tends to underestimate the increase in the cost of living over time. _____ (True/False)

**4.3** Unlike the CPI, the chain-weighted price index for GDP does not include used goods or _____ goods.

**4.4** The single largest component of the basket of goods that comprises the CPI is the category for _____.

**4.5** **Which Professor Is Better Off?** The starting salary for a new assistant economics professor was $15,000 in 1976 and $80,000 in 2005. The value of the CPI for 2005 was 195.3, compared to 56.9 in 1976. In which year did a newly hired professor earn more in real terms?

**4.6** **What Are Comparable Real Salaries?** A job paid $53,000 in 2002. The CPI in 1960 was 29.6, compared to 179.9 in 2002. In 1960, what salary would be comparable to 2002's $53,000 in real terms?

**4.7** **High Prices and Inflation.** Critically evaluate the following statement: "Tokyo is an expensive place to live. They must have a high inflation rate in Japan."

**4.8** **Researching Price Indexes.** Go to the data section of the Web site for the Bureau of Labor Statistics (stats.bls.gov). Contrast the change in the price indexes from 1960 to the present for the overall CPI with the change in some of its components, such as food and beverage and medical care services. What are some of your findings?

## 12.5 | Inflation

**5.1** If a price index is 50 in 1998 and 60 in 1999, the rate of inflation between the two years is _____.

**5.2** Inflation in the United States was higher from 1990 to 2005 than it was from 1970 to 1980. _____ (True/False)

**5.3** Which of the following countries experienced a deflation in the 1990s:
  **a.** United States
  **b.** Japan
  **c.** Canada

**5.4** If the price of gasoline in 1940 was $0.18 a gallon and $2.00 a gallon in 2000, the percentage rate of change for gasoline over this period was _____ percent.

**5.5** **Calculating an Inflation Rate.** A country reports a price index of 55 in 2005 and 60 in 2006. What is the inflation rate between 2005 and 2006?

**5.6** **Price Indexes for the Elderly.** Use the Web to find articles that discuss price indexes that are most appropriate for elderly Americans. How would a finding that the elderly face a different inflation rate affect the debates on Social Security? (Related to Application 4 on page 318.)

## 12.6 | The Costs of Inflation

**6.1** Inflation that is expected is known as _____ inflation.

**6.2** Shoe-leather costs typically increase with rate of inflation. _____ (True/False)

**6.3** Creditors gain from unanticipated inflation. _____ (True/False)

**6.4** Hyperinflation occurs when the inflation rate exceeds _____ percent per month.

**6.5** **Online Shopping and Menu Costs.** How do you think the Internet and online shopping would affect the menu costs of inflation?

**6.6** **Business and Deflation.** Businesses are typically net debtors. What do you believe would happen to them during a major deflation? Explain.

**6.7** **Inflation and ATM Withdrawals.** As the inflation rate increases, would you take more or less money out per ATM visit and why?

# 13

# Why Do Economies Grow?

To understand what economic growth means, consider how the typical American lived in 1783, seven years after the Declaration of Independence was written. According to economic historian Stanley Lebergott,[1] the average U.S. home at that time had no central heat, one fireplace, no plumbing, no hot water, and toilets that were outdoor shacks surrounding a hole in the ground.

Now move ahead well into the nineteenth century. A typical farmer took a bath once a week. Houses had no electricity or gas; a solitary candle provided light at night. There were no refrigerators, no toasters, or any appliances. Bedrooms contained no furniture other than a bed (with no springs); two people slept in what we now consider a single bed. For women, life was particularly hard. They were expected to bake over half a ton of bread a year, kill chickens, and butcher hogs, as well as prepare all vegetables. Canned foods were not readily available until a century later. And you really don't want to hear about medical "science" in those days.

And, just think, only 50 years ago children in the United States were afflicted with polio. Most households did not have television sets, and even those were black and white. What changes will occur in the next 50 years?

- **capital deepening**
  Increases in the stock of capital per worker.

- **technological progress**
  More effcient ways of organizing economic affairs that allow an economy to increase output without increasing inputs.

- **human capital**
  The knowledge and skills acquired by a worker through education and experience and used to produce goods and services.

- **real GDP per capita**
  Gross domestic product per person adjusted for changes in constant prices. It is the usual measure of living standards across time and between countries.

- **growth rate**
  The percentage rate of change of a variable from one period to another.

Our living standards are dramatically different today because of the remarkable growth in GDP per person. Growth in GDP is perhaps the most critical aspect of a country's economic performance. Over long periods, it is the only way to raise the standard of living in an economy.

This chapter begins by looking at some data from both rich and poor countries over the last 30 years. We will see how GDP per capita (meaning per person—every man, woman, and child) compares over this period. We'll then look at how growth occurs. Economists believe that there are two basic mechanisms that increase GDP per capita over the long term. One is **capital deepening**, or increases in an economy's stock of capital (such as buildings and equipment) relative to its workforce. *Technological progress* is the other mechanism by which economies can grow. To economists, **technological progress** specifically means that an economy operates more efficiently, producing more output, but without using any more inputs, such as capital or labor. We'll examine different theories of the origins of technological progress and discuss how to measure its overall importance for the economy. We'll also discuss in detail the role of education, experience, and investments in human beings in fostering economic development, which is called **human capital**.

# 13.1 | ECONOMIC GROWTH RATES

Throughout the world, there are vast differences in standards of living and in rates of economic growth. To understand these differences, we first need to look at the concepts and the tools economists use to study economic growth.

But before we learn how to measure growth, let's take a broad overview of what we mean by *economic growth*. We can understand economic growth by using a tool called the production possibilities curve (PPC). The production possibilities curve shows the set of feasible production options for an economy at a given point of time. In Figure 13.1, we show an economy's trade-off when it comes to producing consumer goods versus military goods. As the economy grows, the entire production possibilities curve shifts outward. This means that the economy can produce more of both goods—that is what we mean by economic growth. Growth also expands the amount of goods available for people to consume. Just think about your own family. A typical family 40 years ago had only one car, whereas today many families have two or three. And, as our chapter-opening story highlights, for many people in history and in the world today, economic growth means a qualitative transformation of their lifestyles.

## Measuring Economic Growth

From earlier chapters, we know that real gross domestic product (GDP) measures in constant prices the total value of final goods and services in a country. Because countries differ in the size of their populations, we want to know a country's real GDP per person, or its **real GDP per capita**.

Real GDP per capita typically grows over time. A convenient way to describe the changes in real GDP per capita is growth rates. The **growth rate** of a variable is the percentage change in that variable from one period to another. For example, to calculate the growth rate of real GDP from year 1 to year 2, suppose real GDP was 100 in year 1 and 104 in year 2. In this case, the growth rate of real GDP would be

$$\text{growth rate} = \frac{(\text{GDP in year 2} - \text{GDP in year 1})}{(\text{GDP in year 1})}$$

$$= \frac{(104 - 100)}{100}$$

$$= \frac{4}{100}$$

$$= 4\% \text{ per year}$$

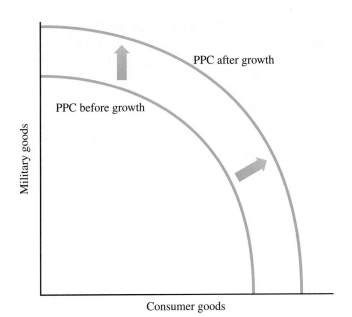

In other words, real GDP grew by 4 percent from year 1 to year 2.

Economies can grow at different rates from one year to the next. But it often is useful to consider what happens when an economy grows at a constant rate, say $g$, for a number of years. Suppose that real GDP for an economy was 100 and that the economy grew at a rate $g$ for $n$ years. How large would the real GDP be after $n$ years? The answer is given by a simple formula:

$$\text{GDP } [n \text{ years later}] = (1 + g)^n \, (100)$$

Example: If the economy starts at 100 and grows at a rate of 4 percent a year for 10 years, output (after 10 years) will be

$$\text{GDP } [10 \text{ years later}] = (1 + .04)^{10} \, (100) = (1.48)(100) = 148$$

which is nearly 50 percent higher than in the first year.

Here's a rule of thumb to help you understand the power of growth rates. Suppose you know the growth rate of real GDP, and it is constant, but you want to know how many years it will take until the level of real GDP doubles. The answer is given by the **rule of 70**:

• **rule of 70**
A rule of thumb that says output will double in 70/$x$ years, where $x$ is the percentage rate of growth.

$$\text{years to double} = \frac{70}{(\text{percentage growth rate})}$$

Example: For an economy that grew at 5 percent a year, it would take

$$\frac{70}{5} = 14 \text{ years}$$

for real GDP to double. (In case you are curious, the rule of 70 is derived by using the mathematics of logarithms.)

## Comparing the Growth Rates of Various Countries

Making comparisons of real GDP or GNP across countries is difficult. Not only do countries have their own currencies, but patterns of consumption and prices can differ sharply between countries. Two examples can illustrate this point. First, because land is scarce in Japan, people live in smaller spaces than do residents of the United States, so the price of housing is higher (relative to other goods) than in the United States. Second, developing countries (such as India or Pakistan) have very different price structures than developed countries. In particular, in developing countries the prices of goods that are not traded—such as household services or land—are relatively cheaper than goods that are traded in world markets. In other words, while all residents of the world may pay the same price for gold jewelry, hiring a cook or household helper is considerably less expensive in India or Pakistan than in the United States.

It is important to take these differences into account. Fortunately, a team of economists led by Robert Summers and Alan Heston of the University of Pennsylvania has devoted decades to developing methods for measuring real GNP across countries. Their procedures are based on gathering extensive data on prices of comparable goods in each country and making adjustments for differences in relative prices and consumption patterns. These methods are now officially used by the World Bank and the International Monetary Fund, two prominent international organizations.

According to these methods, the country with the highest level of income in 2004 was Luxembourg; its real income per capita was $61,220. The United States was second at $39,170, and Norway was third at $38,550.

Table 13.1 lists real GNP per capita for 2004 and the average annual growth rate of GNP per capita between 1960 and 2004 for 11 countries. (GNP is most commonly used in international comparisons.) The United Kingdom, with a GNP per capita of $31,460, follows the United States. Not far behind are Japan, France, and Italy. More representative of typical countries were Mexico and Costa Rica, with GNPs per capita in 2004 of $9,590 and $9,530, respectively. This is less than 25 percent of per capita GNP in the United States. Very poor countries have extremely low GNP per capita. Pakistan, for example, had a GNP per capita of $2,160—less than 6 percent of the GNP per capita of the United States.

In the third column of Table 13.1, notice the differences in growth rates. Consider Japan. In 1960, Japan had a GNP per capita that was only one-half that of France and one-fourth that of the United States. But notice from the third column that Japan's GNP per capita grew on average at 4.10 percent per year during the period, compared to 2.19 percent for the United States and 2.82 percent for France. To place Japan's growth rate for this period into perspective, recall the rule of 70. If an economy grows at an average annual rate of $x$ percent a year, it takes $70/x$ years for output to double. In Japan's case, per capita output was doubling every 70/4.10 years, or approximately every 17 years. At this rate, from the time someone was born to the time he or she reached the age of 34, living standards would have increased by a factor of four—an extraordinary rate of growth. The rule of 70 reinforces the importance of small differences in economic growth rates. A per capita GDP growth rate of 5 percent a year means that the living standard doubles in 14 years. With only 1 percent growth, doubling would take 70 years.

**Table 13.1** | GNP PER CAPITA AND ECONOMIC GROWTH

| Country | GNP Per Capita in 2004 Dollars | Per Capita Growth Rate 1960–2004 |
|---|---|---|
| United States | $39,170 | 2.19% |
| United Kingdom | 31,460 | 2.46 |
| Japan | 30,040 | 4.10 |
| France | 29,320 | 2.82 |
| Italy | 27,860 | 3.00 |
| Mexico | 9,590 | 2.32 |
| Costa Rica | 9,530 | 2.25 |
| India | 3,100 | 2.34 |
| Zimbabwe | 2,180 | 0.58 |
| Pakistan | 2,160 | 1.11 |
| Zambia | 890 | −0.83 |

SOURCES: *World Bank Development Indicators* (2005) and Alan Heston, Robert Summers and Bettina Aten, *Penn World Table* Version 6.1, Center for International Comparisons at the University of Pennsylvania (CICUP), October 2002.

# APPLICATION

**INCREASED GROWTH LEADS TO LESS CHILD LABOR IN DEVELOPING COUNTRIES**

APPLYING THE CONCEPTS #1: How does economic growth affect social indicators such as child labor?

Dartmouth economists Eric V. Edmonds and Nina Pavcnik have studied the factors that lead to changes in child labor in developing countries. Contrary to what many people might think, most child labor occurs in agriculture, with their parents as employers, rather than in manufacturing plants. As the incomes of the parents increase, they tend to rely less on their children and more on substitutes for child labor, such as fertilizer and new machinery. Careful studies in Vietnam revealed a significant drop in child labor during the 1990s, with the bulk of that decrease accounted for by higher family incomes. Their findings suggest that we should think of child labor as a phenomenon that accompanies extreme poverty and that, over time, as economies grow, child labor will tend to disappear. *Related to Exercise 1.9.*

SOURCE: Eric V. Edmonds and Nina Pavcnik, "Child Labor in the Global Economy," *Journal of Economic Perspectives*, vol. 19, no. 1, Winter 2005, pp. 199–220.

The differences in per capita incomes between the developed and developing countries are very large and are also reflected in many different aspects of society. Take, for example, child labor. In the developed world, we disapprove of child labor and wonder how we can work toward its elimination. The answer is relatively simple—more economic growth.

## Are Poor Countries Catching Up?

One question economists ask is whether poorer countries can close the gap between their level of GDP per capita and the GDP per capita of richer countries. Closing this gap is called **convergence**. To converge, poorer countries have to grow at more rapid rates than richer countries. Since 1960, Japan, Italy, and France all have grown more rapidly than the United States and have narrowed the gap in per capita incomes.

Let's look at some evidence provided by two distinguished international economists, Maurice Obstfeld of the University of California, Berkeley, and Kenneth Rogoff of Harvard University. Figure 13.2 plots the average growth rate for 16 currently developed countries from 1870 to 1979 versus the level of per capita income in 1870. Each point represents a different country. Notice that the countries with the lowest initial per capita incomes are plotted higher on the graph. That is, they had higher growth rates than the countries with more income per capita. The downward-sloping line plotted through the points indicates that the countries with higher levels of per capita income in 1870 grew more slowly than countries with lower levels of per capita income. In other words, the tendency was for countries with lower levels of initial income to grow faster and catch up. The graph shows that among the currently developed countries—for example, the United States, France, and the United Kingdom—there was a tendency for convergence over the last century.

> • **convergence**
> The process by which poorer countries close the gap with richer countries in terms of real GDP per capita.

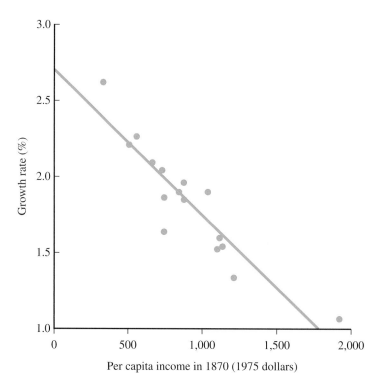

► **FIGURE 13.2**

**Growth Rates Versus Per Capita Income, 1870–1979**

Each point on the graph represents a different currently developed country. Notice that the same countries with the lowest per capita incomes in 1870 (shown along the horizontal axis) are plotted higher on the graph. In other words, the tendency was for countries with lower levels of initial income to grow faster.

*SOURCE: M. Obstfeld and K. Rogoff, Foundations of International Macroeconomics (Cambridge, MA: MIT Press, 1996), Table 7.1.*

Now let's compare the countries that are currently less developed to the advanced industrial countries, using the data in Table 13.1. Here, the picture is not so clear in recent times. While India grew at a faster rate than the United States, Pakistan grew only 1.11 percent per year and fell farther behind advanced economies. In Africa, GNP per capita fell in Zambia, while in Zimbabwe GNP per capita grew less than 1 percent. In general, economists who have studied the process of economic growth in detail find weak evidence that poorer countries are currently closing the gap in per capita income with richer countries.

Indeed, in the last 20 years there has been little convergence. Economist Stanley Fischer, Governor of the Bank of Israel and formerly with the IMF and the Massachusetts Institute of Technology, found that, on average, countries with higher GDP per capita in 1980 grew slightly faster from 1980 to 2000 as compared to countries with lower GDP per capita.[2] African countries, which were among the poorest countries, grew the slowest. However, there were some important exceptions: The two most populous countries, China and India, grew very rapidly. Because these countries contain approximately 35 percent of the world's population, the good news is that living conditions for many people around the globe have improved substantially in the last 20 years.

Many economists thought that as countries developed, inequality would increase among their populations. But recent research challenges this finding.

# 13.2 | CAPITAL DEEPENING

One of the most important mechanisms of economic growth economists have identified is increases in the amount of capital per worker due to capital deepening.

As capital—machines, equipment, and structures—is added to an economy, the workers in the economy will become more productive. In the simplest example, if workers have more machines at their disposal, they will be able to produce more output. A worker in the United States using sophisticated equipment in a

# APPLICATION 2

## GROWTH NEED NOT CAUSE INCREASED INEQUALITY

**APPLYING THE CONCEPTS #2:** Does economic growth necessarily cause more inequality?

For many years, economists believed, following the work of Nobel laureate Simon Kuznets, that as a country develops, inequality within a country followed an inverted "U" pattern—it initially increased as a country developed and then narrowed over time. However, recent research by economists Emmanuel Saez of Harvard and Thomas Piketty, a French economist, casts doubt that this phenomenon is solely the result of growth.

Piketty and Saez looked carefully at data in the United States over the twentieth century. Inequality—as measured by the income share of the top 10 percent of families—increased from 40 percent at the beginning of the 1920s to 45 percent through the end of the Great Depression, consistent with Kuznets's theory. But things changed during World War II. During that time, the share fell to 32 percent by 1944 and remained at that level until the early 1970s, at which time inequality began to again increase.

Piketty and Saez suggest that wage and price controls during World War II reduced differentials in wages and salaries and thereby reduced inequality. Moreover, even after the war these patterns persisted until the 1970s, because society perceived them to be fair. After the 1970s, salaries at the top of the income distribution increased sharply. (Think of the vast sums paid to some major league baseball players or corporate executives.) These findings, as well as related results from other countries, suggest that inequality does not naturally accompany economic development. Social norms and other factors, such as perceived fairness of compensation and the nature of the tax system, also play a role. Moreover, the U.S. experience suggests that these norms can change over time, even within the same country, regardless of growth rates. *Related to Exercise 1.10.*

SOURCE: Thomas Piketty and Emmanuel Saez, "Income Inequality in the United States, 1913–1998," *Quarterly Journal of Economics*, Vol. 118(1), 2003, pp. 1–39.

modern factory, for example, will be able to produce much more output per day than a worker in a developing country who must use less sophisticated equipment. The ability to produce additional output with the added capital will benefit workers. Firms, which own the capital, will find that workers are more productive and will compete with other firms to hire these workers. This competition among firms will raise the wages of workers to reflect their increased productivity. The final result will be that wages for workers will increase as capital per worker increases.

An economy is better off with an increase in the stock of capital. With additions to the stock of capital, workers will enjoy higher wages, and total GDP in the economy will increase. Workers are more productive because each worker has more capital at his or her disposal. But how does an economy increase its stock of capital per worker? The answer is with saving and investment, which we'll discuss next.

• **saving**
Income that is not consumed.

## Saving and Investment

Let's begin with the simplest case: an economy with a constant population, producing at full employment. This particular economy has no government or foreign sector. Output can be purchased only by consumers or by firms. In other words, output consists solely of consumption (C) and investment (I). At the same time, this output generates an amount of income that is equivalent to the amount of output. That is, output (Y) equals income. Any income that is not consumed we call **saving**.

In this economy, saving must equal investment. Here's why: By definition, consumption plus saving equals income:

$$C + S = Y$$

but at the same time income—which is equivalent to output—also equals consumption plus investment:

$$C + I = Y$$

Thus, saving must equal investment:

$$S = I$$

This means that whatever consumers decide to save goes directly into investment. Whatever income individuals do not spend is saving. In turn, those savings go directly into investment.

Next, we need to link the level of investment in the economy to the stock of capital in the economy. The stock of capital depends on two factors: investment and depreciation. The stock of capital increases with any gross investment spending but decreases with depreciation. Why does depreciation decrease the stock of capital? The answer is simple: As capital stock items such as buildings and equipment get older (depreciate), they wear out and become less productive. New investment is needed to replace the buildings and equipment that become obsolete.

Suppose, for example, the stock of capital at the beginning of the year is $10,000. During the year, if there were $1,000 in gross investment and $400 in depreciation, the capital stock at the end of the year would be $10,600 (= $10,000 + $1000 − $400).

It may be helpful to picture the stock of capital as being like a bathtub. The level of water in a bathtub (the stock of capital) depends on the flow of water into the bathtub through the input faucet (gross investment) minus the flow of water out of the bathtub down the drain (depreciation). As long as the flow in exceeds the flow out, the water level in the bathtub (the stock of capital) will increase.

Higher saving, which leads to higher gross investment, will therefore tend to increase the stock of capital available for production. As the stock of capital grows, however, there typically will be more depreciation, because there is more capital (building and equipment) to depreciate. It is the difference between gross investment and depreciation—*net investment*—that ultimately determines the change in the stock of capital for the economy, the level of real wages, and output. In our example, net investment is $1,000 − $400 = $600.

## How Do Population Growth, Government, and Trade Affect Capital Deepening?

So far, we've considered the simplest economy. Let's consider a more realistic economy that includes population growth, a government, and trade.

First, consider the effects of population growth: A larger labor force will allow the economy to produce more total output. However, with a fixed amount of capital and an increasing labor force, the amount of capital per worker will be less. With less capital per worker, output per worker will also tend to be less, because each worker has fewer machines to use. This is an illustration of the principle of diminishing returns.

# PRINCIPLE OF DIMINISHING RETURNS

Suppose that output is produced with two or more inputs and that we increase one input while holding the other inputs fixed. Beyond some point—called the *point of diminishing returns*—output will increase at a decreasing rate.

Consider India, with over a billion people and the world's second most populous country. Although India has a large labor force, the amount of capital per worker is low. With sharp diminishing returns to labor, per capita output in India is low, only $3,100 per person.

The government can affect the process of capital deepening in several ways through its policies of spending and taxation. Suppose the government taxed its citizens so that it could fight a war, pay its legislators higher salaries, or give foreign aid to needy countries. The higher taxes will reduce total income. If consumers save a fixed fraction of their income, total private savings (savings from the nongovernmental sector) will fall. In these cases, the government is not investing the funds it collects and putting those funds into capital formation. It is taxing the private sector to engage in consumption spending. This taxation drains the private sector of savings that would have been used for capital deepening.

Now suppose the government took all the extra tax revenues and invested them in valuable infrastructure, such as roads, buildings, and airports. These infrastructure investments add to the capital stock. If consumers were saving 20 percent of their incomes and the government collected a dollar in taxes from each taxpayer, private saving would fall by 20 cents per taxpayer, but government investment in the infrastructure would increase by a full $1 per taxpayer. In other words, the government "forces" consumers (by taxing them) to invest an additional 80 cents in infrastructure that they otherwise wouldn't have. The net result is an increase in total social saving (private saving plus government saving) of 80 cents per taxpayer.

Finally, the foreign sector can affect capital deepening. An economy can run a trade deficit and import investment goods, such as precision machine tools, to aid capital deepening. The United States, Canada, and Australia built their vast railroad systems in the nineteenth century by running *trade deficits*—selling fewer goods and services to the rest of the world than they were buying—and financing this gap by borrowing. This enabled them to purchase the large amount of capital needed to build their rail networks and grow at more rapid rates by deepening capital. Eventually, these economies had to pay back the funds that were borrowed from abroad by running *trade surpluses*—selling more goods and services to the rest of the world than they were buying from abroad. But because economic growth had increased GDP and wealth, the three countries were able to afford to pay back the borrowed funds. Therefore, this approach to financing deepening capital was a reasonable strategy for them to pursue.

Not all trade deficits promote capital deepening, however. Suppose a country runs a trade deficit because it wants to buy more consumer goods. The country would be borrowing from abroad, but there would be no additional capital deepening—just additional consumption spending. When the country is forced to pay back the funds, there will be no additional GDP to help foot the bill. In order to fund current consumption, the country will be poorer in the future.

## Limits to Capital Deepening

There are natural limits to growth through capital deepening. Capital is subject to diminishing returns just as labor is. With a given labor force, increases in capital will lead to increases in output, but at a diminishing rate. Eventually, growth through capital deepening will cease.

To more fully understand these limits, recall that the stock of capital increases only when there is positive net investment. Remember that net investment equals gross investment minus depreciation. Gross investment depends on the economy's saving rate. Depreciation depends on the total stock of capital that the economy has in place.

As the stock of capital increases, as we have explained, output increases but at a decreasing rate, due to diminishing returns. With a given saving rate, gross investment will also increase along with output, but at a decreasing rate. Depreciation, however, increases directly with the stock of capital. Eventually, the economy reaches a point where gross investment equals depreciation. In other words, just as much water is being drained from the bathtub as is flowing in. At this point, net investment becomes zero.

Therefore, there is a limit to growth through capital deepening, because even though a higher saving rate can increase the level of real GDP, eventually the process comes to a halt. However, it takes time—decades—for this point to be reached. Capital deepening can be an important source of economic growth for a long time.

# 13.3 | THE KEY ROLE OF TECHNOLOGICAL PROGRESS

The other mechanism affecting economic growth is technological progress. Economists use the term *technological progress* in a very specific way: It means that an economy operates more efficiently by producing more output without using any more inputs.

In practice, technological progress can take many forms. The invention of the lightbulb made it possible to read and work indoors at night, the invention of the thermometer assisted doctors and nurses in their diagnoses, and the invention of disposable diapers made life easier at home. All these examples—and you could provide many more—enable society to produce more output without more labor or more capital. With higher output per person, we enjoy a higher standard of living.

Technological progress can be thought of as the birth of new ideas. These new ideas enable us to rearrange our economic affairs and become more productive. Not all technological innovations are necessarily major scientific breakthroughs; some are much more basic. An employee of a soft-drink company who discovers a new and popular flavor for a soft drink is engaged in technological progress, just as scientists and engineers are. Even simple, commonsense ideas from workers or managers can help a business use its capital and labor more efficiently to deliver a better product to consumers at a lower price. For example, a store manager may decide that rearranging the layout of merchandise and location of cash registers helps customers find products and pay for them more quickly and easily. This change is also technological progress. As long as there are new ideas, inventions, and new ways of doing things, the economy can become more productive and per capita output can increase.

## How Do We Measure Technological Progress?

If someone asked you how much of the increase in your standard of living was due to technological progress, how would you answer? Robert Solow, a Nobel laureate in economics from the Massachusetts Institute of Technology, developed a method for measuring technological progress in an economy. As is usual with good ideas, his theory was simple.

Other economists had previously developed methods to measure how the total output in an economy—its real GDP—could be determined by the amount of inputs that were used in the economy, labor and capital, given the current state of technology. Solow recognized that real GDP could increase in an economy for two basic reasons. First, there could be increases in the total amount of labor or capital in the economy. Second, technology could improve, allowing the economy to produce more output with the same levels of inputs.

Solow noted that over any period, we can observe increases in capital, labor, and output. Using these, we can measure technological progress indirectly. We first ask how much of the change in output can be explained by contributions from the changes in the amount of capital and labor that are used. Whatever growth we cannot explain by increases in capital and labor must therefore be caused by increases in technological progress. The method Solow developed to measure the contributions to economic growth from capital, labor, and technological progress is called **growth accounting.**

Table 13.2 illustrates the relative contributions of these growth sources for the U.S. economy from 1929 to 1982 using growth accounting, based on a classic study by the economist Edward Denison. During this period, total output grew at a rate of nearly 3 percent. Because capital and labor growth are measured at 0.56 and 1.34 percent, respectively, the remaining portion of output growth, 1.02 percent, must be due to technological progress. That means that approximately 35 percent of output growth came directly from technological progress.

Other recent estimates give a similar picture of the contribution of technological progress to economic growth. For example, the Bureau of Labor Statistics estimates that between 1987 and 2004 technological progress accounted for 1.4 percentage points of economic growth in the private nonfarm business sector, similar to Denison's estimates.

## Using Growth Accounting

Growth accounting is a useful tool for understanding different aspects of economic growth. Here are three applications of how economists use growth accounting. The first compares growth in Hong Kong and Singapore, the second explores the slowdown in U.S. labor productivity, and the third looks at how the Internet and information technology have affected the U.S. GDP.

| Table 13.2 | SOURCES OF REAL GDP GROWTH, 1929–1982 (AVERAGE ANNUAL PERCENTAGE RATES) |
| --- | --- |
| Growth due to capital growth | 0.56% |
| Growth due to labor growth | 1.34 |
| + technological progress | 1.02 |
| Total output growth | 2.92 |

*SOURCE:* Edward F. Denison, *Trends in Economic Growth 1929–82* (Washington, D.C.: The Brookings Institution, 1985).

- **growth accounting**
  A method to determine the contribution to economic growth from increased capital, labor, and technological progress.

3

# APPLICATION

## HOW GROWTH IN SINGAPORE AND HONG KONG DIFFERED

APPLYING THE CONCEPTS #3: How can we use economic analysis to understand the sources of growth in different countries?

Singapore and Hong Kong have both had phenomenal post–World War II economic growth. From 1980 to 1985, each grew at a rate of approximately 6 percent a year. But a closer examination by Alwyn Young of the University of Chicago revealed that the sources of growth in each country were very different. In Singapore, nearly all the growth was accounted for by increases in labor and capital. Investment levels were extremely high in Singapore, reaching 43 percent as a share of GDP in 1983.

Hong Kong had a much lower investment rate than Singapore—approximately a 20 percent share of GDP—and technological progress made an important contribution. This meant that the residents of Hong Kong could enjoy the same level of GDP as Singapore but consume, not save, a higher fraction of GDP. Residents of Hong Kong were enjoying higher consumption than residents of Singapore were, despite the similarity in growth rates.

The difference in the sources of economic growth between Singapore and Hong Kong may also have important implications for future growth. As we explained a moment ago, there are natural limits to growth through capital deepening. Singapore increased its GDP by increasing its labor inputs and stock of capital. Singapore realized it would eventually find it difficult to keep increasing inputs to production. Economic leaders became concerned that unless they managed to increase their rate of technological progress, their long-term growth prospects would be poor.

In Hong Kong, there is currently a different concern. Technological progress has been the driving force for growth in Hong Kong. Now that it has become part of China, Hong Kong's residents hope its economy will remain free and open to sustain the system that produced technological innovation. *Related to Exercise 3.6.*

SOURCE: Alwyn Young, "A Tale of Two Cities: Factor Accumulation and Technical Change in Hong Kong and Singapore," in *NBER Macroeconomic Annual 1992*, edited by Olivier Blanchard and Stanley Fischer (Cambridge, MA: MIT Press, 1992), pp. 1–53.

# 4

# APPLICATION

## WORLDWIDE FACTORS SLOWED U.S. PRODUCTIVITY GROWTH

**APPLYING THE CONCEPTS #4:** Why did labor productivity in the United States fall sharply during the 1970s and 1980s?

• **labor productivity**
Output produced per hour of work.

One of the common statistics reported about the U.S. economy is **labor productivity**. Defined as output per hour of work, labor productivity is a simple measure of how much a typical worker can produce given the amount of capital in the economy and the state of technological progress. Since 1973, the growth of labor productivity has slowed in the United States and other countries in the world. Table 13.3 shows U.S. productivity growth for different periods since 1959.

The table shows that productivity growth was extremely high during the 1960s. It slowed a bit in the late 1960s, and then slowed dramatically after the oil shocks in the 1970s. In recent years, productivity growth has increased, reaching 2.7 percent from 1994 to 2004. Nonetheless, the rate of productivity growth was very low from the late 1960s to the mid-1990s.

The slowdown in productivity growth has also meant slower growth in real wages and in GDP in the United States since 1973. Figure 13.3 plots real hourly earnings for U.S. workers. The figure shows that real hourly earnings have fallen since 1973. Total compensation, which includes employee benefits such as health insurance, did continue to rise through the 1980s and 1990s as employees received lower wages but higher benefits. However, the rate of growth of total compensation was less than the growth of real hourly earnings in the pre-1973 period.

The decrease in the growth of labor productivity was the primary factor behind this pattern of real wages, because wages can rise with a growing labor force only if output per worker continues to increase. What can explain this decrease in the growth rate? Economists are not short of possible answers. Among the factors, they say, are declines in the education and skills of the workforce; lower levels of investment, and thus a lower level of capital; less spending on infrastructure, such as highways and bridges; increased spending on pollution-control equipment that improves the envi-

| Table 13.3 | U.S. ANNUAL PRODUCTIVITY GROWTH, 1959–2004 |
| --- | --- |

| Years | Annual Productivity Growth Rate |
| --- | --- |
| 1959–1968 | 3.5% |
| 1968–1973 | 2.5 |
| 1973–1980 | 1.2 |
| 1980–1986 | 2.1 |
| 1986–1994 | 1.4 |
| 1994–2004 | 2.7 |

SOURCES: *Economic Report of the President* (Washington, D.C.: U.S. Government Printing Office, 2006) and Bureau of Labor Statistics, Department of Labor, 2006.

▶ **FIGURE 13.3**
**Real Hourly Earnings and Total Compensation for U.S. Employees, 1964–2005**
Real hourly earnings have fallen since 1973. Total compensation, which includes employee benefits, continued to rise through the 1980s and 1990s because even though employees' wages were lower, they received higher benefits.

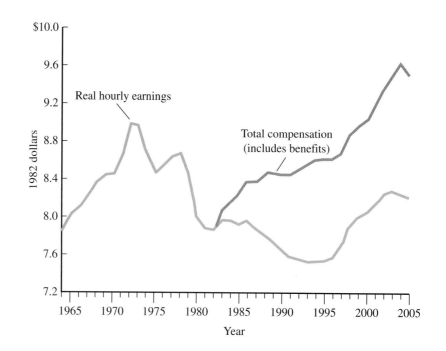

ronment but does not lead to increased output; and the belief that managers are more concerned with producing short-term profits than long-term profits, among lots of other economic and sociological factors. Also, the U.S. economy has become more service oriented during this period, and productivity improvements in services are hard to measure.

Growth accounting has been used to narrow the range of plausible explanations. Using growth accounting methods, economists typically find that the slowdown in labor productivity, in the United States and abroad, cannot be explained by reduced rates of capital deepening. Nor can they be explained by changes in the quality or experience of the labor force. Either a slowdown in technological progress or other factors that are not directly included in the analysis, such as higher worldwide energy prices, must be responsible for the slowdown. Moreover, because the slowdown has been worldwide, it's possible that factors that affect all countries (such as higher energy prices) are responsible rather than factors specific to a single country. Dale Jorgenson, a Harvard economist, has conducted extensive research attempting to link higher energy prices to the slowdown in productivity growth. Not all economists accept this view, however, and so the productivity slowdown remains a bit of a mystery despite the use of growth accounting methods to try to explain it. *Related to Exercise 3.7.*

SOURCE: Dale Jorgenson and C. Doughtery, "International Comparisons of the Sources of Economic Growth," *American Economic Review*, Vol. 86, No. 2, May 1996, pp. 25–29.

# 13.4 | WHAT CAUSES TECHNOLOGICAL PROGRESS?

Because technological progress is an important source of growth, we want to know how it occurs and what government policies can do to promote it. Economists have identified a variety of factors that may influence the pace of technological progress in an economy.

## Research and Development Funding

One way for a country to induce more technological progress in an economy is to pay for it. If the government or large firms employ workers and scientists to advance the frontiers of knowledge in basic sciences, their work can lead to technological progress in the long run. Figure 13.4 presents data on the spending on research and development as a percent of GDP for seven major countries for 1999. The United

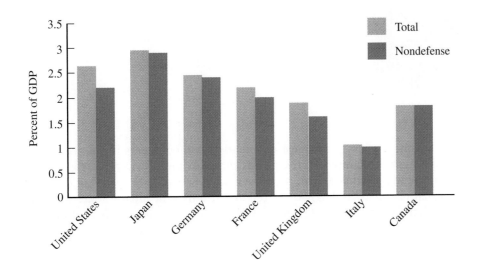

◄ **FIGURE 13.4**
**Research and Development as a Percent of GDP, 1999**
The United States spends more total money than any other country on research and development. However, when the spending is measured as a percentage of each nation's GDP, Japan spends more. A big part of U.S. spending on research and development is in defense-related areas.
*SOURCE: National* Science Foundation, *National Patterns of R&D Resources, 2002, Washington, D.C.*

# APPLICATION

## THE INTERNET AND INFORMATION TECHNOLOGY RAISED PRODUCTIVITY THROUGHOUT THE ECONOMY

APPLYING THE CONCEPTS #5: How did the emergence of the Internet affect economic growth in the United States?

As Table 13.3 shows, U.S. productivity growth did climb in the last half of the 1990s. "New economy" proponents believe the computer and Internet revolution are responsible for the increase in productivity growth. Skeptics wonder, however, whether this increase in productivity growth is truly permanent or just temporary. Higher investment in computer technology began in the mid-1980s, but until recently there was little sign of increased productivity growth. Had the investment in information technology finally paid off?

Robert J. Gordon of Northwestern University used growth accounting methods to shed light on this issue. After making adjustments for the low unemployment rate and high GDP growth rate in the late 1990s, he found that there had been increases in technological progress. In earlier work, he found that these increases were largely confined to the durable goods manufacturing industry, including the production of computers itself. Because the increase in technological progress was confined to a relatively small portion of the economy, Gordon was originally skeptical that we were now operating in a "new economy" with permanently higher productivity growth. However, in subsequent studies he found that productivity growth had spread to other sectors of the economy, such as retail sales and financial institutions.

Other economists as well, also using growth accounting methods, found that technological progress was more widespread throughout the economy, suggesting that the increase was likely to be permanent. Productivity growth continued to be rapid, even during the recessionary period at the beginning of this century, when most economists believed it would slow down. One possible explanation is that it took a substantial period of time before businesses began to harness the use of modern computer technology and the Internet. If productivity growth does continue at its current high rate, we will enjoy more rapid economic growth in the United States and across the globe. *Related to Exercise 3.8.*

SOURCE: Robert J. Gordon, "Exploding Productivity Growth: Contexts, Causes, Implications," Brookings Papers on Economic Activity, 2003(2), pp. 207–298.

States has the highest percentage of scientists and engineers in the world. However, although the United States spends the most money overall, as a percent of GDP, it spends less than Japan. Moreover, a big part of U.S. spending on research and development is in defense-related areas, unlike in Japan. Some economists believe that defense-related research and development is less likely to lead to long-run technological change than nondefense spending; however, many important technological developments, including the Internet, partly resulted from military-sponsored research and development.

## Monopolies That Spur Innovation

The radical notion that monopolies spur innovation was put forth by economist Joseph Schumpeter. In his view, a firm will try to innovate—that is, come up with new products and more efficient ways to produce existing products—only if it reaps a reward. The reward a firm seeks is high profit from its innovations. A high profit can be obtained only if the firm is the sole seller, or monopolist, for the product. Other firms will try to break the firm's monopoly through more innovation, a process Schumpeter called **creative destruction**. Schumpeter believed that by allowing firms to compete to become monopolies, society benefits from increased innovation.

• **creative destruction**
The view that a firm will try to come up with new products and more efficient ways to produce products to earn monopoly profits.

Governments do allow temporary monopolies for new ideas by issuing patents. A *patent* allows the inventor of a product to have a monopoly until the term of the patent expires, which in the United States is now 20 years. With a patent, we tolerate some monopoly power (the power to raise prices that comes with limited competition) in the hope of spurring innovation.

A related idea to patents, which is becoming increasingly important, is the need to protect intellectual property rights. Information technology has made possible the free flow of products and ideas around the world. Publishers of both books and computer software face problems of unauthorized copying, particularly in some developing countries. While the residents of those countries clearly benefit from inexpensive copied books or software, the producers of the books or software in the developed countries will face reduced incentives to enter the market. Even in the United States, pirated music and movies pose a threat to the viability of the entertainment industry. Large and profitable firms may continue to produce despite unauthorized copying, but other firms may be discouraged. The United States has put piracy and unauthorized reproduction among its top agenda items in recent trade talks with several countries.

## The Scale of the Market

Adam Smith stressed that the size of a market was important for economic development. In larger markets, firms have more incentives to come up with new products and new methods of production. Just as Schumpeter suggested, the lure of profits guides the activities of firms, and larger markets provide firms the opportunity to make larger profits. This supplies another rationale for free trade. With free trade, markets are larger, and there is more incentive to engage in technological progress.

## Induced Innovations

Some economists have emphasized that innovations come about through inventive activity designed specifically to reduce costs. This is known as *induced innovation.* For example, during the nineteenth century in the United States, the largest single cost in agriculture was wages. Ingenious farmers and inventors came up with many different machines and methods to cut back on the amount of labor required.

## Education, Human Capital, and the Accumulation of Knowledge

Education can contribute to economic growth in two ways. First, the increased knowledge and skills of people complement our current investments in physical capital. Second, education can enable the workforce in an economy to use its skills to develop new ideas or to copy ideas or import them from abroad. Consider a developing country today. In principle, it has at its disposal the vast accumulated knowledge of the developed economies. But this probably requires a skilled workforce—one reason why many developing countries send their best students to educational institutions in developed countries.

Increasing knowledge and skills are part of human capital—an investment in human beings. Human capital is as important, even more important, than physical capital. Many economists, including Nobel laureate Gary Becker of the University of Chicago, have studied this in detail.

A classic example of human capital is the investment a student makes to attend college. The costs of attending college consist of the direct out-of-pocket costs (tuition and fees) plus the opportunity costs of forgone earnings. The benefits of attending college are the higher wages and more interesting jobs offered to college graduates as compared to high-school graduates. Individuals decide to attend college because these benefits exceed the costs, and it is a rational economic decision. A similar calculation faces a newly graduated doctor who must decide whether to pursue a specialty. Will the forgone earnings of a general physician (which are quite substantial) be worth the time spent learning a specialty that will eventually result in extra income? Investments in health and nutrition can be analyzed within the same framework. The benefits of regular exercise and watching your weight are a healthier lifestyle and energy level than people who do neither.

Human capital theory has two implications for understanding economic growth. First, not all labor is equal. When economists measure the labor input in a country, they must adjust for differing levels of education. These levels of education reflect past investments in education and skills; individuals with higher educational levels will, on average, be more productive. Second, health and fitness also affect productivity. In developing countries, economists have found a strong correlation between the height of individuals (reflecting their health) and the wages that they can earn in the farming sector. At the same time, increases in income through economic growth have led to sharp increases in height and weight.

Human capital theory can also serve as a basis for important public policy decisions. Should a developing country invest in capital (either public or private) or in education? The poorest developing countries lack good sanitation systems, effective transportation systems, and capital investment for agriculture and industry. However, the best use of investment funds may not be for bridges, sewer systems, and roads, but for human capital and education. Studies demonstrate that the returns from investing in education are extremely high in developing countries. The gains from elementary and secondary education, in particular, often exceed the gains from more conventional investments. In developing countries, people having an extra year in school can often raise their wages by 15 to 20 percent a year.

## New Growth Theory

For many years, economists who studied technological progress typically did so independently of economists who studied models of economic growth. But starting in the mid-1980s, several economists, including Nobel laureate Robert E. Lucas of the University of Chicago and Paul Romer, now of Stanford University, began to develop models of growth that contained technological progress as essential features. Their work helped to initiate what is known as **new growth theory**, which accounts for technological progress within a model of economic growth.

In this field, economists study, for example, how incentives for research and development, new product development, or international trade interact with the accumulation of physical capital. New growth theory enables economists to address policy issues, such as whether subsidies for research and development are socially justified and whether policies that place fewer taxes on income earned from investment will spur economic growth or increase economic welfare. Current research in economic growth now takes place within a broad framework that includes explanations of technological progress. As an example, new growth theory suggests that investment in comprehensive education in a developing country will lead to permanent increases in the rate of technological progress as the workforce will be better able to incorporate new ideas and technologies into the workplace.

• **new growth theory**
Modern theories of growth that try to explain the origins of technological progress.

# APPLICATION 6

## A VIRTUOUS CIRCLE: GDP AND HEALTH

**APPLYING THE CONCEPTS #6:** How are economic growth and health related to one another?

As you may have seen in a museum, men and women have grown taller and heavier in the last 300 years. As an example, an average American male adult today stands at approximately 5 feet 10 inches tall, which is nearly 4.5 inches taller than the typical Englishman in the late eighteenth century. Body weights are also substantially higher today. According to Nobel laureate Robert Fogel of the University of Chicago, the average weight of English males in their thirties was about 134 pounds in 1790—20 percent below today's average. A typical Frenchman in his thirties at that time weighed only 110 pounds!

Fogel has argued that these lower weights and heights were due to inadequate food supplies and chronic malnutrition. Not only did lower food supplies lead to smaller physical stature, they also led to a higher incidence of chronic disease. Fogel estimated that the chronic malnutrition caused by limited food supplies at those times limited labor productivity. In France, 20 percent of the labor force lacked enough physical energy to put in more than three hours of light work a day. A high percentage of workers in the society were too frail and ill to contribute much to national output.

Economic growth produced a "virtuous" circle. It increased food supplies, enabling workers to become more productive and increase GDP even more.
*Related to Exercise 4.8.*

SOURCE: Robert William Fogel, *The Escape from Hunger and Premature Death, 1700-2100: Europe, America, and the Third World* (New York: Cambridge University Press, 2004).

Some researchers also suggest the type of education might also matter for technological innovation. Phillipe Aghion of Harvard University and Peter Howitt of Brown University make the case that when a country is far behind the world's technological frontier, it is best for that country to invest in relatively basic education so that the workforce can essentially copy the changes that are occurring in the more advanced economies. But once an economy reaches the world's technological frontier, investment in the most advanced higher education might be most advantageous.[3]

All growth theory today is "new growth theory."

## 13.5 | A KEY GOVERNMENTAL ROLE: PROVIDING THE CORRECT INCENTIVES AND PROPERTY RIGHTS

Governments play a critical role in a market economy. Governments must enforce the rules of the market economy, using its police powers to ensure that contracts are upheld, individual property rights are enforced, and firms can enter safely into economic transactions. Although we may take these features of our economy for granted, not all countries enjoy the benefits of clear enforcement of property rights.

What is the connection between property rights and economic growth? Without clear property rights, there are no proper incentives to invest in the future—the essence of economic growth. Suppose, for example, that you lived on land that needed costly improvements to be made valuable. You might be willing to make the investment in these improvements if you were sure that you would gain the economic benefits from making them. But suppose there was a risk that someone else would reap the benefits—in that case, you would not have incentive to invest.

The absence of clear property rights, unfortunately, is common in many developing countries throughout the world. As many economists have argued, the absence of clear property rights has severely impeded the growth of these economies.

Governments also have a broader role in designing the institutions in a society in which individuals and firms work, save, and invest. Economists have increasingly recognized the importance of these institutions in determining economic growth. For example, as we discussed earlier, the residents of Hong Kong link their rapid economic growth to free and open institutions that provide the right incentives for technological innovations.

# APPLICATION

## LACK OF PROPERTY RIGHTS HINDERS GROWTH IN PERU

**APPLYING THE CONCEPTS #7:** Why are clear property rights important for economic growth in developing countries?

On the hills surrounding Lima, Peru, and many other South American cities, large numbers of residents live in urban slums, many having taken over these lands through "urban invasions." Many families have resided in these dwellings for a long time, and most have basic water, sewage, and electricity. But what these residents don't have is clear titles to their properties.

Hernando DeSoto, a Peruvian economist and author of *The Mystery of Capital,* has studied the consequences of "informal ownership" in detail. He argues that throughout the developing world, property is often not held with clear titles. Without clear evidence of ownership, these owners are not willing to make long-term investments to improve their lives. But there are other important consequences as well.

Economists recognize that strong credit systems—the ability to borrow and lend easily—are critical to the health of developing economies. But without clear title, property cannot be used as collateral (or security) for loans. As a consequence, the poor may in fact be living on very valuable land, but be unable to borrow against that land to start a new business. Also, the types of investments that are made will depend on the availability of credit. Desoto observed that producing palm oil in Peru is very profitable, but it takes time and depends upon the ability to borrow funds. Production of coca paste—an ingredient to cocaine—does not take as much time and does not depend on finance. It is also a plague on the developed world. Switching farmers away from production of coca paste to palm oil also requires improvements in finance, which are very difficult without clear property rights. *Related to Exercise 5.7.*

SOURCE: Hernando DeSoto, *The Mystery of Capital: Why Capitalism Triumphs in the West and Fails Everywhere Else* (New York: Basic Books, 2000).

But, for many countries, growth has been more elusive. For many years, international organizations such as the World Bank—a consortium of countries created to promote development—have tried a variety of diverse methods to assist developing countries. These have included increases in foreign aid, infusions of new machinery, promotion of universal education, and efforts to stem population growth. Despite these efforts, some areas of the world, such as Sub-Saharan Africa, have failed to grow at all.

William Easterly, a former World Bank economist, believes that the World Bank and other international organizations have failed to take into account one of the basic laws of economics: Individuals and firms respond to incentives. According to Easterly, governments in developing countries have failed to provide the proper economic environment that would motivate individuals and firms to take actions that promote economic development.[4] As an example, providing free schooling is not enough—individuals need to know that their investments in education will pay off in the future in terms of higher incomes or better jobs. Without the prospect that education will lead to an improvement in their lives, individuals will not make the effort to obtain an education.

What else can go wrong? Governments in developing countries often adopt policies that effectively tax exports, pursue policies that lead to rampant inflation, and enforce laws that inhibit the growth of the banking and financial sectors. The results are predictable: fewer exports, an uncertain financial environment, and reduced saving and investment. All of these outcomes can cripple an economy's growth prospects. Sometimes these actions are simply based on bad economic advice. Other times, racial or ethnic groups in polarized societies use the economic system to take advantage of their rivals.

What can be done? In Easterly's view, the World Bank and other international organizations need to stop searching for the magic bullet for development. Instead, they should hold governments responsible for creating the proper economic environment. With the right incentives, Easterly believes that individuals and firms in developing countries will take actions that promote economic growth.

# SUMMARY

In this chapter, we explored the mechanisms of economic growth. Although economists do not have a complete understanding of what leads to growth, they regard increases in capital per worker, technological progress, human capital, and governmental institutions as key factors. Here are the main points to remember:

1 *Per capita GDP* varies greatly throughout the world. There is debate about whether poorer countries in the world are converging in per capita incomes to richer countries.

2 Economies grow through two basic mechanisms: *capital deepening* and *technological progress*. Capital deepening is an increase in capital per worker. Technological progress is an increase in output with no additional increases in inputs.

3 Ongoing technological progress will lead to sustained economic growth.

4 Various theories try to explain the origins of technological progress and determine how we can promote it. They include spending on research and development, *creative destruction*, the scale of the market, induced inventions, and education and the accumulation of knowledge, including investments in human capital.

5 Governments can play a key role in designing institutions that promote economic growth, including providing secure property rights.

# KEY TERMS

capital deepening, p. 326

convergence, p. 329

creative destruction, p. 339

growth accounting, p. 335

growth rate, p. 326

human capital, p. 326

labor productivity, p. 336

new growth theory, p. 340

real GDP per capita, p. 326

rule of 70, p. 327

saving, p. 332

technological progress, p. 326

## 13.1 | Economic Growth Rates

**1.1** To gauge living standards across countries with populations of different sizes, economists use _____.

**1.2** In poor countries, the relative prices for nontraded goods (such as household services) to traded goods (such as jewelry) are _____ than in rich countries.

**1.3** Economists who have studied economic growth find only weak evidence for convergence. _____ (True/False)

**1.4** At a 2 percent annual growth rate in GDP per capita, it will take _____ years for GDP per capita to double.

**1.5** **Future Generations.** Some economists say that economic growth involves a trade-off between current generations and future generations. If a current generation raises its saving rate, what does it sacrifice? What will be gained for future generations?

**1.6** **Will the Poorer Country Catch Up?** Suppose one country has a GDP that is one-eighth the GDP of its richer neighbor. But the poorer country grows at 10 percent a year, while the richer country grows at 2 percent a year. In 35 years, which country will have a higher GDP? (*Hint*: Use the rule of 70.)

**1.7** **How Long to Quadruple GDP?** If a country's GDP grows at 3 percent per year, how many years will it take for GDP to increase by a factor of four?

**1.8** **Growth in Per Capita GDP.** The growth rate of real GDP per capita equals the growth rate of real GDP minus the growth rate of the population. If the growth rate of the population is 1 percent per year, how fast must real GDP grow for real GDP per capita to double in 14 years?

**1.9** **Economic Growth and Child Labor.** Why do you think child labor tends to disappear as incomes in developing countries rise? (Related to Application 1 on page 329.)

**1.10** **Economic Growth and Inequality.** Does economic growth automatically lead to increased inequality? Discuss. (Related to Application 2 on page 331.)

**1.11** **Comparing Economic Performance Using International GDP Data.** The Web site for the National Bureau of Economic Research (www.nber.org) contains links to online data, including the Penn World Tables. Using these links, compare the relative growth performance for real GDP per capita of France and Japan from 1950 to 2000. Do the data support the theory of convergence?

## 13.2 | Capital Deepening

**2.1** In an economy with no government sector or foreign sector, saving must equal investment because
**a.** total demand is equal to consumption and investment.
**b.** total income is equal to consumption and saving.
**c.** total income is equal to total demand.
**d.** All of the above.
**e.** None of the above.

**2.2** If everything else is held equal, an increase in the size of the population will _____ total output and _____ per capita output.

**2.3** If the private sector saves 10 percent of its income and the government raises taxes by $200 to finance public investments, total investment—private and public investment—will increase by _____.

**2.4** If a country runs a trade deficit to finance increased current consumption, it will have to reduce consumption in the future to pay back its borrowings. _____ (True/False)

**2.5** **Policies That Promote Capital Deepening.** Which of the following will promote economic growth through capital deepening?
**a.** Higher taxes used to finance universal health care
**b.** Increased imports to purchase new VCRs for consumers
**c.** Increased imports to purchase supercomputers for industry

**2.6** **Limits to Capital Deepening.** Even with a high saving rate, there is a natural limit to capital deepening. Why is there a limit?

**2.7** **Government Spending, Taxes, and Investment.** Suppose a government places a 10 percent tax on incomes and spends half the money from taxes on investment and half on a public consumption goods, such as military parades. Individuals save 20 percent of their income and consume the rest. Does total investment (public and private) increase or decrease in this case?

**2.8** **Trade Deficits and Capital Deepening.** The United States ran large trade deficits during the 1980s and 1990s. How would you determine whether these trade deficits led to increased or decreased capital deepening?

## 13.3 | The Key Role of Technological Progress

**3.1** Robert Solow added _____ to the conventional production function to account for technological change.

**3.2** Once we account for changes in the labor force, _____ is the next biggest source of the growth of GDP in the United States.

**3.3** Hong Kong relied more on capital deepening than Singapore for economic growth. _____ (True/False)

**3.4** According to growth accounting studies, which of the following is a possible reason for the "productivity slowdown" starting in 1973?
a. Reduced rates of capital deepening
b. Changes in the quality or experience of the labor force
c. A slowdown in technological progress or other factors
d. All of the above are possible factors according to growth accounting studies

**3.5** **Measuring Technological Progress in the Health-Care Industry.** Describe how you would measure technological progress in the health-care sector of the economy. How would you account for changes in the quality of health care over time in your analysis?

**3.6** **Economic Growth in Singapore.** Why were some Singapore economists concerned when they learned that a very large fraction of their economic growth was accounted for by capital deepening and not technological progress? (Related to Application 3 on page 335.)

**3.7** **Energy Prices and the Productivity Slowdown.** If increasing energy prices caused the worldwide productivity slowdown beginning in the 1970s, why did increases in energy prices in the first decade of early 2000 apparently not cause a similar slowdown? (Related to Application 4 on page 336.)

**3.8** **Information Technology Spillovers and Economic Growth.** Why would it matter if the productivity gains associated with information technology spill over into other sectors of the economy besides information technology itself? Give a few examples of changes in information technology improving productivity in other sectors of the economy. (Related to Application 5 on page 338.)

**3.9** **Health Insurance, Wages, and Compensation.** In recent years, total compensation of employees—including benefits—has grown, but wages, not including benefits, have not. Explain why this may have occurred, taking into account that many employers provide health insurance to their employees and health-care costs have grown more rapidly than GDP. Is health insurance "free" to employees?

# 13.4 | What Causes Technological Progress?

**4.1** Who invented the theory of creative destruction?
a. Joseph Schumpeter
b. Milton Friedman
c. Robert Gordon
d. John Maynard Keynes

**4.2** Investment in human capital includes purchases of computers used by professors. _____ (True/False)

**4.3** Which of the following may influence technological progress?
a. The scale of the market
b. Monopolies
c. Research and development spending
d. All of the above

**4.4** A worldwide patent and copyright system would _____ the incentive to be innovative.

**4.5** **Cutting the Length of Patents?** Suppose that a group of consumer activists claims that drug companies earn excessive profits because of the patents they have on drugs. The activists advocate cutting the length of time that a drug company can hold a patent to five years. They argue that this will lead to lower prices for drugs because competitors will enter the market after the five-year period. Do you see any drawbacks to this proposal?

**4.6** **Expansion of Free Trade and Technological Innovation.** Explain why the expansion of markets from free trade can lead to increased technological innovation.

**4.7** **How Do We Measure Technological Progress?** If we cannot measure every invention or new idea, how can we possibly measure the contribution to growth of technological progress?

**4.8** **Height and Weight During Rapid Industrialization.** Economic historians have found that the average height of individuals in both the United States and the United Kingdom fell during the mid–nineteenth century before rising again. This was a period of rapid industrialization as well as migration into urban areas. What factors do you think might account for this fall in height and how would it affect your evaluation of economic welfare during the period? (Related to Application 6 on page 341.)

**4.9** **Human Capital Theory and the Age of Law Students.** Most law students tend to be in their twenties and thirties, rather than in their forties. Explain this phenomenon, using the idea of investment in human capital.

# 13.5 | A Key Governmental Role: Providing the Correct Incentives and Property Rights

**5.1** Clear property rights reduce growth in an economy because producers are not able to freely use innovations. _____ (True/False)

**5.2** Which of the following methods has the World Bank *not* tried to assist developing countries?
a. Increases in foreign aid
b. Infusions of new machinery

**c.** Promotion of universal education

**d.** Promotion of population growth

**5.3** The return from education in developing countries is often higher than in developed countries. _____ (True/False)

**5.4** New growth theory suggests that investment in comprehensive education in a developing country will lead to permanent increases in the rate of technological progress. _____ (True/False)

**5.5** **Researching Growth in Africa.** Using the Web site for the World Bank (www.worldbank.org) and other sources, describe the prospects and barriers for economic growth in Africa.

**5.6** **The "Brain Drain" and Incentives for Education.** Some economists are concerned about the "brain drain," the phenomenon in which highly educated workers leave developing countries to work in developed countries. Other economists have argued that "brain drain" could create incentives for others in the country to secure increased education and many of the newly educated might not emigrate. Explain why the "brain drain" could lead to increased education among the remaining residents. How would you test this theory?

**5.7** **Secure Property Rights and Work Outside the Home.** With secure land titles, parents can work outside the home (rather than guarding their property) and earn higher incomes. Explain why this might reduce child labor. (Related to Application 7 on page 342.)

# NOTES

1. Stanley Lebergott, *The Americans* (New York: W.W. Norton, 1984), pp. 65–68.

2. Stanley Fischer, "Globalization and Its Challenges," *American Economic Review Papers and Proceedings*, vol. 93, no. 2, May 2003, pp. 1–32.

3. Phillipe Aghion an Peter Howitt, "Appropiate Growth Theory: A Unifying Framework," December 2005, available at http://www.economics.harvard.edu/faculty/aghion/papers.html. Accessed February, 2006.

4. William Easterly, *The Elusive Quest for Growth: Economists' Adventures and Misadventures in the Tropics* (Cambridge, MA: MIT Press, 2002).

# 14
# Aggregate Demand and Aggregate Supply

As we explained in previous chapters, recessions occur when output fails to grow and unemployment rises. But *why* do recessions occur?

In a sense, recessions are massive failures in economic coordination. For example, during the Great Depression in the 1930s, nearly one-fourth of the U.S. labor force was unemployed. Unemployed workers could not afford to buy goods and services. Factories that manufactured those goods and services had to be shut down because there was little or no demand. As these factories closed, even more

1  What does the behavior of prices in retail catalogs demonstrate about how quickly prices adjust in the U.S. economy?
      *Price Stickiness in Retail Catalogs*

2  How can changes in demand cause a recession? In particular, what factors do economists think caused the 2001 recession?
      *Business Investment, Net Exports, and the 2001 Recession*

3  Do changes in oil prices always hurt the U.S. economy?
      *How the U.S. Economy Has Coped with Oil Price Fluctuations*

workers became unemployed, fueling additional factory shutdowns. This vicious cycle caused the U.S. economy to spiral downward. Similar failures in coordination were happening throughout the world. The worldwide depression continued through the 1930s. How could this destructive chain of events have been halted?

This failure of coordination is not just an historical phenomenon. In 2001, the economy also entered a downturn—although not nearly as severe as the Great Depression. Business activity slowed and many workers lost their jobs. What was the cause of this most recent slow-down of economic activity?

conomies do not always operate at full employment, nor do they always grow smoothly. At times, real GDP grows below its potential or falls steeply, as it did in the Great Depression. Recessions and excess unemployment occur when real GDP falls. At other times, GDP grows too rapidly, and unemployment falls below its natural rate.

"Too slow" or "too fast" real GDP growth are examples of *economic fluctuations*— movements of GDP away from potential output. We now turn our attention to understanding these economic fluctuations, which are also called *business cycles*.

During the Great Depression, there was a failure in coordination. Factories would have produced more output and hired more workers if there had been more demand for their products. In his 1936 book, *The General Theory of Employment, Interest, and Money*, British economist John Maynard Keynes explained that insufficient demand for goods and services was a key problem of the Great Depression. Following Keynes's work, economists began to distinguish between real GDP in the long run, when prices have time to fully adjust to changes in demand, and real GDP in the short run, when prices don't yet have time to fully adjust to changes in demand. During the short run, economic coordination problems are most pronounced. In the long run, however, economists believe the economy will return to full employment, although economic policy may assist it in getting there more quickly.

## 14.1 | STICKY PRICES AND THEIR MACROECONOMIC CONSEQUENCES

Why do recessions occur? One possibility is that large shocks sometimes hit the economy. For example, a developing country depending on agriculture can suffer a loss of its cash crop if there is a prolonged drought. Sharp increases in oil prices can also hurt modern economies that use oil in production and, of course, wars can devastate economies. It is even possible for a series of smaller shocks to have an adverse cumulative effect on an economy.

Led by Keynes, many economists have focused attention on economic coordination problems. Normally, the price system efficiently coordinates what goes on in an economy—even in a complex economy. The price system provides signals to firms as to who buys what, how much to produce, what resources to use, and from whom to buy. For example, if consumers decide to buy fresh fruit rather than chocolate, the price of fresh fruit will rise and the price of chocolate will fall. More fresh fruit and less chocolate will be produced on the basis of these price signals. On a day-to-day basis, the price system works silently in the background, matching the desires of consumers with the output from producers.

But the price system does not always work instantaneously. If prices are slow to adjust, then the proper signals are not given quickly enough to producers and consumers to bring them together. Demands and supplies will not be brought immediately into equilibrium, and coordination can break down.

In modern economies, some prices are very flexible, whereas others are not. In the 1970s, U.S. economist Arthur Okun distinguished between *auction prices*, prices that adjust on a nearly daily basis, and *custom prices*, prices that adjust slowly. Prices for fresh fish, vegetables, and other food products are examples of auction prices— they typically are very flexible and adjust rapidly. Prices for industrial commodities, such as steel rods or machine tools, are custom prices and tend to adjust slowly to changes in demand. As shorthand, economists often refer to slowly adjusting prices as "sticky prices" (just like a door that won't open immediately but sometimes gets stuck).

Steel rods and machine tools are input prices. Like other input prices, the price of labor also adjusts very slowly. Workers often have long-term contracts that do not allow employers to change wages at all during a given year. Union workers, university professors, high school teachers, and employees of state and local governments are all groups whose wages adjust very slowly. As a general rule, there are very few workers in the economy whose wages change quickly. Perhaps movie stars, athletes, and rock stars are the exceptions, because their wages rise and fall with their popularity. But they are far from the typical worker in the economy. Even unskilled, low-wage workers are often protected from a decrease in their wages by minimum-wage laws.

For most firms, the biggest cost of doing business is wages. If wages are sticky, firms' overall costs will be sticky as well. This means that firms' product prices will remain sticky, too. Sticky wages cause sticky prices and hamper the economy's ability to bring demand and supply into balance in the short run.

Typically, firms that supply intermediate goods such as steel rods or other inputs let demand—not price—determine the level of output in the short run. To understand this idea, consider an automobile firm that buys material from a steelmaker on a regular basis. Because the auto firm and the steel producer have been in business with one another for a long time and have an ongoing relationship, they have negotiated a contract that keeps steel prices fixed in the short run.

But suppose that the automobile company's cars suddenly become very popular. The firm needs to expand production, so it needs more steel. Under the agreement made earlier by the two firms, the steel company would meet this higher demand and sell more steel—without raising its price—to the automobile company. As a result, the production of steel is totally determined in the short run by the demand from automobile producers, not by price.

But what if the firm discovered that it had produced an unpopular car and needed to cut back on its planned production? The firm would require less steel. Under the agreement, the steelmaker would supply less steel but not reduce its price. Again, demand—not price—determines steel production in the short run.

Similar agreements between firms, both formal and informal, exist throughout the economy. Typically, in the short run, firms will meet changes in the demand for their products by adjusting production with only small changes in the prices they charge their customers.

What we have just illustrated for an input such as steel applies to workers, who are also "inputs" to production. Suppose that the automobile firm hires union workers under a contract that fixes their wages for a specific period. If the economy suddenly thrives at some point during that period, the automobile company will employ all the workers and perhaps require some to work overtime. If the economy stagnates at some point during that period, the firm will lay off some workers, using only part of the union labor force. In either case, wages are sticky—they will not change during the period of the contract.

Retail prices to consumers, like input prices to producers, are also subject to some "stickiness."

Over longer periods of time, prices do change. Suppose the automobile company's car remains popular for a long time. The steel company and the automobile company will adjust the price of steel on their contract to reflect this increased demand. These price adjustments occur only over long periods. In the short run, demand, not prices, determines output, and prices are slow to adjust.

To summarize, the **short run in macroeconomics** is the period in which prices do not change or do not change very much. In the macroeconomic short run, both formal and informal contracts between firms mean that changes in demand will be reflected primarily in changes in output, not prices.

• **short run in macroeconomics**
The period of time in which prices do not change or do not change very much.

# APPLICATION

**APPLYING THE CONCEPTS #1:** What does the behavior of prices in retail catalogs demonstrate about how quickly prices adjust in the U.S. economy?

To analyze the behavior of retail prices, economist Anil Kashyap of the University of Chicago examined prices in consumer catalogs. In particular, he looked at the prices of 12 selected goods from L.L. Bean, Recreational Equipment Inc. (REI), and The Orvis Company, Inc. Kashyap tracked several goods over time, including several varieties of shoes, blankets, chamois shirts, binoculars, and a fishing rod and fly. He found considerable price stickiness. Prices of the goods that he tracked were typically fixed for a year or more (even though the catalogs came out every six months). When prices did eventually change, he observed a mixture of both large and small changes. During periods of high inflation, prices tended to change more frequently, as might be expected.   *Related to Exercises 1.6 and 1.7.*

SOURCE: Anil Kashyap, "Sticky Prices: New Evidence from Retail Catalogs,"*Quarterly Journal of Economics,* vol. 110, no. 1, 1995, pp. 245–274.

# 14.2 | UNDERSTANDING AGGREGATE DEMAND

In this section, we develop a graphical tool known as the *aggregate demand curve*. Later in the chapter, we will develop the *aggregate supply curve.* Together the aggregate demand and aggregate supply curves form an economic model that will enable us to study how output and prices are determined in both the short run and the long run. This economic model will also provide a framework in which we can study the role the government can play in stabilizing the economy through its spending, tax, and money-creation policies.

## What Is the Aggregate Demand Curve?

*Aggregate demand* is the total demand for goods and services in an entire economy. In other words, it is the demand for currently produced GDP by consumers, firms, the government, and the foreign sector. Aggregate demand is a macroeconomic concept, because it refers to the economy as a whole, not individual goods or markets.

• **aggregate demand curve (AD)**
A curve that shows the relationship between the level of prices and the quantity of real GDP demanded.

The **aggregate demand curve (AD)** shows the relationship between the level of prices and the quantity of real GDP demanded. An aggregate demand curve, AD, is shown in Figure 14.1. It plots the total demand for GDP as a function of the price level. (Recall that the price level is the average level of prices in the economy, as measured by a price index.) At each price level, shown on the *y* axis, we ask what the total quantity demanded will be for all goods and services in the economy, shown on the *x* axis. In Figure 14.1, the aggregate demand curve is downward sloping. As the price level falls, the total quantity demanded for goods and services increases. To understand what the aggregate demand curve represents, we must first learn the components of aggregate demand, why the aggregate demand curve slopes downward, and the factors that can shift the curve.

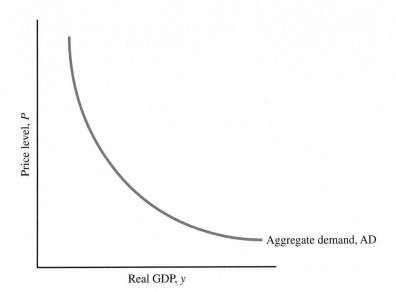

◄ **FIGURE 14.1**
**Aggregate Demand**
The aggregate demand curve plots the total demand for real GDP as a function of the price level. The aggregate demand curve slopes downward, indicating that the quantity of aggregate demand increases as the price level in the economy falls.

## The Components of Aggregate Demand

In our study of GDP accounting, we divided GDP into four components: consumption spending ($C$), investment spending ($I$), government purchases ($G$), and net exports ($NX$). These four components are also the four parts of aggregate demand because the aggregate demand curve really just describes the demand for total GDP at different price levels. As we will see, changes in demand coming from any of these four sources—$C$, $I$, $G$, or $NX$—will shift the aggregate demand curve.

## Why the Aggregate Demand Curve Slopes Downward

To understand the slope of the aggregate demand curve, we need to consider the effects of a change in the overall price level in the economy. First, let's consider the supply of money in the economy. We discuss the supply of money in detail in later chapters, but for now, just think of the supply of money as being the total amount of currency (cash plus coins) held by the public and the value of all deposits in savings and checking accounts. As the price level or average level of prices in the economy changes, so does the purchasing power of your money. This is an example of the real-nominal principle.

### REAL-NOMINAL PRINCIPLE

What matters to people is the real value or purchasing power of money or income, not the face value of money or income.

As the purchasing power of money changes, the aggregate demand curve is affected in three different ways:

- The wealth effect
- The interest rate effect
- The international trade effect

Let's take a closer look at each.

### THE WEALTH EFFECT
The change in the purchasing power of money will affect aggregate demand—the total demand for all goods and services in the economy. As the price level falls, the purchasing power of money increases. When this happens, people holding money find they are better off, or wealthier, and are more willing to spend money on additional goods and services than they had before.

• **wealth effect**
The increase in spending that occurs because the real value of money increases when the price level falls.

The increase in spending that occurs because the real value of money increases when the price level falls is known as the **wealth effect**. Lower prices lead to higher levels of wealth, and higher levels of wealth increase spending on total goods and services. Conversely, when the price level rises, the real value of money decreases, reducing people's wealth and their total demand for goods and services in the economy. When the price level rises, consumers can't simply substitute one good for another that's cheaper, because at a higher price level *everything* is more expensive.

### THE INTEREST RATE EFFECT

With a given supply of money in the economy, a lower price level will lead to lower interest rates. With lower interest rates, both consumers and firms will find it cheaper to borrow money to make purchases. As a consequence, the demand for goods in the economy (consumer durables purchased by households and investment goods purchased by firms) will increase. (We'll explain the effects of interest rates in more detail in later chapters.)

### THE INTERNATIONAL TRADE EFFECT

In an open economy, a lower price level will mean that domestic goods (goods produced in the home country) become cheaper relative to foreign goods, so the demand for domestic goods will increase. For example, if the price level in the United States falls, it will make U.S. goods cheaper relative to foreign goods. If U.S. goods become cheaper than foreign goods, exports from the United States will increase and imports will decrease. Thus, net exports—a component of aggregate demand—will increase.

## Shifts in the Aggregate Demand Curve

A fall in price causes the aggregate demand curve to slope downward because of three factors: the wealth effect, the interest rate effect, and the international trade effect. What happens to the aggregate demand curve if a variable *other* than the price level changes? An increase in aggregate demand means that total demand for all the goods and services contained in real GDP has increased—even though the price level hasn't changed. In other words, increases in aggregate demand shift the curve to the right. Conversely, factors that decrease aggregate demand shift the curve to the left—even though the price level hasn't changed.

Let's look at the key factors that cause these shifts. We will discuss each factor in detail in later chapters:

- Changes in the supply of money
- Changes in taxes
- Changes in government spending
- All other changes in demand

### CHANGES IN THE SUPPLY OF MONEY

An increase in the supply of money in the economy will increase aggregate demand and shift the aggregate demand curve to the right. We know that an increase in the supply of money will lead to higher demand by both consumers and firms. At any given price level, a higher supply of money will mean more consumer wealth and an increased demand for goods and services. A decrease in the supply of money will decrease aggregate demand and shift the aggregate demand curve to the left.

### CHANGES IN TAXES

A decrease in taxes will increase aggregate demand and shift the aggregate demand curve to the right. Lower taxes will increase the income available to households and increase their spending on goods and services—even though the price level in the economy hasn't changed. An increase in taxes will decrease aggregate demand and shift the aggregate demand curve to the left. Higher taxes will decrease the income available to households and decrease their spending.

## CHANGES IN GOVERNMENT SPENDING

At any given price level, an increase in government spending will increase aggregate demand and shift the aggregate demand curve to the right. For example, the government could spend more on national defense or on interstate highways. Because the government is a source of demand for goods and services, higher government spending naturally leads to an increase in total demand for goods and services. Similarly, decreases in government spending will decrease aggregate demand and shift the curve to the left.

## ALL OTHER CHANGES IN DEMAND

Any change in demand from households, firms, or the foreign sector will also change aggregate demand. For example, if the Japanese economy expands very rapidly, and Japanese citizens buy more U.S. goods, U.S. aggregate demand will increase. Or, if households decide they want to spend more, consumption will increase and aggregate demand will increase. Expectations about the future also matter. For example, if firms become optimistic about the future and increase their investment spending, aggregate demand will also increase. However, if firms become pessimistic, they will cut their investment spending and aggregate demand will fall.

When we discuss factors that shift aggregate demand, we must not include any changes in the demand for goods and services that arise from movements in the price level. Changes in aggregate demand that accompany changes in the price level are already included in the curve and do not shift the curve. The increase in consumer spending that occurs when the price level falls from the wealth effect, the interest rate effect, and the international trade effect is in the curve and does not shift it.

Figure 14.2 and Table 14.1 summarize our discussion. Decreases in taxes, increases in government spending, and increases in the supply of money all shift the aggregate demand curve to the right. Increases in taxes, decreases in government spending, and decreases in the supply of money shift it to the left. In general, any increase in demand (not brought about by a change in the price level) will shift the curve to the right. Decreases in demand shift the curve to the left.

**Table 14.1** | FACTORS THAT SHIFT AGGREGATE DEMAND

| Factors That Increase Aggregate Demand | Factors That Decrease Aggregate Demand |
|---|---|
| Decrease in taxes | Increase in taxes |
| Increase in government spending | Decrease in government spending |
| Increase in the money supply | Decrease in the money supply |

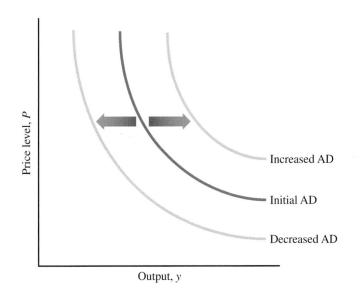

◄ **FIGURE 14.2**
**Shifting Aggregate Demand**
Decreases in taxes, increases in government spending, and an increase in the supply of money all shift the aggregate demand curve to the right. Higher taxes, lower government spending, and a lower supply of money shift the curve to the left.

• **multiplier**
The ratio of the total shift in aggregate demand to the initial shift in aggregate demand.

## How the Multiplier Makes the Shift Bigger

Let's take a closer look at the shift in the aggregate demand curve and see how far changes really make the curve shift. Suppose that the government increases its spending on goods and services by $10 billion. You might think that the aggregate demand curve would shift to the right by $10 billion, reflecting the increase in demand for these goods and services. Initially, the shift will be precisely $10 billion. In Figure 14.3, this is depicted by the shift (at a given price level) from *a* to *b*. But after a brief period of time, total aggregate demand will increase by *more* than $10 billion. In Figure 14.3, the total shift in the aggregate demand curve is shown by the larger movement from *a* to *c*. The ratio of the total shift in aggregate demand to the initial shift in aggregate demand is known as the **multiplier**.

Why does the aggregate demand curve shift more than the initial increase in desired spending? The logic goes back to the ideas of economist John Maynard Keynes. Here's how it works: Keynes believed that as government spending increases and the aggregate demand curve shifts to the right, output will subsequently increase, too. As we saw with the circular flow in Chapter 11, increased output also means increased income for households, as firms pay households for their labor and for supplying other factors of production. Typically, households will wish to spend, or consume, part of that income, which will further increase aggregate demand. It is this additional spending by consumers, over and above what the government has already spent, that causes the further shift in the aggregate demand curve.

The basic idea of how the multiplier works in an economy is simple. Let's say that the government invests $10 million to construct a new federal court building. Initially, total spending in the economy increases by this $10 million paid to a private construction firm. The construction workers and owners are paid $10 million for their work. Suppose the owners and workers spend $6 million of their income on new cars. (As we will see, it does not really matter what they spend it on.) To meet the increased demand for new cars, automobile producers will expand their production and earn an additional $6 million in wages and profits. They, in turn, will spend part of this additional income—let's say, $3.6 million—on televisions. The workers and owners who produce televisions will then spend part of the $3.6 million they earn, and so on, and so on.

To take a closer look at this process, we first need to look more carefully at the behavior of consumers and how their behavior helps to determine the level of aggregate demand. Economists have found that consumer spending depends on the level of income in the economy. When consumers have more income, they want to purchase more goods and services. The relationship between the level of income and consumer spending is known as the **consumption function**:

$$C = C_a + by$$

• **consumption function**
The relationship between the level of income and consumer spending.

► **FIGURE 14.3**
**The Multiplier**
Initially, an increase in desired spending will shift the aggregate demand curve horizontally to the right from *a* to *b*. The total shift from *a* to *c* will be larger. The ratio of the total shift to the initial shift is known as the multiplier.

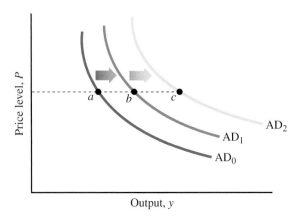

where consumption spending, $C$, has two parts. The first part, $C_a$, is a constant and is independent of income. Economists call this **autonomous consumption spending**.

Autonomous spending is spending that does not depend on the level of income. For example, all consumers, regardless of their current income, will have to purchase some food. The second part, $by$, represents the part of consumption that is dependent on income. It is the product of a fraction, $b$, called the **marginal propensity to consume (MPC)**, and the level of income, or $y$, in the economy. The MPC (or $b$ in our formula) tells us how much consumption spending will increase for every dollar that income increases. For example, if $b$ is 0.6, then for every $1.00 that income increases, consumption increases by $0.60.

Here is another way to think of the MPC: If a household receives some additional income, it will increase its consumption by some additional amount. The MPC is defined as the ratio of additional consumption to additional income, or

$$MPC = \frac{\text{additional consumption}}{\text{additional income}}$$

For example, if the household receives an additional $100 and consumes an additional $70, the MPC will be

$$\frac{\$70}{\$100} = 0.7$$

You may wonder what happens to the other $30. Whatever the household does not spend out of income, it saves. Therefore, the **marginal propensity to save (MPS)** is defined as the ratio of additional savings to additional income:

$$MPS = \frac{\text{additional savings}}{\text{additional income}}$$

The sum of the MPC and the MPS always equals one. By definition, additional income is either spent or saved.

Now we are in a better position to understand the multiplier. Suppose the government increases its purchases of goods and services by $10 million. This will initially raise aggregate demand and income by $10 million. But because income has risen by $10 million, consumers will now wish to increase their spending by an amount equal to the marginal propensity to consume multiplied by the $10 million. (Remember that the MPC tells us how much consumption spending will increase for every dollar that income increases.) If the MPC were 0.6, then consumer spending would increase by $6 million when the government spends $10 million. Thus, the aggregate demand curve would continue to shift to the right by another $6 million in addition to the original $10 million, for a total of $16 million.

But the process does not end there. As aggregate demand increases by $6 million, income will also increase by $6 million. Consumers will then wish to increase their spending by the MPC × $6 million or, in our example, by $3.6 million (0.6 × $6 million). The aggregate demand curve will continue to shift to the right, now by *another* $3.6 million. Adding $3.6 million to $16 million gives us a new aggregate demand total of $19.6 million. As you can see, this process will continue, as consumers now have an additional $3.6 million in income, part of which they will spend again. Where will it end?

Table 14.2 shows how the multiplier works in detail. In the first round, there is an initial increase in government spending of $10 million. This additional demand leads to an initial increase in GDP and income of $10 million. Assuming that the MPC is 0.6, the $10 million of additional income will increase consumer spending by $6 million. The second round begins with this $6 million increase in consumer spending. Because of this increase in demand, GDP and income increase by $6 million. At the end of the second round, consumers will have an additional $6 million; with a MPC of 0.6, consumer spending will therefore increase by 0.6 × $6 million, or $3.6 million.

- **autonomous consumption spending**
  The part of consumption spending that does not depend on income.

- **marginal propensity to consume (MPC)**
  The fraction of additional income that is spent.

- **marginal propensity to save (MPS)**
  The fraction of additional income that is saved.

**Table 14.2 | THE MULTIPLIER IN ACTION**

The initial $10 million increase in aggregate demand will, through all the rounds of spending, eventually lead to a $25 million increase.

| Round of Spending | Increase in Aggregate Demand (millions) | Increase in GDP and Income (millions) | Increase in Consumption (millions) |
|---|---|---|---|
| 1 | $10.00 | $10.00 | $6.00 |
| 2 | 6.00 | 6.00 | 3.60 |
| 3 | 3.60 | 3.60 | 2.16 |
| 4 | 2.16 | 2.16 | 1.30 |
| . | . | . | |
| **Total** | **$25.00** | **$25.00** | **$15.00** |

The process continues in the third round with an increase in consumer spending of $2.16 million. It continues, in diminishing amounts, through subsequent rounds. If we add up the spending in all the (infinite) rounds, we will find that the initial $10 million of spending leads to a $25 million increase in GDP and income. That's 2.5 times what the government initially spent. So in this case, the multiplier is 2.5.

Instead of calculating spending round by round, we can use a simple formula to figure out what the multiplier is:

$$\text{multiplier} = \frac{1}{(1 - \text{MPC})}$$

Thus, in the preceding example, when the MPC is 0.6, the multiplier would be

$$\frac{1}{(1 - 0.6)} = 2.5$$

Now you should clearly understand why the total shift in the aggregate demand curve from *a* to *c* in Figure 9.3 is greater than the initial shift in the curve from *a* to *b*. This is the multiplier in action. The multiplier is important because it means that relatively small changes in spending could lead to relatively large changes in output. For example, if firms cut back on their investment spending, the effects on output would be "multiplied," and this decrease in spending could have a large, adverse impact on the economy.

In practice, once we take into account other realistic factors such as taxes and indirect effects through financial markets, the multipliers are smaller than our previous examples, typically near 1.5 for the U.S economy. This means that a $10 million increase in one component of spending will shift the U.S. aggregate demand curve by approximately $15 million. Knowing the value of the multiplier is important for two reasons. First, it tells us how much shocks to aggregate demand are "amplified." Second, to design effective economic policies to shift the aggregate demand curve, we need to know the value of the multiplier to measure the proper "dose" for policy. In the next chapter, we present a more detailed model of aggregate demand and explain the role for economic policy.

# 14.3 | UNDERSTANDING AGGREGATE SUPPLY

• **aggregate supply curve (AS)**
A curve that shows the relationship between the level of prices and the quantity of output supplied.

Now we turn to the supply side of our model. The **aggregate supply curve (AS)** shows the relationship between the level of prices and the total quantity of final goods and output that firms are willing and able to supply. The aggregate supply curve will complete our macroeconomic picture, uniting the economy's demand for real output with firms' willingness to supply output. To determine both the price level and real GDP, we need to combine *both* aggregate demand and aggregate supply. One slight complication is that because prices are "sticky" in the short run, we need to develop two different aggregate supply curves, one corresponding to the long run and one to the short run.

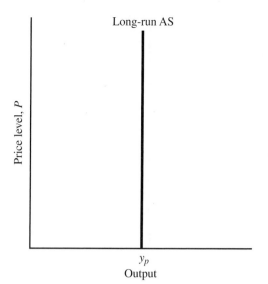

## The Long-Run Aggregate Supply Curve

First we'll consider the aggregate supply curve for the long run, that is, when the economy is at full employment. This curve is also called the **long-run aggregate supply curve**. In previous chapters, we saw that the level of full-employment output, $y_p$, depends solely on the supply of factors—capital, labor—and the state of technology. These are the fundamental factors that determine output in the long run, that is, when the economy operates at full employment.

In the long run, the economy operates at full employment and changes in the price level do not affect employment. To illustrate why this is so, imagine that the price level in the economy increases by 50 percent. That means firms' prices, on average, will also increase by 50 percent. However, so will their input costs. Their profits will be the same and, consequently, so will their output. Because the level of full-employment output does not depend on the price level, we can plot the long-run aggregate supply curve as a vertical line (unaffected by the price level), as shown in Figure 14.4.

### DETERMINING OUTPUT AND THE PRICE LEVEL

We combine the aggregate demand curve and the long-run aggregate supply curve in Figure 14.5. Together, the curves show us the price level and output in the long run when the economy returns to full employment. Combining the two curves will enable us to understand how changes in aggregate demand affect prices in the long run.

The intersection of an aggregate demand curve and an aggregate supply curve determines the price level and equilibrium level of output. At that intersection point, the total amount of output demanded will just equal the total amount supplied by producers—the economy will be in macroeconomic equilibrium. The exact position of the aggregate demand curve will depend on the level of taxes, government spending, and the supply of money, although it will always slope downward. The level of full-employment output determines the long-run aggregate supply curve.

An increase in aggregate demand (perhaps brought about by a tax cut or an increase in the supply of money) will shift the aggregate demand curve to the right, as shown in Figure 14.5. In the long run, the increase in aggregate demand will raise prices but leave the level of output unchanged. In general, shifts in the aggregate demand curve in the long run do not change the level of output in the economy, but only change the level of prices. Here is an important example to illustrate this idea: If the money supply is increased by 5 percent a year, the aggregate demand curve will also shift by 5 percent a year. In the long run, this means that prices will increase by 5 percent a year—that is, there will be 5 percent inflation.

● **long-run aggregate supply curve**
A vertical aggregate supply curve that represents the idea that in the long run, output is determined solely by the factors of production.

**Aggregate Demand and the Long-Run Aggregate Supply**
Output and prices are determined at the intersection of AD and AS. An increase in aggregate demand leads to a higher price level.

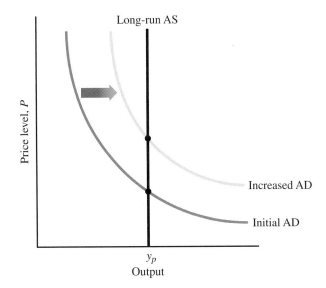

This is the key point about the long run: In the long run, output is determined solely by the supply of human and physical capital and the supply of labor, not the price level. As our model of the aggregate demand curve with the long-run aggregate supply curve indicates, changes in demand will affect only prices, not the level of output.

## The Short-Run Aggregate Supply Curve

In the short run, prices are sticky (slow to adjust) and output is determined primarily by demand. This is what Keynes thought happened during the Great Depression. We can use the aggregate demand curve combined with a **short-run aggregate supply curve** to illustrate this idea. Figure 14.6 shows a relatively flat short-run aggregate supply curve (AS). The short-run aggregate supply curve is relatively flat because in the short run firms are assumed to supply all the output demanded, with small changes in prices. We previously discussed that with formal and informal contracts firms will supply all the output that is demanded with only relatively small changes in prices. The short-run aggregate supply curve has a small upward slope. As firms supply more output, they may have to increase prices somewhat if, for example, they have to pay higher wages to obtain more overtime from workers or pay a premium to obtain some raw materials.

• **short-run aggregate supply curve**
A relatively flat aggregate supply curve that represents the idea that prices do not change very much in the short run and that firms adjust production to meet demand.

▶ **FIGURE 14.6**
**Aggregate Demand and Short-Run Aggregate Supply**
With a short-run aggregate supply curve, shifts in aggregate demand lead to large changes in output but small changes in price.

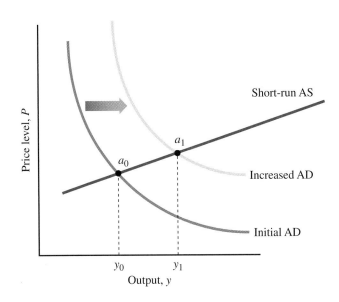

As we just explained, the short-run supply curve is relatively flat because at any point in time we assume that firms supply all the output demanded with relatively small changes in prices. However, the entire short-run supply curve can shift upward or downward as prices adjust to their long-run levels, as we shall see later in this chapter. Our description of the aggregate supply curve is consistent with evidence about the behavior of prices in the economy. Most studies find that changes in demand have relatively little effect on prices within a few quarters. Thus, the aggregate supply curve can be viewed as relatively flat within a limited time. However, changes in aggregate demand will ultimately have an effect on prices.

The intersection of the AD and AS curves at point $a_0$ determines the price level and the level of output. Because the aggregate supply curve is flat, aggregate demand primarily determines the level of output. In Figure 14.6, as aggregate demand increases, the new equilibrium will be at a slightly higher price, and output will increase from $y_0$ to $y_1$.

2

# APPLICATION

## BUSINESS INVESTMENT, NET EXPORTS, AND THE 2001 RECESSION

**APPLYING THE CONCEPTS #2:** How can changes in demand cause a recession? In particular, what factors do economists think caused the 2001 recession?

In 2001, the U.S. economy entered into a recession. To determine what caused the 2001 recession and how it differed from past recessions, economist Kevin Kliesen of the Federal Reserve Bank of St. Louis compared data for recessions over time. Kliesen found that during earlier recessions spending on consumer durables (such as automobiles or refrigerators) decreased, as did new residential housing production. Because both these types of spending are very sensitive to interest rate levels, the data suggested that financial factors and the government's monetary policies were to blame for the recessions.

However, during the 2001 recession spending on consumer durables and new housing production *both* grew throughout the recession. Instead, business investment and net exports dropped. Prior to the recession, there had been large increases in business investment. But following the sharp fall in the stock market in 2000, both investors and firms realized that the economic boom times of the late 1990s were over. As expectations were dashed, firms cut back sharply on their planned investment spending. Net exports fell during the recession for two reasons. First, world economic growth slowed, decreasing the demand for U.S. goods. Second, the value of the dollar increased relative to foreign currencies, making U.S. goods more expensive.

Most forecasters didn't anticipate the drops in business investment and net exports that caused the recession. Indeed, that is the pattern in most recessions: Shocks to aggregate demand are largely unanticipated. That is, after all, why they are called "shocks." *Related to Exercise 3.5.*

SOURCE: Kevin Kliesen, "The 2001 Recession: How Was It Different and What Developments May Have Caused It?" *Federal Reserve Bank of St. Louis Review*, September–October 2003, pp. 23–37.

If the aggregate demand curve moved to the left, output would decrease. If the leftward shift in aggregate demand were sufficiently large, it could push the economy into a recession. Sudden decreases in aggregate demand have been important causes of recessions in the United States. However, the precise factors that shift the aggregate demand curve in each recession will typically differ.

It is important to realize and understand that the level of output where the aggregate demand curve intersects the short-run aggregate supply curve need not correspond to full-employment output. Firms will produce whatever is demanded. If demand is very high and the economy is "overheated," output may exceed full-employment output. If demand is very low and the economy is in a slump, output will fall short of full-employment output. Because prices do not adjust fully over short periods of time, the economy need not always remain at full employment or potential output. With sticky prices, changes in demand in the short run will lead to economic fluctuations and over- and underemployment. Only in the long run, when prices fully adjust, will the economy operate at full employment.

### Supply Shocks

Up to this point, we have been exploring how changes in aggregate demand affect output and prices in the short run and in the long run. However, even in the short run, it is possible for external disturbances to hit the economy and cause the short-run aggregate supply curve to move. **Supply shocks** are external events that shift the aggregate supply curve.

The most notable supply shocks for the world economy occurred in 1973 and again in 1979 when oil prices increased sharply. Oil is a vital input for many companies because it is used to both manufacture and transport their products to warehouses and stores around the country. The higher oil prices raised firms' costs and reduced their profits. To maintain their profit levels, firms raised their product prices.

Figure 14.7 illustrates a supply shock that raises prices. The short-run aggregate supply curve shifts up with the supply shock because firms will supply their output only at a higher price. The AS curve shifts up, raising the price level and lowering the level of output from $y_0$ to $y_1$. Adverse supply shocks can therefore cause a recession (a fall in real output) with increasing prices. This phenomenon is known as **stagflation**, and it is precisely what happened in 1973 and 1979. The U.S. economy suffered on two grounds: rising prices and falling output.

Favorable supply shocks, such as falling prices, are also possible, and changes in oil prices can affect aggregate demand.

• **supply shocks**
External events that shift the aggregate supply curve.

• **stagflation**
A decrease in real output with increasing prices.

▶ **FIGURE 14.7**
**Supply Shock**
An adverse supply shock, such as an increase in the price of oil, will cause the AS curve to shift upward. The result will be higher prices and a lower level of output.

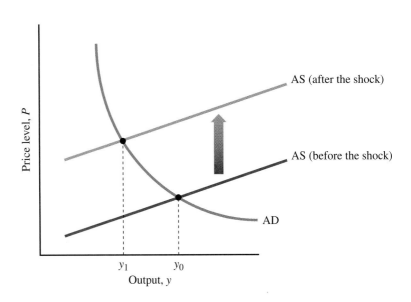

# APPLICATION

**3**

## HOW THE U.S. ECONOMY HAS COPED WITH OIL PRICE FLUCTUATIONS

**APPLYING THE CONCEPTS #3:** Do changes in oil prices always hurt the U.S. economy?

During the 1970s, the world economy was hit with a series of unfavorable supply shocks that raised prices and lowered output, including spikes in oil prices and the prices of many agricultural commodities due to hurricanes, droughts, and floods that destroyed crops or land. As we have discussed, increases in oil prices shift the aggregate supply curve. However, they also have an adverse effect on aggregate demand. Because the United States is a net importer of foreign oil, an increase in oil prices is just like a tax that decreases the income of consumers. As we have seen, an increase in taxes will shift the aggregate demand curve to the left.

However, in the 1990s, things were different—pleasantly different. Between 1997 and 1998, the price of oil on the world market fell from $22 a barrel to less than $13 a barrel. The result was that gasoline prices, adjusted for inflation, were lower than they had ever been in over 50 years. This not only meant cheaper vacations and commuting and an increase in SUV purchases, it also had positive macroeconomic effects. Favorable supply shocks allowed output to rise and prices to fall simultaneously—the best of all worlds.

In 2005, oil prices shot up to $60 a barrel, largely because of increased demand throughout the world, particularly in fast-growing countries such as China and India. Gasoline prices exceeded $3 a gallon. Despite these increases, the economy appeared to absorb these price increases without too much difficulty, and the price increases did not have the adverse effects on aggregate demand as in prior years. Perhaps many years of coping with oil price changes combined with a strong economy made the difference this time.
*Related to Exercises 3.4 and 3.6.*

## 14.4 | FROM THE SHORT RUN TO THE LONG RUN

Up to this point, we have examined how aggregate demand and aggregate supply determine output and prices both in the short run and in the long run. You may be wondering how long it takes before the short run becomes the long run. Here is a preview of how the short run and the long run are connected.

In Figure 14.8, we show the aggregate demand curve intersecting the short-run aggregate supply curve at $a_0$ at an output level $y_0$. We also depict the long-run aggregate supply curve in this figure. The level of output in the economy, $y_0$, exceeds the level of potential output, $y_p$. In other words, this is a boom economy: Output exceeds potential.

What happens during a boom? Because the economy is producing at a level beyond its long-run potential, the level of unemployment will be very low. This will make it difficult for firms to recruit and retain workers. Firms will also find it more

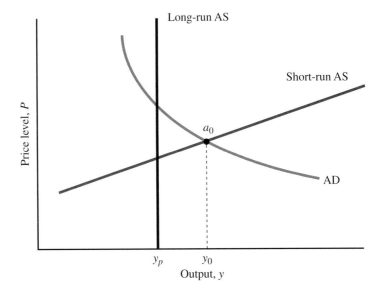

▶ **FIGURE 14.8**
**The Economy in the Short Run**
In the short run, the economy produces at
$y_0$, which exceeds potential output $y_p$.

difficult to purchase needed raw materials and other inputs for production. As firms compete for labor and raw materials, the tendency will be for both wages and prices to increase over time.

Increasing wages and prices will shift the short-run aggregate supply curve upward. Figure 14.9 shows how the short-run aggregate supply curve shifts upward over time. As long as the economy is producing at a level of output that exceeds potential output, there will be continuing competition for labor and raw materials that will lead to continuing increases in wages and prices. In the long run, the short-run aggregate supply curve will keep rising until it intersects the aggregate demand curve at $a_1$. At this point, the economy reaches the long-run equilibrium—precisely the point where the aggregate demand curve intersects the long-run aggregate supply curve.

When the economy is producing below full employment or potential output, the process works in reverse. Unemployment will exceed the natural rate, and there will be excess unemployment. Firms will find it easy to hire and retain workers, and they will offer workers less wages. As firms cut wages, the average wage level in the economy falls. Because wages are the largest component of costs, prices start to fall as well.

The lesson here is that adjustments in wages and prices take the economy from the short-run equilibrium to the long-run equilibrium. This process may take several years, which is why governments may want to use economic policy to speed the process along. We will study economic policy in more detail in the next several chapters.

▶ **FIGURE 14.9**
**Adjusting to the Long Run**
With output exceeding potential, the short-run AS curve shifts upward over time. The economy adjusts to the long-run equilibrium at $a_1$.

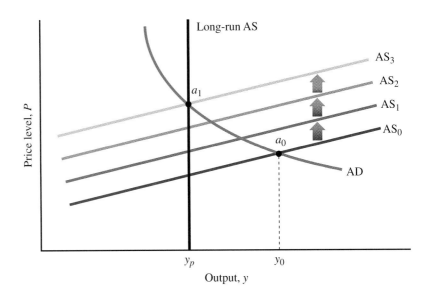

# SUMMARY

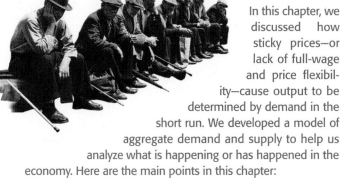

In this chapter, we discussed how sticky prices—or lack of full-wage and price flexibility—cause output to be determined by demand in the short run. We developed a model of aggregate demand and supply to help us analyze what is happening or has happened in the economy. Here are the main points in this chapter:

1 Because prices are sticky in the short run, economists think of GDP as being determined primarily by demand factors in the short run.

2 The *aggregate demand curve* depicts the relationship between the price level and total demand for real output in the economy. The aggregate demand curve is downward sloping because of the wealth effect, the interest rate effect, and the international trade effect.

3 Decreases in taxes, increases in government spending, and increases in the supply of money all increase aggregate demand and shift the aggregate demand curve to the right.

Increases in taxes, decreases in government spending, and decreases in the supply of money all decrease aggregate demand and shift the aggregate demand curve to the left. In general, anything (other than price movements) that increases the demand for total goods and services will increase aggregate demand.

4 The total shift in the aggregate demand curve is greater than the initial shift. The ratio of the total shift in aggregate demand to the initial shift in aggregate demand is known as the *multiplier*.

5 The *aggregate supply curve* depicts the relationship between the price level and the level of output firms supply in the economy. Output and prices are determined at the intersection of the aggregate demand and aggregate supply curves.

6 The *long-run aggregate supply curve* is vertical because, in the long run, output is determined by the supply of factors of production. The *short-run aggregate supply curve* is fairly flat because, in the short run, prices are largely fixed, and output is determined by demand.

7 *Supply shocks* can shift the short-run aggregate supply curve.

8 The short-run aggregate supply curve shifts in the long run, restoring the economy to the full-employment equilibrium.

## KEY TERMS

aggregate demand curve (AD), p. 352

aggregate supply curve (AS), p. 358

autonomous consumption spending, p. 357

consumption function, p. 356

long-run aggregate supply curve, p. 359

marginal propensity to consume (MPC), p. 357

marginal propensity to save (MPS), p. 357

multiplier, p. 356

short-run aggregate supply curve, p. 360

short run in macroeconomics, p. 351

stagflation, p. 362

supply shocks, p. 362

wealth effect, p. 354

## EXERCISES  *Get Ahead of the Curve*

Visit www.myeconlab.com to complete these exercises online and get instant feedback.

### 14.1 | Sticky Prices and Their Macroeconomic Consequences

1.1 Arthur Okun distinguished between *auction* prices, which changed rapidly, and _____ prices, which were slow to change.

1.2 For most firms, the biggest cost of doing business is _____.

1.3 The price system always coordinates economic activity, even when prices are slow to adjust to changes in demand and supply. _____ (True/False)

1.4 Determine whether the wages of each of the following adjust slowly or quickly to changes in demand and supply.
   **a.** Union workers
   **b.** Movie stars
   **c.** University professors
   **d.** Athletes

1.5 **The Internet and Price Flexibility.** The Internet enables consumers to search for the lowest prices of various goods, such as books, music CDs, and airline tickets. Prices for these goods are likely to become more flexible as consumers shop around quickly and easily on the Internet. What types of goods and services do you think may not become more flexible because of the Internet?

**1.6 Properties of Goods Whose Prices Are Sticky.** Give an example of a good or service whose price is sticky. What factors tend to make its price sticky? (Related to Application 1 on page 352.)

**1.7 Retail Price Stickiness in Catalogs.** During periods of high inflation, retail prices in catalogs changed more frequently. Explain why this occurred. (Related to Application 1 on page 352.)

## 14.2 | Understanding Aggregate Demand

**2.1** Which of the following is *not* a component of aggregate demand?
   a. Consumption
   b. Investment
   c. Government expenditures
   d. Depreciation
   e. Net exports

**2.2** In the Great Depression, prices in the United States fell by 33 percent. *Ceteris paribus*, this led to an increase in aggregate demand through three channels: the _____ effect, the interest rate effect, and the international trade effect.

**2.3** President George W. Bush and Congress lowered taxes in 2001. *Ceteris paribus*, this decrease in taxes shifted the aggregate demand curve to the _____.

**2.4** If the MPC is 0.6, the simple multiplier will be _____.

**2.5** Because of other economic factors, such as taxes, the multiplier in the United States is _____ (larger/smaller) than 2.5.

**2.6 What Shifts the Aggregate Demand Curve?** Did the fall in the price level in Japan in the 1990s shift the aggregate demand curve? Why or why not? What factors shift the aggregate demand curve?

**2.7 Calculating the MPC.** In one year, a consumer's income increases by $200 and her consumption increases by $160. What is her marginal propensity to consume?

**2.8 The MPC and Multiplier.** Explain why an increase in the marginal propensity to consume will increase the multiplier.

**2.9 Optimistic Firms and Aggregate Demand.** If firms suddenly become very optimistic about the future, how will that shift the aggregate demand curve?

## 14.3 | Understanding Aggregate Supply

**3.1** The long-run aggregate supply curve is _____ (vertical/horizontal).

**3.2** The short-run aggregate supply curve is relatively flat because prices are _____.

**3.3** Using the long-run aggregate supply curve, a decrease in aggregate demand will _____ prices and _____ output.

**3.4** A negative supply shock, such as higher oil prices, will _____ output and _____ prices in the short run. (Related to Application 3 on page 363.)

**3.5 Nervous Consumers and Economic Fluctuations.** Suppose that households become nervous about the future and decide to increase their saving and decrease their consumption spending. How would this behavior shift the aggregate demand curve? Using the short-run aggregate supply curve, what will happen to prices and output in the short run? Based on the discussion in this chapter, did nervous consumers cause the 2001 recession? (Related to Application 2 on page 361.)

**3.6 Understanding Stagflation.** In 1974, oil prices suddenly increased dramatically and the economy experienced an adverse supply shock. *Ceteris paribus*, what happened to the price level and real GDP? Why is this sometimes called stagflation? (Related to Application 3 on page 363.)

**3.7 The Effect of the Japanese Recession in the United States.** The Japanese economy fell into a recession in the early 1990s. How did that recession shift the aggregate demand curve in the United States? What would be the short-run effect on output and prices? (Hint: If a country falls into a recession, its consumption spending—including its imports—will fall.)

**3.8 What Caused This Recession?** Suppose the economy goes into a recession. The political party in power blames it on an increase in the price of world oil and food. Opposing politicians blame a tax increase that the party in power had enacted. On the basis of aggregate demand and aggregate supply analysis, what evidence should you look at to try to determine what, or who, caused the recession?

**3.9 Increases in Full-Employment Output.** Suppose that in the long run there was a new higher level of full-employment output. What would happen to the level of prices in the economy? (Assume that there is no change in aggregate demand.)

**4.1** Suppose the supply of money increases, causing output to exceed full employment. Prices will _____ and real GDP will _____ in the short run, and prices will _____ and real GDP will _____ in the long run.

**4.2** Consider a decrease in the supply of money that causes output to fall short of full employment. Prices will _____ and real GDP will _____ in the short run, and prices will _____ and real GDP will _____ in the long run.

**4.3** In a boom, real GDP is _____ potential GDP. This implies that unemployment is _____, driving wages _____. This results in a(n) _____ shift of the short-run aggregate supply curve.

**4.4** A negative supply shock temporarily lowers output below full employment and raises prices. After the negative supply shock, real GDP is _____ potential GDP. This implies that unemployment is _____, driving wages _____. This results in a(n) _____ shift of the short-run aggregate supply curve.

**4.5** **What Happens When Aggregate Demand Falls?** Suppose the economy is at full employment and aggregate demand falls. Show the effects on output and prices in the short run. Also show how the short-run aggregate supply curve adjusts over time to bring the economy to the long-run equilibrium.

**4.6** **Government Purchases and Real GDP.** Are increases in government purchases associated with increases in real GDP? A good place to start to find out is the Web site of the Federal Reserve Bank of St. Louis (research.stlouisfed.org/fred2/).

**4.7** **Exports and Real GDP.** Are increases in exports associated with increases in real GDP? A good place to start to find out is the Web site of the Federal Reserve Bank of St. Louis (research.stlouisfed.org/fred2/).

# 15

# Fiscal Policy

During the 1990s, the Japanese economy was in a prolonged recession. Economists proposed many different ideas to try to jump-start the economy. One suggestion was for the Japanese government to issue a certificate entitling each person to the equivalent, in yen, of $200. However, these certificates would be valid only for purchases for one month. After that time, the certificates would be worthless.

The logic behind issuing these time-dated certificates was straightforward. Individuals would feel compelled to rush out and use the certificates within the month. They would therefore immediately purchase

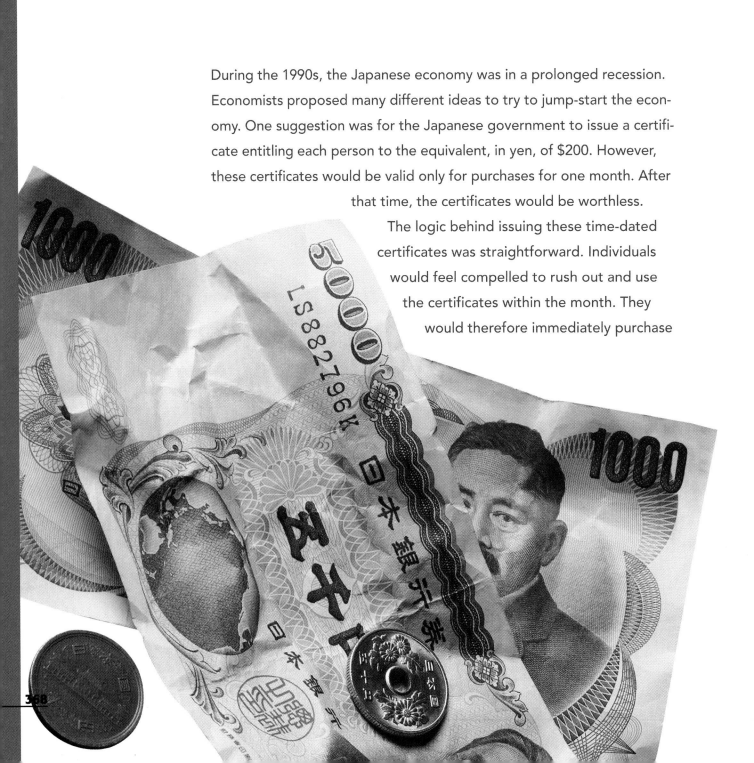

1   Why are the United States and many other countries facing dramatically increasing costs for their government programs?
    *Increasing Life Expectancy and Aging Populations Spur Costs of Entitlement Programs*

2   How does the U.S. government make short- and long-term budget projections?
    *How Governments Use Budget Baselines to Forecast Deficits*

3   How much did the 2001 tax cuts stimulate consumer spending?
    *Surveys Show Much of the 2001 Tax Cuts Were Saved*

goods and services and stimulate demand. Firms would increase production to meet the increased demand, thereby creating more jobs and lifting the economy out of the recession. This is an example, although an unusual one, of government fiscal policy.

• **fiscal policy**
Changes in government taxes and
spending that affect the level of GDP.

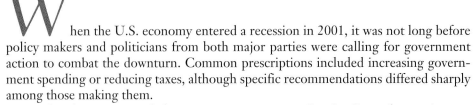

When the U.S. economy entered a recession in 2001, it was not long before policy makers and politicians from both major parties were calling for government action to combat the downturn. Common prescriptions included increasing government spending or reducing taxes, although specific recommendations differed sharply among those making them.

In this chapter, we study how governments can use **fiscal policy**—changes in taxes and spending that affect the level of GDP—to stabilize the economy. We explore the logic of fiscal policy and explain why changes in government spending and taxation can, in principle, stabilize the economy. However, stabilizing the economy in theory is much easier than in actual practice, as we will see.

The chapter also provides an overview of spending and taxation by the federal government. These are essentially the "tools" that the government uses to implement its fiscal policies. We will also examine the federal deficit and begin to explore the controversies surrounding "deficit spending."

One of the best ways to really understand fiscal policy is to see it in action. In the last part of the chapter, we trace the history of U.S. fiscal policy from the Great Depression in the 1930s to the present. As you will see, the public's attitude toward government fiscal policy has not been constant, but has changed sharply over time.

## 15.1 | THE ROLE OF FISCAL POLICY

In the last chapter, we discussed how output and prices are determined where the aggregate demand curve intersects the short-run aggregate supply curve. Over time, we also saw that the short-run aggregate supply curve will shift to bring the economy back to full employment. In this section, we will explore how the government can shift the aggregate demand curve.

### Fiscal Policy and Aggregate Demand

As we discussed in the last chapter, government spending and taxes can affect the level of aggregate demand. Increases in government spending or decreases in taxes will increase aggregate demand and shift the aggregate demand curve to the right. Decreases in government spending or increases in taxes will decrease aggregate demand and shift the aggregate demand curve to the left.

Why do changes in government spending or taxes shift the aggregate demand curve? Recall from our discussion in the last chapter that aggregate demand consists of four components: consumption spending, investment spending, government purchases, and net exports. These four components are the four parts of aggregate demand. Thus, increases in government purchases directly increase aggregate demand because they are a component of aggregate demand. Decreases in government purchases directly decrease aggregate demand.

Changes in taxes affect aggregate demand indirectly. For example, if the government lowers taxes on consumers, they will have more income at their disposal and will increase their consumption spending. Because consumption spending is a component of aggregate demand, aggregate demand will increase as well. Increases in taxes will have the opposite effect. Consumers will have less income at their disposal and decrease their consumption spending. As a result, aggregate demand will decrease. Changes in taxes can also affect businesses and lead to changes in investment spending. Suppose, for example, that the government cuts taxes in such a way as to provide incentives for new investment spending by businesses. Because investment spending is a component of aggregate demand, the increase in investment spending will increase aggregate demand.

In Panel A of Figure 15.1, we show a simple example of fiscal policy in action. The economy is initially operating at a level of GDP, $y_0$, where the aggregate demand curve $AD_0$ intersects the short-run aggregate supply curve AS. This level of output is below the level of full employment or potential output, $y_p$. To increase the level of out-

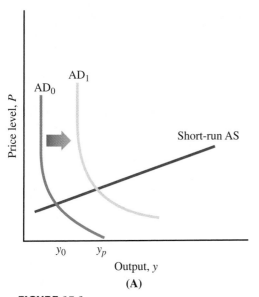
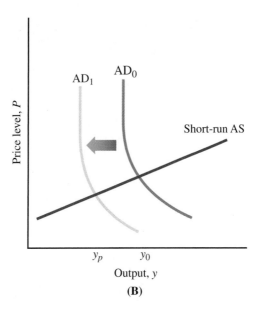

▲ **FIGURE 15.1**
**Fiscal Policy in Action**
Panel A shows that an increase in government spending shifts the aggregate demand curve from $AD_0$ to $AD_1$, restoring the economy to full employment. This is an example of expansionary policy. Panel B shows that an increase in taxes shifts the aggregate demand curve to the left, from $AD_0$ to $AD_1$, restoring the economy to full employment. This is an example of contractionary policy.

put, the government can increase government spending—say, on military goods—which will shift the aggregate demand curve to the right, to $AD_1$. Now the new aggregate demand curve intersects the aggregate supply curve at the full-employment level of output. Alternatively, instead of increasing its spending, the government could reduce taxes on consumers and businesses. This would also shift the aggregate demand curve to the right. Government policies that increase aggregate demand are called **expansionary policies**. Increasing government spending and cutting taxes are examples of expansionary policies.

> **expansionary policies**
> Government policy actions that lead to increases in aggregate demand.

The government can also use fiscal policy to decrease GDP if the economy is operating at too high a level of output, which would lead to the economy overheating and rising prices. In Panel B of Figure 15.1, the economy is initially operating at a level of output, $y_0$, that exceeds full-employment output, $y_p$. An increase in taxes can shift the aggregate demand curve from $AD_0$ to $AD_1$. This shift will bring the economy back to full employment. Alternatively, the government could cut its spending to move the aggregate demand curve to the left. Government policies that decrease aggregate demand are called **contractionary policies**. Decreasing government spending and increasing taxes are examples of contractionary policies.

> **contractionary policies**
> Government policy actions that lead to decreases in aggregate demand.

Both examples illustrate how policy makers use fiscal policy to stabilize the economy. In these two simple examples, fiscal policy seems very straightforward. But as we will soon see, in practice, it is more difficult to implement effective policy.

## The Fiscal Multiplier

Let's recall the idea of the multiplier that we developed in the last chapter. The basic idea of the multiplier is that the final shift in the aggregate demand curve will be larger than the initial increase. For example, if government purchases increased by $10 billion, that would initially shift the aggregate demand curve to the right by $10 billion. However, the total shift in the aggregate demand curve will be larger, say, $15 billion. Conversely, a decrease in purchases by $10 billion may cause a total shift of the aggregate demand curve to the left by $15 billion.

This multiplier effect occurs because an initial change in output will affect the income of households, and thus change consumer spending. For example, an increase in government spending of $10 billion will initially raise household incomes by $10 billion and lead to increases in consumer spending. As we discussed in the last chapter, the precise amount of the increase will depend on the marginal propensity to consume. In turn, the increase in consumer spending will raise output and income further, leading to further increases in consumer spending. The multiplier takes all these effects into account.

As the government develops policies to stabilize the economy, it needs to take the multiplier into account. The total shift in aggregate demand will be larger than the initial shift. As we will see later in this chapter, U.S. policy makers have taken the multiplier into account as they have developed policies for the economy.

## The Limits to Stabilization Policy

As we have seen, the government can use fiscal policy—changes in the level of taxes or government spending—to alter the level of GDP. If the current level of GDP is below full employment or potential output, the government can use expansionary policies, such as tax cuts and increased spending, to raise the level of GDP and reduce unemployment.

Both expansionary and contractionary policies are examples of **stabilization policies**, actions to move the economy closer to full employment or potential output.

It is very difficult to implement stabilization policies for two big reasons. First, there are lags, or delays, in stabilization policy. Lags arise because decision makers are often slow to recognize and respond to changes in the economy, and fiscal policies and other stabilization policies take time to operate. Second, economists simply do not know enough about all aspects of the economy to be completely accurate in all their forecasts. Although economists have made great progress in understanding the economy, the difficulties of forecasting the precise behavior of human beings, who can change their minds or sometimes act irrationally, place limits on our forecasting ability.

### LAGS

Poorly timed policies can magnify economic fluctuations. Suppose that (1) GDP is currently below full employment but will return to full employment on its own within one year and that (2) stabilization policies take a full year to become effective. If policy makers tried to expand the economy today, their actions would not take effect until a year from now. One year from now, the economy would normally, by itself, be back at full employment. But one year from now, if stabilization policies were enacted, the economy would be stimulated unnecessarily, and output would exceed full employment.

Figure 15.2 illustrates the problem caused by lags. Panel A shows an example of successful stabilization policy. The solid line represents the behavior of GDP in the absence of policies. Successful stabilization policies can dampen, that is, reduce in magnitude, economic fluctuations, lowering output when it exceeds full employment and raising output when it falls below full employment. This would be easy to accomplish if there were no lags in policy. The dashed curve shows how successful policies can reduce economic fluctuations.

Panel B shows the consequences of ill-timed policies. Again, assume that policies take a year before they are effective. At the start of year 1, the economy is below potential. If policy makers engaged in expansionary policies at the start of year 1, the change would not take effect until the end of year 1. This would raise output even higher above full employment. Ill-timed stabilization policies can magnify economic fluctuations.

Where do the lags in policy come from? Economists recognize two broad classes of lags: *inside lags* and *outside lags*. **Inside lags** refer to the time it takes to formulate a policy. **Outside lags** refer to the time it takes for the policy to actually work. To help you understand inside and outside lags, imagine that you are steering a large ocean liner and you are looking out for possible collisions with hidden icebergs. The time it

**stabilization policies**
Policy actions taken to move the economy closer to full employment or potential output.

**inside lags**
The time it takes to formulate a policy.

**outside lags**
The time it takes for the policy to actually work.

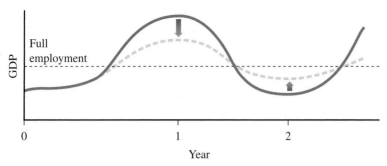

(A) Successful stabilization policy can dampen fluctuations.

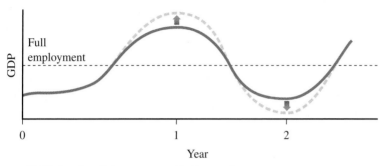

(B) Ill-timed policies can magnify fluctuations.

◄ FIGURE 15.2
Possible Pitfalls in Stabilization Policy
Panel A shows an example of successful stabilization policy. The solid line represents the behavior of GDP in the absence of policies. The dashed line shows the behavior of GDP when policies are in place. Successfully timed policies help smooth out economic fluctuations. Panel B shows the consequences of ill-timed policies. Again, the solid line shows GDP in the absence of policies and the dashed line shows GDP with policies in place. Notice how ill-timed policies make economic fluctuations greater.

takes you to spot an iceberg, communicate this information to the crew, and initiate the process of changing course is the inside lag. Because ocean liners are large and have lots of momentum, it will take a long time before your ocean liner begins to turn; this time is the outside lag.

Inside lags occur for two basic reasons. One reason is that it takes time to identify and recognize a problem. For example, the data available to policy makers may be poor and conflicting. Some economic indicators may look fine, but others may cause concern. It often takes several months to a year before it is clear that there is a serious problem with the economy.

A good example of an inside lag occurred at the beginning of the Great Depression. Although the stock market crashed in October 1929, we know from newspaper and magazine accounts that business leaders were not particularly worried about the economy for some time. Not until late in 1930 did the public begin to recognize the severity of the depression.

The other reason for inside lags is that once a problem has been diagnosed, it still takes time before the government can take action. This delay is most severe for fiscal policy because any changes in taxes or spending must be approved by both houses of Congress and by the president. In recent years, political opponents have been preoccupied with disagreements about the size of the government and the role it should play in the economy, making it difficult to reach a consensus in a timely manner.

For example, soon after he was elected in 1993, President Bill Clinton proposed an expansionary stimulus package as part of his overall budget plan. The package contained a variety of spending programs that were designed to increase the level of GDP and avert a recession. However, the plan was attacked as wasteful and unnecessary, and it did not survive. As it turned out, the stimulus package was not necessary—the economy grew rapidly in the next several years. Nonetheless, this episode illustrates how difficult it is to develop expansionary fiscal policies in time to have the effect we want them to.

Policies are also subject to outside lags—the time it takes for them to become effective. For example, if taxes are cut, it takes time for individuals and businesses to change their spending plans to take advantage of the tax cuts. Therefore, it will take some time before increases in spending will raise GDP. Outside lags in fiscal policy are relatively short. Moreover, the multiplier effects tend to work through the economy rather quickly.

Economists use *econometric models* to replicate the behavior of the economy mathematically and statistically and to assist them in developing economic forecasts. These models can also be used to estimate the length of outside lags. One such model predicts that an increase in government spending will increase GDP by its maximum effect after just six months.

### FORECASTING UNCERTAINTIES

What makes the problem of lags even worse is that economists are not very accurate in forecasting what will happen in the economy. For example, a classic problem that policy makers face when the economy appears to be slowing down is knowing whether the slowdown is temporary or whether it will persist. Unfortunately, stabilization policy cannot be effective without accurate forecasting. If economic forecasters predict an overheated economy and the government adopts a contractionary policy, the result could be disastrous if the economy weakened before the policy took effect. Today, most economic policy makers understand these limitations and are cautious in using activist policies.

# 15.2 | THE FEDERAL BUDGET

The federal budget—the document that describes what the federal government spends and how it pays for that spending—provides the framework for fiscal policy. In this section, we will take a closer look at federal spending and taxation and what happens when one exceeds the other. The federal budget is extremely large, and the programs that the federal government supports are very complex. To give you a sense of the magnitude of the budget, in 2005 total federal spending was approximately 20.2 percent of GDP, or $2.47 trillion. Federal taxes were 17.5 percent of GDP. With a U.S. population of about 300 million, total federal spending amounted to approximately $8,230 per person.

Probably the best way to begin to grasp the scope and complexities of the U.S. federal budget is to look at recent data to see where we spend money and how we raise it. As we explore the budgetary data, keep in mind that the government runs its budget on a *fiscal-year basis*, not a calendar-year basis. Fiscal year 2005, for example, began on October 1, 2004, and ended on September 30, 2005.

States and local governments also provide government services and collect taxes. Some important services, for example, education, are primarily funded by state and local governments, and others, such as welfare and health care for the poor, are funded jointly by the federal government and state governments. However, because our focus in this chapter is on federal fiscal policy, we will concentrate our discussion on federal spending and taxation.

## Federal Spending

Federal spending, spending by the U.S. government, consists of two broad components: federal government purchases of goods and services and transfer payments. As you should recall from our discussion of GDP accounting, only federal government purchases of goods and services are included in GDP. Transfer payments, although an important part of the federal budget, are not a component of GDP because they do not represent any currently produced goods or services.

To study the components of federal spending, we will look at the final data from fiscal year 2005 provided by the Congressional Budget Office, a nonpartisan agency of

**Table 15.1 | FEDERAL SPENDING FOR FISCAL YEAR 2005**

| Category | Outlays (billions) | Percent of GDP |
|---|---|---|
| Total outlays | $2,473 | 20.2% |
| Discretionary spending | 962 | 7.8 |
|   Defense | 493 | 4.0 |
|   Nondefense | 469 | 3.8 |
| Entitlements and mandatory spending | 1,329 | 10.8 |
|   Social Security | 519 | 4.2 |
|   Medicare and Medicaid | 516 | 4.2 |
|   Other programs | 294 | 2.4 |
| Net interest | 182 | 1.5 |

*SOURCE:* Congressional Budget Office, August 2005.

the Congress that provides both budgetary forecasts and historical data on the budget. Table 15.1 provides key data on federal expenditures for fiscal year 2005, both in absolute dollar terms and as a percent of GDP.

Let's begin with the broad categories of the budget. Total spending, or outlays, in fiscal year 2005 were $2,473 billion or approximately 20.2 percent of GDP. Three components of the budget comprise this total: discretionary spending, entitlements and mandatory spending, and net interest.

**Discretionary spending** constitutes all the programs that Congress authorizes on an annual basis that are not automatically funded by prior laws. It includes defense spending and all nondefense domestic spending. When people commonly discuss federal spending, they often focus on this category, which includes the Defense Department, the Environmental Protection Agency, the State Department, the Interior Department, and other agencies. However, discretionary spending is less than 40 percent of total federal spending. Total nondefense spending is less than 4 percent of GDP.

Congress and the president can use discretionary funds directly for activist fiscal policy. To stimulate the economy, they can authorize additional spending by government agencies, or they can urge agencies to accelerate their current spending plans. However, it does take time for bureaucracies to act, and just because Congress authorizes new spending does not mean that the agencies will spend the funds immediately.

**Entitlement and mandatory spending** constitutes all spending that Congress has authorized by prior law. These expenditures must be made by the federal government unless Congress changes the laws. The terms *entitlement* and *mandatory* spending are not totally accurate, however. Individuals are only "entitled" to benefits to the extent that they meet the requirements passed by Congress to collect them. Congress can always change the rules. Similarly, this category of spending is only "mandatory" to the extent that Congress maintains the current programs in place.

Entitlements and mandatory spending are the single-largest component of the federal budget. One of the most familiar programs is **Social Security**, which provides retirement payments to retirees as well as a host of other benefits to widows and families of disabled workers. **Medicare** provides health care to all individuals once they reach the age of 65. **Medicaid** provides health care to the poor, in conjunction with the states. The government provides a range of other programs as well, including additional retirement and disability programs (aside from Social Security) and farm price supports to provide income to farmers. Some of these programs are *means tested*. That is, they are partly based on the income of the recipient. Medicaid, for example, is a means-tested program.

• **discretionary spending**
The spending programs that Congress authorizes on an annual basis.

• **entitlement and mandatory spending**
Spending that Congress has authorized by prior law, primarily providing support for individuals.

• **Social Security**
A federal government program to provide retirement support and a host of other benefits.

• **Medicare**
A federal government health program for the elderly.

• **Medicaid**
A federal and state government health program for the poor.

Net interest is the interest that the government pays the public on the government debt held by the public, for example, U.S. Treasury bonds, bills, and other debt, such as U.S. savings bonds. We will discuss more about how the government borrows money later in the chapter. In fiscal year 2005, total net interest payments to the public were $182 billion, or approximately 1.5 percent of GDP. Total expenditures on net interest are directly related to the total government debt held by the public and the level of interest rates. Increased government debt and higher interest rates will lead to higher net interest payments by the government.

# APPLICATION

## INCREASING LIFE EXPECTANCY AND AGING POPULATIONS SPUR COSTS OF ENTITLEMENT PROGRAMS

**APPLYING THE CONCEPTS #1:** Why are the United States and many other countries facing dramatically increasing costs for their government programs?

As life expectancies increase, the population ages, and new medical technologies become available to help people live longer, economists and budget analysts predict that spending on federal retirement and health programs will grow extremely rapidly. Today, Social Security, Medicare, and Medicaid constitute approximately 9 percent of GDP. Experts estimate that in 2075—when children born today are in their retirement years—spending on these programs will be approximately 21 percent of GDP. This is a larger share of GDP than *all* government spending today! How will our society cope with increased demands for these services?

One possibility is to leave the existing programs in place and just raise taxes to pay for them. This strategy would have two implications: First, if we maintained the federal share of GDP of all other programs, it would mean a large expansion of the federal government, from 20 percent of GDP to 32 percent of GDP. Second, it would mean a very large increase in our tax burden. That would impose burdens on future workers and businesses.

Some economists suggest that the government should save and invest now to increase GDP in the future to reduce the burden on future generations. However, the saving and investment would increase GDP, and entitlement payments would grow right along with it. As a result, the relative burden of taking care of the elderly would not change dramatically.

Another strategy would be to try to reform the entitlement systems, placing more responsibility on individuals and families for their retirement and well-being. For example, we could increase the age at which retirement benefits begin to be paid, and thereby encourage individuals to spend more years in the labor force. Or we could try to reform the health-care system to encourage more competition to reduce health-care expenditures.

All of the changes would be very difficult to make, however. Other countries, including Japan and many in Europe, which have even older populations and low birth rates, will face even more severe challenges and face them earlier than the United States will. Perhaps we can learn from them. Nonetheless, pressures on the federal budget will begin to escalate in the next decade, and policy makers will need to take steps soon to cope with the challenge. *Related to Exercise 2.8.*

**Table 15.2** | SOURCES OF FEDERAL GOVERNMENT REVENUE, FISCAL YEAR 2005

| Category | Receipts (billions) | Percent of GDP |
|---|---|---|
| Total revenue | $2,142 | 17.5% |
| Individual income taxes | 927 | 7.6 |
| Social insurance taxes | 794 | 6.5 |
| Corporate taxes | 269 | 2.2 |
| Estate, excise, and others | 153 | 1.2 |

*SOURCE:* Congressional Budget Office, August 2005.

As the population ages, entitlements and net interest are the fastest-growing component of the federal budget.

## Federal Revenues

The federal government receives its revenue from taxes levied on both individuals and businesses. Table 15.2 shows the revenues the federal government received in fiscal year 2005 in both dollar terms and as a percent of GDP.

Let's review the categories that comprise total federal revenue. The single-largest component of federal revenue is the *individual income tax*. Most everyone is familiar with the federal income tax. Tax returns calculating the tax due by individuals or couples during the prior year must be filed by April 15 of every year. During the year, the federal government collects in advance some of the taxes due by *withholding* a portion of workers' paychecks. Taxpayers not subject to withholding or who earn income through investments must make estimated tax payments each quarter so that the tax due to the federal government is paid evenly over the year in which it is earned.

The second-largest component of federal revenue is *social insurance taxes*, which are taxes levied on earnings to pay for Social Security and Medicare. Today, social insurance taxes are almost as large as individual income taxes, and together they comprise nearly 80 percent of total federal revenue. Unlike individual income taxes, social insurance taxes are paid only on wages and not on income from investments.

Other taxes paid directly by individuals and families include *estate and gift taxes*, *excise taxes*, and *custom duties*. Estate and gift taxes, sometimes known as the "death tax," are levied on the estates and previous gifts of individuals when they pass away. In 2004, estates are taxed only if they exceed $1.5 million—so small estates do not pay this tax—and that threshold is scheduled to increase during this decade. The estate and gift tax raised only 0.2 percent of total federal revenue in 2005, but it generates a great deal of controversy. Opponents of the tax argue that it destroys family-held businesses, such as family farms passed down from one generation to the next. Proponents claim the tax is necessary to prevent "unfair" accumulation of wealth across generations.

The corporate tax is a tax levied on the earnings of corporations. This tax raised less than 13 percent of total federal revenues during fiscal year 2005. The tax was a more important source of revenue in past decades but has declined to today's relatively low level. This decline has been attributed to many factors, including falling corporate profits as a share of GDP, the growth of opportunities for tax shelters, incentives provided by Congress to stimulate business investment and research and development, and complex rules for taxing multinational corporations that operate on a global basis.

The other sources of government revenue are relatively minor. *Federal excise taxes* are taxes levied on the sale of certain products, for example, gasoline, tires, firearms, alcohol, and tobacco. *Custom duties* are taxes levied on goods imported to the United States, such as foreign cars or wines.

## SUPPLY-SIDE ECONOMICS AND THE LAFFER CURVE

Is it possible for a government to cut tax rates yet still raise more revenue? That's a politician's dream. People would face lower tax rates, yet there would be more money for politicians to spend. Economist Arthur Laffer argued in the late 1970s that there was a strong possibility that we could do this in the U.S. economy. Laffer's views influenced many politicians at the time and became the basis for supply-side economics. **Supply-side economics** is a school of thought that emphasizes the role taxes play in the supply of output in the economy. Supply-side economists look not just at the effects of taxes on aggregate demand, as we did earlier in this chapter, but also on aggregate supply. A decrease in tax rates will typically tend to increase the supply of labor and output. Thus, changes in taxes can also shift the aggregate supply curve.

Laffer also developed a model known today as the **Laffer curve**. Suppose a government imposed extremely high tariffs (taxes) on imported goods—tariffs so high that no one could afford to import any goods whatsoever. If this were the case, the government would not collect any revenue from the tariffs. But, if the government cut the rates and individuals began to buy imported goods, the government would start to collect at least some tariff revenue. This was Laffer's point: Lower taxes (tariffs) could actually lead to higher government revenues.

Virtually all economists today believe Laffer's tax revenue idea won't work when it comes to broad-based income taxes or payroll taxes. For these types of taxes, cutting rates from their current levels would simply reduce the revenues that the government collects, because most economists believe that the supply of labor is not as sensitive to changes in tax rates as Laffer believed. But there are some taxes, such as tariffs or taxes on the gains investors' earn by holding stocks and bonds, for which Laffer's claim is plausible.

## The Federal Deficit and Fiscal Policy

The federal government runs a **budget deficit** when it spends more than it receives in tax revenues in a given year. Here is how it works. Suppose a government wishes to spend $100 billion but receives only $95 billion in tax revenue. To actually spend the $100 billion, the government must obtain funds from some source. Facing a $5 billion shortfall, the government will borrow that money from the public. They do so by selling government bonds to the public. A *government bond* is an IOU in which the government promises to pay back the money lent to it with interest. Thus, when the public purchases $5 billion of these bonds, it transfers $5 billion to the government. Later the public will receive the $5 billion back with interest.

If the government collects more in taxes than it wishes to spend in a given year, it is running a **budget surplus**. In this case, the government has excess funds and can buy back bonds previously sold to the public.

You often read about budget forecasts for decades into the future. These forecasts are extremely difficult to make and require explicit assumptions about the future course of economic policy.

## Automatic Stabilizers

Both government spending and tax revenues are very sensitive to the state of the economy. Because tax collections are based largely on individual and corporate income, tax revenues will fall sharply during a recession as national income falls. At the same time, government transfer payments for programs such as unemployment insurance and food stamps will also tend to increase during a recession. The result is higher government spending and lower tax collections and the increased likelihood that the government will run a budget deficit. Similarly, when the economy grows rapidly, tax collections increase and government expenditures on transfer payments decrease, and the likelihood of the federal government running a surplus is greater.

# APPLICATION

## HOW GOVERNMENTS USE BUDGET BASELINES TO FORECAST DEFICITS

**APPLYING THE CONCEPTS #2:** How does the U.S. government make short- and long-term budget projections?

When Congress and the president consider the proper course of fiscal policy, they want to consider the future state of the budget—will there be a deficit or surplus and how big will the deficit or surplus be? But to make these forecasts, it is necessary to make explicit assumptions about what spending and tax policies will be in place. These assumptions are known as *budget baselines*.

For example, for long-term forecasts the Congressional Budget Office (CBO) assumes that mandatory spending will continue as required by law while discretionary spending will remain constant in real terms. For taxes, the CBO also makes its estimates based on current law, taking into account if tax provisions are scheduled to expire in the future. Even if most political observers believe that Congress will not, in fact, let important tax provisions expire, CBO is required to assume so in its budget baseline. For example, if a popular major tax cut is scheduled to expire, CBO might project a balanced budget, but in reality Congress might reestablish the tax cut, with a resulting budget deficit. In general, future budget forecasts should be treated very cautiously. *Related to Exercise 2.9.*

**BUSH 2006 BUDGET: SIMPLY ON THE WRONG TRACK**

| | AMTRAK NEEDS | BUSH BUDGET | FINAL FUNDING | |
|---|---|---|---|---|
| 02 | $955 M | $521 M | $831 M | 13% CUT |
| 03 | $1.2 B | $521 M | $1 B | 13% CUT |
| 04 | $1.8 B | $900 M | $1.2 B | 33% CUT |
| 05 | $1.8 B | $900 M | $1.2 B | 33% CUT |
| 06 | $1.8 B | $0 | ? | |

Now suppose an economy had a balanced federal budget—neither deficit nor surplus. An external shock (such as a dramatic increase in oil prices or drought) then plunged the economy into a recession. Tax revenues fall and expenditures on transfer payments increase, resulting in a budget deficit. Believe it or not, the increased budget deficit actually serves a valuable role in stabilizing the economy. The increased federal budget deficit works through three channels:

1 Increased transfer payments such as unemployment insurance, food stamps, and other welfare payments increase the income of some households, partly offsetting the fall in household income.

2 Other households whose incomes are falling pay less in taxes, which partly offsets the decline in their household income. Because incomes do not fall as much as they would have in the absence of the deficit, consumption spending does not decline as much.

3 Because the corporation tax depends on corporate profits and profits fall in a recession, taxes also fall on businesses. Lower corporate taxes help to prevent businesses from cutting spending as much as they would otherwise during a recession.

The government deficit itself, in effect, offsets part of the adverse effect of the recession and thus helps stabilize the economy.

Similarly, during an economic boom, transfer payments fall and tax revenues increase. This dampens the increase in household income and also the increase in consumption and investment spending that would accompany higher household income and higher corporate profits. Taxes and transfer payments that stabilize GDP without requiring explicit actions by policy makers are called **automatic stabilizers**.

• **automatic stabilizers**
Taxes and transfer payments that stabilize GDP without requiring policy makers to take explicit action.

The great virtue of automatic stabilizers is that they do not require explicit action from the president and Congress to change the law. Given the long inside lags caused by ideological battles in Washington, D.C., over spending, taxes, and the deficit, it is fortunate to have mechanisms in place that dampen economic fluctuations without requiring explicit and deliberative action.

### Are Deficits Bad?

Let's take a closer look at fiscal policy designed to stabilize the economy. If the budget were initially balanced and the economy plunged into a recession, a budget deficit would emerge as tax revenues fell and expenditures increased. To combat the recession, policy makers could then either increase government spending or cut taxes. Both actions, however, would increase the deficit—an important point to remember.

Despite concerns about increasing the deficit, this is precisely the right policy. If policy makers tried to avoid running a deficit by raising taxes or cutting spending, that would actually make the recession worse. The key lesson here is that during a recession, we should focus on what our fiscal policy actions do to the economy, not what they do to the deficit.

Does that mean that concerns about the federal budget deficit are misplaced? No, in the long run, large budget deficits can have an adverse effect on the economy. In the long run, an economy will operate at full employment. The level of output at full employment must be divided between consumption, investment, government spending, and net exports. Suppose, then, that the government cuts taxes for households and runs a deficit. The reduced taxes will tend to increase consumer spending. Consumers may save some of the tax cut, but will consume the rest. However, because in the long run, output is at full employment, some other component of output must be reduced, or crowded out. Crowding out is an example of the principle of opportunity cost.

## PRINCIPLE OF OPPORTUNITY COST
The opportunity cost of something is what you sacrifice to get it.

In this case, we normally expect that the increased consumption spending will come at the sacrifice of reduced investment spending. As we have seen, with reduced investment spending, the economy will grow more slowly in the future. Thus, the budget deficit will increase current consumption but slow the growth of the economy in the future. This is the real concern with prolonged budget deficits.

Another way to understand the concern about long-run deficits is to think of what happens in the financial markets when the government runs large deficits. As the government runs large deficits, it will have to borrow increasing amounts of money from the public by selling U.S. government bonds. In the financial markets, the government will be in increased competition with businesses that are trying to raise funds from the public to finance their investment plans, too. This increased competition from the government will make it more difficult and costly for businesses to raise funds and, as a result, investment spending will decrease.

## 15.3 | FISCAL POLICY IN U.S. HISTORY

The fiscal policies that Congress and the president use have evolved over many years. In this section, we review the historical events that helped create today's U.S. fiscal policies.

## The Depression Era

The basic principles of fiscal policy—using government spending and taxation to stabilize the economy—have been known for many years and, indeed, were discussed in the 1920s. However, it took a long time before economic-policy decisions were based on these principles. Many people associate active fiscal policy in the United States with actions taken by President Franklin Roosevelt during the Great Depression of the 1930s. But this view is misleading, according to E. Cary Brown, a former economics professor at the Massachusetts Institute of Technology.[1]

During the 1930s, politicians did not believe in modern fiscal policy, largely because they feared the consequences of government budget deficits. According to Brown, fiscal policy was expansionary only during two years of the Great Depression, 1931 and 1936. In those years, Congress voted for substantial payments to veterans, over objections of Presidents Herbert Hoover and Franklin Roosevelt. Although government spending increased during the 1930s, taxes increased sufficiently during that same period, with the result that there was no net fiscal expansion.

## The Kennedy Administration

Although modern fiscal policy was not deliberately used during the 1930s, the growth in military spending at the onset of World War II increased total demand in the economy and helped to pull the economy out of its long decade of poor performance. But to see fiscal policy in action, we need to turn to the 1960s. It was not until the presidency of John F. Kennedy during the early 1960s that modern fiscal policy came to be accepted.

Walter Heller, the chairman of the president's Council of Economic Advisers under John F. Kennedy, was a forceful advocate of active fiscal policy. From his perspective, the economy was operating far below its potential, and a tax cut was the perfect medicine to bring the economy back to full employment. When Kennedy entered office, the unemployment rate was 6.7 percent. Heller believed that the unemployment rate at full employment—the "natural rate" of unemployment, that is—was really only about 4 percent. He convinced Kennedy of the need for a tax cut to stimulate the economy, and Kennedy put forth an economic program that was based largely on modern fiscal policy principles.

Two other factors led the Kennedy administration to support the tax cut: First, tax rates were extremely high at the time. The top individual tax rate was 91 percent, compared to about 40 percent today. The corporate tax rate was 52 percent, compared to 35 percent today. Second, Heller convinced Kennedy that even if a tax cut led to a federal budget deficit, it was not a problem. In 1961, the federal deficit was less than 1 percent of GDP, and future projections indicated that the deficit would disappear as the economy grew because of higher tax revenues.

The tax cuts were enacted in February 1964, after Lyndon Johnson became president following Kennedy's assassination. The tax cuts included permanent cuts in rates for both individuals and corporations. Estimating the actual effects that the tax cuts had on the economy is difficult. However, to make a valid comparison, we need to estimate how the economy would have behaved without the tax cuts. What we do know is that the economy grew at a rapid rate following the tax cuts. From 1963 to 1966, both real GDP and consumption grew at rates exceeding 4 percent per year. We cannot rule out the possibility that the economy could have grown just as rapidly without the tax cuts. Nonetheless, the rapid growth during this period suggests that the tax cuts had the effect, predicted by Heller's theory, of stimulating economic growth.

## The Vietnam War Era

The next major use of modern fiscal policy occurred in 1968. As the Vietnam War began and military spending increased, unemployment fell to very low levels. From 1966 to 1969, the overall unemployment rate fell below 4 percent. Policy makers became concerned that the economy was overheating and that this would lead to a higher inflation rate. In 1968, a temporary tax surcharge of 10 percent was enacted to reduce total demand for goods and services. The 10-percent surcharge was a "tax on a tax," so it raised the taxes paid by households by 10 percent. Essentially, the surcharge was specifically designed to be temporary and expired within a year.

The surcharge did not decrease consumer spending as much as economists had initially estimated, however. Part of the reason was that the tax increase was temporary. Economists who have studied consumption behavior have noticed that consumers often base their spending on an estimate of their long-run average income, or **permanent income**, not on their current income.

• **permanent income**
An estimate of a household's long-run average level of income.

For example, consider a salesperson who usually earns $50,000 a year, although her income in any single year might be slightly higher or lower. Knowing that her permanent income is $50,000, she consumes $45,000. If her income in one year is higher than average, say $55,000, she is still likely to consume $45,000 (as if she earned just her normal $50,000) and save the rest.

The temporary, one-year tax surcharge during the Vietnam War had a similar effect. Because consumers knew the surcharge was not permanent, they didn't alter their spending habits very much. The surtax reduced households' savings, not their consumption. The result was a smaller decrease in demand for goods and services than economists anticipated.

During the 1970s, there were many changes in taxes and spending but no major changes in overall fiscal policy. A recession in 1973 led to a tax rebate and other incentives in 1975, but, by and large, changes to fiscal policy were mild.

## The Reagan Administration

The tax cuts enacted during 1981 at the beginning of the first term of President Ronald Reagan were significant. However, they were not proposed to increase aggregate demand. Instead, the tax cuts were justified on the basis of improving economic incentives and increasing the supply of output. In other words, they were supply-side motivated. Taxes can have important effects on the supply of labor, saving, and economic growth. Proponents of the 1981 tax cuts emphasized these particular effects and not increases in aggregate demand. Nonetheless, the tax cuts did appear to increase consumer demand and helped the economy recover from the back-to-back recessions in the early 1980s.

By the mid-1980s, large government budget deficits began to emerge, and policy makers became concerned by them. As the deficits grew and became the focus of attention, interest in using fiscal policy to manage the economy waned. Although there were government spending and tax changes in the 1980s and 1990s, few of them were justified solely as policies to change aggregate demand.

## The Clinton and George W. Bush Administrations

At the beginning of his administration, President Bill Clinton proposed a "stimulus package" that would increase aggregate demand, but it was defeated in Congress. Clinton later successfully passed a major tax increase that brought the budget into balance. By the year 1998, the federal budget actually began to show surpluses rather than deficits, setting the stage for tax cuts.

During his first year in office in 2001, President George W. Bush passed a 10-year tax cut plan that decreased tax rates, in part to eliminate the government surpluses and return revenues to households, but also to stimulate the economy that was slowing down as the high-tech investment boom was ending.

The first year of the tax cut featured tax rebates or refunds of up to $600 per married couple. The refunds were intended to increase aggregate demand.

# APPLICATION

## SURVEYS SHOW MUCH OF THE 2001 TAX CUTS WERE SAVED

**APPLYING THE CONCEPTS #3:** How much did the 2001 tax cuts stimulate consumer spending?

In 2001, approximately 90 million U.S. households received tax rebate checks from the government. These checks were up to $300 for a single taxpayer or $600 for joint, or married, filers. The tax rebate was just the first installment of a multiyear tax reduction for households stemming from a new tax bill passed that year.

According to conventional economic theory, a permanent cut in taxes should largely be spent by households because it represents a new permanent source of income for them. To discover whether in practice households actually spent the tax cuts, Professors Matthew Shapiro and Joel Slemrod surveyed households using the University of Michigan Survey Research Center Monthly Survey. They asked a nationally representative set of households whether they were more likely to spend the rebate, save it, or pay down existing debts (another form of saving). Shapiro and Slemrod surveyed households both when the rebate checks were being mailed and following their arrival.

They found that less than 25 percent of households were likely to spend the rebate—which defied conventional economic wisdom. Moreover, to their surprise, low-income households were no more likely to spend the rebate than higher-income households. According to their results, the tax rebates had only limited success in stimulating aggregate demand.

In analyzing the survey results, Shapiro and Slemrod noted that many households surveyed did not believe that they would receive future rebates of a similar size, despite the change in the tax law. They also speculated that the large fall in the stock market in the two previous years may have made households more financially tentative and inclined to save the tax cut. These results suggest that policy makers need to be cautious in their use of fiscal policy. *Related to Exercise 3.5.*

SOURCE: Matthew Shapiro and Joel Slemrod, "Consumer Response to Tax Rebates," *American Economic Review*, vol. 93, no. 1, March 2003, pp. 381–396.

---

After the September 11, 2001, terrorist attacks, President Bush and Congress became less concerned with balancing the federal budget and authorized new spending programs to provide relief to victims and to stimulate the economy, which had entered into a recession prior to September 11.

In May 2003, President Bush signed another tax bill to stimulate the sluggish economy and, in particular, to increase investment spending. This bill had many distinct features, including moving up some of the previously scheduled cuts in tax rates that were part of the 2001 tax bill, increasing the child tax credit, and lowering taxes on dividends and capital gains.

The combination of the recession, tax cuts, and the increased expenses associated with the wars in Afghanistan and in Iraq in 2003 sharply changed the fiscal landscape

**383**

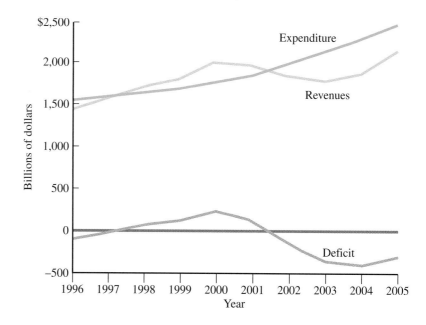

**► FIGURE 15.3**
Federal Taxes, Spending, and Deficits, 1996–2005

again. For fiscal year 2005, the deficit was approximately $331 billion. Other unexpected events, including the federal response to the devastation from Hurricane Katrina, added to the deficit. Figure 15.3 plots the course of spending, taxes, and the deficit since 1996 and shows the recent reemergence of deficits. The prospect of future deficits sharply limits the ability of the U.S. government to conduct expansionary fiscal policy in the near future and will set the background for the political debates in Washington, D.C., for many years to come.

# SUMMARY

This chapter explored the role of government fiscal policy. Using the AD–AS model, we showed how fiscal policy can stabilize the economy. We also discussed the multiplier and the limits to stabilization policy. In addition, the chapter gave us an overview of the federal budget, including spending, revenues, deficits, and surpluses. Finally, we explored how fiscal policy in the United States has changed over time. Here are the key points:

1 Increases in government spending or decreases in taxes will increase aggregate demand.

2 Decreases in government spending or increases in taxes will decrease aggregate demand.

3 Because of the multiplier, the total shift in the aggregate demand curve will be larger than the initial shift. Policy makers need to take the multiplier into account as they formulate policy.

4 Both *inside lags* (the time it takes to formulate policy) and *outside lags* (the time it takes the policy to work) limit the effectiveness of active fiscal policy.

5 The largest component of federal spending is *entitlements and mandatory programs*.

6 The largest components of federal revenues are income taxes and social insurance contributions collected from individuals.

7 Government deficits act as an *automatic stabilizer* that helps to stabilize the economy in the short run.

8 In the short run, fiscal policy actions taken to combat a recession will increase the deficit; in the long run, deficits are a concern because they may lead to crowding out of investment spending.

9 Active fiscal policy has been periodically used in the United States to stimulate the economy; at other times, concerns about deficits have limited the use of fiscal policy.

# KEY TERMS

automatic stabilizers, p. 379

budget deficit, p. 378

budget surplus, p. 378

contractionary policies, p. 371

discretionary spending, p. 375

entitlement and mandatory
     spending, p. 375

expansionary policies, p. 371

fiscal policy, p. 370

inside lags, p. 372

Laffer curve, p. 378

Medicaid, p. 375

Medicare, p. 375

outside lags, p. 372

permanent income, p. 382

Social Security, p. 375

stabilization policies, p. 372

supply-side economics, p. 378

# EXERCISES

Get Ahead of the Curve

Visit www.myeconlab.com to complete these exercises online and get instant feedback.

## 15.1 | The Role of Fiscal Policy

**1.1** To increase aggregate demand, a government can either increase spending or _____ taxes.

**1.2** Contractionary fiscal policy shifts the aggregate demand curve to the _____, _____ prices and _____ real GDP.

**1.3** If the multiplier for government spending is 1.10, then a $110 billion increase in government spending will ultimately shift the demand curve by _____.

**1.4** _____ lags refer to the time it takes for policy makers to recognize an economic problem and take appropriate actions.

**1.5** **A Chinese Experiment.** In 2000, the Chinese government mandated three, one-week holidays throughout the year to stimulate consumer spending. The idea was that these extended vacations would induce the Chinese to spend more of their earnings while on vacation.
   **a.** Using the AD–AS framework, show the mechanism through which the Chinese government believed that the mandated holidays would stimulate the economy.
   **b.** Although consumption spending rose during the vacation period, the data show that consumption fell before and after the vacation. Did the policy work?

**1.6** **Time-Dated Certificates.** The chapter-opening story presented a discussion of a proposal made in Japan to issue time-dated certificates to each person that had to be spent on goods and services within a fixed period or become worthless. Suppose the government was considering whether to issue $400 in time-dated certificates to each household or give each household $400 in cash instead.
   **a.** Which plan would lead to the greatest economic stimulus? How would that depend on the marginal propensity to consume and the fact that this was a one-time program?
   **b.** Which plan do you think the government would find easier to administer?
   **c.** Suppose a household had large credit card debt, which it wished to reduce. Which of the two plans would that household prefer?

**1.7** **The Multiplier and Fiscal Policy.** Why is it important for policy makers to take into account the multiplier as they design fiscal policies?

**1.8** **Fiscal Policy and Inside Lags.** Explain why fiscal policy has very long inside lags.

**1.9** **Financing Budget Deficits.** How does the U.S. government "finance" its budget deficits?

## 15.2 | The Federal Budget

**2.1** Fiscal year 2007 begins on October 1, _____.

**2.2** Discretionary spending is the largest component of federal spending. _____ (True/False)

**2.3** Two examples of entitlement spending are _____ and _____.

**2.4** The two primary sources of federal government revenue are _____ and _____.

**2.5** **The States and Balanced Budgets.** Unlike the U.S. federal government, virtually all states have requirements that they must either plan for or maintain a balanced budget.

**a.** Suppose the national economy experiences a recession. How will this affect the budgets of the states?

**b.** What actions must the states then take to balance the budget?

**c.** Graphically show how these actions, taken together, may destabilize the national economy.

**2.6** **Automatic Stabilizers and Fluctuations in Output.** Because of automatic stabilizers, states with more generous unemployment insurance programs will experience _____ fluctuations in output.

**2.7** **Interest Rate Increases and Government Spending.** In 2005, interest rates in the United States rose. What component of federal spending automatically increased?

**2.8** **Mandatory Spending and Entitlements.** Is "mandatory spending" really mandatory? _____ (yes/no) Explain how mandatory spending differs from discretionary spending. In the face of the coming crisis in entitlement spending, do you believe that mandatory spending will be harder to change than discretionary spending? (Related to Application 1 on page 376.)

**2.9** **Expiring Tax Cuts and Deficit Forecasts.** Suppose a major tax cut that is extremely popular is scheduled to expire in 2011. How would the Congressional Budget Office baseline forecast for revenues differ from a more realistic forecast? (Related to Application 2 on page 379.)

## 15.3 | Fiscal Policy in U.S. History

**3.1** President _____ was the first president to consciously use fiscal policy to stabilize the economy.

**3.2** Fiscal policy was not used very aggressively in the late 1980s and 1990s because of large _____.

**3.3** The U.S. economy witnessed federal budget surpluses in _____.

**3.4** Long-run average income is known as _____ income.

**3.5** **Tax Refunds and Consumer Spending.** In 1999, the Internal Revenue Service began to mail out refund checks because of changes in the tax law in 1998. Economic forecasters predicted that consumption and GDP would increase because of higher refunds on income taxes. Using each of the following assumptions, do you think the forecasters were correct? Answer yes or no. (Related to Application 3 on page 383.)

a. Taxpayers were not aware that they would receive refunds until they had completed their income tax statements.

b. Taxpayers did know that they would receive refunds but, as consumers, based their spending decisions solely on their current levels of income.

c. Taxpayers did know that they would receive refunds and, as consumers, based their consumption decisions on their permanent incomes.

3.6 **The Emergence of Fiscal Surpluses.** What factors led the United States from federal surpluses at the end of the 1990s to deficits in the first decade of 2000?

3.7 **Fiscal Policy for Presidents Roosevelt and Kennedy.** Graphically contrast the effects on prices and real GDP of the fiscal policy of the Kennedy administration in the 1960s and the Roosevelt administration during the Great Depression.

3.8 **College Students and Tax Rebates.** If a college student received a tax rebate, do you think she would be more likely to save it or spend it? How about a middle-aged married man? Explain your reasoning.

3.9 **The Changing Corporate Tax.** Go to the Web site for the Congressional Budget Office (www.cbo.gov) and find historical data on government revenues. Show how the importance of corporate taxes has changed over time.

3.10 **Long-Run Deficit Projections.** The Congressional Budget Office also makes long-run deficit budget projections, extending far into the twenty-first century. What are the main causes of the long-run deficits projected by the CBO?

## NOTES

1. E. Cary Brown, "Fiscal Policy in the 1930s: A Reappraisal," *American Economic Review*, December 1956, Vol. 46, pp. 857–879.

# 16

# Money and the Banking System

As long as there has been paper money, there have been counterfeiters. To combat these counterfeiters (many of whom now just use high-quality photocopiers to recreate money), the U.S. Treasury has introduced one cutting-edge printing technique after another. For example, if you hold up a real $5 dollar bill to the light, you'll notice a faint hologram of Lincoln directly to the right of his printed image. The hologram can't be reproduced easily with photo-copiers, but they are easily visible to cashiers and bank personnel (and anyone else willing to look).

1 What fraction of the stock of U.S. currency is held abroad?
*More Than Half of U.S. Currency Is Held Overseas*

2 Who were the two men who served as chairman of the Federal Reserve from 1979 to 2006 and what were their principal accomplishments?
*Two Recent Major Leaders of the Federal Reserve Board*

3 How did the Fed successfully respond to the major stock market crash in 1987?
*Coping with a Stock Market Crash: Black Monday, 1987*

4 How did the Fed manage to keep the financial system in operation immediately following the attacks on September 11, 2001?
*The Financial System Under Stress: September 11, 2001*

The government must keep innovating to stay ahead. On March 2, 2006, the Federal Reserve banks issued a redesigned $10 note to the public through commercial banks. The notes began circulating immediately in the United States. These notes contained a number of new features as part of an ongoing effort to stay ahead of counterfeiters. These included ink that changes colors as you tilt the bill, watermarks that are visible through both sides of the bills, and a security thread sensitive to ultraviolet light. These may all seem like technological marvels, but the institution of money is even a greater miracle.

The term *money* has a special meaning for economists, so in this chapter we'll look carefully at how money is defined and the role that it plays in the economy. The overall level of money affects the performance of an economy. In Chapter 14, we learned that increases in the money supply increase aggregate demand. In the short run, when prices are largely fixed, this increase will raise total demand and output. But in the long run, continuing money growth leads to inflation.

Our nation's central bank, the Federal Reserve, is responsible for controlling the money supply. In this chapter, we'll see how the Federal Reserve is structured, how it operates, and why it's so powerful.

# 16.1 | WHAT *IS* MONEY?

**money**
Any items that are regularly used in economic transactions or exchanges and accepted by buyers and sellers.

Economists define **money** as any items that are regularly used in economic transactions or exchanges and accepted by buyers and sellers. Let's consider some examples of money used in that way.

We use money regularly every day. In a coffee shop, we hand the person behind the counter some dollar bills and coins, and we receive a cup of coffee. This is an example of an economic exchange: One party hands over currency—the dollar bills and the coins—and the other party hands over goods and services (the coffee). Why do the owners of coffee shops accept the dollar bills and coins in payment for the coffee? The reason is that they will be making other economic exchanges with the dollar bills and coins they accept. Suppose a cup of coffee costs $1.50 and 100 cups are sold in a day. The seller then has $150 in currency. If the coffee costs the seller $100, the seller pays $100 of the currency received and keeps $50 for other expenses and profits. Money makes that possible.

In the real world, transactions are somewhat more complicated. The coffee shop owners take the currency they receive each day, deposit it in bank accounts, and then pay suppliers with checks drawn on those accounts. Clearly, currency is money because it is used to purchase coffee. Checks also function as money because they are used to pay suppliers. In some ancient cultures, precious stones were used in exchanges. In more recent times, gold bars have served as money. During World War II, prisoners of war did not have currency, but they did have rations of cigarettes, so they used them like money, trading them for what they wanted.

## Three Properties of Money

Regardless of what money is used in a particular society, it serves several functions, all related to making economic exchanges easier. Here we discuss three key properties of money.

### MONEY SERVES AS A MEDIUM OF EXCHANGE

**medium of exchange**
Any item that buyers give to sellers when they purchase goods and services.

**barter**
The exchange of one good or service for another.

**double coincidence of wants**
The problem in a system of barter that one person may not have what the other desires.

As our examples illustrate, money is given by buyers to sellers in economic exchanges; therefore, it serves as a **medium of exchange**. Suppose money did not exist and you had a car you wanted to sell to buy a boat. You could look for a person who had a boat and wanted to buy a car and then trade your car directly for a boat. This would be an example of **barter**: the exchange of one good or service for another.

But there are obvious problems with barter. Suppose local boat builders were interested in selling boats but not interested in buying your car. Unless there were a **double coincidence of wants**—that is, unless you wanted to trade a car for a boat, and the boat owner wanted to trade a boat for your car—this economic exchange wouldn't occur. The probability of a double coincidence of wants occurring is very, very tiny. Even if a boat owner wanted a car, he or she might want a different type of car than yours.

By serving as a medium of exchange, money solves this bartering problem. The car owner can sell the car to anyone who wants it and receive money in return. With that money, the car owner can then find someone who owns a boat and purchase the boat for money. The boat owner can use the money in any way he or she pleases. With money, there is no need for a double coincidence of wants. This is why money exists in all societies: It makes economic transactions much easier.

Here is another way to think about this. One of our key principles of economics is that individuals are better off through voluntary exchange.

# PRINCIPLE OF VOLUNTARY EXCHANGE
A voluntary exchange between two people makes both people better off.

Money allows individuals to actually *make* these exchanges. Without money, we would be left with a barter system, and most transactions that make both people better off would not be possible.

## MONEY SERVES AS A UNIT OF ACCOUNT

Money also provides a convenient measuring rod when prices for all goods are quoted in money terms. A boat may be listed for sale at $5,000, a car at $10,000, and a movie ticket at $5. All these prices are quoted in money. We could, in principle, quote everything in terms of movie tickets. The boat would be worth 1,000 tickets, and the car would be worth 2,000 tickets. But because we are using money (and not movie tickets) as a medium of exchange, it is much easier if all prices are expressed in terms of money. A **unit of account** is a standard unit in which prices can be stated and the value of goods and services can be compared. In our economy, money is used as the unit of account because prices are all quoted in terms of money. It is useful to have the medium of exchange also be the unit of account so that prices for all goods and services are quoted in terms of the medium of exchange that is used in transactions—in our case, money.

> • **unit of account**
> A standard unit in which prices can be stated and the value of goods and services can be compared.

## MONEY SERVES AS A STORE OF VALUE

If you sell your car to purchase a boat, you may not be able to purchase the boat immediately. In the meantime, you will be holding the money you received from the sale. Ideally, during that period, the value of the money should not change. What we are referring to here is the function of money as a **store of value**.

Money is actually a somewhat imperfect store of value because of inflation. Suppose inflation is 10 percent a year, which means that all prices rise 10 percent each year. Let's say you sold a tennis racket for $100 to buy 10 CDs worth $100, but that you waited a year to buy them. Unfortunately, at the end of the year, the 10 CDs now cost $110 ($100 × 1.10), or $11 each. With your $100, you can now buy only nine CDs and get $1 in change. Your money has lost some of its stored value.

As long as inflation is low and you do not hold the money for a long time, the loss in its purchasing power won't be a big problem. But as inflation rates increase, money becomes less useful as a store of value.

> • **store of value**
> The property of money that it preserves value until it is used in an exchange.

## Different Types of Monetary Systems

Historically, the world has witnessed different types of monetary systems. The first system is one in which a commodity, such as gold or silver, is used as money, either in the form of bars or coins. This is an example of **commodity money**, in which an actual commodity (gold or silver) serves as money. At some point, governments began issuing paper money. However, the paper money was backed by an underlying commodity, for example, so many ounces of gold. Under a traditional **gold standard**, an individual could present paper money to the government and receive its stated value

> • **commodity money**
> A monetary system in which the actual money is a commodity, such as gold or silver.
>
> • **gold standard**
> A monetary system in which gold backs up paper money.

- **fiat money**
  A monetary system in which money has no intrinsic value but is backed by the government.

- **M1**
  The sum of currency in the hands of the public, demand deposits, other checkable deposits, and travelers' checks.

in gold. In other words, paper money could be exchanged for gold. Prior to 1933 in the United States, individuals could exchange their dollars for gold. President Franklin Roosevelt, however, banned private possession of gold in 1933, although foreign governments could still exchange dollars for gold until 1971. The next step in the evolution of monetary systems was to break the tie between paper money and gold and create a system of *fiat money*. **Fiat money** has no intrinsic value—it is simply created by a government decree. A government will issue paper money and make this money the official legal tender of the society. In the United States today, if you take a $100 bill to the government you will not receive any gold or silver—just another $100 bill in return.

You may wonder what gives money value under a fiat system if it has no intrinsic value. The answer is that the government controls the value of fiat money by controlling its supply in the economy. That is why it is important to prevent counterfeiting, as our chapter-opening story described. In the next chapter, we will see precisely how the government controls the supply of money.

## Measuring Money in the U.S. Economy

In the United States and other modern economies, economic transactions can be carried out in several different ways. In practice, this leads to different measures of money. The most basic measure of money in the United States is called **M1**. It is the sum of currency in the hands of the public, demand deposits, other checkable deposits, and travelers' checks. M1 totaled $1,384 billion in March 2006. Table 16.1 contains the components of M1 and their size; Figure 16.1 shows their relative percentages.

The first part of M1 is currency that is held by the public, that is, all currency held outside of bank vaults. The second component is deposits in checking accounts, called *demand deposits*. Until the 1980s, checking accounts did not pay interest. The third component, other checkable deposits, were introduced in the early 1980s and did pay interest. Today, the distinction between the two types of deposit accounts is not as meaningful because many checking accounts earn interest if the balances are sufficiently high. Finally, traveler's checks are included in M1 because they are regularly used in economic exchanges.

Let's take a closer look at the amount of currency in the economy. Because there are approximately 300 million people in the United States, the $735 billion of cur-

| Table 16.1 | COMPONENTS OF M1, MARCH 2006 |
| --- | --- |
| Currency held by the public | $ 735 billion |
| Demand deposits | 323 billion |
| Other checkable deposits | 319 billion |
| Traveler's checks | 7 billion |
| Total of M1 | 1,384 billion |

*SOURCE:* Federal Reserve Bank of St. Louis.

▶ **FIGURE 16.1**

**Components of M1 for the United States**

Currency is the largest component of M1, the most basic measure of money. Demand and other checkable deposits are the next largest components.
*SOURCE: Federal Reserve Bank of St. Louis.*

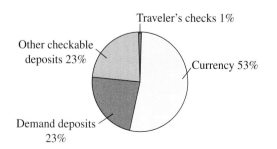

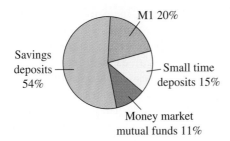

◄ **FIGURE 16.2**
**Components of M2 in the United States**
Savings deposits are the largest component of M2, followed by M1, small deposits, and money market mutual funds.

rency amounts to over $2,450 in currency for every man, woman, and child in the United States. Do you and your friends each have $2,450 of currency?

Most of the currency in the official statistics is not used in ordinary commerce in the United States. Who is using and holding this currency? Some currency is used in illegal transactions such as the drug trade. Few dealers of illegal drugs open bank accounts to deposit currency. In addition, a substantial fraction of U.S. currency is held abroad.

M1 does not include all the assets that are used to make economic exchanges. *M2* is a somewhat broader definition of money that economists use. **M2** includes deposits in saving accounts, deposits in money market mutual funds, and time deposits of less than $100,000. These assets often can't readily be used for exchanges without first being converted to M1. M2 consists of all these investment-like assets plus M1. In March 2006, M2 totaled $6,777 billion. That's about 4.9 times the total of M1. Figure 16.2 shows the relative size of the components of M2.

Economists use different definitions of money because it is not always clear which assets are used primarily as money—that is, which assets are used for

● **M2**
M1 plus other assets, including deposits in savings and loans accounts and money market mutual funds.

# APPLICATION

## MORE THAN HALF OF U.S. CURRENCY IS HELD OVERSEAS

**APPLYING THE CONCEPTS #1:** What fraction of the stock of U.S. currency is held abroad?

According to a report from the U.S. Treasury, between 55 and 60 percent of U.S. currency outstanding is held abroad. About 25 percent of the currency held abroad is located in Latin America, 20 percent in Africa and the Middle East, and about 15 percent in Asia. The remaining 40 percent is held in Europe and countries of the former Soviet Union and their trading partners.

Why do foreigners want to hold U.S. dollars? There are many different reasons. In some countries in Latin America, they circulate with local currency. In other places, they provide a safe store of value. They also provide anonymity to the holder of the currency and are accepted widely throughout the world. Of course, if the United States was not a world economic and political power, dollars would not be held. But as long as the U.S. economy remains strong, there will always be a worldwide demand for dollars. *Related to Exercise 1.11.*

SOURCE: "The Use and Counterfeiting of United States Currency Abroad, Part 2," U.S. Department of the Treasury, March 2003.

economic exchanges and which are used primarily for saving and investing. Money market mutual funds came into existence only in the late 1970s. Some people temporarily "park" their assets in these funds anticipating they will move the funds into riskier, higher-earning stock market investments later. Others may use them to earn interest while avoiding the risks of the stock market or bond market. Sometimes, money market mutual funds are used like regular checking accounts. Other times, they are used like savings accounts. If money market mutual funds are used like checking accounts, they should be considered part of M1. If they are used like savings accounts, however, they should be part of M2. Economists keep an eye on both M1 and M2 because they don't know precisely how all of these money market accounts are being used.

Although credit cards are commonly used in our economy to make transactions, they are not part of the money supply. Here's why: Suppose you have a credit card from the First Union Bank and purchase a new television from an electronics store. As you use your credit card, you are effectively borrowing the amount for the purchase of the television set from the First Union Bank, which, in turn, will pay the electronics store. When you receive your credit card bill, you must begin to pay off the loan from the bank. Credit cards enable you to purchase goods now but use money at a later date to pay for them. The credit card is—unlike money—not a medium of exchange, a unit of account, or a store of value. Credit cards do make it easier to conduct business, but they are not an official part of the money supply.

What about debit cards? If you own a debit card, you can access the funds you have in your checking account when you make the transaction. When you use your debit card to make a purchase—say at a supermarket—it is exactly the same as writing a check. Thus, a debit card works just like a check and is not an independent source of money. The money supply still consists of the balances in checking accounts plus currency held by the public.

# 16.2 | HOW BANKS CREATE MONEY

In this section, we will learn the role that banks play in the creation of money in a modern economy. To understand this role, we first have to look more carefully at the behavior of banks.

### A Bank's Balance Sheet: Where the Money Comes From and Where It Goes

A typical commercial bank accepts funds from savers in the form of deposits, for example, in checking accounts. The bank does not leave all these funds idle, because if it did, it would never make a profit. Instead, the bank turns the money around and loans it out to borrowers. It will be easier to understand how banks create money if we first look at a simplified **balance sheet** for a commercial bank. The balance sheet will show us how the bank raises the money and where it goes after it's been raised.

Balance sheets have two sides: one for assets and one for liabilities. **Liabilities** are the source of funds for the bank. If you open a checking account and deposit your funds in it, the bank is liable for returning the funds to you when you want them. The bank must also pay you interest on the account, if you keep enough money in it. Your deposits are therefore the bank's liabilities. **Assets**, in contrast, generate income for the bank. Loans made by the bank are examples of its assets, because borrowers must pay interest on the loans the bank collects.

When a bank is initially opened, its owners must place their own funds into the bank so it has some startup funds. We call these funds **owners' equity**. If the bank subsequently makes a profit, owners' equity increases; if it loses money, owners' equity decreases.

- **balance sheet**
  An account statement for a bank that shows the sources of its funds (liabilities) as well as the uses of its funds (assets).

- **liabilities**
  The sources of funds for a bank, including deposits and owners' equity.

- **assets**
  The uses of the funds of a bank, including loans and reserves.

- **owners' equity**
  The funds provided to a bank by its owners.

| Assets | Liabilities |
|---|---|
| $ 200 Reserves | $2,000 Deposits |
| $2,000 Loans | $ 200 Owners' equity |
| Total: $2,200 | Total: $2,200 |

◄ **FIGURE 16.3**
**A Balance Sheet for a Bank**
The figure shows a hypothetical balance sheet for a bank holding 10 percent in required reserves, $200. Banks don't earn interest on their reserves, so they will want to loan out any excess of the amounts they are required to hold. This bank has loaned out all of its excess reserves, $2,000.

In Figure 16.3, we show the assets and liabilities of a hypothetical bank. On the liability side, the bank has $2,000 of deposits and owners' equity is $200. Owners' equity is entered on the liability side of the balance sheet because it is a source of the bank's funds. The total source of funds is therefore $2,200—the deposits in the bank plus owners' equity.

On the asset side, the bank holds $200 in **reserves**. These are assets that are not lent out. Reserves can be either cash kept in a bank's vaults or deposits in the nation's central bank, the Federal Reserve. Banks do not earn any interest on these reserves. Hence, they try to keep as little excess reserves on hand as possible and loan out as much as they can. Banks are required by law to hold a specific fraction of their deposits as reserves, called **required reserves**. If a bank chooses to hold additional reserves beyond what is required, these are called **excess reserves**. A bank's reserves are the sum of its required and excess reserves.

In our example, the bank is holding 10 percent of its deposits, or $200, as reserves. The remainder of the bank's assets, $2,000, consists of the loans it has made. By construction, total assets will always equal liabilities, including owners' equity. Balance sheets must therefore always balance.

- **reserves**
  The portion of banks' deposits set aside in either vault cash or as deposits at the Federal Reserve.

- **required reserves**
  The specific fraction of their deposits that banks are required by law to hold as reserves.

- **excess reserves**
  Any additional reserves that a bank holds above required reserves.

## How Banks Create Money

To understand the role that banks play in determining the supply of money, let's suppose that someone walks into the First Bank of Hollywood and deposits $1,000 in cash to open a checking account. Because currency held by the public and checking deposits are both included in the supply of money, the total money supply has not changed with this transaction. The cash deposited into the checking account reduced the currency held by the public by precisely the amount the checking account increased.

Now let's assume that banks are required to keep 10 percent of their deposits as reserves. That means that the **reserve ratio**—the ratio of reserves to deposits—will be 0.1. The First Bank of Hollywood will keep $100 in reserves and make loans totaling $900. The top panel in Figure 16.4 shows the change in First Bank of Hollywood's balance sheet after it has made its loan.

- **reserve ratio**
  The ratio of reserves to deposits.

Suppose the First Bank of Hollywood loans the funds to an aspiring movie producer. The producer opens a checking account at First Bank of Hollywood with the $900 he borrowed. He then buys film equipment from a supplier, who accepts his $900 check and deposits it in the Second Bank of Burbank. The next panel in Figure 16.4 shows what happens to the balance sheet of the Second Bank of Burbank. Liabilities increase by the deposit of $900. The bank must hold $90 in reserves (10 percent of the $900 deposit) and can lend out $810.

Suppose that the Second Bank of Burbank lends the $810 to the owner of a coffeehouse and opens a checking account for her with a balance of $810. She then purchases $810 worth of coffee with a check made out to a coffee supplier, who deposits it into the Third Bank of Venice.

The Third Bank of Venice receives a deposit of $810. It must keep $81 in reserves and can lend out $729. This process continues throughout the Los Angeles area with new loans and deposits. The Fourth Bank of Pasadena will receive a deposit of $729, hold $72.90 in reserves, and lend out $656.10. The Fifth Bank of Compton will receive a deposit of $656.10, and the process goes on.

**Process of Deposit Creation: Changes in Balance Sheets**

The figure shows how an initial deposit of $1,000 can expand the money supply. The first three banks in the figure loaned out all of their excess reserves and the borrowers deposited the full sum of their loans. In the real world, though, people hold part of their loans as cash and banks don't necessarily loan out every last dime of their excess reserves. Consequently, a smaller amount of money will be created than what's shown here.

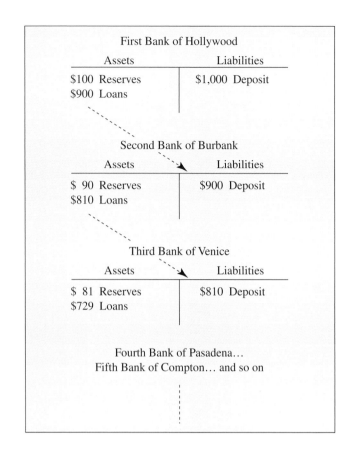

## How the Money Multiplier Works

The original $1,000 cash deposit has created checking account balances throughout Los Angeles. What's the total amount? Adding up the new accounts in all the banks (even the ones we have not named), we have

$$\$1,000 + \$900 + \$810 + \$729 + 656.10 + \cdots = \$10,000$$

How did we come up with this sum? There is a simple formula that can give us the answer:

total increase in checking account balance throughout all banks

$$= (\text{initial cash deposit}) \times \frac{1}{(\text{reserve ratio})}$$

In our example, the reserve ratio is 0.1, so the increase in checking account balances is 1/0.1, or 10 times the initial cash deposit. The initial $1,000 deposit led to a total increase in checking account balances of $10,000 throughout all of the banks.

Recall that the money supply, M1, is the sum of deposits at commercial banks plus currency held by the public. Therefore, the change in the money supply, M1, will be the change in deposits in checking accounts plus the change in currency held by the public. Notice that we referred to "change," meaning an increase or decrease. Here's why: In our example, the public, represented by the person who initially made the $1,000 deposit at the First Bank of Hollywood, holds $1,000 less in currency. However, deposits increased by $10,000. Therefore, the money supply, M1, increased by $9,000 ($10,000 − $1,000). No single bank lent out more than it had in deposits. Yet for the banking system as a whole, the money supply expanded by a multiple of the initial cash deposit.

The term *1/reserve ratio* in the formula is called the **money multiplier**. It tells us what the total increase in checking account deposits would be for any initial cash

• **money multiplier**
The ratio of the increase in total checking account deposits to an initial cash deposit.

deposit. Recall the multiplier for government spending. An increase in government spending led to larger increases in output through the multiplier. The government-spending multiplier arose because additional rounds of consumption spending were triggered by an initial increase in government spending. In the banking system, an initial cash deposit triggers additional rounds of deposits and lending by banks. This leads to a multiple expansion of deposits.

As of 2006 in the United States, banks were required to hold 3 percent in reserves against checkable deposits between $7.8 million and $48.3 million and 10 percent on all checkable deposits exceeding $48.3 million. Because large banks would face a 10-percent reserve requirement on any new deposits, you might think, on the basis of our formula, that the money multiplier would be approximately 10.

However, the money multiplier for the United States is between two and three—much smaller than the value of 10 implied by our simple formula. The primary reason is that our formula assumed that all loans made their way directly into checking accounts. In reality, people hold part of their loans as cash. The cash that people hold is not available for the banking system to lend out. The more money people hold in cash, the lower the amount they have on deposit that can be loaned out again. This decreases the money multiplier. The money multiplier would also be less if banks held excess reserves. We can represent these factors in a money multiplier ratio, but it will not be as simple as the one we introduced here.

## How the Money Multiplier Works in Reverse

The money-creation process also works in reverse. Suppose you go to your bank and ask for $1,000 in cash from your checking account. The bank must pay you the $1,000. The bank's liabilities fall by $1,000, but its assets must also fall by $1,000. Withdrawing your $1,000 means two things at the bank: First, if the reserve ratio is 0.1, the bank will reduce its reserves by $100. Second, your $1,000 withdrawal minus the $100 reduction in reserves means that the bank has $900 less to lend out. The bank will therefore reduce its loans by $900. With fewer loans, there will be fewer deposits in other banks. The money multiplier working in reverse decreases the money supply.

You may wonder how a bank goes about reducing its outstanding loans. If you had borrowed from a bank to invest in a project for your business, you would not want the bank phoning you, asking for its funds, which are not lying idle, but are invested in your business. Banks do not typically call in outstanding loans from borrowers. Instead, if banks cannot tap into their excess reserves when their customers want to withdraw cash, they have to make fewer new loans. In these circumstances, a new potential borrower would find it harder to obtain a loan from the bank.

Up to this point, our examples have always started with an initial cash deposit. However, suppose that Paul receives a check from Freda and deposits it into his bank. Paul's bank will eventually receive payment from Freda's bank. When it does, it will initially have an increase in both deposits and reserves—just as if a cash deposit were made. Because Paul's bank has to hold only a fraction of the deposits as reserves, it will be able to make loans with the remainder.

However, there is one crucial difference between this example, in which one individual writes a check to another, and our earlier example, in which an individual makes a cash deposit: When Paul receives the check from Freda, the money supply will not be changed in the long run. Here's why: When Freda's check is deposited in Paul's bank, the money supply will begin to expand, but when Freda's bank loses its deposit, the money supply will start to contract. The expansions and contractions offset each other when private citizens and firms write checks to one another.

In the next chapter, we will see how the Federal Reserve (commonly called the "Fed") can *change* the money supply to stabilize the economy. In the remainder of this chapter, we'll look at the structure of the Federal Reserve and the critical role that it plays as a central bank stabilizing the financial system.

# 16.3 | A BANKER'S BANK: THE FEDERAL RESERVE

The Federal Reserve System was created in 1913 after a series of financial panics in the United States. Financial panics can occur when there is bad news about the economy or the stability of financial institutions. During these panics, numerous bank runs occurred, depleting the funds on hand that could be loaned out. Severe economic downturns followed.

Congress created the Federal Reserve System to be a **central bank**, or "a banker's bank." When it was created, one of the Fed's primary jobs was to serve as a **lender of last resort**. When banks need to borrow money during a financial crisis, they can turn to the central bank as "a last resort" for these funds. As an example, if a bank experienced a run, the Federal Reserve would lend it the funds it needed.

The Federal Reserve has several key functions. Let's briefly describe them.

### THE FED SUPPLIES CURRENCY TO THE ECONOMY

Working through the banking system, the Federal Reserve is responsible for supplying currency to the economy. Although currency is only one component of the money supply, if individuals prefer to hold currency rather than demand deposits, the Federal Reserve and the banking system will facilitate the public's preferences.

### THE FED PROVIDES A SYSTEM OF CHECK COLLECTION AND CLEARING

The Federal Reserve is responsible for making our system of complex financial transactions "work." This means that when Paul writes Freda a check, the Federal Reserve oversees the banks to ensure that Freda's bank receives the funds from Paul's bank. This is known as *check clearing*. As our economy moves to more electronic transactions, the Federal Reserve provides oversight over these transactions as well.

### THE FED HOLDS RESERVES FROM BANKS AND OTHER DEPOSITORY INSTITUTIONS AND REGULATES BANKS

As we have seen, banks are required to hold reserves with the Federal Reserve System. The Federal Reserve also serves as a regulator to banks to ensure that they are complying with rules and regulations. Ultimately, the Federal Reserve wants to ensure that the financial system is safe.

### THE FED CONDUCTS MONETARY POLICY

One of the important responsibilities of the Federal Reserve is to conduct **monetary policy**, the range of actions that influence the level of real GDP or inflation.

Virtually all countries have central banks. The Indian central bank is known as the Reserve Bank of India. In the United Kingdom, the central bank is the Bank of England. Central banks serve as lenders of last resort to the banks in their countries and also help to control the level of economic activity. If the economy is operating at a level that's "too hot" or "too cold," they can manipulate the money supply to fend off economic problems. We'll see how central banks use monetary policy to influence real GDP or inflation and fend off economic problems in the next chapter.

## The Structure of the Federal Reserve

When members of Congress created the Federal Reserve System, they were aware the institution would be very powerful. Consequently, they deliberately created a structure that attempted to disperse the power, moving it away from major U.S. financial centers (such as New York) to other parts of the country. They divided the United States into 12 Federal Reserve districts, each of which has a **Federal Reserve Bank**. These district banks provide advice on monetary policy, take part in decision making on monetary policy, and act as a liaison between the Fed and the banks in their districts.

Figure 16.5 shows where each of the 12 Federal Reserve Banks is located. At the time the Fed was created, economic and financial power in this country was concen-

**central bank**
A banker's bank: an official bank that controls the supply of money in a country.

**lender of last resort**
A central bank is the lender of last resort, the last place, all others having failed, from which banks in emergency situations can obtain loans.

**monetary policy**
The range of actions taken by the Federal Reserve to influence the level of GDP or inflation.

**Federal Reserve Bank**
One of 12 regional banks that are an official part of the Federal Reserve System.

▲ **FIGURE 16.5**
**Locations of the 12 Federal Reserve Banks**
The 12 Federal Reserve banks are scattered across the United States. These district banks serve as a liaison between the Fed and the banks in their districts. Hawaii and Alaska are in the twelfth district, which is headquartered in San Francisco.

trated in the East and the Midwest. This is no longer true. What major Western city does not have a Federal Reserve Bank? It is, of course, Los Angeles. Although financial power is no longer concentrated in the East and Midwest, the locations of the Federal Reserve Banks still reflect the Fed's historical roots.

There are two other subgroups of the Fed in addition to the Federal Reserve Banks. The **Board of Governors of the Federal Reserve** is the second subgroup. It is the true seat of power in the Federal Reserve System. Headquartered in Washington, D.C., the seven members of the board are appointed for 14-year terms by the president. The chairperson of the Board of Governors serves a four-year term. As the principal spokesperson for monetary policy in the United States, what the chairperson says, or might say, is carefully observed or anticipated by financial markets throughout the world. The chairperson and the seven members must also be confirmed by the Senate.

The third subgroup of the Fed is the **Federal Open Market Committee (FOMC)**, which makes decisions about monetary policy The FOMC is a 12-person board consisting of the seven members of the Board of Governors, the president of the New York Federal Reserve Bank, plus the presidents of four other regional Federal Reserve Banks. (The presidents of the regional banks other than New York serve on a rotating basis; the seven nonvoting bank presidents attend the meetings and offer their opinions.) The chairperson of the Board of Governors also serves as the chairperson of the FOMC. The FOMC makes the actual decisions on changes in the money supply. Its members are assisted by vast teams of professionals at the Board of Governors and at the regional Federal Reserve Banks. The structure of the Federal Reserve System is depicted in Figure 16.6.

On paper, monetary policy-making power appears to be spread throughout the government and the country. In practice, however, the Board of Governors, and especially the chairperson, has the real control. The Board of Governors operates with considerable independence. Presidents and members of Congress can bring political pressures on the Board of Governors, but 14-year terms tend to insulate the members from external pressures.

The current chairman of the Federal Reserve is Benjamin S. Bernanke, who began his term on February 1, 2006. He will have a high standard to meet, because his two predecessors were very strong and talented chairmen.

• **Board of Governors of the Federal Reserve**
The seven-person governing body of the Federal Reserve System in Washington, D.C.

• **Federal Open Market Committee (FOMC)**
The group that decides on monetary policy: It consists of the seven members of the Board of Governors plus five of 12 regional bank presidents on a rotating basis.

**The Structure of the Federal Reserve System**
The Federal Reserve System in the United States consists of the Federal Reserve Banks, the Board of Governors, and the Federal Open Market Committee (FOMC). The FOMC is responsible for making monetary policy decisions.

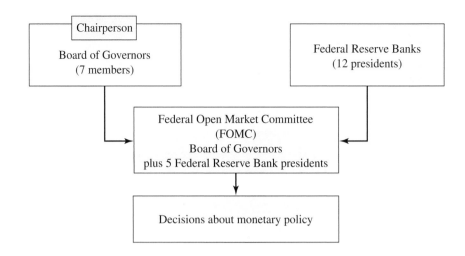

2

# APPLICATION

## TWO RECENT MAJOR LEADERS OF THE FEDERAL RESERVE BOARD

**APPLYING THE CONCEPTS #2:** Who were the two men who served as chairman of the Federal Reserve between 1979 to 2006 and what were their principal accomplishments?

The two chairmen before the current chairman, Benjamin Bernanke, were Paul Volcker, who served from 1979 to 1987, and Alan Greenspan, who served from 1987 to 2006. In their day, each was the country's major figure in monetary policy.

Paul Volcker was appointed by President Jimmy Carter, who sought an established banker to help combat inflation. Volcker, who served as the president of the New York Federal Reserve Bank, took a pay cut to come to Washington to fight inflation. A tall, imposing figure who smoked cigars, Volcker was relentless in his fight against inflation. Although he tamed inflation, the economy was forced through a period of high interest rates and a severe recession. As we will explain in the next few chapters, reducing inflation from high levels typically does require the economy to experience a recession.

In 1987, President Ronald Reagan appointed Alan Greenspan. Greenspan was first tested by the 1987 stock market crash and steered the economy away from a recession. Over the following years, he successfully guided monetary policy. Except for the recessions in the early 1990s and in 2001, the economy grew smoothly and inflation remained under control. During the mid-1990s, the Federal Reserve allowed the economy to grow at a faster rate than most economists believed possible, but the gamble paid off, and there was no resurgence of inflation. In 1999 and 2000, the Federal Reserve may have tightened monetary policy prematurely, contributing to the subsequent economic contraction. Nonetheless, Greenspan's performance has earned near universal praise, and one author deemed him the "maestro."
*Related to Exercise 3.9.*

### The Independence of the Federal Reserve

Countries differ in the degree to which their central banks are independent of political authorities. In the United States, the chairperson of the Board of Governors is required to report to Congress on a regular basis, but in practice, the Fed makes its own decisions and later informs Congress what it did. The chairperson of the Federal Reserve also often meets with members of the executive branch to discuss economic affairs. The central banks in both the United States and the United Kingdom operate with considerable independence of elected officials. In other countries, the central bank is part of the treasury department of the government and potentially subject to more direct political control. There is a lively debate among economists and political scientists as to whether countries with more independent central banks (banks with less external political pressure) experience less inflation. Central banks that are not independent will always be under pressure to help finance their country's government deficits by creating money. We'll see in a later chapter that when central banks succumb to this pressure, the result is inflation. Independence, on the other hand, typically means less inflation.

# 16.4 | WHAT THE FEDERAL RESERVE DOES DURING A FINANCIAL CRISIS

As the lender of last resort, the Fed can quell disturbances in the financial markets. Let's look at two historical examples.

# APPLICATION

## COPING WITH A STOCK MARKET CRASH: BLACK MONDAY, 1987

**APPLYING THE CONCEPTS #3:** How did the Fed successfully respond to the major stock market crash in 1987?

On October 19, 1987, known as "Black Monday," the Dow Jones index of the stock market fell a dramatic 22.6 percent in one day. Similar declines were felt in other indexes and stock markets around the world. These declines shocked both businesses and investors. In just 24 hours, many people and firms found themselves much less wealthy. The public began to worry that banks and other financial institutions—to protect their own loans and investments—would call in borrowers' existing loans and stop making new ones. A sharp drop in available credit could, conceivably, plunge the economy into a deep recession.

Alan Greenspan had just become chairman of the Federal Reserve that year. As a sophisticated economist with historical knowledge of prior financial crises, he recognized the seriousness of the situation. He quickly issued a public statement in which he said that the Federal Reserve stood ready to provide liquidity to the economy and the financial system. Banks were told that the Fed would let them borrow liberally. In fact, the Fed provided liquidity to such an extent that interest rates even fell. As a result of Greenspan's action, "Black Monday" did not cause a recession in the United States. *Related to Exercise 4.6.*

## THE FINANCIAL SYSTEM UNDER STRESS: SEPTEMBER 11, 2001

**APPLYING THE CONCEPTS #4:** How did the Fed manage to keep the financial system in operation immediately following the attacks on September 11, 2001?

The Fed was tested again on September 11, 2001, following the terrorist attacks against the United States. Many financial firms keep little cash on hand and expect to borrow on a daily basis to pay their ongoing bills and obligations. When the financial markets closed after September 11, many of these firms were in trouble. Unless some actions were taken quickly, these firms would default on their debts, leading to payment problems for other firms and further defaults. To prevent a default avalanche, the Federal Reserve immediately took a number of steps to provide additional funds to the financial system.

The first tool that the Federal Reserve used was to allow banks to borrow more. In regular times, the volume of these direct loans from the Federal Reserve is not very large. On Wednesday, September 12, total lending to banks rose to $45.5 *billion*, up from just $99 million the week before.

In normal times, the Federal Reserve System serves as a clearinghouse for checks. A bank will bring checks it receives from customers to the Federal Reserve and receive immediate credit on its accounts. The Federal Reserve then debits the account of the bank upon which the check was written. The difference between the credits and the debits extended by the Federal Reserve is called the "Federal Reserve float." Immediately following September 11, the Federal Reserve allowed this float to increase sharply from $2.9 billion to $22.9 billion. These actions effectively put an additional $20 billion into the banking system.

The Federal Reserve also purchased government securities in the marketplace and, as a result, put $30 billion into the hands of private citizens and their banks. It also arranged to provide dollars to foreign central banks such as the Bank of England to meet their own needs and the needs of their own banks to facilitate any dollar transactions they had during this crisis. Taken together, all these actions increased the credit extended by the Federal Reserve by over $90 billion. This massive response by the Federal Reserve prevented a financial panic that could have had devastating effects on the world economy. *Related to Exercise 4.7.*

# SUMMARY

We began this chapter by examining the role money plays in the economy and how economists define money. We then looked at the flow of money in and out of banks and saw how banks can create money with deposits and loans. Finally, we examined the structure of the Federal Reserve and the key roles that central banks can play during financial crises. Here are the main points you should remember from this chapter:

1 *Money* consists of anything that is regularly used to make exchanges. In modern economies, money consists primarily of currency and deposits in checking accounts.

2 Banks are financial intermediaries that earn profits by accepting deposits and making loans. Deposits, which are liabilities of banks, are included in the money supply.

3 Banks are required by law to hold a fraction of their deposits as reserves, either in cash or in deposits with the Federal Reserve. Total reserves consist of *required reserves* plus *excess reserves*.

4 If there is an increase in reserves in the banking system, the supply of money will expand by a multiple of the initial deposit. This multiple is known as the *money multiplier*.

5 Decisions about the supply of money are made at the *Federal Open Market Committee* (FOMC), which includes the seven members on the Board of Governors and the president of the

New York Federal Reserve Bank, as well as four of the 11 other regional bank presidents, who serve on a rotating basis.

6 In a financial crisis like those that occurred in 1987 and 2001, the Fed can help stabilize the economy. Recent Fed chairmen Paul Volcker and Alan Greenspan have been powerful and important figures in the national economy.

## KEY TERMS

assets, p. 394

balance sheet, p. 394

barter, p. 390

Board of Governors of the Federal Reserve, p. 399

central bank, p. 398

commodity money, p. 391

double coincidence of wants, p. 390

excess reserves, p. 395

Federal Open Market Committee (FOMC) , p. 399

Federal Reserve Bank, p. 398

fiat money, p. 392

gold standard, p. 391

lender of last resort, p. 398

liabilities, p. 394

M1, p. 392

M2, p. 393

medium of exchange, p. 390

monetary policy, p. 398

money, p. 390

money multiplier, p. 396

owners' equity, p. 394

required reserves, p. 395

reserve ratio, p. 395

reserves, p. 395

store of value, p. 391

unit of account, p. 391

## EXERCISES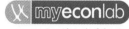

*Get Ahead of the Curve*

Visit www.myeconlab.com to complete these exercises online and get instant feedback.

### 16.1 | What *Is* Money?

1.1 Money solves the problem of double coincidence of wants that would regularly occur under a system of _____.

1.2 Money is an imperfect store of value because of _____.

1.3 Deposits in checking accounts are included in the definition of money because they are a very liquid asset. _____ (True/False)

1.4 M1 is _____ (greater/less) than M2.

1.5 Money market mutual funds are hard to classify in a definition of money because they are only held to facilitate transactions. _____ (True/False)

1.6 So much U.S. currency is in global circulation because it is a safe asset compared to assets denominated in foreign currency. _____ (True/False)

1.7 **Debit Cards.** In recent years, debit cards have become popular. Debit cards allow the holder of the card to pay a merchant for goods and services directly from a checking account. How do you think the introduction of debit cards affected the amount of currency in the economy? How about the amount of checking account deposits?

1.8 **Traveler's Checks.** Why are traveler's checks classified as money? What factors are beginning to make them obsolete?

1.9 **California Money?** In 1992, the state of California ran out of funds and could not pay its bills. It issued IOUs, called *warrants*, to its workers and suppliers. Only large banks and credit unions accepted the warrants. Should these warrants be viewed as money?

1.10 **Credit Cards.** Why aren't credit cards part of the money supply?

1.11 **Inflation and Currency Held Abroad.** Suppose inflation in the United States rose to around 7 percent a year. How do you think this would affect the demand for U.S. currency by foreigners? (Related to Application 1 on page 393.)

1.12 **Using Gold as Money.** Some societies have used gold as money. What are the advantages and disadvantages of using gold coins?

1.13 **Currency and Underground Economy.** Search the Web for articles on the "currency and the underground economy." How have various authors used estimates of currency to measure the underground economy?

### 16.2 | How Banks Create Money

2.1 Banks are required by law to keep a fraction of their deposits as _____.

2.2 Banks prefer to keep reserves rather than make loans because they receive a higher interest rate. _____ (True/False)

**2.3** If the reserve ratio is 0.2 and a deposit of $100 is made into a bank, the bank can lend out _____.

**2.4** If the reserve ratio is 0.2, the simplified money multiplier will be _____ .

**2.5** **Bad Loans to South America.** During the 1980s, U.S. banks made loans to South American countries. Many of these loans turned out to be worthless. How did this affect the assets, liabilities, and owners' equity of these banks?

**2.6** **Banks Versus Insurance Companies.** Both insurance companies and banks are financial intermediaries. Why do macroeconomists study banks more intensively than insurance companies?

**2.7** **Understanding M1 and M2.** If you write a check from your checking account to your money market account, what happens to M1 and M2?

**2.8** **Cash Withdrawals and Changes in the Money Supply.** If a customer withdrew $2,000 in cash from a bank and the reserve ratio was 0.2, by how much could the supply of money eventually be reduced?

**2.9** **Understanding Multiple Expansion.** If no single bank can lend out more than it has, how does multiple expansion of deposits actually occur?

**2.10** **Looking for Trends in the Money Supply.** Go to the Web site of the Federal Reserve Bank of St. Louis (research.stlouisfed.org/fred2/). Look carefully at the components of M1 and M2 over the last 10 years. What trends do you see?

# 16.3 | A Banker's Bank: The Federal Reserve

**3.1** The Federal Reserve is the "_____ of last resort."

**3.2** The San Francisco Federal Reserve Bank is the only one in the West because San Francisco outbid Los Angeles to be its host. _____ (True/False)

**3.3** The _____ votes on monetary policy.

**3.4** _____ -year terms help ensure the political independence of the Board of Governors.

**3.5** The two Federal Reserve chairmen that preceded Ben Bernanke were _____ and _____.

**3.6** **The Treasury Secretary and the Fed.** Occasionally, some economists or politicians suggest that the Secretary of the Treasury become a member of the Federal Open Market Committee. How do you think this would affect the operation of the Federal Reserve?

**3.7** **Independent Central Banks.** What are the pros and cons of having an independent central bank?

**3.8** **The President of the New York Federal Reserve Bank.** The president of the New York Federal Reserve Bank is always a voting member of the Federal Open Market Committee. Given your understanding of the conduct of monetary policy, why is this true?

**3.9** **The Tougher Job?** Although Alan Greenspan presided over the Fed for a longer period of time and dealt with a stock market crisis, many economists believe that Paul Volker had a tougher job during his time as chairman of the Federal Reserve. Explain why they hold this belief. (Related to Application 2 on page 400.)

# 16.4 | What the Federal Reserve Does During a Financial Crisis

**4.1** Alan Greenspan supplied _____ to the banking system during the stock market crash of 1987 to avoid a crisis.

**4.2** The "float" in the banking system is the difference between the Federal Reserve's _____ and _____ when clearing checks.

**4.3** Two actions that the Fed took after September 11, 2001, to ensure the financial system operated smoothly were _____ and _____.

**4.4** **Required Reserves During the Great Depression.** During the Great Depression, banks held excess reserves because they were concerned that depositors might be more inclined to withdraw funds from their accounts. At one point, the Fed became concerned about the "excess" reserves and raised the reserve requirements for banks.
   **a.** Assuming that banks were holding excess reserves for precautionary purposes, do you think they would continue to want to hold excess reserves even after reserve requirements were raised? Explain.
   **b.** What do you think happened to the money supply after the Fed raised reserve requirements?

**4.5** **Crisis in the Short-Term Credit Market.** In 1973, several major companies went bankrupt and were not going to be able to pay interest on their short-term loans. This caused a crisis in the market. There was concern that the short-term credit market would collapse, and that even healthy corporations would not be able to borrow. How do you think the Fed should have handled that situation?

**4.6** **Banks During a Stock Market Crisis.** When the stock market crashes and investors lose their funds, banks may reduce lending to these investors because their net worth has been reduced. They may even want them to repay their loans immediately. What effect would this have on the supply of money? Should the Fed counteract this? (Related to Application 3 on page 401.)

**4.7** **Check Clearing and September 11.** How did the Federal Reserve manipulate the check-clearing process to increase liquidity in response to the potential financial crisis following the terrorist attacks of September 11, 2001? (Related to Application 4 on page 402.)

# ECONOMIC EXPERIMENT

## Money Creation

This experiment demonstrates the money-creation process. Students act like bankers and investors. Bankers loan money to investors, who then buy machines that produce output. The experiment is divided into several separate days. On each day, all loans are executed in the morning, all deposits happen over the lunch hour, and all machines are purchased in the afternoon. Each bank can receive only one deposit and issue only one loan. The interest rate paid to depositors and the interest rate paid by borrowers are negotiable. The experiment starts when the instructor deposits $625 from the sale of a government bond into a bank.

## Bank Actions

The sequence of possible bank actions on a given day is as follows:

1. Early morning: Count money. Check for excess reserves, including deposits from the previous noon.

2. Middle morning: Loan out any excess reserves in a single loan to a borrower and negotiate an interest rate for the loan. The loan is executed by writing a bank check to the borrower.

3. Noon: Receive a deposit (bank check deposited into a checking account).

4. Afternoon: Relax, golf.

## Rules for Banks

The rules for banks are as follows:

1. For each $1 deposited, you must hold $0.20 in reserve.

2. If you don't issue a loan, you can earn 3 percent by investing overseas.

## Investor Actions

The sequence of possible investor actions on a given day is as follows:

1. Early morning: Sleep in while bankers count their money.

2. Middle morning: Borrow money from a bank and negotiate an interest rate for the loan.

3. Noon: Deposit the loan at the bank of your choice and negotiate an interest rate for the deposit.

4. Afternoon: Buy machines from Machine Inc., paying with a personal check.

## Investor Payoffs

Each machine costs $1, generates $1.10 worth of output, and then expires.

As the students play, the instructor keeps track of the model economy on a tally sheet, which shows the money-creation process in action, round by round.

What role do the return on overseas investment (3 percent) and the return from owning a machine ($1.10 on a $1.00 investment) play in this experiment?

## MONEY-CREATION EXPERIMENT: TALLY SHEET

| Bank Receiving Deposit | Amount Deposited | Interest Rate on Deposit | Amount Loaned | Interest Rate on Loan | Amount Added to Reserves | Change in Money Supply |
|---|---|---|---|---|---|---|
| | | | | | | |
| | | | | | | |
| | | | | | | |
| | | | | | | |
| | | | | | | |
| | | | | | | |
| | | | | | | |
| | | | | | | |
| | | | | | | |
| | | | | | | |
| | | | | | | |
| | | | | | | |
| | | | | | | |

# 17

# Monetary Policy

On February 1, 2006, Ben S. Bernanke took the reigns as the new chairman of the Federal Reserve. His immediate predecessors, Alan Greenspan and Paul Volcker, gained their experience and expertise working on Wall Street and in banking, respectively. In contrast, Bernanke had an academic career. As a former chairman of the Economics Department at Princeton University, Bernanke was known as an academic whose scholarly work focused on the Great Depression and the role of monetary policy in controlling inflation. Although he had little direct experience in financial markets, he did have experience in economic policy and monetary policy. Before his appointment as chairman, Bernanke was chairman of the

**1** What happens to interest rates when the economy recovers from a recession?
*Rising Interest Rates During an Economic Recovery*

**2** Is it better for decisions about monetary policy to be made by a single individual or by a committee?
*The Effectiveness of Committees*

**3** Can changes in the way central banks are governed affect inflation expectations?
*Increased Political Independence for the Bank of England Lowered Inflation Expectations*

President's Council of Economic Advisers from June 2005 to January 2006 and a member of the Board of Governors of the Federal Reserve System from 2002 to 2005.

Bernanke took office with a robust economy and modest inflation; however, there were warning signs of potential problems: a low U.S. savings rate, a historically large trade deficit, and looming government deficits as the baby boomers retire. As a student of economic history, Bernanke understands one thing: He will undoubtedly have to deal with novel situations that no one had dreamed of before.

In this chapter, we will learn why everyone is so interested in what the Federal Reserve is about to do. In the short run, when prices don't have enough time to change and we consider them temporarily fixed, the Federal Reserve can influence interest-rate levels in the economy. When the Federal Reserve lowers interest rates, investment spending and GDP increase because the cost of funds is cheaper. Conversely, when the Fed increases interest rates, investment spending and GDP decrease because the cost of funds is higher. In the long run, however, the Federal Reserve does not have this power to control real GDP. In the long run, changes in the money supply will only affect inflation.

# 17.1 | THE MONEY MARKET

• **money market**
The market for money in which the amount supplied and the amount demanded meet to determine the nominal interest rate.

The **money market** is the market for money where the amount supplied and the amount demanded meet to determine the nominal interest rate. Recall that the nominal interest rate is the stated or quoted interest rate before adjusting for inflation. We begin by learning the factors that determine the public's demand for money. Once we understand what affects the demand for money, we can see how the actions of the Federal Reserve determine the supply of money. Then we'll see how the demand and supply of money together determine interest rates.

## The Demand for Money

• **transaction demand for money**
The demand for money based on the desire to facilitate transactions.

Let's think of money as simply one part of wealth. Suppose your total wealth is valued at $1,000. In what form will you hold your wealth? Should you put all your wealth into the stock market? Or perhaps into the bond market? Or should you hold some of your wealth in money, that is, currency and deposits in checking accounts?

### INTEREST RATES AFFECT MONEY DEMAND
If you invest in assets such as stocks or bonds, you will generally earn income on them. *Stocks* are shares in the ownership of a corporation. There are two sources of income from stocks: dividends paid to their owners out of the profits of the corporation, and the typical increase in their value over time. Bonds pay interest. Thus, both stocks and bonds provide returns to investors. If you hold your wealth in currency or in a checking account, however, you will receive either no interest or very low interest. And if inflation rises sharply, you might even lose money. Holding your wealth as money in currency or a checking account means that you sacrifice some potential income.

Money does, however, provide a valuable service. It facilitates transactions. If you go to a grocery store to purchase cereal, the store will accept currency or a check, but you won't be able to pay for cereal with your stocks and bonds. People hold money primarily for this basic reason: Money makes it easier to conduct everyday transactions. Economists call this reason for holding money the **transaction demand for money**.

To understand the demand for money, we rely on the principle of opportunity cost.

## PRINCIPLE OF OPPORTUNITY COST
The opportunity cost of something is what you sacrifice to get it.

The opportunity cost of holding money is the return that you could have earned by holding your wealth in other assets. We measure the opportunity cost of holding money by the interest rate. Suppose that the interest rate available to you on a long-term bond is 6 percent per year. If you hold $100 of your wealth in the form of this bond, you'll earn $6 a year. If you hold currency instead, you'll earn no interest. So the opportunity cost of holding $100 in currency is $6 per year, or 6 percent per year.

As interest rates increase in the economy, the opportunity cost of holding money also increases. Economists have found that as the opportunity cost of holding money increases, the public demands less money. The quantity demanded of money will decrease with an increase in interest rates.

In Figure 17.1, we draw a demand for money curve, $M^d$, as a function of the interest rate. At higher interest rates, individuals will want to hold less money than they will at lower interest rates because the opportunity cost of holding money is higher. As interest rates rise from $r_0$ to $r_1$, the quantity of money demanded falls from $M_0$ to $M_1$.

### THE PRICE LEVEL AND GDP AFFECT MONEY DEMAND

The demand for money also depends on two other factors. One is the overall price level in the economy. The demand for money will increase as the level of prices increases. If prices for your groceries are twice as high, you will need twice as much money to purchase them. The amount of money people typically hold during any time period will be closely related to the dollar value of the transactions that they make. This is an example of the real-nominal principle in action.

## REAL-NOMINAL PRINCIPLE

What matters to people is the real value of money or income—its

purchasing power—not the face value of money or income.

The other factor that influences the demand for money is the level of real GDP or real income. It seems obvious that as income increases, individuals and businesses will make more purchases. In the same way, as real GDP increases, individuals and businesses will make more transactions. To facilitate these transactions, they will want to hold more money.

Figure 17.2 shows how changes in prices and GDP affect the demand for money. Panel A shows how the demand for money shifts to the right as the price level increases. At any interest rate, people will want to hold more money as prices increase. Panel B shows how the demand for money shifts to the right as real GDP increases. At

► **FIGURE 17.2**
**Shifting the Demand for Money**
Changes in prices and real GDP shift the demand for money.

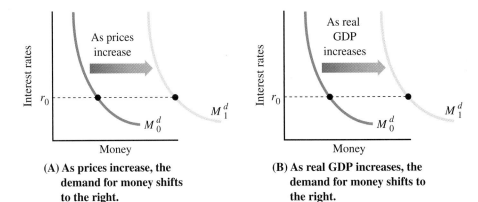

(A) As prices increase, the demand for money shifts to the right.

(B) As real GDP increases, the demand for money shifts to the right.

any interest rate, people will want to hold more money as real GDP increases. These graphs both show the same result. An increase in prices or an increase in real GDP will increase money demand.

### OTHER COMPONENTS OF MONEY DEMAND

Traditionally, economists have identified other motives besides transactions for individuals or firms to hold money. If you hold your wealth in the form of property, such as a house or a boat, it is costly to sell the house or boat on short notice if you need to obtain funds. These forms of wealth are **illiquid**, meaning that they are not easily transferable into money. If you hold your wealth in currency or checking accounts, you do not have this problem. Economists recognize that individuals have a **liquidity demand for money**. People want to hold money so they can make transactions on quick notice.

During periods of economic volatility, investors might not want to hold stocks and bonds because their prices might fall. Instead, they might convert them into holdings that fall into the M2 category, such as savings accounts and money market funds. These investments earn lower interest rates but are less risky than stocks and bonds, whose prices can fluctuate. This demand for "safer" assets is called the **speculative demand for money**. For example, after the stock market began to fall in 2000, individuals became very uncertain about the future and shifted their funds from the stock market to money market mutual funds. This shift of assets from stocks to money temporarily increased M2. When the market started to recover, some investors shifted funds back into the stock market, decreasing M2 in the economy.

In summary, individuals hold money for three motives: to facilitate transactions, to provide liquidity, and to reduce risk. The amount of money they want to hold will depend on interest rates, the level of real GDP, and the price level.

- **illiquid**
  Not easily transferable to money.

- **liquidity demand for money**
  The demand for money that represents the needs and desires individuals and firms have to make transactions on short notice without incurring excessive costs.

- **speculative demand for money**
  The demand for money that arises because holding money over short periods is less risky than holding stocks or bonds.

## 17.2 | HOW THE FEDERAL RESERVE CAN CHANGE THE MONEY SUPPLY

As we discussed in the last chapter, the banking system as a whole can expand the money supply only if new reserves come into the system. As we saw, when private citizens and firms write checks to one another, there will be no net change in the supply of money. Because the total amount of reserves in the system is unchanged, the money supply cannot expand. There is one organization, however, that has the power to change the total amount of reserves in the banking system: the Federal Reserve.

## Open Market Operations

The Fed can increase or decrease the total amount of reserves in the banking system through **open market operations**, which are the purchase or sale of U.S. government securities by the Fed. There are two types of open market operations:

- In **open market purchases**, the Fed buys government bonds from the private sector.
- In **open market sales**, the Fed sells government bonds to the private sector.

To understand how the Fed can increase the supply of money, let's trace what happens after an open market purchase. Suppose the Federal Reserve purchases $1 million worth of government bonds currently owned by the private sector. The Fed writes a check for $1 million and presents it to the party who sold the bonds. The Federal Reserve now owns those bonds. The party who sold the bonds then deposits the $1 million in its bank.

Here is the key to how the supply of money increases when the Fed purchases government bonds: As we explained in the last chapter, each bank must keep an account with the Fed containing both its required and excess reserves. The check written against the Federal Reserve increases the bank's total reserves, essentially giving it more money to lend out. In this case, the bank's account balance increases by $1 million. If the reserve requirement is 10 percent, the bank must keep $100,000 in reserves, but it can now lend out $900,000 from its excess reserves. Basically, when the Fed buys bonds, the proceeds go out into the economy. Open market purchases of bonds therefore increase the money supply.

The Federal Reserve has powers that ordinary citizens and even banks do not have. The Fed can write checks against itself to purchase government bonds without having any explicit "funds" in its account for the purchase. Banks accept these checks because they count as part of their total reserves.

As you might expect, open market sales will, conversely, decrease the supply of money. Suppose the Federal Reserve sells $1 million worth of government bonds to a Wall Street firm. The firm will pay for the bonds with a check for $1 million drawn on its bank and give this check to the Federal Reserve. The bank must either hand over $1 million in cash or, more likely, reduce its total reserves with the Federal Reserve by $1 million. When the Fed sells bonds, it is basically taking the money exchanged for them out of the hands of the public. Open market sales therefore decrease the money freely available in the economy.

In summary, if the Federal Reserve wishes to increase the money supply to stimulate the economy (perhaps it is operating too sluggishly), it buys government bonds from the private sector in open market purchases. If the Fed wishes to decrease the money supply to slow the economy down (perhaps it is growing too quickly and inflation is occurring), it sells government bonds to the private sector in open market sales.

## Other Tools of the Fed

Open market operations are by far the most important way in which the Federal Reserve changes the supply of money. There are two other ways in which the Fed can change the supply of money, which we'll discuss next.

### CHANGING RESERVE REQUIREMENTS

Another way the Fed can change the money supply is by changing the reserve requirements for banks. If the Fed wishes to increase the supply of money, it can reduce banks' reserve requirements so they have more money to lend out. This would expand the money supply. To decrease the supply of money, the Federal Reserve can raise reserve requirements.

Changing reserve requirements is a powerful tool, but the Federal Reserve doesn't use it very often because it disrupts the banking system. Suppose a bank is required to hold exactly 10 percent of its deposits as reserves and that it has loaned the

- **open market operations**
  The purchase or sale of U.S. government securities by the Fed.

- **open market purchases**
  The Fed's purchase of government bonds from the private sector.

- **open market sales**
  The Fed's sale of government bonds to the private sector.

other 90 percent. If the Federal Reserve suddenly increases its reserve requirement to 20 percent, the bank would be forced to call in or cancel many of its loans. Its customers would not like this! Today, the Fed doesn't make sharp changes in reserve requirements. It did in the past, including during the Great Depression, because it mistakenly believed that the banks were holding too much in excess reserves. Banks, however, were holding additional reserves because they wanted to protect themselves from bank runs. As a result, after the increase in required reserves, banks increased their reserves even more, further reducing the supply of money to the economy.

**CHANGING THE DISCOUNT RATE**

Another way the Fed can change the money supply is by changing the *discount rate*. The **discount rate** is the interest rate at which banks can borrow directly from the Fed. Suppose a major customer comes to the bank and asks for a loan. Unless the bank could find an additional source of funds, it would have to refuse to make the loan. Banks are reluctant to turn away major customers. They first try to borrow reserves from other banks through the **federal funds market**, a market in which banks borrow and lend reserves to and from one another. If the rate—called the **federal funds rate**— seemed too high to the bank, it could borrow directly from the Federal Reserve at the discount rate. By changing the discount rate, the Federal Reserve can influence the amount of borrowing by banks. If the Fed raises the discount rate, banks will be discouraged from borrowing reserves because it has become more costly. Lowering the discount rate will induce banks to borrow additional reserves.

In principle, the Federal Reserve could use the discount rate as a tool independent of monetary policy. That is, it could lower the discount rate to expand the money supply and raise the discount rate to reduce the money supply. Today, the Fed follows a policy of keeping the discount rate close to the federal funds rate to avoid large swings in borrowed reserves by banks. In the past, changes in the discount rate, however, were quite visible to financial markets. Participants in the financial markets often interpreted these changes as revealing clues about the Fed's intentions for future monetary policy.

# 17.3 | HOW INTEREST RATES ARE DETERMINED: COMBINING THE DEMAND AND SUPPLY OF MONEY

Combining the demand for money, determined by the public, with the supply of money, determined by the Fed, we can see how interest rates are determined in the short run in a demand-and-supply model of the money market.

Figure 17.3 depicts a model of the money market. The supply of money is determined by the Federal Reserve, and we assume for simplicity that it is independent of

**• discount rate**
The interest rate at which banks can borrow from the Fed.

**• federal funds market**
The market in which banks borrow and lend reserves to and from one another.

**• federal funds rate**
The interest rate on reserves that banks lend each other.

▶ **FIGURE 17.3**
**Equilibrium in the Money Market**
Equilibrium in the money market occurs at an interest rate of $r^*$, at which the quantity of money demanded equals the quantity of money supplied.

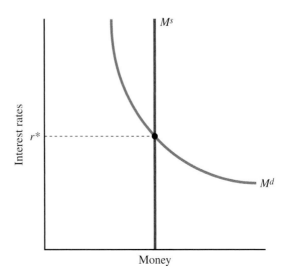

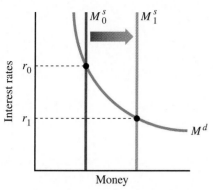
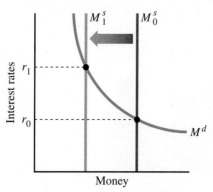

**(A) An open market purchase shifts the supply of money to the right and leads to lower interest rates.**

**(B) An open market sale shifts the supply of money to the left and leads to higher interest rates.**

interest rates. We represent this independence by a vertical supply curve for money, $M^s$. In the same graph, we draw the demand for money $M^d$. Market equilibrium occurs where the demand for money equals the supply of money, at an interest rate of $r^*$.

At this equilibrium interest rate $r^*$, the quantity of money demanded by the private sector equals the quantity of money supplied by the Federal Reserve. What happens if the interest rate is higher than $r^*$? At a higher interest rate, the quantity of money demanded would be less than the fixed quantity supplied, so there would be an excess supply of money. In other markets, excess supplies cause the price to fall. It's the same here. The "price of money" in the market for money is the interest rate. If the interest rate were below $r^*$, the demand for money would exceed the fixed supply: There would be an excess demand for money. As in other markets when there are excess demands, the price rises. Here, the "price of money," or the interest rate, would rise until it reached $r^*$. As you can see, money-market equilibrium follows the same logic as any other economic equilibrium.

We can use this simple model of the money market to understand the power of the Federal Reserve. Suppose the Federal Reserve increases the money supply through an open market purchase of bonds. In Panel A of Figure 17.4, an increase in the supply of money shifts the money supply curve to the right, leading to lower interest rates. A decrease in the money supply through the Fed's open market sale of bonds, as depicted in Panel B of Figure 17.4, decreases the supply of money, shifting the money supply curve to the left and increasing interest rates.

We can also think of the process from the perspective of banks. Recall our discussion of money creation through the banking system. After the Fed's open market purchase of bonds, some of the money the Fed paid for the bonds gets deposited into banks. Banks will want to make loans to consumers and businesses with that money, because holding it in their reserves with the Fed earns them no interest. To entice people to borrow, banks will lower the interest rates they charge on their loans. After an open market purchase of bonds by the Fed, interest rates will fall throughout the entire economy.

Now we understand why potential new homeowners—as well as businesspeople and politicians—want to know what the Federal Reserve is likely to do in the near future. The Fed exerts direct control over interest rates in the short run. If the Fed decides interest rates should be lower, it buys bonds in the open market to increase the supply of money. If the Fed wants higher interest rates, it sells bonds in the open market to decrease the money supply.

# 17.4 | INTEREST RATES AND HOW THEY CHANGE INVESTMENT AND OUTPUT (GDP)

For the Fed, higher or lower interest rates are just a means to an end. The Fed's ultimate goal is to change output—either to slow or speed the economy by influencing aggregate demand.

# APPLICATION

## RISING INTEREST RATES DURING AN ECONOMIC RECOVERY

**APPLYING THE CONCEPTS #1:** What happens to interest rates when the economy recovers from a recession?

Economists have often noticed that as an economy recovers from a recession, interest rates start to rise. And, in general, interest rates tend to rise as the economy grows quickly. An example of this occurred during 2005, when interest rates on three-month Treasury bills rose from 2.3 percent at the beginning of the year to 3.9 percent at the end of the year, as real GDP grew very rapidly.

Some observers think this is puzzling because they associate higher interest rates with lower output. Why should a recovery be associated with higher interest rates?

The simple model of the money market helps explain why interest rates can rise during an economic recovery. One key to understanding this phenomenon is that the extra income being generated by firms and individuals during the recovery will increase the demand for money. Because the demand for money increases while the supply of money remains fixed, interest rates rise.

Another factor is that the Federal Reserve itself may want to raise interest rates as the economy grows rapidly to avoid overheating the economy. In this case, the Fed cuts back on the supply of money to raise interest rates. In both cases, however, the public should expect rising interest rates during a period of economic recovery and rapid GDP growth. *Related to Exercise 3.4.*

To show how the Fed affects the interest rate, which in turn affects investment (a component of GDP), and finally, GDP itself, we combine our demand and supply for money with a curve that shows how investment spending is related to interest rates. This is shown in Figure 17.5. Panel A in Figure 17.5 shows how interest rates are determined by the demand and supply for money. It is identical to Figure 17.3 on page 412, which we studied earlier. The graph shows us the equilibrium interest rate for money.

Panel B shows a downwards sloping relationship between interest rates and investment spending. In other words, the graph shows that as interest rates fall, investment spending in the economy will increase. Why is there this negative relationship between interest rates and investment? Firms have a number of investment projects that they could undertake which all have payoffs in the future. These projects all require firms to either use their own funds or borrow funds in order to undertake the investments. The opportunity cost to the firms of these funds is the interest rate that they could earn by simply investing the funds in the financial markets. As interest rates in the economy fall, so does the opportunity cost of the funds needed for investment. With a lower opportunity cost, investments become more attractive to firms and total investment in the economy will increase. Conversely, as interest rates rise, the opportunity cost of funds increases and investment spending will decrease. Now let's combine Panel A and Panel B. We can see that at the equilibrium interest rate $r^*$ the level of investment in the economy will be given by $I^*$.

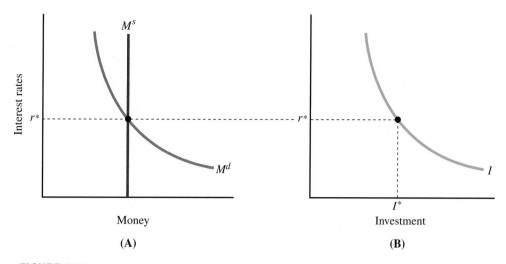

▲ **FIGURE 17.5**
**The Money Market and Investment Spending**
The equilibrium interest rate $r^*$ is determined in the money market. At that interest rate, investment spending is given by $I^*$.

We should note that consumption as well as investment can depend on interest rates. That is, spending on consumer durables, such as automobiles and refrigerators, will also depend negatively on the rate of interest. Consumer durables are really investment goods for the household: If you buy an automobile, you incur the cost today and receive benefits, such as the ability to use the car, in the future. As interest rates rise, the opportunity costs of investing in the automobile will rise. Consumers will respond to the increase in the opportunity cost by purchasing fewer cars. In this chapter, we discuss how changes in interest rates affect investment, but keep in mind that the purchases of consumer durables are affected too.

In Figure 17.6, we show the effects of an increase in the money supply using our money market and investment graphs. As the supply of money increases, interest rates fall from $r_0$ to $r_1$. With lower interest rates, investment spending will increase from $I_0$ to $I_1$. This increase in investment spending will then increase aggregate demand—the total demand for goods and services in the economy—and shift the aggregate demand curve to the right.

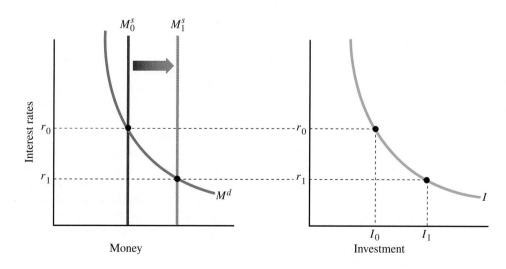

◄ **FIGURE 17.6**
**Monetary Policy and Interest Rates**
As the money supply increases, interest rates fall from $r_0$ to $r_1$. Investment spending increases from $I_0$ to $I_1$.

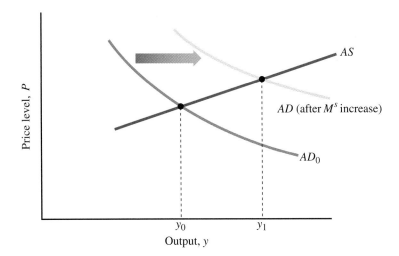

We show the shift of the aggregate demand curve in Figure 17.7. With the increase in aggregate demand, both output ($y$) and the price level ($P$) in the economy as a whole will increase in the short run. Thus, by reducing interest rates, the Fed affects output and prices in the economy.

In summary, when the Fed increases the money supply, it leads to lower interest rates and increased investment spending. In turn, a higher level of investment spending will ultimately lead to a higher level of GDP.

| open market bond purchases | → | increase in money supply | → | fall in interest rates | → | rise in investment spending | → | increase in GDP |
|---|---|---|---|---|---|---|---|---|

The Fed can also use its influence to increase interest rates, which will have the exact opposite effect. Investment spending will fall, along with aggregate demand. The aggregate demand curve will shift to the left, and the price level and output in the economy will fall, too. We can again represent this entire sequence of events:

| open market bond sale | → | decrease in money supply | → | rise in interest rates | → | fall in investment spending | → | decrease in GDP |
|---|---|---|---|---|---|---|---|---|

## Monetary Policy and International Trade

We have been discussing monetary policy without taking into account international trade or international movements of financial funds across countries. Once we bring in these considerations, we will see that monetary policy operates through an additional route.

Suppose the Federal Reserve lowers U.S. interest rates through an open market purchase of bonds. As a result, investors in the United States will be earning lower interest rates and will seek to invest some of their funds abroad. To invest abroad, they will need to sell their U.S. dollars and buy the foreign currency of the country where they intend to invest. This will affect the **exchange rate**—the rate at which one currency trades for another currency in the market. As more investors sell their dollars to buy foreign currency, the exchange rate will fall. A fall in the exchange rate or a decrease in the value of a currency is called **depreciation of a currency**. Lower U.S. interest rates brought on by the Fed will

• **exchange rate**
The rate at which currencies trade for one another in the market.

• **depreciation of a currency**
A decrease in the value of a currency.

**416**

cause the dollar to depreciate. This will ultimately change the demand and supply of goods and services around the globe because it will make U.S. goods cheaper than foreign goods. Let's see why.

In this case, the lower value of the dollar will mean that U.S. goods become relatively cheaper on world markets. Suppose that the exchange rate were two Swiss francs to the dollar, meaning you would receive two Swiss francs for every dollar you exchanged. If a U.S. machine sells for $100,000, it will cost 200,000 Swiss francs. Now suppose the value of the dollar depreciates so that one dollar now buys only one Swiss franc. The same U.S. machine will now cost Swiss residents half of what they used to pay for it—just 100,000 francs instead of 200,000. In other words, the lower value of the dollar makes U.S. goods cheaper for foreigners. As a result, foreign residents will want to buy more U.S. goods, and U.S. companies will want to export more goods to meet the higher foreign demand.

That's the good news about the lower value of the U.S. dollar. The bad news is that the lower value of the dollar will make it more expensive for U.S. residents to buy foreign goods. If the exchange rate were still two Swiss francs to the dollar as it originally was at the outset of our example, Swiss chemicals with a price tag of 60,000 francs would cost a U.S. resident $30,000. If the exchange rate of the dollar depreciates to one franc per dollar, however, the same chemicals will cost twice as much—$60,000. As the dollar depreciates, imports become more expensive, and U.S. residents tend to import fewer of them.

Let's recap this: As the exchange rate for the U.S. dollar falls, U.S. goods become cheaper and foreign goods become more expensive. The United States then exports more goods and imports fewer goods. *Net* exports increase, in other words. This increase in net exports increases the demand for U.S. goods and increases GDP. Remember that this all began with an open market purchase of bonds by the Fed that increased the money supply. Here is the sequence of events:

open market bond purchase → increase in money supply → fall in interest rates → fall in exchange rate → increase in net exports → increase in GDP

The three new links in the sequence are from interest rates to exchange rates, from exchange rates to net exports, and from net exports to GDP.

This sequence also works in reverse. If the Fed conducts an open market sale of bonds, U.S. interest rates rise. As a result, foreign investors earning lower interest rates elsewhere will want to move their money to the United States where they can earn a higher return. As they buy more U.S. dollars, the exchange rate for the dollar will increase, and the dollar will increase in value. An increase in the value of a currency is called **appreciation of a currency**. The appreciation of the dollar will make U.S. goods more expensive for foreigners and imports cheaper for U.S. residents. Suppose the exchange rate for the U.S. dollar appreciates, and each dollar can now be exchanged for three Swiss francs instead of two. The same machine the Swiss had to pay 200,000 francs for when the exchange rate was one dollar to two francs now costs 300,000 francs. The Swiss chemicals U.S. residents bought for $30,000 will now cost them less—just $20,000.

When U.S. interest rates rise as a result of an open market sale by the Fed, we expect exports to decrease and imports to increase, decreasing net exports. The decrease in net exports will reduce the demand for U.S. goods and lead to a fall in output. Here is the sequence of events:

- **appreciation of a currency**
  An increase in the value of a currency.

open market bond sale → decrease in money supply → rise in interest rates → rise in exchange rate → decrease in net exports → decrease in GDP

To summarize, an increase in interest rates will reduce both investment spending (including consumer durables) and net exports. A decrease in interest rates will increase investment spending and net exports. As you can see, monetary policy in an open economy is even more powerful than monetary policy used in a closed economy.

The Fed and other central banks are well aware of the power they have to influence exchange rates and international trade. For countries that depend extensively on international trade—such as Canada and Switzerland—the effects of monetary policy on exchange rates are critical to their economic well-being.

# 17.5 | MONETARY POLICY CHALLENGES FOR THE FED

Now that we have seen how changes in the money supply affect aggregate demand, we can see that the government has two different types of tools to change the level of GDP in the short run: The government can use either fiscal policy—changes in the level of taxes or government spending—or monetary policy—changes in the supply of money and interest rates—to alter the level of GDP.

If the current level of GDP is below full employment or potential output, the government can use expansionary policies such as tax cuts, increased spending, or increases in the money supply to raise the level of GDP and reduce unemployment. If the current level of GDP exceeds full employment or potential output, the economy will overheat, and the rate of inflation will increase. To avoid this overheating, the government can use contractionary policies to reduce the level of GDP back to full employment or potential output.

In Chapter 15, we explored some of the limitations of stabilization policy. We saw that fiscal policy is subject to lags and fraught with complications because political parties have different ideas about what the government should or should not do, and it takes them time to reach agreement. Monetary policy also has its complications.

## Lags in Monetary Policy

Recall that there are two types of lags in policy. *Inside lags* are the time it takes for policy makers to formulate and implement policy changes. *Outside lags* are the time it takes for policy to actually work.

The inside lags for monetary policy are relatively short compared to those for fiscal policy. The FOMC meets eight times a year and can decide on major policy changes at any time and very quickly. It can even give the chairperson of the Board of Governors some discretion to make changes between meetings.

Of course, it does take time for the people working at the Fed to recognize that problems are beginning to occur in the economy. A good example is the 1990 recession. In 1990, Iraq invaded Kuwait. After the invasion, there was some concern that higher oil prices and the uncertainty of the political situation in Kuwait would trigger a recession in the United States, which, of course, is heavily dependent on oil. However, Alan Greenspan, the chairman of the Federal Reserve, testified before Congress as late as October 1990 that the economy had not yet slipped into a recession. Not until that December did Greenspan declare that the economy had entered into a recession. Yet, looking back, we now know that the recession had actually started five months earlier, in July.

Decisions about monetary policy are made by a committee. How does this affect the effectiveness of monetary policy?

The outside lags related to monetary policy, however, are quite long. Most econometric models predict that an interest rate cut will take at least two years for most of its effects to be felt. This delay means that for the Fed to conduct successful monetary policy, it must be able to forecast accurately two years in the future! A study by two economists, David and Christina Romer of the University of California, Berkeley, suggests that the Federal Reserve actually makes more accurate inflation forecasts

# APPLICATION 2

## THE EFFECTIVENESS OF COMMITTEES

**APPLYING THE CONCEPTS #2:** Is it better for decisions about monetary policy to be made by a single individual or by a committee?

When Professor Alan Blinder returned to teaching after serving as vice-chairman of the Federal Reserve from 1994 to 1996, he was convinced that committees were not effective for making decisions about monetary policy. However, no research had been done on this topic. With another researcher, Blinder developed an experiment to see whether individuals or groups make better decisions and who makes them more rapidly.

The type of experiment Blinder and his colleague developed was designed to explore how quickly individuals and groups could distinguish changes in underlying trends from random events. For example, if unemployment were to rise in one month, such a rise could be a temporary aberration or it could be the beginning of a recession. Changing monetary policy would be a mistake if the rise were temporary, but waiting too long to change policy would be costly if the change were permanent. Who is better at making these sorts of determinations?

The results of the experiment showed that committees perform better than individuals. Committees make decisions as quickly and are more accurate than individuals making decisions by themselves. Moreover, committee decisions were not simply related to the average performance of the individuals who composed the committee—the actual *process* of having meetings and discussions appears to have improved the group's overall performance. *Related to Exercise 5.8.*

SOURCE: Alan Krueger, "Economic Scene: A Study Shows Committees Can Be More Than the Sum of Their Members," *New York Times*, December 7, 2000, p. C2.

than the private sector does, and that it is somewhat better at forecasting output as well.[1] They attribute the Fed's success to its large staff and access to more extensive information than private-sector forecasters have.

However, the Fed has difficulty predicting when recessions are about to occur. As an example, in May 2000, the Fed—fearing a rise in inflation—raised the federal funds rate from 6.00 to 6.50 percent. Yet, on January 3, 2001, the Fed reversed itself and restored the rate to 6.00 percent, because it feared a recession. It was too little—and too late—to prevent the 2001 recession.

Because of the long outside lags for monetary policy and difficulties in forecasting the economy, many economists believe that the Fed should not take a very active role in trying to stabilize the economy. Instead, they recommend that the Fed concentrate on keeping the inflation rate low and stable.

## Expectations of Inflation

An economy can, in principle, operate at full employment with any inflation rate. No "magic" inflation rate is necessary to sustain full employment. To understand this point, consider the long run when the economy operates at full employment. As we have seen, in the long run, changes in aggregate demand only affect prices and not output. If the Federal Reserve increases the money supply at 5 percent a year, prices in the economy will rise by 5 percent a year. That is, annual inflation will be 5 percent.

Suppose inflation continued for a long time at this rate. After a while, everyone in the economy would begin to expect that the 5 percent annual inflation that had occurred in the past would continue into the future. Economists call these beliefs *expectations of inflation*. People's expectations of inflation affect all aspects of economic life. For example, automobile producers will expect to increase the price of their products by 5 percent every year. They will also expect their costs—of labor and steel, for example—to increase by 5 percent a year. Workers will begin to believe that the 5 percent increases in their wages will be matched by a 5 percent increase in the prices of the goods they buy. Continued inflation becomes the normal state of affairs, and people "build it into" their daily decision-making process. For example, they expect the price of a car to be 5 percent higher next year.

This is also true in financial markets. Both borrowers and lenders will want to take into account any ongoing inflation. When there is inflation, economists make a distinction between the interest rate quoted in the market, which is called the *nominal interest rate*, and the *real interest rate*, which is what you actually earn after inflation has taken into account. The real rate is what determines investment spending in the economy.

The nominal interest rate is equal to the real interest rate plus the inflation rate:

$$\text{nominal rate} = \text{real rate} + \text{inflation rate}$$

If the real rate of interest is 2 percent per year and the inflation rate is 5 percent for the year, the nominal rate of interest is 7 percent (5 + 2).

In the short run, the inflation rate is normally slow to change and the Fed can usually affect real rates of interest by changing nominal rates. But in the long run, the Fed has little control over real interest rates—which are primarily determined by savings and investment—and only affects the inflation rate.

Central bankers must take into account expectations of inflation. They must be aware of the long-run implications of their actions even as they make decisions about short-term policy. For example, suppose the Fed wanted to lower real rates of interest in order to fight a recession. If the participants in the financial market believed that this was only a short-term action, then expectations of inflation would not change and the Fed could effectively conduct its stabilization policy through normal monetary policy. However, if market participants believed that the Fed would continue to engage in expansionary policy in the future, this could trigger an increase in expected inflation and lead to higher nominal interest rates, without any change in real interest rates. Workers and firms might start to build higher inflation expectations into their decisions, creating even more difficulties for the Fed. Thus, to be effective, the Fed must signal to financial markets that it is prepared to keep the inflation rate constant in the long run, even as it engages in expansionary policy in the short run.

Central banks use different tools to signal their commitment to keeping inflation in check. Speeches or statements by central bankers sometimes are effective. Central banks with a high degree of political independence are generally believed by financial markets to be more reliable in fighting inflation. And, in some countries, central banks have set explicit inflation targets to insure their credibility. The current Chairman of the Federal Reserve, Ben Bernanke, has written favorably about the gains to a central bank from setting explicit inflation targets.

# APPLICATION

## INCREASED POLITICAL INDEPENDENCE FOR THE BANK OF ENGLAND LOWERED INFLATION EXPECTATIONS

**APPLYING THE CONCEPTS #3:** Can changes in the way central banks are governed affect inflation expectations?

On May 6, 1997, the Chancellor of Exchequer in Great Britain, Gordon Brown, announced a major change in monetary policy. From that time forward, the Bank of England would be more independent from the government. Although the government would still retain the authority to set the overall goals for policy, the Bank of England would be free to pursue its policy goals without direct political control.

Mark Spiegel, an economist with the Federal Reserve Bank of San Francisco, studied how the British bond market reacted to the policy change. Spiegel did this by comparing the interest rates changes on two types of long-term bonds: bonds that are automatically adjusted (or indexed) for inflation and bonds that are not. The difference between the two interest rates primarily reflects expectations of inflation. Thus, if the gap narrowed following the policy announcement, this would be evidence that the new policy reduced expectations of inflation. If it did not, the announced policy would have had no effect on inflation expectations.

After the announcement, the gap narrowed. Based on this evidence, he concluded that the announcement did, indeed, cause expectations about inflation to fall by about half a percentage point. *Related to Exercise 5.9.*

SOURCE: "British Central Bank Independence and Inflation Expectations," *Federal Reserve Bank of San Francisco Economic Letter*, November 28, 1997.

## SUMMARY

This chapter showed how monetary policy affects aggregate demand and the economy in the short run. Together, the demand for money by the public and the supply of money determined by the Federal Reserve determine interest rates. Changes in interest rates will in turn affect investment and output. In the international economy, interest rates also affect exchange rates and net exports. Still, there are limits to what effective monetary policies can do. Here are the main points of the chapter:

1 The demand for money depends negatively on the interest rate and positively on the level of prices and real GDP.

2 The Fed can determine the supply of money through *open market purchases and sales,* changing reserve requirements, or changing the discount rate. Open market operations are the primary tool the Fed uses to implement monetary policy.

3 The level of interest rates is determined in the *money market* by the demand for money and the supply of money.

4 To increase the level of GDP, the Federal Reserve buys bonds on the open market. To decrease the level of GDP, the Federal Reserve sells bonds on the open market.

5 An increase in the money supply will decrease interest rates, increase investment spending, and increase output. A decrease in the money supply will increase interest rates, decrease investment spending, and decrease output.

6 In an open economy, a decrease in interest rates will depreciate the local currency and lead to an increase in net exports. Conversely, an increase in interest rates will appreciate the local currency and lead to a decrease in net exports.

7 Both lags in economic policies and the need to influence inflation expectations in the long run make successful monetary policy difficult in practice.

appreciation of a currency, p. 417

depreciation of a currency, p. 416

discount rate, p. 412

exchange rate, p. 416

federal funds market, p. 412

federal funds rate, p. 412

illiquid, p. 410

liquidity demand for money, p. 410

money market, p. 408

open market operations, p. 411

open market purchases, p. 411

open market sales, p. 411

speculative demand for money, p. 410

transaction demand for money, p. 408

EXERCISES  Visit www.myeconlab.com to complete

*Get Ahead of the Curve* these exercises online and get instant feedback.

## 17.1 | The Money Market

**1.1** We measure the opportunity cost of holding money with _____.

**1.2** The quantity of money demanded will _____ (increase/decrease) as interest rates rise.

**1.3** The principle of _____ suggests that the demand for money should increase as prices increase.

**1.4** Currency is a(n) _____ asset and IBM stocks are a(n) _____ asset.

**1.5** **Checking Account Interest Rates.** During the 1980s, banks started to pay interest (at low rates) on checking accounts for the first time. Given what you know about opportunity costs, how would interest paid on checking affect the demand for money?

**1.6** **Pegging Interest Rates.** Suppose the Federal Reserve wanted to fix, or "peg," the level of interest rates at 6 percent per year. Using a simple demand-and-supply graph, show how increases in money demand would change the supply of money if the Federal Reserve pursued the policy of this fixed interest rate. Use your answer to explain this statement: "If the Federal Reserve pegs interest rates, it loses control of the money supply."

**1.7** **Money Demand and Nominal Interest Rates.** We know that investment spending depends on real interest rates. Yet the demand for money will depend on nominal interest rates, not on real interest rates. Can you explain why money demand should depend on nominal rates?

**1.8** **Examples of Liquidity Demand.** Define the *liquidity demand for money* and give an example from your own experience of the liquidity demand for money.

## 17.2 | How the Federal Reserve Can Change the Money Supply

**2.1** To increase the supply of money, the Fed should _____ bonds.

**2.2** Increasing reserve requirements _____ the supply of money.

**2.3** Banks trade reserves with one another in the _____ market.

**2.4** Banks borrow from the Fed at the _____ rate.

**2.5** **Purchasing Foreign Currency.** What would happen to the supply of money if the Fed purchased foreign currency held by the public?

**2.6** **Bankers and Reserve Requirements.** If you were a banker, why would you be concerned if the Fed were to increase reserve requirements for deposits?

**2.7** **Borrowing from the Market, Not the Fed.** As a banker, you can borrow either at the discount rate from the Fed or from the federal funds market. What factors might lead you to prefer to borrow from the federal funds market?

## 17.3 | How Interest Rates Are Determined: Combining the Demand and Supply of Money

**3.1** Interest rates typically fall in a recession because the demand for money depends _____ on changes in real income.

**3.2** Through its effect on money demand, an increase in prices will _____ interest rates.

**3.3** Open market purchases lead to rising bond prices and _____ interest rates.

**3.4** **Recessions and Interest Rates.** The economy starts to head into a recession. Using a graph of the money market, show what happens to interest rates. (Related to Application 1 on page 414.)

**3.5** **Market Crashes and Increased Demand for Liquidity.** If following the stock market crash of 1987, investors suddenly became more cautious and wanted additional liquidity, what effects would this have had in the money market and on interest rates?

**3.6** **Rising Prices and the Money Market.** Draw a graph of the money market to show the effects of an increase in prices on interest rates.

**4.1** When the Federal Reserve sells bonds on the open market, it leads to _____ (higher/lower) levels of investment and output in the economy.

**4.2** To increase the level of output, the Fed should conduct an open market _____ (sale/purchase) of bonds.

**4.3** An open market purchase _____ the supply of money, which _____ interest rates, which _____ investment, and finally results in a(n) _____ in output.

**4.4** An increase in the supply of money will _____ (appreciate/depreciate) a country's currency.

**4.5** **Interest Rates, Durable Goods, and Nondurable Goods.** Refrigerators and clothing are to some extent durable. Explain why the decision to purchase a refrigerator is likely to be more sensitive to interest rates than the decision to buy clothing.

**4.6** **Where Is Monetary Policy Stronger?** In an open economy, changes in monetary policy affect both interest rates and exchange rates. Comparing the United States and Switzerland, in which country would monetary policy have a more significant effect on GDP through changes in exchange rates?

**4.7** **Tracing the Effects of a Decline in the Money Supply.** In 1981, the Federal Reserve reduced the growth rate of the money supply. Draw the appropriate graphs to illustrate the effects of a decrease in the supply of money on interest rates, investment, and aggregate demand.

## 17.5 | Monetary Policy Challenges for the Fed

**5.1** _____ (Inside/Outside) lags are longer for the Fed.

**5.2** Experimental evidence shows us that individuals perform _____ than committees in making monetary policy decisions.

**5.3** The Fed has no influence over expectations of inflation. _____ (True/False)

**5.4** **Playing the Praise and Blame Game.** The Federal Reserve leaders like to take credit for good economic performance. If there are lags in policies, explain why they may not deserve all the credit (or blame) for their economic policies.

**5.5** **Asset Prices as a Guide to Monetary Policy?** Some central bankers have looked at asset prices, such as prices of stocks, to guide monetary policy. The idea is that if stock prices begin to rise, it might signal future inflation or an overheated economy. Are there any dangers to using the stock market as a guide to monetary policy?

**5.6** **What Information Does the Fed Use?** The Federal Reserve uses both econometric models as well as other, more general information about the economy to make decisions about monetary policy. To see what some of this general information looks like, go to the Web site for the Federal Reserve Open Market Committee (FOMC) (www.federalreserve.gov/fomc) and read the report of the Beige Book (a briefing book named for the color of its cover). What type of information is provided in the Beige Book?

**5.7** **International Influences on Fed Policy.** As international trade becomes more important, monetary policy becomes more heavily influenced by developments in the foreign exchange markets. Go to the Web page of the Federal Reserve (www.federalreserve.gov) and read some recent speeches given by Fed officials. Do international considerations seem to affect policy makers in the United States today?

**5.8** **Committee Size and Policy.** An experiment showed that a committee can make better decisions than individuals. How might the size of a committee affect the quality of decision making? What might be the benefits of a larger committee and what might be its costs? (Related to Application 2 on page 419.)

**5.9** **Inflation Targets for a Central Bank** What would be the advantages to a central bank from setting an explicit inflation target? Can you think of any disadvantages? (Related to Application 3 on page 421.)

## NOTES

1. Christina D. Romer and David H. Romer, "Federal Reserve Information and the Behavior of Interest Rates," 2000, *The American Economic Review*, Vol. 90, no. 3. pp. 429–457.

# 18

# International Trade and Finance

Look at the label on your shirt or your tie. Chances are it was made in China, Indonesia, or another developing country. If you own a $100 pair of brand-name athletic shoes it was probably assembled somewhere in the Far East, perhaps Vietnam or Cambodia. We are no longer surprised to learn this, because many major companies locate their key production facilities abroad.

But somehow, we are still astonished that when we make a service call to fix a problem on our personal computer, we may end up be

MADE IN CHINA
FABRIQUÉ EN CHINE
SIZE : WM

1 How many jobs are lost to outsourcing (the shift of production to other countries)?
   *Moving Jobs to Different States and Different Countries*

2 Does the protection of one domestic industry harm another?
   *Candy Cane Makers Move to Mexico for Cheap Sugar*

3 Do tariffs (taxes) on imported goods hurt the poor disproportionately?
   *The Impact of Tariffs on the Poor*

4 What are the most pressing current issues in today's trade negotiations?
   *Ongoing Trade Negotiations*

5 Why did a group of European countries adopt a common currency?
   *The First Decade of the Euro*

speaking to a technical representative in Bangalore, India. And certainly many sophisticated jobs are now performed outside the United States. High-tech firms in Silicon Valley in California often have their computer code written in India or other countries around the globe. How will these changes in our global economy affect our lives in the United States? And how will these global changes affect the world's financial system?

O ur world is becoming increasingly global, which creates wonderful new opportunities but also poses new challenges for citizens and their governments throughout the world. Many people are uneasy about the consequences of free trade with foreign countries and are concerned about the changes that will occur in terms of jobs, industries, and the international financial system. This chapter explores the underlying basis for international trade and how this is managed through the world financial system. It also explores the tensions that naturally occur with free trade and the policy options that governments have to manage our new global system. Let's begin by understanding why people want to trade with one another.

# 18.1 | COMPARATIVE ADVANTAGE AND EXCHANGE

As we saw earlier in the book, a market is an institution or arrangement that enables people to buy and sell things. The alternative to buying and selling in markets is to be self-sufficient, with each of us producing everything we need for ourselves. Rather than going it alone, most of us specialize: We produce one or two products for others and then exchange the money we earn for the products we want to consume.

### Specialization and the Gains from Trade

We can explain how people can benefit from specialization and trade with a simple example of two people and two products. Suppose that the crew of the television show *Survivor* finishes filming a season of episodes on a remote tropical island, and when the crew returns to the mainland two people miss the boat and are left behind. The two real survivors produce and consume two goods, coconuts and fish. The first row of Table 18.1 shows their production possibilities. Each day Fred can either gather 2 coconuts or catch 6 fish, while Kate can either gather 1 coconut or catch 1 fish.

We'll show that the two survivors will be better off if each person specializes in one product and then exchanges with the other person. We can use one of the key principles to explore the rationale for specialization.

# PRINCIPLE OF OPPORTUNITY COST
The opportunity cost of something is what you sacrifice to get it.

Fred's opportunity cost of a coconut is 3 fish—that's how many fish he could catch in the time required to gather 1 coconut. Similarly, his opportunity cost of a fish is one-third coconut, the number of coconuts he could gather in the time required to catch 1 fish. For Kate, the opportunity cost of a coconut is 1 fish, and the opportunity cost of a fish is 1 coconut.

To demonstrate the benefits of exchange, let's imagine that both people are initially self-sufficient, with each producing enough of both goods to satisfy their own desires. Suppose there are 6 workdays per week. If Fred initially devotes 2 days per

Table 18.1 | PRODUCTIVITY AND OPPORTUNITY COSTS

|  | Fred | | Kate | |
|---|---|---|---|---|
|  | Coconuts | Fish | Coconuts | Fish |
| Output per day | 2 | 6 | 1 | 1 |
| Opportunity cost | 3 fish | 1/3 coconut | 1 fish | 1 coconut |

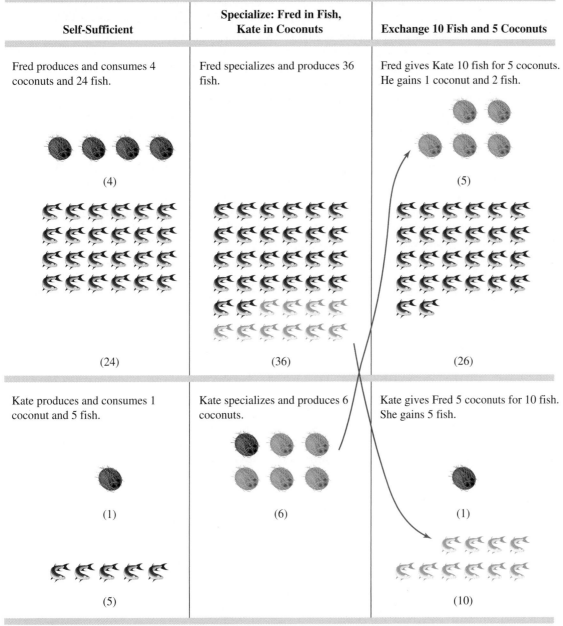

| Self-Sufficient | Specialize: Fred in Fish, Kate in Coconuts | Exchange 10 Fish and 5 Coconuts |
|---|---|---|
| Fred produces and consumes 4 coconuts and 24 fish. | Fred specializes and produces 36 fish. | Fred gives Kate 10 fish for 5 coconuts. He gains 1 coconut and 2 fish. |
| (4) | | (5) |
| (24) | (36) | (26) |
| Kate produces and consumes 1 coconut and 5 fish. | Kate specializes and produces 6 coconuts. | Kate gives Fred 5 coconuts for 10 fish. She gains 5 fish. |
| (1) | (6) | (1) |
| (5) | | (10) |

▲ **FIGURE 18.1**
**Specialization and the Gains from Trade**

week to gathering coconuts and 4 days per week to catching fish, he will produce and consume 4 coconuts (2 per day times 2 days) and 24 fish (6 per day times 4 days) per week. This is shown in the first column of Figure 18.1. If Kate initially devotes 1 day per week to coconuts and 5 days per week to fish, she will produce and consume 1 coconut and 5 fish per week.

Specialization will increase the total output of our little survivor economy. It is sensible for each person to specialize in the good for which he or she has a lower opportunity cost. We say that a person has a **comparative advantage** in producing a particular product if he or she has a lower opportunity cost than another person:

• Fred has a comparative advantage producing fish because his opportunity cost of fish is one-third coconut per fish, compared to 1 coconut per fish for Kate.

• **comparative advantage**
The ability of one person or nation to produce a good at a lower opportunity cost than another person or nation.

• Kate has a comparative advantage in coconuts because her opportunity cost of coconuts is 1 fish per coconut, compared to 3 fish per coconut for Fred.

The second column of Figure 18.1 shows what happens to production when the two people specialize: Fred produces 36 fish and Kate produces 6 coconuts. The total output of both goods increases: The number of coconuts increases from 5 to 6, and the number of fish increases from 29 to 36. Specialization increases the output of both goods because both people are focusing on what they do best.

If specialization is followed by exchange, both people will be better off. Suppose Fred and Kate agree to exchange 2 fish per coconut. Fred could give up 10 fish to get 5 coconuts. As shown in the third column of Figure 18.1, that leaves him with 5 coconuts and 26 fish. Compared to the self-sufficient outcome, he has more of both goods—one more coconut and 2 more fish. If Kate gives up 5 coconuts to get 10 fish, that leaves her with 1 coconut and 10 fish, which is better than her self-sufficient outcome of one coconut and 5 fish. Specialization and exchange make both people better off, illustrating one of the key principles of economics:

## PRINCIPLE OF VOLUNTARY EXCHANGE

A voluntary exchange between two people makes both people better off.

### Comparative Advantage Versus Absolute Advantage

We've seen that it is beneficial for each person to specialize in the product for which he or she has a comparative advantage—a lower opportunity cost. You may have noticed that Fred is more productive than Kate in producing both goods. Fred requires a smaller quantity of resources (less labor time) to produce both goods, so he has an **absolute advantage** in producing both goods. Despite his absolute advantage, Fred gains from specialization and trade because he has a comparative advantage in fish. Fred is twice as productive as Kate in producing coconuts, but six times as productive in producing fish. By relying on Kate to produce coconuts, Fred frees up time to spend producing fish, the good for which he has the larger productivity advantage over Kate. The lesson is that specialization and exchange result from comparative advantage, not absolute advantage.

**• absolute advantage**
The ability of one person or nation to produce a product at a lower resource cost than another person or nation.

## 18.2 | COMPARATIVE ADVANTAGE AND INTERNATIONAL TRADE

The lessons of comparative advantage and specialization apply to trade between nations. Each nation could be self-sufficient, producing all the goods it consumes, or it could specialize in products for which it has a comparative advantage. Even if one nation is more productive than a second nation in producing all goods, trade will be beneficial if the first nation has a bigger productivity advantage in one product— that is, if one nation has a comparative advantage in some product. An **import** is a product produced in a foreign country and purchased by residents of the home country. An **export** is a product produced in the home country and sold in another country.

Many people are skeptical about the idea that international trade can make everyone better off. President Abraham Lincoln expressed his discomfort with importing goods:[1]

> I know if I buy a coat in America, I have a coat and America has the money—If I buy a coat in England, I have the coat and England has the money.

What President Lincoln didn't understand is that when he buys a coat in England, he sends dollars to England, and the dollars don't just sit there, but eventually are

**• import**
A product produced in a foreign country and purchased by residents of the home country.

**• export**
A product produced in the home country and sold in another country.

# APPLICATION

## MOVING JOBS TO DIFFERENT STATES AND DIFFERENT COUNTRIES

**APPLYING THE CONCEPTS #1:** How many jobs are lost to outsourcing (the shift of production to other countries)?

When a domestic firm shifts part of its production to a different country, we say that the firm is *outsourcing* or *offshoring*. Mattel's Barbie doll is a classic example of outsourcing, with production occurring in Saudi Arabia, Taiwan, Japan, China, Indonesia, Malaysia, Europe, and the United States. In the modern global economy, transportation and communication costs are relatively low, so firms can spread production across many countries. By taking advantage of the comparative advantages of different countries, a firm can produce its product at a lower cost, charge a lower price, and sell more output.

In recent years, outsourcing has received a lot of attention as firms shift service functions overseas. The reduction of communication costs and the standardization of software have allowed firms to outsource business services such as customer service, telemarketing, document management, and medical transcription. Firms shift these functions overseas to reduce production costs, allowing them to sell their products at lower prices. Some recent studies of outsourcing have reached a number of conclusions:[4]

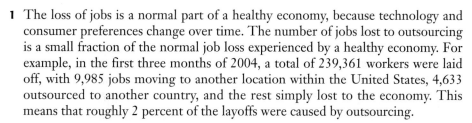

1 The loss of jobs is a normal part of a healthy economy, because technology and consumer preferences change over time. The number of jobs lost to outsourcing is a small fraction of the normal job loss experienced by a healthy economy. For example, in the first three months of 2004, a total of 239,361 workers were laid off, with 9,985 jobs moving to another location within the United States, 4,633 outsourced to another country, and the rest simply lost to the economy. This means that roughly 2 percent of the layoffs were caused by outsourcing.

2 The jobs lost to outsourcing are at least partly offset by jobs gained through *insourcing*, jobs that are shifted from overseas to the United States.

3 The cost savings from outsourcing are substantial, leading to lower prices for consumers and more output for firms. The jobs gained from increased output at least partly offset the jobs lost to outsourcing.

*Related to Exercises 2.3 and 2.5.*

SOURCE: U.S. Bureau of Labor Statistics, "Extended Mass Layoffs Associated with Domestic and Overseas Relocations, First Quarter 2004," June 2004.

# APPLICATION

## CANDY CANE MAKERS MOVE TO MEXICO FOR CHEAP SUGAR

**APPLYING THE CONCEPTS #2:** Does the protection of one domestic industry harm another?

About 90 percent of the world's candy canes are consumed in the United States, and until recently most candy canes were produced domestically. Domestic producers were closer to consumers, so they had lower transportation costs and lower prices than their foreign competitors. Domestic firms used their superior access to consumers to dominate the market.

In recent years, the domestic production of candy canes has decreased as firms have shut plants in the United States and opened new ones in Mexico. In 2003, Spangler Candy Company of Bryan, Ohio, shifted half of its production to a plant in Juarez, Mexico. The company opened the Mexico plant because the cost of sugar, the key ingredient in candy, is only $0.06 per pound in Mexico, compared to $0.21 in the United States. The shift to Mexico saves the firm about $2.7 million per year on sugar costs. The high price of sugar has caused other candy manufacturers to shift their operations overseas. Since 1998, the Chicago area, the center of the U.S. confection industry, has lost about 3,000 candy-production jobs.

Why is the price of sugar in the United States so high? The government protects the domestic sugar industry from foreign competition by restricting sugar imports. As a result, the supply of sugar in the United States is artificially low and the price is artificially high. In this case, the protection of jobs in one domestic industry reduces jobs in another domestic industry.

*Related to Exercises 2.4 and 2.6.*

SOURCE: "Sugar Costs Give Candy Cane Makers a Bitter Aftertaste," *Chicago Tribune*, December 25, 2003, p. 14.

sent back to the United States to buy goods produced by American workers. In the words of economist Todd Buchholz, the author of *New Ideas from Dead Economists:*[2]

> Money may not make the world go round, but money certainly goes around the world. To stop it prevents goods from traveling from where they are produced most inexpensively to where they are desired most deeply.

### Movie Exports

Although many people think of exports in terms of farm products, such as corn and wheat, and manufactured products, such as airplanes and satellites, one of the leading U.S. exports is movies. The U.S. film industry employs about 350,000 Americans, and almost two-thirds of its revenue comes from films exported to countries around the world. Figure 18.2 shows the distribution of box office revenue from different parts of the world. Between 2001 and 2004, total export revenue from movies increased from $8.6 billion to $15.7 billion, with the largest increases in Europe and the Middle East.[3] By comparison, each year the United States exports about $25 billion worth of aircraft and spacecraft and about $12 billion worth of wheat, rice, and corn.

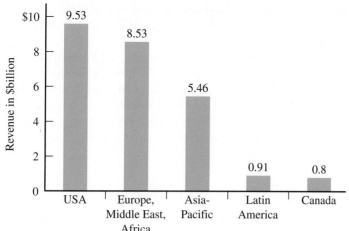

◄ **FIGURE 18.2**
**International Box Office Revenue for U.S. Films, 2004**
*SOURCE:* Author's computations based on MPA Worldwide Market Research, MPA Snapshot Report: 2004 International Theatrical Market (Motion Picture Association, March 2005).

# 18.3 | PROTECTIONIST POLICIES

Now that you know the basic rationale for specialization and trade, we can explore the effects of public policies that restrict it. Despite the advantages of trade, governments restrict it to protect domestic industries or jobs in those industries. We will consider four common import-restriction policies: an outright ban on imports, an import quota, voluntary export restraints, and a tariff.

## Import Bans

To show how an import ban affects the market, let's start with an unrestricted market—no import ban. Figure 18.3 shows the market for shirts in Chipland, a nation with a comparative advantage in producing computer chips, not shirts. The domestic supply curve shows the quantity of shirts supplied by firms in Chipland. Looking at point *b*, we see that Chipland firms will not supply any shirts unless the price is at least $17 per shirt. The total supply curve for shirts, which shows the quantity supplied by both domestic firms and foreign firms (in Shirtland), lies to the right of the domestic supply curve. At each price, the total supply of shirts exceeds the domestic supply because foreign firms supply shirts, too. Point *c* shows the free-trade equilibrium. The demand curve from domestic residents intersects the total supply curve at a price of

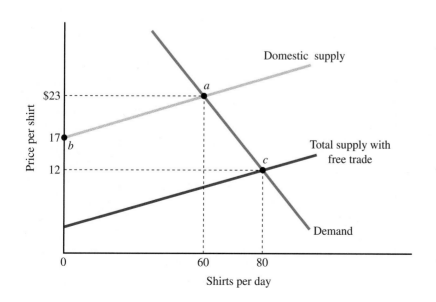

◄ **FIGURE 18.3**
**Effects of an Import Ban**
In the free-trade equilibrium, demand intersects the total supply curve at point *c*, with a price of $12 and a quantity of 80 shirts. If shirt imports are banned, the equilibrium is shown by the intersection of the demand curve and the domestic supply curve (point *a*). The price increases to $23.

$12 per shirt and a quantity of 80 shirts. Because this price is below the minimum price for domestic firms, domestic firms produce no shirts, and all the shirts in Chipland are imported from Shirtland.

What will happen if Chipland bans imported shirts? Foreign suppliers will disappear from the shirt market, so the total supply of shirts will be the domestic supply. In Figure 18.3, point *a* shows the equilibrium when Chipland bans imported shirts: The domestic demand curve intersects the domestic supply curve at a price of $23 per shirt and a quantity of 60 shirts. In other words, the decrease in supply resulting from the import ban increases the price consumers have to pay for shirts and decreases the quantity available for them to buy.

## Quotas and Voluntary Export Restraints

• **import quota**
A government-imposed limit on the quantity of a good that can be imported.

An alternative to an import ban is an **import quota**—a government-imposed limit on the quantity of a good that can be imported. An import quota is a restrictive policy that falls between free trade and an outright ban: Imports are cut, but not eliminated. For example, if a quota were put on shirts, the price consumers would have to pay would fall somewhere between the price they would pay with free trade ($12 per shirt, as in our example) and the price they would pay if imported shirts were banned ($23 per shirt). Where exactly the price would fall would depend on how high or low the quotas are.

• **voluntary export restraint (VER)**
A scheme under which an exporting country voluntarily decreases its exports.

Import quotas are illegal under international trading rules. To get around these rules, an exporting country will sometimes agree to a **voluntary export restraint (VER)**. A VER is similar to an import ban. When an exporting nation adopts a VER, it decreases its exports to avoid having to face even more restrictive trade policies importing countries might be tempted to impose on them. Although VERs are legal under global-trade rules, they violate the spirit of international free-trade agreements. In any case, quotas and VERs have the same effect. Like a quota, a VER increases the price of the restricted good, making it more feasible for domestic firms to participate in the market.

Figure 18.4 shows the effect of an import quota or VER. Starting from the free-trade equilibrium at point c, an import quota will shift the total supply curve to the left: At each price there will be a smaller quantity of shirts supplied because foreign suppliers aren't allowed to supply as many. The total supply curve when there is an import quota or VER will lie between the domestic supply curve and the total supply curve under free trade. The equilibrium under an import quota or VER occurs at point *d*, where the demand curve intersects the total supply curve under an import limitation. The $20 price per shirt with the import quota exceeds the $17 minimum

▶ **FIGURE 18.4**
**Market Effects of a Quota, a VER, or a Tariff**
An import quota shifts the supply curve to the left. The market moves upward along the demand curve to point *d*, which is between point *c* (free trade) and *a* (an import ban). We can reach the same point with a tariff that shifts the total supply curve to the same position.

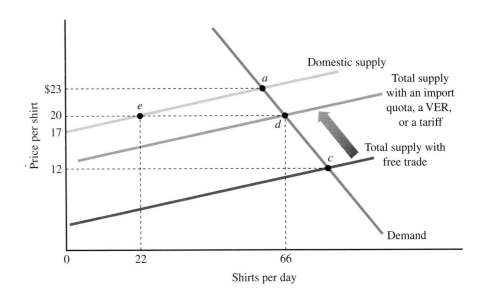

price of domestic firms, so domestic firms supply 22 shirts (point *e*). Under a free-trade policy, they would have supplied no shirts.

A quota or a VER produces winners and losers. The winners include foreign and domestic shirt producers. In our example, foreign firms can sell shirts at a price of $20 instead of $12 each, and the price is high enough for domestic firms to participate in the market. This generates benefits for the firms and their workers. The losers are consumers, who pay a higher price for shirts. In some cases, the government issues **import licenses** to some citizens, who can then buy shirts from foreign firms at a low price, such as $12, and sell the shirts at the higher domestic price, $20. Because import licenses provide profits to the holder, they are often awarded to politically powerful firms or individuals. Moreover, because they are so valuable, some people may bribe government officials for the licenses.

We know that consumers pay higher prices for goods that are subject to protectionist policies, but how much more? Here is one example. In the United States, voluntary export restraints on Japanese automobiles in 1984 increased the price of a Japanese car by about $1,300 and the price of a domestic car by about $660.[5]

An alternative to a quota or a VER is an import **tariff**, which is a tax on an imported good. Tariffs have the same effect as quotas and VERs. We know from our earlier discussions that a tax shifts the supply curve to the left and increases the equilibrium price. In Figure 18.4, suppose the tariff shifts the total supply curve with free trade so that it intersects the domestic demand curve at point *d*. In other words, we reach the same point we reached with the quota: Consumers pay the same $20 price per shirt, and domestic firms produce the same quantity: 22 shirts.

There is one fundamental difference between a quota and a tariff. An import quota allows importers to buy shirts from foreign suppliers at a low price—say, $12 per shirt—and sell them for $20 each, the artificially high price. In other words,

- **import licenses**
  Rights, issued by a government, to import goods.

- **tariff**
  A tax on imported goods.

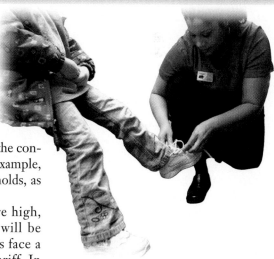

# APPLICATION

## THE IMPACT OF TARIFFS ON THE POOR

**APPLYING THE CONCEPTS #3:** Do tariffs (taxes) on imported goods hurt the poor disproportionately?

Economists have found that tariffs in the United States fall most heavily on lower-income consumers. In the United States, tariffs are very high on textiles, apparel items, and footwear. These goods represent a higher fraction of the consumption of lower-income households than higher-income households. For example, footwear accounts for 1.3 percent of the expenditure of lower-income households, as compared to 0.5 percent for higher-income households.

Moreover, even within these categories of goods for which tariffs are high, the highest tariffs fall on the cheapest products—precisely those that will be purchased by lower-income consumers. For example, low-priced sneakers face a 32-percent tariff, whereas expensive track shoes face only a 20-percent tariff. In general, to protect U.S. industries, tariffs are highest on labor-intensive goods—goods that use relatively more labor than capital. But these goods tend to be lower priced. That is why tariffs do fall disproportionately on the poor. *Related to Exercise 3.7.*

SOURCE: *Economic Report of the President 2006,* Chapter 7, available online at www.gpoaccess.gov/eop/download.html, accessed June, 2006.

importers make money from the quota. Under a tariff, the government gets the money, collecting $8 per shirt from foreign suppliers. Citizens in Chipland will prefer the tariff to the quota because the government can use the revenue from the tariff to cut other taxes or expand public programs.

In the real world, tariffs can have major effects. One trade expert estimated that cutting industrial tariffs by 50 percent would increase the output of the world's economy by $270 billion per year. Similar easing of tariffs on agricultural products would cut the world's food bill by $100 billion.[6] Tariffs also appear to disproportionately affect the poor.

# 18.4 | A BRIEF HISTORY OF INTERNATIONAL TARIFF AND TRADE AGREEMENTS

Today, the average U.S. tariff is 4.6 percent of the value of imported goods, a rate that is close to the average tariffs in Japan and most European nations but very low by historical standards. As we noted earlier, when the Smoot–Hawley tariffs were implemented in the 1930s, the average U.S. tariff was a whopping 59 percent of a product's price. Tariffs are lower today because several international agreements subsequently reduced them.

The first major international trade agreement following World War II was the **General Agreement on Tariffs and Trade (GATT)**. This agreement was initiated in 1947 by the United States and 23 other nations and now has over 149 members. Nine rounds of GATT negotiations over tariffs and trade regulations have taken place, resulting in progressively lower tariffs for the member nations. The last completed set of negotiations, the Uruguay round (1994), decreased tariffs by about one-third of the previous level. In 1995, the **World Trade Organization (WTO)** was formed to enforce GATT and other international trade agreements. Under GATT's "most favored nation" provision, a country that reduces tariffs for one nation must do so for all members of GATT. This provision helps reduce tariffs throughout the world.

A new round of trade negotiations began in Doha, Qatar, in 2001. This round focused on many issues especially relevant to developing countries.

In addition to the large group of nations involved in the WTO, other nations have formed trade associations to lower trade barriers and promote international trade. Here are some of the most well-known agreements:

- The North American Free Trade Agreement (NAFTA) took effect in 1994 and will be implemented over a 15-year period. The agreement will eventually eliminate all tariffs and other trade barriers between Canada, Mexico, and the United States.

- The European Union (EU) was designed to remove all trade barriers within Europe and create a single market. Initially, the EU consisted of just six countries: Belgium, Germany, France, Italy, Luxembourg, and the Netherlands. Denmark, Ireland, and the United Kingdom joined in 1973; Greece in 1981; Spain and Portugal in 1986; and Austria, Finland, and Sweden in 1995. In 2004, the biggest ever enlargement took place with 10 new countries joining the EU.

- The leaders of 18 Asian nations have formed an organization called Asian Pacific Economic Cooperation (APEC). In 1994, APEC signed a nonbinding agreement to reduce trade barriers among these nations.

- The proposed U.S.-Central America Free Trade Agreement (CAFTA) would promote trade liberalization between the United States and five Central American countries: Costa Rica, El Salvador, Guatemala, Honduras, and Nicaragua. Modeled after the North American Free Trade Agreement (NAFTA), CAFTA must be approved by the U.S. Congress and by National Assemblies in the Central American countries before it becomes law.

**• General Agreement on Tariffs and Trade (GATT)**
An international agreement established in 1947 that has lowered trade barriers between the United States and other nations.

**• World Trade Organization (WTO)**
An organization established in 1995 that oversees GATT and other international trade agreements, resolves trade disputes, and holds forums for further rounds of trade negotiations.

# 4

# APPLICATION

## ONGOING TRADE NEGOTIATIONS

**APPLYING THE CONCEPTS #4:** What are the most pressing current issues in today's trade negotiations?

The focus of the latest round of trade negotiations was to help the developing countries by opening up trade in agriculture, as well as to continue to reduce barriers in manufacturing throughout the globe. The comparative advantage of many developing countries lies in agriculture, but the developed countries, such as those in both Europe and the United States, still provide subsidies and protection to their agriculture industries. Subsidies to exports lower world prices, and thereby make it more difficult for developing countries to compete in world markets. Although the number of farmers has decreased in developed countries, they remain politically powerful, particularly in Europe.

The Doha rounds have proceeded through a number of meetings of negotiators in Cancun, Geneva, Paris, and Hong Kong. In the Hong Kong meeting in December 2005, negotiators agreed in principle to eliminate all export subsidies for agriculture exports by the year 2013. This was an important accomplishment, but many more details and issues need to be negotiated before the Doha round can come to a fruitful conclusion. *Related to Exercise 4.7.*

Some economists are concerned that these regional trade agreements may stand in the way of broader international trade agreements under GATT. Although regional agreements may lead to reduced tariffs for neighboring or member countries, they do little to promote efficiency across the globe. For example, a Belgian firm may find it easier to sell goods in France than a firm from South America that has a lower cost of production.

# 18.5 | HOW EXCHANGE RATES ARE DETERMINED

Now we turn to how the international financial system manages trade in both goods and in financial assets. The first step is to examine how the value of a currency is determined in world markets. We then look at the factors that can change the value of a currency.

## What Are Exchange Rates?

To conduct international transactions between countries with different currencies, it is necessary to exchange one currency for another. The **exchange rate** is defined as the price at which we can exchange one currency for another.

Suppose a U.S. songwriter sells the rights of a hit song to a Japanese producer. The U.S. songwriter agrees to accept $50,000. If the exchange rate between the U.S. dollar and Japanese yen is 100 yen per dollar, it will cost the Japanese producer

• **exchange rate**
The price at which currencies trade for one another in the market.

• **euro**
The common currency in Europe.

• **appreciation of a currency**
An increase in the value of a currency relative to the currency of another nation.

• **depreciation of a currency**
A decrease in the value of a currency relative to the currency of another nation.

5,000,000 yen to purchase the rights to the song. Because international trade occurs between nations with different currencies, the exchange rate—the price at which one currency trades for another currency—is a crucial determinant of trade. Fluctuations in the exchange rate can have a huge impact on what goods countries import or export and the overall trade balance.

Throughout this chapter, we will measure the exchange rate in units of foreign currency per U.S. dollar, that is, as "100 Japanese yen per dollar or 0.8 euro per dollar." The **euro** is the common currency in Europe. With these exchange rates, you would receive 100 yen for each dollar, but only 0.8 euro for each dollar.

We can think of the exchange rate as the price of dollars in terms of foreign currency. An increase in the value of a currency relative to the currency of another nation is called an **appreciation of a currency**. If the exchange rate between the dollar and the yen increases from 100 yen per dollar to 110 yen per dollar, one dollar will purchase more yen. Say, for instance, you've taken a trip to Japan for spring break. Because the dollar has appreciated, your dollar will exchange for more yen. You will now have more yen to spend on Japanese goods—say, MP3 players, DVD players, or entertainment—than you would have before the dollar appreciated. The dollar has become more expensive in terms of yen. Its price has risen, in other words. Because the dollar has increased in value, we say that the dollar has appreciated against the yen.

A **depreciation of a currency** is a decrease in the value of a currency relative to the currency of another nation. If the exchange rate falls from 100 to 90 yen per dollar, you'll get fewer yen for each dollar you exchange. Japanese goods—whose prices remain the same in Japanese yen—will become more expensive to U.S. residents. You'll have to use more dollars to obtain the yen to purchase the same MP3 and DVD players. The price of dollars in terms of yen has fallen, in other words, so we say that the dollar has depreciated against the yen.

Be sure you understand that if one currency appreciates, the other must depreciate. If the dollar appreciates against the yen, for example, the yen must depreciate against the dollar. You'll get more yen in exchange for the dollar, but now when you trade your yen back, you'll get fewer dollars. For example, if the dollar appreciates from 100 to 110 yen per dollar, when you trade 100 yen back into U.S. currency, no longer will you get $1.00—you'll get just $0.91. Conversely, if the dollar depreciates against the yen, the yen must appreciate against the dollar. If the dollar depreciates from 100 yen to 90 yen per dollar, when you trade back 100 yen, you'll get $1.11, rather than just $1.00.

The exchange rate enables us to convert prices in one country to values in another country. A simple example illustrates how an exchange rate works. If you want to buy a watch from France, you need to know what it would cost. You call the store in France and are told that the watch sells for 240 euros. The store owners live in France and want to be paid in euros. To figure out what it will cost you in dollars, you need to know the exchange rate between euros and dollars. If the exchange rate is 0.8 euro per dollar, the watch would cost you $300:

$$\frac{240 \text{ euros}}{0.8 \text{ euro per dollar}} = \$300$$

If the exchange rate is one euro per dollar, the watch would cost only $240. As you can see, changes in the exchange rate will affect the prices of goods purchased on world markets and partly determine the pattern of imports and exports throughout the world.

### How Demand and Supply Determine Exchange Rates

How are exchange rates determined? The exchange rate between U.S. dollars and euros is determined in the foreign-exchange market, the market in which dollars trade for euros. To understand this market, we can use demand and supply. In Figure 18.5, we plot the demand and supply curves for dollars in exchange for euros.

The supply curve is the quantity supplied of dollars in exchange for euros. Individuals or firms that want to buy European goods or assets will need to exchange dollars for euros. The supply curve is drawn under the assumption that as euros

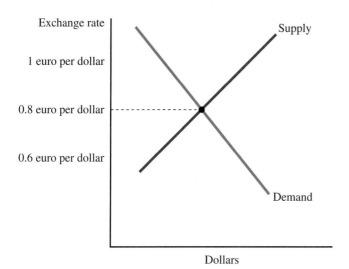

◄ **FIGURE 18.5**
**The Demand for and Supply of
U.S. Dollars**
Market equilibrium occurs where the
demand for U.S. dollars equals the supply.

become cheaper, total spending on European goods and assets will increase. Therefore, the supply curve slopes upward: As the value of the dollar increases, more dollars will be supplied to the currency market in exchange for euros.

The demand curve represents the quantity demanded of dollars in exchange for euros. Individuals or firms in Europe that want to buy U.S. goods or assets must trade euros for dollars. For example, to visit Disneyland in California, a German or French family must exchange euros for dollars. As the exchange rate for the U.S. dollar falls, dollars become cheaper in terms of euros. This makes U.S. goods and assets less expensive for European residents, because each euro buys more U.S. dollars. As U.S. goods and assets become cheaper, we assume that more European residents will want to trade euros for dollars. Therefore, the demand curve for dollars in exchange for euros slopes downward: Total demand for dollars will increase as the price of the dollar falls, or depreciates, against the euro.

Equilibrium in the market for foreign exchange occurs where the demand curve intersects the supply curve. In Figure 18.5, equilibrium occurs at an exchange rate of 0.8 euro per dollar. At this price, the willingness to trade dollars for euros just matches the willingness to trade euros for dollars. The foreign exchange market is in balance, and the price of euros in terms of a dollar is $1.25.

Price of euros per dollar in equilibrium:

$$0.8 \text{ euro per dollar} = \frac{1 \text{ dollar}}{0.8 \text{ euro}} = 1.25 \text{ dollars per euro, or } \$1.25 \text{ per euro}$$

Now, however, suppose the demand and supply forces between dollars and euros change. If the exchange rate, $e$, increases, the dollar buys *more* euros—the price of dollars in terms of euros increases, in other words. For example, if $e$ increases from 0.8 euro per dollar to 1 euro per dollar, the dollar has become more valuable—meaning that it has appreciated against the euro. Be sure you see both sides of the same exchange coin: If the dollar appreciates against the euro, then the euro must depreciate against the dollar. So, if the exchange rate increases from 0.8 to 1 euro per dollar, what will the price of a single euro be now?

When the dollar appreciates, each euro is worth less. In this case, the price of the euro would fall from $1.25 per euro to $1.00 per euro.

Dollar appreciates:

$$1.0 \text{ euro per dollar} = \frac{1 \text{ dollar}}{1 \text{ euro}} = 1.0 \text{ dollar per euro, or } \$1.00 \text{ per euro}$$

If the exchange rate falls from 0.8 euro to 0.6 euro per dollar, the dollar has depreciated in value against the euro—the price of dollars in terms of euros has decreased, in other words. When the dollar depreciates, each euro is worth more. In this case, the price of the euro would rise from $1.25 to $1.67.

Dollar depreciates:

$$0.6 \text{ euro per dollar} = \frac{1 \text{ dollar}}{0.6 \text{ euro}} = 1.67 \text{ dollars per euro, or } \$1.67 \text{ per euro}$$

## Changes in Demand or Supply

Changes in demand or changes in supply will change equilibrium exchange rates. In Figure 18.6, we show how an increase in demand, a shift of the demand curve to the right, will increase, or appreciate, the exchange rate. U.S. dollars will become more expensive relative to euros as the price of U.S. dollars in terms of euros increases.

Two factors will shift the demand curve for dollars: First, higher U.S. interest rates will lead to an increased demand for dollars. With higher returns in U.S. markets, investors throughout the world will want to buy dollars to invest in U.S. assets. The other factor, lower U.S. prices, will also lead to an increased demand for dollars. For example, if prices at Disneyland fell, there would be an overall increase in the demand for dollars, because more tourists would want to visit Disneyland.

Figure 18.7 shows the effects of an increase in the supply of dollars, a shift in the supply curve to the right. An increase in the supply of dollars will lead to a fall, or depreciation, of the value of the dollar against the euro. What will cause the supply of dollars to increase? Again, the same two factors: interest rates and prices. Higher European interest rates will lead U.S. investors to purchase European bonds or other interest-paying assets. Purchasing European bonds will require U.S. investors to supply dollars for euros, which will drive down the exchange rate for dollars. Lower European prices will also lead to an increase in the supply of dollars for euros.

Let's summarize the key facts about the foreign exchange market, using euros as our example:

1 The demand curve for dollars represents the demand for dollars in exchange for euros. The curve slopes downward. As the dollar depreciates, there will be an increase in the quantity of dollars demanded in exchange for euros.

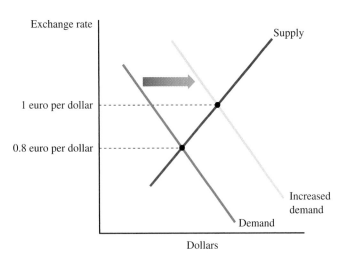

▲ **FIGURE 18.6**
**Shifts in the Demand for U.S.Dollars**
An increase in the demand for dollars will increase (appreciate) the dollar's exchange rate. Higher U.S. interest rates or lower U.S. prices will increase the demand for dollars.

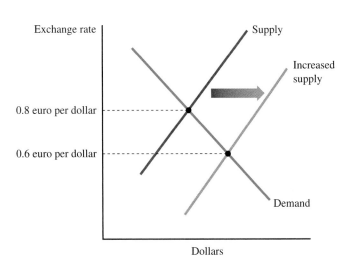

▲ **FIGURE 18.7**
**Shifts in the Supply of U.S. Dollars**
An increase in the supply of dollars will decrease (depreciate) the dollar exchange rate. Higher European interest rates or lower European prices will increase the supply of dollars.

**2** The supply curve for dollars is the supply of dollars in exchange for euros. The curve slopes upward. As the dollar appreciates, there will be an increase in the quantity of dollars supplied in exchange for euros.

**3** Increases in U.S. interest rates and decreases in U.S. prices will increase the demand for dollars, leading to an appreciation of the dollar.

**4** Increases in European interest rates and decreases in European prices will increase the supply of dollars in exchange for euros, leading to a depreciation of the dollar.

Let's apply these ideas to a concrete example. In Chapter 11, we discussed that in recent years the United States has been running a large trade deficit. What does this mean for the foreign exchange market? A U.S. trade deficit means that we are buying more goods from abroad than we are selling. This means that the supply of dollars from trade is less than the demand for dollars from trade. The reason that the foreign exchange market remains in equilibrium despite the trade deficit is that we have an offsetting surplus in the demand and supply for assets (stocks and bonds). Foreign countries have been purchasing more U.S. assets than we are purchasing foreign assets. As a result of the U.S. surplus in asset transactions, the foreign exchange market remains in equilibrium, despite U.S. trade deficits. Through their increased net purchases of U.S. assets, foreign countries now own a greater share of U.S. assets—but this is the price we pay for our large trade deficits.

# 18.6 | FIXED AND FLEXIBLE EXCHANGE RATES

To set the stage for understanding exchange rate systems, let's recall what happens when a country's exchange rate appreciates—increases in value. There are two distinct effects:

**1** The increased value of the exchange rate makes imports less expensive for the residents of the country where the exchange rate appreciated. For example, if the U.S. dollar appreciates against the euro, European watches will become less expensive for U.S. consumers. U.S. consumers would like an appreciated dollar, because it would lower their cost of living.

**2** The increased value of the exchange rate makes U.S. goods more expensive on world markets. A U.S. exchange appreciation will increase imports, such as European watches, but decrease exports, such as California wine.

Because exports fall and imports rise, net exports (exports minus imports) will decrease. Similarly, when a country's exchange rate depreciates, there are two distinct effects:

**1** For example, if the U.S. dollar depreciated against the Japanese yen, Japanese imports would become more expensive in the United States, thereby raising the cost of living in the United States.

**2** At the same time, U.S. goods would become cheaper in world markets. U.S. exports will rise and imports will fall, so net U.S. exports will increase.

## Fixing the Exchange Rate

Sometimes countries do not want their exchange rate to change. They may want to avoid sharp rises in the cost of living for their citizens when their currency depreciates, or they may want to keep net exports from falling when their currency appreciates. To prevent the value of the currency from changing, governments can enter the foreign exchange market to try to influence the price of foreign exchange. Economists call these efforts to influence the exchange rate **foreign exchange market intervention**.

In the United States, the Treasury Department has the official responsibility for foreign exchange intervention, though it operates in conjunction with the Federal Reserve. In other countries, governments also intervene in the foreign exchange market. To influence the price at which one currency trades for another, governments have to affect the demand or supply for their currency. To increase the value of its cur-

• **foreign exchange market intervention**
The purchase or sale of currencies by government to influence the market exchange rate.

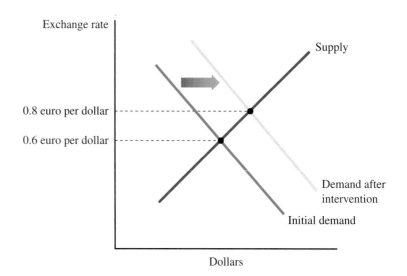

► **FIGURE 18.8**
**Government Intervention to Raise the Price of the Dollar**
To increase the price of dollars, the U.S. government sells euros in exchange for dollars. This shifts the demand curve for dollars to the right.

rency, a government must increase the currency's demand. To decrease the value of its currency, the government must increase its supply.

In Figure 18.8, we show how governments can fix, or peg, the price of a currency. Suppose the U.S. and European governments want the exchange rate to be 0.8 euro per dollar. The price at which demand and supply are currently equal, however, is only 0.6 euro per dollar. To increase the price of the U.S. dollar, the governments will need to increase the dollar's demand. To do this, either government—the United States or European banks—or both, can sell euros for dollars in the foreign exchange market. This will shift the demand curve for dollars to the right until the price of dollars rises to 0.8 euro per dollar.

Conversely, if the governments want to lower the price of the dollar relative to euros, they will buy euros in exchange for dollars. By selling dollars for euros, they increase the supply of dollars. The price of the dollar therefore falls while the price of the euro increases. Note that to affect the price of the euro against the dollar, the U.S. government must exchange euros for dollars. The government will acquire and accumulate euros anytime it tries to raise the price of euros. To raise the price of the dollar, which lowers the value of the euro, the U.S. government must sell some of the euros it has accumulated. But what would happen if the United States had no euros to sell? The United States could borrow euros from European governments or persuade them to sell euros for dollars.

## Fixed Versus Flexible Exchange Rates

Next, we discuss two different types of exchange rate systems. Then we take a brief look at historical U.S exchange rate policy and developments in exchange rates in the world today.

### FLEXIBLE EXCHANGE RATE SYSTEM

• **flexible exchange rate system**
A currency system in which exchange rates are determined by free markets.

If exchange rates are determined in free markets, we have a **flexible exchange rate system**. Under a pure flexible exchange rate system, the price of a currency will rise if the demand increases more than supply and will fall if supply increases more than demand. As we have seen, a variety of factors can determine exchange rates, including foreign and domestic interest rates as well as foreign and domestic prices. Other factors, including market psychology, can also affect the value of a nation's currency. Whatever its source, an increase in the demand for currency will raise its price. We have also seen that governments may intervene to prevent currency from changing its value. In the most extreme case, there would be no change in the value of a currency.

### FIXED EXCHANGE RATES

Whether you are in California, New York, or Indiana, all prices are quoted in dollars. No one asks whether your dollar came from San Francisco or Miami. Within the United States, a dollar is a dollar. Suppose, though, that every state had its own currency. There might be a California dollar (with a picture of the Golden Gate Bridge), an Oregon dollar (showing pictures of tall trees), and a Florida dollar (showing Disney World, of course). In principle, these dollars might trade at different rates, depending on the demand and supply of one state's dollar relative to the supply and demand for another state's dollar. For example, the Texas dollar might be worth more than the Michigan dollar, trading for 1.2 Michigan dollars.

Think how much more complicated it would be to do business. To buy goods from a mail-order company in Maine, you would have to find out the exchange rate between your state's dollar and the Maine dollar. Any large business operating in all 50 states would be overwhelmed trying to keep track of all exchange rate movements across the states. The economy would become less efficient because individuals and businesses would have to focus a lot of their attention on exchange rates.

These same ideas apply across nations. Wouldn't it be nice if all countries either used the same currency or fixed their exchange rates against one another so that no one would have to worry about exchange rate movements? Currency systems in which governments try to keep constant the values of their currencies against one another are called **fixed exchange rate systems**. After World War II, the countries of the world operated under a fixed exchange system known as Bretton Woods. The Bretton Woods system was named after the town in New Hampshire where the representatives of each nation met in 1944 and agreed to adopt this system. The system centered around the United States: All countries fixed or pegged their currencies against the U.S. dollar.

In a typical fixed exchange rate system, every country that pegs its rate to a central country's exchange rate must intervene in the foreign exchange market when necessary to keep its exchange rate constant. For example, a government would have to intervene if, at the fixed exchange rate, the private demand and supply for its currency were unequal.

## BALANCE OF PAYMENTS DEFICITS AND SURPLUSES

Suppose the supply of a country's currency exceeds the demand at the fixed exchange rate. An excess supply of a country's currency at the fixed exchange rate is known as a balance of payments deficit. A **balance of payments deficit** will occur whenever there is a trade deficit that is not matched by net sales of assets to foreigners by the private sector. For example, a trade deficit of $100 billion with net sales of assets to foreigners of only $80 billion would mean that there is an excess supply of $20 billion. With an excess supply of a country's currency in the currency market, that currency would fall in value without any intervention. To prevent the currency from depreciating in value and to maintain the fixed exchange rate, the government would have to sell foreign currency and buy its own currency. As you saw from our foreign exchange intervention discussion, if a country sells foreign exchange, its holdings of foreign exchange will fall. So you can see that when a country runs a balance of payments deficit, it has decreased its holdings of foreign exchange.

It's also very possible that the demand for a country's currency will exceed its supply at the fixed exchange rate. An excess demand for a country's currency at the fixed exchange rate is known as a **balance of payments surplus**. A balance of payments surplus arises when there is a trade surplus that is not matched by net purchases of foreign assets by the private sector. With an excess demand for a country's currency, it will rise in value without any intervention. To prevent its currency from appreciating—to maintain the fixed exchange rate, in other words—the government will have to buy foreign currency and sell its own. Because it is buying foreign exchange, its holdings of foreign exchange will increase. From this discussion, you should be able to see that when a country runs a balance of payments surplus, it has increased its holding of foreign exchange.

Under a fixed exchange rate system, countries that run persistent balance of payments deficits or balance of payments surpluses must take corrective actions. If domestic policy actions, such as changing taxes, government spending, or the money supply, do not cure the problem, a country will eventually have to change the level at which the exchange rate is fixed. A country that faces a balance of payments deficit can lower the value at which the currency is pegged to increase its net exports, a process called a **devaluation**. Conversely, a country that faces a balance of payments surplus can increase the value at which its currency is pegged and reduce its net exports, a process called **revaluation**.

• **fixed exchange rate system**
A system in which governments peg exchange rates to prevent their currencies from fluctuating.

• **balance of payments deficit**
Under a fixed exchange rate system, a situation in which the supply of a country's currency exceeds the demand for the currency at the current exchange rate.

• **balance of payments surplus**
Under a fixed exchange rate system, a situation in which the demand of a country's currency exceeds the supply for the currency at the current exchange rate.

• **devaluation**
A decrease in the exchange rate to which a currency is pegged under a fixed exchange rate system.

• **revaluation**
An increase in the exchange rate to which a currency is pegged under a fixed exchange rate system.

### The U.S. Experience with Fixed and Flexible Exchange Rates

As we discussed earlier, after World War II the countries of the world adopted the Bretton Woods fixed exchange rate system. In the 1970s, the Bretton Woods system was replaced by the current system—a flexible exchange rate system—in which supply and demand primarily determine exchange rates.

If a fixed exchange rate system makes it easier to trade, why did it break down in the early 1970s? Fixed exchange rate systems provide benefits, but they require countries to maintain similar economic policies—especially to maintain similar inflation rates and interest rates. To understand this, suppose the exchange rate between the United States and Germany were fixed, but the United States has an annual inflation rate of 6 percent compared to 0 percent in Germany. Because prices in the United States would be rising by 6 percent per year, the U.S. real exchange rate (that is, the exchange rate adjusted for changes in prices in both countries) against Germany would also be increasing at 6 percent per year. This difference in their real exchange rates over time would cause a trade deficit to emerge in the United States as U.S. goods became more expensive on world markets—including in Germany. As long as the differences in inflation continued and the exchange rate remained fixed, the U.S. real exchange rate would continue to appreciate, and the U.S. trade deficit would grow even worse. Clearly, this course of events would have to be halted under an agreed-upon fixed exchange rate system.

In the late 1960s, inflation in the United States began to exceed inflation in other countries, and a U.S. balance of payments deficit emerged—just as in our example. In 1971, President Nixon surprised the world and devalued the U.S. dollar against the currencies of all the other countries. This was a sharp departure from the rules underlying Bretton Woods. Nixon hoped that a one-time devaluation of the dollar would alleviate the U.S. balance of payments deficit and maintain the underlying system of fixed exchange rates.

However, the U.S. devaluation did not stop the U.S. balance of payments deficit. Germany tried to maintain the mark's fixed exchange rate with the U.S. dollar by purchasing U.S. dollars in the foreign exchange market. What Germany was doing was importing inflation from the United States. With the U.S. balance of payments deficit continuing, Germany was required to buy U.S. dollars to keep the mark from appreciating. Germany bought U.S. dollars with German marks. Those German marks were then put into circulation. The German supply of marks in Germany therefore increased, and this increase in marks raised the inflation rate in Germany.

Private-sector investors knew that Germany did not wish to run persistent trade surpluses and import U.S. inflation. They bet that Germany would revalue the mark against the dollar—that is, raise the value of the mark against the dollar. They bought massive amounts of German assets, trading their dollars for marks to purchase them because they thought the mark's value would eventually sharply increase. Their actions forced the German government to buy even *more* dollars to force the price of the mark upward and keep it pegged to the dollar. The resulting flow of financial capital into Germany was so massive that the German government eventually gave up all attempts to keep its exchange rate fixed to the dollar. Instead, it let the exchange rate be determined in the free market. This was the end of the Bretton Woods system.

### Exchange Rate Systems Today

The flexible exchange rate system has worked well enough since the breakdown of Bretton Woods. World trade has grown at a rapid rate. Moreover, the flexible exchange rate system has seamlessly managed many diverse situations, including two major oil shocks in the 1990s, large U.S. budget deficits in the 1980s, and large Japanese and Chinese trade surpluses in the last 15 years.

During the Bretton Woods period, many countries placed restrictions on the flows of financial capital by, for example, not allowing their residents to purchase foreign assets or by limiting foreigners' purchases of domestic assets. By the 1970s, these restrictions began to be eliminated, and private-sector transactions in assets grew rapidly. With massive amounts of funds being traded in financial markets, it becomes very difficult to fix, or peg, an exchange rate.

# 5

# APPLICATION

## THE FIRST DECADE OF THE EURO

APPLLYING THE CONCEPTS #5: Why did a group of European countries adopt a common currency?

January 1, 1999, was the day 11 European countries agreed to use a common currency. Austria, Belgium, Finland, France, Germany, Ireland, Italy, Luxembourg, the Netherlands, Portugal, and Spain irrevocably fixed their exchange rates to the euro. In 2002, euro notes and coins were actually put into circulation. Beginning July 1, 2002, French francs, German marks, Italian lira, and other national currencies ceased to be used.

A European central bank manages the monetary affairs related to the euro. It plays a role similar to the role the Federal Reserve Bank plays in the United States. The countries in the European Union no longer conduct their own independent monetary policy. Because the countries are no longer able to make monetary policy, fiscal policy has become the only remaining tool for macroeconomic stabilization.

Not all the European countries joined this system. Fearing a possible loss of independence, the United Kingdom, Denmark, and Sweden decided not to join the system initially. Greece initially did not meet some of the European Union's fiscal criteria necessary to join, but did become a member in 2001. Economists will carefully watch this experiment unfold in the twenty-first century. The jury is still out on whether adopting a common currency was a wise economic move for the countries that joined the new regime. Will the benefits of a larger market outweigh the disadvantages of having one monetary policy for all the members? *Related to Exercise 6.8.*

Nonetheless, countries whose economies are closely tied together might want the advantages of fixed exchange rates. One way to avoid some of the difficulties of fixing exchange rates between countries is to abolish individual currencies and establish a single currency. This is precisely what a group of European countries decided to do. They adopted a single currency, the euro, throughout Europe and a single central bank to control the supply of the currency. With a single currency, European countries hope to capture the benefits of serving a large market like the United States does with its single currency.

The United Kingdom decided to remain outside this European single currency system. Its currency, like the U.S. dollar and the Japanese yen, now floats against each of those currencies and the euro. Many other countries have tied their exchange rate to either the dollar or the yen. Some economists believe that the world will eventually settle into three large currency blocs: the euro, the dollar, and the yen.

In this chapter, we discussed the benefits of specialization and trade, and the trade-offs associated with protectionist policies. We also explored how exchange rates are determined and how the world's financial system facilitates trade. Here are the main points of the chapter:

1 If one country has a *comparative advantage* vis-à-vis another country in producing a particular good (a lower opportunity cost), specialization and trade will benefit both countries.

2 An import ban or an *import quota* increases prices, protecting domestic industries, but domestic consumers pay the price.

3 A *tariff*, a tax on imports, generates revenue for the government, whereas an *import quota*—a limit on imports—generates revenue for foreigners or importers.

4 *Exchange rates* are currently determined in foreign *exchange markets* by supply and demand.

5 Governments can attempt to change the value of currencies by buying or selling currencies in the foreign exchange market. Purchasing a currency will raise its value; selling a currency will decrease its value.

6 A system of *fixed exchange rates* can provide a better environment for business but requires that countries keep their inflation rates and interest rates within narrow limits.

## KEY TERMS

absolute advantage, p. 428

appreciation of a currency, p. 436

balance of payments deficit, p. 441

balance of payments surplus, p. 441

comparative advantage, p. 427

depreciation of a currency, p. 436

devaluation, p. 441

euro p. 436

exchange rate, p. 435

export, p. 428

fixed exchange rate system, p. 441

flexible exchange rate system, p. 440

foreign exchange market intervention, p. 439

General Agreement on Tariffs and Trade (GATT), p. 434

import, p. 428

import licenses, p. 433

import quota, p. 432

revaluation, p. 441

tariff, p. 433

voluntary export restraint (VER), p. 432

World Trade Organization (WTO), p. 434

## EXERCISES

Visit www.myeconlab.com to complete
*Get Ahead of the Curve*     these exercises online and get instant feedback.

### 18.1 | Comparative Advantage and Exchange

**1.1** Consider an accounting firm with two accountants.
  **a.** Fill the blanks in the following table.

| | Quigley | | Slokum | |
| --- | --- | --- | --- | --- |
| | *Financial Statements* | *Tax Returns* | *Financial Statements* | *Tax Returns* |
| Output per hour | 2 | 8 | 1 | 1 |
| Opportunity cost | | | | |

  **b.** Quigley has a comparative advantage in _____, while Slokum has a comparative advantage in _____.

**1.2** Mike, the manager of a car wash, is more productive at washing cars than any potential workers he could hire. Should he wash all the cars himself? _____ (Yes/No)

**1.3** Adam Smith listed three reasons for specialization to increase productivity: (1) _____; (2) _____; and (3) _____.

**1.4** President Lincoln's discomfort with imports resulted from his failure to recognize that money sent to England eventually _____.

**1.5** **Exchange in an Island Economy.** Robin and Terry are stranded on a deserted island and consume two products, coconuts and fish. In a day, Robin can catch 2 fish or gather 8 coconuts, and Terry can catch 1 fish or gather 1 coconut.
  **a.** Use these numbers to prepare a table like Table 18.1 on page 426. Which person has a comparative advantage in fishing? Which person has a comparative advantage in gathering coconuts?
  **b.** Suppose that each person is initially self-sufficient. In a six-day week, Robin produces and consumes 32

coconuts and 4 fish, and Terry produces and consumes 4 coconuts and 2 fish. Show that specialization and exchange (at a rate of 3 coconuts per fish) allows Robin to consume more coconuts and the same number of fish and allows Terry to consume more coconuts and the same number of fish. Illustrate your answer with a graph like Figure 18.1 on page 427.

**1.6 Technological Innovation and Exchange**. Recall the example of Fred and Kate shown in Table 18.1 on page 426. Suppose a technological innovation, such as a rope ladder, increases the coconut productivity of both people: Fred can now produce 3 coconuts per day, while Kate can now produce 2 coconuts per day. Their productivity for fish has not changed. Suppose they agree to trade 1 coconut for each fish. Will both people gain from specialization and trade?

**1.7 Comparative Advantage in Teaching**. Professor Kirby is a better teacher than Professor Jones for both an undergraduate course (U) and a graduate course (G). Teaching performance is measured by the average score on students' standardized tests:

| | Professor Kirby | Professor Jones |
|---|---|---|
| Average Score in Undergraduate Course | 48 | 24 |
| Average Score in Graduate Course | 60 | 20 |

a. If each professor teaches one course and the objective is to maximize the sum of the test scores, which course should each professor teach?
b. Is your answer to (a) consistent with Kirby teaching the course for which she has the larger productivity advantage over Jones?

## 18.2 | Comparative Advantage and International Trade

**2.1** Outsourcing leads to _____ prices for consumers.

**2.2** In the first three months of 2004, the number of jobs moving to another state was _____ (larger/smaller) than the number of jobs moving to another country.

**2.3** Approximately what percentage of job losses in the first 3 months of 2004 were caused by outsourcing—2, 10, or 25 percent? (Related to Application 1 on page 429.)

**2.4** Candy cane manufacturers are shutting plants in the United States and moving to Mexico because import restrictions have caused higher _____ prices in the United States. (Related to Application 2 on page 430.)

**2.5 Outsourcing and Net Job Losses**. Consider a software firm that employs programmers and customer-service workers. Suppose the firm shifts its customer-service activities to a call center in another country, and 300 customer-service workers lose their jobs. In addition, suppose the outsourcing reduces the firm's overall production cost by 20 percent, allowing the company to cut the price of its software by 20 percent. Explain why the net loss of jobs from the firm's outsourcing will be fewer than 300 jobs. (Related to Application 1 on page 429.)

**2.6 The Steel Industry Versus the Appliance Industry**. Suppose the United States limits the imports of steel to protect its domestic steel industry. Explain the implications of the import restrictions on industries such as appliance manufacturers who use steel as an input. (Related to Application 2 on page 430.)

**2.7 Data on Exports and Imports**. Access the *Statistical Abstract of the United States* on the Internet and download the tables in the section entitled "Foreign Commerce and Aid." One of the tables lists U.S. exports and imports by selected Standard Industrial Trade Classification (SITC) commodity. Fill the blanks in the following table for the most recent year listed in the table.

| Commodity | Export Value ($ millions) | Import Value ($ millions) | Net Exports = Exports – Imports ($ millions) |
|---|---|---|---|
| Coffee | | | |
| Corn | | | |
| Soybeans | | | |
| Airplanes | | | |
| Footwear | | | |
| Vehicles | | | |
| Crude oil | | | |

**2.8 Trade Balances by Country**. Access the *Statistical Abstract of the United States* on the Internet and download the tables in the section entitled "Foreign Commerce and Aid." One of the tables lists U.S. exports and imports and merchandise trade balance by country. Fill the blanks in the following table for the most recent year listed in the table.

| Country | Exports ($ millions) | General Imports ($ millions) | Merchandise Trade Balance ($ millions) |
|---|---|---|---|
| Australia | | | |
| China | | | |
| Italy | | | |
| Japan | | | |
| Mexico | | | |
| Netherlands | | | |
| Saudi Arabia | | | |
| Singapore | | | |

## 18.3 | Protectionist Policies

**3.1** If a country bans the importation of a particular good, the market equilibrium is shown by the intersection of the _____ curve and the _____ curve.

**3.2** The equilibrium price under an import quota is _____ (above/below) the price that occurs with an import ban and _____ (above/below) the price that occurs with free trade.

**3.3** From the perspective of consumers, a _____ (tariff/quota) is better.

**3.4** Threatening to impose a tariff on a country's exports if it doesn't open up its markets to trade is an example of a _____ policy.

**3.5** **Incentives for Smuggling.** If a country bans imports, smugglers may try to penetrate its markets. Suppose Chipland bans shirt imports, causing some importers to bribe customs officials who "look the other way" as smugglers bring shirts into the country. Your job is to combat shirt smuggling. Use the information in Figure 18.3 on page 431 to answer the following questions:
   **a.** Suppose importers can sell their shirts on the world market at a price of $12 per shirt. How much is an importer willing to pay to get customs officials to look the other way?
   **b.** What sort of change in trade policy would make your job easier?

**3.6** **Tariffs on Steel Imports.** When the United States placed a tariff on steel imports in 2002, foreign producers naturally complained. But there were also complaints from U.S. firms operating in other industries. Why would other types of firms strongly object to the tariffs on U.S. steel imports?

**3.7** **Tariffs and the Poor.** Historically, apparel and textiles were subject to high tariffs. Explain why this might hurt low-income consumers more than high-income consumers. (Related to Application 3 on page 433.)

**3.8** **The Political Dynamics of Tariffs and Quotas.** Suppose the president of a nation proposes that it switch from a system of import quotas to a system of tariffs, with the idea that the switch will not affect the quantity of goods imported. Who will be in favor of the switch? Who will oppose it? Would you expect the proponents and the opponents to have the same political influence on the president?

## 18.4 | A Brief History of International Tariff and Trade Agreements

**4.1** The latest trade round is called the _____ round.

**4.2** The _____ was formed in 1995 to oversee GATT.

**4.3** NAFTA is a free trade agreement between the United States, Mexico, and _____.

**4.4** The average tariff rate in the United States is roughly _____ percent.

**4.5** **A Major Change in U.S. Trade Policy?** In Chapter 7 of the 2006 *Economic Report of the President* (www.gpoaccess.gov/eop/download.html), the authors of the report discuss the important changes that occurred in 1934 under the Reciprocal Trade Agreements Act. They contend that it began to move the United States to a policy of more open trade after the Smoot–Hawley tariffs. Identify the key changes enacted in 1934.

**4.6** **Expansion in the European Union.** When the EU originated, member countries generally had similar standards of living. However, with the most recent expansion of the EU, countries that were less developed joined the developed countries. What implications might the entry of the new countries have for wage inequality within the more established European countries?

**4.7** **Tracking Current Trade Talks.** Go to the Web site for the World Trade Organization (www.wto.org) and briefly summarize the current status of ongoing trade negotiations. (Related to Application 4 on page 435.)

## 18.5 | How Exchange Rates Are Determined

**5.1** The dollar _____ against the euro when banks in Europe cut interest rates.

**5.2** If the dollar appreciates against the euro, then the euro also _____ against the dollar.

**5.3** The dollar _____ against the euro when the inflation rate in the United States increases.

**5.4** A shift in the demand for euros and away from dollars will _____ the dollar against the euro.

**5.5** **Using Demand and Supply Analysis.** Draw a demand and supply graph for British pounds to determine the effects of the following on the exchange rate between the British pound and the Japanese yen. (The vertical axis will be yen per pound.)
   **a.** An increase in Japanese interest rates
   **b.** An increase in the price of British goods
   **c.** An increase in British interest rates

**5.6** **The Effects of Policy Changes in Japan.** Until the early 1980s, Japan required its large insurance companies to invest all of their vast holdings in Japanese securities. At the prompting of the United States, Japan relaxed the restrictions and allowed the companies to invest anywhere in the world. What effect do you think this had on the yen/dollar exchange rate and the trade balance between the two countries?

**5.7** **Exchange Rate and Rumors of a Coup.** Suppose there are rumors that there is about to be a military coup in a South American country. Explain what you think will happen to that country's exchange rate.

**6.1** The government _____ foreign currency for dollars if it wants to peg the exchange rate at a higher rate than would normally prevail in the market.

**6.2** If there is an excess supply of a country's currency at the fixed exchange rate, there is a balance of payments _____.

**6.3** The Bretton Woods agreement broke down during the decade of the _____.

**6.4** When European countries joined together to create the euro, they no longer were able to conduct independent _____ policy.

**6.5** **Expectations of Depreciation and Investing**. Individuals wishing to invest in Turkey in 2006 had two choices. They could invest in bonds that would pay returns in 2007 in Turkish lira and earn 14.7 percent. Or they could invest in Turkish bonds that would pay returns in U.S. dollars but earn only 5.2 percent. From this data, what do you think the market believes is the expected rate of depreciation of the Turkish lira against the U.S. dollar? Explain.

**6.6** **Pressures on the Bank of England**. During the late 1980s, the United Kingdom had fixed exchange rates with other countries in Europe, including Germany. To fight inflationary pressures after East Germany and West Germany were reunited, the German central bank raised interest rates sharply.

**a.** Let's figure out why the United Kingdom had to raise interest rates along with Germany. First, if the United Kingdom did not raise interest rates, what would investors do with their funds? Second, what effect would this movement of funds have had on the British pound? To prevent these changes in the British pound, what would the British central bank have had to do?

**b.** Speculators in foreign exchange believed that the Bank of England would not raise interest rates. Why did speculators sell British pounds in massive amounts? Why did this force the British government to abandon its fixed exchange rate with Germany?

**6.7** **Uncovering U.S. Exchange Rate Policy**. Suppose the United States reported that the U.S. Treasury had increased its holdings of foreign currencies from last year. What does this tell you about the foreign exchange policies of the United States during the last year?

**6.8** **Monetary and Exchange Rate Issues for the European Central Bank**. Go to the Web site of the European Central Bank (www.ecb.int). Identify three important issues facing the European Central Bank that are currently being debated. How do these discussions relate to the value of the euro versus the dollar? (Related to Application 5 on page 443.)

## NOTES

1. Todd G. Buchholz, *New Ideas from Dead Economists* (New York: Penguin, 1999), p. 75.

2. Buchholz, p. 76.

3. MPA Worldwide Market Research, *MPA Snapshot Report: 2004 International Theatrical Market* (Motion Picture Association, March 2005).

4. Buchholz, p. 21.

5. *A Review of Recent Developments in the U.S. Automobile Industry, Including an Assessment of the Japanese Voluntary Restraint Agreements* (Washington, D.C.: U.S. International Trade Commission, February 1985).

6. Gary C. Hufbauer, "The Benefits of Open Markets and the Costs of Trade Protection and Economic Sanction," ACCF Center for Policy Research, available online at www.accf.org/ publications/reports/ sr-benefits-openmarkets1997.html. Accessed June, 2006.

# Glossary

**Absolute advantage** The ability of one person or nation to produce a product at a lower resource cost than another person or nation.

**Accounting cost** The explicit costs of production.

**Accounting profit** Total revenue minus accounting cost.

**Adverse-selection problem** A situation in which the uninformed side of the market must choose from an undesirable or adverse selection of goods.

**Aggregate demand curve (AD)** A curve that shows the relationship between the level of prices and the quantity of real GDP demanded.

**Aggregate supply curve (AS)** A curve that shows the relationship between the level of prices and the quantity of output supplied.

**Anticipated inflation** Inflation that is expected.

**Appreciation of a currency** An increase in the value of a currency relative to the currency of another nation.

**Assets** The uses of the funds of a bank, including loans and reserves.

**Asymmetric information** A situation in which one side of the market—either buyers or sellers—has better information than the other.

**Automatic stabilizers** Taxes and transfer payments that stabilize GDP without requiring policy makers to take explicit action.

**Autonomous consumption spending** The part of consumption spending that does not depend on income.

**Average fixed cost (AFC)** Fixed cost divided by the quantity produced.

**Average variable cost (AVC)** Variable cost divided by the quantity produced.

**Balance of payments deficit** Under a fixed exchange rate system, a situation in which the supply of a country's currency exceeds the demand for the currency at the current exchange rate.

**Balance of payments surplus** Under a fixed exchange rate system, a situation in which the demand of a country's currency exceeds the supply for the currency at the current exchange rate.

**Balance sheet** An account statement for a bank that shows the sources of its funds (liabilities) as well as the uses of its funds (assets).

**Barrier to entry** Something that prevents firms from entering a profitable market.

**Barter** The exchange of one good or service for another.

**Board of Governors of the Federal Reserve** The seven-person governing body of the Federal Reserve System in Washington, D.C.

**Break-even price** The price at which economic profit is zero; price equals average total cost.

**Budget deficit** The amount by which government spending exceeds revenues in a given year

**Budget surplus** The amount by which government revenues exceed government expenditures in a given year.

**Capital deepening** Increases in the stock of capital per worker.

**Cartel** A group of firms that act in unison, coordinating their price and quantity decisions.

**Central bank** A banker's bank: an official bank that controls the supply of money in a country.

**Ceteris paribus** The Latin expression meaning other variables being held fixed.

**Chain-weighted index** A method for calculating changes in prices that uses an average of base years from neighboring years.

**Change in demand** A shift of the demand curve caused by a change in a variable other than the price of the product.

**Change in quantity demanded** A change in the quantity consumers are willing and able to buy when the price changes; represented graphically by movement along the demand curve.

**Change in quantity supplied** A change in the quantity firms are willing and able to sell when the price changes; represented graphically by movement along the supply curve.

**Change in supply** A shift of the supply curve caused by a change in a variable other than the price of the product.

**Commodity money** A monetary system in which the actual money is a commodity, such as gold or silver.

**Comparative advantage** The ability of one person or nation to produce a good at a lower opportunity cost than another person or nation.

**Complements** Two goods for which a decrease in the price of one good increases the demand for the other good.

**Concentration ratio** The percentage of the market output produced by the largest firms.

**Constant returns to scale** A situation in which the long-run total cost increases proportionately with output, so average cost is constant.

**Constant-cost industry** An industry in which the average cost of production is constant; the long-run supply curve is horizontal.

**Consumer Price Index** A price index that measures the cost of a fixed basket of goods chosen to represent the consumption pattern of a typical consumer.

**Consumption expenditures** Purchases of newly produced goods and services by households.

**Consumption function** The relationship between the level of income and consumer spending.

**Contestable market** A market with low entry and exit costs.

**Contractionary policies** Government policy actions that lead to decreases in aggregate demand.

**Convergence** The process by which poorer countries close the gap with richer countries in terms of real GDP per capita.

**Cost-of-living adjustments (COLAs)** Automatic increases in wages or other payments that are tied to the CPI.

**Creative destruction** The view that a firm will try to come up with new products and more efficient ways to produce products to earn monopoly profits.

**Cross-price elasticity of demand** A measure of the responsiveness of demand to changes in the price of a another good; equal to the percentage change in the quantity demanded of one good ($X$) divided by the percentage change in the price of another good ($Y$).

**Cyclical unemployment** Unemployment that occurs during fluctuations in real GDP.

**Deflation** Negative inflation or falling prices of goods and services.

**Demand schedule** A table that shows the relationship between the price of a product and the quantity demanded, *ceteris paribus*.

**Depreciation of a currency** A decrease in the value of a currency relative to the currency of another nation.

**Depreciation** Reduction in the value of capital goods over a one-year period due to physical wear and tear and also to obsolescence; also called *capital consumption allowance*.

**Depression** The common name for a severe recession.

**Devaluation** A decrease in the exchange rate to which a currency is pegged under a fixed exchange rate system.

**Diminishing returns** As one input increases while the other inputs are held fixed, output increases at a decreasing rate.

**Discount rate** The interest rate at which banks can borrow from the Fed.

**Discouraged workers** Workers who left the labor force because they could not find jobs.

**Discretionary spending** The spending programs that Congress authorizes on an annual basis.

**Diseconomies of scale** A situation in which the long-run average cost of production increases as ouput increases.

**Dominant strategy** An action that is the best choice for a player, no matter what the other player does.

**Double coincidence of wants** The problem in a system of barter that one person may not have what the other desires.

**Duopolists' dilemma** A situation in which both firms in a market would be better off if both chose the high price, but each chooses the low price.

**Duopoly** A market with two firms.

**Economic cost** The opportunity cost of the inputs used in the production process; equal to explicit cost plus implicit cost.

**Economic growth** Sustained increases in the real GDP of an economy over a long period of time.

**Economic model** A simplified representation of an economic environment, often employing a graph.

**Economic profit** Total revenue minus economic cost.

**Economics** The study of choices when there is scarcity.

**Economies of scale** A situation in which the long-run average cost of production decreases as output increases.

**Elastic demand** The price elasticity of demand is greater than one.

**Entitlement and mandatory spending** Spending that Congress has authorized by prior law, primarily providing support for individuals.

**Entrepreneurship** The effort used to coordinate the factors of production—natural resources, labor, physical capital, and human capital—to produce and sell products.

**Euro** The common currency in Europe.

**Excess demand (shortage)** A situation in which, at the prevailing price, the quantity demanded exceeds the quantity supplied.

**Excess reserves** Any additional reserves that a bank holds above required reserves.

**Excess supply (surplus)** A situation in which at the prevailing price the quantity supplied exceeds the quantity demanded.

**Exchange rate** The price at which currencies trade for one another in the market.

**Expansion** The period after a trough in the business cycle during which the economy recovers.

**Expansionary policies** Government policy actions that lead to increases in aggregate demand.

**Explicit cost** The actual monetary payment for inputs.

**Export** A good produced in the home country (for example, the United States) and sold in another country.

**External benefit** A benefit from a good experienced by someone other than the person who buys the good.

**External cost of production** A cost incurred by someone other than the producer.

**Factors of production** The resources used to produce goods and services; also known as *production inputs*.

**Federal funds market** The market in which banks borrow and lend reserves to and from one another.

**Federal funds rate** The interest rate on reserves that banks lend each other.

**Federal Open Market Committee (FOMC)** The group that decides on monetary policy: It consists of the seven members of the Board of Governors plus five of 12 regional bank presidents on a rotating basis.

**Federal Reserve Bank** One of 12 regional banks that are an official part of the Federal Reserve System.

**Fiat money** A monetary system in which money has no intrinsic value but is backed by the government.

**Firm-specific demand curve** A curve showing the relationship between the price charged by a specific firm and the quantity the firm can sell.

**Fiscal policy** Changes in government taxes and spending that affect the level of GDP.

**Fixed cost (FC)** Cost that does not vary with the quantity produced.

**Fixed exchange rate system** A system in which governments peg exchange rates to prevent their currencies from fluctuating.

**Flexible exchange rate system** A currency system in which exchange rates are determined by free markets.

**Foreign exchange market intervention** The purchase or sale of currencies by government to influence the market exchange rate.

**Free rider** A person who gets the benefit from a good but does not pay for it.

**Frictional unemployment** Unemployment that occurs with the normal workings of the economy, such as workers taking time to search for suitable jobs and firms taking time to search for qualified employees.

**Full employment** The level of unemployment that occurs when the unemployment rate is at the natural rate.

**Game theory** The study of decision making in strategic situations.

**Game tree** A graphical representation of the consequences of different actions in a strategic setting.

**GDP deflator** An index that measures how the prices of goods and services included in GDP change over time.

**General Agreement on Tariffs and Trade (GATT)** An international agreement established in 1947 that has lowered trade barriers between the United States and other nations.

**Gold standard** A monetary system in which gold backs up paper money.

**Government purchases** Purchases of newly produced goods and services by local, state, and federal governments.

**Grim-trigger strategy** A strategy where a firm responds to underpricing by choosing a price so low that each firm makes zero economic profit.

**Gross domestic product (GDP)** The total market value of final goods and services produced within an economy in a given year.

**Gross investment** Total new investment expenditures.

**Gross national product** GDP plus net income earned abroad.

**Growth accounting** A method to determine the contribution to economic growth from increased capital, labor, and technological progress.

**Growth rate** The percentage rate of change of a variable from one period to another.

**Human capital** The knowledge and skills acquired by a worker through education and experience and used to produce goods and services.

**Hyperinflation** An inflation rate exceeding 50 percent per month.

**Illiquid** Not easily transferable to money.

**Implicit cost** The opportunity cost of inputs that do not require a monetary payment.

**Import licenses** Rights, issued by a government, to import goods.

**Import quota** A government-imposed limit on the quantity of a good that can be imported.

**Import** A good produced in a foreign country and purchased by residents of the home country (for example, the United States).

**Income effect for leisure demand** The change in leisure time resulting from a change in real income caused by a change in the wage.

**Income elasticity of demand** A measure of the responsiveness of demand to changes in consumer income; equal to the percentage change in the quantity demanded divided by the percentage change in income.

**Increasing-cost industry** An industry in which the average cost of production increases as the total output of the industry increases; the long-run supply curve is positively sloped.

**Individual demand curve** A curve that shows the relationship between the price of a good and quantity demanded by an individual consumer, *ceteris paribus*.

**Individual supply curve** A curve showing the relationship between price and quantity supplied by a single firm, *ceteris paribus*.

**Indivisible input** An input that cannot be scaled down to produce a smaller quantity of output.

**Inelastic demand** The price elasticity of demand is less than one.

**Inferior good** A good for which an increase in income decreases demand.

**Inflation rate** The percentage rate of change in the price level.

**Inflation** Sustained increases in the average prices of all goods and services.

**Input-substitution effect** The change in the quantity of labor demanded resulting from an increase in the price of labor relative to the price of other inputs.

**Inside lags** The time it takes to formulate a policy.

**Intermediate goods** Goods used in the production process that are not final goods and services.

**Labor force participation rate** The percentage of the population over 16 years of age that is in the labor force.

**Labor force** The total number of workers, both the employed and the unemployed.

**Labor productivity** Output produced per hour of work.

**Labor** Human effort, including both physical and mental effort, used to produce goods and services.

**Laffer curve** A relationship between the tax rates and tax revenues that illustrates that high tax rates could lead to lower tax revenues if economic activity is severely discouraged.

**Law of demand** There is a negative relationship between price and quantity demanded, *ceteris paribus*.

**Law of supply** There is a positive relationship between price and quantity supplied, *ceteris paribus*.

**Learning effect** The increase in a person's wage resulting from the learning of skills required for certain occupations.

**Lender of last resort** A central bank is the lender of last resort, the last place, all others having failed, from which banks in emergency situations can obtain loans.

**Liabilities** The sources of funds for a bank, including deposits and owners' equity.

**Limit pricing** The strategy of reducing the price to deter entry.

**Liquidity demand for money** The demand for money that represents the needs and desires individuals and firms have to make transactions on short notice without incurring excessive costs.

**Long-run aggregate supply curve** A vertical aggregate supply curve that reflects the idea that in the long run, output is determined solely by the factors of production.

**Long-run average cost (LAC)** The long-run cost divided by the quantity produced.

**Long-run demand curve for labor** A curve showing the relationship between the wage and the quantity of labor demanded over the long run, when the number of firms in the market can change and firms can modify their production facilities.

**Long-run marginal cost (LMC)** The change in long-run cost resulting from a one-unit increase in output.

**Long-run market supply curve** A curve showing the relationship between the market price and quantity supplied in the long run.

**Long-run total cost (LTC)** The total cost of production when a firm is perfectly flexible in choosing its inputs.

**Low-price guarantee** A promise to match a lower price of a competitor.

**M1** The sum of currency in the hands of the public, demand deposits, other checkable deposits, and travelers' checks.

**M2** M plus other assets, including deposits in savings and loans accounts and money market mutual funds.

**Macroeconomics** The study of the nation's economy as a whole; focuses on the issues of inflation, unemployment, and economic growth.

**Marginal benefit** The additional benefit resulting from a small increase in some activity.

**Marginal change** A small, one-unit change in value.

**Marginal cost** The additional cost resulting from a small increase in some activity.

**Marginal product of labor** The change in output from one additional unit of labor.

**Marginal propensity to consume (MPC)** The fraction of additional income that is spent.

**Marginal propensity to save (MPS)** The fraction of additional income that is saved.

**Marginal revenue** The change in total revenue from selling one more unit of output.

**Marginal-revenue product of labor (MRP)** The extra revenue generated from one additional unit of labor; *MRP* is equal to the price of output times the marginal product of labor.

**Market demand curve** A curve showing the relationship between price and quantity demanded by all consumers, *ceteris paribus*.

**Market equilibrium** A situation in which the quantity demanded equals the quantity supplied at the prevailing market price.

**Market power** The ability of a firm to affect the price of its product.

**Market supply curve for labor** A curve showing the relationship between the wage and the quantity of labor supplied.

**Market supply curve** A curve showing the relationship between the market price and quantity supplied by all firms, *ceteris paribus*.

**Marketable pollution permits** A system under which the government picks a target pollution level for a particular area, issues just enough pollution permits to meet the pollution target, and allows firms to buy and sell the permits; also known as a *cap-and-trade system*.

**Means-tested program** A government spending program that provides assistance to those whose income falls below a certain level.

**Medicaid** A federal and state government health program for the poor.

**Medicare** A federal government health program for the elderly.

**Medium of exchange** Any item that buyers give to sellers when they purchase goods and services.

**Menu costs** The costs associated with changing prices and printing new price lists when there is inflation.

**Merger** A process in which two or more firms combine their operations.

**Microeconomics** The study of the choices made by households, firms, and government and how these choices affect the markets for goods and services.

**Minimum efficient scale** The output at which scale economies are exhausted.

**Minimum supply price** The lowest price at which a product will be supplied.

**Mixed market** A market in which goods of different qualities are sold for the same price.

**Monetary policy** The range of actions taken by the Federal Reserve to influence the level of GDP or inflation.

**Money market** The market for money in which the amount supplied and the amount demanded meet to determine the nominal interest rate.

**Money multiplier** The ratio of the increase in total checking account deposits to an initial cash deposit.

**Money** Any items that are regularly used in economic transactions or exchanges and accepted by buyers and sellers.

**Monopolistic competition** A market served by many firms that sell slightly different products.

**Monopoly** A market in which a single firm sells a product that does not have any close substitutes.

**Moral hazard** A situation in which one side of an economic relationship takes undesirable or costly actions that the other side of the relationship cannot observe.

**Multiplier** The ratio of the total shift in aggregate demand to the initial shift in aggregate demand.

**Nash equilibrium** An outcome of a game in which each player is doing the best he or she can, given the action of the other players.

**National income** The total income earned by a nation's residents both domestically and abroad in the production of goods and services.

**Natural monopoly** A market in which the economies of scale in production are so large that only a single large firm can earn a profit.

**Natural rate of unemployment** The level of unemployment at which there is no cyclical unemployment. It consists of only frictional and structural unemployment.

**Natural resources** Resources provided by nature and used to produce goods and services.

**Negative relationship** A relationship in which two variables move in opposite directions.

**Net exports** Exports minus imports.

**Net investment** Gross investment minus depreciation.

**Network externalities** The value of a product to a consumer increases with the number of other consumers who use it.

**New growth theory** Modern theories of growth that try to explain the origins of technological progress.

**Nominal GDP** The value of GDP in current dollars.

**Nominal value** The face value of an amount of money.

**Normal good** A good for which an increase in income increases demand.

**Normative analysis** Answers the question "What *ought to be?*"

**Open market operations** The purchase or sale of U.S. government securities by the Fed.

**Open market purchases** The Fed's purchase of government bonds from the private sector.

**Open market sales** The Fed's sale of government bonds to the private sector.

**Opportunity cost** What you sacrifice to get something.

**Output effect** The change in the quantity of labor demanded resulting from a change in the quantity of output produced.

**Outside lags** The time it takes for the policy to actually work.

**Owners' equity** The funds provided to a bank by its owners.

**Patent** The exclusive right to sell a new good for some period of time.

**Peak** The date at which a recession starts.

**Perfectly competitive market** A market with many sellers and buyers of a homogeneous product and no barriers to entry.

**Perfectly elastic demand** The price elasticity of demand is infinite.

**Perfectly elastic supply** The price elasticity of supply is infinite.

**Perfectly inelastic demand** The price elasticity of demand is zero.

**Perfectly inelastic supply** The price elasticity of supply is zero.

**Permanent income** An estimate of a household's long-run average level of income.

**Personal disposable income** Personal income that households retain after paying taxes.

**Personal income** Income, including transfer payments, received by households.

**Physical capital** The stock of equipment, machines, structures, and infrastructure that is used to produce goods and services.

**Pollution tax** A tax or charge equal to the external cost per unit of pollution.

**Positive analysis** Answers the question "What is?" or *"What will be?"*

**Positive relationship** A relationship in which two variables move in the same direction.

**Predatory pricing** A pricing scheme under which a firm decreases the price to drive rival firms out of business and increases the price when rival firms leave the market.

**Price discrimination** The practice of selling a good at different prices to different consumers.

**Price elasticity of demand ($E_d$)** A measure of the responsiveness of the quantity demanded to changes in price; equal to the absolute value of the percentage change in quantity demanded divided by the percentage change in price.

**Price elasticity of supply** A measure of the responsiveness of the quantity supplied to changes in price; equal to the percentage change in quantity supplied divided by the percentage change in price.

**Price taker** A buyer or seller that takes the market price as given.

**Price fixing** An arrangement in which firms conspire to fix prices.

**Private cost of production** The production cost borne by a producer, which typically includes the costs of labor, capital, and materials.

**Private good** A good that is consumed by a single person or household; a good that is rival in consumption and excludable.

**Private investment expenditures** Purchases of newly produced goods and services by firms.

**Product differentiation** The process used by firms to distinguish their products from the products of competing firms.

**Production possibilities curve** A curve that shows the possible combinations of products that an economy can produce, given that its productive resources are fully employed and efficiently used.

**Public good** A good that is available for everyone to consume, regardless of who pays and who doesn't; a good that is nonrival in consumption and nonexcludable.

**Quantity demanded** The amount of a product that consumers are willing and able to buy.

**Quantity supplied** The amount of a product that firms are willing and able to sell.

**Real GDP per capita** Gross domestic product per person adjusted for changes in constant prices. It is the usual measure of living standards across time and between countries.

**Real GDP** A measure of GDP that controls for changes in prices.

**Real value** The value of an amount of money in terms of what it can buy.

**Recession** Commonly defined as six consecutive months of declining real GDP.

**Rent seeking** The process of using public policy to gain economic profit.

**Required reserves** The specific fraction of their deposits that banks are required by law to hold as reserves.

**Reserve ratio** The ratio of reserves to deposits.

**Reserves** The portion of banks' deposits set aside in either vault cash or as deposits at the Federal Reserve.

**Revaluation** An increase in the exchange rate to which a currency is pegged under a fixed exchange rate system.

**Rule of 70** A rule of thumb that says output will double in $x$ years, where $x$ is the percentage rate of growth.

**Saving** Income that is not consumed.

**Scarcity** The resources we use to produce goods and services are limited.

**Seasonal unemployment** The component of unemployment attributed to seasonal factors.

**Shoe-leather costs** Costs of inflation that arise from trying to reduce holdings of cash.

**Short run in macroeconomics** The period of time in which prices do not change or do not change very much.

**Short-run aggregate supply curve** A relatively flat aggregate supply curve that represents the idea that prices do not change very much in the short run and that firms adjust production to meet demand.

**Short-run average total cost (ATC)** Short-run total cost divided by the quantity of output; equal to *AFC* plus *AVC*.

**Short-run demand curve for labor** A curve showing the relationship between the wage and the quantity of labor demanded over the short run, when the firm cannot change its production facility.

**Short-run marginal cost (MC)** The change in short-run total cost resulting from a one-unit increase in output.

**Short-run market supply curve** A curve showing the relationship between market price and the quantity supplied in the short run.

**Short-run supply curve** A curve showing the relationship between the market price of a product and the quantity of output supplied by a firm in the short run.

**Short-run total cost (TC)** The total cost of production when at least one input is fixed; equal to fixed cost plus variable cost.

**Shut-down price** The price at which the firm is indifferent between operating and shutting down; equal to the minimum average variable cost.

**Signaling effect** The information about a person's work skills conveyed by completing college.

**Slope of a curve** The vertical difference between two points (the *rise*) divided by the horizontal difference (the *run*).

**Social cost of production** Private cost plus external cost.

**Social Security** A federal government program to provide retirement support and a host of other benefits.

**Speculative demand for money** The demand for money that arises because holding money over short periods is less risky than holding stocks or bonds.

**Stabilization policies** Policy actions taken to move the economy closer to full employment or potential output.

**Stagflation** A decrease in real output with increasing prices.

**Store of value** The property of money that it preserves value until it is used in an exchange.

**Structural unemployment** Unemployment that occurs when there is a mismatch of skills and jobs.

**Substitutes** Two goods for which an increase in the price of one good increases the demand for the other good.

**Substitution effect for leisure demand** The change in leisure time resulting from a change in the wage (the price of leisure) relative to the price of other goods.

**Sunk cost** A cost that a firm has already paid or committed to pay, so it cannot be recovered.

**Supply schedule** A table that shows the relationship between the price of a product and quantity supplied, *ceteris paribus*.

**Supply shocks** External events that shift the aggregate supply curve.

**Supply-side economics** A school of thought that emphasizes the role that taxes play in the supply of output in the economy.

**Tariff** A tax on imported goods.

**Technological progress** More efficent ways of organizing economic affairs that allow an economy to increase output without increasing inputs.

**Thin market** A market in which some high-quality goods are sold but fewer than would be sold in a market with perfect information.

**Tie-in sales** A business practice under which a business requires a consumer of one product to purchase another product.

**Tit-for-tat** A strategy where one firm chooses whatever price the other firm chose in the preceding period.

**Total revenue** The money a firm generates from selling its product.

**Total-product curve** A curve showing the relationship between the quantity of labor and the quantity of output produced, *ceteris paribus*.

**Trade deficit** The excess of imports over exports.

**Trade surplus** The excess of exports over imports.

**Transaction demand for money** The demand for money based on the desire to facilitate transactions.

**Transfer payments** Payments from governments to individuals that do not correspond to the production of goods and services.

**Trough** The date at which output stops falling in a recession.

**Trust** An arrangement under which the owners of several companies transfer their decision-making powers to a small group of trustees.

**Unanticipated inflation** Inflation that is not expected.

**Unemployment insurance** Payments unemployed people receive from the government.

**Unemployment rate** The percentage of the labor force that is unemployed.

**Unit elastic demand** The price elasticity of demand is one.

**Unit of account** A standard unit in which prices can be stated and the value of goods and services can be compared.

**Value added** The sum of all the income—wages, interest, profits, and rent—generated by an organization. For a firm, we can measure value added by the dollar value of the firm's sales minus the dollar value of the goods and services purchased from other firms.

**Variable cost (VC)** Cost that varies with the quantity produced.

**Variable** A measure of something that can take on different values.

**Voluntary export restraint (VER)** A scheme under which an exporting country voluntarily decreases its exports.

**Wealth effect** The increase in spending that occurs because the real value of money increases when the price level falls.

**World Trade Organization (WTO)** An organization established in 1995 that oversees GATT and other international trade agreements, resolves trade disputes, and holds forums for further rounds of trade negotiations.

# Photo Credits

**COVER:** J. W. Burkey/Image Bank/Getty Images.

**CHAPTER 01:** Page 2, Gilles Mingasson/Getty Images, Inc - Liaison; Page 3, Kari Erik Marttila Photography; Page 4, EPA / ARLEEN NG/Landov LLC; Page 11, Getty Images - Photodisc; Page 12, © Keren Su / CORBIS All Rights Reserved.

**CHAPTER 02:** Page 28, SuperStock, Inc.; Page 31, Jon Riley/Stone/Getty Images; Page 34, Corbis/Reuters America LLC; Page 37, © George Hall / CORBIS All Rights Reserved; Page 39, © Tim Tadder / CORBIS All Rights Reserved.

**CHAPTER 03:** Page 48, The Image Works; Page 68, Corbis Royalty Free; Page 69, Corbis Royalty Free; Page 70, Corbis Royalty Free; Page 71, © Reinhard Eisele / CORBIS All Rights Reserved; Page 72, © James L. Amos / CORBIS All Rights Reserved.

**CHAPTER 04:** Page 78, Adam Rountree/AP Wide World Photos; Page 86, © Roy Morsch / CORBIS All Rights Reserved; Page 87, SIMON MAINA / AFP / Getty Images; Page 88, AP, Los Angeles county Dept. of Public Health; Page 91, © Russ Munn / CORBIS All Rights Reserved; Page 92 © Premium Stock/Corbis/All rights reserved; Page 101, Zigy Kaluzny/Getty Images Inc. - Stone Allstock; Page 103, Nelson Hancock © Rough Guides.

**CHAPTER 05:** Page 108, Andrzej Gorzkowski; Page 123, Animals/Earth Scenes.

**CHAPTER 06:** Page 130, Lynn Sladky/AP Wide World Photos; Page 140, Corbis Royalty Free; Page 143, © Viviane Moos / CORBIS All Rights Reserved; Page 145, Getty Images, Inc.; Page 146, AP Wide World Photos; Page 148, AP Wide World Photos.

**CHAPTER 07:** Page 156, David Young-Wolff/PhotoEdit Inc.; Page 164, AGE Fotostock America, Inc.; Page 166, Jeffrey Coolidge/Getty Images - Iconica; Page 169, Joseph Barrak /Agence France Presse/ Getty Images; Page 170, Corbis Royalty Free; Page 170, AP Wide World Photos.

**CHAPTER 08:** Page 180, Tony Dejak/AP Wide World Photos; Page 181, Ed Andrieski/AP Wide World Photos; Page 193, Getty Images, Inc.; Page 195, Don Bryan/AP Wide World Photos; Page 200, Roberto Benzi/AGE Fotostock America, Inc.; Page 205, © Paul Chinn / CORBIS All Rights Reserved; Page 208, © Ariel Skelley / CORBIS All Rights Reserved; Page 210, Scott Morgan / Taxi / Getty Images.

**CHAPTER 09:** Page 220, dpa / Carsten Rehder/Landov LLC; Page 228, Ron Redfern © Dorling Kindersley; Page 229, Duane Burleson/AP Wide World Photos; Page 229, John Guistina/Getty Images - Iconica; Page 232, Getty Images, Inc.; Page 234, Darrell G. Gulin/DRK Photo; Page 239, © George Steinmetz / CORBIS All Rights Reserved; Page 242, JEFF HAYNES/AFP/Getty Images; Page 244, © Lester Lefkowitz / CORBIS All Rights Reserved; Page 245, © Frans Lanting / CORBIS All Rights Reserved.

**CHAPTER 10:** Page 254, Stockdisc/Getty Images, Inc.; Page 261, Photo Researchers, Inc.; Page 264, © David De La Paz / CORBIS All Rights Reserved; Page 265, Michael Newman/PhotoEdit Inc.; Page 267, Getty Images, Inc.; Page 269, Michael Newman/PhotoEdit Inc.

**CHAPTER 11:** Page 280, Mehdi Chebil/Alamy.com; Page 281, Alamy.com; Page 292, © James Leynse / CORBIS All Rights Reserved; Page 297, Beth A. Keiser/AP Wide World Photos; Page 299, Corbis Royalty Free.

**CHAPTER 12:** Page 304, Ted S. Warren/AP Wide World Photos; Page 307, Poppy Berry/Corbis Zefa Collection; Page 309, AGE Fotostock America, Inc.; Page 313, Corbis Royalty Free; Page 318, Getty Images, Inc.

**CHAPTER 13:** Page 324, Richard Cummins/CORBIS Images.com; Page 325, SuperStock, Inc.; Page 329, Getty Images, Inc.; Page 331, © Lorenzo Ciniglio / CORBIS All Rights Reserved; Page 335, Vincent Yu/AP Wide World Photos; Page 338, Rick Wilking/Corbis/Reuters America LLC; Page 341, H. Rumph, Jr./AP Wide World Photos; Page 342, © Greg Smith / CORBIS All Rights Reserved.

**CHAPTER 14:** Page 348, AP Wide World Photos; Page 349, © Joseph Schwartz/CORBIS All Rights Reserved; Page 352, © Dale C. Spartas / CORBIS All Rights Reserved; Page 361, Rudi Von Briel/PhotoEdit Inc.; Page 363, © Axel Koester / CORBIS All Rights Reserved.

**CHAPTER 15:** Page 368, Ingram Publishing/Superstock Royalty Free; Page 376, Carlos Javier Sanchez/AP Wide World Photos; Page 379, Nam Y. Huh/AP Wide World Photos; Page 383, Daniel Hulshizer/AP Wide World Photos.

**CHAPTER 16:** Page 388, U.S. Treasury / HO/Landov LLC; Page 393, Vincent Thian/AP Wide World Photos; Page 400, Getty Images, Inc.; Page 401, Peter Morgan/AP Wide World Photos; Page 402, © Sandy Felsenthal / CORBIS All Rights Reserved.

**CHAPTER 17:** Page 406, David Scull / Bloomberg News/Landov LLC; Page 414, Getty Images, Inc.; Page 419, Britt Leckman/AP Wide World Photos; Page 421, Getty Images, Inc.

**CHAPTER 18:** Page 424, Pearl Bucknall; Page 429, AP Wide World Photos; Page 430, © Lew Robertson / CORBIS All Rights Reserved; Page 433, Dior Azcuy/AP Wide World Photos; Page 435, © Adrian Bradshaw / CORBIS All Rights Reserved; Page 443, Raymond Reuter/Corbis/Sygma.

# Index

Key terms and the page on which they are defined appear in **boldface.**